Mobil
Travel Guide®

NEW ENGLAND

ACKNOWLEDGMENTS

We gratefully acknowledge the help of our representatives for their efficient and perceptive inspections of the lodging and dining establishments listed, the establishments' proprietors for their cooperation in showing their facilities and providing information about them, and the many users of previous editions who have taken the time to share their experiences. Mobil Travel Guide is also grateful to all the talented writers who contributed entries to this book.

Front and back cover images: ©iStockPhoto.com

All maps: created by Mapping Specialists

The information contained herein is derived from a variety of third-party sources. Although every effort has been made to verify the information obtained from such sources, the publisher assumes no responsibility for inconsistencies or inaccuracies in the data or liability for any damages of any type arising from errors or omissions.

Neither the editors nor the publisher assume responsibility for the services provided by any business listed in this guide or for any loss, damage or disruption in your travel for any reason.

ISBN: 9-780841-60863-4   Manufactured in Canada

10 9 8 7 6 5 4 3 2 1

TABLE OF CONTENTS

WRITTEN IN THE STARS   4

STAR RATINGS   6

INTRODUCTIONS   9

NEW ENGLAND

CONNECTICUT   10-46

MAINE   47-116

MASSACHUSETTS   117-249

NEW HAMPSHIRE   250-284

RHODE ISLAND   285-303

VERMONT   304-347

INDEX   348

★
★
★
★
★

WRITTEN IN THE STARS

Because time is precious and the travel industry is ever-changing, having accurate, reliable travel information at your fingertips has never been more important. With this in mind, Mobil Travel Guide has provided invaluable insight to travelers through its Star Rating system for more than 50 years.

The Mobil Corporation (known as Exxon Mobil Corporation since a 1999 merger) began producing the Mobil Travel Guide books in 1958 following the introduction of the U.S.-interstate highway system in 1956. The first edition covered only five Southwestern states. Since then, our books have become the premier travel guides in North America, covering all 50 states and Canada, and beginning in 2008, international destinations such as Hong Kong and Beijing.

Today, the concept of a "five-star" experience is one that permeates the collective conciousness, but few people realize it's one that originated with Mobil. We created our star rating system to give travelers an easy-to-recognize quality scale for choosing where to stay, dine and spa. Based on an objective process, we make recommendations to our readers that we believe will enhance the quality and value of their travel experiences. Our trusted Mobil One- to Five-Star rating system is the oldest and most respected lodging and restaurant inspection and rating program in North America. Most hoteliers, restaurateurs and industry observers favorably regard the rigor of our inspection program and understand the prestige and benefits that come with receiving a Mobil Star rating.

The Mobil Travel Guide process of rating each establishment includes unannounced inspections, incognito evaluations and a review of unsolicted comments from the general public. We inspect more than 500 attributes at each property we visit, from cleanliness to the condition of the rooms and public spaces, to employee attitude and courtesy. It's a system that rewards those properties that strive for and achieve excellence each year. And the very best properties raise the bar for those that wish to compete with them.

Only facilities that meet Mobil Travel Guide's standards earn the privilege of being listed in the guide. Properties are continuously updated, and deteriorating, poorly managed establishments are removed. We wouldn't recommend that you visit a hotel, restaurant or spa that we wouldn't want to visit ourselves.

★
★
★
★

★★★★★The Mobil Five-Star Award indicates that a property is one of the very best in the country and consistently provides gracious and courteous service, superlative quality in its facility and a unique ambience. The lodgings and restaurants at the Mobil Five-Star level consistently continue their commitment to excellence, doing so with grace and perseverance.

★★★★The Mobil Four-Star Award honors properties for outstanding achievement in overall facility and for providing very strong service levels in all areas. These award winners provide a distinctive experience for the ever-demanding and sophisticated consumer.

★★★The Mobil Three-Star Award recognizes an excellent property that provides full services and amenities. This category ranges from exceptional hotels with limited services to elegant restaurants with a less formal atmosphere.

★★The Mobil Two-Star property is a clean and comfortable establishment that has expanded amenities or a distinctive environment. These properties are an excellent place to stay or dine.

★The Mobil One-Star property is limited in its amenities and services but provides a value experience while meeting travelers' expectations. The properties should be clean, comfortable and convenient.

We do not charge establishments for inclusion in our guides. We have no relationship with any of the businesses and attractions we list and act only as a consumer advocate. We do the investigative legwork so that you won't have to.

Restaurants and hotels—particularly small chains and stand-alone establishments—change management or even go out of business with surprising quickness. Although we make every effort to continuously update information, we recommend that you call ahead to make sure the place you've selected is still open.

STAR RATINGS

MOBIL RATED HOTELS

Whether you're looking for the ultimate in luxury or the best bang for your travel buck, we have a hotel recommendation for you. To help you pinpoint properties that meet your needs, Mobil Travel Guide classifies each lodging by type according to the following characteristics.

★★★★★The Mobil Five-Star hotel provides consistently superlative service in an exceptionally distinctive luxury environment. Attention to detail is evident throughout the hotel, resort or inn, from bed linens to staff uniforms.

★★★★The Mobil Four-Star hotel provides a luxury experience with expanded amenities in a distinctive environment. Services may include automatic turndown service, 24-hour room service and valet parking.

★★★The Mobil Three-Star hotel is well appointed, with a full-service restaurant and expanded amenities, such as a fitness center, golf course, tennis courts, 24-hour room service and optional turndown service.

★★The Mobil Two-Star hotel is considered a clean, comfortable and reliable establishment that has expanded amenities, such as a full-service restaurant.

★The Mobil One-Star lodging is a limited-service hotel, motel or inn that is considered a clean, comfortable and reliable establishment.

For every property, we also provide pricing information. The pricing categories break down as follows:

$ = Up to $150

$$ = $151-$250

$$$ = $251-$350

$$$$ = $351 and up

All prices quoted are accurate at the time of publication; however, prices cannot be guaranteed.

MOBIL RATED RESTAURANTS

Every restaurant in this book has been visited by Mobil Travel Guide's team of experts and comes highly recommended as an outstanding dining experience.

★★★★★The Mobil Five-Star restaurant offers one of few flawless dining experiences in the country. These establishments consistently provide their guests with exceptional food, superlative service, elegant décor and exquisite presentations of each detail surrounding a meal.

★★★★The Mobil Four-Star restaurant provides professional service, distinctive presentations and wonderful food.

★★★The Mobil Three-Star restaurant has good food, warm and skillful service and enjoyable décor.

★★The Mobil Two-Star restaurant serves fresh food in a clean setting with efficient service. Value is considered in this category, as is family friendliness.

★The Mobil One-Star restaurant provides a distinctive experience through culinary specialty, local flair or individual atmosphere.

Because menu prices can fluctuate, we list a pricing category rather than specific prices. The pricing categories are defined as follows, per diner, and assume that you order an appetizer or dessert, an entrée and one drink:

$ = $15 and under

$$ = $16-$35

$$$ = $36-$85

$$$$ = $86 and up

★
★
★
★
★

MOBIL RATED SPAS

Mobil Travel Guide's spa ratings are based on objective evaluations of hundreds of attributes. About half of these criteria assess basic expectations, such as staff courtesy, the technical proficiency and skill of the employees and whether the facility is clean and maintained properly. Several standards address issues that impact a guest's physical comfort and convenience, as well as the staff's ability to impart a sense of personalized service. Additional criteria measure the spa's ability to create a completely calming ambience.

★★★★★The Mobil Five-Star spa provides consistently superlative service in an exceptionally distinctive luxury environment with extensive amenities. The staff at a Mobil Five-Star spa provides extraordinary service beyond the traditional spa experience, allowing guests to achieve the highest level of relaxation and pampering. These spas offer an extensive array of treatments, often incorporating international themes and products. Attention to detail is evident throughout the spa, from arrival to departure.

★★★★The Mobil Four-Star spa provides a luxurious experience with expanded amenities in an elegant and serene environment. Throughout the spa facility, guests experience personalized service. Amenities might include, but are not limited to, single-sex relaxation rooms where guests wait for their treatments, plunge pools and whirlpools in both men's and women's locker rooms, and an array of treatments, including a selection of massages, body therapies, facials and a variety of salon services.

★★★The Mobil Three-Star spa is physically well appointed and has a full complement of staff.

INTRODUCTION

If you've been a reader of Mobil Travel Guides, you may have noticed a new look and style in our guidebooks. Since 1958, Mobil Travel Guide has assisted travelers in making smart decisions about where to stay and dine. Fifty-one years later, our mission has not changed: We are committed to our rigorous inspections of hotels, restaurants and, now, spas, to help you cut through all the clutter, and make easy and informed decisions on where you should spend your time and budget. Our team of anonymous inspectors are constantly on the road, sleeping in hotels, eating in restaurants and making spa appointments, evaluating hundreds of standards to determine a property's star rating.

As you read these pages, we hope you get a flavor of the places included in the guides and that you will feel even more inspired to visit and take it all in. We hope you'll experience what it's like to stay in a guest room in the hotels we've rated, taste the food in a restaurant or feel the excitement at an outdoor music venue. We understand the importance of finding the best value when you travel, and making the most of your time. That's why for more than 50 years, Mobil Travel Guide has been the most trusted name in travel.

If any aspect of your accommodation, dining, spa or sight-seeing experience motivates you to comment, please contact us at Mobil Travel Guide, 200 W. Madison St., Suite 3950, Chicago, IL 60606, or send an email to info@mobiltravelguide.com Happy travels.

★
★
★
★
★

CONNECTICUT

WHEN SOME PEOPLE THINK OF CONNECTICUT, THEY ENVISION KHAKI-CLAD MILLIONAIRES sipping martinis on manicured Greenwich lawns. Others call to mind the state's manageable capital city, Hartford, home to insurance companies galore and the country's first newspaper. Still others think of charming Mystic and the southeastern coastal area that has been wildly popular ever since Julia Roberts' star performance in *Mystic Pizza*. And some will picture the state's quiet northwestern and northeastern corners, full of rambling old farmhouses and hilly country roads. All, of course, would be correct.

A region of around three-million residents, Connecticut has much diversity and much to offer discerning travelers. For starters, the Constitution State has the mildest climate in New England and many historic tree-lined towns. It also has an entire southern border on Long Island Sound and an eponymous river. Adriaen Block sailed into the latter in 1614; Connecticut's first colonists soon followed, settling Hartford, Windsor and Wethersfield. The state hosted myriad important Revolutionary and Civil War events, and is home to many famous inventors.

FUN FACTS

Connecticut originates from a Mohegan word meaning "place of the long tidal river."

The state song of Connecticut is *Yankee Doodle*.

Connecticut has the most million-dollar homes in the Northeast and the second most in the nation.

George W. Bush and Katharine Hepburn were both born in Connecticut.

Today, Connecticut's industry revolves around agriculture, manufacturing and insurance. But most travelers will continue to remember it fondly as a beautiful state full of grand old summer homes, endless green pastures, soft sand beaches and the occasional fleet of megayachts.

Information: www.tourism.state.ct.us

AVON

This town on the Farmington River dates to 1645. The town has historic churches, buildings and even a covered bridge.

Information: Greater Hartford Tourism District, 31 Pratt St., Hartford, 860-244-8180, 800-793-4480; www.town.avon.ct.us

WHAT TO SEE AND DO
FARMINGTON VALLEY ARTS CENTER
25 Arts Center Lane, Avon, 860-678-1867; www.fvac.net
Located in a historic stone explosives plant, these twenty studios are now occupied by artists. The onsite Fisher Gallery features guest-curated exhibits and handmade crafts, gifts and artwork. January-October: Wednesday-Saturday, Sunday afternoons; November-December: daily 9 a.m.-5 p.m.

CONNECTICUT

★
★★
★★
★

CLASSIC CONNECTICUT

Situated halfway between New York City and Boston, the fabled town of Mystic is one of Connecticut's top tourist destinations. Having read that, you might be imagining swarms of camera-toting day-trippers. And you'd be right, sort of. Mystic in the summer can be tough to navigate, but Mystic in the winter, spring and fall is a charming, uncrowded spot. The ever-popular Seaport Museum and Aquarium are must-visits, as is the nearby Foxwoods Resort, the world's largest gambling casino. But more than anything, Mystic is a great place to start your state exploration. The surrounding seaside, hills, cities and farming communities are, for the most part, picture perfect.

From Mystic, take I-95 to Old Lyme, home of the Florence Griswold Art Museum and Rocky Neck State Park beach. Cross the bridge into Old Saybrook, and follow Highway 9 to Essex, a picturesque village with shops and restaurants. The Connecticut River Museum is located here, as is the departure point for the Valley Railroad, which runs along the river. Follow scenic Highway 154 to Chester, and take the country's oldest continuous ferry—don't worry, it carries cars—across to Gillette Castle in East Haddam. Or continue over the bridge for a great view of the Victorian Goodspeed Opera House, a destination in its own right. You can return via Highway 9 or take the scenic way: Highway 82 to Highway 156 to I-95, back along the eastern side of the river. Continue west on I-95 to Hammonasset Beach State Park in Madison. Then head down Highway 1, past the town's classic historic homes, to Guilford, site of the Henry Whitfield State Museum.

★Abolitionist Harriet Beecher Stowe lived in Hartford.

★The city is known as the insurance capital of the world, with many major insurance companies headquartered in Hartford.

HOTEL

★★★AVON OLD FARMS HOTEL

279 Avon Mountain, Avon, 860-677-1651, 800-836-4000; www.avonoldfarmshotel.com
Avon has many "authentic," rusty (yes, that's rusty, not rustic) *bed and breakfasts.* If you're looking for quaint yet comfortable, check into the Avon Old Farms Hotel instead. The sweeping 160-room property is low on kitschy charm and high on functionality and service. Twenty landscaped acres, brass chandeliers and white canopied beds save the property from business-retreat banality. A lively outdoor pool scene adds further life to the mountainside hotel. 160 rooms. Complimentary continental breakfast. High-speed Internet access. Restaurant. Fitness center. Free newspaper. Pool. $

RESTAURANTS

★★★AVON OLD FARMS INN

Routes 10 and 44, Avon, 860-677-2818, 860-674-2434; www.avonoldfarmsinn.com
Set in a 1757 stagecoach stop building, this stone-walled eatery is themed accordingly. Old stirrups and bridles hang from the ceiling, and the floors and walls are built from smooth stone. Entrées range from hearty (filet mignon, short ribs) to healthy

(spinach salad, tomato-basil linguine); the menu also includes a few kosher options. American menu. Lunch, dinner, Sunday brunch. Bar. Children's menu. **$$**

★★DAKOTA
225 W. Main St., Avon, 860-677-4311; www.dakotarestaurant.com
Seafood, steak menu. Dinner. Bar. Children's menu, Sunday brunch. **$$**

BRIDGEPORT
Bridgeport is a manufacturing town through and through, but heavy industry doesn't always mean ugly aesthetics. An urban, gritty charm runs through the city's streets and there is a vibrant cultural scene. Settled in 1639, Bridgeport was home to world-famous ringleader P. T. Barnum, founder of the Ringling Brothers and Barnum and Bailey Circus. It wasn't altogether uncommon, way back when, to catch a glimpse of his elephants pulling a plow through the town's fields.

WHAT TO SEE AND DO
BARNUM MUSEUM
820 Main St., Bridgeport, 203-331-1104; www.barnum-museum.org
On display are memorabilia from P. T. Barnum's life and circus career, including arti-facts relating to Barnum's General Tom Thumb and Jenny Lind and a scale model of the three-ring circus. Tuesday-Saturday 10 a.m -4:30 p.m.; Sunday noon-4:30 p.m.

CONNECTICUT'S BEARDSLEY
Beardsley Park, 1875 Noble Ave., Bridgeport, 203-394-6565; www.beardsleyzoo.org
The state's only zoo covers 30 acres and houses more than 200 animals. Daily 9 a.m.-4 p.m.; closed Thanksgiving, Christmas Day, New Year's Day.

DISCOVERY MUSEUM AND PLANETARIUM
4450 Park Ave., Bridgeport, 203-372-3521; www.discoverymuseum.org
This kid-friendly spot has a planetarium; 120 hands-on science and art exhibits; a children's museum; and the Challenger Learning Center. Tuesday-Sunday.

SPECIAL EVENT
BARNUM FESTIVAL
1070 Main St., Bridgeport, 203-367-8495, 866-867-8495; www.barnumfestival.com
Commemorates the life of P. T. Barnum. March-September.

HOTELS
★★HOLIDAY INN
1070 Main St., Bridgeport, 203-334-1234, 888-465-4329; www.holiday-inn.com
235 rooms. High-speed Internet access. Restaurant, bar. Airport transportation avail-able. Pool. Pets accepted, fee. Fitness center. Free newspaper. **$**

★★★TRUMBULL MARRIOTT MERRITT PARKWAY
180 Hawley Lane, Trumbull, 203-378-1400, 800-682-4095; www.marriott.com
323 rooms. High-speed Internet access. Restaurant, bar. Pets not accepted. Free newspaper. **$$**

CONNECTICUT

★
★
★
★
★

CLINTON

This popular beach town, which overlooks Long Island Sound, is equidistant to New York and Boston.

Information: Chamber of Commerce, 50 E. Main St., Clinton, 860-669-3889;
www.clintonct.com

WHAT TO SEE AND DO
CHAMARD VINEYARDS

115 Cow Hill Road, Clinton, 860-664-0299, 800-371-1609;
www.chamard.com

A 15-acre vineyard and winery offers chardonnay, pinot noir, merlot and other varieties. Tours and tastings. Wednesday-Saturday.

CHATFIELD HOLLOW STATE PARK

381 Route 80, Killingworth, 860-663-2030; www.ct.gov

Nearly 550 acres sit in a heavily wooded hollow peppered by natural caves that once provided shelter for Native Americans. Onsite pond, swimming, fishing; hiking, ice-skating, picnicking.

STANTON HOUSE

63 E. Main St., Clinton, 860-669-2131;
www.clintonct.com

This 13-room house connected to a general store is the site of Yale University's first classroom. Exhibits include period furnishings; antique American and Staffordshire dinnerware; a weapon collection; and the bed used by the Marquis de Lafayette during an 1824 visit. June-September, by appointment.

HOTEL
★CLINTON MOTEL

163 E. Main St., Clinton, 860-669-8850

15 rooms. High-speed Internet access. Outdoor pool. Pets accepted. **$**

RESTAURANT
★LOG CABIN RESTAURANT AND LOUNGE

232 Boston Post Road, Clinton, 860-669-6253

Italian menu. Lunch, dinner. Bar. Children's menu. **$**

DANBURY

This western Connecticut town's history is replete with patriotic pride. During the American Revolution, it was a supply depot and the site of a Continental Army hospital. Originally settled by eight Norwalk families seeking fertile land, the city was once the hub of the hat industry. Danbury native Zadoc Benedict is credited with opening the first factory in 1790—it made three hats a day. Things have since sped up.

Information: Housatonic Valley Tourism District, 30 Main St., Danbury,
203-743-0546, 800-841-4488; www.danbury.org

★
★
★
★
★

WHAT TO SEE AND DO
CANDLEWOOD LAKE
35 E. Hayestown Road, Danbury

Connecticut's largest lake is more than 14 miles long and, with more than 60 miles of shoreline, extends one finger into Danbury. Swimming, fishing, boating; picnicking, concession. Fees for some activities.

SPECIAL EVENTS
CHARLES IVES CENTER FOR THE ARTS
Mill Plain Road, Danbury, 203-837-9226; www.ivesconcertpark.com

Outdoor classical, country, folk, jazz and pop concerts on Western Connecticut State University's Westside campus. July-early September: Friday-Sunday.

TASTE OF GREATER DANBURY
Danbury Green, Green Ives and White streets, Danbury, 203-792-1711;
www.citycenterdanbury.com

Food vendors, live music and children's games draw crowds together year after year at this outdoor festival. September.

HOTELS
★★ETHAN ALLEN HOTEL
21 Lake Ave., Danbury, 203-744-1776, 800-742-1776; www.ethanallenhotel.com

200 rooms. Restaurant, bar. Airport transportation available. High-speed Internet access. **$**

★★HOLIDAY INN
80 Newtown Road, Danbury, 203-792-4000, 888-465-4329;
www.holiday-inn.com

114 rooms. High-speed Internet access. Restaurant, bar. Airport transportation available. **$**

★★★SHERATON DANBURY HOTEL
18 Old Ridgebury Road, Danbury, 203-794-0600, 800-325-3535;
www.danburyplaza.com

Conveniently located just three miles from Danbury Airport, this Sheraton has comfortably outfitted guest rooms, and onsite restaurant and fitness room. Amenities include nightly turndown service, and if you just can't get away from work, rooms feature large desks. 242 rooms. Restaurant, bar. **$**

SPECIALTY LODGING
THE HOMESTEAD INN
5 Elm St., New Milford, 860-354-4080; www.homesteadct.com

14 rooms. Complimentary continental breakfast. High-speed Internet access. Free local calls. **$**

RESTAURANTS
★★CIAO CAFÉ AND WINE BAR
2B Ives St., Danbury, 203-791-0404; www.ciaocafetwosteps.com

Italian menu. Lunch, dinner. Bar. Reservations recommended. Outdoor seating. **$$**

★THE HEARTH
Route 7, Brookfield, 203-775-3360
American menu. Lunch, dinner. Closed Monday, February. Bar. Children's menu. **$$**

★★TWO STEPS DOWNTOWN GRILLE
5 Ives St., Danbury, 203-794-0032; www.ciaocafetwosteps.com
American, Southwestern menu. Lunch, dinner, Sunday brunch. Bar. Children's menu. Outdoor seating. **$$**

ESSEX

Twelve years ago, its tree-lined Main Street helped win Essex the honor of "The Best Small Town in America." Not much has changed since then. The peaceful Eastern Connecticut village of 6,000 exudes storybook charm in the form of its brick post office, antique shops and 1700s-era ship captain's houses.
Information: Connecticut River Valley & Shoreline Visitors Council,
393 Main St., Middletown, 860-347-0028, 800-486-3346; www.cttourism.org

WHAT TO SEE AND DO
CONNECTICUT RIVER MUSEUM
67 Main St., Essex, 860-767-8269; www.ctrivermuseum.org
Housed in the last remaining steamboat dock building on the Connecticut River, the museum features exhibits that celebrate the rich cultural heritage and natural resources of the river valley, including the only full-size operating replica of the *Turtle*, America's first successful submarine. Tuesday-Sunday 10 a.m.-5 p.m.

VALLEY RAILROAD
1 Railroad Ave., Essex, 860-767-0103; www.essexsteamtrain.com
A scenic 12-mile steam train excursion along the Connecticut River to Chester, with an optional one-hour Connecticut River cruise. Early May-late October, days vary; also Christmas trips.

SPECIAL EVENT
DEEP RIVER ANCIENT MUSTER AND PARADE
Devitt's Field, Main Street, Deep River, 860-388-7575
Approximately 60 fife and drum players recall the Revolutionary War period. Third Saturday in July.

HOTELS
★★★COPPER BEECH INN
46 Main St., Ivoryton, 860-767-0330, 888-809-2056; www.copperbeechinn.com
Travelers looking for a romantic New England getaway should check into this charming 1889 Victorian inn. Once the residence of a prominent ivory importer, the country retreat is set on sprawling wooded grounds. 13 rooms. Children over 12 years only. Complimentary full breakfast. Restaurant. Closed a week in January. **$$**

★★★★★

★★★GRISWOLD INN

36 Main St., Essex, 860-767-1776; www.griswoldinn.com

Known to locals as "the Griz," this 1776 inn is known for its lavish English-style Sunday buffet breakfast (order a mimosa). The rooms and suites are full of fresh flowers and antiques. 31 rooms. Complimentary continental breakfast. Restaurant. **$$**

RESTAURANTS

★★★COPPER BEECH INN

46 Main St., Ivoryton, 860-767-0330, 888-809-2056; copperbeechinn.com

Much like its namesake inn, the restaurant is all soft elegance and warm romance. Patrons here dine on hearty, French country fare amidst fresh flowers, sparkling silver and soft candlelight. American, French menu. Dinner. Bar. Jacket required. Closed Monday. Reservations recommended. **$$$**

★★SAGE AMERICAN BAR & GRILL

129 W. Main St., Chester, 860-526-9898; www.sageamerican.com

Seafood, steak menu. Dinner. Children's menu. Outdoor seating. **$$**

FARMINGTON

Home to the erstwhile "finishing school" Miss Porter's, Farmington is one of New England's most bucolic towns. During the early 1800s, the small city bustled with silversmiths, tinsmiths, cabinetmakers, clockmakers and carriage builders.

Information: Greater Hartford Tourism District, 234 Murphy Road, Hartford, 860-244-8181, 800-793-4480; www.farmington-ct.org

WHAT TO SEE AND DO

HILL-STEAD MUSEUM

35 Mountain Road, Farmington, 860-677-4787; www.hillstead.org

A Colonial Revival-style country house designed by Theodate Pope in collaboration with McKim, Mead and White contains industrialist A. A. Pope's collection of French Impressionist paintings. Tuesday-Sunday. May-October 10 a.m.-5 p.m. November-April 11 a.m.-4 p.m.

STANLEY-WHITMAN HOUSE

37 High St., Farmington, 860-677-9222; www.stanleywhitman.org

This 1720 home is one of the finest early 18th-century houses in the United States. May-October: Wednesday-Sunday noon-4 p.m.; November-April: Saturday-Sunday afternoons, also by appointment.

SPECIAL EVENT

FARMINGTON ANTIQUES WEEKEND

Polo Grounds, Farmington, 860-677-7862; www.farmingtonantiquesweekend.com

More than 600 dealers descend on the town for one of the largest annual antique events in the state. Mid-June and early September.

HOTELS

★★CENTENNIAL INN SUITES

5 Spring Lane, Farmington, 860-677-4647, 800-852-2052;
www.centennialinn.com

112 rooms, all suites. Complimentary continental breakfast. High-speed Internet access. Free local calls. Pets accepted. **$$**

★★★THE FARMINGTON INN OF GREATER HARTFORD

827 Farmington Ave., Farmington, 860-677-2821, 800-648-9804;
www.farmingtoninn.com

72 rooms. Complimentary continental breakfast. Wireless Internet access. Restaurant, bar. Business center. **$**

★★★HARTFORD MARRIOTT FARMINGTON

15 Farm Springs Road, Farmington, 860-678-1000,
800-228-9190; www.marriott.com

Close enough to downtown to be convenient, yet far enough away from the city center to be peaceful, this modern Marriott pampers business travelers and leisure guests alike with a full range of amenities, including two swimming pools and a tennis court. 374 rooms. High-speed Internet access. Restaurant, bar. Free local calls. **$$**

RESTAURANTS

★★APRICOT'S

1593 Farmington Ave., Farmington, 860-673-5405,

American menu. Lunch, dinner, brunch. Bar. Casual attire. Reservations recommended. Outdoor seating. **$$**

★STONEWELL

354 Colt Highway, Farmington, 860-677-8855; www.thestonewell.com

American menu. Lunch, dinner. Bar. Children's menu. Casual attire. **$$**

GREENWICH

Possibly the state's most talked about town, Greenwich has long been home to hedge fund barons, ladies who lunch and other well-moneyed folk. Its proximity to New York City—28 miles from Times Square—and the sea—oceanfront megamansions dot the coastline—has made this settlement of 58,000 one of the most coveted places to live, anywhere. Even those without an "it" address can stroll Greenwich's leafy, photo-friendly 18th-century streets, shop in its Manhattan-worthy boutiques and maybe even catch a glimpse of a millionaire.

Information: Chamber of Commerce, 21 W. Putnam Ave., Greenwich,
203-869-3500; www.greenwichchamber.com

WHAT TO SEE AND DO

AUDUBON CENTER

613 Riversville Road, Greenwich, 203-869-5272;
www.greenwich.audubon.org

This 522-acre sanctuary includes a self-guided nature trail. Daily.

★
★
★
★

BRUCE MUSEUM

1 Museum Drive, Greenwich, 203-869-0376; www.brucemuseum.org

The arts and sciences museum features exhibits, lectures, concerts and educational programs. Tuesday-Saturday 10 a.m.-5 p.m., Sunday 1-5 p.m. Closed Monday and major holidays.

BUSH-HOLLEY HOUSE

39 Strickland Road, Cos Cob, 203-869-6899; www.hstg.org

This former residence of a successful 18th-century farmer became the site of the Cos Cob art colony at the turn of the century. Current exhibits include late 18th-century Connecticut furniture; paintings by Childe Hassam, Elmer Livingston MacRae and John Henry Twachtman; sculptures by John Rogers; and pottery by Leon Volkmar. Tuesday-Sunday, afternoons.

PUTNAM COTTAGE/KNAPP TAVERN

243 E. Putnam Ave., Greenwich, 203-869-9697; www.putnamcottage.org

Near this tavern, Revolutionary General Israel Putnam made a daring escape from the Redcoats in 1779. The onsite museum now has an herb garden and a restored barn April-December: Sunday 1-4 p.m.; also by appointment.

HOTELS

★★★THE DELAMAR

500 Steamboat Road, Greenwich, 203-661-9800; www.thedelamar.com

The award-winning Delamar looks more like a Lake Como mansion than an old Connecticut retreat. Its sprawling cream-colored façade hides an interior rich with original artwork, sparkling chandeliers, ornate sconces and a plethora of marble. Overlooking the Greenwich Marina, the property has 82 rooms filled with up-to-date electronics, luxe Italian linens and cast-iron tubs. Even pooches get pampered here with the resort's "sophisticated pet" program. 82 rooms. Children over 12 years only. Restaurant, bar. Free parking. Pets accepted. Spa. $$$

★★★HOMESTEAD INN

420 Field Point Road, Greenwich, 203-869-7500; www.homesteadinn.com

Renovated by Greenwich hoteliers Thomas and Theresa Henkelmann, the inn—and its accompanying three-star restaurant—is a study in old-school sumptuous elegance. The rooms at the Homestead Inn aren't called rooms—they're called "chambers." And the lodging at this renovated 1799 inn is anything but average: second- and third-floor suites have imported furniture, Frette linens and original artwork, plus heated bathroom floors. 18 rooms. Closed two weeks in March. Children over 12 years only. Restaurant, bar. $$$$$

★★★HYATT REGENCY GREENWICH

1800 E. Putnam Ave., Old Greenwich, 203-637-1234, 800-633-7313; www.greenwich.hyatt.com

Before magazine giant Condé Nast moved to Manhattan, the *Vogue* and *Glamour* publisher was headquartered at 1800 E. Putnam. Now a Hyatt, the building has retained much of its early glamour with an elegant atrium-style lobby with ponds, stone walls and an impressive array of trees, plants and flowers. Guest rooms are spacious and feature Internet access, bath robes and plush pillows. 373 rooms. Wireless Internet access. Restaurant, bar. Business center. $$$

SPECIALTY LODGINGS

HARBOR HOUSE INN
165 Shore Road, Old Greenwich, 203-637-0145; www.hhinn.com
23 rooms. Complimentary continental breakfast. $

STANTON HOUSE INN
76 Maple Ave., Greenwich, 203-869-2110; www.shinngreenwich.com
24 rooms. Complimentary continental breakfast. $$

RESTAURANTS

★★★JEAN-LOUIS
61 Lewis St., Greenwich, 203-622-8450; www.restaurantjeanlouis.com
Sophisticated and elegant with professional service to match, this cozy restaurant has a menu grounded in the precision of French classicism. The décor is decidedly Parisian as well—the serving china and candle lamps were all custom-made in France. The chef works directly with local farmers for the freshest ingredients, and in addition to the à la carte menu, the restaurant offers tastings, petit tastings, plus vegetarian and vegan menus. French menu. Lunch, dinner. Closed Sunday; also first two weeks of August. Business casual attire. Reservations recommended. $$$

★★★L'ESCALE
500 Steamboat Road, Greenwich, 203-661-4600;
www.lescalerestaurant.com
This French-Mediterranean restaurant earns its stars by re-creating the Mediterranean on the North Atlantic shore with a stone fireplace and terra-cotta floors to warm the dining room and light-filtering thatched bamboo to shade the patio. The menu from Francois Kwaku-Dongo includes a salad of caramelized leeks and chanterelles; apple- and prune-paired foie gras; and crispy duck breast. The eatery has become quite a gathering place for locals and travelers alike, and it's no wonder why—L'Escale allows guests to sail to dinner and tie up their yachts at its waterfront dock. French, Mediterranean menu. Breakfast, lunch, dinner, Sunday brunch. Bar. Business casual attire. Reservations recommended. Valet parking. Outdoor seating. $$$

★★TERRA RISTORANTE ITALIANO
156 Greenwich Ave., Greenwich, 203-629-5222; www.terraofgreenwich.com
Italian menu. Lunch, dinner. Bar. Business casual attire. Reservations recommended. Outdoor seating. $$$

★★THAT LITTLE ITALIAN RESTAURANT
228-230 Mill St., Greenwich, 203-531-7500; www.greenwichtlir.com,
www.tlirgreenwich.com
Italian menu. Lunch, dinner. Closed Monday. Casual attire. Outdoor seating. $$

CONNECTICUT

★
★
★
★

★★★THOMAS HENKELMANN

420 Field Point Road, Greenwich, 203-869-7500;
www.thomashenkelmann.com

German-born, French-trained chef Thomas Henkelmann's eatery proffers clever takes on traditional French fare. The formal spot's lobster bisque is Henkelmann's specialty—a rich, creamy concoction full of sweet and savory flavors. Service is discreet and attentive, and well-cared-for gardens are ideal for an after dinner stroll. French menu. Breakfast, lunch, dinner. Closed Sunday; also two weeks in March. Bar. Jacket required. Reservations recommended. Valet parking. $$$$

GROTON

To the military minded, the town of Groton is synonymous with the submarine. It was here, in 1912, that the General Dynamics Corporation built the world's first diesel-powered sub. The first nuclear-powered one appeared here some four decades later. Today, the town hosts a U.S. naval base and several scientific research plants.

Information: Connecticut's Mystic & More, 470 Bank St., New London,
860-444-2206, 800-863-6569; www.town.groton.ct.us

WHAT TO SEE AND DO

FORT GRISWOLD BATTLEFIELD STATE PARK

57 Fort St., Groton, 860-445-1729;
www.ct.gov

The park includes a 135-foot monument to 88 Revolutionary soldiers slain by British troops under the command of Benedict Arnold. Park, daily. Monument and museum, Memorial Day-Labor Day: daily; Labor Day-Columbus Day: Saturday-Sunday.

HISTORIC SHIP *NAUTILUS* AND SUBMARINE *FORCE* MUSEUM

Naval Submarine Base New London, 1 Crystal Lake Road,
Groton, 860-694-3174, 800-343-0079;
www.ussnautilus.org

The permanent home of the *Nautilus*, the world's first nuclear-powered submarine. Self-guided and audio tours are available, as well as museum exhibits depicting history of the US Submarine *Force*. May-October: 9 a.m.-5 p.m.; November-April: 9 a.m.-4 p.m.; closed Tuesday year-round, closed Thanksgiving, Christmas Day and New Years' Day.

HOTEL

★★★MYSTIC MARRIOTT HOTEL AND SPA

625 North Road, Groton, 860-446-2600, 800-228-9290; www.marriott.com

Just outside the historic seafaring town of Mystic, this full-service hotel is a perfect base for exploring the Mystic Aquarium or the nearby Foxwoods and Mohegan Sun casinos. Guest rooms and suites are sophisticated and show off a continental flair. The centerpiece of the hotel is the Elizabeth Arden Red Door Spa, favored for its superior treatments and fine service. 285 rooms. High-speed Internet access. Two restaurants, bar. Airport transportation available. Pets not accepted. $$

RESTAURANTS
★★★OCTAGON
625 North Road, Groton, 860-326-0360;
www.waterfordgrouprestaurants.com
Located in the Mystic Marriott Hotel & Spa, this upscale steak house serves prime cuts in sleek surroundings. Filet mignon, New York strip steak and Kobe sirloin are on the menu as well as lighter choices like sesame-crusted tuna, seared salmon with Maryland lump crab and grilled swordfish. The wine list, winner of *Wine Spectator*'s Award of Excellence, features more than 200 varietals. Steak menu. Breakfast, dinner. Bar. Children's menu. Business casual attire. Reservations recommended. Valet parking. $$$

★★VINES
625 North Road, Groton, 860-446-2600,
www.waterfordgrouprestaurants.com
American menu. Lunch, dinner. Bar. Children's menu. Casual attire. Valet parking. $$

GUILFORD
Guilford was settled by a group of Puritans who followed the Reverend Henry Whitfield here from England. After repeated runs for political office, one of the residents, Samuel Hill, gave rise to the expression "run like Sam Hill."
Information: Chamber of Commerce, 63 Whitfield St., Guilford, 203-453-9677;
www.guilfordct.com

WHAT TO SEE AND DO
HENRY WHITFIELD STATE MUSEUM
248 Old Whitfield St., Guilford, 203-453-2457; www.whitfieldmuseum.com
This 1639 house is the oldest in the state. April-mid-December: Wednesday-Sunday 10 a.m.-4:30 p.m.

HYLAND HOUSE
84 Boston St., Guilford, 203-453-9477
Restored and furnished in 17th-century period, this 1660 house has an herb garden and guided tours. Early June-October: Tuesday-Sunday.

THOMAS GRISWOLD HOUSE MUSEUM
171 Boston St., Guilford, 203-453-3176
A fine example of a saltbox house, this 1775 home has period gardens and a restored working blacksmith shop. Early June-October: Tuesday-Sunday; winter by appointment.

HOTEL
★TOWER SUITES MOTEL
320 Boston Post Road, Guilford, 203-453-9069
14 rooms, all suites. $

CONNECTICUT

★
★
★
★
★

HARTFORD

Connecticut's capital city falls, appropriately enough, in the center of the state. Settled in 1633 on the region's eponymous river, Hartford has deep democratic roots. When Brit Sir Edmund Andros tried to seize the state's own declaration of independence, loyal citizen Joseph Wadsworth hid the charter in a hollow tree. The secret stashing place is still known as the Charter Oak, and Hartford still exhibits creative spirit. *The Hartford Courant*, founded in 1764, is the oldest continuously published newspaper in the United States. The daily regularly covers the city's booming insurance and education industries.

Information: Greater Hartford Convention & Visitors Bureau, 1 Civic Center Plaza, Hartford, 860-728-6789, 800-446-7811; www.enjoyhartford.com

WHAT TO SEE AND DO

BUTLER-MCCOOK HOMESTEAD AND MAIN STREET HISTORY CENTER

396 Main St., Hartford, 860-522-1806; www.ctlandmarks.org

This preserved house, occupied by four generations of one family (1782-1971), has possessions dating back 200 years, a collection of Victorian toys, Japanese armor and a Victorian garden. Wednesday-Sunday.

HARRIET BEECHER STOWE CENTER

77 Forest St., Hartford, 860-522-9258;
www.harrietbeecherstowecenter.org

The restored Victorian cottage of the author of *Uncle Tom's Cabin* contains original furniture and memorabilia. Tours. Monday-Saturday 9:30 a.m.-4:30 p.m., Sunday noon-4:30 p.m.

MARK TWAIN HOUSE

351 Farmington Ave., Hartford, 860-247-0998; www.marktwainhouse.org

Tom Sawyer, *Huckleberry Finn* and other books were published while Samuel Clemens (Mark Twain) lived in this three-story Victorian mansion featuring the decorative work of Charles Comfort Tiffany and the Associated Artists. Tours. May-October and December: daily; rest of year: Monday, Wednesday-Sunday.

MUSEUM OF CONNECTICUT HISTORY

Connecticut State Library, 231 Capitol Ave., Hartford, 860-757-6335

Exhibits include the Colt Collection of Firearms; Connecticut artifacts, including the original 1662 Royal Charter; and portraits of Connecticut's governors. The library features law, social sciences, history, genealogy collections and official state archives. Monday-Saturday.

NOAH WEBSTER FOUNDATION AND HISTORICAL SOCIETY

227 S. Main St., West Hartford, 860-521-5362; www.noahwebsterhouse.org

This 18th-century homestead was the birthplace of America's first lexicographer, writer of the *Blue-Backed Speller* and the *American Dictionary*. Thursday-Monday 1-4 p.m.

★
★
★
★
★

OLD STATE HOUSE

800 Main St., Hartford, 860-522-6766

The oldest state house in the nation was designed by Charles Bulfinch. The restored Senate chamber has a Gilbert Stuart portrait of George Washington. Monday-Saturday.

STATE CAPITOL

210 Capitol Ave., Hartford, 860-240-0222; www.cga.ct.gov

Take guided one-hour tours of the restored, gold-domed capitol building and the contemporary legislative office building. Monday-Friday.

UNIVERSITY OF HARTFORD

200 Bloomfield Ave., West Hartford, 860-768-4100; www.hartford.edu

An independent institution with 6,844 students on a 320-acre campus. Many free concerts, operas, lectures and art exhibits.

WADSWORTH ATHENEUM MUSEUM OF ART

600 Main St., Hartford, 860-278-2670; www.wadsworthatheneum.org

This is one of the nation's oldest continuously operating public art museums with more than 40,000 works of art spanning 5,000 years. Exhibits include 15th- to 20th-century paintings; American furniture; sculpture, porcelains; English and American silver, the Amistad Collection of African-American art; and changing contemporary exhibits. Wednesday-Sunday. Thursday and Saturday mornings. Free admission.

HOTELS

★★CROWNE PLAZA

50 Morgan St., Hartford, 860-549-2400, 877-227-6963;
www.crowneplaza.com

350 rooms. Restaurant, bar. Airport transportation available. **$**

★★★GOODWIN HOTEL

1 Haynes St., Hartford, 860-246-7500, 800-922-5006; www.goodwinhotel.com

This luxury hotel is among Hartford's best, and its downtown location across from the Civic Center makes it a popular choice with business travelers. Built in 1881 for business tycoon J. P. Morgan, the red brick Queen Anne-style building has rooms and suites with a masculine, clubby décor. The boys' club appeal extends to the Goodwin's two eateries. 124 rooms. Restaurant, bar. **$$**

★★HOLIDAY INN

363 Roberts St., East Hartford, 860-528-9611, 888-465-4329;
www.holiday-inn.com

130 rooms. Wireless Internet access. Restaurant, bar. **$**

★★★SHERATON HARTFORD HOTEL

100 E. River Drive, East Hartford, 860-528-9703, 888-530-9703; www.sheraton.com

215 rooms. Restaurant, bar. **$$**

CONNECTICUT

★
★
★
★

RESTAURANTS

★★BUTTERFLY

831 Farmington Ave., West Hartford, 860-236-2816

Chinese menu. Lunch, dinner. Sunday brunch. Bar. **$$**

★★★CARBONE'S

588 Franklin Ave., Hartford, 860-296-9646; www.carbonesct.com

Hearty Italian dishes and friendly service have kept Carbone's a longtime Hartford favorite. Need evidence? Take a look at the entrance walls, plastered with many autographed pictures of politicians, sports figures and other satisfied customers. Italian menu. Lunch, dinner. Closed Sunday. Bar. Casual attire. Reservations recommended. **$$$**

★HOT TOMATOES

1 Union Place, Hartford, 860-249-5100; www.hottomatos.net

American menu. Lunch, dinner, late-night. Bar. Casual attire. Outdoor seating. **$$**

★★★MAX DOWNTOWN

185 Asylum St., Hartford, 860-522-2530; www.maxrestaurantgroup.com

Lively and central, Max Downtown is a hit with staffers from the nearby Capitol Building. Many other city dwellers make the pilgrimage to the New American spot as well, eager to partake in its upscale atmosphere, extensive wine list and inventive cuisine. American menu. Lunch, dinner, late-night. Bar. Business casual attire. Reservations recommended. Valet parking. **$$$**

★★PEPPERCORN'S GRILL

357 Main St., Hartford, 860-547-1714; www.peppercornsrestaurant.com

Italian menu. Lunch, dinner, late-night. Closed Sunday; also one week in summer. Bar. Business casual attire. Reservations recommended. Valet parking. Outdoor seating. **$$$**

★RESTAURANT BRICCO

78 LaSalle Road, West Hartford, 860-233-0220; www.restaurantbricco.com

Italian, Mediterranean menu. Lunch, dinner. Children's menu. Outdoor seating. **$$**

LAKEVILLE

Like many of its New England neighbors, Lakeville played a key part in the American Revolution. The town's blast furnace—once owned by Ethan Allen—cast scores of guns used by soldiers to fight the British. In 1843, the furnace was torn down and the first knife manufacturing plant took its place. The Hotchkiss School is nearby.

Information: www.lakevillect.com

WHAT TO SEE AND DO

HOLLEY-WILLIAMS HOUSE

15 Millerton Road, Lakeville, 860-435-3878; www.ctvisit.com

The museum is full of 18th- and 19th-century history, including a 1768 iron-master's home and a Holley Manufacturing Company pocketknife exhibit from 1876. Mid-June-Labor Day: Saturday-Sunday and holiday afternoons; also by appointment.

SPECIAL EVENTS

MUSIC MOUNTAIN SUMMER MUSIC FESTIVAL
Music Mountain Road, Falls Village, 860-824-7126; www.musicmountain.org
Performances by well-known ensembles and guest artists; jazz series. Mid-June-early
September: Saturday-Sunday.

ROAD RACING CLASSIC
497 Lime Rock Road, Lakeville, 800-722-3577; www.limerock.com
The Mohegan Sun Grand Prix and NASCAR Busch North 200 events are held the
same weekend. Memorial Day weekend.

HOTELS

★★INN AT IRON MASTERS
229 N. Main St., Lakeville, 860-435-9844; www.innatironmasters.com
28 rooms. Restaurant, bar. **$**

★★★INTERLAKEN INN
74 Interlaken Road, Lakeville, 860-435-9878, 800-222-2909;
www.interlakeninn.com
This century-old inn has rooms furnished with antiques. There's an onsite spa and
restaurant. Activities include tennis, ping-pong and an outdoor heated pool. 80 rooms.
Restaurant. **$**

SPECIALTY LODGING

WAKE ROBIN INN
106 Sharon Road, Lakeville, 860-435-2000; www.wakerobininn.com
This stately inn has been in operation since 1914. Rooms are traditionally decorated,
some with canopied beds. 38 rooms. **$$**

LITCHFIELD
Home to the country's first law school, Litchfield sits on a plateau above the Naug-
atuck Valley. For the most part, the industrial revolution bypassed the quiet hamlet;
its most famous citizens include the Reverend Henry Ward Beecher and his sister,
Harriet Beecher Stowe, author of *Uncle Tom's Cabin*.
Information: Litchfield Hills Visitors Bureau, Litchfield, 860-567-4506;
www.litchfieldhills.com

WHAT TO SEE AND DO

HAIGHT-BROWN VINEYARD AND WINERY
29 Chestnut Hill Road, Litchfield, 800-577-9463
One of the few vineyards to grow vinifera-grapes in New England, Haight is Con-
necticut's first winery. Tours, tastings. Daily.

LITCHFIELD HISTORY MUSEUM
7 South St., Litchfield, 860-567-4501; www.litchfieldhistoricalsociety.org
Onsite is an outstanding collection of American art and artifacts from the 18th to 21st
centuries. Mid-April-November: Tuesday-Sunday.

CONNECTICUT

★
★
★
★
☆

TAPPING REEVE HOUSE

82 South St., Litchfield, 860-567-4501

A retrospective of 19th-century Litchfield through the lives of the students who attended the Litchfield Law School and the Litchfield Female Academy; graduates include Aaron Burr and John C. Calhoun. Mid-April-November: Tuesday-Sunday.

TOPSMEAD STATE FOREST

46 Chase Road, Litchfield, 860-567-5694;
www.ct.gov

This 511-acre forest includes an English Tudor mansion overlooking a 40-acre wildlife preserve. Second and fourth weekends of June-October.

HOTEL

★★★LITCHFIELD INN

432 Bantam Road, Litchfield, 860-567-4503, 800-499-3444;
www.litchfieldinnct.com

32 rooms. Complimentary continental breakfast. Restaurant, bar. **$**

RESTAURANTS

★SENOR PANCHOS

7 Village Green Drive, Litchfield, 860-567-3663;
www.senor-panchos.com

Mexican menu. Lunch, dinner. Casual attire. **$$**

★★VILLAGE RESTAURANT

25 West St., Litchfield, 860-567-8307

American menu. Lunch, dinner, Sunday brunch. Bar. Children's menu. **$$**

★★★WEST STREET GRILL

43 West St., Litchfield, 860-567-3885

Owner James O'shea has created the improbable: a trendy hotspot that appeals to both second-home New Yorkers and local residents. American menu. Lunch, dinner. Bar. Children's menu. Reservations recommended. **$$$**

MADISON

This beachfront central Connecticut town has a quaint main street lined with boutiques, coffee shops and bed and breakfasts.

Information: Chamber of Commerce, 22 Scotland Ave., Madison, 203-245-7394,
Tourism Office, 12 School St., Madison, 203-245-5659; www.madisonct.com

WHAT TO SEE AND DO

ALLIS-BUSHNELL HOUSE AND MUSEUM

853 Boston Post Road, Madison, 203-245-4567; www.museumsusa.org

Period rooms with four-corner fireplaces, doctor's office and equipment, costume exhibits and shipbuilding tools are all inside this 1785 house. May-October: Wednesday, Friday-Saturday, limited hours; other times by appointment.

HAMMONASSET BEACH STATE PARK

1288 Boston Post Road, Madison, 203-245-2785

This beach covers more than 900 acres and has a two-mile-long stretch on Long Island Sound. Saltwater swimming, scuba diving, fishing, boating, hiking, picnicking and camping are available.

HOTEL

★★MADISON BEACH HOTEL

94 W. Wharf Road, Madison, 203-245-1404; www.madisonbeachhotel.com

35 rooms. Closed January-February. Complimentary continental breakfast. Restaurant, bar. **$**

RESTAURANTS

★★★CAFÉ ALLEGRE

725 Boston Post Road, Madison, 203-245-7773; www.allegrecafe.com

Italian menu. Lunch, dinner. Closed Monday. Bar. Children's menu. Outdoor seating. **$$**

★★FRIENDS AND COMPANY

11 Boston Post Road, Madison, 203-245-0462

Seafood, steak menu. Lunch, dinner. Sunday brunch. Closed last Monday in June. Bar. Children's menu. **$$**

MANCHESTER

Locals brag their town is like a "city of village charm." They might be right: Manchester's 50,000 citizens live on streets out of another era, ones filled with leafy trees and restored 18th-century homes. The spot was once the silk capital of the Western world and is still a major manufacturing center.

Information: Greater Manchester Chamber of Commerce, 20 Hartford Road, Manchester, 860-646-2223; www.manchesterchamber.com

WHAT TO SEE AND DO

CHENEY HOMESTEAD

106 Hartford Road, Manchester, 860-647-9983; www.manchesterhistory.org

This is the birthplace of the brothers who launched the state's once-promising silk industry. Friday-Sunday.

CONNECTICUT FIREMEN'S HISTORICAL SOCIETY FIRE MUSEUM

230 Pine St., Manchester, 860-649-9436

Located in a 1901 firehouse, this museum has antique firefighting equipment and memorabilia, leather fire buckets, hoses, helmets, hand-pulled engines, a horse-drawn hose wagon, and old prints and lithographs. Mid-April-mid-November: Friday-Sunday.

HOTELS

★BEST VALUE INN-MANCHESTER

400 Tolland Turnpike, Manchester, 860-643-1555, 888-315-2378; www.bestvalueinn.com

32 rooms. **$**

CONNECTICUT

★CLARION HOTEL

191 Spencer St., Manchester, 860-643-5811, 800-992-4004;
www.clarionsuites.com

104 rooms, all suites. Complimentary full breakfast. Airport transportation available. **$**

RESTAURANTS

★★★CAVEY'S FRENCH RESTAURANT

45 E. Center St., Manchester, 860-643-2751

This family-run restaurant has been a Connecticut landmark since the 1930s. On the lower level of a two-story building (the upstairs holds the same family's Italian restaurant), Cavey's serves seasonal, contemporary French cuisine in a charming atmosphere. French menu. Dinner. Closed Sunday-Monday. Bar. **$$$**

★★★CAVEY'S ITALIAN RESTAURANT

45 E. Center St., Manchester, 860-643-2751

The Italian counterpart to Cavey's French Restaurant, this Italian eatery located above French, offers a menu of Northern Italian food. Dishes like veal piccata and chicken tetrazzini are served in an elegant dining room with the same personalized and friendly service you'll find downstairs. Italian menu. Dinner. Closed Sunday-Monday. Bar. **$$**

MYSTIC

The town of Mystic, a shipbuilding and whaling center from the 17th-19th centuries, sits on both sides of its eponymous river. Its name is derived from the Pequot, "Mistuket."

Information: Tourist Information Center, Olde Mystic Village,
860-536-1641; Connecticut's Mystic & More, 470 Bank St., New London,
860-444-2206, 800-863-6569; www.mysticcountry.com

WHAT TO SEE AND DO

DENISON HOMESTEAD

120 Pequotsepos Road, Mystic, 860-536-9248

This 1717 home is full of heirlooms from 11 generations of a single family. Guided tour. Mid-May-mid-October: Thursday-Monday afternoons; rest of year, by appointment.

MYSTIC AQUARIUM

55 Coogan Blvd., Mystic, 860-572-5955; www.mysticaquarium.org

The exhibits here feature more than 6,000 live specimens from around the world. Demonstrations with dolphins, sea lions, and the only whales in New England delight young and old alike, as does Seal Island, an outdoor exhibit of seals and sea lions in natural settings, and the penguin pavilion. The facility also includes Dr. Robert Ballard's Institute for Exploration, which is dedicated to searching the deep seas for lost ships. The museum's Challenge of the Deep exhibit allows patrons to use state-of-the-art technology to re-create the search for the *Titanic* or explore the biology of undersea ocean vents. Daily; hours vary by season.

MYSTIC SEAPORT
75 Greenmanville Ave., Mystic, 860-572-5315; www.visitmysticseaport.org
This 17-acre complex is the nation's largest maritime museum, dedicated to preservation of 19th-century oceanic history. Visitors may board the 1841 wooden whale ship *Charles W. Morgan*, square-rigged ship *Joseph Conrad*, or fishing schooner *L. A. Dunton*. The collections also include some 400 smaller vessels; a representative seaport community with historic homes and waterfront industries; a working shipyard, children's museum and planetarium. May-October: daily.

HOTELS
★COMFORT INN
48 Whitehall Ave., Mystic, 860-572-8531, 800-572-9339; www.comfortinn.com
120 rooms. Complimentary continental breakfast. Wireless Internet access. Free continental breakfast, coffee. Local calls, newspaper. $$

★★★HILTON MYSTIC
20 Coogan Blvd., Mystic, 860-572-0731, 800-774-1500; www.hilton.com
On a quiet side road near the noisy Olde Mystic Village, and just one block from Interstate 95 (I-95), this business-oriented hotel is all about location. Shopping outlets, the Seaport Museum and the aquarium are all nearby. Not into fighting through the tourist hoards? Stay inside and mellow out at the hotel pool. 183 rooms. Wireless Internet access. Restaurant, bar. Children's activity center. $$

★★★INN AT MYSTIC
3 Williams Ave., Mystic, 860-536-9604, 800-237-2415; www.innatmystic.com
This five-building property is the only Connecticut inn that overlooks both Mystic Harbor and Long Island Sound. Its five buildings are spread over 15 manicured acres, in the center of which sits the 1904 Classical Revival mansion where Lauren Bacall and Humphrey Bogart honeymooned. Inside, the rooms come with period furnishings, whirlpools, orchard views. 68 rooms. Restaurant, bar. $$

★★★WHALER'S INN
20 E. Main St., Mystic, 860-536-1506, 800-243-2588; www.whalersinnmystic.com
Homey, comfortable and located in the heart of historic Mystic, the Whaler's Inn is ideal for those seeking a very upscale New England bed and breakfast experience. The 1865 Colonial clapboard comes complete with a wide front porch and rocking chairs. Rooms are outfitted with Waverly wall coverings, four-poster beds and wing-back chairs, and the large bathrooms have pedestal sinks and whirlpool tubs. Each guest room has a breathtaking view of the scenic Mystic River; lucky guests will snag suites with private verandas. 49 rooms. Complimentary continental breakfast. Restaurant, bar. $$

CONNECTICUT

★
★
★
★
★

SPECIALTY LODGING

THE OLD MYSTIC INN

52 Main St., Old Mystic, 860-572-9422; www.oldmysticinn.com

Built in 1784, the Old Inn is set in a serene neighborhood a few miles from downtown Mystic. The rooms in the main house feature Early American décor, antiques, private baths and fireplaces. The carriage house has four guest rooms with private entrances. Eight rooms. Children over 15 years only. Complimentary full breakfast. **$$**

RESTAURANTS

★★★BRAVO BRAVO

20 E. Main St., Mystic, 860-536-3228; www.ckrestaurantgroup.com

This local favorite, located at the seaside Whaler's Inn, serves creative gourmet dishes. Thanks to floor-to-ceiling windows, the spacious dining room is bright and inviting. Italian menu. Lunch, dinner. Bar. Casual attire. Reservations recommended. **$$**

★★★FLOOD TIDE

3 Williams Avenue, Mystic, 860-536-8140, 800-237-2415; www.mysticinns.com

Complimentary hors d'oeuvres are served in the piano lounge at this waterfront restaurant. The gourmet dishes, Sunday brunch and harbor views are all worth the trip. American, Continental menu. Breakfast, lunch, dinner, Sunday brunch. Bar. Children's menu. Casual attire. Reservations recommended. Outdoor seating. **$$$**

★★GO FISH

Olde Mistick Village, Mystic, 860-536-2662

Seafood menu. Lunch, dinner. Bar. Casual attire. Reservations recommended. **$$**

★MYSTIC PIZZA

56 W. Main St., Mystic, 860-536-3700; www.mysticpizza.com

Pizza. Lunch, dinner. Casual attire. **$**

★★SEAMEN'S INNE

105 Greenmanville Ave., Mystic, 860-572-5303; www.seamensinne.com

American, seafood menu. Lunch, dinner. Bar. Children's menu. Casual attire. Reservations recommended. Outdoor seating. **$$**

NEW HAVEN

New Haven is an unlikely cultural center. Part gritty metropolis of 130,000, part educational mecca, the city has long struggled with its split personality. Much of the action revolves around Yale University, which hosts some 10,000 students and countless more employees. No doubt every Yalie knows the historical importance of his adopted city: It was here that Eli Whitney worked out the principles of mass production and where Revolutionary War hero Nathan Hale studied. Just 75 miles from New York City, New Haven is a park-filled industrial city on the rise.

Information: Greater New Haven Convention & Visitors Bureau,
169 Orange St., New Haven, 203-777-8550, 800-332-7829;
www.visitnewhaven.com, www.cityofnewhaven.com

CONNECTICUT

WHAT TO SEE AND DO

AMISTAD MEMORIAL

165 Church St., New Haven

This 14-foot bronze relief sculpture is a unique three-sided form that depicts a trio of significant episodes in the life of Joseph Cinque, one of 50 Africans kidnapped in Sierra Leone and slated for sale in Cuba in 1839. His ship was secretly rerouted to Long Island Sound, after which a fierce battle for the would-be slaves' freedom ensued in New Haven. Two years later, their victory was won.

EAST ROCK PARK

Orange and Cold Spring Streets, New Haven, 203-946-6086;
www.cityofnewhaven.com

The city's largest park includes the Pardee Rose Gardens, a bird sanctuary, hiking trails, athletic fields, tennis courts and picnic grounds. April-November: daily; rest of year: Saturday-Sunday and holidays.

FORT NATHAN HALE PARK AND BLACK ROCK FORT

36 Woodward Ave., New Haven, 203-946-8790; www.fort-nathan-hale.org

Federal guns kept British warships out of the harbor in 1812. Since then, Black Rock Fort has been restored and archaeological excavations are in progress. The Civil War-era Fort Nathan Hale has also been reconstructed. Both offer spectacular views of the harbor. Memorial Day-Labor Day: daily.

GROVE STREET CEMETERY

227 Grove St., New Haven, 203-787-1443; www.grovestreetcemetery.org

This was the first cemetery in the United States to be divided into family plots. Noah Webster, Charles Goodyear, Eli Whitney and many early settlers of the area are buried here.

LIGHTHOUSE POINT PARK

2 Lighthouse Point Road, New Haven, 203-946-8005; www.cityofnewhaven.com

The 82-acre park on Long Island Sound has an 1840 lighthouse, restored antique carousel, bird sanctuary, bathhouse, boat ramp and beach. Daily.

NEW HAVEN GREEN

Church and Elm Streets, New Haven
www.pps.org

In 1638, these 16 acres were laid out, making New Haven the first planned city in America. On the town common are three churches: United, Trinity Episcopal and Center Congregational. The latter is a masterpiece of American Georgian architecture.

PARDEE-MORRIS HOUSE

325 Lighthouse Road, New Haven, 203-562-4183

Built in 1750, burned by the British in 1779 and rebuilt in 1780, this house has American period furnishings and a kitchen garden. June-August: Saturday-Sunday.

CONNECTICUT

★
★
★
★
☆

PEABODY MUSEUM OF NATURAL HISTORY

170 Whitney Ave., New Haven, 203-432-5050

The museum has exhibits of mammals, invertebrate life, Plains and Connecticut Native Americans, meteorites, minerals, birds of Connecticut and several life-size dinosaurs, including a 60-foot-long brontosaurus reconstructed from original fossil material. Daily.

YALE UNIVERSITY

149 Elm St., New Haven, 203-432-2300; www.yale.edu

Founded by 10 Connecticut ministers and named for Elihu Yale, an early donor to the school, Yale is widely recognized as one of the best universities in the country. Walking tours are conducted daily by undergraduate students. Weekdays 10:30 a.m., 2 p.m.; Saturday-Sunday 1:30 p.m.

SPECIAL EVENTS

NEW HAVEN SYMPHONY ORCHESTRA

Woolsey Hall, College and Grove streets, New Haven, 203-776-1444

A series of concerts by leading artists. October-May.

YALE REPERTORY THEATER

1120 Chapel St., New Haven, 203-432-1234, 800-833-8134; www.yale.edu/yalerep

The Yale Repertory Theater prides itself on creating bold and passionate theatrical productions. The troupe often includes artistic leaders; four of the productions have won the Pulitzer Prize. Early October-mid-May.

HOTELS

★★COURTYARD BY MARRIOTT

30 Whalley Ave., New Haven, 203-777-6221, 800-228-9290; www.courtyard.com

160 rooms. Restaurant, bar. $

★★★OMNI NEW HAVEN HOTEL

155 Temple St., New Haven, 203-772-6664, 800-843-6664; www.omnihotels.com

This hotel is close to Yale University's campus, making it a popular choice for parents helping their kids move to college. After all the heavy lifting, the plush beds and feather pillows are heaven-sent. There's also a bar and restaurant in which to refuel. 305 rooms. Restaurant, bar. $$

SPECIALTY LODGING

THREE CHIMNEYS

1201 Chapel St., New Haven, 203-789-1201, 800-443-1554;
www.threechimneysinn.com

This lovely historic inn, built in the 1870s, is one block from Yale University. Guest rooms feature canopy beds with Edwardian bed drapes. 11 rooms. Complimentary full breakfast. $$

RESTAURANT

★INDOCHINE PAVILION

1180 Chapel St., New Haven, 203-865-5033

Vietnamese menu. Lunch, dinner. Closed Monday. Bar. $$

NEW LONDON

New London has one of the finest deep-water ports on the Atlantic coast. From the first days of the republic well into the 21st century, the small city has been a seagoing community. Whalers once amassed fortunes here, and townspeople still welcome ships of all kinds—submarines, cutters, yachts, cruisers—home. Today, the economy has veered somewhat onshore, to steel, medicine and high-tech product manufacturing plants.

Information: Connecticut's Mystic & More, 470 Bank St.,
New London, 860-444-2206, 800-863-6569; www.mysticcountry.com

WHAT TO SEE AND DO

EUGENE O'NEILL THEATER CENTER
305 Great Neck Road, Waterford, 860-443-5378; www.oneilltheatercenter.org
The complex includes the O'Neill Playwrights Conference, O'Neill Critics Institute, O'Neill Music Theater Conference, O'Neill Puppetry Conference and the National Theater Institute. There are staged readings of new plays and musicals during summer at the Barn Theater, Amphitheater and Instant Theater. June-August.

JOSHUA HEMPSTEAD HOUSE
11 Hempstead Court, New London, 860-443-7949; www.viamichelin.co.uk
This is the oldest house in the city. The Hempstead family diary details life in the house during colonial times. Mid-May-mid-October: Thursday-Sunday afternoons.

LYMAN ALLYN ART MUSEUM
625 Williams St., New London, 860-443-2545; www.lymanallyn.org
More than 15,000 works are on display; the collection includes Contemporary, Modern and Early American fine arts. Tuesday-Saturday 10 a.m.-5 p.m., Sunday 1-5 p.m. Closed Mondays and major holidays.

MONTE CRISTO COTTAGE
325 Pequot Ave., New London, 860-443-5378; www.oneilltheatercenter.org
The restored boyhood home of playwright and Nobel prize winner Eugene O'Neill. Mid-June-Labor Day: Tuesday-Saturday.

NATHANIEL HEMPSTEAD HOUSE
11 Hempstead Court, New London, 860-443-7949; www.baysider.com
One of the state's two surviving examples of mid-18th-century cut-stone architecture. Mid-May-mid-October: Thursday-Sunday afternoons.

OCEAN BEACH PARK
1225 Ocean Ave., New London, 800-510-7263; www.ocean-beach-park.com
Swim in the ocean or an Olympic-sized pool (with a waterslide). There's also a boardwalk, amusement arcade and mini-golf. Saturday before Memorial Day-Labor Day: daily.

CONNECTICUT

★
★
★
★

SHAW PERKINS MANSION

11 Blinman St., New London, 860-443-1209

The Naval headquarters for the state during the Revolutionary War is now a genealogical and historical library.

US COAST GUARD ACADEMY

31 Mohegan Ave., New London, 860-444-8444; www.cga.edu

The school houses 800 active cadets. The Visitors' Pavilion has a multimedia show (May-October daily); the museum includes the 295-foot-long ship *Eagle*. Friday-Sunday, when in port; limited hours.

SPECIAL EVENTS

CONNECTICUT STORYTELLING FESTIVAL

Connecticut College, 270 Mohegan Ave., New London, 860-439-2764;
www.connstorycenter.org

Nationally acclaimed artists lead readings, workshops and concerts. Late April.

SAILFEST

New London City Pier, Bank St., New London, 860-443-1879; www.sailfest.org

Arts and crafts and food vendors line the streets downtown while people of all ages browse, eat and enjoy the three stages of entertainment. The largest fireworks show on the East Coast takes place on Saturday night. One weekend in early July.

HOTEL

★★RADISSON HOTEL NEW LONDON

35 Governor Winthrop Blvd., New London,
860-443-7000, 888-201-1718; www.radisson.com

120 rooms. Restaurant, bar. Airport transportation available. $

NORWALK

Norwalk's growth was heavily influenced by Long Island Sound. The city evolved rapidly from an agricultural community to a major seaport, then to a manufacturing center known for high-fashion hats, corsets and clocks. The Sound still plays an important part in Norwalk's development, providing beauty, recreation and, of course, oysters.

Information: Coastal Fairfield County Convention & Visitors Bureau,
297 West Ave., Norwalk, 203-853-7770, 800-866-7925; www.coastalct.com

WHAT TO SEE AND DO

HISTORIC SOUTH NORWALK (SONO)

Washington and Water streets, South Norwalk, 800-866-7925;
www.visitfairfieldcountyct.com

The 19th-century waterfront neighborhood has historical buildings, unique shops art galleries and restaurants.

LOCKWOOD-MATHEWS MANSION MUSEUM

295 West Ave., Norwalk, 203-838-9799; www.lockwoodmathewsmansion.org

This 60-room Victorian mansion was built by financier LeGrand Lockwood and features a 42-foot-tall skylit rotunda, ornamented doors, carved marble and inlaid woodwork, period furnishings and a mechanical music exhibit. Mid-March-December: Wednesday-Sunday noon-4 p.m.; rest of year by appointment only.

MARITIME AQUARIUM AT NORWALK
10 N. Water St., Norwalk, 203-852-0700; www.maritimeaquarium.org
A hands-on maritime museum with a shark touch tank and a harbor seal pool, plus 125 species and an IMAX screen. Daily.

MILL HILL HISTORIC PARK
2 E. Wall St., Norwalk, 203-846-0525; www.geocities.com/Heartland/Trail/8030
The complex of historic Early American buildings includes the Town House Museum (circa 1835), Fitch House Law Office (circa 1740) and a schoolhouse (circa 1826). Memorial Day-Labor Day: Sunday 1-4 p.m.

SPECIAL EVENTS
INTERNATIONAL IN-WATER BOAT SHOW
Norwalk Cove Marina, 48 Calf Pasture Beach Road, Norwalk,
212-984-7000; www.boatshownorwalk.com
The show features more than 750 of the newest and most innovative performance boats, sailboats and sailing yachts. Guests at this waterside boat show can also try scuba diving, view a restored classic boat or grab a drink at the Sand Bar. Third weekend in September.

OYSTER FESTIVAL
Veteran's Park, Seaview Ave., East Norwalk, 800-866-7925;
www.visitfairfieldcountyct.com, www.seaport.org
Featuring appearances from tall ships and vintage oyster boats, this festival has regularly drawn 60,000 visitors a year since it began in 1978. More than 3,000 volunteers make the festival possible each year and many local nonprofit groups benefit. Weekend after Labor Day.

ROUND HILL HIGHLAND GAMES
Cranbury Park, Kensett Road, Norwalk, 800-866-7925; www.roundhill.org
A heritage celebration with Highland dancing, pipe bands, caber tossing, clan tents and Scottish and American food. Late June or early July.

SONO ARTS CELEBRATION
Washington and South Main Streets, South Norwalk,
203-866-7916; www.sonoarts.org
Juried crafts, kinetic sculpture race, entertainment, concessions and a block party make up this celebration in historic South Norwalk. First weekend in August.

HOTELS
★★DOUBLETREE CLUB HOTEL
789 Connecticut Ave., Norwalk, 203-853-3477, 800-222-8733; www.doubletree.com
268 rooms. Wireless Internet access. Restaurant, bar. $

CONNECTICUT

★
★
★
★
★

★★FOUR POINTS BY SHERATON

426 Main Ave., Norwalk, 203-849-9828, 800-329-7466; www.fourpoints.com

127 rooms. Restaurant, bar. Free high-speed Internet access. Fitness center. Indoor pool, outdoor pool. **$$**

★★★THE SILVERMINE TAVERN

194 Perry Ave., Norwalk, 203-847-4558; www.silverminetavern.com

This country inn was established in 1929, and it's still going strong with its white-picket-fence charm. Expect rooms outfitted with antiques and four-poster beds, plus hospitality from the staff that's as charming as the colonial decor. 10 rooms. Closed Tuesday, September-May. Complimentary continental breakfast. Restaurant, bar. Sunday brunch, lunch, dinner. **$$**

RESTAURANTS

★★★PASTA NOSTRA

116 Washington St., South Norwalk, 203-854-9700; www.pastanostra.com

Reservations are a must at this restaurant, which was a former pasta retail store. The highest quality ingredients go into the menu selections, and there is an extensive wine list to choose from. Italian menu. Dinner. Closed Sunday-Tuesday. Casual attire. Reservations recommended. **$$$**

★★SILVERMINE TAVERN

194 Perry Ave., Norwalk, 203-847-4558, 888-693-9967; www.silverminetavern.com

American menu. Lunch, dinner, late-night, Sunday brunch. Closed Tuesday; also Monday in January-April. Bar. Children's menu. Casual attire. Reservations recommended. Outdoor seating. **$$$**

NORWICH

Norwich was one of the first chartered cities in Connecticut and since the end of the 18th century, it has been a leader in area industrial development. The colony's first paper mill was opened here in 1766, and the first cut nails in America were Norwich-made in 1772. The city of nearly 40,000 is divided into three distinct sections: Norwichtown to the northwest; a business section near the Thames docks; and a central residential area that showcases many 19th-century homes.

Information: Connecticut's Mystic and More, 470 Bank St., New London, 860-444-2206, 800-863-6569; www.mysticcountry.com

WHAT TO SEE AND DO

INDIAN LEAP

Yantic and Sachem streets, Norwich, 860-886-4683

These falls were a favorite resort and outpost of the Mohegans. Legend has it that a band of Narragansetts, during the 1643 Battle of Great Plains, came upon the falls while fleeing the Mohegans (more popularly known as the Mohicans). Many were forced to jump off the cliffs and into the chasm below.

ROYAL MOHEGAN BURIAL GROUNDS

Sachem and Washington streets, Norwich, 860-862-6390; www.mohegan.nsn.us

The resting place of Uncas, chief of the Mohicans.

TANTAQUIDGEON INDIAN MUSEUM
1819 Norwich-New London Turnpike, Uncasville, 860-848-9145
Works of Mohegan and other New England tribes, past and present. May-November: Monday-Friday 10 a.m.-3 p.m.

SPECIAL EVENT
BLUE GRASS FESTIVAL
Strawberry Park, 42 Pierce Road, Preston, 860-886-1944, 888-794-7944;
www.strawberrypark.net
You can either come for the day or make reservations for a campsite and enjoy four days of bluegrass music. Past performers have included Rhonda Vincent, the Tim O'Brien Band and the Waybacks. Late May-early June.

HOTEL
★★★THE SPA AT NORWICH INN
607 W. Thames St., Norwich, 860-886-2401, 800-275-4772;
www.thespaatnorwichinn.com
From the outside, this property looks just like any other posh New England country inn. Step across the Norwich Inn's threshold, though, and you'll be transported to a very bucolic paradise. The property has 42 acres of grounds to roam, plus a 32-treatment-room spa. Offerings include the requisite massage and facials, but also more cutting-edge treatments like hydrotherapy and energy work. 65 rooms. Restaurant, bar. Golf. Fitness center, fitness guide. Outdoor pool, indoor pool. $

RESTAURANT
★★KENSINGTON
607 W Thames St., Norwich, 860-886-2401, 866-410-5942
American menu. Breakfast, lunch, dinner, Sunday brunch. Bar. Outdoor seating. $$$

OLD LYME
Lore has it that sea captains, flush from their huge hauls, once owned and occupied every Old Lyme house. The town's modern inhabitants are a more sophisticated (though no less loaded) lot. The sleepy village, with its restored manors and safe, tree-lined streets, has become a classier mini-Greenwich for summering New Yorkers. Artsy types come here for the local design scene; tourists flock here for the seaside vistas. Only a privileged few get to stay year-round.
Information: Connecticut's Mystic and More, 470 Bank St.,
New London, 860-444-2206, 800-863-6569; www.mysticcountry.com

WHAT TO SEE AND DO
FLORENCE GRISWOLD MUSEUM
96 Lyme St., Old Lyme, 860-434-5542; www.flogris.org
This stately late-Georgian mansion housed America's most celebrated art colony at the turn of the century. Paintings by Willard Metcalf, Childe Hassam and other artists are on display. Krieble Gallery: Tuesday-Saturday 10 a.m.-5 p.m., Sunday 1-5 p.m.; Chadwick Studio: mid-May-October.

CONNECTICUT

★★★★

HOTELS

★★★BEE AND THISTLE INN

100 Lyme St., Old Lyme, 860-434-1667, 800-622-4946;
www.beeandthistleinn.com

This 1756 inn is widely recognized by savvy travelers as one of the state's most romantic getaways. The antique-decorated rooms are cozy and clean, and the service is precise but never fawning. 11 rooms. Closed two weeks in January. Children over 12 years only. Restaurant, bar. Spa. Wireless Internet access. **$**

★★★OLD LYME INN

85 Lyme St., Old Lyme, 860-434-2600, 800-434-5352; www.oldlymeinn.com

Located in the town's historic district, this classic bed and breakfast is close to Essex, Mystic Seaport, Mystic Aquarium and several local art galleries. Most guests, however, choose to stay put in their sumptuous rooms or watch the sunset from a deep Adirondack chair on the sweeping front lawn. 13 rooms. Complimentary continental breakfast. Restaurant, bar. **$$**

RESTAURANTS

★★★BEE AND THISTLE INN

100 Lyme St., Old Lyme, 860-434-1667, 800-622-4046; www.beeandthistleinn.com

Romance is alive and well in the Bee and Thistle's white table-clothed main dining room. The formal, candlelit scene looks like something out of an Austen novel. But the food is all 21st-century—Chef Kristofer Rowe blends fresh produce with first-rate seafood and steak for hearty but arty meals. American menu. Breakfast, lunch, dinner, Sunday brunch. Bar. Closed two weeks in January. Complimentary continental breakfast. **$$$**

★★★OLD LYME INN

85 Lyme St, Old Lyme, 860-434-2600, 800-434-5352; www.oldlymeinn.com

The meat-heavy menu and clubhouse-like décor of the inn's grill room gives way to the dining room's more sophisticated appeal. The real draw here, though, are the mouth-watering homemade desserts like triple chocolate silk tower and "meltaway" chocolate cake. American menu. Lunch, dinner. brunch. Bar. **$$$**

OLD SAYBROOK

This shabby chic town at the mouth of the Connecticut River is full of magnificent second homes. Originally the site of Yale College, it's the third-oldest named community in the state.

Information: Chamber of Commerce, 146 Main St., Old Saybrook,
860-388-3266; Connecticut Valley Tourism Commission, 393 Main
St., Middletown, 860-347-0028; www.oldsaybrookct.com

WHAT TO SEE AND DO

FORT SAYBROOK MONUMENT PARK

Highway154, Saybrook Point, Old Saybrook, 860-395-3152;
www.oldsaybrookct.org

An 18-acre park with remains of Fort Saybrook, the state's first military fortification. Daily.

GENERAL WILLIAM HART HOUSE

350 Main St., Old Saybrook, 860-388-2622; oldsaybrook.com/history

The 1767 Georgian-style residence of well-to-do New England merchant and politician William Hart features eight corner fireplaces, one of which is decorated with Sadler and Green transfer-print tiles illustrating *Aesop's Fables*. Mid-June-Labor Day: Friday-Sunday 1-4 p.m.

SPECIAL EVENTS

ARTS AND CRAFTS SHOW

Town Green, Main St., Old Saybrook, 860-388-3266; www.oldsaybrookct.com

More than 200 artists and craftspersons. Last full weekend in July.

CHRISTMAS TORCHLIGHT PARADE

Main Street, Old Saybrook, 860-388-3266; www.connecticutblues.com

Forty fife and drum corps march down Main Street on the second Saturday in December.

HOTELS

★★★SAYBROOK POINT INN AND SPA

2 Bridge St., Old Saybrook, 860-395-2828, 800-243-0212;www.saybrook.com

Water views of Long Island Sound and the Connecticut River provide a postcard-perfect backdrop to this seaside getaway. Like many area inns, guest rooms here are replete with 18th-century period-style furnishings and accessories. 62 rooms. Restaurant, bar. Pool. Breakfast. Fitness center. Pets accepted. $$

★★★WATER'S EDGE RESORT AND CONFERENCE CENTER

1525 Boston Post Road, Westbrook, 860-399-5901, 800-222-5901;
www.watersedge-resort.com

Located on Long Island Sound, there's fun for the whole family at the Water's Edge Resort. Kids have their own activity center, but adults can also partake in myriad activities including softball, face painting, scavenger hunts, kite flying, football, horseshoes and volleyball. 32 rooms. Restaurant, bar. Children's activity center. Beach. Spa. $$

RESTAURANT

★★DOCK AND DINE

College St., Old Saybrook, 860-388-4665; www.dockdinect.com

Seafood, steak menu. Lunch, dinner. Closed Monday-Tuesday Mid-October-mid-April. Bar. Children's menu. $$

★
★
★
★
★

RIDGEFIELD

It's not exactly Paris, but this southwestern Connecticut town *does* have a rare Champs Elysées-style boulevard. Ninety-nine feet wide, the street is lined with trees and stately houses. It was here that, in 1777, a pretraitorous Benedict Arnold set up barricades and fought the Battle of Ridgefield.

Information: Chamber of Commerce, 9 Bailey Ave., Ridgefield,

203-438-5992, 800-386-1708; Housatonic Valley Tourism Commission,

30 Main St., Danbury, 203-743-0546, 800-841-4488;

www.ridgefieldchamber.org

WHAT TO SEE AND DO
ALDRICH CONTEMPORARY ART MUSEUM
258 Main St., Ridgefield, 203-438-4519; www.aldrichart.org
The museum has changing exhibits and a sculpture garden. Tuesday-Sunday noon-5 p.m.

KEELER TAVERN MUSEUM
132 Main St., Ridgefield, 203-438-5485; www.keelertavernmuseum.org
A restored 18th-century tavern, stagecoach stop and home that was once revolutionary patriot headquarters. A British cannonball is still embedded in the wall. Wednesday, Saturday-Sunday 1-4 p.m.

HOTELS
★★★THE ELMS INN
500 Main St., Ridgefield, 203-438-2541; www.elmsinn.com
Established in 1799, this is the oldest continuously run inn in the state. No creaky stairs and peeling paint here—the property has been lovingly restored and now boasts historic appeal (antique furnishings, old-world charm) and modern conveniences (wireless Internet access, dry cleaning). 23 rooms. Complimentary continental breakfast. Restaurant, bar. Wireless Internet access. Free weekday newspaper. $$$

★★★STONEHENGE INN
35 Stonehenge Road, Ridgefield, 203-438-6511; www.stonehengeinn-ct.com
Set on a swan-filled lake, Stonehenge looks like an old white rambling farmhouse. Inside rooms are elegant and service is top-notch. 16 rooms. Complimentary continental breakfast. Restaurant, bar. $$

★★★WEST LANE INN
22 West Lane, Ridgefield, 203-438-7323; www.westlaneinn.com
This country inn has comfortably decorated rooms with televisions, VCRs and refrigerators. Breakfast is served each morning in the breakfast room or on the terrace. 18 rooms. Complimentary continental breakfast. Restaurant. $$

RESTAURANTS
★★★THE ELMS
500 Main St., Ridgefield, 203-438-9206; www.elmsinn.com
A roaring fireplace sets the tone at the Elms, where award-wining chef Brendan Walsh creates standout "Yankee Cuisine." Dishes include pulled wild boar and lobster Shepherd's pie. American menu. Lunch, dinner. Closed Monday-Tuesday. Reservations recommended. Outdoor seating. $$

★★★STONEHENGE
35 Stonehenge Road, Ridgefield, 203-438-6511; www.stonehengeinn-ct.com
The restaurant's tranquil scenery and attentive service make it popular among locals and tourists alike. Menu highlights include pan-seared scallops and shrimp, and a buttery fresh steamed lobster. French menu. Dinner. Reservations recommended. Valet parking. $$$

★
★
★
★
★

★VENICE RESTAURANT
125 Cops Hill Road, Ridgefield, 203-438-3333
Italian menu. Lunch, dinner. Bar. Children's menu. Casual attire. Outdoor seating. **$$**

STAMFORD

Stamford is so close to New York, some label the growing city an out-of-state suburb. But while it does have several resident commuters, not all its professionals travel to Manhattan. More than 20 *Fortune* 500 companies are headquartered here, making Stamford a booming business town in its own right with pretty marinas and beaches on Long Island Sound.
Information: Chamber of Commerce, 733 Summer St., Stamford, 203-359-4761; www.stamfordchamber.com

WHAT TO SEE AND DO
BARTLETT ARBORETUM AND GARDENS
151 Brookdale Road, Stamford, 203-322-6971; www.bartlett.arboretum.uconn.edu
Collections of dwarf conifers, rhododendrons, azaleas, wildflowers, perennials and witches brooms are open to the public, as are ecology trails and the natural woodlands surrounding the gardens. Gardens daily 8:30 a.m.-sunset; visitors center Monday-Friday 8:30 a.m.-4:30 p.m.; greenhouse Monday-Friday 9:30 a.m.-11 a.m.

HOTELS
★★HOLIDAY INN
700 E. Main St., Stamford, 203-358-8400, 888-465-4329; www.holiday-inn.com
383 rooms. Wireless Internet access. Restaurant, bar. Indoor pool, outdoor pool. Pets accepted. Complimentary breakfast. Airport transportation available. Kids eat free. **$**

★★★SHERATON STAMFORD HOTEL
2701 Summer St., Stamford, 203-359-1300, 800-325-3535; www.sheraton.com/stamford
The Sheraton is 45 minutes from Manhattan, but most guests never make it into the city, preferring to explore Connecticut's fabled Gold Coast instead. Cream-colored walls, blue and white furnishings and lots of plants lend a coastal theme to the hotel. Pets are welcome here, thanks to the resort's "Love that Dog" program. 448 rooms. Wireless Internet access. Restaurant, bar. Airport transportation available. Fitness center. Business center. **$$$**

★★★STAMFORD MARRIOTT HOTEL & SPA
243 Tresser Blvd., Stamford, 203-357-9555, 800-732-9689; www.marriott.com
This hotel's biggest draw might be its prime location—right across the street from the Stamford Town Center Mall. If you can't find anything you like in those 130 stores, don't worry: The Marriott is also close to the Palace Theater, Playland Amusement Park, and the Whitney Museum. Bring your pooch and check in to the onsite spa (canines get their own Pet Travel Kits). 506 rooms. High-speed Internet access. Two restaurants, bar. Airport transportation available. **$$$**

★
★
★
★

★★★THE WESTIN STAMFORD

1 Stamford Place, Stamford, 203-967-2222, 888-627-7154;
www.westinstamford.com

The Westin's quick, efficient service and central downtown location make it a hit with business travelers. New York culture vultures often stop in on their way to soak in some New England charm. 462 rooms. Wireless Internet access. Restaurant, bar. **$$**

RESTAURANTS

★CRAB SHELL

46 Southfield Ave., Stamford, 203-967-7229; www.crabshell.com

American, seafood menu. Lunch, dinner. Bar. Casual attire. Outdoor seating. **$$**

★★FIO'S RISTORANTE

299 Long Ridge Road, Stamford, 203-964-9802;
www.fiosristorante.com

Italian menu. Lunch, dinner. Bar. Casual attire. Reservations recommended. Outdoor seating. **$$$**

★★IL FALCO

59 Broad St., Stamford, 203-327-0002; www.ilfalco.com

Italian menu. Lunch, dinner. Closed Sunday. Bar. Casual attire. Valet parking. **$$$**

★★LA BRETAGNE

2010 W. Main St., Stamford, 203-324-9539;
www.labretagnerestaurant.com

Continental, French menu. Lunch, dinner. Closed Sunday. Bar. Business casual attire. Reservations recommended. **$$$**

WASHINGTON

With its prime location in posh Litchfield County, Washington is a favorite destination for antiquing. Quaint churches and historic buildings dot the rolling landscape.
Information: www.washingtonct.org

WHAT TO SEE AND DO

HISTORICAL MUSEUM OF GUNN MEMORIAL LIBRARY

5 Wykeham Road, Washington, 860-868-7756; www.gunnlibrary.org

This house, built in 1781, contains collections and exhibits on area history, paintings, furnishings, gowns, dolls, dollhouses and tools. Thursday-Saturday 10 a.m.-4 p.m.; also by appointment.

INSTITUTE FOR AMERICAN INDIAN STUDIES

38 Curtis Road, Washington, 860-868-0518; www.birdstone.org

A museum of Northeastern Woodland Indian artifacts with a permanent exhibit hall. Exhibits include changing Native American art displays, a replicated indoor longhouse, an outdoor replicated Algonkian village and a simulated archaeological site. Monday-Saturday 10 a.m.-5 p.m., Sunday noon-5 p.m.

CONNECTICUT

★
★
★
★

HOTEL

★★★★★THE MAYFLOWER INN
118 Woodbury Road, Washington, 860-868-9466; www.mayflowerinn.com
This country inn, located less than two hours from New York City, evokes the feeling and quiet elegance of an English countryside hotel. Set on 28 acres of rolling hills, streams and lush gardens, guest rooms and suites are swathed in luxurious fabrics and feature four-poster, canopied beds, 18th- and 19th-century art and modern touches like flatscreen TVs. The dining room's seasonal menu makes good use of fresh, local ingredients with dishes such as organic Atlantic salmon with fresh veggies. The tap room has a more casual menu of Vermont cheddar-topped burgers and lemon-rosemary chicken. The sprawling spa is superlative. 24 rooms. Children over 12 years only. Wireless Internet access. Restaurant, bar. Spa. $$$$

SPA

★★★★★THE MAYFLOWER SPA
118 Woodbury Road, Washington, 860-868-9466; www.mayflowerinn.com
The 20,000-square-foot Mayflower Spa, opened in 2006, features the same classic design, elegant furnishing and quiet luxury of its namesake inn. Those who come for the full spa experience receive a pre-arrival consultation to create a schedule of pampering services and fitness and nutrition classes. The spa has an indoor heated pool and mosaic-domed whirlpool. A wide variety of classes range from kickboxing to ballet. Private yoga classes and Pilates studios are also available. And guests are provided with goodies including yoga mats, MP3 players, loungewear and even rain boots.

WESTPORT

Much like neighboring Greenwich, Westport is home to several uber-successful corporate warriors. It's also full of thriving small businesses and notable actors and illustrators. The town is surrounded by wooded hills and Long Island Sound beaches, making it a pretty, if pricey, place to live.
Information: Westport/Weston Chamber of Commerce, 60 Church Lane, Westport, 203-227-9234; www.westportchamber.com

SPECIAL EVENT

LEVITT PAVILION FOR THE PERFORMING ARTS
Jesup Green, 260 Compo Road South, Westport, 203-226-7600; www.levittpavilion.com
Nightly free outdoor performances of jazz, pop, rock, dance and children's music. Late June-early August.

HOTELS

★★★INN AT NATIONAL HALL
2 Post Road W, Westport, 203-221-1351, 800-628-4255; www.innatnationalhall.com
This distinctive inn sits along the banks of the Saugatuck River and is within walking distance to shops, galleries and the beach. Slightly quirky with an *Alice in Wonderland* feel, the 1873 Italianate property has only 15 individually designed rooms decorated in vibrant themes (the Watermelon Room, the Equestrian Suite). River views add an enchanting touch to the accommodations, and several chambers boast soaring two-story

CONNECTICUT

★
★
★
★

ceilings and crystal chandeliers. 15 rooms. Complimentary continental breakfast. Restaurant. Pool. Beach. Pets accepted. High-speed Internet access. Airport transportation available. $$$

★★WESTPORT INN

1595 Post Road East, Westport, 203-259-5236, 800-446-8997; www.westportinn.com
116 rooms. Restaurant, bar. Breakfast. Wireless Internet access. Fitness center. Heated indoor pool. Pet friendly. $

SPECIALTY LODGINGS

THE INN AT LONGSHORE

260 Compo Road South, Westport, 203-226-3316; www.innatlongshore.com
Rooms at this sprawling country inn are simply decorated with antique furnishings. 12 rooms. Complimentary continental breakfast. Restaurant, bar. $

RESTAURANTS

★★★COBB'S MILL INN

12 Old Mill Road, Weston, 203-227-7221, 800-640-9365; www.cobbsmillinn.com
At the Cobb's Mill Inn, excellent service merges with an elegant, historic ambience. The cuisine is beautifully presented, and the setting is a rustic, cozy barn. Seafood, steak menu. Lunch, dinner. Bar. Valet parking. Brunch. $$$

★★NISTICO'S RED BARN

292 Wilton Road, Westport, 203-222-9549; www.redbarnrestaurant.com
American menu. Lunch, dinner, brunch. Children's menu. Valet parking. Outdoor seating. $$$

★
★★
★★
★★
★

WETHERSFIELD

Wethersfield, "the most ancient town in Connecticut," has a rich heritage. Settled by a group of Massachusetts colonists, it became the commercial center of the Connecticut River communities and an important post in the American colonies-West Indies trade route. Agriculture, especially corn, rye and red onion, was Wethersfield's main industry. During the American Revolution, notable figures such as George Washington and Count de Rochambeau came to Wethersfield to craft war plans.

Information: Wethersfield Historical Society, 150 Main St., Wethersfield, 860-529-7656; www.wethhist.org

WHAT TO SEE AND DO

BUTTOLPH-WILLIAMS HOUSE

249 Broad St., Wethersfield, 860-529-0460
This restored 1700 building contains a fine collection of pewter, delft, fabrics, period furniture. May-October: Wednesday-Monday, limited hours.

DINOSAUR STATE PARK

400 West St., Rocky Hill, 860-529-8423; www.dinosaurstatepark.org
While excavating the site of a new building, construction crews discovered a stone slab bearing three-toed tracks of dinosaurs; eventually, more than 2,000 prints were unearthed. The building project was cancelled and the 65-acre area was designated a

state park. Visitors can examine the crisscrossing tracks and view a skeletal cast and life-size models of the area's prehistoric inhabitants. Tuesday-Sunday.

HURLBURT-DUNHAM HOUSE
150 Main St., Wethersfield, 860-529-7656; www.wethhist.org/sites.html
A Georgian house updated in Italianate style. Rich in decoration, it includes original Rococo Revival wallpapers, painted ceilings and a varied collection of furniture. Mid-March-mid-May and mid-October-December 25: Saturday-Sunday.

WEBB-DEANE-STEVENS MUSEUM
211 Main St., Wethersfield, 860-529-0612; www.webb-deane-stevens.org
The museum consists of three 18th-century houses that stand at the center of old Wethersfield: the Joseph Webb house, the Silas Deane house and the Isaac Stevens house. They have been restored and reflect the different lives of their owners—a merchant, a diplomat and a tradesman. May-October: Wednesday-Monday; rest of year: Saturday-Sunday.

HOTEL
★BEST WESTERN CAMELOT INN
1330 Silas Deane Highway, Wethersfield, 860-563-2311,
888-563-3930; www.bestwestern.com
112 rooms. Complimentary continental breakfast. Bar. Fitness center. Pets accepted. Pool, whirlpool. High-speed Internet access. $

WINDSOR LOCKS
Located on the Connecticut River, this town is home to Bradley International Airport.
Information: Chamber of Commerce, Windsor Locks, 860-623-9319; www.wmch.com

WHAT TO SEE AND DO
NEW ENGLAND AIR MUSEUM
36 Perimeter Road, Windsor Locks, 860-623-3305; www.neam.org
One of the largest and most comprehensive collections of aircraft and aeronautical memorabilia in the world is located right next to Bradley International Airport. More than 80 aircraft, including bombers, fighters, helicopters and gliders, are on display; some date back to 1909. There's also a jet fighter cockpit simulator. Daily.

NODEN-REED HOUSE & BARN
58 West St., Windsor Locks, 860-627-9212
Situated in a 19th-century house and a barn are an antique sleigh bed, taffeta evening dress, wedding dress, antique quilts, kitchen utensils and newspapers and periodicals from the 1800s. May-October: Sunday afternoons.

OLD NEWGATE PRISON
115 Newgate Road, East Granby, 860-653-3563; www.eastgranby.com
Here, a 1707 copper mine was converted to a Revolutionary prison for Tories. It then became a state prison. Check out self-guided tour of underground caverns where the prisoners once lived. Mid-May-October: Wednesday-Sunday. 10 a.m.-4:30 p.m.

CONNECTICUT

HOTELS

★★DOUBLETREE HOTEL

16 Ella Grasso Turnpike, Windsor Locks, 860-627-5171, 800-222-8733;
www.doubletree.com

200 rooms. Restaurant, bar. Airport transportation available. Fitness center. Pets accepted. Pool, whirlpool. High-speed Internet accepted. Business center. **$**

★HOMEWOOD SUITES

65 Ella Grasso Turnpike, Windsor Locks, 860-627-8463, 800-225-5466;
www.homewoodsuites.com

132 rooms, all suites. Complimentary continental breakfast. Airport transportation available. Fitness center. Pets accepted. Pool, whirlpool. High-speed Internet access. Free local calls. Business center. **$**

★★★SHERATON BRADLEY AIRPORT HOTEL

1 Bradley International Airport, Windsor Locks, 860-627-5311, 877-422-5311;
www.sheraton.com/bradleyairport

This hotel is well-situated near Bradley Airport, and short drive south brings you to Hartford. Guest rooms are comfortable affairs, with the Sheraton's signature Sweet Sleeper beds and soft, warm duvets. Room amenities include parking on the premises and a computer work station. 237 rooms. Restaurant, bar. Fitness center. Indoor pool, whirlpool. High-speed Internet access. Pets accepted. Business center. **$**

46

CONNECTICUT

★
★
★
★
★

MAINE

MAYBE IT'S THE FLAT YANKEE TWANG OR THE SALTY SEA AIR. WHATEVER IT IS, THERE IS something about Maine. With the highest tides in the country and a temperature that ranges from -46 F to 105 F, Maine is a popular state to visit year-round. There are 6,000 lakes and ponds and 3,500 miles of seacoast (though the water can be a bit chilly, with temperatures steady in summer in the 50s).

In 1604, St. Croix Island became Maine's first settlement, but it only lasted one winter. Another early settlement was established near Pemaquid Point, but it was the short-lived Popham Colony, at the mouth of the Kennebec River, that built America's first transatlantic trader in 1607, called the *Virginia*. Maine was a part of Massachusetts until 1820, when it was officially admitted to the Union.

Today, Maine is a vast playground of natural beauty, populated (in some places sparsely) by hearty Mainers who earn their stripes by surviving the long, dark winters. Most of Maine's 17.6 million acres of forest are open for public recreational use, including more than 580,000 acres owned by the state. Acadia National Park is one of the nation's wildest and most beautiful areas, now filled with a resurgent bald eagle population. Other wildlife can easily be seen in Maine, from the large numbers of seals and porpoises that swim in the waters off Penobscot Bay in summer to the pods of migratory whales that pass through each year.

In summer, the state swells with visitors who come to feast on lobster, sail the rugged, rocky coast, poke through antique shops in achingly quaint towns or even take a plunge in the perennially chilly coastal waters. Celebrities and the merely shockingly wealthy—including Martha Stewart, the Bush family, Stockard Channing, John Travolta and Stephen King—keep compounds here in places like Kennebunkport and Bar Harbor and occasionally add a dash of glamour to what is typically a humble, down-to-earth population.

Of course, fall rivals summer for the most popular time to visit New England's largest state and that's because of the resplendent display of autumn leaves the landscape produces each year. Tourists who come (in droves) during this time are called "leaf-peepers." The state's inns, restaurants and roads are usually packed to capacity in September and October.

Local residents muddle through the summer and autumn crowds and dream of quiet, snowy winters, when they have the charms of this great state (mostly) to themselves again.

Information: www.visitmaine.com

FUN FACTS

Nearly 90% of the nation's lobster supply is caught off the coast of Maine.

Maine has more than 5,000 miles of coastline—more than California.

Maine grows more blueberries than any other state.

ACADIA NATIONAL PARK

The rocky coastline and thick woodlands filled with wildlife make Acadia National Park a favorite spot to visit in Maine. The park takes up almost half of Mount Desert Island and has smaller areas on Isle au Haut, Little Cranberry Island, Baker Island, Little Moose Island and part of the mainland at Schoodic Point. Created by the force of glaciers, the coastal area has countless valleys, lakes and mountains.

Although small compared with other national parks, Acadia is one of the most visited parks in the country and the only national park in the northeastern United States. A 27-mile-loop road connects the park's eastern sights on Mount Desert Island, and ferry services take travelers to some of the smaller islands. Visitors can explore 1,530-foot Cadillac Mountain, the highest point on the Atlantic Coast of the United States, watch waves crash against Thunder Hole, or swim in the ocean at various coastal beaches. A road to the summit of Cadillac provides views of Frenchman, Blue Hill and Penobscot bays.

Mount Desert Island was founded by the French explorer Samuel de Champlain in 1604. Shortly thereafter, French Jesuit missionaries settled there until driven off by an armed vessel from Virginia. This was the first act of overt warfare between France and England for control of North America. Until 1713, the island was a part of French Acadia and it wasn't until after the Revolutionary War that it was officially settled. In 1916, a portion of the area was proclaimed Sieur de Monts National Monument. It was changed to Lafayette National Park in 1919, and finally, in 1929, it was enlarged and renamed Acadia National Park.

Like all national parks, Acadia is a wildlife sanctuary, where bald eagles are thriving. Fir, pine, spruce, many hardwoods and hundreds of varieties of wildflowers flourish. There are more than 120 miles of trails, and park rangers take visitors on various walks and cruises, pointing out and explaining the natural, cultural and historical features of the park. Forty-five miles of carriage roads offer bicyclists scenic rides through Acadia. Copies of ranger-led programs and trail maps are available at the visitor center.

There is saltwater swimming at Sand Beach and freshwater swimming at Echo Lake. Snowmobiles are allowed in some areas, and cross-country skiing is available. Most facilities are open Memorial Day-September. Portions of the park are open year-round, and the picnic grounds are open May-October. Limited camping is available at two park campgrounds: Blackwoods, open year-round, requires reservations from mid-June-mid-September; and Seawall, open late May-late September, is on a first-come, first-served basis. The park headquarters, 2½ miles west of Bar Harbor on Highway 233, provides visitor information.

AUGUSTA

Augusta, the capital of Maine, was settled in 1628 when settlers from Plymouth established a trading post on the site of Cushnoc, a Native American village. Soon after, in 1754, Fort Western was built to protect settlers against Native American raids, and from that, the settlement grew. Located 39 miles from the sea, Augusta is at the head of navigation on the Kennebec River.

Information: Kennebec Valley Chamber of Commerce,
21 University Drive, 207-623-4559; www.augustamaine.com

WHAT TO SEE AND DO

BLAINE HOUSE

State and Capitol streets, Augusta, 207-287-2301;
www.maine.gov/museum/collections/index.html

This is the 1833 house of James G. Blaine, Speaker of the U.S. House of Representatives and an 1884 presidential candidate. Since 1919, this 28-room house has been the official residence of Maine's governors. Originally built in Federal-style, it was remodeled several times and today appears semi-colonial. Tours available. Tuesday-Thursday, limited hours.

MAINE STATE MUSEUM

83 State House Station, Augusta, 207-287-2301; www.state.me.us/museum

Exhibits of Maine's natural environment, prehistory, social history and manufacturing heritage. Daily Monday-Friday 9 a.m.-5 p.m., Saturday 10 a.m.-4 p.m., Sunday closed.

OLD FORT WESTERN

City Center Plaza, 16 Cony St., Augusta, 207-626-2385; www.oldfortwestern.org

Fort complex built in 1754 by Boston merchants; main house and reproduction blockhouse, watch boxes and palisade. Costumed staff interprets 18th-century life on the Kennebec River. Memorial Day-Labor Day, daily; after Labor Day-Columbus Day, Saturday-Sunday, limited hours.

STATE HOUSE

83 State House Station, Augusta, 207-287-2301

The original design for this impressive building was by Charles Bulfinch (architect of the Massachusetts State House), and dates back to the early 1800s. Remodeled and enlarged in 1910, it rises majestically above Capitol Park and the Kennebec River. On its 185-foot dome is a statue, designed by W. Clark Noble, of a classically robed woman bearing a pine bough torch. Monday-Friday.

HOTELS

★★★BEST WESTERN SENATOR INN & SPA

284 Western Ave., Augusta, 207-622-5804, 877-772-2224; www.senatorinn.com

This hotel is the perfect jumping-off point for exploring Acadia or Maine's western mountains. Or Stay put and enjoy the colonial charm of the rooms, the relaxing spa (complete with its own Jurlique store) or the American cuisine at the restaurant Cloud 9. 125 rooms. Pets accepted, some restrictions; fee. Complimentary full breakfast. Wireless Internet access. Restaurant, bar. Children's activity center. Fitness room. Spa. Pool, whirlpool. $$

49

MAINE

★
★
★
★

★COMFORT INN

281 Civic Center Drive, Augusta, 207-623-1000, 800-808-1188; www.comfortinn.com

99 rooms. Pets accepted. Complimentary continental breakfast. Restaurant, bar. Fitness room. Indoor pool, whirlpool. Complimentary Wireless Internet access. **$**

★QUALTIY INN & SUITES

65 Whitten Road, Augusta, 207-622-3776, 800-237-8466; www.augustaqualityinn.com

58 rooms. Complimentary continental breakfast. Fitness center. Outdoor pool. **$**

SPECIALTY LODGING
WINGS HILL INN

9 Dry Point Drive, Rome, 207-495-2400, 866-495-2400; www.wingshillinn.com

Renovated farmhouse built in 1800. Eight rooms. Complimentary full breakfast. **$**

BAILEY ISLAND

Located at the end of Highway 24, along the northern shore of Casco Bay, Bailey Island is the most popular of the 365 Calendar Islands. Together with Orr's Island—to which it's connected by a cribstone bridge—Bailey is a resort and fishing center. Originally called "New waggin" by an early trader from Kittery, Bailey Island was renamed after Deacon Timothy Bailey of Massachusetts, who banished early settlers and claimed the land for himself. Bailey Island and Orr's Island partially enclose an arm of Casco Bay called Harpswell Sound—the locale of John Whittier's poem "The Dead Ship of Harpswell" and of Harriet Beecher Stowe's "Pearl of Orr's Island."

Information: Chamber of Commerce of the Bath-Brunswick Region,
59 Pleasant St., Brunswick, 207-725-8797; www.midcoastmaine.com

★
★
★
★
★

WHAT TO SEE AND DO
GIANT STAIRCASE

Ocean Street, off Route 24

Natural rock formation dropping 200 feet in steps to ocean. Scenic overlook area.

SPECIALTY LODGING
LOG CABIN ISLAND INN

5 Log Cabin Lane, Bailey Island, 207-833-5546; www.logcabin-maine.com

Eight rooms. Log cabin; panoramic view of bay. Closed November-March. Complimentary full breakfast. Restaurant. Pool. **$**

RESTAURANT
★COOK'S LOBSTER HOUSE

Garrison Cove Road, Bailey Island, 207-833-2818; cookslobster.com

Seafood menu. Lunch, dinner. Bar. Children's menu. Outdoor seating. Dockage. **$$$**

BANGOR

In 1604, Samuel de Champlain sailed up the Penobscot River to what is now Bangor and reported that the area was "most pleasant and agreeable," the hunting good and the oak trees impressive. Started as a harbor town, Bangor turned to lumber when the railroads picked up much of the shipping business. In 1842, it became the second-largest lumber port in the country.

Bangor received its name by mistake. An early settler, Reverend Seth Noble, was sent to register the new town under its chosen name of Sunbury. When officials asked Noble for the name, he thought they were asking him for the name of a tune he was humming and he replied "Bangor." Today, the city is the third largest in Maine and is a trading and distribution center.

Information: Bangor Convention and Visitors Bureau, 40 Harlow St., Bangor, 207-947-5205; www.bangorcvb.org

WHAT TO SEE AND DO
BANGOR MUSEUM AND CENTER FOR HISTORY
159 Union St., Bangor, 207-942-1900
Features exhibits of regional artifacts and the Quipus collection of historic clothing. Tuesday-Saturday.

COLE LAND TRANSPORTATION MUSEUM
405 Perry Road, Bangor, 207-990-3600; www.colemuseum.org
The Cole Museum showcases the history of transportation in the American Northeast. The museum houses one of the largest collections of snow removal equipment found in one place anywhere in the country, as well as a cache of military vehicles. A great place to take children, this museum has more than 20,000 visitors go through its turnstiles each year to see the permanent collection of local railroad pieces, and cars and trucks, uniquely designed to traverse the streets of Bangor. Historic photographs of Maine are also on display. May-mid-November, daily 9 a.m.-5 p.m.

MONUMENT TO PAUL BUNYAN
Bass Park, Main Street, Bangor
A 31-foot-tall statue commemorates the legendary lumberjack.

HOTELS
★FAIRFIELD INN
300 Odlin Road, Bangor, 207-990-0001, 800-228-2800; www.fairfieldinn.com
153 rooms. Complimentary continental breakfast. Fitness room. Indoor pool, whirlpool. Complimentary onsite parking. High-speed Internet access. **$**

★★HOLIDAY INN
404 Odlin Road, Bangor, 207-947-0101, 800-799-8651; www.holiday-inn.com
123 rooms. Pets accepted, some restrictions. Restaurant, bar. Outdoor pool, indoor pool. Airport transportation available. High-speed Internet access. **$**

SPECIALTY LODGING
THE LUCERNE INN
2517 Main Road, Dedham, 207-843-5123, 800-325-5123; www.lucerneinn.com
This is a colonial-style farmhouse with a connecting stable; it was established as an inn in 1814. 31 rooms. Complimentary continental breakfast. Restaurant. Outdoor pool. **$$**

RESTAURANT
★CAPTAIN NICK'S SEAFOOD HOUSE
1165 Union St., Bangor, 207-942-6444
Seafood menu. Lunch, dinner. Bar. Children's menu. Casual attire. **$$**

51

MAINE

★
★
★
★
☆

BAR HARBOR

Bar Harbor, the largest village on Mount Desert Island, has a summer population of more than 20,000 and is headquarters for the surrounding summer resort area. The island, which includes most of Acadia National Park, is mainly rugged granite, with many bays and inlets for sailing. In the mid-1800s, socially prominent figures, including publisher Joseph Pulitzer, had elaborate summer cottages built on the island. However, prosperity ended with the Great Depression, World War II and the Great Fire of 1947, which destroyed many of the estates and scorched more than 17,000 acres. As a result, instead of just evergreens, the forests in the area now have younger, more varied trees bearing red, yellow and orange leaves in fall.

Information: Chamber of Commerce, 93, Cottage St., 207-288-5103;
www.barharborinfo.com

WHAT TO SEE AND DO

ABBE MUSEUM

26 Mount Desert St., Bar Harbor, 207-288-3519; www.abbemuseum.org

This museum holds an extensive collection of Native American artifacts. The original location in Acadia National Park (open Memorial Day-mid-October) now houses exhibits on the archaeology of Maine and the history of the Abbe. Daily 9 a.m.-6 p.m.; closed January.

BAR HARBOR HISTORICAL SOCIETY MUSEUM

33 Ledgelawn Ave., Bar Harbor, 207-288-0000; www.barharborhistorical.org

Collection of early photographs of hotels, summer cottages and Green Mountain cog railroad; hotel registers from the early to late 1800s; maps, scrapbook of the 1947 fire. Mid-June-October, Monday-Saturday 1-4 p.m.; closed Sundays and holidays.

BAR HARBOR WHALE WATCH COMPANY

1 West St., Bar Harbor, 207-288-2386, 888-533-9253; www.whalesrus.com

Offers a variety of cruises aboard catamarans *Friendship V* or *Helen H* to view whales, seal, puffin, osprey and more. Also offers nature cruises and lobster and seal-watching. Cruises vary in length and destination. May-October daily. Depart from Bluenose Ferry Terminal.

FERRY SERVICE TO YARMOUTH, NOVA SCOTIA

121 Edens St., Bar Harbor, 207-288-3395; www.catferry.com

Passenger and car carrier *Cat Ferry* makes three-hour trips.

THE JACKSON LABORATORY

600 Main St., Bar Harbor, 207-288-6000; www.jax.org

An internationally known mammalian genetics laboratory conducting research relevant to cancer, diabetes, AIDS, heart disease, blood disorders, birth defects, aging, and normal growth and development. Audiovisual and lecture programs. Early June-late August.

MAINE

★
★★
★★
★

LOBSTER HATCHERY

1351 State Highway 3, Bar Harbor, 207-244-7330; www.theoceanarium.com

Young lobsters are hatched from eggs to ½ inch in length and then returned to the ocean to supplement the supply; guides narrate process. Mid-May-late October, Monday-Saturday.

HOTELS

★ACADIA INN

98 Eden St., Bar Harbor, 207-288-3500, 800-638-3636; www.acadiainn.com

95 rooms. Closed mid-November-March. Complimentary continental breakfast. Outdoor pool, whirlpool. Wireless Internet access. **$$**

★★★BAR HARBOR HOTEL-BLUENOSE INN

90 Eden St., Bar Harbor, 207-288-3348, 800-445-4077; www.bluenoseinn.com

From its hilltop location on Mount Desert Island, this hotel offers scenic views of Frenchman Bay. Explore nearby Acadia National Park or walk down to the dock and catch the *Cat Ferry* for a day trip to Yarmouth, Nova Scotia. The guest rooms feature traditional four-poster beds and balconies and include mini-refrigerators, CD and DVD players and bathrobes. Enjoy gourmet dining in the Rose Garden Restaurant. 98 rooms. Closed November-mid-April. Wireless Internet access. Restaurant, bar. Fitness room. Pool, whirlpool. Business center. **$$**

★★BAR HARBOR INN

Newport Drive, Bar Harbor, 207-288-3351, 800-248-3351; www.barharborinn.com

153 rooms. Pets accepted, some restrictions; fee. Complimentary continental breakfast. Restaurant, bar. Fitness room. Pool. Beach access. Wireless Internet access. **$$**

★BAR HARBOR MOTEL

100 Eden St., Bar Harbor, 207-288-3453, 800-388-3453; www.barharbormotel.com

70 rooms. Closed mid-October-mid-May. Pool. **$**

★★★THE BAYVIEW

111 Eden St., Bar Harbor, 207-288-5861, 800-356-3585; www.thebayviewbarharbor.com

Located directly on the water, this 8-acre inn is within five minutes of the town's center, but still offers a private setting. There are three buildings, including condos for guests on longer stays. Guest rooms are spacious and feature French doors which lead to wide, private decks overlooking the water. Luxurious furnishings, including four-poster beds, inlaid wood tables and armoires provide a residential feel. 26 rooms. Complimentary full breakfast. Wireless Internet access. Fitness room. Tennis. Airport transportation available. Business center. Closed November-mid-May. **$$**

★BEST WESTERN INN

452 Route 3, Bar Harbor, 207-288-5823, 800-937-8376; www.bestwesterninn.com

70 rooms. Closed November-April. Pets accepted, some restrictions. Complimentary continental breakfast. Pool. High-speed Internet access. **$$**

★
★
★
★
★

★★HARBORSIDE HOTEL & MARINA

55 West St., Bar Harbor, 207-288-5033, 800-328-5033; www.theharborsidehotel.com
187 rooms. Closed November-March. Complimentary continental breakfast. Restaurant, bar. Fitness room. Pool, whirlpool. $$

★★HOLIDAY INN

123 Eden St., Bar Harbor, 207-288-9723, 800-234-6835; www.barharborregency.com
280 rooms. Closed November-April. Wireless Internet access. Three restaurants, two bars. Fitness room. Pool, whirlpool. Tennis. $$

★★QUALITY INN

40 Kebo St., Bar Harbor, 207-288-5403, 800-282-5403; www.qualityinn.com
75 rooms. Closed November-mid-April. Pool, whirlpool. Bar. Golf. $$

★WONDER VIEW INN

50 Eden St., Bar Harbor, 207-288-3358, 888-439-8439; www.wonderviewinn.com
79 rooms. Closed November-April. Pets accepted, some restrictions; fee. Restaurant, bar. Pool. $$

SPECIALTY LODGINGS

BALANCE ROCK INN

21 Albert Meadow, Bar Harbor, 207-288-2610, 800-753-0494;
www.balancerockinn.com
23 rooms. Closed late October-early May. Pets accepted; fee. Complimentary full breakfast. Internet access. Whirlpool. $$

BAR HARBOR GRAND HOTEL

269 Main St., Bar Harbor, 207-288-5226, 888-766-2529; www.barharborgrand.com
70 rooms. Complimentary continental breakfast. Closed December-April. High-speed Internet access. Fitness room. $

BLACK FRIAR INN

10 Summer St., Bar Harbor, 207-288-5091; www.blackfriarinn.com
This inn is decorated with Victorian style furniture and fabrics. Seven rooms. Children over 12 years only. Complimentary full breakfast. $

CASTELMAINE

39 Holland Ave., Bar Harbor, 207-288-4563, 800-338-4563; www.castlemaineinn.com
Tucked away on a quiet side street, this inn is a Victorian-style house, circa 1886, located one mile from Acadia National Park and within walking distance of the ocean. It was once the summer residence of the Austro-Hungarian ambassador. 17 rooms. Closed November-April. Complimentary continental breakfast. Whirlpool. Wireless Internet access. $

CLEFTSTONE MANOR

92 Eden St., Bar Harbor, 207-288-8086, 888-288-4951; www.cleftstone.com
This Victorian inn is set on terraced grounds and is located less than one mile from downtown Bar Harbor. The inn was once owned by the Blair family of Washington,

★
★
★
★
★

D.C. 16 rooms. Children over 10 years only. Complimentary full breakfast. Closed November-April. **$**

INN AT BAY LEDGE

150 Sand Point Road, Bar Harbor, 207-288-4204; www.innatbayledge.com

This inn, built in 1907, is located at the top of an 80-foot cliff on Mount Desert Island near Acadia National Park. 10 rooms. Children over 16 years only. Complimentary full breakfast. Closed late October-April. Whirlpool. Bar. **$$$**

MANOR HOUSE INN

106 West St., Bar Harbor, 207-288-3759, 800-437-0088;
www.barharbormanorhouse.com

This is a restored historic Victorian mansion, which dates back to 1887. 18 rooms. Children over 12 years only. Complimentary full breakfast. Pets not accepted. **$$**

MIRA MONTE INN & SUITES

69 Mount Desert St., Bar Harbor, 207-288-4263, 800-553-5109; www.miramonte.com

This is a restored Victorian home on 2½ acres with wraparound porch and period furnishings. 16 rooms. Closed mid-October-April. Complimentary full breakfast. **$$**

THORNHEDGE INN

47 Mount Desert St., Bar Harbor, 207-288-5398, 877-288-5398;
www.thornhedgeinn.com

This Queen Anne-style inn is located in the Historic Corridor District of Bar Harbor, close to many shops, galleries and restaurants. It was built in 1900 by the publisher of Louisa May Alcott's *Little Women* as a summer cottage. 13 rooms. **$**

RESTAURANTS

★124 COTTAGE STREET

124 Cottage St., Bar Harbor, 207-288-4383

American menu. Dinner. Closed November-May. Bar. Children's menu. Outdoor seating. **$$**

★★MAGGIE'S

6 Summer St., Bar Harbor, 207-288-9007; www.maggiesbarharbor.com

International menu. Dinner. Casual attire. Reservations recommended. Outdoor seating. Closed Sunday; late October-mid-June. Bar. **$$**

★★★READING ROOM

Newport Drive, Bar Harbor, 207-288-3351, 800-248-3351; www.barharborinn.com

Located on the oceanfront, this restaurant offers a panoramic view of the harbor and docks through large windows. Seafood is the star of the menu, with everything from lobster pie to local diver sea scallops available. American menu. Breakfast, lunch, dinner, Sunday brunch. Bar. Children's menu. Casual attire. Reservations recommended. Valet parking. Closed December-March. Wireless Internet access. Fitness room. **$$$**

★
★
★
★
★

★ROUTE 66
21 Cottage St., Bar Harbor, 207-288-3708; www.bhroute66.com
American menu. Lunch, dinner. Bar. Children's menu. Casual attire. Reservations recommended. Outdoor seating. Closed mid-October to mid-May. **$$**

★★SEASONS
51 Rodick St., Bar Harbor, 207-288-5117
American menu. Dinner. Bar. Children's menu. Casual attire. Outdoor seating. Closed mid-November to late-March. **$$**

BATH

For more than two centuries, Bath has been a shipbuilding center on the west bank of the Kennebec River. The Bath Iron Works, which dates to 1833, began building ships in 1889. It has produced destroyers, cruisers, a battleship, pleasure craft and steamers, and now also produces patrol frigates. Altogether, Bath has launched more than 4,000 ships from its shores. Several mansions, built when Bath was a great seaport, still stand.

BAXTER STATE PARK

While serving as a legislator and as governor of Maine, Percival P. Baxter wanted to create a wilderness park around Mount Katahdin—Maine's highest peak (5,267 feet). Rebuffed by voters but not deterred, Baxter bought the land with his own money and deeded to the state of Maine a 201,018-acre park "to be forever left in its natural, wild state." The park can be reached from Greenville via paper company roads, from Millinocket via Highway 157, or from Patten via Highway 159.

The Park Authority operates the following campgrounds: Katahdin Stream, Abol and Nesowadnehunk, Roaring Brook (Roaring Brook Road), Chimney Pond (by trail 3.3 miles beyond Roaring Brook), Russell Pond (Wassataquoik Valley, seven miles by trail beyond Roaring Brook), South Branch Pond (at outlet of Lower South Branch Pond), Trout Brook Farm (Trout Brook Crossing). There are cabins ($17/person/night) at Daicey Pond off Nesowadnehunk Road and at Kidney Pond. All areas except Chimney, Kidney and Daicey ponds have tent space, and all areas except Trout Brook Farm, Kidney and Daicey ponds have lean-tos ($6/person/night), water (unprotected, should be purified), and primitive facilities (no indoor plumbing, no running water; some springs); bunkhouses ($7/night) at some campgrounds. Children under 7 stay free throughout the park.

Reservations should be made by mail (and paid in full) in advance. For detailed information, contact the Reservation Clerk, Baxter State Park, 64 Balsam Drive, Millinocket. Swimming, fishing, canoes for rent are available at Russell Pond, South Branch Pond, Daicey Pond, Kidney Pond and Trout Brook farm.

The park is open for camping mid-May to mid-October. No pets or motorcycles are permitted. Vehicles exceeding 7 feet wide, 9 feet high or 22 feet long will not be admitted.
Information: 18 miles northwest of Millinocket, 207-723-5140

★
★★
★★
★

A restored 19th-century business district, waterfront park and public landing are also part of the city.

Information: Chamber of Commerce of the Bath-Brunswick Region,
45 Front St., 207-443-9751; www.midcoastmaine.com

WHAT TO SEE AND DO
FORT POPHAM MEMORIAL
Popham Beach, Highway 209, 207-389-1335
Construction of the fort began in 1861. It was never finished, and it was garrisoned in 1865-1866. It remains an impressive masonry structure with gun emplacements. Picnic tables. May-November, daily.

MAINE MARITIME MUSEUM
243 Washington St., Bath, 207-443-1316; www.mainemaritimemuseum.org
Maritime History Building has exhibits of maritime art and artifacts, ship models and paintings. Tours of original shipyard buildings, demonstrations of sea-faring techniques (seasonal); waterfront picnic area and playground. Museum store. Daily 9:30 a.m.-5 p.m.

POPHAM COLONY
Highway 209 on Sabino Head
In 1607, the first American vessel, the *Virginia*, was built here by colonists who shortly thereafter returned to England. On the hilltop nearby is Fort Baldwin, built during World War I. A 70-foot tower offers a panoramic view of the coast and the Kennebec River.

HOTELS
★★HOLIDAY INN
139 Richardson St., Bath, 207-443-9741, 800-465-4329; www.holiday-inn.com
141 rooms. Pets accepted, some restrictions. Restaurant, bar. Fitness room. Pool, whirlpool. High-speed Internet access. **$**

SPECIALTY LODGINGS
GALEN C. MOSES HOUSE
1009 Washington St., Bath, 207-442-8771, 888-442-8771; www.galenmoses.com
This inn, built in 1874, is on the National Register of Historic Houses. It features a Victorian interior and stained-glass windows. All the rooms are decorated with antiques. Six rooms. Children over 12 years only. Complimentary full breakfast. Pets accepted, some restriction. **$$**

RESTAURANTS
★MAE'S CAFÉ AND BAKERY
160 Center St., Bath, 207-442-8577
American menu. Breakfast, lunch, dinner. Casual attire. Outdoor seating. **$$**

★TASTE OF MAINE
Highway 1, Woolwich, 207-443-4554; www.tasteofmaine.com
Seafood, steak menu. Lunch, dinner. Children's menu. Outdoor seating. Closed late December-mid-March. **$$**

MAINE

BELFAST

Belfast, named for the city in Northern Ireland, was settled in 1770 by Irish and Scottish immigrants. An old seaport on the west shore of Penobscot Bay, Belfast is also a hub of small boat traffic to the bay islands. It is the seat of Waldo County.

Information: Chamber of Commerce, 17 Main St., 207-338-5900;
www.belfastmaine.org

WHAT TO SEE AND DO
LAKE ST. GEORGE STATE PARK
278 Belfast Augusta Road, Liberty, 207-589-4255;
www.state.me.us

The park covers more than 360 acres. Swimming, bathhouse, lifeguard, fishing, boating (ramp, rentals); snowmobiling permitted, picnicking, camping. May 15-October 1; fee.

HOTEL
★BELFAST HARBOR INN
91 Searsport Ave., Belfast, 207-338-2740, 800-545-8576; www.belfastharborinn.com

61 rooms. Pets accepted, some restrictions; fee. Complimentary continental breakfast. Restaurant. Pool. **$**

SPECIALTY LODGING
PENOBSCOT BAY INN
192 Northport Ave., Belfast, 207-338-5715, 800-335-2370; www.penobscotbayinn.com

This turn-of-the-century country inn overlooks the bay. 19 rooms. Pets accepted, some restrictions; fee. Complimentary full breakfast. Reservations recommended. **$$**

RESTAURANTS
★★DARBY'S
155 High St., Belfast, 207-338-2339; www.darbysrestaurant.com

International menu. Lunch, dinner. Bar. Children's menu. Casual attire. Reservations recommended. **$$**

★YOUNG'S LOBSTER POUND
2 Fairview St., Belfast, 207-338-1160

Seafood menu. Breakfast, lunch, dinner. Outdoor seating. Casual attire. Reservations recommended. **$$**

BETHEL

Bethel, on both banks of the winding Androscoggin River, is built on Oxford Hills and is backed by the rough foothills of the White Mountains. In addition to being a year-round resort, it's an educational and wood products center. One of Maine's leading preparatory schools, Gould Academy (founded in 1836), is located here, as is Sunday River ski resort, one of New England's snowiest ski areas.

Information: Chamber of Commerce, 207-824-2282, 800-442-5826;
www.bethelmaine.com

★
★
★
★

WHAT TO SEE AND DO

CARTER'S X-COUNTRY SKI CENTER

Intervale Road, Bethel, 207-824-3880; www.cartersxcski.com

One thousand acres with 55 kilometers of groomed cross-country trails. Rentals, lessons, lounge, shop, two lodges. December-March. Daily 10 a.m.-5 p.m.

DR. MOSES MASON HOUSE MUSEUM

14 Broad St., Bethel, 207-824-2908; www.bethelhistorical.org

Restored 1813 home of prominent congressman who served during Andrew Jackson's administration. Antique furnishings, early American murals. July-Labor Day, Tuesday-Sunday 1-4 p.m.; rest of year, by appointment.

GRAFTON NOTCH STATE PARK

Highway 2, 207-824-2912;
www.state.me.us

The Appalachian Trail passes through the notch; interpretive displays, scenic view, picnicking; fishing. May 15-October 15; fee.

SUNDAY RIVER SKI RESORT

Sunday River Road, Bethel, 207-824-3000, 800-543-2754; www.sundayriver.com

Nine quad, four triple, two double chairlifts (including four High-speed detachables and one surface lift); patrol, school, rentals, ski shop; snowmaking; cafeterias, restaurants; bars. 127 runs; longest run is three miles; vertical drop 2,340 feet. Mid-November-mid-April, daily. 100 cross-country trails adjacent. Mountain biking May-Labor Day, daily. Labor Day-late October, weekends.

HOTELS

★★★BETHEL INN & COUNTRY CLUB

On the Common, Bethel, 207-824-2175, 800-654-0125; www.bethelinn.com

This hotel features rooms in a three traditional colonial buildings as well as a series of luxury townhouses, perfect for families visiting the nearby slopes. In summer, there is a championship golf course designed by architect Geoffrey Cornish. 60 rooms. Pets accepted, some restrictions; fee. Restaurant, bar. Children's activity center. Fitness room. Pool, whirlpool. Golf. Tennis. $$

★★★THE BRIAR LEA INN AND RESTAURANT

150 Mayville Road, Bethel, 207-824-4717, 877-311-1299; www.briarleainn.com

Built in the 1850s, this inn has a farmhouse atmosphere, with rooms decorated in vintage prints and antiques. The onsite pub and restaurant, the Jolly Drayman, is modeled after similar pubs in England and serves a wide selection of English, Irish and local beers. Six rooms. Pets accepted, some restrictions; fee. Complimentary full breakfast. Restaurant. $

★NORSEMAN INN

134 Mayville Road, Bethel, 207-824-2002; www.norsemaninn.com

31 rooms. Complimentary continental breakfast. $$

★
★
★
★

RESTAURANT

★S. S. MILTON

43 Main St., Bethel, 207-824-2589

Seafood, steak menu. Lunch (May-October), dinner. Closed Tuesday. Children's menu. Casual attire. Reservations recommended. Outdoor seating. **$$**

BLUE HILL

Named for a nearby hill that delivers a beautiful view of Mount Desert Island, Blue Hill evolved from a thriving seaport to a summer colony known for its crafts and antiques. Mary Ellen Chase, born here in 1887, wrote about Blue Hill in *A Goodly Heritage* and *Mary Peters*.

Information: Blue Hill Peninsula Chamber of Commerce, 207-374-3242;
www.bluehillme.com

WHAT TO SEE AND DO

HOLT HOUSE

Water Street, Blue Hill, 207-326-8250; www.bluehillhistory.org

One of the oldest houses in Blue Hill; now home of the Blue Hill Historical Society, which features town memorabilia. July-September, Tuesday, Friday, Saturday 11 a.m.-2 p.m.

RACKLIFFE POTTERY

132 Elsworth Road, Blue Hill, 207-374-2297; www.rackliffepottery.com

Family manufactures wheel-thrown dinnerware from native red-firing clay. Open workshop. July-August, daily; rest of year, Monday-Saturday.

ROWANTREES POTTERY

84 Union St., Union, 207-374-5535

Manufactures functional pottery and wheel-thrown handcrafted dinnerware. June-September, Monday-Saturday; closed holidays.

HOTEL

★★★BLUE HILL INN

40 Union St., Blue Hill, 207-374-2844, 800-826-7415; www.bluehillinn.com

This federal-style house at the tip of the bay has operated as a bed and breakfast since 1840 and is on the National Register of Historic Places. For a more private retreat choose one of the quaint guest rooms or the adjacent Cape House suite. 12 rooms. Restaurant. Airport transportation available. Wireless Internet access. **$$**

BOOTHBAY HARBOR

Native Americans were paid 20 beaver pelts for the area encompassing Boothbay Harbor. Today, it's a protected harbor, a haven for boatmen and the scene of well-attended regattas several times a summer. Boothbay Harbor, on the peninsula between the Sheepscot and Damariscotta rivers, shares the peninsula and adjacent islands with a dozen other communities, including Boothbay (settled 1630), of which it was once a part.

Information: Boothbay Harbor Region Chamber of Commerce,
207-633-2353, 800-266-8422; www.boothbayharbor.com

MAINE

WHAT TO SEE AND DO

BOOTHBAY RAILWAY VILLAGE

586 Wiscasset Road, Highway 27, Boothbay, 207-633-4727; www.railwayvillage.org

Historical Maine exhibits of rural life, railroads and antique autos and trucks. Rides on a coal-fired, narrow-gauge steam train to an antique vehicle display. Also on exhibit are displays of early fire equipment, a general store, a one-room schoolhouse and two restored railroad stations. Mid-June to mid-October, daily.

BOOTHBAY REGION HISTORICAL SOCIETY MUSEUM

72 Oak St., Boothbay Harbor, 207-633-0820; www.boothbayhistorical.org

Artifacts of Boothbay Region. July-Labor Day, Wednesday-Saturday 10 a.m.-2 p.m.; rest of year, Friday-Saturday.

SPECIAL EVENT

WINDJAMMER DAYS

192 Townsend Ave., Boothbay Harbor, 207-633-2353; www.boothbayharbor.com

Old schooners that previously sailed the trade routes and now cruise the Maine coast sail en masse into harbor. Waterfront food court, entertainment, street parade, children's activities. Late June.

HOTELS

★★BROWN'S WHARF MOTEL

121 Atlantic Ave., Boothbay Harbor, 207-633-5440, 800-334-8110;
www.brownswharfinn.com

70 rooms. Pets not accepted, Restaurant, bar. Closed November-April. Wireless Internet access. $

★★FISHERMAN'S WHARF INN

22 Commercial St., Boothbay Harbor, 207-633-5090, 800-628-6872;
www.fishermanswharfinn.com

54 rooms. Closed November-May. Complimentary full breakfast. Wireless Internet access. Restaurant, bar. Valet parking. $$

★★★SPRUCE POINT INN

88 Grandview Ave., Boothbay Harbor, 207-633-4152, 800-553-0289;
www.sprucepointinn.com

Located on a quiet peninsula on the east side of Boothbay Harbor, this retreat is the perfect getaway for families, groups and couples. Activities include swimming in salt and freshwater pools, kayaking, bicycling, fishing and hiking trails. 85 rooms. Closed mid-October-mid-May. Pets accepted. Wireless Internet access. Two restaurants, bar. Children's activity center. Fitness room, fitness classes available. Spa. Pool, whirlpool. Tennis. Business center. $$

★TUGBOAT INN

80 Commercial St., Boothbay Harbor, 207-633-4434, 800-248-2628;
www.tugboatinn.com

64 rooms. Restaurant, bar. Closed December-mid-March. $

★
★
★
★
★

SPECIALTY LODGINGS

1830 ADMIRAL'S QUARTERS INN

71 Commercial St., Boothbay Harbor, 207-633-2474, 800-644-1878;
www.admiralsquartersinn.com

Built in 1830, this sprawling inn has ocean views. Seven rooms. Children over 12 years only. Complimentary full breakfast. Closed mid-December-mid-February. High-speed Internet access. **$$**

ANCHOR WATCH BED AND BREAKFAST

9 Eames Road, Boothbay Harbor, 207-633-7565; www.anchorwatch.com

This inn is located on Boothbay Harbor and has its own private pier. Five rooms. Children over 9 years only. Complimentary full breakfast. **$$**

FIVE GABLES INN

107 Murray Hill Road, East Boothbay, 207-633-4551, 800-451-5048;
www.fivegablesinn.com

This inn, built in 1890, features Victorian décor. 15 rooms. Closed November-mid-May. Children over 12 years only. Complimentary full breakfast. **$**

HARBOUR TOWNE INN ON THE WATERFRONT

71 Townsend Ave., Boothbay Harbor, 207-633-3934, 800-722-4240;
www.harbourtowneinn.com

Located in a historic Victorian house, this bed and breakfast has views of the ocean. 12 rooms. Complimentary continental breakfast. Private parking. **$$**

HOWARD HOUSE LODGE

347 Townsend Ave., Boothbay Harbor, 207-633-3933, 800-466-6697;
www.howardhouselodge.com

This country, chalet-style building is set in a wooded area. 14 rooms. Complimentary full breakfast. Free Wireless Internet access. **$**

KENNISTON HILL INN

Wiscasset Road, Boothbay, 207-633-2159, 800-992-2915; www.kennistonhillinn.com

This restored colonial-style farmhouse, which dates to 1786, is decorated with antiques. 10 rooms. Children over 10 years only. Complimentary full breakfast. Free Wireless Internet. Reservations recommended. **$$**

RESTAURANTS

★★★88 GRANDVIEW

88 Grandview, Boothbay Harbor, 207-633-4152, 800-553-0289;
www.sprucepointinn.com

At this restaurant, located inside the Spruce Point Inn tables are covered with crisp white linens and are set with fine china. Seating is also provided on the enclosed sun-porch and outdoor deck with umbrella-topped tables overlooking the Atlantic Ocean. Dishes include candied duck breast and beef with Bordelaise sauce. A pianist performs nightly. Continental menu. Dinner. Bar. Business casual attire. Reservations recommended. Outdoor seating. Closed late October-mid-May. **$$$**

★ANDREW'S HARBORSIDE RESTAURANT

12 Bridge St., Boothbay Harbor, 207-633-4074; www.andrewsharborside.com

American, seafood menu. Breakfast, lunch, dinner. Bar. Children's menu. Casual attire. Reservations recommended. Closed mid-October-Mother's Day. $$

★BLUE MOON CAFÉ

54 Commercial St., Boothbay Harbor, 207-633-2349;
www.bluemoonboothbayharbor.com

American menu. Breakfast, lunch. Casual attire. Outdoor seating. Closed November-March. $

★★CHINA BY THE SEA

96 Townsend Ave., Boothbay Harbor, 207-633-4449; www.chinabythesea.net

Chinese menu. Lunch, dinner. Bar. Children's menu. Casual attire. Reservations recommended. $$

★★CHOWDER HOUSE

22 Granary Way, Boothbay Harbor, 207-633-5761

Seafood, barbecue menu. Lunch, dinner. Bar. Casual attire. Outdoor seating. June-mid-September; closed October-May. Reservations recommended. $

★★FISHERMAN'S WHARF INN

22 Commercial St., Boothbay Harbor, 207-633-5090, 800-628-6872;
www.fishermanswharfinn.com

American, seafood menu. Lunch, dinner. Bar. Children's menu. Casual attire. Reservations recommended. Valet parking. Outdoor seating. Closed mid-October-mid-May. $$

BRIDGTON

This community between Long and Highland lakes is within easy reach of Pleasant Mountain (2,007 feet), a recreational area that offers skiing as well as a magnificent view of 50 lakes. Bridgton also has many unique craft and antiques shops located within a 2-mile radius of the town center.

Information: Bridgton Lakes Region Chamber of Commerce, 207-647-3472;
www.mainelakeschamber.com

WHAT TO SEE AND DO

GIBBS AVENUE MUSEUM

44 Gibbs Ave., Bridgton, 207-647-3699; www.bridgtonhistory.org

Headquarters of Bridgton Historical Society. Permanent exhibits include narrow-gauge railroad memorabilia; Civil War artifacts; and a Sears "horseless carriage" from 1911. Special summer exhibits. Genealogy research facility includes Bridgton and Saw River railroad documents. September-June, by appointment; rest of year, Monday-Friday afternoons.

SHAWNEE PEAK SKI AREA

119 Mountain Road, Bridgton, 207-647-8444; www.shawneepeak.com

Quad, two triple, double chairlift; snowmaking, school, rentals, patrol; nursery; restaurant, cafeteria, bar. Longest run 1½ miles; vertical drop 1,350 feet. Night skiing. December-March, daily.

HOTEL
★★★THE INN AT LONG LAKE

15 Lake House Road, Naples, 207-693-6226, 800-437-0328; www.innatlonglake.com

The early 1900s style of this Lakes Region inn fits right in with the ambience of historic Naples Village. Amenities include country breakfasts, cozy common rooms and a landscaped backyard. 16 rooms. Closed January-March. Complimentary continental breakfast. Wireless Internet access. Bar. **$$**

RESTAURANT
★BLACK HORSE TAVERN

26 Portland St., Bridgton, 207-647-5300; www.theblackhorsetavern.com

Seafood, steak menu. Lunch, dinner, Sunday brunch. Bar. Children's menu. **$$**

BRUNSWICK

Once a lumbering center and later a mill town, Brunswick is now mainly concerned with trade, health care and education. It is the home of Bowdoin College and Brunswick Naval Air Station. The city lies northeast of a summer resort area on the shores and islands of Casco Bay. Federalist mansions along Federal Street and Park Row recall Brunswick's past.

Information: Chamber of Commerce of the Bath-Brunswick Region,
59 Pleasant St., 207-725-8797; www.midcoastmaine.com

WHAT TO SEE AND DO
BOWDOIN COLLEGE

1 College St., Brunswick, 207-725-3000; www.bowdoin.edu

Nathaniel Hawthorne, Henry Wadsworth Longfellow, Robert Peary, Franklin Pierce and Joan Benoit Samuelson graduated from this small liberal arts college, which was established in 1794.

JOSHUA L. CHAMBERLAIN MUSEUM

226 Maine St., Brunswick, 207-729-6606;
www.community.curtislibrary.com

This is the former residence of Maine's greatest Civil War hero, four-term Governor of Maine and president of Bowdoin College. Guided tours. May-October, Tuesday-Sunday.

PEARY-MACMILLAN ARCTIC MUSEUM

Hubbard Hall, Bowdoin College, 9500 College Station, Brunswick,
207-725-3416; www.bowdoin.edu

Exhibits relating to Arctic exploration, ecology and Inuit (Eskimo) culture. Tuesday-Sunday.

PEJEPSCOT HISTORICAL SOCIETY MUSEUM

159 Park Row, Brunswick, 207-729-6606; www.curtislibrary.com

Regional historical museum housed in an 1858 sea captain's home; changing exhibits, research facilities. Monday-Saturday 10 a.m-4 p.m.

SKOLFIELD-WHITTIER HOUSE

161 Park Row, Brunswick, 207-729-6606; www.community.curtislibrary.com

An 18-room Victorian structure last occupied in 1925; furnishings and housewares of three generations. Guided tours. Memorial Day-Columbus Day, Tuesday-Saturday.

THOMAS POINT BEACH

29 Meadow Road, Brunswick, 207-725-6009; www.thomaspointbeach.com

Swimming, lifeguard. Picnicking, tables, fireplaces. Snack bar; gift shop, arcade, playground; camping (fee). Memorial Day-Labor Day, daily.

HOTELS
★★★CAPTAIN DANIEL STONE INN

10 Water St., Brunswick, 207-725-9898, 877-573-5151;
www.captaindanielstoneinn.com

This 1819 Federal style inn, housed in a sea captain's home, has been elegantly restored to include modern amenities. The onsite restaurant is a local favorite for its seafood dishes, including plenty of fresh lobster. 34 rooms. Complimentary continental breakfast. Restaurant, bar. **$$**

★COMFORT INN

199 Pleasant St., Brunswick, 207-729-1129, 877-424-6423; www.comfortinn.com

77 rooms. Complimentary continental breakfast. Wireless Internet access. Fitness room. **$**

RESTAURANT
★GREAT IMPASTA

42 Maine St., Brunswick, 207-729-5858; www.thegreatimpasta.com

Italian menu. Lunch, dinner. Bar. **$$**

BUCKSPORT

Although originally settled in 1762, the Penobscot Valley town of Bucksport was so thoroughly burned by the British in 1779 that it was not resettled until 1812. On the east bank of the Penobscot River, Bucksport is a shopping center for the area, but is primarily an industrial town with an emphasis on paper manufacturing. The Waldo Hancock Bridge crosses the Penobscot to Verona Island. Nearby Castine is home to the Maine Maritime Academy and is one of the oldest settlements in New England.

Information: Bucksport Chamber of Commerce, 207-469-6818; www.allmaine.com

WHAT TO SEE AND DO
ACCURSED TOMBSTONE

Buck Cemetery, Main and Hinks streets, near Verona Island Bridge, Bucksport

The granite obelisk over grave of founder Jonathan Buck bears an indelible mark in the shape of a woman's leg—said to have been put there by a witch whom he had hanged.

★
★
★
★
☆

WILSON MUSEUM

107 Perkins St., Castine, 207-326-9247; www.wilsonmuseum.org

Prehistoric, historic, geologic and art exhibits Late May-September: Tuesday-Sunday. On grounds is John Perkins House, Hearse House, Blacksmith Shop. Memorial Day, May 27-September 30, daily, 2-5 p.m.

SPECIALTY LODGINGS

CASTINE INN

33 Main St., Castine, 207-326-4365; www.castineinn.com

Built in 1898, this elegant inn has 17 rooms decorated in a simple, crisp style. Gourmet breakfasts are served in the inn's dining room each morning. 17 rooms. Closed November-April. Children over 8 years only. Complimentary full breakfast. Restaurant, bar. $$

PENTAGOET INN

26 Main St., Castine, 207-326-8616, 800-845-1701; www.pentagoet.com

Victorian main building built in 1894 with smaller, colonial annex (circa 1770); library and sitting room, antiques, period furnishings. 16 rooms. Closed November-April. Pets accepted, some restrictions; fee. Complimentary full breakfast. Restaurant, bar. Wireless Internet access. $

CALAIS

This town, nestled on the border of Maine and New Brunswick, has a unique distinction—it is located exactly halfway between the North Pole and the equator. The 45th Parallel passes a few miles south of town. A marker on Highway 1 near Perry indicates the spot.

Information: Calais Regional Chamber of Commerce, 39 Union St.,
207-454-2308, 888-422-3112; www.visitcalais.com

WHAT TO SEE AND DO

MOOSEHORN NATIONAL WILDLIFE REFUGE

Charlotte Road, Calais, 207-454-7161; www.fws.gov

Glacial terrain with forests, valleys, lakes, bogs and marshes. Abundant wildlife. Fishing, hiking, hunting, cross-country skiing, bird-watching. Daily.

ST. CROIX ISLAND INTERNATIONAL HISTORIC SITE

Highway 1, St. Croix River; accessible only by boat, 207-454-3871; www.nps.gov/sacr

In 1604, French explorers Pierre Duguaf and Samuel de Champlain, leading a group of approximately 75 men, selected this as the site of the first attempted European settlement on the Atlantic Coast north of Florida. Information shelter; no facilities. Daily.

SPECIAL EVENT

INTERNATIONAL FESTIVAL WEEK

207-454-2308, 888-422-3112

Celebration of friendship between Calais and St. Stephen, New Brunswick; entertainment, concessions, contests, fireworks, parade. Early August.

RESTAURANT
★WICKACHEE
282 Main St., Calais, 207-454-3400

American menu. Breakfast, lunch, dinner. Children's menu. Casual attire. Closed Sunday. **$**

CAMDEN

Used as the backdrop for the 1950s movie *Peyton Place*, Camden is the quintessential New England coastal town. Its unique setting makes it a popular four-season resort area. Activities include sailing, kayaking, swimming, camping, hiking, and in winter, skiing on a mountain with views of the ocean. The poet Edna St. Vincent Millay began her career in Camden.

Information: Camden-Rockport-Lincolnville Chamber of Commerce, 207-236-4404; www.camdenme.org

WHAT TO SEE AND DO
CAMDEN HILLS STATE PARK
280 Belfast, Camden, 207-236-3109; www.state.me.us/cgi-bin/doc/parks/find_one_name.pl?park_id=14

Maine's third-largest state park, surrounding 1,380-foot Mount Megunticook. Road leads to Mount Battie (800 feet). Spectacular view of coast. Hiking, picnic facilities, camping. May 15-October 15, fee. Memorial Day-Columbus Day.

CAMDEN OPERA HOUSE
29 Elm St., Camden, 207-236-7963; www.camdenoperahouse.com

Elm Street Theater with musical and theatrical performances and concerts.

CAMDEN SNOW BOWL
Hosmer Pond Road, Camden, 207-236-3438; www.camdensnowbowl.com

Double chairlift, two T-bars; patrol, school, rentals; toboggan chute and rentals; snow-boarding; snowmaking; snack bar, lodge. Views of the ocean from the top of the mountain. Late December-mid-March, daily.

CONWAY HOMESTEAD-CRAMER MUSEUM
Highway 1 and Conway Road, Camden, 207-236-2257

Authentically restored 18th-century farmhouse. Collection of carriages, sleighs and farm implements in old barn; blacksmith shop, privy and herb garden. Mary Meeker Cramer Museum contains paintings, ship models, quilts; costumes, documents and other memorabilia; changing exhibits. July-August, Monday-Thursday.

MAINE STATE FERRY SERVICE
McKay St., and Highway 1, Lincolnville Beach, 207-789-5611

Twenty-minute trip to Islesboro (Dark Harbor) on the *Margaret Chase Smith*. Mid-May-late October, weekdays, nine trips; Sunday, eight trips; rest of year, six trips daily.

MAINE

★
★
★
★
★

WINDJAMMER SAILING

Camden Harbor, 800-807-9463; www.sailmainecoast.com

Old-time schooners leave from Camden and Rockport Harbors for half- to six-day trips along the coast of Maine. May-October. For further information, rates, schedules or reservations, contact the Maine Windjammer Association.

SPECIAL EVENTS

BAY CHAMBER CONCERTS

Rockport Opera House, Central St., Rockport, 207-236-2823;
www.baychamberconcerts.org

Classical music performances by Vermeer Quartet and guest artists. July-August, Thursday-Friday evenings. Jazz musicians perform September-June (one show each month) Monday-Friday, 9 a.m.-5 p.m.

WINDJAMMER WEEKEND

Camden Harbor, 207-236-4404; www.windjammerweekend.com

Celebration of Maine's windjammer fleet; fireworks. Labor Day weekend.

HOTELS

★BEST WESTERN CAMDEN RIVERHOUSE HOTEL

11 Tannery Lane, Camden, 207-236-0500, 800-755-7483; www.camdenmaine.com

35 rooms. Pets accepted, some restrictions; fee. Complimentary continental breakfast. Fitness room. Pool, whirlpool. Free Wireless Internet access. **$$**

★★★BLUE HARBOR HOUSE, A VILLAGE INN

67 Elm St., Camden, 207-236-3196, 800-248-3196; www.blueharborhouse.com

Built in 1768 as the home of the first Camden settler, James Richards, guest rooms are now filled with quilts and antiques. Enjoy a hearty breakfast before hiking Camden Hills State Park or taking a Penobscot Bay boat ride. 11 rooms. Complimentary full breakfast. Whirlpool. Wireless Internet access. **$$**

★★★CAMDEN HARBOUR INN

83 Bayview Street, Camden, 800-236-4266; www.camdenharbourinn.com

Influenced by its international owners, Camden Harbour Inn offers guests impeccable service, luxurious amenities and lovely views. Guests can expect to be spoiled with fine linens and towels, a king-size pillow-top mattress, luxe bathrobes, flat-screen TV and complimentary breakfast from the fine Natalie's restaurant. 18 rooms, 4 suites. Complimentary Wireless Internet access. Complimentary full gourmet breakfast. Restaurant, bar. Spa.

★★CEDAR CREST MOTEL

115 Elm St., Camden, 207-236-4839, 800-422-4964; www.cedarcrestmotel.com

37 rooms. Closed November-April. Restaurant. Pool. Wireless Internet access. **$**

SPECIALTY LODGINGS

CAMDEN WINDWARD HOUSE

6 High St., Camden, 207-236-9656, 877-492-9656; www.windwardhouse.com

This 1854 inn is located in the center of Camden's historic district, within walking distance to many restaurants, shops and Camden Harbor. Mount Battie and Camden Hills State Park are nearby. Eight rooms. Children over 12 years only. Complimentary full breakfast. Guest parking. Bar. **$$**

ELMS BED AND BREAKFAST

84 Elm St., Camden, 207-236-6060, 800-388-6000; www.elmsinn.net

This Federal-style home built in 1806 features a lighthouse theme. Seven rooms. Children over five years only. Complimentary full breakfast. **$$**

HAWTHORN INN

9 High St., Camden, 207-236-8842, 866-381-3647; www.camdenhawthorn.com

This 1894 Victorian inn is conveniently located near Camden's downtown area. The rooms all have private baths, and some have fireplaces, whirlpools and private decks with harbor views. 10 rooms. Closed January. Children over 12 years only. Complimentary full breakfast. Internet access. Pets not accepted. **$$**

INN AT OCEAN'S EDGE

Highway 1, Camden, 207-236-0945; www.innatoceansedge.com

This contemporary inn overlooks Penobscot Bay. Spacious rooms feature four-poster king beds. Most rooms have an ocean view. 30 rooms. No children under 14. Complimentary full breakfast. Fitness room. **$$**

INN AT SUNRISE POINT

Highway 1, Camden, 207-236-7716, 800-435-6278; www.sunrisepoint.com

This oceanfront hideaway is just minutes from Camden Harbor. Guests can choose to stay in a restored 1920s Maine-style cottage or in the main house. Breakfast is served in the conservatory and afternoon hors d'oeuvres are available in the library.. 13 rooms. Children over 12 years only. Complimentary full breakfast. Whirlpool. Free Wireless Internet access. Pets not accepted. **$$$**

THE LODGE AND COTTAGES AT CAMDEN HILLS

Highway 1, Camden, 207-236-8478, 800-832-7058; www.thelodgeatcamdenhills.com

This inn is located near Camden Hills State Park. Some rooms have fireplaces, Jacuzzi tubs or kitchens. 14 rooms. Pets accepted, some restrictions; fee. Reservations recommended. **$$**

MAINE STAY BED AND BREAKFAST

22 High St., Camden, 207-236-9636; www.mainestay.com

Farmhouse built in 1802; barn and carriage house. Antiques include a 17th-century samurai chest. Eight rooms. Children over 12 years only. Complimentary full breakfast. Pets not accepted. High-speed Internet access. **$$**

MAINE

★
★
★
☆
☆

NORUMBEGA INN

63 High St., Camden, 207-236-4646; www.norumbegainn.com

This stone castle-by-the-sea was designed and built by the inventor of duplex telegraphy and is located near Penobscot Bay. Offering panoramic views of the ocean, the property has been fully restored and is furnished with modern conveniences. Each room has a king bed, private bath and evening turndown service is provided. 13 rooms. Children over 7 years only. Complimentary full breakfast. **$$**

THE VICTORIAN BY THE SEA

Sea View Drive, Lincolnville, 207-236-3785, 800-382-9817; www.victorianbythesea.com

This Victorian summer cottage was built in 1881. Seven rooms. Children over 12 years only. Complimentary full breakfast. Free Wireless Internet access. **$$**

WHITEHALL INN

52 High St., Camden, 207-236-3391, 800-789-6565; www.whitehall-inn.com

Spacious old resort inn (1834); poet Edna St. Vincent Millay gave a reading here in 1912. 50 rooms. Closed mid-October-mid-May. Restaurant, bar. Tennis. Complimentary full breakfast. **$$**

RESTAURANTS

★★ATLANTICA

1 Bayview Landing, Camden, 207-236-6011; www.atlanticarestaurant.com

Seafood menu. Dinner. Bar. Business casual attire. Reservations recommended. Outdoor seating. Closed Tuesday in winter; also month of January or March. **$$$**

★★THE LOBSTER POUND

Highway 1, Lincolnville Beach, 207-789-5550; www.lobsterpoundmaine.com

American, seafood menu. Lunch, dinner. Children's menu. Casual attire. Reservations recommended. Closed November-April. Daily May-October. **$$**

★★★NATALIE'S

83 Bayview Street, Camden, 207-236-7008, 800-236-4266;
www.camdenharbourinn.com/natalies.htm

Relish harbor views from the wraparound porch or windows in the 20th-century Parisian bistro-inspired restaurant. Chef Lawrence Klang's menu changes seasonally and is influenced by French, Italian, and classic American cuisine. And you can expect the freshest ingredients in everything from your roasted butternut squash soup to your porcini-dusted sea scallops to your crème brulée. French menu. Dinner. Bar. Casual attire. Reservations recommended. Outdoor seating. $24-46.

★★PETER OTT'S

16 Bayview St., Camden, 207-236-4032

Seafood, steak menu. Dinner. Bar. Children's menu. Casual attire. Closed major holidays. **$$**

★
★
★
★
★

★★★VINCENT'S
52 High St., Camden, 207-236-3391, 800-789-6565; www.whitehall-inn.com
Located in the quaint Whitehall Inn, this restaurant attracts visitors and local residents alike. The cuisine is New American with a healthy focus on seafood. Dine in the main dining room, the glass-enclosed dining porch, the seasonal side patio or order bar food in the adjacent lounge. American, seafood, steak menu. Breakfast, dinner. Bar. Business casual attire. Reservations recommended. Outdoor seating. Daily. $$

★★WATERFRONT
40 Bayview St., Camden, 207-236-3747; www.waterfrontcamden.com
Originally a boat shed, this restaurant is located on Camden Harbor with docking and access for boaters and has specialized in presenting fresh regional seafood in both traditional and adventurous ways for more than 25 years. The décor includes open, beamed ceilings, hanging lanterns and a double fireplace; the outdoor deck is the place to be for an exceptional harbor view. Seafood, steak menu. Lunch, dinner. Bar. Children's menu. Casual attire. Outdoor seating. Daily. $$

CARIBOU

Caribou, the nation's northeasternmost city, is primarily an agricultural area but has become a center for manufacturing. The area's many lakes are perfect for swimming, fishing, boating and camping.
Information: Chamber of Commerce, 24 Sweden St., 800-722-7648, 207-498-6156; www.cariboumaine.net

WHAT TO SEE AND DO
CARIBOU HISTORICAL CENTER
Highway 1, Caribou, 207-498-2556; www.cariboumaine.net
Museum devoted to history of northern Maine. June-August, Thursday-Saturday; rest of year, by appointment.

NYLANDER MUSEUM
657 Main St., Caribou, 207-493-4209; www.nylandermuseum.org
Fossils, rocks, minerals, butterflies and shells collected by Olof Nylander, Swedish-born geologist and naturalist; early man artifacts; changing exhibits. Gift shop. Memorial Day-Labor Day, Tuesday-Saturday 12:30-4:30 p.m.; rest of year, by appointment.

HOTEL
★★CARIBOU INN & CONVENTION CENTER
19 Main St., Caribou, 207-498-3733, 800-235-0466; www.caribouinn.com
73 rooms. Restaurant, bar. Indoor pool, whirlpool. Airport transportation available. Fitness center. Pets accepted. Reservations recommended. $

RESTAURANTS
★JADE PALACE
Skyway Plaza, Caribou, 207-498-3648
American, Chinese menu. lunch, dinner. Bar. $$

MAINE

★
★
★
★
★

★RENO'S
117 Sweden St., Caribou, 207-496-5331
American, Italian menu. Breakfast, lunch, dinner. Children's menu. **$**

CENTER LOVELL

This community on Kezar Lake is close to the New Hampshire border and the White Mountain National Forest. The surrounding region is rich in gems and minerals.

HOTEL
★★QUISISANA LODGE
Pleasant Point Road, Center Lovell, 207-925-3500; www.quisisanaresort.com
16 rooms. Restaurant. Private sand beaches. Tennis. Closed September-May. **$$$**

SPECIALTY LODGINGS
ADMIRAL PEARY HOUSE
27 Elm St., Fryeburg, 207-935-3365, 877-423-6779; www.admiralpearyhouse.com
Located in the oldest village in the White Mountains of western Maine, this bed and breakfast—named after the discoverer of the North Pole—sits on 10 acres of landscaped lawns and gardens. Seven rooms. Complimentary full breakfast. Whirlpool. Tennis. Airport transportation available. Free wireless Internet access. **$**

OXFORD HOUSE INN
548 Main St., Fryeburg, 207-935-3442, 800-261-7206; www.oxfordhouseinn.com
This turn-of-the-century mission-style house is now a bed and breakfast with comfortably furnished rooms. A full gourmet breakfast is prepared for guests each morning. Four rooms. Complimentary full breakfast. Free Wireless Internet access. Pets not accepted.

RESTAURANT
★★OXFORD HOUSE INN
548 Main St., Fryeburg, 207-935-3442, 800-261-7206; www.oxfordhouseinn.com
Seafood, steak menu. Dinner. Bar. Children's menu. Reservations recommended. Outdoor seating. Closed Monday-Wednesday in winter and spring. **$$**

CHEBEAGUE ISLANDS

Little Chebeague and Great Chebeague islands, off the coast of Portland in Casco Bay, were once a favorite camping spot of various tribes. The Native Americans had a penchant for clams, and the first European settlers found heaps of clamshells scattered across the land. Those shells were later used to pave many of the islands' roads, some of which still exist today.

Great Chebeague, six miles long and approximately three miles wide, is connected to Little Chebeague at low tide by a sandbar. There are various locations for swimming. Additionally, both islands are easy to explore on foot or bicycle. At one time, Great Chebeague was home to a prosperous fishing and shipbuilding community, and it was a quarrying center in the late 1700s. Today, it receives hundreds of visitors every summer.

Information: www.chebeague.org

WHAT TO SEE AND DO
CASCO BAY LINES
56 Commercial St., Portland, 207-774-7871; www.cascobaylines.com
From Portland, Commercial and Franklin streets; one-hour crossing. Daily.

CHEBEAGUE TRANSPORTATION
123 Roy Hill Road, Chebeague Island, 207-846-3700; www.chebeaguetrans.com
From Cousins Island, near Yarmouth; 15-minute crossing. Daily. Off-site parking with shuttle to ferry.

CRANBERRY ISLES
The Cranberry Isles, named because of the rich, red cranberry bogs that once covered Great Cranberry Isle, lie off the southeast coast of Mount Desert Island. There are five islands in the group: Little and Great Cranberry, Sutton, Bear and Baker. Great Cranberry, the largest, covers about 900 acres. Baker Island is part of Acadia National Park, and Sutton is privately owned. In 1830, the islands petitioned the state to separate from Mount Desert Island.
Information: www.cranberryisles.com

WHAT TO SEE AND DO
ISLESFORD HISTORICAL MUSEUM
Main Street, and Sand Beach Road, Cranberry Isles, 207-244-9224;
www.mainemuseums.org
Exhibits on local island history from 1604. Mid-June-September, daily.

DAMARISCOTTA
Damariscotta, whose name is an Abenaki word meaning "river of many fishes," has a number of colonial, Greek Revival and pre-Civil War houses. With the neighboring city of Newcastle across the Damariscotta River, this is a trading center for a seaside resort region extending to Pemaquid Point and Christmas Cove.
Information: Chamber of Commerce, 207-563-8340; www.damariscottaregion.com

WHAT TO SEE AND DO
CHAPMAN-HALL HOUSE
Main and Church Streets, Damariscotta,
Restored 1754 house with original-whitewash kitchen, period furniture; local shipbuilding exhibition. July-early September, Monday-Saturday.

COLONIAL PEMAQUID STATE PARK
Colonial Pemaquid Road, New Harbor, 207-677-2423
Excavations have uncovered foundations of a jail, tavern and private homes. Fishing, boat ramp; picnicking; free parking. Memorial Day-Labor Day, daily.

FORT WILLIAM HENRY STATE MEMORIAL
New Harbor, 207-677-2423
Reconstructed 1692 fort tower; museum contains relics, portraits, maps and copies of Native American deeds. Memorial Day-September: daily.

MAINE

PEMAQUID POINT LIGHTHOUSE PARK

Pemaquid Lighthouse, New Harbor, 207-677-2494; www.lighthouse.cc

Includes an 1827 lighthouse that towers above the pounding surf (not open to public); Fishermen's Museum housed in old lightkeeper's dwelling; art gallery; recreational facilities. Memorial Day-Columbus Day, daily; rest of year, by appointment.

HOTELS

★★★THE BRADLEY INN

3063 Bristol Road, New Harbor, 207-677-2105, 800-942-5560; www.bradleyinn.com

This inn, built by a sea captain for his bride in 1880, is located at the tip of Pemaquid Peninsula close to John's Bay and the Pemaquid Lighthouse. Nearby activities include golfing, fishing, boating, walks on the beach, a winery, nature area and fine restaurants. 16 rooms. Closed January-March. Complimentary full breakfast. Restaurant. $$$

★★★NEWCASTLE INN

60 River Road, Newcastle, 207-563-5685, 800-832-8669; www.newcastleinn.com

Overlooking gardens and the Damariscotta River, this Federal-style 1850 inn offers rooms and suites with four-poster or canopy beds, sitting areas or fireplaces. A four-course dinner preceded by complimentary hors d'oeuvres is served in one of the two dining rooms. 15 rooms. Children over 12 years only. Restaurant, bar. Free Wireless Internet access. Complimentary full breakfast. $$

SPECIALTY LODGINGS

THE BRANNON BUNKER INN

349 Highway 129, Walpole, 207-563-5941, 800-563-9225; www.brannonbunkerinn.com

The area's first bed and breakfast, rooms feature simply furnished with quilts and antique furniture. Eight rooms. Pets accepted, some restrictions; fee. Complimentary continental breakfast. $$

DOWN EASTER INN

220 Bristol Road, Damariscotta, 207-563-5332, 207-563-1134; www.downeasterinn.com

This 1785 Greek Revival farmhouse was built by a ship chandler whose ancestors were among the first settlers of Bristol. 22 rooms. Complimentary continental breakfast. Restaurant. Closed Columbus Day-Memorial Day. $

DEER ISLE

A bridge over Eggemoggin Reach connects these islands to the mainland. There are two major villages here—Deer Isle (the older) and Stonington. Lobster fishing and tourism are the backbone of the economy and fishing, sailing, tennis and golf are available in the area.

Information: Deer Isle/Stonington Chamber of Commerce, Stonington, 207-348-6124 (in season); www.deerisle.com

WHAT TO SEE AND DO
ISLE AU HAUT

Reached by ferry from Stonington, much of this island—with hills more than 500 feet tall, forested shores and cobblestone beaches—is in Acadia National Park.

ISLE AU HAUT BOAT SERVICES

Seabreeze Ave., Stonington, 207-367-6516; www.isleauhaut.com
Service to the island and excursion trips available.

HOTELS
★★GOOSE COVE LODGE

300 Goose Cove Road, Sunset, 207-348-2508, 800-728-1963;
www.goosecovelodge.com
21 rooms. Children's activity center. Closed mid-October-April. Pets not accepted. **$**

★★★PILGRIMS INN

20 Main St., Deer Isle, 207-348-6615; www.pilgrimsinn.com
This restored historic wood frame building was built in 1793 and has eight-foot-wide fireplaces. Nearby are galleries and a famous art school. The chef prepares meals from local seafood, produce and fresh-grown ingredients from the garden. 16 rooms. Closed November-mid-May. Restaurant.Complimentary continental breakfast. Wireless Internet access. Pets accepted, some restrictions; fee.

EASTPORT

At the southern end of Passamaquoddy Bay, Eastport is a community with 150-year-old houses and ancient elms. The average tide at Eastport is approximately 18 feet, although tides up to 25 feet have been recorded here. Eastport was the site of one of the country's first tide-powered electric generating projects, and while it was never completed, it resulted in the construction of two tidal dams. The city is also the nation's aquaculture capital, where millions of salmon and trout are raised in pens in the chilly off-shore waters.

Information: 207-853-4644; www.eastport.net

WHAT TO SEE AND DO
BARRACKS MUSEUM

74 Washington St., Eastport
This 1822 building once served as the officers' barracks for a nearby fort, which was held by British troops during the War of 1812. Memorial Day-Labor Day, Wednesday-Saturday afternoons.

OLD SOW WHIRLPOOL

Between Moose and Deer Islands, www.oldsowwhirlpool.com
One of the largest in the Western Hemisphere; most active three hours before high tide.

PASSAMAQUODDY INDIAN RESERVATION

Highway 190, Perry, 207-853-2551
In 1604, Samuel de Champlain was the first European to encounter members of this Algonquin tribe. Festivals and ceremonies throughout the year.

MAINE

★
★
★
★
★

SPECIALTY LODGINGS
TODD HOUSE

1 Capen Ave., Eastport, 207-853-2328

This authentic New England Cape once housed soldiers during the War of 1812. It is near the ocean and has views of the bay. Eight rooms. Pets accepted; fee. Complimentary continental breakfast. **$**

WESTON HOUSE BED AND BREAKFAST

26 Boyton St., Eastport, 207-853-2907, 800-853-2907;
www.westonhouse-maine.com

This restored 19th-century residence has a sitting room with an authentic tin ceiling. Rooms are comfortably decorated with antiques. Four rooms. No children allowed. Complimentary full breakfast. Pets not accepted. **$**

ELLSWORTH

This is the shire town and trading center for Hancock County—which includes some of the country's choicest resort territory, including Bar Harbor. In the beginning of the 19th-century, Ellsworth was the second-largest lumber shipping port in the world.

Information: Chamber of Commerce, 163 High St., Ellsworth, 207-667-5584;
www.ellsworthchamber.org

WHAT TO SEE AND DO
LAMOINE STATE PARK

23 State Park Road, Ellsworth, 207-667-4778;
www.state.me.us/cgi-bin/doc/parks/find_one_name.pl?park_id=16

A 55-acre recreation area around beach on Frenchman Bay. Fishing; boating; picnicking, camping. Memorial Day-mid-October, daily. Standard fees.

STANWOOD SANCTUARY (BIRDSACRE) AND HOMESTEAD MUSEUM

289 High St., Ellsworth, 207-667-8460; www.birdsacre.com

Trails, ponds and picnic areas on a 130-acre site. Museum collections include mounted birds, nests and eggs. Wildlife rehabilitation center with shelters for injured birds, including hawks and owls. Museum was the home of pioneer ornithologist, photographer and writer Cordelia Stanwood (1865-1958). Sanctuary and rehabilitation center daily; Homestead Museum and Nature Center from June-September 10-4 p.m.

HOTEL
★★HOLIDAY INN

215 High St., Ellsworth, 207-667-9341, 888-465-4329; www.ichotelsgroup.com

103 rooms. Pets accepted, some restrictions; fee. Restaurant, bar. Fitness room. Pool, whirlpool. Tennis. Parking available. **$**

FORT KENT

Fort Kent, at the northern end of famous Highway 1 (the other end is at Key West, Florida), is the chief community of Maine's "far north." A bridge across the St. John River leads to Clair, New Brunswick. The town is a lumbering, farming, hunting and

★
★
★
★
★

fishing center. Canoeing, downhill and cross-country skiing, as well as snowmobiling are popular here. A campus for the University of Maine is located here.

Information: Fort Kent Chamber of Commerce, 291 W. Main St.,
207-834-5354, 800-733-3563; www.fortkentchamber.com

WHAT TO SEE AND DO
FORT KENT BLOCKHOUSE
North edge of town, 207-941-4014
www.hps.gov/maac/planyourvisit/blockhouse.htm
Built in 1839 during the Aroostook Bloodless War with Britain, and used as a guard post. Restored; antique hand tools in museum; interpretive displays. Picnicking. Memorial Day-Labor Day, daily.

FORT KENT HISTORICAL SOCIETY MUSEUM AND GARDENS
54 W. Main St., Fort Kent, 207-834-5121; www.visitmaine.com
Former Bangor and Aroostook railroad station, built in early 1900s, now houses historical museum. Usually last two weeks in June-August, Tuesday-Friday.

LONESOME PINE TRAILS
Forest Avenue, Fort Kent, 207-834-5202
Thirteen trails, 2,300-foot slope with 500-foot drop; beginners slope and tow; rope tow, T-bar; school, patrol, rentals; lodge, concession. (December-April)

SPECIAL EVENT
CAN AM CROWN SLED DOG RACES
West Main Street, Fort Kent, 207-834-3312, 800-733-3563; www.can-am.sjv.net
Three races (30, 60 and 250-mile) begin on Main Street and finish at the Lonesome Pine Ski Lodge. Late February-early March.

FREEPORT
Freeport is a historic seaside town that played a part in Maine's early history—papers were signed here separating the state from Massachusetts in 1820. Today the town is known as a destination for shopping. It's home to dozens of outlets and the renowned flagship L. L. Bean clothing and sporting goods store, which stays open 24 hours a day, selling everything from kayaks to bikes, thermal underwear to colorful fleece jackets.

Information: Freeport Merchants Association, 23 Depot St., 207-865-1212, 800-865-1994;
www.freeportusa.com

WHAT TO SEE AND DO
ATLANTIC SEAL CRUISES
25 Main St., South Freeport. Depart from Town Wharf, 207-865-6112;
www.freeportusa.org/freeportmember116.html
Cruises aboard a 40-foot, 28-passenger vessel on Casco Bay to Eagle Island and Robert E. Peary house museum; also seal and bird-watching trips, fall foliage sightseeing cruises. Schedules vary. Tickets can be purchased at Main Street office. Hours 8 a.m.-7 p.m.

MAINE

★
★
★
★
★

FACTORY OUTLET STORES

42-28 Main St., Freeport, 800-865-1994; www.freeportusa.com

Freeport is home to more than 170 outlet stores and centers that offer brand-name merchandise at discounted prices, including the famous L. L. Bean clothing and sporting goods flagship store, which stays open 24 hours a day.

MAST LANDING SANCTUARY

20 Gilsland Farm Road, Falmouth, 207-781-2330;
www.maineaudubon.org/about/contact.shtml

A 140-acre area maintained by the Maine Audubon Society. Hiking, cross-country skiing. Daily.

HOTELS

★★BEST WESTERN FREEPORT INN

31 Highway 1, Freeport, 207-865-3106, 800-780-7234; www.bestwestern.com

80 rooms. Pets accepted, some restrictions. Restaurant. Two outdoor pools. High-speed Internet access. $$

★CASCO BAY INN

107 Highway 1, Freeport, 207-865-4925, 800-570-4970; www.cascobayinn.com

45 rooms. Closed mid-December-mid-April. High-speed Internet access. Golf. $

★★★HARRASEEKET INN

162 Main St., Freeport, 207-865-9377, 800-342-6423; www.harraseeketinn.com

Three structures make up the inn: the Federalist House (1798), the Early Victorian House (1850) and a modern, colonial-style inn. Spacious guest rooms are decorated with antiques and feature mahogany furnishings, and quarter canopy beds with heirloom bedspreads and have cozy fireplaces. Complimentary tea is served in the paneled drawing room each afternoon, and there is a complimentary breakfast buffet each morning. This inn is located just two blocks from the L.L. Bean flagship store and the town's more than 170 shopping outlets. 84 rooms. Pets accepted, some restrictions; fee. Complimentary full breakfast. Restaurant, bar. Indoor pool. Airport transportation available. $$

SPECIALTY LODGINGS

BREWSTER HOUSE BED & BREAKFAST

180 Main St., Freeport, 207-865-4121, 800-865-0822; www.brewsterhouse.com

Built in 1888, this waterfront inn has rooms decorated with fresh floral prints and antique furniture. Seven rooms. Children over 8 years only. Complimentary full breakfast. Free Wireless Internet access. Pets not accepted. $$$

FREEPORT CLIPPER INN

181 Main St., Freeport, 207-865-9623, 866-866-4002; www.freeportclipperinn.com

This restored Greek Revival Cape home (circa 1840) features colonial furnishings. Seven rooms. Children over 12 years only. Complimentary full breakfast. Pool. Complimentary Wireless Internet access. $

KENDALL TAVERN BED AND BREAKFAST

213 Main St., Freeport, 207-865-1338, 800-341-9572; www.kendalltavern.com

This bed and breakfast is located at the north end of Freeport. Built in 1832, the first floor was opened as a tavern, and a second story was added years later. Guest rooms feature antiques and handmade quilts. Each morning, a country-style breakfast is served in the dining room. Seven rooms. Children over 8 years only. Complimentary full breakfast. Pets accepted, restrictions; fee. $$

ROYALSBOROUGH INN AT BAGLEY HOUSE

1290 Royalsborough Road, Durham, 207-865-6566, 800-765-1772; www.royalsboroughinn.com

Restored 1772 country inn; wood beams, wide pine floors, original beehive oven. Eight rooms. Complimentary full breakfast. Pets not accepted. $$

WHITE CEDAR INN

178 Main St., Freeport, 207-865-9099, 800-853-1269; www.whitecedarinn.com

Former home of Arctic explorer Donald MacMillan. Seven rooms. Pets accepted, some restrictions; fee, Children over 8 years only. Complimentary full breakfast. Free wirless Internet access. Reservations recommended. $

RESTAURANTS

★CORSICAN

9 Mechanic St., Freeport, 207-865-9421; www.corsicanrestaurant.com

Italian, seafood menu. Lunch daily, dinner Monday-Saturday. Closed holidays. Children's menu. Casual attire. Reservations recommended. $$

★GRITTY MCDUFF'S

187 Lower Main St., Freeport, 207-865-4321; www.grittys.com

American, seafood menu. Lunch, dinner, late-night. Bar. Children's menu. Casual attire. Outdoor seating. $$

★★JAMESON TAVERN

115 Main St., Freeport, 207-865-4196; www.jamesontavern.com

Seafood, steak menu. Lunch, dinner. Bar. Children's menu. Casual attire. Reservations recommended. Outdoor seating. $$

★LOBSTER COOKER

39 Main St., Freeport, 207-865-4349; www.lobstercooker.net

Seafood menu. Lunch, dinner. Children's menu. Casual attire. Outdoor seating. $$

★★★THE MAINE DINING ROOM

162 Main St., Freeport, 207-865-9377, 800-342-6423; www.harraseeketinn.com

This restaurant, located in the Harraseeket Inn, offers a cozy atmosphere, enhanced by two wood-burning fireplaces and windows overlooking the gardens. Organic and homegrown foods shine on the menu, and the wine selection is one of the largest in Maine. American menu. Breakfast, dinner, brunch. Bar. Business casual attire. Reservations recommended. Pets accepted. $$$

MAINE

★
★
★
★

GREENVILLE

Greenville is a starting point for trips into the Moosehead Lake region. Until it was incorporated in 1836, it was known as Haskell in honor of its founder Nathaniel Haskell.

Information: Moosehead Lake Region Chamber of Commerce, 207-695-2702, 888-876-2778; www.mooseheadlake.org

WHAT TO SEE AND DO
MOOSEHEAD MARINE MUSEUM

North Main Street, Greenville, 207-695-2716; www.katahdincruises.com/museum.html
Located on the steamboat *Katahdin*, berthed in East Cove. Exhibits of the steamboat era and the Kineo Hotel; cruises available. July-Columbus Day.

HOTELS
★CHALET MOOSEHEAD LAKEFRONT MOTEL

Birch Street, Greenville, 207-695-2950, 800-290-3645; www.mooseheadlodging.com
27 rooms. Pets accepted, some restrictions; fee. Whirlpool. $

★INDIAN HILL MOTEL

127 Moosehead Lake Road, Greenville, 207-695-2623, 800-771-4620; www.mooseheadlodging.com
15 rooms. Pets not accepted. $

SPECIALTY LODGINGS
GREENVILLE INN

40 Norris St., Greenville, 207-695-2206, 888-695-6000; www.greenvilleinn.com
13 rooms. Complimentary continental breakfast. Restaurant, bar. Pets not accepted. $$

THE LODGE AT MOOSEHEAD LAKE

368 Lily Bay Road, Greenville, 207-695-4400, 800-825-6977; www.lodgeatmooseheadlake.com
At this romantic retreat, lodge rooms and adjacent carriage house suites are adorned with charming rustic interiors including hand-carved poster beds. Most guest rooms feature sunset views over the water and Squaw Mountain. Explore nearby Lily Bay State Park or take part in the year-round recreations of the lake and surrounding wilderness. Five rooms. Children over 14 years only. Complimentary full breakfast. Pets accepted. $$$$

KENNEBUNK

The inland sister to tony beach town Kennebunkport, this village is equally visually appealing and quaint. At one time, the original settlement that was to become Kennebunk used to be a part of Wells. When Maine separated from Massachusetts in 1820, Kennebunk separated from Wells. Once a shipbuilding community on the Mousam and Kennebunk Rivers, today Kennebunk is the business center for the summer resort area that includes Kennebunkport and Kennebunk Beach.

Information: Chamber of Commerce, 17 Western Ave., 207-967-0857; www.kkcc.maine.org

WHAT TO SEE AND DO
BRICK STORE MUSEUM
117 Main St., Kennebunk, 207-985-4802; www.brickstoremuseum.org

A block of restored 19th-century buildings including William Lord's Brick Store; exhibits of fine and decorative arts, historical and maritime collections. Tuesday-Friday, 10 a.m.-4.30 p.m., Saturday 10 a.m.-1 p.m. Parking available.

SPECIALTY LODGINGS
ARUNDEL MEADOWS INN
Rte 1, Arundel, Kennebunk, 207-985-3770; www.arundelmeadowsinn.net

This restored farmhouse (built in1827) is decorated with antiques and features expansive gardens. Seven rooms. Children over 12 years only. Complimentary full breakfast. Outdoor pool. **$**

THE BEACH HOUSE
211 Beach Ave., Kennebunk Beach, 207-967-3850; www.beachhseinn.com

This inn (circa 1890) is located on Kennebunk Beach, just two miles from Kennebunkport. Rooms are crisp and contemporary, with plush duvet-topped beds. Afternoon tea is served in the sitting room, which has a view of the ocean. 34 rooms. Complimentary continental breakfast. Reservations recommended. **$$$$**

THE KENNEBUNK INN
45 Main St., Kennebunk, 207-985-3351; www.thekennebunkinn.com

Built in 1799, this cozy inn features turn-of-the-century décor. 22 rooms. Pets accepted, some restrictions; fee. Complimentary continental breakfast. Restaurant. Wireless Internet access. **$**

RESTAURANTS
★FEDERAL JACK'S RESTAURANT AND BREW PUB
8 Western Ave., Kennebunk, 207-967-4322; www.federaljacks.com

American, seafood menu. Lunch, dinner, late-night. Bar. Children's menu. Casual attire. Outdoor seating. Daily. **$$**

★★★GRISSINI
27 Western Ave., Kennebunk, 207-967-2211; www.restaurantgrissini.com

Grissini offers Tuscan cooking in an airy, loft-like setting. Features include a large stone fireplace, an open kitchen and an outdoor garden dining area. Italian menu. Dinner. Bar. Casual attire. Reservations recommended. Outdoor seating. **$$**

★★THE KENNEBUNK INN
45 Main St., Kennebunk, 207-985-3351; www.thekennebunkinn.com

American, seafood menu. Lunch, dinner, brunch. Bar. Children's menu. Casual attire. Reservations recommended. Outdoor seating. **$$$**

MAINE

★
★
★
★
★

★★★WINDOWS ON THE WATER

12 Chase Hill Road, Kennebunk, 207-967-3313, 800-773-3313;
www.windowsonthewater.com

This local favorite opened in 1985 and is family-owned and -operated. The menu features plenty of meat dishes (filet mignon and parmesan-crusted rack of lamb), but the specialty here is fresh, sustainable fish and seafood, from native striped bass to day boat sea scallops. American menu. Lunch, dinner. Children's menu. Casual attire. Reservations recommended. Outdoor seating. $$$

KENNEBUNKPORT

At the mouth of the Kennebunk River, this quaint coastal town is a favorite summer destination of well-heeled New Englanders. The Bush family has its warm-weather compound here, and generations of bluebloods have checked into the historic Colony Hotel and walked along the beach to Walker's Point. In fall and winter, the town is equally appealing, with its many boutiques, restaurants and charming inns as diversions.

Information: Chamber of Commerce, 17 Western Ave., Kennebunk,
207-967-0857; www.kkcc.maine.org

WHAT TO SEE AND DO
SCHOOL HOUSE

135 N. St., Kennebunkport, 207-967-2751; www.kporthistory.org

(1899) Headquarters of the Kennebunkport Historical Society. Houses collections of genealogy, photographs, maritime history and many artifacts and documents on Kennebunkport's history. Tuesday-Friday.

★
★
★
★

HOTELS
★★THE BREAKWATER INN AND HOTEL

127-131 Ocean Ave., Kennebunkport, 207-967-5333; www.thebreakwaterinn.com

37 rooms. Complimentary continental breakfast. Restaurant. Spa. $$$

★★★THE COLONY HOTEL

140 Ocean Ave., Kennebunkport, 207-967-3331, 800-552-2363;
www.thecolonyhotel.com/maine

Located on a rock promontory overlooking the Atlantic Ocean and the mouth of the Kennebec River, this hotel features a heated saltwater pool, beach and gardens. Other nearby activities include golf, tennis, kayaking, bicycling, boating, shopping and touring art galleries. Maine lobster and local seafood are the focus at the hotel's restaurant. 125 rooms. Pets accepted; fee. Restaurant, bar. Beach. Outdoor pool. Closed November-mid-May. $$

★★★KENNEBUNKPORT INN

One Dock Square, Kennebunkport, 207-967-2621, 800-248-2621;
www.kennebunkportinn.com

Built by a wealthy tea and coffee merchant in 1899, the Victorian mansion was renovated to be an inn in 1926. Conveniently located in the heart of the historic seaport of Kennebunkport, this inn is an easy walk to the harbor and all the shops and galleries of Dock Square. Guest rooms feature period antiques and reproductions, high four-post

beds, elegant fabrics and floral carpeting. 49 rooms. Complimentary continental break-
fast. Wireless Internet access. Restaurant, bar. Spa. Outdoor pool. $$$

★★★NONANTUM RESORT

95 Ocean Ave., Kennebunkport, 207-967-4050, 800-552-5651;
www.nonantumresort.com

This is one of the oldest operating inns in the state. The beach is nearby, as is the Bush
family compound for those hoping to glimpse the 41st or 43rd presidents. Maine
seafood is the specialty at the onsite restaurant. 111 rooms. Restaurant, bar. Outdoor
pool. Closed mid-November-April. Free local phone calls. $

★RHUMB LINE MOTOR LODGE

Ocean Avenue, Kennebunkport, 207-967-5457, 800-337-4862;
www.rhumblinemaine.com

59 rooms. Complimentary continental breakfast. Bar. Fitness room. Indoor pool, out-
door pool, whirlpool. Wireless Internet access. Spa. Fitness center. $

★★★★THE WHITE BARN INN

37 Beach Ave., Kennebunkport, 207-967-2321; www.whitebarninn.com

A cluster of cottages, restored barns and a circa-1860s house make up this quaint spot
on the coast of Maine. The charming rooms and suites are decorated with antiques
and feature wood-burning fireplaces, whirlpool tubs, and flatscreen TVs. Simple
pleasures here include relaxing by the stone swimming pool, riding a bike along the
coast, experiencing a spa treatment and having afternoon tea by the fire in the com-
fortable sitting room. The inn has one of the region's most acclaimed restaurants,
which serves New England cuisine in a rustic, candlelit setting. 25 rooms. Compli-
mentary full breakfast. Wireless Internet access. Restaurant, bar. Spa. Outdoor pool.
Business center. $$$$

SPECIALTY LODGINGS

BUFFLEHEAD COVE

Bufflehead Cove Lane, Kennebunkport, 207-967-3879; www.buffleheadcove.com

This secluded Victorian inn is spacious and old-fashioned. Close to downtown Ken-
nebunkport, guests can leisurely explore the local beaches or visit the numerous restau-
rants, art galleries, antique shops and old bookstores. Six rooms. Children over 11 years
only. Complimentary full breakfast. $$$

CAPE ARUNDEL INN

208 Ocean Ave., Kennebunkport, 207-967-2125; www.capearundelinn.com

This Victorian-style 1890 inn features turn-of-the-century décor and overlooks the
seacoast. 14 rooms. Complimentary continental breakfast. Restaurant. Closed mid-
December-mid-April. $$

CAPTAIN FAIRFIELD INN

8 Pleasant St., Kennebunkport, 207-967-4454, 800-322-1928;
www.captainfairfield.com

This Federal-style 1813 historic bed and breakfast is at the heart of Kennebunkport.
Guest rooms are decorated with antique and period furniture and each has its own

private bath and sitting area. The inn is surrounded by towering trees and gardens and overlooks the river and harbor. It is within walking distance to shops and art galleries, as well as the ocean and a variety of restaurants. Nine rooms. Children over 6 years only. Complimentary full breakfast. Wireless Internet access. **$$**

THE CAPTAIN JEFFERDS INN

5 Pearl St., Kennebunkport, 207-967-2311, 800-839-6844;
www.captainjefferdsinn.com
This historic inn built in 1804 has been fully restored and is furnished with antiques and period reproductions. All rooms have private baths, fresh flowers, down-filled comforters and fireplaces. A complimentary three-course breakfast is included as are afternoon refreshments. 15 rooms. Pets accepted, some restrictions; fee. Children over 8 years only. Complimentary full breakfast. Closed last two weeks in December. **$$$**

THE CAPTAIN LORD MANSION

6 Pleasant St., Kennebunkport, 207-967-3141, 800-522-3141; www.captainlord.com
Set on an acre of gardens, this inn is decorated with a worldly mix of period furnishings and different themes. Repeat visitors are rewarded with an engraved stone in the Memory Garden after their tenth stay. 17 rooms. Children over 12 years only. Complimentary full breakfast. **$**

ENGLISH MEADOWS INN

141 Port Road, Kennebunkport, 207-967-5766, 800-272-0698;
www.englishmeadowsinn.com
Victorian farmhouse (1860) and attached carriage house. 12 rooms. Pets accepted, some restrictions; fee. Complimentary full breakfast. Closed January. **$**

MAINE STAY INN & COTTAGES AT THE MELVILLE WALKER HOUSE

34 Maine St., Kennebunkport, 207-967-2117, 800-950-2117; www.mainestayinn.com
This 19th-century bed and breakfast (1860) is located in the residential area of Kennebunkport's historic district, near the harbor and beach. 17 rooms. Complimentary full breakfast. **$$$**

OLD FORT INN

8 Old Fort Ave., Kennebunkport, 207-967-5353, 800-828-3678; www.oldfortinn.com
This inn has guest rooms in a turn-of-the-century carriage house built of red brick and local stone. There is a tennis court and heated freshwater pool onsite. Located just one block from the Atlantic Ocean, guests can explore nearby beaches, boutiques and art galleries. 16 rooms. Complimentary full breakfast. Outdoor pool. Tennis. Closed mid-December-mid-April. Pool. **$$$$**

TIDES INN BY THE SEA

252 Kings Highway, Kennebunkport, 207-967-3757; www.tidesinnbythesea.com
Built as an inn in 1899. Original guest book on display; signatures include Theodore Roosevelt and Sir Arthur Conan Doyle. 22 rooms. Complimentary continental breakfast. Restaurant. Closed mid-October-mid-May. **$$$**

★
★
★
★
☆

YACHTSMAN LODGE & MARINA

57 Ocean Ave., Kennebunkport, 207-967-2511; www.yachtsmanlodge.com

30 rooms. Pets accepted, some restrictions; fee. Complimentary continental breakfast. Closed December-April. **$**

RESTAURANTS

★BARTLEY'S DOCKSIDE

Western Avenue, Kennebunkport, 207-967-5050; www.bartleys-dockside.com

Seafood menu. Lunch, dinner. Children's menu. Casual attire. Outdoor seating. **$$**

★★THE BELVIDERE ROOM

252 Kings Highway, Kennebunkport, 207-967-3757; www.tidesinnbythesea.com

American menu. Dinner. Closed Tuesday; also mid-October-mid-May. Bar. Children's menu. Casual attire. Reservations recommended. **$$**

★★THE LANDING HOTEL & RESTAURANT

21 Ocean Ave., Kennebunkport, 207-967-4221, 866-967-4221;
www.thelandinghotelandrestaurant.com

American, Seafood menu. Lunch, dinner. Closed late October-early May. Bar. Children's menu. Casual attire. Outdoor seating. **$$**

★MABEL'S LOBSTER CLAW

124 Ocean Ave., Kennebunkport, 207-967-2562

Seafood menu. Lunch, dinner. Children's menu. Casual attire. Reservations recommended. Outdoor seating. Closed November-early April. **$$**

★NUNAN'S LOBSTER HUT

9 Mills Road, Kennebunkport, 207-967-4362

Seafood menu. Dinner. Casual attire. Closed Columbus Day-May. **$$**

★★★STRIPERS

131-133 Ocean Ave., Kennebunkport, 207-967-5333; www.thebreakwaterinn.com

Its décor makes the restaurant feel like a modern seaside cottage, with a soft green banquette, steel-rimmed tabletops and a see-through aquarium wall that divides the entry from the main dining room. The menu includes options such as local Kennebunkport oysters, farm-raised striped bass, halibut and scallops. Located within the Breakwater Inn and Spa, Stripers is close to Dock Square's shops and galleries. Seafood menu. Dinner, brunch. Bar. Business casual attire. Reservations recommended. Valet parking. Outdoor seating. Closed late October-early April. **$$$**

★★★★★THE WHITE BARN INN RESTAURANT

37 Beach Ave., Kennebunkport, 207-967-2321; www.whitebarninn.com

A New England classic, this charming candlelit space inside the White Barn Inn is

MAINE

★
★
★
★

bedecked with fresh flowers and white linen-topped tables. Chef Jonathan Cartwright creates delicious regional dishes accented with a European flair. The four-course prix fixe menu changes weekly, highlighting seafood from Maine's waters as well as native game and poultry. The vast wine selection complements the cuisine, and a rolling cheese cart offers some of the best local artisans' products. American menu. Bar. Jacket required. Reservations recommended. Valet parking. No disabled facilities. Dinner. Closed three weeks in January. $$$$

SPA

★★★★SPA AT WHITE BARN INN
37 Beach Ave., Kennebunkport, 207-967-2321; www.whitebarninn.com
Though located in a traditional New England country inn, the Spa at White Barn Inn delivers minimalism without compromising luxury. Guests can request a light-of-the-moon plunge, which is a fizz of marine pebbles infused with mandarin orange and lemon essential oils, or an aroma sea bath. The nearby Kennebunk River provides the materials used in the spa's signature stone massage, while natural marine algae and Maine sea salts are incorporated into the body wraps.

KINGFIELD
Located in the valley of the Carrabassett River, Kingfield once had several lumber mills. The town was named after William King, Maine's first governor, and was the birthplace of F. E. and F. O. Stanley, the twins who developed the Stanley Steamer. Canoeing, hiking and downhill skiing are available in nearby areas.

WHAT TO SEE AND DO
CARRABASSETT VALLEY SKI AREA
Sugarloaf Access Road, Kingfield, 207-237-2000; www.sugarloaf.com
Approximately 50 miles of ski touring trails. Center offers lunch (daily); school, rentals; skating rink (fee), rentals; trail information area; shop. Half-day rates. Early December-late April, daily.

★
★★
★★
★★
★

SUGARLOAF/USA SKI AREA
Sugarloaf Access Road, Kingfield, 207-237-2000, 800-843-5623
This ski area features two quad, triple, eight double chairlifts; T-bar; school, patrol, rentals; snowmaking; lodge; restaurants, coffee shop, cafeteria, bars; nursery; bank, health club, shops. There are also Six Olympic runs, 45 miles of trails; longest run 3½ miles; vertical drop 2,820 feet. 65 miles of cross-country trails. Early November-May, daily.

HOTELS
★★★GRAND SUMMIT RESORT HOTEL
5091 Access Road, Kingfield, 207-237-2222, 800-843-5623; www.sugarloaf.com
Each room in this hotel has a view of the mountains and features oak furniture and brass fixtures. Guests can partake in skiing and golfing activities nearby. The hotel is located at the base of the slopes, making a great getaway for snow bunnies and families. 120 rooms. Restaurant, bar. Fitness room. Whirlpool. Golf, 18 holes. Tennis. Ski-in/ski-out. $

★★THE HERBERT GRAND HOTEL

Main Street, Kingfield, 207-265-2000, 800-843-4372; www.herbertgrandhotel.com

33 rooms. Pets accepted; fee. Complimentary continental breakfast. Restaurant. Free wireless Internet access. **$**

★★SUGARLOAF INN

Highway 27, Kingfield, 207-237-6814, 800-843-5623; www.sugarloaf.com/inn

42 rooms. Restaurant, bar. Indoor pool, outdoor pool, whirlpool. Golf. Tennis. Ski-in/ski-out. **$**

RESTAURANT
★★LONGFELLOW'S

247 Main St., Kingfield, 207-265-4394

American, seafood menu. Lunch, dinner. Children's menu. Outdoor seating. **$**

KITTERY

This old sea community has built ships since its early days. Kittery men built the *Ranger*, which sailed to France under John Paul Jones with the news of Burgoyne's surrender. Across the Piscataqua River from Portsmouth, New Hampshire, Kittery is the home of the Portsmouth Naval Shipyard.

Information: Greater York Region Chamber of Commerce, 1 Stonewall Lane, Kittery, 207-363-4422; www.yorkme.org

WHAT TO SEE AND DO
FORT FOSTER PARK

Northeast via Highway 103 to Gerrish Island, 207-439-3800; www.kittery.org

A 92-acre park with picnicking, pavilion; beach; baseball field; fishing pier. Cross-country skiing in winter. Entrance fee per individual and per vehicle. June-August, daily; May and September, Saturday-Sunday.

HAMILTON HOUSE

40 Vaughan Lanes, South Berwick, 207-384-2454; www.spnea.org

Redecorated at the turn of the century, the inn has a mixture of antiques, painted murals and country furnishings to emulate America's colonial past, The Georgian house overlooks the Salmon Falls River, and has a perennial garden, flowering trees and shrubs, and garden cottage. Tours: June-mid-October, Wednesday-Sunday afternoons.

KITTERY HISTORICAL AND NAVAL MUSEUM

Highway 1 and Rogers Road, Kittery, 207-439-3080

Exhibits portray history of U.S. Navy and Kittery—Maine's oldest incorporated town—as well as southern Maine's maritime heritage. June-October, Tuesday-Saturday.

SARAH ORNE JEWETT HOUSE

5 Portland St., South Berwick, 207-384-2454; www.spnea.org/visit/homes/jewett.htm

Novelist Sarah Orne Jewett spent most of her life in this 1774 Georgian residence. The interior was restored to re-create the appearance of the house during her time

(1849-1909), and still contains some original 18th- and 19th-century wallpaper and fine paneling. Her bedroom-study has been left as she had arranged it. June-mid-October, Friday-Sunday.

HOTEL
★COACHMAN INN
380 Highway 1, Kittery, 207-439-4434, 800-824-6183; www.coachmaninn.net
43 rooms. Complimentary continental breakfast. Outdoor pool. High-speed Internet access. **$**

RESTAURANTS
★CAP'N SIMEON'S GALLERY
90 Pepperell Road, Kittery Point, 207-439-3655; www.capnsimeons.com
Located in a 17th-century boathouse, this restaurant features nautical décor. There are views of the pier and lighthouses, and entertainment is offered on weekends. Seafood menu. Lunch, dinner, Sunday brunch. Bar. Children's menu. Casual attire. **$$**

★★WARREN'S LOBSTER HOUSE
11 Water St., Kittery, 207-439-1630; www.lobsterhouse.com
Seafood menu. Lunch, dinner. Sunday brunch. Bar. Children's menu. Casual attire. Valet parking. Outdoor seating. **$$**

LEWISTON

Maine's second-largest city is 30 miles up the Androscoggin River from the sea, directly across the river from its sister city of Auburn. Known as the Twin Cities, both are strong manufacturing communities. Lewiston was the first of the two cities to harness the water power of the Androscoggin Falls, but both cities make good use of the river.
Information: Androscoggin County Chamber of Commerce,
179 Lisbon St., 207-783-2249; www.androscoggincounty.com

WHAT TO SEE AND DO
BATES COLLEGE
56 Campus Ave., Lewiston, 207-786-6255; www.bates.edu
(1855) New England's oldest and the nation's second-oldest coeducational institution of higher learning; originally the Maine State Seminary, it was renamed after a prominent Boston investor. Liberal arts and sciences. On its well-landscaped campus are the Edmund S. Muskie Archives (1936 alumnus, former Senator and U.S. Secretary of State) and a beautiful chapel containing a handcrafted tracker-action organ.

SPECIAL EVENT
FESTIVAL DE JOIE
190 Birch St., Lewiston, 207-782-6231; www.festivaldejoie.org
Celebration of Lewiston and Auburn's Franco-American heritage. Features ethnic songs, dancing, cultural activities and traditional foods. Late July-early August.

HOTEL
★★RAMADA INN
490 Pleasant St., Lewiston, 207-784-2331, 800-272-6232; www.ramadamaine.com
117 rooms. Complimentary continental breakfast. Restaurant, bar. Fitness room. Indoor pool, whirlpool. Business center. **$**

LUBEC
Quoddy Head State Park, the easternmost point in the United States, is located in Lubec. There is a lighthouse here, as well as the Franklin D. Roosevelt Memorial Bridge, which stretches over Lubec Narrows to Campobello Island. Roosevelt summered here throughout much of his childhood and into his adult years.

WHAT TO SEE AND DO
ROOSEVELT CAMPOBELLO INTERNATIONAL PARK
459 Highway 774, New Brunswick, 506-752-2922; www.nps.gov/roca
Canadian property jointly maintained by Canada and the United States. Approximately 2,800 acres, it includes the 11-acre estate where Franklin D. Roosevelt had his summer home and was stricken with poliomyelitis. Self-guided tours of 34-room house, interpretive guides available, films shown in visitor center, picnic sites in natural area, observation platforms and interpretive panels at Friar's Head. No camping. Saturday before Memorial Day-October 31, daily.

SPECIALTY LODGING
HOME PORT INN
45 Main St., Lubec, 207-733-2077, 800-457-2077; www.homeportinn.com
Built in 1880. Seven rooms. Complimentary continental breakfast. Restaurant. Closed mid-October-late May. **$**

RESTAURANT
★★HOME PORT INN
45 Main St., Lubec, 207-733-2077; www.homeportinn.com
American menu. Dinner. Casual attire. Reservations recommended. Closed November-April. **$$**

MILLINOCKET
Maine's tallest peak, Mount Katahdin rises over Baxter State Park, the origin point of the Appalachian Trail. Millinocket provides the closest base for exploring this outdoor wilderness area, where sightings of moose and even the Northern Lights are common.
Information: Katahdin Area Chamber of Commerce, 1029 Central St.,
207-723-4443; www.katahdinmaine.com; from 9 a.m.-4 p.m.

HOTELS
★★BEST VALUE HERITAGE MOTOR INN-MILLINOCKET
935 Central St., Millinocket, 207-723-9777; www.heritageinnmaine.com
49 rooms. Pets accepted. Complimentary continental breakfast. Restaurant, bar. Fitness room. Pool. Free wireless Internet access. **$**

MAINE

★
★
★
★

★★KATAHDIN INN
740 Central St., Millinocket, 207-723-4555, 877-902-4555; www.katahdininn.com
82 rooms. Pets accepted, some restrictions. Complimentary continental breakfast. Bar. Fitness room. Pool, whirlpool. $

★★PAMOLA MOTOR LODGE
973 Central St., Millinocket, 207-723-9746; www.pamolamotorlodge.com
29 rooms. Complimentary continental breakfast. Restaurant, bar. Outdoor pool, whirlpool. $

MONHEGAN ISLAND

Monhegan Plantation, nine miles out to sea, approximately two miles long and one mile wide, is devoted to lobsters and summer visitors. Rockwell Kent and Milton Burns were among the first of many artists to summer here. Today, the warm-weather population is about 20 times the year-round number. There is more work in winter—by special law, lobsters may be trapped in Monhegan waters only from January to June. This gives them the other six months to fatten. Thus, Monhegan lobsters command the highest prices.

Leif Ericson may have landed on here in AD 1000. In its early years, Monhegan Island was a landmark for sailors, and by 1611 it was well-known as a general headquarters for European fishermen, traders and explorers. For a time, the island was a pirate den. Small compared with other Maine islands, Monhegan is a land of contrasts. On one side of the island, sheer cliffs drop 150 feet to the ocean below, while on the other side Cathedral Woods offers visitors a quiet forest to explore.

★
★★
★
☆

WHAT TO SEE AND DO
MONHEGAN LIGHTHOUSE/MUSEUM
1 Lighthouse Hill, Monhegan Island, 207-596-7003; www.monheganmuseum.org
Historic lighthouse has been in operation since 1824; automated since 1959.

NORTHEAST HARBOR

This coastal village is located on Mount Desert Island, a land of rocky coastlines, forests and lakes. The island is reached from the mainland by a short bridge.

WHAT TO SEE AND DO
FERRY SERVICE
33 Main St., Cranberry Isles, 207-244-3575
Connects Northeast Harbor with the Cranberry Isles; three-mile, 30-minute crossing. Summer: daily; rest of year: schedule varies.

WOODLAWN MUSEUM (THE BLACK HOUSE)
172 Surrey Road, Northeast Harbor, 207-667-8671; www.woodlawnmuseum.com
Circa-1820 Federal house built by a local landowner; antiques. Garden; carriage house with old carriages and sleighs. May-October: Tuesday-Sunday; rest of year: by appointment.

HOTEL

★★★ASTICOU INN

15 Peabody Drive, Northeast Harbor, 207-276-3344, 800-258-3373;
www.asticou.com

Rooms at this sprawling Victorian inn are decorated with oriental rugs and traditional furniture. The grounds include beautifully landscaped gardens as well as clay tennis courts and an outdoor heated pool. 31 rooms. Off season, Monday-Friday. In season: daily. Closed mid-September-mid-June. Restaurant, bar. Outdoor pool. Tennis. Heated swimming pool. Free Wi-Fi. Free shuttle service available. Spa. **$$$**

SPECIALTY LODGING

MAISON SUISSE INN

Kimball Lane and Main Street, Northeast Harbor, 207-276-5223, 800-624-7668;
www.maisonsuisse.com

This restored, single-style 1892 summer cottage was once a speakeasy during Prohibition. 15 rooms. Pets accepted, some restrictions. Complimentary full breakfast. Closed November-April. **$$$**

RESTAURANT

★DOCKSIDER

14 Sea St., Northeast Harbor, 207-276-3965

Seafood menu. Lunch, dinner. Children's menu. Casual attire. Outdoor seating. Closed Columbus Day-mid-May. **$$**

NORWAY

Norway was founded by English settlers in the late 1700s. This tiny hamlet is known for its picturesque, rolling hills.

Information: Oxford Hills Chamber of Commerce, 213 Main St.,
South Paris, 207-743-2281; www.oxfordhillsmaine.com

MAINE

WHAT TO SEE AND DO

PENNESSEEWASSEE LAKE

Interseaction of Route 117/188 and Route 26

This seven-mile-long lake covering 922 acres received its name from the Native American words meaning "sweet water." Swimming, beaches, waterskiing; brown trout, bass and perch fishing; boating (marina, rentals, launch). Ice skating. Contact Chamber of Commerce.

★
★★
★★
★
★

HOTEL

★★★WATERFORD INNE

258 Chadbourne Road, Waterford, 207-583-4037; www.waterfordinn.com

At this 19th-century eight-room farmhouse, the rooms are decorated in fresh country prints and simple farmhouse-style furniture. Meanwhile, the restaurant is a cozy welcoming spot that serves hearty, satisfying dishes like crab and leek bisque, and pork chops with apples. The inn is surrounded by fields and woods. Eight rooms. Pets accepted; fee. Complimentary full breakfast. Restaurant. **$**

RESTAURANT
★★MAURICE RESTAURANT FRANCAIS
109 Main St., South Paris, 207-743-2532; www.mauricerestaurant.com
French menu. Bar. Lunch, Tuesday-Friday, Sunday, dinner. **$$**

OGUNQUIT

Maine's "stern and rockbound coast" becomes a sunny strand here with a great white beach that stretches for three miles. The Ogunquit public beach is one of the finest on the Atlantic offering marine views of Perkins Cove and attracting a substantial art colony.

Information: Chamber of Commerce, 207-646-2939; www.ogunquit.org

WHAT TO SEE AND DO
OGUNQUIT MUSEUM OF AMERICAN ART
543 Shore Road, Ogunquit, 207-646-4909; www.ogunquitmuseum.org
20th-century American sculpture and painting. Museum overlooks the ocean and sculpture gardens. July-mid-October, daily.

SPECIAL EVENT
OGUNQUIT PLAYHOUSE
10 Highway 1, Northeast Harbor, 207-646-2402; www.ogunquitplayhouse.org
Established in the early 1930s. Top plays and musicals with professional actors. Late June-Labor Day weekend.

HOTELS
★★★ANCHORAGE BY THE SEA
125 Shore Road, Ogunquit, 207-646-9384; www.anchoragebythesea.com
This property has a prime location directly on the ocean. Rooms are comfortable and have views of the sea. 212 rooms. Complimentary continental breakfast. Restaurant. Pool, whirlpool. Free wireless Internet access. **$**

★THE BEACHMERE INN
62 Beachmere Place, Ogunquit, 207-646-2021, 800-336-3983;
www.beachmereinn.com
53 rooms. Complimentary continental breakfast. Closed mid-December-April. Beach. Wireless Internet access. **$$**

★★GORGES GRANT HOTEL
449 Main St., Ogunquit, 207-646-7003, 800-646-5001; www.ogunquit.com
81 rooms. Closed mid-December-March. Restaurant. Fitness room. Pool, whirlpool. Beach. Golf. Wireless Internet access. Breakfast. **$**

★★THE GRAND HOTEL
276 Shore Road, Ogunquit, 207-646-1231, 800-806-1231; www.thegrandhotel.com
28 rooms. Complimentary continental breakfast. Pool. Closed September-March. Wireless Internet access. **$**

★JUNIPER HILL INN

336 Main St., Ogunquit, 207-646-4501, 800-646-4544; www.ogunquit.com

100 rooms. Fitness room. Indoor pool, two outdoor pools, two whirlpools. Wireless Internet access. Free Breakfast. **$**

★★MEADOWMERE

Highway 1, Ogunquit, 207-646-9661, 800-633-8718; www.meadowmere.com

145 rooms. Complimentary continental breakfast. Restaurant. Fitness room. Indoor pool, outdoor pool, whirlpool. **$$**

★THE MILESTONE

687 Main St., Ogunquit, 207-646-4562, 800-646-6453; www.ogunquit.com

70 rooms. Fitness room. Outdoor pool, whirlpool. Closed November-March. Wireless Internet access. Breakfast. **$**

★RIVERSIDE

50 Riverside Lane, Ogunquit, 207-646-2741; www.riversidemotel.com

38 rooms. Complimentary continental breakfast. Closed November-mid-April. **$**

★THE TERRACE BY THE SEA

23 Wharf Lane, Ogunquit, 207-646-3232; www.terracebythesea.com

36 rooms. Complimentary continental breakfast. Outdoor pool. Closed January-February. **$**

SPECIALTY LODGINGS

HARTWELL HOUSE

312 Shore Road, Ogunquit, 207-646-7210, 800-235-8883;
www.hartwellhouseinn.com

At this countryside bed and breakfast, most rooms have French doors leading to terraces or balconies that overlook the gardens. A full gourmet breakfast and afternoon tea are served daily. This inn is only minutes away from a summer resort. 16 rooms. Children over 14 years only. Complimentary full breakfast. **$$**

THE PINE HILL INN

14 Pine Hill Road South, Ogunquit, 207-361-1004, 724-730 1484;
www.pinehillsinn.com

Turn-of-the-century cottage with sun porch. Six rooms. Children over 12 years only. Complimentary full breakfast. **$**

RESTAURANTS

★★★98 PROVENCE

262 Shore Road, Ogunquit, 207-646-9898; www.98provence.com

The cottage-like setting provides a warm, comfortable atmosphere. This welcoming country French restaurant offers an appealing menu in a small clapboard house with classics like fisherman soup or escargot. French menu. Dinner. Bar. Casual attire. Closed Tuesday; mid-December-mid-April. **$$**

★★★ARROWS

Berwick Road, Ogunquit, 207-361-1100; www.arrowsrestaurant.com

This idyllic restaurant housed in an 18th-century farmhouse is a seasonal dining destination. Co-owners and co-chefs Clark Frasier and Mark Gaier bake their own breads, grow their own organic vegetables and offer a creative and elegant menu. American menu. Dinner. Bar. Business casual attire. Reservations recommended. Closed Monday; also December-early April. Valet parking. $$$

★BARNACLE BILLY'S

Perkins Cove, Ogunquit, 207-646-5575, 800-866-5575; www.barnbilly.com

Lobster tank. Seafood menu. Lunch, dinner. Casual attire. Valet parking. Outdoor seating. Reservations recommended. $$

★★BILLY'S ETC.

Oarweed Cove Road, Ogunquit, 207-646-4711; www.barnbilly.com

American, seafood menu. Lunch, dinner. Closed November-mid-April. Bar. Valet parking. Outdoor seating. Reservations recommended. $$

★★BLUE ELEPHANT

309 Shore Road, Ogunquit, 207-641-2028, 866-646-7064; www.seaviewmotel.com

Thai menu. Dinner. Bar. Casual attire. Reservations recommended. Outdoor seating. $$

★★★CLAY HILL FARM

220 Clay Hill Road, Cape Neddick, 207-361-2272; www.clayhillfarm.com

This restaurant, housed in a historic 1780 farmhouse, is located on 30 acres of protected woodlands and certified by the National Wildlife Association as a wildlife habitat and bird sanctuary. The menu features fresh and seasonal dishes such as basil roasted haddock with tomato, cured olives and artichoke hearts. Seafood menu. Dinner. Bar. Valet parking. Closed Monday-Wednesday, November-April. Garden breakfast. $$$

★★GYPSY SWEETHEARTS

30 Shore Road, Ogunquit, 207-646-7021; www.gypsysweethearts.com

International menu. Dinner. Bar. Casual attire. Reservations recommended. Outdoor seating. Closed Monday. $$

★★★JONATHAN'S

92 Bourne Lane, Ogunquit, 207-646-4777; www.jonathansrestaurant.com

This restaurant is located in a house surrounded by gardens that was once the home of the owner's parents. It serves dishes created with fresh, seasonal ingredients (many of the fruits and vegetables come from the restaurant's own farm, as does the lamb.) American menu. Dinner. Bar. Casual attire. Closed Monday. $$

★★NO. FIVE-O

50 Shore Road, Ogunquit, 207-646-5001; www.five-oshoreroad.com

American menu. Dinner. Bar. Casual attire. Reservations recommended. Outdoor seating. Closed December 24-28, late February-late March. $$

★OARWEED COVE
Oarweed Road, Ogunquit, 207-646-4022; www.oarweed.com
American, seafood menu. Lunch, dinner. Bar. Children's menu. Casual attire. Valet parking. Outdoor seating. Closed mid-October-early May. **$$**

★OGUNQUIT LOBSTER POUND
504 Main St., Ogunquit, 207-646-2516
Seafood menu. Dinner. Closed mid-November-mid-February. Bar. Children's menu. Casual attire. Outdoor seating. **$$**

★★OLD VILLAGE INN
250 Main St., Ogunquit, 207-646-7088; www.theoldvillageinn.com
This cozy and romantic restaurant features Victorian décor and is located in a mid-19th-century inn. American menu. Dinner. Bar. Children's menu. **$$**

★★S. W. SWAN BISTRO
309 Shore Road, Ogunquit, 207-646-7210; www.swanbistro.com
American, French menu. Dinner. Bar. Casual attire. Reservations recommended. Outdoor seating. **$$$**

OLD ORCHARD BEACH

This popular beach resort, 12 miles south of Portland, is a longtime favorite on the Maine Coast. It has a crescent beach seven miles long and about 700 feet wide.
Information: Chamber of Commerce, 207-934-2500, 800-365-9386;
www.oldorchardbeachmaine.com

WHAT TO SEE AND DO
THE PIER
Old Orchard Beach
Extends 475 feet into the harbor; features shops, boutiques, restaurant. May-September, daily.

MAINE

★
★
★
★
★

HOTELS
★THE EDGEWATER
57 W. Grand Ave., Old Orchard Beach, 207-934-2221, 800-203-2034;
www.janelle.com
35 rooms. Closed mid-November-mid-March. Outdoor pool. Daily. **$**

★THE GULL MOTEL INN & COTTAGES1
89 W. Grand Ave., Old Orchard Beach, 207-934-4321, 877-662-4855;
www.gullmotel.com
25 rooms. Outdoor pool. Closed mid-October-April. Pets not accepted. **$**

★HORIZON
2 Atlantic Ave., Old Orchard Beach, 207-934-2323, 888-550-1745;
www.horizonmotel.com
14 rooms, all suites. Closed mid-October-April. **$**

★ROYAL ANCHOR RESORT

203 E. Grand Ave., Old Orchard Beach, 207-934-4521, 800-934-4521;
www.royalanchor.com

40 rooms. Complimentary continental breakfast. Outdoor pool. Tennis. Closed mid-October-April. **$**

SPECIALTY LODGING
ATLANTIC BIRCHES INN

20 Portland Ave., Old Orchard Beach, 207-934-5295, 888-934-5295;
www.atlanticbirches.com

Restored Victorian house. 10 rooms. Complimentary continental breakfast. Outdoor pool. Internet access. **$**

RESTAURANTS
★★BELL BUOY RESTAURANT

24 Old Orchard St., Old Orchard Beach, 207-934-2745

American, seafood menu. Breakfast, dinner. Bar. Children's menu. Casual attire. Reservations recommended. **$$**

★★CAPTAIN'S GALLEY RESTAURANT

168 Saco Ave., Old Orchard Beach, 207-934-1336;
www.captainsgalleyrestaurant.com

Seafood, steak menu. Breakfast, lunch, dinner. Bar. Children's menu. Casual attire. **$$**

★★★JOSEPH'S BY THE SEA

55 W. Grand Ave., Old Orchard Beach, 207-934-5044; www.josephsbythesea.com

American, seafood menu. Breakfast, dinner. Bar. Casual attire. Reservations recommended. Outdoor seating. Closed December 21, Thanksgiving Day, April; hours vary in May, November-December. **$$**

★★OCEANSIDE GRILLE AT THE BRUNSWICK

39 W. Grand Ave., Old Orchard Beach, 207-934-4873; www.thebrunswick.com

American, seafood menu. Lunch, dinner, late-night. Bar. Casual attire. Reservations recommended. Outdoor seating. **$$**

ORONO

The Penobscot River flows through this valley town, which is named after Native American chief Joseph Orono. The "Maine Stein Song" was popularized here in the 1930s by Rudy Vallee.

Information: Bangor Region Chamber of Commerce, 519 Main St., Bangor,
207-947-0307; www.bangorregion.com

WHAT TO SEE AND DO
UNIVERSITY OF MAINE-ORONO

5703 Alumni Hall, Orono, 207-581-1110; www.umaine.edu

This is the largest of seven campuses of the University of Maine system. On campus is Jordan Planetarium (207-581-1341).

RESTAURANT
★★MARGARITA'S
15 Mill St., Orono, 207-866-4863; www.margs.com
American, Mexican menu. Lunch, dinner. Bar. Children's menu. Casual attire. **$$**

PORTLAND

Maine's largest city is located on Casco Bay and dotted with islands that are popular with summer visitors. Because of its size, affordable housing and free-spirited feel, Portland is increasingly popular as an alternative to the nation's biggest cities (and absorbs plenty of Boston refugees). It's a city of fine elms, stately old homes, historic churches and charming streets. Portland was raided by Native Americans several times before the Revolution. In 1775, it was bombarded by the British, who afterward burned the town. Another fire in 1866 wiped out large sections of the city. Henry Wadsworth Longfellow, the famed poet who lived in Portland, remarked that the ruins reminded him of Pompeii.

Information: Convention & Visitors Bureau of Greater Portland,
245305 Commercial St., 207-772-5800; www.visitportland.com

WHAT TO SEE AND DO
CHILDREN'S MUSEUM OF MAINE
142 Free St., Portland, 207-828-1234; www.childrensmuseumofme.org
Hands-on museum where interactive exhibits allow children to become a Maine lobsterman, storekeeper, computer expert or astronaut. Memorial Day-Labor Day, daily; rest of year, Tuesday-Saturday, 10 a.m.-5 p.m. Sunday, noon-5 p.m. Admission: $8 per person.

MAINE HISTORY GALLERY
489 Congress St., Portland, 207-774-1822; www.mainehistory.com
Features Museum's Collection of more than 2,000 paintings, prints and other original works of art, and approximately 8,000 artifacts. Collection includes costume and textiles, decorative arts, Native American artifacts and archaeological material, political items and military artifacts. Changing programs and exhibits trace the history of life in Maine. Gallery talks and hands-on workshops also offered. (Daily) Monday-Saturday 10 a.m.-5 p.m. Sunday noon-5 p.m.

PORTLAND HEAD LIGHTHOUSE MUSEUM
1000 Shore Road, Cape Elizabeth, 207-799-2661; www.portlandheadlight.com
Said to be first lighthouse authorized by the United States and the oldest lighthouse in continuous use; erected in 1791 on orders from George Washington. June-October, daily. November-December and April-May, weekends. 10 a.m.-4 p.m., Admission: adults $2, children $1.

PORTLAND MUSEUM OF ART
7 Congress Square, Portland, 207-775-6148; www.portlandmuseum.org
Collections of American and European paintings, sculpture, prints and decorative art; State of Maine Collection with works by artists from and associated with Maine; John Whitney Payson Collection (Renoir, Monet, Picasso and others). Free admission Friday

MAINE

★
★
★
★
☆

evenings. May-October: daily; November-April: Tuesday-Sunday 10 a.m.-5 p.m., Friday 10 a.m.-9 p.m., closed on New Year's Day, Thanksgiving, Christmas Day.

PORTLAND OBSERVATORY

138 Congress St., Portland, 207-774-5561; www.portlandlandmarks.org/observatory
This 1807 octagonal, shingled landmark is the last surviving 19th-century signal tower on the Atlantic. There are 102 steps to the top. Memorial Day-Columbus Day, daily.

TATE HOUSE

1267 Westbrook St., Portland, 207-774-6177; www.tatehouse.org
A 1755 Georgian structure built by George Tate, mast agent for the British Navy. Furnished and decorated in the period of Tate's residence, 1755-1800; 18th-century herb gardens. Mid-June-mid-October: Tuesday-Sunday 10 a.m.-4 p.m.; weekends through October 31. Adults $7, seniors $5, children $2.

VICTORIA MANSION

109 Danforth St., Portland, 207-772-4841; www.victoriamansion.org
One of the finest examples of 19th-century architecture surviving in the United States. Opulent 1858 Victorian interior includes frescoes, carved woodwork and stained and etched glass. May-October, Monday-Saturday 10 a.m.-4 p.m.; closed Memorial Day.

WADSWORTH-LONGFELLOW HOUSE

489 Congress St., Portland, 207-772-1807;
www.mainehistory.org/house_overview.shtml
Boyhood home of Henry Wadsworth Longfellow. Built in 1785 by the poet's grandfather, General Peleg Wadsworth, it is maintained by the Maine Historical Society. Contains furnishings, portraits and personal possessions of the family. June-mid-October, daily.

SPECIAL EVENTS
NEW YEAR'S EVE PORTLAND

582 Congress St., Portland, 207-772-5800
Fifteen indoor and many outdoor locations. More than 90 performances, mid-afternoon-mid-night; a citywide, nonalcoholic celebration with parade and fireworks. December 31.

OLD PORT FESTIVAL

549 Congress St., Portland, 207-772-6828; www.portlandmaine.com
Celebration of Portland's restored waterfront district between Commercial Street and Congress Street. This one-day event features a parade, entertainment and food. Early June.

SIDEWALK ART SHOW

14 Ocean Great Way, Portland, 207-772-5800; www.visitportland.com
Exhibits extend along Congress Street from Congress Square to Monument Square. Third Saturday in August.

HOTELS

★★BEST WESTERN MERRY MANOR INN

700 Main St., South Portland, 207-774-6151, 800-780-7234;
www.merrymanorinn.com

153 rooms. Pets accepted. Wireless Internet access. Restaurant. Fitness room. Outdoor pool, children's pool, whirlpool. Airport transportation available. Business center. **$**

★★★BLACK POINT INN

510 Black Point Road, Scarborough, 207-883-2500, 800-258-0003;
www.blackpointinn.com

This seaside resort is located on a hill at the tip of Prout's Neck with the natural rugged beauty of the Maine coast on three sides. Each room has period wallpaper and both porcelain and crystal lamps. Many of the rooms and cottages were former sea captains' homes. 65 rooms. Closed December-April. Pets accepted, some restrictions; fee. Restaurant, bar. Fitness room. Beach. Indoor pool, outdoor pool, whirlpool. Airport transportation available. Free high-speed Internet access. **$$$**

★★★EASTLAND PARK HOTEL

157 High St., Portland, 207-775-5411, 888-671-8008; www.eastlandparkhotel.com

202 rooms. Pets accepted; fee. Wireless Internet access. Restaurant, bar. Fitness room. Airport transportation available. Business center. **$$**

★★EMBASSY SUITES

1050 Westbrook St., Portland, 207-775-2200, 800-753-8767;
www.embassysuitesportland.com

This hotel is located close to the Portland International Jetport and the Maine Mall (complimentary shuttle service is provided to both). Guest rooms feature a separate sitting area and sleeping room, plush beds, two small desks and a wet bar with microwave. An evening manager's reception (with a three-piece band) is offered on Thursdays. 119 rooms, all suites. Pets accepted. Complimentary full breakfast. Wireless Internet access. Restaurant, bar. Fitness room. Indoor pool, whirlpool. Business center. Airport transportation available. Complimentary parking. **$$**

★HAMPTON INN

171 Philbrook Ave., South Portland, 207-773-4400, 800-426-7866;
www.portlandhamptoninn.com

117 rooms. Pets accepted; fee. Complimentary continental breakfast. High-speed Internet access. Airport transportation available. Indoor pool. Fitness room. **$**

★★HOLIDAY INN

88 Spring St., Portland, 207-775-2311, 800-345-5050; www.innbythebay.com

239 rooms. Free wireless Internet access. Restaurant, bar. Fitness room. Indoor pool. Airport transportation available. Business center. Complimentary parking. **$$**

★★★INN BY THE SEA

40 Bowery Beach Road, Cape Elizabeth, 207-799-3134, 800-888-4287;
www.innbythesea.com

This all-suite resort property is near the historic city of Portland on the coast. Every

★
★
★
★
★

guest room has a porch or deck with a view of the ocean. Guests can enjoy a number of recreational activities such as an outdoor pool, tennis, shuffleboard, walking or jogging and volleyball. Amenities include terrycloth robes and turndown service with a 24-hour business and concierge service. 57 rooms, all suites. Pets accepted, some restrictions. Restaurant. Outdoor pool. Tennis. **$$**

★★★PORTLAND HARBOR HOTEL

468 Fore St., Portland, 207-775-9090, 888-798-9090; www.portlandharborhotel.com

This hotel is located in the Old Port district of downtown Portland, a fully restored area of Victorian buildings that is now restaurants, shops and galleries, just one block from the waterfront. A boutique hotel, it exudes European style and charm. An enclosed garden patio with a fountain is just off the lobby dining room. Guest rooms feature toile spreads, custom mattresses with fine linens, feather pillows and duvets, and a two-level desk with leather chair. 97 rooms. Pets accepted, some restrictions; fee. Wireless Internet access. Restaurant, bar. Fitness room. Airport transportation available. Business center. **$$**

★★★PORTLAND MARRIOTT AT SABLE OAKS

200 Sable Oaks Drive, South Portland, 207-871-8000, 800-752-8810; www.marriott.com

Just a few miles from the Portland International Jetport and close to historic downtown Portland, this hotel is situated on a hill in a surprisingly rural setting. A small pond with a fountain and covered portico welcomes guests at the hotel entry. Nearby activities include golf, jogging, tennis, a spa and the beach. 227 rooms. Pets accepted, some restrictions; fee. Wireless Internet access. Two restaurants, bar. Fitness room. Indoor pool, whirlpool. Golf, 18 holes. Airport transportation available. Business center. Complimentary parking. **$$**

★★★PORTLAND REGENCY HOTEL & SPA

20 Milk St., Portland, 207-774-4200, 800-727-3436; www.theregency.com

This small European-style hotel is located in Portland's Old Port waterfront district, surrounded by galleries, shops and restaurants. A circular brick driveway leads guests to the historic red brick building, which was built in 1895. The lobby and public rooms hold true to the hotel's heritage, with mahogany woodwork, Victorian furnishings and a "map room" with burgundy leather chairs. The period décor in the guest rooms includes two- or four-poster beds and antique or reproduction dressers, tables and desks. The spa offers a complete selection of treatments. 95 rooms. Wireless Internet access. Restaurant, bar. Fitness room. Spa. Whirlpool. Airport transportation available. Business center. Valet parking. **$$**

SPECIALTY LODGINGS

INN AT SAINT JOHN

939 Congress St., Portland, 207-773-6481, 800-636-9127; www.innatstjohn.com

Built in 1896; European motif, antiques. 39 rooms. Pets accepted, some restrictions. Complimentary continental breakfast. Airport transportation available. Restaurants. Wireless Internet access. **$**

INN ON CARLETON

46 Carleton St., Portland, 207-775-1910, 800-639-1779; www.innoncarleton.com

This brick townhouse was built in 1869. Six rooms. Children over 9 years only. Complimentary full breakfast. **$$**

POMEGRANATE INN

49 Neal St., Portland, 207-772-1006, 800-356-0408; www.pomegranateinn.com

This inn built in 1884 is small, yet sophisticated and located in the historic Western Promenade neighborhood. Antiques and art dot the property. There is also an urban garden for guests to enjoy. Located a short walk to the midtown arts district and there are museums, art galleries, boat rides, fine restaurants and recreational activities nearby. Eight rooms. Children over 16 years only. Complimentary full breakfast. **$$**

RESTAURANTS

★★★BACK BAY GRILL

65 Portland St., Portland, 207-772-8833; www.backbaygrill.com

Located in downtown Portland in a restored 1888 pharmacy, this local favorite offers innovative cuisine and an intimate dining room. The pressed-tin ceiling adds to the ambience of the cozy rooms. The daily menu features fresh locally sourced foods (the restaurant is a member of the Maine Organic Farmers Growers Association) and emphasizes high-quality ingredients. Special dinners are offered with a prix fixe menu (wine tastings, wine dinners, lobster evenings). American menu. Dinner. Closed Sunday. Bar. Business casual attire. Reservations recommended. **$$$**

★★DI MILLO'S FLOATING RESTAURANT

25 Long Wharf, Portland, 207-772-2216; www.dimillos.com

American, seafood menu. Lunch, dinner, late-night. Bar. Children's menu. Casual attire. Reservations recommended. Outdoor seating. **$$**

★★EGGSPECTATION

125 Western Ave., South Portland, 207-871-7000; www.eggspectationusa.com

American menu. Breakfast, lunch, dinner. Bar. Children's menu. Casual attire. Reservations recommended. Outdoor seating. Daily. **$$**

★★FORE STREET

288 Fore St., Portland, 207-775-2717; www.forestreet.biz

Seafood, steak menu. Dinner. Bar. Casual attire. Reservations recommended. **$$**

★NEWICK'S SEAFOOD

740 Broadway, South Portland, 207-799-3090, 877-439-0255; www.newicks.com

Seafood menu. Lunch, dinner. Bar. Children's menu. Casual attire. Closed Monday (off-season). **$**

★★★PARK KITCHEN

422 N.W. Eighth Ave., Portland, 503-223-7275; www.parkkitchen.com

Located in a historic building along the North Park blocks, the food here is influenced by the seasons, with dishes such as lamb cassoulet making an appearance in winter, while salmon with cucumber and caraway is a summer specialty. Wines

MAINE

★
★
★
★
★

and microbrews are recommended for each entrée that chef Scott Dolich creates at this welcoming restaurant, which features an open kitchen. American menu, other. Lunch, dinner. Brunch. Bar. Children's menu. Casual attire. Reservations recommended. Outdoor seating. Closed Monday. **$$**

★★RIBOLITA
41 Middle St., Portland, 207-774-2972
Italian menu. Dinner. Children's menu. Casual attire. Reservations recommended. Outdoor seating. Closed Sunday-Monday. **$$**

★★★THE ROMA CAFÉ
769 Congress St., Portland, 207-773-9873; www.theromacafe.com
Located in a circa-1887 Victorian mansion, this restaurant features small dining rooms with fireplaces, a beautiful carved wood staircase and beveled glass windows in a charming atmosphere. Menu offerings include seafood, lobster and Italian dishes. Italian, seafood menu. Lunch, dinner. Bar. Casual attire. Reservations recommended. Closed Sunday-Monday. **$$**

★★★STREET & CO.
33 Wharf St., Portland, 207-775-0887
Located in the Old Port District on a cobblestone street, this 19th-century building was formerly a fish warehouse. The décor is upscale rustic, with exposed bricks, original plank hardwood flooring and beamed ceilings. Tables are heavy black stone slabs with rough-hewn wood legs. A fully open kitchen is opposite the center dining room, which offers large windows that open to the street. Only seafood is served, along with the freshest seasonal organic produce. American, seafood menu. Dinner. Bar. Casual attire. Reservations recommended. **$$$**

★★TYPHOON! ON BROADWAY
410 S.W. Broadway, Portland, 503-244-8285; www.typhoonrestaurants.com
Thai menu. Lunch, dinner. Casual attire. Reservations recommended. Outdoor seating. **$$**

★★WALTER'S CAFÉ
15 Exchange St., Portland, 207-871-9258; www.walterscafe.com
International menu. Lunch, dinner. Bar. Business casual attire. Reservations recommended. **$$**

RANGELEY
There are 40 lakes and ponds within 10 miles of Rangeley. The six lakes that form the Rangeley chain—Rangeley, Cupsuptic, Mooselookmeguntic, Aziscoos, Upper Richardson and Lower Richardson—are spread over a wide area and give rise to the Androscoggin River. Some of Maine's highest mountains rise beside the lakes. The development of ski and snowmobiling areas has turned this summer vacation spot into a year-round resort.
Information: Rangeley Lakes Chamber of Commerce, 207-864-5364, 800-685-2537; www.rangeleymaine.com

WHAT TO SEE AND DO
RANGELEY LAKE STATE PARK
South Shore Drive, Rangeley, 207-864-3858; www.state.me.us/doc/parks
More than 690 acres on Rangeley Lake. Swimming, fishing, boating (ramp, floating docks); snowmobiling permitted; picnicking, camping. May 15-October 1. Standard fees.

WILHELM REICH MUSEUM
19 Dodge Pond Road, Rangeley, 207-864-3443; www.wilhelmreichmuseum.org
Unusual stone building housing scientific equipment, paintings and other memorabilia of this physician-scientist; slide presentation, nature trail, discovery room. July-August, Wednesday-Sunday 1-5 p.m.; September, Sunday only 1-5 p.m.; rest of year, by appointment. Admission: adults $6, children under 12 free.

HOTELS
★★COUNTRY CLUB INN
1 Country Club Drive, Rangeley, 207-864-3831; www.countryclubinnrangeley.com
19 rooms. Pets accepted, some restrictions; fee. Restaurant, bar. Outdoor pool. Airport transportation available. Closed April, November. Dinner, sports. **$$**

★★★RANGELEY INN
2443 Main St., Rangeley, 207-864-3341, 800-666-3687; www.rangeleyinn.com
The year-round resort offers skiing and snowmobiling in the winter and swimming and boating in the summer. This restored inn is located within the mountain lake wilderness of the Longfellow mountains of western Maine. Moose and loons can be spotted nearby. 50 rooms. Pets accepted, some restrictions; fee. Restaurant, bar. Dining room. **$**

RESTAURANT
★★★RANGELEY INN
2443 Main St., Rangeley, 207-864-3341; www.rangeleyinn.com
This romantic inn has been open for more than 90 years. Enjoy an elegant dinner in the main dining room, which showcases an ornate tin ceiling and chandeliers. Then retire to the pub that has a crackling fire in the fireplace and local microbrews on tap. American, seafood menu. Breakfast, dinner. Bar. Children's menu. Outdoor seating. Closed Sunday-Thursday; also April-May. **$**

ROCKLAND
This town on Penobscot Bay is the banking and commercial center of the region and the seat of Knox County. It is also the birthplace of poet Edna St. Vincent Millay. Its economy is geared to the resort trade, but there is commercial fishing and light industry. It is the railhead for the whole bay. Supplies for boats, public landing and guest moorings are here.
Information: Rockland-Thomaston Area Chamber of Commerce,
207-596-0376, 800-562-2529; www.therealmaine.com

WHAT TO SEE AND DO
FARNSWORTH ART MUSEUM AND WYETH CENTER
16 Museum St., Rockland, 207-596-6457; www.farnsworthmuseum.org
Cultural and educational center for the region. Collection of more than 10,000 works of 18th- to 20th-century American art. Center houses personal collection of Wyeth family (N.C., Andrew and Jamie) art and archival material. Memorial Day-Columbus Day, daily; rest of year, Tuesday-Sunday 10 a.m.-5 p.m.; closed Thanksgiving, Christmas and New Year Day.

MAINE LIGHTHOUSE MUSEUM
1 Park Drive, Rockland, 207-594-3301; www.mainelighthousemuseum.com
A large collection of lighthouse lenses and artifacts; Civil War collection. Museum shop. Daily. Admission: adults $5, seniors $4, children under 12 free.

MAINE STATE FERRY SERVICE
517A Main St., Rockland, 207-596-2202; www.state.me.us/mdot/opt/ferry/215-info.php
Ferries make a 15-mile (1 hour, 15-minute) trip to Vinalhaven and a 12½-mile (1 hour, 10-minute) trip to North Haven. (All year, two to three trips daily.) Also a 23-mile (2 hour, 15-minute) trip to Matinicus Island once a month.

WINDJAMMERS
Maine Windjammer Association, 800-807-9463; www.sailmainecoast.com
Twelve old-time schooners sail out for three to six days following the same basic route through Penobscot Bay into Blue Hill and Frenchman's Bay, stopping at small villages and islands along the way. Each ship carries an average of 30 passengers. For further information, rates, schedules or reservations, contact the Maine Windjammer Association. Memorial Day-Columbus Day.

SPECIAL EVENTS
MAINE LOBSTER FESTIVAL
Harbor Park, or at the public landing, Rockland, 207-596-0376, 800-562-2529;
www.mainelobsterfestival.com
A five-day event centered on Maine's chief marine creature, with a huge tent cafeteria serving lobster and other seafood. Parade, harbor cruises, maritime displays, bands, entertainment. First weekend in August.

SCHOONER DAYS & NORTH ATLANTIC BLUES FESTIVAL
Rockland Harbor, 207-596-0376
Three-day festival celebrating Maine's maritime heritage, featuring a parade of the area's fleet of historic schooners, plus arts, entertainment, concessions, fireworks, blues bands and club crawl. Weekend after July 4.

HOTELS
★★★CAPTAIN LINDSEY HOUSE INN
5 Lindsey St., Rockland, 207-596-7950, 800-523-2145; www.lindseyhouse.com
This inn (built in 1830) is located in downtown Rockland, close to galleries, shops and the waterfront. The guest rooms have furnishings from around the world. 10 rooms. Children over 10 years only. Complimentary continental breakfast. Restaurant. $$

★GLEN COVE MOTEL
Highway 1, Glen Cove, 207-594-4062, 800-453-6268; www.glencovemotel.com
36 rooms. Outdoor pool. Closed February. Tennis. **$**

★★★SAMOSET RESORT
220 Warrenton St., Rockport, 207-594-2511, 800-341-1650; www.samoset.com
Named for the chief of the Pemaquid Indians who greeted the Pilgrims, this inn has welcomed guests since 1889. It is a year-round resort set on 230 ocean-side acres of the rugged coast of Maine. 178 rooms. Restaurant, bar. Children's activity center. Fitness room. Indoor pool, outdoor pool, whirlpool. Tennis. **$$**

SPECIALTY LODGINGS
CRAIGNAIR INN
5 Third St., Spruce Head, 207-594-7644, 800-320-9997; www.craignair.com
Built in 1930; boarding house converted to an inn in 1947. 21 rooms. Pets accepted, some restrictions; fee. Complimentary full breakfast. Restaurant. **$**

LAKESHORE INN
184 Lakeview Drive, Rockland, 207-594-4209, 866-540-8800; www.lakeshorebb.com
This Colonial New England farmhouse was built in 1767. Four rooms. Children over 12 years only. Complimentary full breakfast. Whirlpool. Internet access. Restaurant. **$$**

RESTAURANTS
★HARBOR VIEW
Thomaston Landing, Thomaston, 207-354-8173
Seafood, steak menu. Lunch, dinner. Bar. Outdoor seating. Closed Sunday-Monday (November-April). **$$**

MAINE

★★★PRIMO
2 S. Main St., Rockland, 207-596-0770; www.primorestaurant.com
An ardent supporter of sustainable agriculture, chef Melissa Kelly uses mostly local, organic produce (much of it grown on the restaurant's farm) and incorporates vegetables, even in meat dishes. The menu, which changes weekly, draws from coastal Italy and France, and features everything from asparagus soup with goat cheese to olive oil-poached salmon with bitter greens and beets to wood-roasted oysters. Co-owner and pastry chef Price Kushner contributes equally savory desserts. American menu. Dinner. Bar. Casual attire. Reservations recommended. Closed Tuesday. Restaurant. **$$$**

ROCKWOOD
This town is located on the shores of Moosehead Lake, the state's largest lake. Though the area is rustic and largely unspoiled, it's a favorite of hikers, campers and tourists.

WHAT TO SEE AND DO
NORTHERN OUTDOORS, INC.
Martins Pond and Highway 201, Rockwood, 207-663-4466, 800-765-7238;
www.northernoutdoors.com
Specializes in outdoor adventures including whitewater rafting on Maine's Kennebec, Penobscot and Dead rivers (May-October). Also snowmobiling (rentals), hunting, and resort facilities, rock climbing and freshwater kayak touring. Internet access.

WILDERNESS EXPEDITIONS, INC.
Rockwood, 207-534-2242, 800-825-9453; www.birches.com
Whitewater rafting on the Kennebec, Penobscot and Dead rivers; also canoe trips and ski tours. May-September: daily. Hunting. Dinner.

HOTEL
★★MOOSEHEAD MOTEL
16 Moosehead Motel Lane, Rockwood, 207-997-3800;
www.maineguide.com/moosehead/motel
14 rooms. Restaurant. Pets not accepted. Free parking. $

RUMFORD
This papermill town is located in the valley of the Oxford Hills, where the Ellis, Swift and Concord rivers flow into the Androscoggin. The spectacular Penacook Falls of the Androscoggin are right in town. Rumford serves as a year-round resort area.
Information: River Valley Chamber of Commerce, 10 Bridge St.,
207-364-3241; www.rivervalleychamber.com

★
★★
★★
★★

WHAT TO SEE AND DO
MOUNT BLUE STATE PARK
Highway 142, Weld, 207-585-2347
Recreation areas on Lake Webb include swimming, bathhouse, lifeguard, fishing, boating (ramp, rentals); hiking trail to Mount Blue, cross-country skiing, snowmobiling permitted, picnicking, camping. Memorial Day-Labor Day.

HOTEL
★BLUE IRIS MOTOR INN
1405 U.S. Route 2, Rumford, 207-364-4495, 800-601-1515;
www.blueiris.50megs.com
13 rooms. Outdoor pool. $

SACO
Saco, on the east bank of the Saco River, was originally called Pepperellboro, until its name was changed in 1805. Saco is only four miles from the ocean.
Information: Biddeford/Saco Chamber of Commerce, 110 Main St., 207-282-1567;
www.biddefordsacochamber.com

WHAT TO SEE AND DO
DYER LIBRARY & SACO MUSEUM
371 Main St., Saco, 207-283-3861; www.sacomuseum.org
Public library has arts and cultural programs. Museum features local history, decorative and fine art; American paintings, ceramics, glass, clocks and furniture; changing exhibits. Tuesday-Friday. Admission: adults $4, seniors $3, children under 6 free.

RESTAURANT
★★CASCADE INN
941 Portland Road, Saco, 207-283-3271
American, seafood menu. Lunch, dinner. Bar. Children's menu. Reservations recommended. $$

SCARBOROUGH
Scarborough contains some industry, but it is primarily a farming community and has been for more than 300 years. It is also a bustling tourist town during the summer months as vacationers descend upon nearby beaches and resorts. The first Anglican church in Maine is here, as is painter Winslow Homer's studio, now a national landmark.
Information: Convention & Visitors Bureau of Greater Portland,
245 Commercial St., Portland, 207-772-5800; www.visitportland.com

WHAT TO SEE AND DO
SCARBOROUGH MARSH AUDUBON CENTER
Pine Point Road, Scarborough, 207-883-5100; www.maineaudubon.org
Miles of nature and waterway trails through marshland area; canoe tours, special programs. Mid-June-Labor Day: daily, 9.30 a.m.-5.30 p.m.

HOTELS
★FAIRFIELD INN
2 Cummings Road, Scarborough, 207-883-0300, 800-228-2800;
www.fairfieldinn.com
120 rooms. Complimentary continental breakfast. Outdoor pool. High-speed Internet access. Complimentary parking. $

★TOWNEPLACE SUITES BY MARRIOTT PORTLAND SCARBOROUGH
700 Roundwood Drive, Scarborough, 207-883-6800, 800-491-2268;
www.towneplacesuites.com
95 rooms. Pets accepted; fee. Fitness room. Outdoor pool. Free High-speed Internet access. Complimentary parking. $

SEARSPORT
On the quiet upper reaches of Penobscot Bay, this is an old seafaring town. In the 1870s, at least 10 percent of the captains of the U.S. Merchant Marines lived here. The village abounds with antiques shops and is sometimes referred to as the "antique capital of Maine."
Information: Chamber of Commerce, Main Street, 207-548-6510;
www.searsportme.com

MAINE

★
★
★
★

PENOBSCOT MARINE MUSEUM

5 Church St., Searsport, 207-548-2529; www.penobscotmarinemuseum.org

Old Town Hall (1845), Merithew House (circa 1860), Fowler-True-Ross House (1825), Phillips Library and Carver Memorial Gallery. Ship models, marine paintings, American and Asian furnishings. Memorial Day weekend-mid-October: daily; rest of year, Monday-Saturday 9.30 a.m.-5.30 p.m. Admission: adults $8, children $3, children under six free.

SEBAGO LAKE

The second-largest of Maine's lakes, this is perhaps the most popular, partly because of its proximity to Portland. About 12 miles long and 8 miles wide, it lies among wooded hills. Boats can travel a total of more than 40 miles from the south end of Sebago Lake, through the Songo River to the north end of Long Lake. Numerous resort communities are hidden in the trees along the shores. Sebago, home of the landlocked salmon (*Salmo sebago*), is also stocked with lake trout.

WHAT TO SEE AND DO
MARRETT HOUSE AND GARDEN

Highway 25, Standish, 207-642-3032

Built in 1789 in Georgian style, but later enlarged and remodeled in the Greek Revival fashion; period furnishings; farm implements. Coin from Portland banks was stored here during the War of 1812, when it was thought that the British would take Portland. Perennial and herb garden. Tours June-October first Saturday of the month.

HOTEL
★★★MIGIS LODGE

Highway 302, South Casco, 207-655-4524; www.migis.com

This property is set on more than 100 acres of wooded land on the shore of a lake. A gift shop sells crafts from Maine. Wood for the fireplace in each guest room is delivered daily and there are handmade quilts on every bed and fresh flowers in the room. 58 rooms. Closed mid-October-May. Restaurant, bar. Children's activity center. Fitness room. Beach. Tennis. Airport transportation available. $$$

SKOWHEGAN

Skowhegan, on the Kennebec River, is surrounded by beautiful lakes. Shoes, paper pulp and other wood products are made here. In the village's center, there is a 12-ton, 62-foot-high Native American carved of native pine by Bernard Langlais. Skowhegan is the birthplace of Margaret Chase Smith, who served three terms in the U.S. House of Representatives and four terms in the Senate.

Information: Chamber of Commerce, 23 Commercial St. Skowhegan,
207-474-3621, 888-772-4392; www.skowheganchamber.com

WHAT TO SEE AND DO
HISTORY HOUSE

40 Elm St., Skowhegan, 207-474-6632

(1839) Old household furnishings; museum contains books, china, dolls and documents. Mid-June-mid-September: Tuesday-Friday afternoons.

SPECIAL EVENT
SKOWHEGAN STATE FAIR
Madison Avenue, Fairgrounds, Skowhegan, 207-474-2947;
www.skowheganstatefair.com

One of the oldest in the country, since 1818. One-mile-long midway, stage shows, harness racing; contests, exhibits. August.

RESTAURANT
★★HERITAGE HOUSE
182 Madison Ave., Skowhegan, 207-474-5100
Seafood, steak menu. Lunch, dinner. Bar. Casual attire. $$

SOUTHWEST HARBOR

This is a prosperous, working seacoast village on Mount Desert Island. There are lobster wharves, where visitors can watch about 70 fishermen bring in their catch, and many shops where boats are constructed. Visitors can also rent sailboats and power boats in Southwest Harbor to explore the coves and islands; hiking trails and quiet harbors offer relaxation.

Information: Chamber of Commerce, South West Harbor,
207-244-9264, 800-423-9264; www.acadia.net/swhtrcoc

WHAT TO SEE AND DO
CRANBERRY COVE BOATING COMPANY
207-244-5882
Cruise to Cranberry Islands. See native wildlife and learn island history. Six departures daily. Departs from Upper Town Dock. Mid-June-mid-September, daily.

MAINE STATE FERRY SERVICE
Grandville Road, Bass Harbor, 207-244-3254; www.maine.gov
Ferry makes six-mile (40-minute) trip to Swans Island and 8¼-mile (50-minute) trip to Frenchboro (limited schedule). Swans Island (all-year, one to six trips daily).

MOUNT DESERT OCEANARIUM
172 Clark Point Road, Southwest Harbor, 207-244-7330; www.theoceanarium.com
More than 20 tanks with Gulf of Maine marine creatures. Touch tank permits animals to be picked up. Exhibits on tides, seawater, plankton, fishing gear, weather. Inquire for information on special events. Mid-May-mid-October: Monday-Saturday.

WENDELL GILLEY MUSEUM
4 Herrick Road, Southwest Harbor, 207-244-7555; www.wendellgilleymuseum.org
Art and natural history museum featuring a collection of bird carvings by local artist Wendell Gilley; changing exhibits of local and historical art; films. June-October, Tuesday-Sunday 10 a.m.-4 p.m., May and November-December, Friday-Sunday 10 a.m.-4 p.m., closed Monday-Thursday. Admission: adults $5, children $2.

SPECIALTY LODGINGS
THE CLARK POINT INN
109 Clark Point Road, Southwest Harbor, 207-244-9828, 888-775-5953;
www.clarkpointinn.com
An 1857 Captain's house; deck with harbor view. Five rooms. Closed mid-October-April. Children over 8 years only. Complimentary full breakfast. Bar. High-speed Internet access. **$$**

KINGSLEIGH INN
373 Main St., Southwest Harbor, 207-244-5302; www.kingsleighinn.com
Built in 1904, wraparound porch. Eight rooms. Children over 10 years only. Complimentary full breakfast. Bar. Wireless Internet access. Hiking. Dinner. **$**

RESTAURANT
★BEAL'S LOBSTER PIER
182 Clark Point Road, Southwest Harbor, 207-244-3202; www.bealslobster.com
Seafood menu. Lunch, dinner. Casual attire. Outdoor seating. **$$**

WATERVILLE
A large Native American village once occupied the west bank of the Kennebec River where many of Waterville's factories now stand. An important industrial town, Waterville is the center of the Belgrade and China lakes resort area. Manufactured goods include men's and women's shirts, paper and molded-pulp products and woolens.

Information: Mid-Maine Chamber of Commerce, One Post Office
Square, 207-873-3315; www.midmainechamber.com

WHAT TO SEE AND DO
COLBY COLLEGE
4601 Mayflower Hill Drive, Waterville, 207-872-3000; www.colby.edu
This 714-acre campus, established in 1813, includes an art museum in the Bixler Art and Music Center (daily; free); a Walcker organ designed by Albert Schweitzer in Lorimer Chapel; and books, manuscripts and letters of Maine authors Edwin Arlington Robinson and Sarah Jewett in the Miller Library. Monday-Friday; free.

REDINGTON MUSEUM
62 Silver St., Waterville, 207-872-9439
Waterville Historical Society collection includes 18th- and 19th-century furnishings, manuscripts, Civil War and Native American relics; historical library; children's room; apothecary museum. Mid-May-Labor Day, Tuesday-Saturday.

TWO-CENT FOOTBRIDGE
Front Street, Waterville
One of the few remaining former toll footbridges in the United States.

MAINE

★
★
★
★

HOTELS

★★BEST WESTERN WATERVILLE INN

356 Main St., Waterville, 207-873-3335, 800-780-7234; www.bestwestern.com

86 rooms. Pets accepted. Restaurant, bar. Outdoor pool. Business center, fitness center. Pets accepted. $

★★HOLIDAY INN

375 Upper Main St., Waterville, 207-873-0111, 888-465-4329; www.holiday-inn.com

139 rooms. Pets accepted, some restrictions. Restaurant, bar. Fitness room. Indoor pool, whirlpool. $

RESTAURANTS

★BIG G'S DELI

581 Benton Ave., Winslow, 207-873-7808; www.big-g-s-deli.com

Deli menu. Breakfast, lunch, dinner. Children's menu. $

★★JOHN MARTIN'S MANOR

54 College Ave., Waterville, 207-873-5676; www.johnmartinsmanor.com

American, seafood menu. Lunch, dinner. Bar. Children's menu. Casual attire. Reservations recommended. $

★WEATHERVANE

470 Kennedy Memorial Drive, Waterville, 207-873-4522, 800-654-4369;
www.weathervaneseafoods.com

Seafood menu. Lunch, dinner. Children's menu. Casual attire. Reservations recommended. $$

WELLS

One of the oldest English settlements in Maine, Wells includes Moody, Wells Beach and Drake's Island. It was largely a farming center with some commercial fishing, until the resort trade began in the 20th-century. Charter boats, surfcasting and pier fishing attract anglers; there are also seven miles of beaches for swimming.

Information: Chamber of Commerce, 207-646-2451; www.wellschamber.org

MAINE

★
★
★
★

WHAT TO SEE AND DO

RACHEL CARSON NATIONAL WILDLIFE REFUGE

Highway 9, Wells, 207-646-9226; www.fws.gov/rachelcarson

Approximately 5,000 acres of salt marsh and coastal edge habitat; more than 250 species of birds may be observed during the year. Visitor center; one-mile interpretive nature trail. All year, sunrise-sunset.

WELLS NATURAL ESTUARINE RESEARCH RESERVE

342 Laudholm Farm Road, Wells, 207-646-1555; www.wellsreserve.org

Approximately 1,600 acres of fields, forest, wetlands and beach. Laudholm Farm serves as visitor center. Programs on coastal ecology and stewardship, exhibits and tours. Reserve (daily). Visitor center. May-October, daily; rest of year, Monday-Friday. Monday-Saturday 10 a.m.-4 p.m., Sunday noon-4 p.m.

HOTELS
★GARRISON SUITES

1099 Post Road, Wells, 207-646-3497, 800-646-3497; www.garrisonsuites.com

47 rooms. Pets accepted, some restrictions. Outdoor pool, whirlpool. Closed mid-October-April. **$**

★★VILLAGE BY THE SEA

1373 Post Road, Wells, 207-646-1100, 800-444-8862; www.vbts.com

73 rooms, all suites. Indoor pool, outdoor pool. Fitness center. Free wireless Internet access. **$$**

RESTAURANTS
★★GREY GULL

475 Webhannet Drive, Wells, 207-646-7501; www.thegreygullinn.com

American menu. Dinner. Bar. Children's menu. Casual attire. Reservations recommended. **$$**

★HAYLOFT

Highway 1, Moody, 207-646-4400

American, seafood menu. Breakfast, lunch, dinner, brunch. Children's menu. Casual attire. **$$**

★LITCHFIELD'S

2135 Post Road, Wells, 207-646-5711; www.litchfields-restaurant.com

American menu. Lunch, dinner. Bar. Children's menu. Casual attire. **$$**

★★LORD'S HARBORSIDE

352 Harbor Road, Wells, 207-646-2651; www.lordsharborside.com

Seafood menu. Lunch, dinner. Bar. Children's menu. Casual attire. Pool. Closed Tuesday. **$$**

★MAINE DINER

2265 Post Road, Wells, 207-646-4441; www.mainediner.com

American menu. Breakfast, lunch, dinner, brunch. Children's menu. Casual attire. **$$**

★★STEAKHOUSE

1205 Post Road, Wells, 207-646-4200; www.the-steakhouse.com

Steak menu. Dinner. Bar. Children's menu. Casual attire. Reservations recommended. Closed Monday. **$$**

WISCASSET

Many artists and writers live here in beautiful old houses put up in the golden days of clipper-ship barons and sea captains. Chiefly a summer resort area built around its harbor, Wiscasset is half as populous as it was in 1850. Wiscasset is home to the remains of two ancient wooden schooners, which were hauled into the harbor in 1932.

WHAT TO SEE AND DO

LINCOLN COUNTY MUSEUM AND OLD JAIL

133 Federal St., Wiscasset, 207-882-6817; www.planetware.com

First penitentiary built in the District of Maine in 1809-1811. Jailer's house has changing exhibits, relics of Lincoln County. June and September: Saturday-Sunday; July-August: Tuesday-Sunday.

NICKELS-SORTWELL HOUSE

121 Main St., Wiscasset, 207-882-7169;
www.historicnewengland.org/visit/homes/nickels.htm

Classic Federal-style elegance. Built in 1807 for a shipmaster in the lumber trade, William Nickels, it was used as a hotel between 1820 and 1900. The mansion was then bought by Mayor Alvin Sortwell of Cambridge, Massachusetts, as a private home. Graceful elliptical stairway; many Sortwell family furnishings; restored garden. June-mid-October, Friday-Sunday. Tours: on the hours 11 a.m.-4 p.m. Admission: $5.

POWNALBOROUGH COURTHOUSE

Route 128, Cedar Grove Road, Dresden, 207-882-6817;
www.lincolncountyhistory.org

Oldest pre-Revolutionary courthouse in Maine. Three-story 1761 building houses furnished courtroom, spinning room, tavern, bedrooms, parlor and kitchen. Nature trails along river; picnic areas; Revolutionary cemetery. Museum: June and September: Saturday-Sunday; July-August: Tuesday-Sunday; October-May: by appointment.

SPECIALTY LODGINGS

COD COVE INN

22 Cross Road, Edgecomb, 207-882-9586, 800-882-9586; www.codcoveinn.com

Located high on a hill, this New England-style inn overlooks the Sheepscott River and the harbor. The grounds include a flowering garden with gazebo, outdoor swimming pool and whirlpool. Area activities include lighthouse touring, antique shopping, whale-watching or dining on lobster. 30 rooms. Complimentary continental breakfast.

SQUIRE TARBOX INN

1181 Main Road, Westport Island, 207-882-7693, 800-818-0626;
www.squiretarboxinn.com

Restored 18th-century farmhouse situated on working dairy goat farm. 11 rooms. Pets accepted, some restrictions. Complimentary full breakfast. Restaurant. Closed January-March. $$

RESTAURANT

★★LE GARAGE

15 Water St., Wiscasset, 207-882-5409; www.legaragerestaurant.com

Seafood, steak menu. Lunch, dinner. Bar. $$

YARMOUTH

Yarmouth is a quaint New England village 10 miles north of Portland. There are many well-maintained older homes and specialty shops. It is linked by a bridge to Cousins Island in the bay.

Information: Chamber of Commerce, 158 Main St., 207-846-3984; www.yarmouthmaine.org

WHAT TO SEE AND DO
EARTHA

2 DeLorme Drive, Yarmouth, 207-846-7025; www.delorme.com

World's largest globe. Three stories high, Eartha is the largest printed image of the Earth ever created and spins in the lobby of the DeLorme Map Company. Daily.

YARMOUTH HISTORICAL SOCIETY MUSEUM

215 Main St., Yarmouth, 207-846-6259; www.yarmouth.me.us

Two galleries with changing exhibits of local and maritime history, fine and decorative arts. Local history research room; historical lecture series. July-August: Monday-Friday afternoons; rest of year: Tuesday-Saturday.

SPECIAL EVENT
CLAM FESTIVAL

158 Main St., Yarmouth, 207-846-3984; www.clamfestival.com

Celebration of soft-shelled clams. Arts and crafts, entertainment, parade, fireworks. Third weekend in July.

RESTAURANT
★★ROYAL RIVER GRILLHOUSE

106 Lafayette St., Yarmouth, 207-846-1226; www.royalrivergrillhouse.com

American menu. Lunch, dinner, Sunday brunch. Bar. Children's menu. Outdoor seating. $$

YORK

Originally named Agamenticus by the Plymouth Company, the area was settled in 1624, chartered as a city—the first in America—in 1641 and renamed Gorgeanna. Following a reorganization in 1652, the "city" in the wilderness took the name York. The present-day York area includes York Village, York Harbor, York Beach and Cape Neddick.

Information: Greater York Region Chamber of Commerce, 1 Stonewall Lane, 207-363-4422; www.yorkme.org

WHAT TO SEE AND DO
EMERSON-WILCOX HOUSE

York and Lindsey Roads, York

Built in 1742, with later additions. Served at various times as a general store, tavern and post office, as well as the home of two of the town's prominent early families. Now contains a series of period rooms dating to 1750; antique furnishings.

JOHN HANCOCK WAREHOUSE

York and Lindsey Roads, York, 207-363-4974;
www.oldyork.org/buildings/hancock.html
Owned by John Hancock until 1794, this is one of the earliest surviving customs houses in Maine. Used now to interpret the maritime history of this coastal village. Mid-June-mid-October: Tuesday-Saturday afternoons.

OLD GAOL

Lindsay Road, York
Built in 1719 with 18th-century additions. One of the oldest English public buildings in the United States, it was used as a jail until 1860. Dungeons and cells for felons and debtors, as well as galleries of local historical artifacts and late 1800s photography exhibit.

OLD YORK HISTORICAL SOCIETY

140 Lindsay Road, York, 207-363-4974; www.oldyork.org
Tours of seven buildings dating to the early 1700s. (Mid-June-September) Visitor orientation and tickets at Jefferds Tavern. Administration Office houses museum offices (Monday-Friday) and historical and research library.

SAYWARD-WHEELER HOUSE

9 Barrell Lane, York Harbor, 207-384-2454; www.spnea.org/visit/homes/sayward.htm
Home of the 18th-century merchant and civic leader Tory Jonathan Sayward. Tours. June-October: first Saturday of the month.

HOTELS

★★ANCHORAGE MOTOR INN

265 Long Beach Ave., York Beach, 207-363-5112; www.anchorageinn.com
179 rooms. Bar. Fitness room. Two indoor pools, two outdoor pools, whirlpool. Sun and Surf Restaurant & Beachside Deck. $

★★★STAGE NECK INN

8 Stage Neck Road, York Harbor, 207-363-3850, 800-340-1130; www.stageneck.com
This inn is located on an ocean-bound peninsula in York Harbor. The resort offers a beach and is also close to the Kittery outlet malls, antiques shops, art galleries and historic attractions of York. 58 rooms. Restaurant, bar. Fitness room. Beach. Indoor pool, outdoor pool, whirlpool. Tennis. Water pool. Sandy Beach. Free in-room High-speed Internet access. Spa treatments. $$

SPECIALTY LODGINGS

DOCKSIDE GUEST QUARTERS

22 Harris Island Road, York, 207-363-2868, 888-860-7428; www.docksidegq.com
25 rooms. Restaurant, bar. Closed weekdays late October-December, March-Memorial Day, December-February. $$

EDWARDS HARBORSIDE INN

Stage Neck Road, York Harbor, 207-363-3037; www.edwardsharborside.com
Turn-of-the-century house with period furnishings. Nine rooms. Complimentary continental breakfast. Beach. $$$

MAINE

★
★
★
★
★

YORK HARBOR INN

Coastal Highway 1A, York Harbor, 207-363-5119, 800-343-3869;
www.yorkharborinn.com

54 rooms. Complimentary continental breakfast. Restaurant, bar. Whirlpool. High-speed Internet access. Beach. **$$**

RESTAURANTS

★★DOCKSIDE

22 Harris Island Road, York, 207-363-2722, 888-860-7428; www.docksidegq.com

Seafood, steak menu. Lunch, dinner. Bar. Casual attire. Reservations recommended. Outdoor seating. Closed Monday; day after Columbus Day-late May. **$$**

★★FAZIO'S ITALIAN

38 Woodbridge Road, York, 207-363-7019; www.fazios.com

Italian menu. Dinner. Bar. Children's menu. Casual attire. Reservations recommended. Pool. **$$**

★★★YORK HARBOR INN

Highway 1A, York Harbor, 207-363-5119; www.yorkharborinn.com

Antique furnishings, floral wallpaper and lace curtains add to the ambience of this quaint, colonial inn.The menu features local seafood, much of it caught close to the restaurant. Seafood menu. Dinner, Sunday brunch. Children's menu. Casual attire. Reservations recommended. Closed Monday-Thursday (fall-spring). **$$**

116

MAINE

★
★★
★★
★★
★

MASSACHUSETTS

TO SOME, "NEW ENGLAND" MEANS ONE THING: MASSACHUSETTS. OVER FIVE CENTURIES, the Bay State has become the region's emblematic poster child—one rich in historical personality and modern diversions. Case in point: explorer John Cabot (his ancestors would become the ultimate Boston Brahmins) landed on these shores in 1497, just 5 years after Columbus' famed cross-Atlantic trip. The legendary Mayflower soon followed, establishing roots in what would become an area of American greats. Paul Revere, John Hancock, Sam Adams and, of course, the Kennedys all hailed from Massachusetts. So did literary giants like Ralph Waldo Emerson, Henry David Thoreau and Emily Dickenson. But for all its historical heft—it was local patriots who jump-started the American Revolution—the Bay State is not stuck in the past.

Boston, the biggest city in New England, is a lively metropolis, home to booming businesses and the fiercely followed Red Sox. Its residents live in a cross-section of neighborhoods along the (newly clean!) Charles River. The North End, the city's Little Italy, bursts with gelaterias and red sauce-heavy trattorias; the South End, by contrast, is awash in chic clothing boutiques and avant-garde eateries. To the west, north and south of the city stretch verdant, upscale suburbs and quiet, laid-back beach towns. Farther west, along the Massachusetts-New York border is the Berkshires, a county so steeped in arts, culture and culinary experiences, it has become a go-to destination for people several states over.

And then there's Cape Cod and the Islands—Nantucket and Martha's Vineyard—a few of America's most sought-after summer spots. The area's hundreds of miles of coastline and soft, white-sand beaches are a vacationers' paradise. Locals live in gray-shingled homes in small beach hamlets and for the most part, welcome visitors to their postcard-perfect Main Streets. The vibe is Puritan modern, slightly conservative but fun loving.

It is often said that every town in Massachusetts has a small part in the American story. A statewide trip takes travelers from Plymouth Rock, where it all began, to the battle of Bunker Hill, to the philosopher favorite Walden Pond, to the academic powerhouse Cambridge, to the industrial savvy Lowell, to the constantly innovating Boston. Indeed, the whole state is a melting pot of old traditions and modern ideas, lived out along a breathtaking coastline and myriad quiet hill villages.

★ FUN FACTS

The first computer was developed in 1928 at the Massachusetts Institute of Technology (M.I.T.)

Cranberry juice is the state beverage of Massachusetts.

The Boston terrier, a cross between an English bulldog and an English terrier, was the first purebred dog to be developed in the U.S.

Ruth Wakefield invented the chocolate chip cookie at the Tollhouse Inn in Whitman, Massachusetts.

AMHERST

This storied Central Massachusetts town exudes academia. More than half its citizens are students (the other half might be professors), and its former natives include such scholarly types as Eugene Field, Emily Dickinson, Robert Frost and Noah Webster. The seat of Amherst College and the crown jewel of the University of Massachusetts system, this is a town filled with life, culture and ideas.

Information: Chamber of Commerce, 409 Main St., Amherst,
413-253-0700; www.amherstchamber.com

WHAT TO SEE AND DO
AMHERST COLLEGE
100 Boltwood Ave., Amherst, 413-542-2000; www.amherst.edu
One of the best liberal arts colleges in the country, Amherst enrolls some 1,550 students. On a tree-shaded green in the middle of town, its Robert Frost Library owns approximately half of Emily Dickinson's poems, as well as materials by Wordsworth, Eugene O'Neill and others.

EMILY DICKINSON MUSEUM: THE HOMESTEAD AND THE EVERGREENS
280 Main St., Amherst, 413-542-8161; www.emilydickinsonmuseum.org
The Homestead was the birthplace and home of poet Emily Dickinson; the Evergreens housed her brother and his family. Select rooms are open for tours on a first-come, first-served basis. March-May, September-October, Wednesday-Saturday 1-5 p.m.; June-August, Wednesday-Saturday 10 a.m.-5 p.m., Sunday 1-5 p.m.; November-mid-December, Wednesday, Saturday 1-5 p.m.

ERIC CARLE MUSEUM OF PICTURE BOOK ART
125 W. Bay Road, Amherst, 413-658-1100; www.picturebookart.org
This 40,000-square-foot facility opened in 2002 as the first museum in the United States exclusively devoted to children's picture book art. Its founder, Eric Carle, has illustrated more than 70 picture books, including *The Very Hungry Caterpillar* which has been published in more than 30 languages and has sold more than 18 million copies. Tuesday-Friday 10 a.m.-4 p.m., Saturday 10 a.m.-5 p.m., Sunday noon-4 p.m.

UNIVERSITY OF MASSACHUSETTS
Massachusetts Avenue and North Pleasant Street, Amherst,
413-545-0111; www.umass.edu
Founded in 1863, and with 24,000 students, UMass-Amherst is the state's major facility of public higher education. It has more than 150 buildings on a 1,450-acre campus. Tours. Daily.

HOTEL
★HOWARD JOHNSON
401 Russell St., Hadley, 413-586-0114; www.hojo.com
100 rooms. Complimentary full breakfast. Business center. Fitness center. Pets accepted. Pool. Wireless Internet access. **$**

SPECIALTY LODGINGS

ALLEN HOUSE VICTORIAN INN

599 Main St., Amherst, 413-253-5000; www.allenhouse.com

Seven rooms. Children over 10 years only. Complimentary full breakfast. Wireless Internet access. **$**

LORD JEFFERY INN

30 Boltwood Ave., Amherst, 01002. 413-253-2576, 800-742-0358;
www.lordjefferyinn.com

48 rooms. Two restaurants, Bar. Wireless Internet access. **$**

ANDOVER

The seat of Boston's northern suburbs is a picturesque small city bursting with brick homes and quiet charm. Many of its residents commute to jobs in Boston. Many others are connected to the legendary Phillips Andover Academy—known simply as Andover—the posh prep school which is also the oldest incorporated school in the country.

Information: Merrimack Valley Chamber of Commerce, 264 Essex St.,
Lawrence, 978-686-0900; www.merrimackvalleychamber.com

WHAT TO SEE AND DO

PEABODY MUSEUM

175 Main St., Andover, 978-749-4490; www.andover.edu

This Native American archaeological museum has exhibits on the physical and cultural evolution of man and the prehistoric archaeology of New England, the Southwest, Mexico and the Arctic. Monday-Friday 8 a.m.-5 p.m., by appointment only.

PHILLIPS ANDOVER ACADEMY

180 Main St., Andover, 978-749-4000; www.andover.edu

Nearly 1,100 students make up this co-ed boarding school for grades 9-12. Notable alumni include photographer Walker Evans, poet Oliver Wendell Holmes, child-rearing expert Benjamin Spock and actor Humphrey Bogart. The campus sits on 450 acres with 170 buildings. The Cochran Sanctuary, a 65-acre landscaped area, has walking trails, a brook and two ponds. Daily.

HOTELS

★★★ANDOVER INN

4 Chapel Ave., Andover, 978-475-5903, 800-242-5903; www.andoverinn.com

Located on the campus of Phillips Andover Academy, this neo-Georgian country inn was built in 1930 to provide lodging for visiting parents and alumni. The rooms are all decorated in period furnishings and cozy accents. 23 rooms. Restaurant. Bar. Wireless Internet access. Complimentary continental breakfast. **$**

★★ANDOVER WYNDHAM HOTEL

123 Old River Road, Andover, 978-975-3600; www.wyndham.com

293 rooms. Restaurant. Bar. Airport transportation available. High-speed Internet access. Pets accepted. **$$**

MASSACHUSETTS

★
★
★
★
☆

★★LA QUINTA INN & SUITES ANDOVER

131 River Road, Andover, 978-685-6200; www.lq.com

179 rooms. Complimentary continental breakfast. Restaurant. Fitness center. Pets accepted. High-speed Internet access. Indoor swimming pool. Spa. **$**

RESTAURANT
★CHINA BLOSSOM

946 Osgood St., North Andover, 978-682-2242; www.chinablossom.com

Chinese menu. Lunch, dinner. Bar. **$$**

BOSTON

With the culture of Chicago, the beauty of San Francisco and the diversity of Paris, Boston is the social, financial, educational, historical, culinary and sports center of New England. It should be no surprise that its nickname is "the Hub," and most state happenings revolve around what's going on in this port city of some 600,000 citizens. America's early settlers moved here in the mid-1600s; their legacy is still very much alive in the old Colonials of Charlestown and narrow, winding streets of the North End. Paul Revere's fabled ride, and indeed the Revolution itself, started here, giving Boston bragging rights over nearly every other American city.

Visitors can retrace Revere and other early patriots' steps along the Freedom Trail, a three-hour walking route that encapsulates much of the area's history. Current citizens, though, leave the past to tourists and obsess instead over the Boston Red Sox and New England Patriots, two championship teams known as much for their die-hard fans as for their athletic prowess. Fenway Park, the oldest U.S. baseball stadium and home to the legendary Green Monster, hosts the Red Sox—visitors would do well to take in a game here while in town. Afterward, they can explore the city's neighborhoods, from the upscale Beacon Hill to the bursting-with-life North End to the formerly Irish, rapidly gentrifying South Boston (i.e. the "Southie" so well portrayed in local son Matt Damon's *Good Will Hunting*.)

Boston is perhaps best known for its top-tier universities—a whopping 100 in all—the most famous of which include Harvard, M.I.T., Boston University and the Berklee School of Music. During the academic year, students canvas Commonwealth Avenue and the Back Bay's Newbury Street shopping district, lending the whole city a youthful, energetic vibe (though older residents love to complain about the youngsters' rowdiness).

Students, locals and tourists alike love strolling through this walking city—possibly because of Boston drivers' rightful reputation as the worst in the world—especially along the landscaped Charles River Esplanade. The 18-mile-long waterside stretch has walking, running and biking trails, boathouses, tennis courts and myriad shaded benches. On a summer day, the spot is packed with Bostonians getting exercise and checking out the evolving city skyline.

Information: Greater Boston Convention & Visitors Bureau, 2 Copley Place,
617-536-4100, 888-733-2678; www.bostonusa.com

WHAT TO SEE AND DO
BOSTON AFRICAN AMERICAN NATIONAL HISTORIC SITE

14 Beacon St., Boston, 617-742-5415; www.nps.gov/boaf

Built by free black Bostonians in 1806, the building was an educational and religious center and site of the founding of the New England Anti-Slavery Society in 1832.

★
★
★
★
☆

May-September: daily; rest of year: Monday-Saturday. The Meeting house is the starting point for the Black Heritage Trail, a walking tour conducted by the National Park Service that takes guests past black history-related sites.

BOSTON BALLET
19 Clarendon St., Boston, 617-695-6955; www.bostonballet.com
The Boston Ballet offers classic and contemporary performances by a company of some of the finest dancers in the world. If you're visiting in late November or December, don't miss *The Nutcracker,* performed annually before more than 140,000 people—that's the largest ballet audience in the world. Performances held October-May.

BOSTON BRUINS
TD Banknorth Garden, 100 Legends Way,
Boston, 617-624-1000; www.bostonbruins.com
One of the great hockey traditions in the NHL, the Bruins were one of the league's founding six teams.

BOSTON CELTICS
226 Causeway St., Fourth Floor, Boston, 866-423-5849;
www.nba.com/celtics
With 17 championships notched in its belt, Boston's pro basketball team has won more NBA titles than any other franchise. October-June.

BOSTON COLLEGE
140 Commonwealth Ave., Chestnut Hill, 617-552-8000; www.bc.edu
This huge Catholic college of 14,500 students has a major presence in the city, thanks in part to its top-ranked basketball, hockey and football teams. The school's main campus in Chestnut Hill is full of old stone manors with stained-glass windows.

BOSTON COMMON
Beacon and Tremont Streets, Boston
The oldest public park in the United States, the Boston Common is steeped in history. In the 1640s, farmers used the Common as a cattle pasture; later, the colonial militia used it to train soldiers. Colonists gathered here to hear speeches, witness public hangings and watch spirited fencing duels. Today, the Common's 45 acres are still a vibrant city center—an ideal place to stroll, in-line skate, play Frisbee, catch a free concert or enjoy a picnic. In the winter, the park's famous Frog Pond freezes over into a public ice skating rink. Daily.

BOSTON HARBOR ISLANDS NATIONAL RECREATION AREA
408 Atlantic Ave., Suite 225, Boston, 617-223-8666;
www.bostonharborislands.areaparks.com
This national park is actually made up of several Boston Harbor islands, some open to the public, some private. Take the ferry to Georges Island; from there, a free water taxi sails you to Lovells, Peddocks, Gallops, Grape and Bumpkin islands. Each is unique, with features such as sand dunes, freshwater ponds and native wildlife. Camp on Lovells and Peddocks islands with a permit from the Metropolitan District Commission. May-mid-October.

MASSACHUSETTS

★
★
★
★
★

BOSTON PUBLIC GARDEN

Arlington, Boylston, Charles and Beacon Streets, Boston,
617-522-1966; www.swanboats.com

Adjacent to the Boston Common, this is the first botanical garden in the United States, with 24 acres featuring a splendid variety of flowers and ornamental shrubs. It's also home to the city's famous Swan Boats, which visitors can rent for a 15-minute paddled ride around the garden's lagoon.

BOSTON PUBLIC LIBRARY

700 Boylston St., Boston, 617-536-5400; www.bpl.org

The stunning Italian Renaissance building by Charles McKim includes a central courtyard and fountain. Other highlights include mural decorations, bronze doors, sculptures and several reading rooms, including the Bates Room, where visitors study and surf the Internet in silence. Monday-Thursday 9 a.m.-9 p.m.; Friday-Saturday 9 a.m.-5 p.m.

BOSTON RED SOX

Fenway Park, 4 Yawkey Way, Boston, 617-267-9440;
www.redsox.mlb.com

Going to Fenway isn't just about watching the Red Sox, it's about steeping yourself in tradition. Built in 1901, the park is home to the Green Monster, the infamous 37-foot, left-field wall. Cy Young pitched a perfect game at Fenway in 1904, and in 1914, young Babe Ruth joined the home team. Today's 2004 and 2007 World Series Champs are no less impressive. Regular tours. March-October.

BOSTON SYMPHONY ORCHESTRA/BOSTON POPS

301 Massachusetts Ave., Boston, 617-266-1492; www.bso.org

Symphony Hall is said to have perfect acoustics, a draw that packs the house despite lofty ticket prices. Both the old-school Boston Symphony Orchestra and the livelier Boston Pops perform here, when they're not giving free outdoor concerts on the Charles River Esplanade. BSO performances October-April; Pops performances May-early July, mid-late-December.

BOSTON TEA PARTY SHIP AND MUSEUM

300 Congress St., Boston, 617-338-1773;
www.bostonteapartyship.com

The museum ship is a replica of one of the three famous boats docked in the harbor the night of the Boston Tea Party. In 2001, the museum was badly damaged by a fire and closed for renovations. It's scheduled to reopen in the fall of 2009.

BOSTON UNIVERSITY

One Silber Way, Boston, 617-353-2300; www.bu.edu

A college of more than 28,000 students, B.U. encompasses an entire area of the city (not the least of which is the "B.U. Beach," a riverside strip of grassy lawn typically littered with sunbathing students). The Mugar Memorial Library houses the papers of Dr. Martin Luther King Jr., Robert Frost, Isaac Asimov and other writers and artists.

MASSACHUSETTS

★
★
★
★
★

BUNKER HILL MONUMENT

43 Monument Square, Charlestown, 617-242-5641; www.nps.gov

Standing 221 feet high (that's 294 steps, with no elevator), the Bunker Hill Monument marks the site of the first major battle of the Revolutionary War. It was here that American Colonel William Prescott ordered his troops not to fire until "you see the whites of their eyes," so that bullets would not be wasted. Daily.

CHARLES RIVER ESPLANADE

This flat, smooth asphalt path runs for 18 miles along the Charles River, from Boston to Cambridge to Watertown. During the summer months, active types stroll, jog, bike or blade the Esplanade; lazier locals picnic or sunbathe along both sides of the river. On a clear day, the river and skyline views are magnificent—some of the best in Boston. Rent a bike at Back Bay Bikes & Boards (336 Commonwealth Ave., 617-247-2336; www.backbaybicycles.com), Community Bicycle Supply (496 Tremont St., Boston, 617-542-8623; www.communitybicycle.com), Cambridge Bicycle (259 Massachusetts Ave., Cambridge, 617-876-6555) or Ata Cycle (1773 Massachusetts Ave., Cambridge, 617-354-0907; www.atabike.com). Rent rollerblades at Beacon Hill Skate Shop, (135 Charles St., 617-482-7400) or Blades Board & Skate (Boston and Cambridge, 617-437-6300; www.blades.com).

CHILDREN'S MUSEUM OF BOSTON

300 Congress St., Boston, 617-426-6500; www.bostonkids.org

With interactive exhibits on science, technology, art and culture, the Children's Museum lives up to its billing as "Boston's best place for kids 0-10." A kid-size construction site includes a mini artists' studio, real loom and weaving area, full-size wigwam and rock climbing area. Saturday-Thursday 10 a.m.-5 p.m., Friday 10 a.m.-9 p.m.

COMMUNITY BOATING

21 David Mugar Way, Boston, 617-523-1038;
www.community-boating.org

Community Boating runs the largest and oldest public sailing program in the country. Purchasing a two-day membership means unlimited use of boats, plus sailing, windsurfing or kayaking instruction. April-November: daily; closed December-March.

COPLEY PLACE

100 Huntington Ave., Boston, 617-369-5000;
www.shopcopleyplace.com

With more than 100 stores and a central glass atrium, Copley Place is all about upscale shopping and dining. Stores include Barneys, Neiman Marcus, Louis Vuitton, Christian Dior and Gucci. Daily.

COPP'S HILL BURYING GROUND

Hull and Snow Hill Streets, Boston, 617-635-4505; www.cityofboston.gov

This is the second-oldest burying ground in Boston. Robert Newman, who hung the lanterns in the steeple of Old North Church, is buried here, as is the Puritan Mather family and African Americans from the nearby New Guinea Community, who lie in unmarked graves. Daily.

MASSACHUSETTS

★
★
★
★
★

DUCK TOURS

3 Copley Place, Suite 310, Boston, 617-267-3825;
www.bostonducktours.com

This long-standing Boston tradition takes you from land to sea in a World War II half-boat, half-truck vehicle known as a Duck. Your conDUCKtor starts the 80-minute tour near the Boston Common and drives through the city before diving into the Charles River. April-November: on the hour from 9 a.m. to one hour before sunset.

FANEUIL HALL MARKETPLACE

4 S. Market Building, Fifth floor Boston, 617-523-1300;
www.faneuilhallmarketplace.com

Faneuil Hall is more than just a shopping center: It has operated as a local marketplace since 1742, when wealthy merchant Peter Faneuil built and donated the area to the city. Today, it buzzes with tourists catching street performances or snacking on treats from indoor food mall Quincy Market. Daily.

FRANKLIN PARK GOLF COURSE (WILLIAM J. DEVINE GOLF COURSE)

1 Circuit Drive, Dorchester, 617-265-4084; www.sterlinggolf.com

This 6,009-yard, par-70 golf course is the second-oldest public golf course in the country. Rates are reasonable, especially for kids under 18, and club rentals are just $10. The course is wide open but demanding, with some steep hills. Daily dawn-dusk; closed for snow and inclement weather.

FRANKLIN PARK ZOO

1 Franklin Park Road, Dorchester, 617-541-5466;
www.zoonewengland.org

The medium-sized zoo has "Bird's World," an indoor/outdoor aviary complex with natural habitats; an African tropical forest; a hilltop range with camels, antelopes and zebras; and a children's zoo. Daily.

FREEDOM TRAIL

99 Chauncy St., Suite 401 617-242-5642; www.thefreedomtrail.org

This two- to three-hour walking tour takes visitors past some of Boston's most famous historical sites. It begins at the Boston Common and ends at the Bunker Hill Monument in Charlestown. Red bricks or red paint mark the trail, which you can follow on your own (free brochures are available) or with guided assistance.

GRANARY BURYING GROUND

Tremont and Bromfield Streets, Boston, 617-635-4505;
www.cityofboston.gov

Revolutionary War heroes Paul Revere, John Hancock, Samuel Adams and Peter Faneuil (whose headstone is misspelled as "Peter Funal") lie here. The name comes from a grain storage building (a granary) that used to sit nearby. Daily 9 a.m.-7 p.m.

HAYMARKET

Blackstone Street, Boston

Rain or shine, winter or summer, Bostonians flock to Haymarket and its outdoor stalls for the freshest fruits, vegetables and seafood around.

★
★
★
★
★

INSTITUTE OF CONTEMPORARY ART

100 Northern Ave., Boston, 617-478-3100; www.icaboston.org

In late 2006 the ICA moved into its brand-new waterfront South Boston building. The four-floor museum now has a sizable theater with walls of glass, a large outdoor deck and several galleries showing permanent and temporary collections. Tuesday-Sunday.

ISABELLA STEWART GARDNER MUSEUM

280 The Fenway, Boston, 617-566-1401; www.gardnermuseum.com

The museum is housed in the 19th-century home of Isabella Stewart Gardner. Collections include paintings and sculptures from around the world. On weekends in fall, winter and spring, look for free afternoon concerts. Tuesday-Sunday; concerts late September-May.

KING'S CHAPEL AND BURYING GROUND

58 Tremont St., Boston, 617-227-2155; www.cityofboston.gov

King's Chapel, started by the Massachusetts Royal Governor, has held church services at its location longer than any other church in the United States. When the congregation outgrew the church in 1754, a new building was erected around the old, which was then dismantled. The Burying Ground next door is the oldest cemetery in Boston. Daily; closed Sunday-Friday in winter.

125

L'ARTE DI CUCINARE

6 Charter St., Boston, 617-523-6032; www.cucinare.com

Michele Topor, a 30-year resident of the North End and passionate gourmet chef, leads 3½-hour tours of the North End Italian markets. Reservations are required, and each tour is limited to 13 people. Wednesday, Friday-Saturday.

LOUIS BOSTON

234 Berkeley St., Boston, 617-262-6100, 800-225-5135; www.louisboston.com

This men's and women's clothing emporium is considered among the finest in the world. Housed in the historic former museum of science building, the buyers here stock the shelves with hard-to-find labels from designers who are ahead of their time. Monday-Wednesday 11 a.m.-6 p.m., Thursday-Saturday 11 a.m.-7 p.m.

LOUISBURG SQUARE

Louisburg Square, Beacon Hill

This lovely little residential square is one of Boston's most coveted addresses. Louisa May Alcott, William Dean Howells and other famous Bostonians—including current Senator John Kerry—have had homes here.

MDC MEMORIAL HATCH SHELL

On the Charles River, between Storrow Drive and the water, 617-626-4970; www.mass.gov/dcr/hatch_events.htm

Packing as much as possible into the summer months, the Hatch Shell offers free entertainment nearly every night of the week. Offerings range from dance performances to rock concerts to the Boston Pops Fourth of July celebration. Early June-early September.

MASSACHUSETTS

★
★
★
★

MINUTEMAN COMMUTER BIKEWAY

www.minutemanbikeway.org

Begins near Alewife (T) station, goes through Lexington and Arlington and ends at Bedford. This 11-mile bike path looks like a miniature highway, complete with on- and off-ramps, a center line and traffic signs. The trail mimics portions of Paul Revere's famous ride. Daily.

MOTHER CHURCH, THE FIRST CHURCH OF CHRIST, SCIENTIST CHRISTIAN SCIENCE CENTER

210 Massachusetts Ave., Boston, 617-450-2000; www.tfccs.com

This is the headquarters of the Christian Science Monitor, and the home of the Mapparium, a walk-through stained-glass globe. Daily.

MUSEUM AT THE JOHN FITZGERALD KENNEDY LIBRARY

617-514-1600, 866-535-1960; www.jfklibrary.org

Designed by I. M. Pei, the library is one of the most beautiful contemporary works of architecture in the country. Daily 9 a.m.-5 p.m.

MUSEUM OF AFRO AMERICAN HISTORY

14 Beacon St., Boston, 617-725-0022; www.afroammuseum.org

The Museum of Afro American History preserves and exhibits the contributions of African-American Bostonians and New Englanders during colonial settlement and the Revolutionary War. The museum also features workshops for kids and adults, a public lecture series, storytelling for children, and poet and author visits. Monday-Saturday 10 a.m.-4 p.m.

MUSEUM OF FINE ARTS

465 Huntington Ave., Boston, 617-267-9300; www.mfa.org

The MFA, Boston's answer to New York's Metropolitan Museum of Art, combines classic and contemporary art with ancient artifacts. The grand white-stone building is practically an exhibit in itself. Monday-Tuesday and Saturday-Sunday 10 a.m.-4:45 p.m., Wednesday-Friday till 9:45 p.m.

MUSEUM OF SCIENCE

1 Science Park, Charles River Dam and Storrow Drive, Boston, 617-723-2500; www.mos.org

The MOS's entertaining exhibitions include a T. rex model (complete with 58 teeth), presentations with live animals at the Wright Theater, a chick hatchery, and a lighthouse that explains light, optics and color. Also onsite is the Charles Hayden Planetarium. Saturday-Thursday 9 a.m.-5 p.m., Friday till 9 p.m.

NEWBURY STREET

1-361 Newbury St., Boston, www.newbury-st.com

There's no better shopping street in New England than Newbury. Independent boutiques and well-known chain shops sell everything from baby gear to kitchen equipment to truffles to artwork. The street is also home to scores of spas and cafés, making it a one-stop shopping, eating and pampering destination.

NEW ENGLAND AQUARIUM

Central Wharf, Boston, 617-973-5200; www.neaq.org

The aquarium has a colorful array of dolphins, sea lions, penguins, turtles, sharks, eels, harbor seals and fish from around the world. Every 90 minutes, sea lions perform. There's also an IMAX theater. Monday-Friday 9 a.m.-5 p.m., Saturday-Sunday, holidays till 6 p.m.

NEW ENGLAND AQUARIUM WHALE WATCHES

Central Wharf, Boston, 617-973-5206; www.neaq.org/visit/ww.tickets.html

Stellwagen Bank, 25 miles from Boston, is a terrific area for whale-watching. From Boston, the New England Aquarium's tour takes you out to the feeding grounds of a variety of whales, many of which are endangered. Purchase tickets in advance. Boston Harbor Cruises (617-227-4321; www.bostonharborcruises.com) and Beantown Whale Watch (617-542-8000; www.beantownwhalewatch.com) also operate whale cruises in Boston. Mid-April-late October.

NICHOLS HOUSE MUSEUM

55 Mount Vernon St., Boston, 617-227-6993;
www.nicholshousemuseum.org

Typical 1804 domestic architecture of Beacon Hill from its era; one of two homes on Beacon Hill open to the public. Attributed to Charles Bulfinch; antique furnishings and art from America, Europe and the Orient from the 17th to early 19th centuries. Collection of Rose Standish Nichols, landscape designer and writer. May-October: Tuesday-Saturday noon-4 p.m.; November-April: Thursday-Saturday noon-4 p.m.

OLD NORTH CHURCH

193 Salem St., Boston, 617-523-6676; www.oldnorth.com

Old North Church is the oldest church in Boston. On April 18, 1775, church sexton Robert Newman hung two lanterns in the steeple to signal that the British Army was heading up the Charles River. When Paul Revere saw the signal, he jumped on his horse and rode to Lexington to warn the militia. The next day, the shot heard round the world was fired on Lexington Green, officially beginning the Revolutionary War. Daily.

OLD SOUTH CHURCH

645 Boylston St., Boston, 617-536-1970; www.oldsouth.org

A church community since 1669, Old South Church has a medieval architectural style that boasts impressive mosaics, stained glass and cherry woodwork. Worship held Sunday.

OLD SOUTH MEETING HOUSE

310 Washington St., Boston, 617-482-6439;
www.oldsouthmeetinghouse.org

The most important date in Old South's history is December 16, 1773, when 5,000 colonists gathered at the church to protest the British tax on tea and decide on a course of action. From there, the men dressed as Native Americans, snuck onto three ships laden with tea, and dumped the cargo overboard. Daily.

MASSACHUSETTS

OLD STATE HOUSE/SITE OF BOSTON MASSACRE

206 Washington St., Boston, 617-720-1713;
www.bostonhistory.org

The Old State House was originally built as the headquarters of the British government in Boston. It is now the city's oldest surviving public building. Inside, a museum exhibits the prominent role the building played in the American Revolution. In 1770, British troops shot into a crowd that had gathered here to hear a proclamation; the fallen are memorialized by a small circle of paving stones (it now sits under dense city traffic). Daily 9 a.m.-5 p.m.

PARK STREET CHURCH

1 Park St., Boston, 617-523-3383; www.parkstreet.org

William Lloyd Garrison delivered his first antislavery address here in 1829. The church is often called "Brimstone Corner" because brimstone for gunpowder was stored here during the War of 1812. Mid-June-August: limited hours; Sunday services all year.

PAUL REVERE HOUSE

19 N. Square, Boston, 617-523-2338; www.paulreverehouse.org

Built in 1680, the well-preserved Paul Revere House is Boston's oldest building. It still includes authentic furnishings and offers a rare glimpse of colonial life. Here, Paul Revere plied his silversmith trade and sold his wares, often in exchange for food or livestock. His successful ride to Lexington on April 18, 1775, was immortalized by Henry Wadsworth Longfellow in "The Midnight Ride of Paul Revere." Mid-April-late October: daily 9:30 a.m.-5:15 p.m.; early November-mid-April: daily 9:30 a.m.-4:15 p.m.; closed Monday in January-March.

SAMUEL ADAMS BREWERY

30 Germania St., Boston, 617-522-9080;
www.samueladams.com/contact_tour.aspx

Take a tour of the Boston Beer Museum and discover the critical details of the brewing process. While you're at it, sample a few Samuel Adams microbrews. (Tours Thursday-Saturday)

THE SHOPS AT THE PRUDENTIAL CENTER

800 Boylston St., Boston, 800-746-7778;
www.prudentialcenter.com

This indoor shopping mall includes Saks Fifth Avenue, Club Monaco, Barnes and Noble and more. Daily.

STATE HOUSE

24 Beacon St., Boston, 617-727-3676;
www.cityofboston.gov/freedomtrail/Massachusettshouse.asp

The Massachusetts State House is an architectural marvel, with a golden dome sheathed in 23-carat gold leaf (the original state house's was copper). Designed by Charles Bulfinch and built on land owned by John Hancock, Paul Revere helped lay the cornerstones on July 4, 1795. Monday-Friday 10 a.m.-3:30 p.m.

MASSACHUSETTS

★
★
★
★
★

SUFFOLK DOWNS

111 Waldemar Ave., East Boston, 617-567-3900;
www.suffolkdowns.com

Seabiscuit once won at Suffolk Downs, a local track that's been operating since 1935. The track offers pari-mutuel betting, which unlike casino gambling, doesn't involve betting against the house, only against other spectators. Daily.

TRINITY CHURCH

206 Clarendon St., Boston, 617-536-0944;
www.trinitychurchboston.org

This Henry Hobson Richardson-built church was inspired by Phillips Brooks, the ninth rector of Trinity Church and author of the Christmas carol, "O Little Town of Bethlehem." Daily.

USS CONSTITUTION

Charlestown Navy Yard, Boston National Historical Park, One Constitution Road,
Boston, 617-242-7511; www.cityofboston.gov

The oldest commissioned warship in the world got the nickname "Old Ironsides" during the War of 1812. Some 600 miles off the coast of Boston, it engaged the British HMS *Guerriere* in battle. While the *Guerriere* was badly damaged, cannonballs merely bounced off the *Constitution's* sides, as if they were made of iron (really, they're three layers of oak). In 1830, the ship was saved from the scrap heap because of public response to Oliver Wendell Holmes' poem "Old Ironsides." It was restored in 1925. May-September, daily 9 a.m.-6 p.m., October-April, daily 10 a.m.-5 p.m.

WANG THEATER/THE SHUBERT THEATER

265 and 270 Tremont St., Boston, 617-482-9393; www.citicenter.org

Broadway shows, theater productions, dance and opera companies, and musical performers appear at the 3,600-seat Wang Theater, a world-class venue for the performing arts. The Shubert hosts an impressive array of quality local theater, dance and opera productions, many of which appeal to children.

SPECIAL EVENTS

BOSTON MARATHON

617-236-1652; www.bostonmarathon.org

The notoriously hilly and difficult Boston marathon is one of the most famous footraces in the world. To qualify, runners must have already posted an acceptable time in another marathon. (But that doesn't stop thousands of "scabs" from jumping into the race behind the pros.) Most of the city shuts down for the day, as fans line the route and cheer like crazy. Third Monday in April.

FIRST NIGHT BOSTON

617-542-1399; www.firstnight.org

First Night is Boston's New Year's Eve celebration. The alcohol-free event begins with a Mardi Gras-style Grand Procession and features more than 250 performances in both indoor and outdoor venues. Those who can stay awake are treated to a fireworks display at midnight.

MASSACHUSETTS

HOTELS

★BEST WESTERN ROUNDHOUSE SUITES

891 Massachusetts Ave., Boston, 617-989-1000, 888-468-3562;
www.bestwestern.com

92 rooms. Pets accepted. Complimentary continental breakfast. Airport transportation available. Fitness center. High-speed Internet access. **$**

★★★★★BOSTON HARBOR HOTEL

70 Rowes Wharf, Boston, 617-439-7000, 800-752-7077; www.bhh.com

Occupying an idyllic waterfront location, this quiet, luxurious hotel is located across from Boston's financial district and along a stretch of land that was once dominated by an elevated highway. The staff at this full-service property is attentive. Rooms and suites are draped in rich colors—it's worth paying extra for a room with a view. In the summer, live music, dancing and an outdoor movie night take place on the hotel's outdoor patio. The hotel's Meritage restaurant is the domain of chef Daniel Bruce, whose dishes consist of the freshest local ingredients and are paired with wines by the glass or bottle from around the world. The Rowes Wharf water taxi whisks guests straight to the airport, avoiding Boston's notorious traffic. 230 rooms. High-speed Internet access. Three restaurants, two bars. Airport transportation available. **$$$$**

★★★BOSTON MARRIOTT COPLEY PLACE

110 Huntington Ave., Boston, 617-236-5800, 877-901-2079;
www.copleymarriott.com

An enclosed walkway connects the Marriot to the shops and restaurants of the Prudential Center and Copley Place, as well as to the meeting rooms of the Hynes Convention Center. Just minutes from the Museum of Fine Arts and Newbury Street, the Marriot has one of the largest ballrooms in New England and boasts a sushi bar as one of its three restaurants. 1,147 rooms. High-speed Internet access. Three restaurants, two bars. **$$**

★★★BOSTON MARRIOTT LONG WHARF

296 State St., Boston, 617-227-0800, 800-228-9290; www.marriott.com

Adjacent to Faneuil Hall and near the Fleet Center, this mid-20th-century hotel has rooms with stunning harbor or city skyline views. It's also a short walk to the Harbor Islands ferry, whale-watching boats or a water taxi stand. A nautical theme is used throughout with grand interior murals depicting Long Wharf fishermen, and a railing system that mimics that of a cruise ship. At Tia's on the Waterfront, the hotel's popular restaurant, a bucket of steamed clams and a bottle of cold beer on the patio is summertime heaven. 402 rooms. High-speed Internet access. Restaurant, bar. Airport transportation available. Indoor swimming pool. Fitness center. Unlimited local phone calls. **$$**

★★★THE COLONNADE HOTEL

120 Huntington Ave., Boston, 617-424-7000, 800-962-3030;
www.colonnadehotel.com

One of Back Bay's more family-friendly hotels, the Colonnade's big claim to fame is its roof-top pool—the only such swimming hole in the city. The 11th-floor area is typically full of bikini-clad beautiful people and the Who's Who on Boston's media scene.

The pool is fully catered for lunch and happy hour—the onsite bar makes great frozen cocktails—and, because of its guests-and-VIPs-only weekday policy, is generally free of crowds. 285 rooms. Wireless Internet access. Restaurant, bar. **$$$**

COPLEY SQUARE HOTEL

47 Huntington Ave., Boston, 617-536-9000; www.copleysquarehotel.com

One of Boston's most recognizable landmark hotels (the signature red sign can be seen from almost anywhere in Back Bay) got a major makeover. Upgrades restored its historic charm and lend a modern boutique-hotel feel to the 143-room hotel. New features include contemporary light fixtures, fabrics and glossy details in the lobby. At press time, the hotel was scheduled to re-open in late 2008. 143 rooms. Two restaurants, two bars. Wireless Internet access. Pets accepted. **$$**

★★COURTYARD MARRIOTT BOSTON TREMONT HOTEL

275 Tremont St., Boston, 617-426-1400, 800-321-2211; www.marriott.com

315 rooms. Wireless Internet access. Business center. Fitness center. **$$$**

★★DOUBLETREE GUEST SUITES

400 Soldiers Field Road, Boston, 617-783-0090, 800-222-8733; www.doubletree.com

308 rooms, all suites. Restaurant. Bar. Swimming pool. Business center. Wireless Internet access. Whirlpool. Pets accepted. **$**

★★★THE ELIOT HOTEL

370 Commonwealth Ave., Boston, 617-267-1607, 800-443-5468; www.eliothotel.com

This 95-room European-style boutique hotel is located just off the Massachusetts Turnpike in the Back Bay, convenient to shopping, entertainment and cultural sites. A quiet elegance pervades the lobby and most of the newly renovated accommodations are spacious suites with pull-out sofas, French bedroom doors, Italian marble baths and down comforters. The Eliot is also home to the critically acclaimed Clio and Uni restaurants, which serve contemporary French-American and Japanese cuisine, respectively. 95 rooms. Wireless Internet access. Restaurant, bar. **$$$**

★★★THE FAIRMONT COPLEY PLAZA BOSTON

138 St., James Ave., Boston, 617-267-5300, 800-441-1414; www.fairmont.com

Conveniently situated in the heart of the Theater District, this landmark 1925 hotel is also within walking distance of the Back Bay and South End. Named after the American painter John Singleton Copley, the Fairmont is traditional and elegant. The lobby has an exquisite high-domed ceiling and dramatic marble pillars, and is decorated with ornate furnishings as well as elaborate rugs. Watching over all of this is Catie Copley, the hotel's resident black Labrador, who's happy to be petted or taken for walks by guests. 383 rooms. High-speed Internet access. Restaurant, bar. Fitness center. **$$$**

★
★
★
★
★

★★★★★FOUR SEASONS HOTEL BOSTON

200 Boylston St., Boston, 617-338-4400, 800-330-3442;
www.fourseasons.com

The Four Seasons has a prime location overlooking the Public Garden and Boston Common. The renovated contemporary lobby, complete with a dramatic yellow marble and black granite floor, gleams. Antiques, fine art, sumptuous fabrics, period furniture and sleek technology such as flatscreen televisions and wireless Internet access bring the guest rooms and suites up to date. Attentive service heightens the experience. Canines are also pampered, and there's even a convenient dog-walking service. The Bristol Lounge is where Boston's power players come to celebrate their success. 273 rooms. High-speed Internet access. Two restaurants, two bars. Airport transportation available. Fitness center. Pool. Business center. $$$$

★HARBORSIDE INN OF BOSTON

185 State St., Boston, 617-723-7500, 888-723-7565;
www.harborsideinnboston.com

54 rooms. Wireless Internet access. Closed one week in late December. $$

★★★HILTON BOSTON BACK BAY

40 Dalton St., Boston, 617-236-1100, 800-445-8667; www.hilton.com

Built in the age of glass-box towers, this business-oriented hotel is conveniently located across the street from the Hynes Convention Center. A recent renovation enhanced the hotel's amenities and upped the square footage of existing guest rooms. To further cater to its hard-working clients, the Hilton added excellent desks, a top-notch fitness club and a 24-hour business center. 385 rooms. Wireless Internet access. Restaurant, two bars. Fitness center. Pool, whirlpool. Business center. Pets accepted. $$$

★★★HILTON BOSTON LOGAN AIRPORT

1 Hotel Drive, Boston, 617-568-6700, 800-445-8667; www.hilton.com

Experiencing one of Logan's many layovers? Check into the Hilton, one of the airport's most convenient and comfortable hotels. A skybridge connects terminals, and the hotel runs free shuttles to the airport subway stop and water taxi dock. The rooms, with their ruddy wood furniture and stocked minibars, are comfortably familiar spots to wait out a flight delay. 599 rooms. Wireless Internet access. Two restaurants, bar. Airport transportation available. Fitness center. Business center. Pool, whirlpool. Pets accepted. $$$

★★HOLIDAY INN SELECT-GOVERNMENT CENTER

5 Blossom St., Boston, 617-742-7630, 800-465-4329;
www.holiday-inn.com

303 rooms. Wireless Internet access. Restaurant, bar. Fitness center. Outdoor pool. $

★★HOTEL 140

140 Clarendon St., Boston, 617-585-5600, 800-714-0140;
www.hotel140.com

54 rooms. High-speed Internet access. Business center. Restaurant. Fitness room. Complimentary continental breakfast. Pets not accepted. $$

★
★
★
★
★

★★★HOTEL COMMONWEALTH

500 Commonwealth Ave., Boston, 617-933-5000, 866-784-4000;
www.hotelcommonwealth.com

In the heart of once-funky, now-yuppie Kenmore Square, this property is a modern mammoth that stretches an entire block. The hotel anchors the neighborhood with its gallery of upscale boutiques—don't miss the first-floor chocolatier—and two terrific restaurants. Rooms are furnished with oversized French Empire writing desks, Frette linens, Egyptian cotton blankets, pillow-top mattresses, and they have gleaming marble bathrooms. Fenway Park is around the corner and the Boston University campus begins a few yards up the street. 150 rooms. Wireless Internet access. Two restaurants, two bars. In-room spa. $$$

★★★HYATT HARBORSIDE

101 Harborside Drive, Boston, 617-568-1234, 800-233-1234; www.hyatt.com

Another good Logan Airport lodging, this hotel has a friendly staff, spacious guest rooms and a meeting facility designed with the business traveler in mind. Stranded guests can enjoy the indoor lap pool or the health and fitness center, both of which have scenic waterfront and Boston skyline views. 270 rooms. Wireless Internet access. Restaurant, bar. Airport transportation available. Business center. Indoor pool. Fitness center. $$

★★★HYATT REGENCY BOSTON FINANCIAL DISTRICT

1 Ave., de Lafayette, Boston, 617-912-1234, 800-233-1234; www.hyatt.com

When Hyatt took over this former Swisshotel, it kept much of the latter's elegant décor (as well as its discounted weekend packages). Principally a business hotel, it sits a block off Boston Common at the intersection of the financial and theater districts. Trendy restaurants and nightclubs of the Ladder District are just steps away. Antique furniture, marble floors and Waterford crystal chandeliers in public areas suggest Old World refinement. Many upper-level corner suites have city views, and 500 rooms. Wireless Internet access. Restaurant, bar. Business center. Indoor pool. $$$

MASSACHUSETTS

★★★INTERCONTINENTAL BOSTON

510 Atlantic Ave., Boston, 617-747-1000, 800-972-3381;
www.intercontinentalboston.com

Located in a new high-rise building in Boston's financial district, this luxury hotel is one of the city's most contemporary in design. The lobby has soaring ceilings, sleek furniture and working fireplaces. Rooms feature plush duvet-topped beds, marble bathrooms with deep soaking tubs and flatscreen TVs. The hotel's Rumba bar (which spotlights rums from around the world) and 24-hour Miel restaurant are hotspots for drinking and dining. 424 rooms. Restaurant, bar. Business center. Fitness center. Indoor pool. Pets accepted, some restrictions. Valet parking only. Spa. $$$

★★★THE LANGHAM BOSTON

250 Franklin St., Boston, 617-451-1900, 800-791-7781; www.langhamhotels.com

Near Faneuil Hall, the Freedom Trail and the North End, the Langham (formerly Le Meridien) is a perfect base for retracing the steps of famous patriots. The hotel's signature red awnings give way to a grand lobby done up in jewel tones. The guest rooms are equally delightful—many offer wonderful views of Post Office Square. Frequented by politicos and business power players, the Julien Bar, with its "101 Martini Menu," is one of the most popular hotel bars in the city. 325 rooms. High-speed Internet access. Restaurant, bar. Airport transportation available. $$$

★★★LENOX HOTEL

61 Exeter St., Boston, 617-536-5300, 800-225-7676; www.lenoxhotel.com

This downtown landmark is one of Boston's finest lodgings. The European-style hotel's lobby has a beautifully ornate ceiling with gilded moldings. Well-appointed guest rooms exude elegance and style. Large windows are draped in blue and gold; and some rooms have working wood-burning fireplaces. The hotel has won awards for environmental awareness. 212 rooms. Wireless Internet access. Restaurant, bar. $$$

★★★MILLENNIUM BOSTONIAN HOTEL

26 N. St., Boston, 617-523-3600, 800-343-0922; www.millenniumhotels.com

Right across from touristy Faneuil Hall, the Millennium is ideal for visitors who don't want to walk far to see historic attractions. At this downtown hotel, guest rooms vary from tiny to palatial; be sure to inquire carefully when booking. City Hall is nearby, so plenty of local business gets accomplished in the lobby bar. Guests also receive a discount at the adjacent Aveda Spa. 201 rooms. High-speed Internet access. Restaurant, bar. Pets not accepted. Business center. Fitness center. $$$

★★★NINE ZERO HOTEL

90 Tremont St., Boston, 617-772-5800, 866-646-3937; www.ninezero.com

When Kimpton bought out this downtown boutique hotel last year, Nine Zero lost much of its independent character. But the chain has done a lot to spruce up its property and amenities. The lobby and suites are a modern mix of nickel, chrome, stainless steel and glass, and the property offers wireless Internet access. Luxe amenties include Frette linens, goose-down comforters and pillows, and local beauty guru Mario Russo's bath products. 190 rooms. Restaurant, bar. Pets accepted. $$$

★★★OMNI PARKER HOUSE

60 School St., Boston, 617-227-8600, 800-843-6664; www.omnihotels.com

The Parker House, which gave the world its eponymous dinner rolls and the Boston cream pie, is the oldest continuously operating hotel in the United States. The plush lobby and dining room, which date from just before World War I, are good examples of Edwardian excess. The guest rooms are up to modern standards, as are the sleek fitness room and private, convenient business center. 551 rooms. High-speed Internet access. Restaurant, bar. Fitness center. $$$

★RAMADA INN

800 Morrissey Blvd., Boston, 617-287-9100; www.ramada.com

174 rooms. Business center. Fitness center. Free High-speed Internet access. Swimming pool. Restaurant. $

MASSACHUSETTS

★★★★THE RITZ-CARLTON, BOSTON COMMON
10 Avery St., Boston, 617-574-7100, 800-241-3333; www.ritzcarlton.com

Located near the city's theater district and overlooking the country's oldest public space, the Ritz-Carlton, Boston Common is convenient for business and leisure travelers alike. The guest rooms and suites have a distinctly serene feel with muted tones and polished woods. After a night of indulgence, guests often head to the massive Sports Club/LA, the city's most exclusive health club. Dogs are welcomed in style with the Pampered Pet Package, which includes bowls, biscuits and a personalized dog tag. 193 rooms. High-speed Internet access. Restaurant, bar. Business center. Fitness center. Pets accepted. $$$$

★★★SEAPORT HOTEL
1 Seaport Lane, Boston, 800-440-3318, 877-732-7678;
www.seaportboston.com

It may look a bit like a beached ocean liner, but the Seaport is solidly grounded with modern rooms and impressive amenities. An above-ground, covered walkway joins the property with the World Trade Center; as such, it's home to many conferences, conventions and sales events. The Seaport's health club is large and well equipped, and the restaurant is one of Boston's best for upscale seafood. By 2010, developers promise the surrounding area will be packed with shops, restaurants and galleries (right now it's a bit barren). 426 rooms. High-speed Internet access. Restaurant bar. Airport transportation available. Pool. Fitness center. Business center. Pets accepted. $$$

★★★SHERATON BOSTON HOTEL
39 Dalton St., Boston, 617-236-2000, 800-325-3535;
www.sheraton.com/boston

Ideally located in the historic Back Bay and adjacent to the Hynes Convention Center, this hotel offers guests attentive service in an elegant atmosphere. 1,216 rooms. High-speed Internet access. Two restaurants, bar. Pool. Fitness center. Business center. Pets accepted. $$$

★★★★TAJ BOSTON
15 Arlington St., Boston, 617-536-5700, 877-482-5267; www.tajhotels.com

Boston's hotel scene changed forever last year when the Taj hotel chain bought out the old Ritz Carlton on Arlington Street. In the lobby, the property looks much the same— "wedding cake" ceiling details, elaborate moldings, lavish carpets and graceful marble staircases. The guest rooms are still heavenly, with feather beds, soft robes, Molton Brown amenities and luxe marble bathrooms (suites include wood-burning fireplaces *and* a fireplace butler service). And the oldest tradition of all, the hotel's proper afternoon tea, is still going strong. 273 rooms. High-speed Internet access. Restaurant, two bars. Fitness center. Business center. Complimentary morning newspaper. $$$$

★★★WESTIN COPLEY PLACE
10 Huntington Ave., Boston, 617-262-9600, 800-937-8461;
www.westin.com/copleyplace

Rising 36-stories above the Copley Mall, this hotel is a great home base from which to explore Newbury Street, the Back Bay and the South End. Rooms are what you'd

★
★
★
★
★

expect from a Westin—a notch above those of the other major chains. 803 rooms. High-speed Internet access. Three restaurant, three bars. Airport transportation available. Pets accepted. Pool. Fitness center. Business center. $$$

★★★★XV BEACON
15 Beacon St., Boston, 617-670-1500, 877-982-2226; www.xvbeacon.com

This turn-of-the-century Beaux-Arts building on Beacon Hill belies the sleek décor found within. Original artwork commissioned specifically for the hotel by well-known artists adorns the walls. The eclectic guest rooms and suites are decorated in a palette of rich chocolate browns, blacks and creams. Rooms feature canopy beds with luxurious Italian linens and gas fireplaces covered in cool stainless steel. Completed in crisp white with simple fixtures, the bathrooms are a modernist's dream. The cuisine at the Federalist is delicious and fresh, and the restaurant's wine list is extensive and impressive. 61 rooms. High-speed Internet access. Restaurant. Bar. Airport transportation available. Pets accepted. Exercise. Spa. Fitness room. $$$$

SPECIALTY LODGINGS

CHARLES STREET INN
94 Charles St., Boston, 617-314-8900, 877-772-8900; www.charlesstreetinn.com

Step into the past without sacrificing modern conveniences at this charming city inn. The street-level reception and staircases are rather tight, but rooms are large and regal enough to qualify as decadent. Expect to find working fireplaces, massive antique armoires and heavily draped canopy beds in most. The hotel's location is ideal for exploring Beacon Hill, downtown or Back Bay on foot after a continental breakfast bounty is delivered to your door. Nine rooms. Wireless Internet access. Complimentary continental breakfast. $$$

GRYPHON HOUSE
9 Bay State Road, Boston, 617-375-9003, 877-375-9003;
www.gryphonhouseboston.com

More of a luxury bed and breakfast than a hotel, this circa-1895 brownstone stands at the juncture of Back Bay and Fenway. Each room is about the size of a studio apartment, has a working gas fireplace and wet bar, and is decorated in the Victorian style. The Kenmore subway stop, Boston University and Fenway Park are just moments away. Eight rooms. Complimentary continental breakfast. Wireless Internet access. $$

NEWBURY GUEST HOUSE
261 Newbury St., Boston, 617-437-7666, 800-437-7668;
www.newburyguesthouse.com

A string of residences along upper Newbury Street was linked with indoor staircases and hallways to create this Back Bay bed and breakfast. Rooms tend to be on the small side, in part because private bathrooms were added when conversions were made. The décor is eclectic. A good value for its location; just ask for a rear-facing room to escape street noise. 32 rooms. Complimentary full breakfast. Wireless Internet access. $$

RESTAURANTS

★★ABE & LOUIE'S

793 Boylston St., Boston, 617-536-6300;
www.abeandlouies.com

Steak menu. Lunch, dinner, brunch. Bar. Casual attire. Reservations recommended. Valet parking. Outdoor seating. **$$$**

★★★AQUITAINE

569 Tremont St., Boston, 617-424-8577;
www.aquitaineboston.com

Owned by the Aquitaine Group, this hip, modern boîte is an offshoot of fellow South End restaurant Metropolis café. Regulars rave about the steak frites. The wine list is intriguing, and the staff helpful. But what really makes this Tremont spot a must-visit is its creative, delicious Sunday brunch. French bistro menu. Dinner, brunch. Bar. Casual attire. Reservations recommended. Valet parking. **$$**

★★★★AUJOURD'HUI

200 Boylston St., Boston, 617-338-4400, 617-423-0154;
www.fourseasons.com

With floor-to-ceiling windows overlooking Boston's Public Garden, Aujourd'hui is a beautiful spot for a business lunch or an intimate dinner. Tables are set with Italian damask linens and decorated with antique plates and fresh flowers. The kitchen aims to please here, and turns out an innovative selection of seasonal modern French fare prepared with regional ingredients. The predominantly American wine list complements the kitchen's talent. A menu with lighter dishes is also available. French menu. Dinner, Sunday brunch. Bar. Children's menu. Business casual attire. Reservations recommended. Valet parking. **$$$**

★★★AURA

1 Seaport Lane, Boston, 617-385-4300; www.seaporthotel.com

This casually elegant waterfront restaurant is based in the Seaport Hotel. So it's no surprise its menu focuses on fish—New England clam chowder, pan-roasted Maine diver scallops, Mediterranean-style swordfish and a seared loin of yellowfin tuna all make appearances. Desserts include maple ricotta cheesecake with Concord grape sorbet and a bittersweet chocolate tart with caramel ice cream. Seafood menu. Breakfast, lunch, dinner, late-night, brunch. Bar. Children's menu. Business casual attire. Valet parking. **$$$**

★★B & G OYSTERS LTD

550 Tremont St., Boston, 617-423-0550; www.bandgoysters.com

Seafood menu. Lunch, dinner. Casual attire. Valet parking. Outdoor seating. Closed holidays. **$$$**

★★BOB'S SOUTHERN BISTRO

604 Columbus Ave., Boston, 617-536-6204; www.bobssouthernbistro.com

American menu. Dinner, brunch. Bar. Casual attire. Reservations recommended. Closed holidays. **$$**

★
★
★
★

★★BONFIRE

50 Park Plaza, Boston, 617-262-3473; www.bonfiresteakhouse.com

Steak menu. Bar. Business casual attire. Reservations recommended. Valet parking. $$$

★★BRASSERIE JO

120 Huntington Ave., Boston, 617-425-3240; www.brasseriejoboston.com

French menu. Breakfast, lunch, dinner, late-night, brunch. Bar. Children's menu. Casual attire. Reservations recommended. Valet parking. Outdoor seating. $$

★★★BRAVO RESTAURANT

465 Huntington Ave., Boston, 617-369-3474; www.mfa.org

This bold-colored dining hall is located on the second story of the Museum of Fine Arts. The restaurant's contemporary design reflects the museum's galleries of modern art (a few works are displayed on the eatery's walls). The chef incorporates fresh, local ingredients into an eclectic American menu. A wine tasting is offered on the last Wednesday of each month. Eclectic American menu. Lunch, dinner, brunch. Bar. Children's menu. Business casual attire. Reservations recommended. Outdoor seating. $$$

★★BROWN SUGAR CAFÉ-FENWAY

129 Jersey St., Boston, 617-266-2928; www.brownsugarcafe.com

Thai menu. Lunch, dinner. Casual attire. Outdoor seating. $$

★★THE BUTCHER SHOP

552 Tremont St., Boston, 617-423-4800; www.thebutchershopboston.com

International menu. Lunch, dinner, brunch. Children's menu. Casual attire. Valet parking. $$$

★★★THE CAPITAL GRILLE

359 Newbury St., Boston, 617-262-8900; www.thecapitalgrille.com

Dark walls and an extensive single-malt Scotch list make this high-roller-frequented steakhouse a man's spot through and through. Its generous portions of well-marbled steak, creamed spinach and buttery mashed potatoes are hearty enough for the hungriest diner. The house specialty is the gargantuan dry-aged porterhouse. Weighing in at 24 juicy, bold ounces, it should come with its own defibrillator. Steak menu. Dinner. Bar. Business casual attire. Reservations recommended. Valet parking. $$$

★★CARMEN

33 N. Square, Boston, 617-742-6421; www.carmenboston.com

Mediterranean menu. Lunch, dinner. Closed Monday. Bar. Casual attire. $$

★★CASA ROMERO

30 Gloucester St., Boston, 617-536-4341; www.casaromero.com

Mexican menu. Dinner, Sunday brunch. Bar. Outdoor seating. $$$

★★CHAU CHOW CITY

81 Essex St., Boston, 617-338-8158

Chinese menu. Lunch, dinner, late-night. Bar. Children's menu. Casual attire. Reservations recommended. $$

★CHEERS

84 Beacon St., Boston, 617-227-9605; www.cheersboston.com

American menu. Lunch, dinner. Bar. Children's menu. Casual attire. $$

★★CIAO BELLA

240A Newbury St., Boston, 617-536-2626; www.ciaobella.com

Italian menu. Lunch, dinner. Bar. Casual attire. Reservations recommended. Valet parking. Outdoor seating. $$$

★★CLARKE'S TURN OF THE CENTURY

21 Merchants Row, Boston, 617-227-7800

American menu. Lunch, dinner, late-night. Bar. Casual attire. $$

★★★★CLIO

370 Commonwealth Ave., Boston, 617-536-7200; www.cliorestaurant.com

Fresh fish plays a big role in chef/owner Ken Oringer's culinary symphony. For those who prefer their seafood raw, Clio has a separate sashimi bar, Uni, that features a pricey selection of rare fish from around the world. The rooms are perpetually packed with Boston's media and financial elite. French, Pan-Asian menu. Breakfast, dinner. Bar. Business casual attire. Reservations recommended. Valet parking. Closed Monday. $$$

★★DAVIDE

326 Commercial St., Boston, 617-227-5745; www.davideristorante.com

Italian menu. Dinner. Bar. Valet parking. $$

★★★DAVIO'S

75 Arlington St., Boston, 617-357-4810; www.davios.com

This northern Italian steakhouse has been a Boston institution for more than 20 years. Its large dining room features dramatic high ceilings, contemporary décor and imposing columns, and an open kitchen lets diners watch chef Steve DiFillippo at work. Favored dishes include grilled porterhouse veal chops, hand-rolled potato gnocchi and a rich chocolate cake. Davio's To-Go Shop, serving delicious takeout such as pizza, sandwiches and dessert, is located next door. Italian menu. Lunch, dinner, late-night. Bar. Children's menu. Business casual attire. Reservations recommended. Valet parking. $$$

★DURGIN PARK

340 Faneuil Hall Marketplace, Boston, 617-227-2038;
www.durgin-park.com

American menu. Lunch, dinner. Bar. Children's menu. Casual attire. Outdoor seating. $$

MASSACHUSETTS

★
★
★
★
★

★★★EASTERN STANDARD

528 Commonwealth Ave., Boston, 617-532-9100;
www.easternstandardboston.com

With its prime location in the middle of newly buzzing Kenmore Square, this restaurant mixes classic French bistro décor and food with a cavernous space (that's usually packed to the rafters). The menu reads like a greatest hits of beloved comfort food dishes, from steak frites to meatloaf and mashed potatoes, viener schnitzel to beef short rib bourguignon (though there are also raw bar offerings for those in search of lighter fare). The outdoor seating is a prime warm weather people-watching spot, and the bar is renowned for its expert versions of classic cocktails. American. Breakfast, lunch, dinner. Valet parking. Outdoor dining. **$$**

★★EXCELSIOR

272 Boylston St., Boston, 617-426-7878;
www.excelsiorrestaurant.com/home

American menu. Dinner, late-night. Bar. Casual attire. **$$$**

★★FILIPPO

283 Causeway St., Boston, 617-742-4143; www.filipporistorante.com

Italian menu. Lunch, dinner. Bar. Children's menu. Valet parking. Closed Monday-Tuesday. **$$$**

★★FRANKLIN CAFÉ

278 Shawmut Ave., Boston, 617-350-0010; www.franklincafe.com

American menu. Dinner, late-night. Bar. Casual attire. **$$**

★★GINZA

16 Hudson St., Boston, 617-338-2261; www.ginzaboston.com

Japanese menu. Lunch, dinner, late-night. Casual attire. Closed Thanksgiving. **$$**

★★★GRILL 23 & BAR

161 Berkeley St., Boston, 617-542-2255; www.grill23.com

We all know the formula at steakhouses: lots of beef paired with lots of testosterone, served up in a dark, wood-paneled boys club. Grill 23 serves lots of beef (seven juicy USDA Prime sirloin cuts) and ample testosterone (handsome, suited men line the bar), but this high-energy spot is anything but staid. Set in the historic Salada Tea Building, the vast space has sculptured ceilings, Corinthian columns and marble floors. It also has several nonsteak options in the form of a raw bar; lobster, shrimp, and clam entrées; caviar, sashimi and ceviche options; and plenty of lamb and poultry. Seafood, steak menu. Dinner. Bar. Business casual attire. Reservations recommended. Valet parking. **$$$**

★★★HAMERSLEY'S BISTRO

553 Tremont St., Boston, 617-423-2700;
www.hamersleysbistro.com

For two decades, chef Gordon Hamersley has packed diners in nightly with his perfectly executed, seasonally influenced French bistro fare. The house specialty, chicken roasted with garlic, lemon and parsley is the perfect example of how simple food can shine. The kitchen also offers a weekly vegan special that could tantalize even the most ardent carnivore. Hamersley's eclectic wine list changes with the seasons, as does the menu. An attentive staff completes the experience. French bistro menu. Dinner. Bar. Casual attire. Reservations recommended. Valet parking. Outdoor seating. $$$

★★THE HUNGRY I

71 1/2 Charles St., Boston, 617-227-3524

French bistro menu. Lunch, dinner, Sunday brunch. Bar. Business casual attire. Reservations recommended. Valet parking. Outdoor seating. $$$

★★★ICARUS

3 Appleton St., Boston, 617-426-1790;
www.icarusrestaurant.com

In a converted 1860s building, this South End standard is popular in the winter, when its cozy, wood-paneled ambiance warms chilly customers. Chef Chris Douglas prepares a seasonal American menu, full of flavorful dishes like slow-roasted tomato soup with Timson cheese panini, polenta with braised exotic mushrooms and duck in a cider and bourbon sauce. Come Friday nights, when a live jazz band takes the stage, the intimate bar is the place to be. American menu. Dinner. Bar. Valet parking. $$$$

★JASPER WHITE'S SUMMER SHACK

50 Dalton St., Boston, 617-867-9955;
www.summershackrestaurant.com

Seafood menu. Lunch, dinner. Bar. Children's menu. Casual attire. $$

★★JIMMY'S HARBORSIDE

242 Northern Ave., Boston, 617-423-1000; www.jimmysharborside.com

Seafood menu. Lunch, dinner. Bar. Children's menu. Casual attire. Reservations recommended. Valet parking. Outdoor seating. $$

★★KASHMIR

279 Newbury St., Boston, 617-536-1695; www.kashmirspices.com

Indian menu. Lunch, dinner. Casual attire. Reservations recommended. Valet parking. Outdoor seating. $$

★★★★LE'ESPALIER

774 Boylston St., Boston, 617-262-3023; www.lespalier.com

This Back Bay institution moved from a 19th-century townhouse to a tony spot adjacent to the Mandarin Oriental in fall 2008, but managed to hold onto the bulk of its intimate charm. Dining here brings you back to another era (when men still wore coats and ties to dinner) and chef/proprietor Frank McClelland's prix fixe menu only embellishes the experience: The dishes are a mix of French-influenced, traditional New England recipes like roasted Vermont rabbit with potato gnocchi and peas, and butter-poached Maine lobster with braised pork belly and sweet corn. His tasting menus can be amped up with caviar courses and an overflowing fromage cart, and the monster wine list puts plenty of stellar bottles alongside a few choices under $50. French menu. Dinner, Saturday tea. $$$$

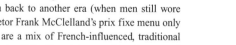

★★LALA ROKH

97 Mount Vernon St., Boston, 617-720-5511; www.lalarokh.com

Persian menu. Lunch, dinner. Business casual attire. **$$**

★★LES ZYGOMATES

129 S St., Boston, 617-542-5108; www.winebar.com

French menu. Lunch, dinner. Bar. Casual attire. Reservations recommended. Valet parking. Closed Sunday. **$$$**

★★★LOCKE-OBER

3 Winter Place, Boston, 617-542-1340; www.lockeober.com

Established in 1875, Boston's famed Locke-Ober is a city icon. Once a stomping ground for various foodies, financiers, politicians and local glitterati, the restaurant makes traditional American fare feel exciting. With chef/co-owner Lydia Shire, even slightly passé dishes like beef Stroganoff made with hand-cut egg noodles and onion soup gratine taste fresh. Don't miss the signature Indian pudding for dessert. American menu. Lunch, dinner. Bar. Business casual attire. Reservations recommended. Valet parking. Closed Sunday. **$$$**

★★LUCIA

415 Hanover St., Boston, 617-367-2353; www.luciaboston.com

Italian menu. Lunch, dinner. Bar. Casual attire. Reservations recommended. Valet parking. **$$**

★★★MAMMA MARIA

3 N. Square, Boston, 617-523-0077; www.mammamaria.com

Mamma Maria just might be one of the North End's best trattorias. Filled nightly with celebrities and savvy locals, the romantic spot set in an early 19th-century brick townhouse, serves a contemporary Italian menu that features seasonal ingredients and steers clear of heavy, cheesy, red-sauced pastas. Italian menu. Dinner. Bar. Casual attire. Valet parking. **$$$**

★★★MASA

439 Tremont St., Boston, 617-338-8884; www.masarestaurant.com

This lively Southwestern restaurant is located on the edge of the South End near Chinatown and the theater districts. Its lively bar area overlooks a chandelier-lit dining room, decorated with exposed brick walls, large mirrors, black-and-white checkered floors and flowing drapes. The spicy cuisine includes tapas, dinner and brunch menus. The margaritas are killer. Southwestern menu. Dinner. Bar. Casual attire. Reservations recommended. Valet parking. Outdoor seating. **$$**

★★★★MERITAGE

70 Rowes Wharf, Boston, 617-439-3995, 800-752-7077; www.bhh.com

Chef Daniel Bruce's passion is mixing wine with food. Accordingly, his Meritage, located in the Boston Harbor Hotel, offers more than 900 bottles. Eclectic, seasonal dishes are paired with wine flavors rather than varietals, progressing from light to heavy. Fennel-cured smoked salmon is matched with sparkling wines, while the herb-and-mustard-marinated filet comes with a pairing of robust reds. All menu items are available as large or small plates. International menu. Dinner, Sunday brunch. Bar. Business casual attire. Reservations recommended. Valet parking. Closed Monday. **$$$**

★★★THE METROPOLITAN CLUB

1210 Boylston St., Chestnut Hill, 617-731-0600; www.metclubandbar.com

Think all-American steakhouse next door meets modern urban night club and you've got The Met Club. Chef Todd Winer's specialties include a Myer rib eye for two, a bone-in veal parmigiana and a halibut for two with Italian pistachio butter. The sultry bar and lounge offers sexy cocktails and tempting snacks, including white garlic lobster pizza and Tokyo kobe miniwiches. Modern steakhouse menu. Sunday brunch, lunch, dinner. Bar. Casual attire. Reservations recommended. Valet parking. No credit cards accepted. **$$$**

★★★MIEL

510 Atlantic Ave., Boston, 617-747-1000, 800-327-0200; www.intercontinentalboston.com

Miel—French for honey—is a sunny Provençal brasserie. On the ground floor of the new InterContinental Boston, the 24-hour restaurant looks out over the revitalized waterfront. In warmer months, guests can dine on an outdoor patio. Inside, the yellow half-moon-shaped room has wrought-iron chandeliers, tile floors and a large stone hearth, plus a whole wall of olive oil jars. In addition to French classics such as Pistou soup and bouillabaisse, the chef sets up a raw bar daily. French menu. Breakfast, lunch, dinner, late-night. Bar. Casual attire. Reservations recommended. Valet parking. Outdoor seating. **$$$**

★MIKE'S CITY DINER

1714 Washington St., Boston, 617-267-9393; www.mikescitydiner.com

American menu. Breakfast, lunch. Casual attire. **$**

★★★MISTRAL

223 Columbus Ave., Boston, 617-867-9300; www.mistralbistro.com

Although the vaulted ceilings and sophisticated décor may scream glam, chef/owner Jamie Mammanno's creative yet uncomplicated cuisine departs from those expectations. Menu items such as tuna tartare, grilled thin-crust pizzas and skillet-roasted Cornish game hen are complemented by a superb wine list. French, Mediterranean menu. Dinner. Bar. Casual attire. Reservations recommended. Valet parking. **$$$**

★★NEPTUNE OYSTER

63 Salem St, Boston, 617-742-3474; www.neptuneoyster.com

Seafood menu. Lunch, dinner. Bar. Casual attire. **$$**

★★★★NO. 9 PARK

9 Park St., Boston, 617-742-9991; www.no9park.com

In the shadow of the State House on historic Beacon Hill sits No. 9 Park. Chef/owner Barbara Lynch's effort to support top-of-the-line local producers is evident—many ingredients are identified by farm on the menu. Perfectly prepared with a healthy dose of flavor and style, Lynch's modern European fare runs the gamut from beef to fish to

MASSACHUSETTS

venison to pheasant. Wine director Cat Silirie selects a thoughtful and unique list, and trains the friendly waitstaff to be as knowledgeable as she is. French, Mediterranean menu. Lunch, dinner. Bar. Business casual attire. Reservations recommended. Valet parking. Closed Sunday. $$$

★★★THE OAK ROOM

138 St., James Ave., Boston, 617-267-5300; www.theoakroom.com

This Old World steakhouse in the Fairmont Copley Plaza is steeped in Edwardian charm, as evidenced by the restored carved-plaster ceiling, baroque woodwork and garnet-red draperies. The perpetual, boisterous crowd of twenty- and thirty-somethings love the Oak Room's hearty grilled fish and beef tenderloin, oysters Rockefeller and clams casino. American menu. Breakfast, lunch, dinner, Sunday brunch. Bar. Children's menu. Business casual attire. Reservations recommended. Valet parking. $$$

★★★THE PALM

200 Dartmouth St., Boston, 617-867-9292; www.thepalm.com

"Let them eat meat!" might be an apt phrase to hang on a wall at The Palm. The local branch of the New York City favorite attracts financial moguls and out-of-town dealmakers looking to talk shop over copious amounts of perfectly seared prime beef. Tempting dessert trays include perennial favorites such as six-layer chocolate cake and carrot cake. Steak menu. Lunch, dinner. Bar. Children's menu. Casual attire. Reservations recommended. Valet parking. $$$

★★★PARKER'S

60 School St., Boston, 617-227-8600; www.omnihotels.com

Charles Dickens and Ralph Waldo Emerson ate here when they were in town, and John F. Kennedy's grandfather made Parker's the de facto headquarters of Massachusetts pols. The historical spot still attracts a cross-section of diners with a combination of classic and modern fare: steak au poivre with flaming tableside presentation is offered alongside pomegranate-glazed chicken, and salad selections include a "retro" chilled Iceberg wedge and an arugala salad with pancetta, Parmesan and lemon-basil oil. American menu. Breakfast, lunch, dinner. Bar. Children's menu. Casual attire. Reservations recommended. Closed Sunday. $$$

★PEKING TOM'S

25 Kingston St., Boston, 617-482-6282; www.kingstonstation.com

Chinese menu. Lunch, dinner. Bar. Casual attire. $$

★★PHO REPUBLIQUE

1415 Washington St., Boston, 617-262-0005;
www.phorepublique.net

Vietnamese menu. Dinner, late-night. Bar. Casual attire. $$

★★★RADIUS

8 High St., Boston, 617-426-1234; www.radiusrestaurant.com

Radius is a chic, slick, modern space decked in silver and red décor. Chef Michael Schlow shows off inspired modern French cooking with spare (read: no heavy sauces) dishes prepared with infused oils, emulsions, juices, vegetable purées and reductions. Dishes are well-textured and balanced and dessert is a heavenly experience. French menu. Lunch, dinner. Bar. Business casual attire. Reservations recommended. Valet parking. Closed Sunday. $$$

★★THE RED FEZ

1222 Washington St., Boston, 617-338-6060; www.theredfez.com

Middle Eastern menu. Dinner, late-night, Sunday brunch. Bar. Casual attire. Outdoor seating. $$

★★RISTORANTE TOSCANO

47 Charles St., Boston, 617-723-4090; www.toscanoboston.com

Italian menu. Lunch, dinner. Bar. Business casual attire. Reservations recommended. Valet parking. Closed Sunday. $$

★★★SAGE

1395 Washington St., Boston, 617-248-8814; www.sageboston.com

This teeny spot got a big upgrade last year when it traded its 35-seat North End space for roomy new digs in the South End. The interior is still rustic and cozy—just a bit more bustling—and chef/owner Anthony Susis is still serving modern Italian fare, including handmade pastas like gnocchi and ravioli. Italian menu. Dinner. Casual attire. Reservations recommended. Closed Sunday. $$$

★★SONSIE

327 Newbury St., Boston, 617-351-2500; www.sonsieboston.com

International menu. Breakfast, lunch, dinner, late-night, brunch. Bar. Casual attire. Reservations recommended. Valet parking. Outdoor seating. $$

★★★SORRELINA

1 Huntington Ave., Boston, 617-412-4600; www.sorellinaboston.com

It's hard to decide which lends more to the wow factor at this Back Bay restaurant: the sleek, contemporary design or the sophisticated Italian food. Cork floors, a white quartzite-terrazzo bar and low banquettes (all the better to see and be seen) make the room decidedly sexy. Though classics like spaghetti or veal Milanese make an appearance on the menu, chef/owner Jamie Mammano (also the talent behind Boston's Teatro, the Federalist and Mistral restaurants) dresses them up with gulf shrimp and chiles or saffron risotto. The exemplary wine list is punctuated by hard-to-find Italian bottles and balanced out with American and French selections. Italian. Dinner. Valet parking. $$$

★★TAPEO

266 Newbury St., Boston, 617-267-4799; www.tapeo.com

Spanish, tapas menu. Dinner. Bar. Casual attire. Reservations recommended. Outdoor seating. $$

★★TARANTA

210 Hanover St., Boston, 617-720-0052; www.tarantarist.com

Peruvian, Italian menu. Dinner. Casual attire. $$$

★★TERRAMIA

98 Salem St., Boston, 617-523-3112; www.terramiaristorante.com

Italian menu. Dinner. Children's menu. Reservations recommended. $$$

★★★TOP OF THE HUB

800 Boylston St., Boston, 617-536-1775; www.topofthehub.net

If sweeping views are your thing, you'll want to add Top of the Hub to your short list of Boston must-visits. Located in Back Bay, this special-occasion spot specializes in elegant and romantic dining on the top floor of the Prudential building. The New American menu takes some chances, but for the most part stays true to the seasons, featuring a wide selection of fish, game, pork and beef. Main courses, such as the slow-roasted pork tenderloin (enough to feed a family of four), are ample; be prepared to share. American menu. Lunch, dinner. Bar. Business casual attire. Reservations recommended. $$$

★★TREMONT 647/SISTER SOREL

647 Tremont St., Boston, 617-266-4600; www.tremont647.com

American menu. Dinner, brunch. Bar. Casual attire. Outdoor seating. $$

★★★TROQUET

140 Boylston St., Boston, 617-695-9463; www.troquetboston.com

The marriage of food and wine is the focus of this authentic Back Bay bistro. For example, owners Chris and Diane Campbell match flights of Sauvignon Blanc with a tangy fried goat cheese arugula salad and sweet Merlots with leg of lamb. As a result, dinner becomes an education as well as a fine gastronomical experience. American, French menu. Dinner. Bar. Business casual attire. Reservations recommended. Valet parking. Closed Sunday-Monday. $$$

★★★UNION BAR AND GRILLE

1357 Washington St., Boston, 617-423-0555; www.unionrestaurant.com

With leather banquettes and blazingly white tablecloths, Union Bar and Grille caps the gentrification of the South End's Washington Street. Stephen Sherman, the Culinary Institute of America-trained chef, produces a seasonally shifting menu that incorporates trendy dishes like tuna with grilled fennel, but also includes updated New England classics such as lobster tossed with corn and chanterelle mushrooms, and rack of lamb drizzled with fig sauce. The wine list is heavy on California and New Zealand whites. Pastry chef Joshua Steinberg's dessert menu gives diners a spot of chocolate on almost every plate. American menu. Dinner, Sunday brunch. Bar. Casual attire. Valet parking. $$$

★★UNION OYSTER HOUSE

41 Union St., Boston, 617-227-2750; www.unionoysterhouse.com

Seafood menu. Lunch, dinner, late-night. Bar. Children's menu. Casual attire. Reservations recommended. Valet parking. $$

★★★VIA MATTA

79 Park Plaza, Boston, 617-422-0008; www.viamattarestaurant.com

Michael Schlow, Christopher Myers and Esti Parsons, the savvy team behind Radius, are the folks you can thank for opening Via Matta, a trendy Italian eatery across from

★
★
★
☆

the Park Plaza Hotel. The place buzzes with energy, especially at lunch, as the city's power players sip Italian wine and nosh on lightly breaded Chicken Milanese. The hotspot has a shaded outdoor patio, as well as Enoteca, a candle-lit bar area perfect for drinks and small plates. Be sure to save room for dessert—Schlow's panna cotta might be the best in Boston. Italian menu. Lunch, dinner. Bar. Casual attire. Reservations recommended. Valet parking. Outdoor seating. Closed Sunday. **$$$**

BRAINTREE

This city, just south of Boston, is the site of second President John Adams' estate. Though Adams was away for much of their marriage, first as a European ambassador during the Revolutionary War, and later in Philadelphia as president, his wife Abigail stayed behind and helped the farm and homestead flourish.

Information: South Shore Chamber of Commerce, 36 Miller Stile Road, Quincy,
617-479-1111; www.southshorechamber.org

WHAT TO SEE AND DO
ABIGAIL ADAMS HOUSE
180 Norton St., Weymouth, 781-335-4205; www.abigailadamsbirthplace.org
The birthplace of Abigail Smith Adams, daughter of a local clerygyman, wife of President John Adams, mother of President John Quincy Adams. July-Labor Day: Tuesday-Sunday.

GILBERT BEAN MUSEUM
786 Washington St., Braintree, 781-848-1640; www.braintreehistorical.org
This house contains 17th- and 18th-century furnishings, military exhibits and local-historical displays. Tuesday-Wednesday, Saturday-Sunday 10 a.m.-4:30 p.m.

HOTELS
★★HOLIDAY INN
1374 N. Main St., Randolph, 781-961-1000, 800-465-4329; www.holiday-inn.com
158 rooms. Restaurant, bar. Pets not accepted. **$**

★HOLIDAY INN EXPRESS
909 Hingham St., Rockland, 781-871-5660; www.rocklandhi.com
76 rooms. Complimentary continental breakfast. **$**

★★★SHERATON BRAINTREE HOTEL
37 Forbes Road, Braintree, 781-848-0600, 800-325-3535;
www.sheraton.com/braintree
Just 12 miles from Logan International Airport and near the JFK library and Bayside Exposition Center, the Sheraton Braintree is a good choice for those who want to visit Boston without paying the city's sky-high hotel rates. Relax in the indoor or outdoor pool, sauna and steam rooms or enjoy an invigorating workout at the extensive onsite health club that has racquetball, aerobics and Nautilus machines. 396 rooms. Restaurant, bar. **$**

RESTAURANT
★★CAFFE BELLA
19 Warren St., Randolph, 781-961-7729
Italian menu. Dinner. Closed Sunday. Bar. **$$$**

BREWSTER

This quiet community on the inner arm of the Cape is dominated by miles of beautiful Cape Cod Bay beaches. Soft sand, gentle waves and plenty of shallow tide pools make Brewster an ideal family getaway.

Information: Cape Cod Chamber of Commerce, Highways 6 and 13, Hyannis, 508-362-3225, 888-332-2732; www.capecodchamber.org

WHAT TO SEE AND DO

CAPE COD MUSEUM OF NATURAL HISTORY

869 Highway, 6A, Brewster, 508-896-3867; www.ccmnh.org

Here are exhibits on wildlife and ecology, plus a library, lectures, field walks and trips to Monomoy Island. Daily 10 a.m.-4 p.m.

CAPE COD REPERTORY THEATER COMPANY

3299 Highway, 6A, Brewster, 508-896-1888; www.caperep.org

With both an indoor and outdoor theater, this troupe offers children's performances on Tuesday and Friday mornings in July and August. In addition, you'll find productions for the whole family in the outdoor theater in the woods near Nickerson State Park.

NEW ENGLAND FIRE & HISTORY MUSEUM

1439 Main St., Brewster, 508-896-5711

This six-building complex houses an extensive collection of firefighting equipment. Also on hand are a diorama of Chicago's 1871 fire, antique engines, the world's only 1929 Mercedes-Benz fire engine, a life-size reproduction of Ben Franklin's firehouse, a 19th-century blacksmith shop, and the largest apothecary in the country (that's 664 gold-leaf bottles of medicine). Memorial Day weekend-Labor Day, Monday-Saturday 10 a.m.-4 p.m., Sunday noon-4 p.m.; mid-September-Columbus Day, weekends.

NICKERSON STATE PARK

3488 Highway, 6A, Brewster, 508-896-3491; www.mass.gov

Nickerson State Park offers an unusual experience on Cape Cod: densely wooded areas that show no signs of the typical marshy Cape regions. The park has camping, challenging hiking trails, an eight-mile bike path, fishing, swimming, canoeing and bird-watching. Daily.

OCEAN EDGE GOLF COURSE

2660 Highway, 6A, Brewster, 508-896-9000; www.oceanedge.com

This beautiful golf course, just a stone's throw from the ocean, offers 6,665 yards of manicured greens, plus five ponds for challenging play. Greens fees drop considerably in the off-season, and lessons from PGA pros are often available. Daily; closed for snow and inclement weather.

HOTEL

★★★OCEAN EDGE RESORT

2907 Main St., Brewster, 508-896-9000, 800-343-6074; www.oceanedge.com

This sprawling 19th-century English country manor offers guests an oasis of comfort and privacy on Cape Cod Bay. Resort activities include golf, tennis, swimming, hiking and biking. Kids are welcome, but romantics shouldn't shy away—the estate is big enough for every type of family. 406 rooms. Restaurant, bar. Children's activity center. Airport transportation available. $$

SPECIALTY LODGINGS

BRAMBLE INN
2019 Main St., Brewster, 508-896-7644; www.brambleinn.com
Eight rooms. Children over 8 years only. Complimentary full breakfast. Restaurant. Closed January-April. $

BREWSTER BY THE SEA
716 Main St., Brewster, 508-896-3910, 800-892-3910;
www.brewsterfarmhouseinn.com
Eight rooms. Children over 10 years only. Complimentary full breakfast. High-speed Internet access. Spa. Pool. $

CAPTAIN FREEMAN INN
15 Breakwater Road, Brewster, 508-896-7481, 800-843-4664;
www.captainfreemaninn.com
12 rooms. Children over 10 years only. Complimentary full breakfast. Airport transportation available. Pets not accepted. $

ISAIAH CLARK HOUSE
1187 Main St., Brewster, 508-896-2223, 800-822-4001; www.isaiahclark.com
Seven rooms. Children over 10 years only. Complimentary full breakfast. Pets not accepted. $

THE OLD MANSE INN
1861 Main St., Brewster, 508-896-3149, 866-896-3149;
www.oldmanseinn.com
Nine rooms. Complimentary full breakfast. $$

OLD SEA PINES INN
2553 Main St., Brewster, 508-896-6114; www.oldseapinesinn.com
24 rooms. Children over eight years only (except in family suites). Complimentary full breakfast. Pets not accepted. $

RESTAURANTS

★★★BRAMBLE INN
2019 Main St., Brewster, 508-896-7644; www.brambleinn.com
Chef/owner Ruth Manchester delights guests with creative cuisine and heartwarming hospitality at this cozy eatery in Brewster's historic district. The four quaint dining rooms, including an enclosed porch, make the Bramble Inn a perfect choice for a romantic dinner. American menu. Dinner. Bar. Business casual attire. Reservations recommended. Closed January-April. $$$

★★BREWSTER FISH HOUSE
2208 Main St., Brewster, 508-896-7867; www.ccmenus.com/brewstermenus
American, seafood menu. Lunch, dinner. Closed December-April. $$$

★BREWSTER INN AND CHOWDER HOUSE

1993 Main St., Brewster, 508-896-7771;
www.ccmenus.com/brewstermenus

American menu. Lunch, dinner. Bar. Casual attire. Outdoor seating. $$

★★★CHILLINGSWORTH

2449 Main St., Brewster, 508-896-3640, 800-430-3640;
www.chillingsworth.com

The grand 300-year-old Chillingsworth Foster estate sprawls along the edge of the King's Highway. For the last 30 years, its restaurant has been synonymous with epicurean eating on Cape Cod. The formal dining rooms, furnished in antiques, are spread through the central house. The seven-course dinner is a contemporary interpretation of classic French cuisine—seared veal steak with truffle risotto, for example, or lobster with sautéed spinach and fennel. Plan to dress up and spend the whole evening munching (quicker, lighter fare can be had in the more casual bistro on a glassed-in porch). French menu. Lunch, dinner. Bar. Reservations recommended. Outdoor seating. Closed Monday; also December-mid-May. $$$

BROOKLINE

What started out as a commuter community has blossomed into a booming city in its own right. Directly to the east of Boston, Brookline began in the 1600s as a summer oasis for wealthy merchants and politicians. Centuries later, the town was still attracting notable Americans—Frederick Law Olmsted and John F. Kennedy both lived here (the latter's boyhood home is now open to the public). Today, Brookline's much-envied, Victorian-lined shady streets are home to moneyed families and one of the best school systems in the Boston area. Washington Square, Coolidge Corner and Brookline Village, with their shops, eateries and bars, attract younger residents and out-of-towners alike.

Information: www.townofbrooklinemass.com

WHAT TO SEE AND DO

JOHN F. KENNEDY NATIONAL HISTORIC SITE

83 Beals St., Brookline, 617-566-7937; www.nps.gov/jofi

The birthplace and childhood home of the nation's 35th president has been restored to its 1917 state. Ranger-guided tours. May-October, Wednesday-Sunday 10 a.m.-4:30 p.m.

RESTAURANTS

★★★THE FIREPLACE

1634 Beacon St., Brookline, 617-975-1900;
www.fireplacerest.com

Thanks to its yuppified neighborhood, the Fireplace can seem like a cross between *Friends* and *Cheers,* where everyone knows everyone else, and half the diners are just stopping to chat and sip a glass of Sancerre. Hungry patrons are devoted to the hearty fare—braised brisket, grilled halibut, gingerbread pudding—much of it made from scratch in the wood-fired oven or smoke box. The eponymous hearth provides welcome warmth and added coziness in winter months. American, seafood menu. Lunch, dinner, brunch. Children's menu. Casual attire. $$

★★★FUGAKYU

1280 Beacon St., Brookline, 617-734-1268;

Fugakyu stands out among all of Brookline's many sushi spots. Its Coolidge Corner location is huge and heavy on the blonde wood-white screen décor. Larger parties can reserve private tatami rooms—complete with rice paper walls and sliding doors—and choose from a menu of soups, tempuras, stir-fries, noodles, pickle plates, sushi, sashimi, maki rolls and tableside braises. Diners rave about the tempura-fried green tea ice cream dessert topped with just a dab of red-bean paste. Japanese, sushi menu. Lunch, dinner, late-night. Reservations recommended. Closed Sunday.

★RUBIN'S KOSHER DELICATESSEN

500 Harvard St., Brookline, 617-731-8787; www.rubinskosher.com

Kosher deli menu. Breakfast, lunch, dinner. Sunday-Thursday. Closed Saturday; Jewish holidays. **$**

★★WASHINGTON SQUARE TAVERN

714 Washington St., Brookline, 617-232-8989;
www.washingtonsquaretavern.com

American menu. Dinner, Sunday brunch. Bar. Casual attire. **$$**

CAMBRIDGE

Across the Charles River from Boston, Cambridge seems a world away. Though connected to the state capital, and often lumped in with it geographically, the "People's Republic of Cambridge," as locals have christened it, has a decidedly different vibe. Famous for its universities (Harvard, M.I.T.), bustling squares and ethnically diverse residents (at least 80 different nations are represented by the city's public school kids), the area is a melting pot of people and ideas. The gritty, nightclub-filled streets of Central Square run into the vibrant back roads of Harvard Square and the mansion-lined Brattle Street (actor John Malkovich lives here), which in turn leads into safe, family-friendly Huron Village. Farther to the east is Inman Square, a multicultural neighborhood overflowing with cafés, eateries and sweet little shops. Most of the city is easily accessible by public bus or train; those with more stamina should consider walking these historic, but very much alive, streets.

Information: Chamber of Commerce, 859 Massachusetts Ave.,
617-876-4100; www.cambcc.org.

WHAT TO SEE AND DO
CAMBRIDGE ANTIQUE MALL

201 Monsigenur O'Brien Highway, Cambridge, 617-868-9655;
www.marketantique.com

Stroll through five floors of antique furniture, books, artwork, toys, clothing and more. Tuesday-Sunday 11 a.m.-6 p.m.

CHRIST CHURCH

0 Garden St., Cambridge, 617-876-0200; www.cccambridge.org

Dating back to 1759, this Episcopal Church building is the oldest in Cambridge. The fine Georgian colonial designed by Peter Harrison was used as a barracks during the Revolution. Daily.

MASSACHUSETTS

★
★
★
★

FORMAGGIO KITCHEN

244 Huron Ave., Cambridge, 617-354-4750; www.formaggiokitchen.com

Whether you consider yourself a *gourmet* or a *gourmand*, you'll easily lose yourself in this culinary playground. With a selection of 200 artisan cheeses, fine pastas, international chocolates, exotic spices, mouthwatering snacks and Italian coffees, the famed Formaggio Kitchen is a food-lover's dream.

HARVARD MUSEUM OF NATURAL HISTORY

26 Oxford St., Cambridge, 617-495-3045; www.hmnh.harvard.edu

The Harvard Museum of Natural History is three museums in one: A botanical museum examines the study of plants, the museum of zoology examines the study of animals and a geological museum examines the study of rocks and minerals. All three explore the evolution of science and nature throughout time. Daily 9 a.m.-5 p.m.

HARVARD UNIVERSITY

24 Quincy St., Cambridge, www.harvard.edu
Information center: 1350 Massachusetts Ave., Cambridge, 617-495-1573

America's oldest university was founded in 1636. Two years later, when a minister named John Harvard died and bequested half his estate to the school, the college was named for him. The prototypical brick- and quad-filled campus spans Harvard and Radcliffe colleges, as well as 10 graduate and professional schools.

MASSACHUSETTS

HARVARD UNIVERSITY ART MUSEUMS

32 Quincy St., Cambridge, 617-495-9400; www.artmuseums.harvard.edu

Visit three museums in one: the Fogg Art Museum (including wide-ranging collections of paintings and sculpture), the Busch-Reisinger Museum (which features mostly German art) and the Arthur M. Sackler Museum (ancient art, plus Asian and Islamic collections). Admission to one museum covers all three; allow a half day for all. Free on Wednesdays and Saturdays until noon. Daily.

★
★
★
★
☆

LIST VISUAL ARTS CENTER AT MIT

Wiesner Building, 20 Ames St., Cambridge, 617-253-4680; listart.mit.edu

The museum has changing exhibits of contemporary art. The MIT campus also has an outstanding permanent collection of outdoor sculpture, including works by Calder, Moore and Picasso, and significant architecture, including buildings by Aalto, Pei and Saarinen. October-June, daily.

LONGFELLOW NATIONAL HISTORIC SITE

105 Brattle St., Cambridge, 617-876-4491; www.nps.gov/long

This Georgian-style house built in 1759 was Washington's headquarters during the 1775-1776 siege of Boston, and Henry Wadsworth Longfellow's home from 1837 until his death in 1882. Wednesday-Sunday 10 a.m.-4:30 p.m.

MASSACHUSETTS INSTITUTE OF TECHNOLOGY

77 Massachusetts Ave., Cambridge, 617-253-1000; www.mit.edu

M.I.T. remains one of the greatest science and engineering schools in the world. On the Charles River, the campus' 135 acres house impressive neoclassic and modern buildings. Monday-Friday.

MIT MUSEUM

265 Massachusetts Ave., Cambridge, 617-253-5927; web.mit.edu

Collections and exhibits interpret the Institute's social and educational history, developments in science and technology, and the interplay of technology and art. Tuesday-Friday 10 a.m.-5p.m., Saturday-Sunday noon-5 p.m.; closed Monday.

PEABODY MUSEUM OF ARCHAEOLOGY AND ETHNOLOGY

11 Divinity Ave., Cambridge, 617-496-1027

The Peabody Museum, one of the oldest anthropology museums in the world, traces human cultural history in the Western Hemisphere. Daily.

RADCLIFFE COLLEGE'S SCHLESINGER LIBRARY CULINARY COLLECTION

10 Garden St., Cambridge, 617-495-8647; www.radcliffe.edu/schles

Through Radcliffe's culinary collection, you'll have access to more than 9,000 cookbooks. Although you can't borrow from the library, you can still tap into the books of some of the world's greatest chefs, including Samuel Narcisse Chamberlain, Julia Child and Sophie Coe. Monday-Friday.

SPECIAL EVENT
HEAD OF THE CHARLES REGATTA

2 Gerry's Landing Road, Cambridge, 617-868-6200; www.hocr.org

More than 300,000 spectators from all over the world descend on Boston for this three-mile rowing race that involves 7,000 athletes and 1,470 rowing shells. Olympic and World champions race each other on the Charles River, while countless fans tailgate and cheer along the shore.

HOTELS
★★A CAMBRIDGE HOUSE BED AND BREAKFAST INN

2218 Massachusetts Ave., Cambridge, 617-491-6300, 800-232-9989;
www.acambridgehouse.com

15 rooms. Complimentary continental breakfast. Wireless Internet access. **$$**

★★BEST WESTERN HOTEL TRIA

220 Alewife Brook Parkway, Cambridge, 617-491-8000, 866-333-8742;
www.bestwestern.com

69 rooms. Complimentary continental breakfast. High-speed Internet access. Restaurant, bar. Fitness center. Pool. Pets accepted (fee). **$**

★★BOSTON MARRIOTT CAMBRIDGE

2 Cambridge Center, Cambridge, 617-494-6600, 800-228-9290;
www.marriott.com

433 rooms. High-speed Internet access. Two restaurants, two bars. **$$**

★★★CHARLES HOTEL

1 Bennett St., Cambridge, 617-864-1200, 800-882-1818;
www.charleshotel.com

Celebrities, politicians and visiting dignitaries (not to mention the wealthy parents of Harvard students) all stay at the Charles, one of Boston's most beloved hotels. The guest

★
★
★
★
★

rooms mix Shaker-inspired design with a multitude of modern amenities such as three two-line phones, Bose Wave radios, TVs in the bathrooms and more. Dine in either of its two restaurants, and be sure to tune into the sweet sounds of jazz at the Regattabar, where swinging national bands hit the stage. In winter, the hotel's courtyard becomes an ice-skating rink, while various community events, such as a farmer's market, take place here in the summer. 294 rooms. Wireless Internet access. Restaurant, bar. Spa. Pets accepted (fee). $$$

★★★HOTEL MARLOWE

25 Edwin H. Land Blvd., Cambridge, 617-868-8000, 800-825-7140;
www.hotelmarlowe.com

The Marlowe sets itself apart from other East Cambridge lodgings with its whimsical palette of crimson, deep blue and bright gold. Surrounded by luxury condos and a shopping mall, this modern hotel is less than a block from the Museum of Science. Amenities are top of the line (Frette linens, Aveda bath products), the in-room Sony PlayStations amuse youngsters, and the pet-friendly vibe is a big plus for animal lovers. 236 rooms. Wireless Internet access. Restaurant, bar. Airport transportation available. Valet parking. Pets accepted. $$$

★★★HYATT REGENCY CAMBRIDGE

575 Memorial Drive, Cambridge, 617-492-1234, 800-633-7313;
www.hyatt.com

From the lavishly appointed lobby (with a large open atrium and glass elevators) to the spacious guest rooms to the darling gazebo in the well-maintained courtyard, this hotel makes patrons feel at home. Its Charles River location is 15 minutes from both Harvard Square and downtown Boston. 469 rooms. Wireless Internet access. Restaurant, bar. $$

★★★THE INN AT HARVARD

1201 Massachusetts Ave., Cambridge, 617-491-2222, 800-458-5886;
www.theinnatharvard.com

Acclaimed postmodernist Cambridge architect Graham Gund showed great restraint in creating this neoclassical structure at the edge of Harvard Square. Guest rooms have a casual, homey feel, but a four-story atrium turns the reception area into a soaring library and lounge area. The university frequently books many of the rooms for visiting scholars and dignitaries; just be sure to make reservations months ahead of a graduation or alumni weekend. 111 rooms. Wireless Internet access. Restaurant, bar. $$

★★★LE MERIDIEN

20 Sidney St., Cambridge, 617-577-0200;
www.starwoodhotels.com/lemeridien

This high-tech-themed hotel identifies closely with the similarly named school—it even incorporates printed circuit-board designs into the bedroom furniture. Predictably, the hotel is wired every which way, with lightning-quick Internet access and Sony PlayStations in all guest rooms. The spot also functions as a conference and meeting center for cutting-edge companies in media, biotech, robotics and computing. 210 rooms. Free wireless Internet access. Business center. Restaurant, bar. $$

★★★ROYAL SONESTA HOTEL BOSTON

40 Edwin Land Blvd., Cambridge, 617-806-4200, 800-766-3782;
www.sonesta.com/boston

Perched on the Charles River, this hotel boasts panoramic Boston skyline views, hand-somely appointed guest rooms and a state-of-the-art health spa with massage thera-pists, reflexology and a poolside sun deck. The property is adjacent to the Museum of Science and is within walking distance to the CambridgeSide Galleria, an indoor shopping mall. 400 rooms. Wireless Internet access. Two restaurants, two bars. Business center. $$$

RESTAURANTS

★★BLUE ROOM

1 Kendall Square, Cambridge, 617-494-9034; www.theblueroom.net

Mediterranean menu. Dinner, Sunday brunch. Bar. Casual attire. Reservations recommended. Outdoor seating. $$$

★★CASABLANCA

40 Brattle St., Cambridge, 617-876-0999; www.casablanca-restaurant.com

Mediterranean menu. Lunch, dinner, brunch. Bar. Casual attire. Reservations recommended. $$$

★★CHEZ HENRI

1 Shepard St., Cambridge, 617-354-8980; www.chezhenri.com

Cuban menu, French menu. Dinner. Bar. $$$

★★★CRAIGIE ON MAIN

853 Main St., Cambridge, 617-497-5511; www.craigiestreetbistrot.com

Chef Tony Maws often hits nearby farmers markets to create "market menus" on the day items become available. He's fanatical about crafting dishes from scratch and using organic ingredients whenever possible. A decent-sized wine list is filled almost completely with organic producers as well. French bistro, International menu. Dinner. Casual attire. Reservations recommended. Closed Monday-Tuesday; also late June-early July. $$

★★EAST COAST GRILL & RAW BAR

1271 Cambridge St., Cambridge, 617-491-6568; www.eastcoastgrill.net

Seafood menu. Dinner, Sunday brunch. Bar. Casual attire. $$

★★THE ELEPHANT WALK

2067 Mass Ave., Cambridge, 617-492-6900; www.elephantwalk.com

French, Pacific-Rim/Pan-Asian menu. Dinner. Bar. Children's menu. Casual attire. Reservations recommended. $$$

★★★HARVEST

44 Brattle St., Cambridge, 617-868-2255; www.harvestcambridge.com

Harvest's rustic ambiance—pewter tableware, dried flowers, sturdy, dark wood—is at odds with the building's modern exteriors. Inside, classic American dishes (don't

MASSACHUSETTS

★
★
★
★

miss the nightly risotto) are served from an open kitchen in the family-friendly dining room. American menu. Lunch, dinner, Sunday brunch. Children's menu. Outdoor seating. $$$

★★HELMAND

143 First St., Cambridge, 617-492-4646
Afghan menu. Dinner. Bar. $$

★★★OLEANA

134 Hampshire St., Cambridge, 617-661-0505;
www.oleanarestaurant.com
Mediterranean menus are a dime a dozen in the Boston area, but few chefs coax out the cuisine's diverse influences as well as Oleana's chef/owner Ana Sortun. She matches Middle Eastern almonds with herbs from Provence in a chicken dish, and branches out with the likes of a Basque-influenced venison with caramelized turnip. Regulars enjoy the scallops with basmati-pistachio pilaf from the menu. The outdoor patio and fireplace-lit indoor rooms are inviting. Eastern Mediterranean menu. Dinner. Bar. Casual attire. Reservations recommended. Outdoor seating. $$$

★★★★RIALTO

1 Bennett St., Cambridge, 617-661-5050;
www.rialto-restaurant.com
Fresh from a complete redesign, this second floor Charles Hotel eatery is more popular than ever. Chef/owner Jody Adams's distinctive brand of boldly flavored Mediterranean-inspired fare has also been reimagined, but her honest, straightforward approach and dedication to fresh, seasonal produce remains. Her Italian-heavy menu is a full of complimentary flavors and the wine list is well-rounded. Mediterranean menu. Dinner. Bar. Business casual attire. Reservations recommended. Valet parking. $$$

CAPE COD

The invention of the automobile changed Cape Cod from a group of isolated fishing villages, large estates and cranberry bogs into one of the world's prime resort areas. Today, the seaside region's population more than triples during the summertime, when 200,000 year-round residents prepare for nearly 500,000 visitors. Since World War II, hundreds of hotels and resorts have opened to accommodate the hordes of tourists (good luck finding a last-minute room in August), but the quaint villages themselves have remained virtually unchanged.

Seventy miles long, the Cape is a peninsula land mass in the shape of a bent arm and clenched fist. Buzzards Bay and the Cape Cod Canal mark the beginning of the Cape, Chatham and Nauset beaches are at its "elbow," and Provincetown, or P-town to those in the know, lies at its northern tip. Because the Cape extends 30 miles offshore and into the warm Gulf Stream, its climate is notably gentler than that of the mainland. As an added bonus, many Cape towns have two beaches—one bay-side, one ocean-side, both covered with fine, soft sand. All in all, the Cape's coastline stretches for a never-ending 560 miles.

★★★SALTS
798 Main St., Cambridge, 617-876-8444; www.saltsrestaurant.com

Located between Kendall Square and Central Square, this tiny neighborhood place has a quiet and cozy atmosphere. Romantics looking for special-occasion dining can't go wrong at Salts, where the focus is on local, organic produce. A mostly French menu pairs well with a list of some 200 French and American wines.
Contemporary American menu. Dinner. Business casual attire. Reservations recommended. Closed Sunday-Monday. $$$

★★SANDRINE'S
8 Holyoke St., Cambridge, 617-497-5300; www.sandrines.com

French bistro menu. Lunch, dinner. Bar. Business casual attire. Reservations recommended. $$$

CHATHAM

Chatham is among the hubs of the Cape's social scene. Though tourists are hard to distinguish from blue-blooded locals, look closely. Year-rounders are most likely the ones sipping lemonade on the porches of their comfortable estates that look out over Pleasant Bay and Nantucket Sound. Monomoy Island, an unattached sand bar that stretches 10 miles into the sea, was once a haunt of "moon-cussers"—beach pirates who lured vessels aground with false lights.
Information: Chamber of Commerce, Chatham, 888-332-2732;
www.capecodchamber.org

WHAT TO SEE AND DO
CHATHAM LIGHT
Bridge and Main Streets, Chatham, 508-430-0628;
www.chathamlighthouserealty.com

This quintessential Cape lighthouse has been through many incarnations and restorations, but has always offered a superb view of the Atlantic and the seals on the beach below. Daily.

MONOMOY NATIONAL WILDLIFE REFUGE
Monomoy Island, Chatham, 508-945-0594; www.monomoy.fws.gov

The refuge is 2,750 acres of bird-lover's paradise. The spectacle is greatest in spring, when the inhabitants exhibit bright plumage while breeding.

HOTELS
★★★THE BRADFORD OF CHATHAM
26 Cross St., Chatham, 508-945-1030, 888-242-8426;
www.bradfordinn.com

38 rooms. Children over 12 only. Complimentary full breakfast. $$

★★★CHATHAM BARS INN
297 Shore Road, Chatham, 508-945-0096, 800-527-4884;
www.chathambarsinn.com

Built in 1814, this grand Cape Cod landmark has managed to maintain most of its historic charm without falling into disrepair. The guest rooms have 180-degree views

★
★
★
★
★

of Pleasant Bay; well-maintained gardens and a private beach (one of the few in the area) are just outside. The resort recently added a large, state-of-the-art spa that offers plenty of pampering. 205 rooms. Wireless Internet access. Four restaurants, two bars. Children's activity center. Beach. Airport transportation available. $$$$

★THE CHATHAM MOTEL
1487 Main St., Chatham, 508-945-2630, 800-770-5545;
www.chathammotel.com
32 rooms. Closed November-April. $

★CHATHAM SEAFARER
2079 Main St., Chatham, 508-432-1739, 800-786-2772;
www.chathamseafarer.com
20 rooms. Pool. $

★★★CHATHAM WAYSIDE INN
512 Main St., Chatham, 508-945-5550, 800-242-8426; www.waysideinn.com
This classic village inn dates back to the 1860s, as evidenced by the lobby's original knotty pine flooring. The informal and cozy property has 56 large, clean and comfortable rooms—a few have private balconies and jetted tubs. The grounds are within walking distance to the water and the town center. 56 rooms. Restaurant, bar. $$$

★★★CRANBERRY INN
359 Main St., Chatham, 508-945-9232, 800-332-4667; www.cranberryinn.com
Located in the historic district, this elegant inn offers guests all the comforts of home. Relax in the well-appointed guest rooms or enjoy the picturesque view of a windmill while lazing in one of the Kennedy rocking chairs set along the expansive front porch. 19 rooms. Children over 12 years only. Complimentary full breakfast. Golf. $

★★★PLEASANT BAY VILLAGE RESORT
1191 Orleans Road, Chatham, 508-945-1133, 800-547-1011;
www.pleasantbayvillage.com
From the exquisitely arranged rock garden, where a waterfall cascades into a stone-edged pool filled with colorful koi, to the lavish gardens, this six-acre woodland retreat offers timeless tranquility. Many rooms have private patios, grills and screened-in porches. 58 rooms. Closed late October-April. Wireless Internet access. Restaurant. $$

★★★QUEEN ANNE INN
70 Queen Anne Road, Chatham, 508-945-0394, 800-545-4667;
www.queenanneinn.com
34 rooms. Complimentary continental breakfast. Restaurant. Closed January. $

★★★WEQUASSETT INN
On Pleasant Bay, Chatham, 508-432-5400, 800-225-7125; www.wequassett.com
This country inn-resort hybrid appeals to antique lovers and activity junkies alike. Located on 22 acres, the full-service spot overlooks Pleasant Bay and the Atlantic

MASSACHUSETTS

★
★
★
★
★

Ocean. Suites take a cosmopolitan slant on country décor. Take advantage of the prestigious private Cape Cod National Golf Club. 104 rooms. Wireless Internet access. Two restaurants, bar. Children's activity center. Beach. Airport transportation available. Closed December-March. $$$$

SPECIALTY LODGINGS

CAPTAIN'S HOUSE INN
369-377 Old Harbor Road, Chatham, 508-945-0127, 800-315-0728;
www.captainshouseinn.com
Once a sea captain's estate, this pretty inn was built in 1839 and features period wall-papers, Williamsburg antiques and elegantly refined Queen Anne chairs. Many of the guestrooms are named for the ships that once sailed the nearby seas. 16 rooms. Children over 12 only. Complimentary full breakfast. Pool. Fitness center. $$

MOSES NICKERSON HOUSE INN
364 Old Harbor Road, Chatham, 508-945-5859, 800-628-6972;
www.mosesnickersonhouse.com
In 1839, whaling captain Moses Nickerson built the house that's home to this quaint bed and breakfast. Seven rooms. Children over 10 years only. Complimentary full breakfast. $

OLD HARBOR INN
22 Old Harbor Road, Chatham, 508-945-4434, 800-942-4434;
www.chathamoldharborinn.com
Built in 1933, this former residence of a prominent doctor has been renovated and is furnished with a blend of antiques and modern conveniences. Eight rooms. Children over 14 years only. Complimentary full breakfast. $

RESTAURANTS

★★CHATHAM SQUIRE
487 Main St., Chatham, 508-945-0945; www.thesquire.com
Seafood menu. Lunch, dinner. Bar. Children's menu. Casual attire. $$

★★IMPUDENT OYSTER
15 Chatham Bars Ave., Chatham, 508-945-3545
Seafood menu. Lunch, dinner. Bar. Children's menu. Casual attire. Reservations rec-ommended. $$$

★★PATE'S
1260 Main St., Chatham, 508-945-9777; www.patesrestaurant.com
American menu. Dinner. Bar. Children's menu. Casual attire. Closed February-March. $$

★★★★TWENTY-EIGHT ATLANTIC
Pleasant Bay Road, Chatham, 508-432-5400, 800-225-7125; www.wequassett.com
Black truffle risotto, truffled salmon tartare and a petite clambake are among the enticing entrées offered at this waterfront restaurant located in the Wequassett Resort.

MASSACHUSETTS

★
★
★
★
★

The large, open dining room features featuring wide views of Pleasant Bay. American menu. Breakfast, lunch, dinner. Bar. Children's menu. Business casual attire. Reservations recommended. Outdoor seating. Closed December-March. $$$

★★VINING'S BISTRO
595 Main St., Chatham, 508-945-5033;
International menu. Dinner. Casual attire. Closed in winter. $$

CONCORD

About as old-school New England as it gets, Concord (along with neighboring Lexington) boasts the title "Birthplace of the Republic." A litany of American literary greats—Ralph Waldo Emerson, Henry David Thoreau, Nathanial Hawthorne, Louisa May Alcott—once called this country town home. The area got its name from the unusual "peace and concord" between its colonial settlers and the native population in the 17th century.

Information: Concord Chamber of Commerce, 15 Walden St., Concord,
978-369-3120; www.concordchamberofcommerce.org

WHAT TO SEE AND DO

CODMAN HOUSE

Codman Road, Lincoln, 781-259-8843
Originally a two-story, L-shaped Georgian mansion, this 1740 house was more than doubled in size by Federal merchant John Codman to imitate an English-country residence. June-mid-October, 1st Saturday of each month, tours: 11 a.m.-4 p.m.

CONCORD MUSEUM
200 Lexington Road, Concord, 978-369-9763;
www.concordmuseum.org
On display are period rooms, galleries of domestic artifacts and decorative arts chronicling the history of Concord from Native American habitation to the present. Exhibits include Ralph Waldo Emerson's study, Henry David Thoreau's belongings used at Walden Pond and Paul Revere's signal lantern. Daily.

DECORDOVA MUSEUM & SCULPTURE PARK
51 Sandy Pond Road, Lincoln, 781-259-8355;
www.decordova.org
This museum has an eclectic collection of paintings, posters, photography, sculpture and media. The Sculpture Park displays large contemporary sculptures throughout 35 wooded acres. In early June, rain or shine, the museum sponsors the Annual Art in the Park Festival and Art Sale. Tuesday-Sunday 11 a.m.-5 p.m.

DRUMLIN FARM EDUCATION CENTER
208 S. Great Road, Lincoln, 781-259-2200;
www.massaudubon.org/Nature_Connection/Sanctuaries/Drumlin_Farm/index.php
A demonstration farm with domestic and native creatures, gardens and hayrides. Tuesday-Sunday. March 1-October 31: 9 a.m.-5 p.m.; November 1-February 28: 9 a.m.-4 p.m., Closed on Monday holidays, Thanksgiving, Christmas Eve, Christmas Day and New Year's Day.

★
★
★
★
☆

FRUITLANDS MUSEUMS

102 Prospect Hill Road, Harvard, 978-456-3924;
www.fruitlands.org

The Fruitlands Farmhouse contains the furniture, books, and memorabilia of the Alcott family and the Transcendentalists. The Shaker Museum has furniture and handicrafts, and the Picture Gallery American primitive portraits and paintings by Hudson River School artists. The American Indian Museum shows prehistoric artifacts and Native American art. Mid-May-October, Monday-Friday 11 a.m.-4 p.m., Saturday-Sunday until 5 p.m.

GREAT MEADOWS NATIONAL WILDLIFE REFUGE

Lincoln Street, and 73 Weir Hill Road, Sudbury Center, 978-443-4661;
www.fws.gov/northeast/greatmeadows

Great Meadows combines terrific dirt trails with a wildlife refuge that attracts more than 200 species of birds, including the magnificent great blue heron. Daily dawn-dusk.

GROPIUS HOUSE

68 Baker Bridge Road, Lincoln, 781-259- 8098; www.spnea.org

This was the family home of Bauhaus architect Walter Gropius and the first building he designed after arriving in the United States in 1937. June-October, first Saturday of the month. Tours: 11 a.m.-4 p.m.

161

MINUTE MAN NATIONAL HISTORICAL PARK

174 Liberty St., Concord, 978-369-6993; www.nps.gov/mima

The park consists of 900 acres along the Battle Road between Lexington and Concord. Walk the 5½-mile Battle Road Trail, stop at Hartwell Tavern to see reenactments of colonial life and continue to North Bridge, the site of the first battle of the Revolutionary War (a.k.a., the shot heard round the world). Spring, summer, fall: daily; winter: Saturday-Sunday.

OLD MANSE

269 Monument St., Concord, 978-369-3909; www.thetrustees.org

This was the parsonage of Concord's early ministers, including Reverend William Emerson, Ralph Waldo Emerson's grandfather. Nathaniel Hawthorne lived here for a time and made it the setting for *Mosses from an Old Manse.* Mid-April-October, Monday-Saturday 10 a.m.-5 p.m.

ORCHARD HOUSE

399 Lexington Road, Concord, 978-369-4118; www.louisamayalcott.org

Louisa May Alcott wrote *Little Women* here. Open year-round, hours vary seasonally.

RALPH WALDO EMERSON HOUSE

28 Cambridge Turnpike, Concord, 978-369-2236;
www.rwe.org/emersonhouse

This was Ralph Waldo Emerson's home from 1835 to 1882. Mid-April-late October, Thursday-Saturday 10 a.m.-4:30 p.m, Sunday from 1 p.m.

MASSACHUSETTS

★
★
★
☆

SLEEPY HOLLOW CEMETERY

Bedford Street, Concord; www.concordnet.org/Pages/ConcordMA_Cemetery/sleepy

The Alcotts, Ralph Waldo Emerson, Nathaniel Hawthorne, Margaret Sidney, Daniel Chester French and Henry David Thoreau are buried here.

WALDEN POND STATE RESERVATION

915 Walden St., Concord, 978-369-3254; www.mass.gov/dcr/parks/walden

Henry David Thoreau, the American writer and naturalist, made Walden Pond famous when he lived in a nearby rustic cabin for two years. The cabin still stands and is part of the park's collection. A 1½-mile trail circles the pond, perfect for hiking, running or swimming. Get here early—before 11 a.m.—the lot closes once it's full. Daily.

WAYSIDE

455 Lexington Road, Concord; www.nps.gov/archive/mima/wayside/Planfrm1.htm

Well-known 19th-century authors Nathaniel Hawthorne, the Alcotts and Margaret Sidney, author of the *Five Little Peppers* books, lived here. May-October.

SPECIAL EVENT

PATRIOT'S DAY PARADE

Concord, 978-369-3120, 888-733-2678; www.concordnet.org

Patriot's Day commemorates the Battle of Lexington and Concord, which marked the beginning of the Revolutionary War on April 18, 1775. Schools and many businesses close, and the entire city celebrates. Watch parades and reenactments of the night of Paul Revere's famous ride, and at noon the famous Boston Marathon begins in Hopkinton. Third Monday in April, one-day-only event.

HOTELS

★BEST WESTERN AT HISTORIC CONCORD

740 Elm St., Concord, 978-369-6100, 800-780-7234;
www.bestwestern.com

106 rooms. Complimentary continental breakfast. Pets accepted; fee, High-speed Internet access. Pool. Fitness center. $

★★★COLONIAL INN

48 Monument Square, Concord, 978-369-9200, 800-370-9200;
www.concordscolonialinn.com

Henry David Thoreau's family once owned the property, which has been an inn since 1889. Anchoring the western edge of Monument Square in historic Concord, the Colonial Inn is a short walk to the town's shops and cafés. Guest rooms are individually decorated and have been updated with four-poster beds. There are a variety of dining venues, including the main restaurant (for breakfast, lunch, dinner and Sunday brunch), outdoor porch (formal High Tea) and a rustic colonial tavern (beers, live jazz). 56 rooms. Wireless Internet access. Two restaurants, two bars. $$

★★★HAWTHORNE INN

462 Lexington Road, Concord, 978-369-5610; www.concordmass.com

Built in 1870, the Hawthorne Inn is less than a mile east of the village center. The pink house is surrounded by gardens and its neighbors include Minuteman National

Historic Park and the Wayside and Orchard houses. Nineteenth-century antiques, original artwork, Japanese woodcuts, pre-Columbian pottery, a kitschy collection of salt and pepper shakers, and books and old maps are displayed throughout the hotel. Seven rooms. Complimentary continental breakfast. Wireless Internet access. **$$**

★★HOLIDAY INN
242 Adams Place, Boxborough, 978-263-8701;
www.holiday-inn.com
143 rooms. Restaurant, bar. Pets accepted, fee. **$**

RESTAURANT
★★COLONIAL INN
48 Monument Square, Concord, 978-369-2373, 800-370-9200;
www.concordscolonialinn.com
American menu. Breakfast, lunch, dinner, Sunday brunch. Bar. Children's menu. Casual attire. Reservations recommended. Outdoor seating. **$$**

DANVERS

Settlers from Salem looking for more farmland founded this small industrial town. In 1692, Danvers was the scene of some of the most severe witchcraft hysteria—in all, 20 people were put to death here.

Information: North Shore Chamber of Commerce, 5 Cherry Hill Drive,
Danvers, 978-774-8565; www.northshorechamber.org

WHAT TO SEE AND DO
GLEN MAGNA FARMS
Ingersoll Street, Danvers, 978-774-9165;
www.glenmagnafarms.org
A 20-room mansion with 1790-1890 furnishings and Chamberlain garden, this Derby summer house was built by Samuel McIntire. May-July: by appointment only.

REBECCA NURSE HOMESTEAD
149 Pine St., Danvers, 978-774-8799; www.rebeccanurse.org
This house, an excellent example of the New England saltbox style, was the homestead of Rebecca Nurse, a saintly woman accused of and executed for witchcraft in 1692. Mid-June-mid-September, Tuesday-Sunday; mid-September-October, weekends; rest of year: by appointment.

WITCHCRAFT VICTIMS MEMORIAL
176 Hobart St., Danvers,
The memorial includes the names of those who died, as well as quotes from eight victims.

HOTELS
★★COURTYARD BY MARRIOTT
275 Independence Way, Danvers, 978-777-8630, 800-321-2211;
www.courtyard.com
120 rooms. High-speed Internet access. Restaurant, bar. **$**

MASSACHUSETTS

★
★
★
★
★

★DAYS INN
152 Endicott St., Danvers, 978-777-1030, 800-329-7466; www.daysinn.com
129 rooms. Complimentary continental breakfast. High-speed Internet access. Pool. Pets not accepted. **$**

★★★SHERATON FERNCROFT RESORT
50 Ferncroft Road, Danvers, 978-777-2500, 800-325-3535; www.sheraton.com
This hotel boasts luxurious guest rooms, world class dining and a state-of-the-art, fully-staffed business center. Be pampered at the salon and day spa, enjoy a game of golf on the 18-hole Robert Trent Jones-designed course, or lounge in the indoor pool. 367 rooms. High-speed Internet access. Restaurant, bar. Airport transportation available. **$$**

RESTAURANT
★★THE HARDCOVER
15-A Newbury St., Danvers, 978-774-1223; www.barnsiderrestaurants.com
Seafood, steak menu. Dinner. Bar. Children's menu. **$$$**

DEERFIELD

Twice destroyed by French and Native American attacks and almost forgotten by history, Deerfield was once the northwest frontier of New England. Today, it remains unspoiled by big business or big buildings, populated instead by historic homes, vast meadowlands and the nationally acclaimed prep school Deerfield Academy. The tiny village boasts one of the most beautiful lanes in America known simply as "The Street," a mile-long stretch of 80 houses dating from the 18th and early 19th centuries.
Information: Historic Deerfield, 84B Old Main St., Deerfield,
413-774-5581; www.historic-deerfield.org

WHAT TO SEE AND DO
HISTORIC DEERFIELD
Highways 5 and 10, Deerfield, 413-774-5581; www.historic-deerfield.org
The town's main street maintains 14-historic houses furnished with collections of antique furniture, silver, ceramics and textiles. A 28,000-square-foot Collections Study Center features changing exhibits. Daily walking tours and antique forums and workshops are available. Daily 9:30 a.m-4:30 p.m.

MEMORIAL HALL MUSEUM
10 Memorial St., Deerfield, 413-774-3768; www.deerfield-ma.org/museum.htm
Built in 1798, Deerfield Academy's first building contains colonial furnishings and Native American relics. May-October, daily 11 a.m.-5 p.m.

HOTEL
★★★DEERFIELD INN
81 Old Main St., Deerfield, 413-774-5587, 800-926-3865;
www.deerfieldinn.com
Early guests once pulled up to this historic inn by stagecoach; a few years later, visitors arrived on trolleys. Today, customers pull in behind the wheels of sleek German

MASSACHUSETTS

★
★
★
★
★

sports cars. The 1884 inn itself, however, hasn't changed much—the sitting parlors still exhibit period wallpaper and antiques, and the 10 main rooms remain cozy with New England quaintness. Updates include sparkling bathrooms, four-poster beds and a 13-room barn annex. Though it's said an old-town ghosts wander its halls, the inn is perpetually packed; some Deerfield Academy parents book graduation rooms four years in advance. 23 rooms. Complimentary full breakfast. Two restaurants, bar. **$$**

RESTAURANTS

★★★DEERFIELD INN
81 Old Main St., Deerfield, 413-774-5587, 800-926-3865;
www.deerfieldinn.com
The aforementioned inn's dining room is among the finest—and only—dining options in the area. Reservations are a must, as Deerfield students typically pack the place on weeknights and weekends. The menu of classic New England cuisine changes seasonally. American menu. Breakfast, dinner. Bar. Children's menu. Business casual attire. Reservations recommended. **$$**

★★★SIENNA
6B Elm St., Deerfield, 413-665-0215; www.siennarestaurant.com
This contemporary 45-seat restaurant serves American cooking marked by French technique. Chef and owner Karl-Braverman creates dishes influenced by seasonally available ingredients, such as duck with white potato, blood orange, bok choy and Spanish vinegar demi glace. American menu. Dinner. Closed Sunday and Tuesday. **$$**

DENNIS

Dennis is the seat of "the Dennises," a group of Cape Cod communities that includes Dennisport, East Dennis, South Dennis and West Dennis. It was here in 1816 that Henry Hall developed the commercial cultivation of cranberries. The town is well-known for its laid-back vibe and pristine beaches.
Information: Chamber of Commerce, 238 Swan River Road, Dennis,
508-398-3568; www.dennischamber.com

WHAT TO SEE AND DO

JOSIAH DENNIS MANSE
77 Nobscusset Road, Dennis, 508-385-3528; www.dennishistsoc.org
The restored home of the minister for whom the town was named has antiques, a Pilgrim chest, a children's room, a spinning and weaving exhibit and a maritime wing. July-August, Tuesday and Thursday.

SPECIAL EVENT

CAPE PLAYHOUSE
820 Main St., Dennis, 508-385-3911, 877-385-3911;
www.capeplayhouse.com
The Cape Playhouse hosts both established Broadway stars and up-and-coming actors for two-week runs of musicals, comedies and dramatic plays. It's the oldest professional summer theater in the United States. On summer Friday mornings, it has special children's performances like puppetry, storytelling and musicals. The complex also

houses the Cape Museum of Fine Arts, the Playhouse Bistro and the Cape Cinema. Late June-Labor Day.

HOTELS

★HUNTSMAN MOTOR LODGE

829 Main St., West Dennis, 508-394-5415, 800-628-0498;
www.thehuntsman.com
25 rooms. $

★★LIGHTHOUSE INN

1 Lighthouse Inn Road, West Dennis, 508-398-2244; www.lighthouseinn.com
63 rooms. Restaurant, bar. Children's activity center. Beach. Closed mid-October-late May. $$

★SESUIT HARBOR

1421 Main St., East Dennis, 508-385-3326, 800-359-0097;
www.sesuitharbormotel.com
20 rooms. Complimentary continental breakfast. $

★★SOUNDINGS SEASIDE RESORT

79 Chase Ave., Dennisport, 508-394-6561; www.thesoundings.com
102 rooms. Restaurant. Beach. Closed mid-October-mid-May. $$

★★THREE SEASONS MOTOR LODGE

421 Old Wharf Road, Dennisport, 508-398-6091;
www.threeseasonsmotel.com
61 rooms. Wireless Internet access. Restaurant. Beach. Closed November-April. $$

SPECIALTY LODGINGS

BY THE SEA GUESTS

57 Chase Ave., Dennisport, 508-398-8685, 800-447-9202;
www.bytheseaguests.com
On a beachfront road facing Nantucket Sound, this inn has clean, bright rooms with chenille bedspreads and fine-art prints. The property's large veranda provides great scenery for morning alfresco meals. 12 rooms. Complimentary full breakfast. Beach. Pets not accepted. $$

CORSAIR AND CROSSRIP OCEANFRONT

41 Chase Ave., Dennisport, 508-398-2279; www.corsaircrossrip.com
46 rooms. Complimentary continental breakfast. Wireless Internet access. Children's activity center. Beach. Closed late October-mid-April. $$

ISAIAH HALL BED AND BREAKFAST INN

152 Whig St., Dennis, 508-385-9928, 800-736-0160;
www.isaiahhallinn.com
This 1857 farmhouse has rooms decorated with antiques and oriental rugs. 10 rooms. Children over seven years only. Complimentary continental breakfast. Closed November-mid-April. $

RESTAURANTS

★BOB'S BEST SANDWICHES
613 Main St., Dennisport, 508-394-8450
Deli menu. Breakfast, lunch. Children's menu. Casual attire. Outdoor seating. $

★★CLANCY'S
8 Upper County Road, Dennisport, 508-394-6661;
www.clancysrestaurant.com
American menu. Lunch, dinner, Sunday brunch. Bar. Children's menu. Casual attire. Valet parking. Outdoor seating. $$

★★LA SCALA
106 Depot St., Dennisport, 508-398-3910; www.lascalaoncapecod.com
Italian menu. Dinner. Bar. Children's menu. Casual attire. Reservations recommended. $$

★★★RED PHEASANT INN
905 Main St., Dennis, 508-385-2133, 800-480-2133; www.redpheasantinn.com
Housed in a 200-year-old barn, this restaurant delights romantics and gourmands alike with its quaint surroundings and fine food. The American menu consists of fish and meat specialties; lamb and game offerings change nightly. The 300-bottle wine list is enough to impress the most demanding connoisseurs. American menu. Dinner. Bar. Reservations recommended. Valet parking. $$$

★★SCARGO CAFÉ
799 Main St., Dennis, 508-385-8200, 888-355-0112;
www.scargocafe.com
International menu. Lunch, dinner. Bar. Children's menu. Casual attire. Outdoor seating. $$

★★SWAN RIVER SEAFOOD
5 Lower County Road, Dennisport, 508 394 4466, 800-448-7926;
www.swanriverrestaurant.com
Seafood menu. Lunch, dinner. Bar. Children's menu. Casual attire. Reservations recommended (parties of six or more). Outdoor seating. Closed mid-October-mid-May. $$

★
★
★
★
★

EASTHAM
The *Mayflower* party met its first Native Americans in this quintessential Cape Cod town. Today, the Bay-side spot is famous for Nauset Beach, a sprawling expanse of white sand that was once a ship graveyard.
Information: Chamber of Commerce, Eastham, 508-240-7211, 508-255-3444;
www.easthamchamber.com

WHAT TO SEE AND DO
EASTHAM HISTORICAL SOCIETY
190 Samoset Road, Eastham, 508-255-0558; www.easthamhistorical.org
This museum, housed in an 1869 schoolhouse, has Native American artifacts and farming and nautical implements. July-August: Monday-Friday afternoons.

EASTHAM WINDMILL
Windmill Green, Eastham, 508-240-7211; www.easthamhistorical.org
This is the oldest windmill on the Cape; built in 1680, it was restored in 1936. Late June-Labor Day: daily.

HOTELS
★CAPTAIN'S QUARTERS
5000 Route 6North Eastham, 508-255-5686, 800-327-7769;
www.captains-quarters.com
75 rooms. Closed mid-November-mid-April. Complimentary continental breakfast. $

★★FOUR POINTS BY SHERATON
3800 Highway 6, Eastham, 508-255-5000, 800-533-3986; www.fourpoints.com
107 rooms. Wireless Internet access. Restaurant, bar. Airport transportation available. $

★★THE INN AT THE OAKS
3085 County Road, Eastham, 508-255-1886, 877-255-1886;
www.inattheoaks.com
10 rooms. Complimentary full breakfast. $$

SPECIALTY LODGINGS
THE PENNY HOUSE INN
4885 County Road, Eastham, 508-255-6632, 800-554-1751;
www.pennyhouseinn.com
12 rooms. Children over eight years only. Complimentary full breakfast. Spa. $$

THE WHALEWALK INN
220 Bridge Road, Eastham, 508-255-0617, 800-440-1281; www.whalewalkinn.com
16 rooms. Children over 12 only. Complimentary full breakfast. $$$

FALL RIVER
In 1892, blue-collar Fall River was the site of one of the most famous murder trials in American history, after Lizzie Borden allegedly killed her father and stepmother with an axe (she was acquitted). Since then, the city has maintained a gritty, urban persona, thanks to its numerous industrial mills and factories.
Information: Fall River Area Chamber of Commerce, 200 Pocasset St.,
Fall River, 508-676-8226; www.fallriverchamber.com

WHAT TO SEE AND DO
BATTLESHIP COVE
5 Water St., Fall River, 508-678-1100
Onsite at the Cove are five World War II-era naval ships; the *Lionfish,* a World War II attack submarine; and the battleship USS *Massachusetts.* Commissioned in 1942, the latter was active in the war's European and Pacific theaters and now houses the state's official World War II and Gulf War Memorial. Also here are *PT Boat 796, PT Boat 617* and the destroyer *USS Joseph P. Kennedy Jr.,* which saw action in the Korean, Vietnam and Cuban conflicts. Daily 9 a.m.-6 p.m.

★
★
★
★
★

The Spa Where Luxury Meets The Active Life

. . . .

Less Than 2 hours from New York

MAYFLOWER
Inn & Spa

118 Woodbury Road, Washington, Connecticut 06793
860.868.9466 www.mayflowerinn.com

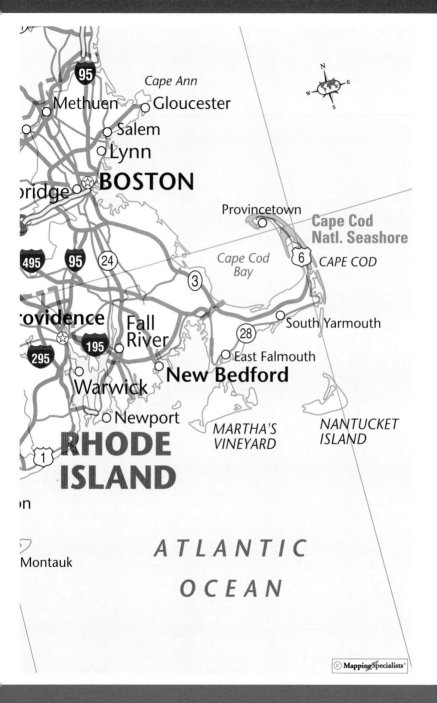

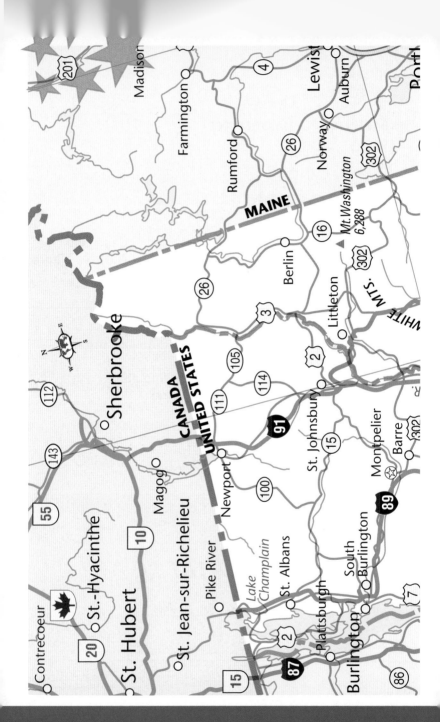

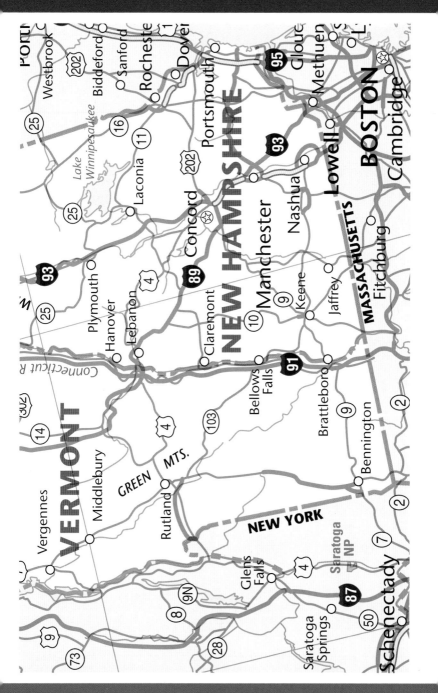

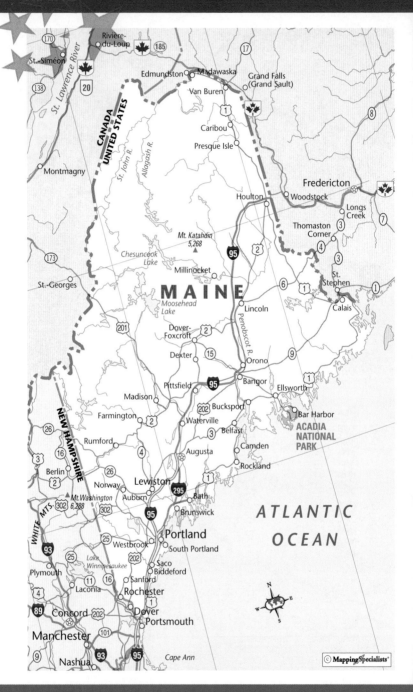

The Center for Hospitality Research

Hospitality Leadership Through Learning

The Cornell School of Hotel Administration's
world-class faculty explores new ways
to refine the practice of hospitality
management.

Our research drives better results.
Better strategy.
Better management.
Better operations.

See our work at:
www.chr.cornell.edu

537 Statler Hall • hosp_research@cornell.edu • 607.255.9780

Cornell University
School of Hotel Administration

FALL RIVER HISTORICAL SOCIETY

451 Rock St., Fall River, 508-679-1071; www.lizzieborden.org

The 16-room Victorian mansion exhibits displays on the Fall River Steamship Line, dolls, fine art, glassware, costumes and Lizzie Borden trial artifacts. April-May, October-November, Tuesday-Friday; June-September, Tuesday-Sunday; December, Monday.

LIZZIE BORDEN BED AND BREAKFAST

92 Second St., Fall River, 508-675-7333; www.lizzie-borden.com

In 1892, Lizzie Borden's father and stepmother were found murdered in their Fall River Greek Revival house. Borden was tried for the murder, but acquitted. Enterprising souls have turned the house into a bed and breakfast, where guests can learn about the murders over a breakfast similar to the one the Bordens ate before their deaths, and even spend a chilling night in the supposedly haunted house.

HOTELS

★HAMPTON INN

53 Old Bedford Road, Westport, 508-675-8500, 800-426-7866;
www.hamptoninn.com

133 rooms. Complimentary continental breakfast. Airport transportation available. Pool. Fitness center. Business center. High-speed Internet access. $

★QUALITY INN

1878 Wilbur Ave., Somerset, 508-678-4545, 800-228-5151;
www.qualityinn.com

104 rooms. Complimentary continental breakfast. Pets accepted, High-speed Internet access. $

RESTAURANTS

★★THE BACK EDDY

1 Bridge Road, Westport, 508-636-6500; www.thebackeddy.com

American, seafood menu. Dinner. Casual attire. Closed January-March. $$$

★★WHITE'S OF WESTPORT

66 State Road, Wesport, 508-675-7185;
www.lafrancehospitality.com

Seafood, steak menu. Lunch, dinner. Bar. Children's menu. $$

FALMOUTH

Falmouth, on the southwest corner of the Cape, boasts a whopping 68 miles of coastline and 12 public beaches. Its pride and joy is the Woods Hole Oceanographic Institution, the largest independent marine study facility in the world. Ferries run from Falmouth to Martha's Vineyard, but many vacationers make this upscale Cape town their final vacation destination.

Information: Cape Cod Chamber of Commerce, Hyannis,
508-362-3225, 888-227-3263; www.capecodchamber.org

MASSACHUSETTS

★
★
★
★
★

WHAT TO SEE AND DO

ASHUMET HOLLY & WILDLIFE SANCTUARY

Ashumet and Currier Roads, Falmouth, 508-362-1426;
www.massaudubon.org

This is a Massachusetts Audubon Society-run 45-acre wildlife preserve with a holly trail, herb garden and observation beehive. Daily dawn-dusk.

BRADLEY HOUSE MUSEUM

573 Woods Hole Road, Woods Hole, 508-548-7270

Featured is a model of Woods Hole circa 1895, an audiovisual show of local history, and restored ships. July-August, Tuesday-Saturday; June and September, Wednesday, Saturday; schedule may vary.

CAPE COD KAYAK

1270 Highway 28A, Cataumet, 508-563-9377;
www.capecodkayak.com

This outfitter runs guided kayak tours on area lakes, rivers and harbors. Experienced kayakers can rent boats and head out on their own for up to a week. March-November; closed December-February.

SPECIAL EVENT

FALMOUTH ROAD RACE

661 E. Main St., Falmouth, 508-540-7000;
www.falmouthroadrace.com

Starting in Woods Hole and winding back into Falmouth Heights, this hilly and hot course meanders past breathtaking scenery. The 7.1-mile race has been called the Best USA Road Race by *Runners World* magazine. Entry is by lottery; those who don't get in typically join the more than 70,000 spectators who line the course. Third Sunday in August.

HOTELS

★★★COONAMESSETT INN

311 Gifford St., Falmouth, 508-548-2300;
www.capecodrestaurants.org

North of town, in a shady, wooded area, lies the Coonamessett Inn. The property's five buildings are spread out over six landscaped acres that also host a barn, carriage house and caretaker's cottage. Sandy beaches, harbors and myriad antique shops are all nearby. The inn's rooms are spacious, with pine furniture, sitting areas, oversized closets, fresh flowers and refrigerators. Take advantage of the complimentary continental breakfast and/or try dinner at the inn's seasonal restaurant. 28 rooms. Complimentary continental breakfast. Wireless Internet access. Restaurant, bar. Airport transportation available. $

★NAUTILUS MOTOR INN

539 Woods Hole Road, Woods Hole, 508-548-1525, 800-654-2333;
www.nautilusinn.com

54 rooms. Closed late October-mid-April. $

★★★NEW SEABURY RESORT AND CONFERENCE CENTER

Rock Landing Road, New Seabury, 508-477-9111, 800-999-9033;
www.newseabury.com

This resort is also a residential community. It sits on 2,300 recreation-filled acres and offers rentals from early March to early January. Villa development began in 1962 and it now consists of two golf courses, 16 tennis courts and private beaches. 160 rooms. Restaurant, bar. Children's activity center. Airport transportation available. **$**

★★RAMADA INN

40 N. Main St., Falmouth, 508-457-0606, 888-744-5394;
www.innonthesquare.com

72 rooms. Restaurant, bar. **$**

★RED HORSE INN

28 Falmouth Heights Road, Falmouth, 508-548-0053, 800-628-3811;
www.redhorseinn.com

22 rooms. **$**

★★SEA CREST RESORT

350 Quaker Road, North Falmouth, 508-540-9400, 800-225-3110;
www.seacrest-resort.com

266 rooms. Restaurant, bar. Children's activity center. Beach. **$$**

SPECIALTY LODGINGS
CAPTAIN TOM LAWRENCE HOUSE

75 Locust St., Falmouth, 508-540-1445, 800-266-8139;
www.captaintomlawrence.com

Vaulted ceilings, hardwood floors and a spiral staircase add to the romantic, old-world charm of this inn located within walking distance of the town's main street. Built in 1861, it is a former whaling captain's home. Seven rooms. Complimentary full breakfast. Closed January. **$$**

ELM ARCH INN

26 Elm Arch Way, Falmouth, 508-548-0133; www.elmarchinn.com

This former whaling captain's house was built in 1810. It was attacked by the British in 1814; the hole where the cannonball hit is still visible in the dining area. 24 rooms. **$**

GRAFTON INN

261 Grand Ave. South, Falmouth, 203-531-5065;
www.graftoninn.com

10 rooms. Children over 16 years only. Complimentary full breakfast. **$$**

INN ON THE SOUND

313 Grand Ave., Falmouth, 508-457-9666, 800-564-9668;
www.innonthesound.com

10 rooms. Children over 18 years only. Complimentary full breakfast. **$$**

MASSACHUSETTS

★
★
★
★
★

MOSTLY HALL

27 Main St., Falmouth, 508-548-3786, 800-682-0565;
www.mostlyhall.com

This 1849 plantation-style house is the only one of its kind on Cape Cod. Six rooms. Children over 16 years only. Complimentary full breakfast. **$**

THE PALMER HOUSE INN

81 Palmer Ave., Falmouth, 508-548-1230, 800-472-2632;
www.palmerhouseinn.com

This 1901 Queen Anne-style inn and guesthouse welcomes visitors year-round. The Shining Sea Bikeway, ferries to the islands and beaches are all nearby. 16 rooms. Children over 10 years only. Complimentary full breakfast. **$$**

WILDFLOWER INN

167 Palmer Ave., Falmouth, 508-548-9524, 800-294-5459;
www.wildflower-inn.com

Rooms at this intimate inn feature whirlpool baths, kitchenettes and period furniture. Six rooms. Complimentary full breakfast. **$$**

RESTAURANTS

★FALMOUTH RESTAURANT

457 Main St., Falmouth, 508-540-0060

American menu. Breakfast, lunch, dinner. Children's menu. Casual attire. **$**

★THE FLYING BRIDGE

220 Scranton Ave., Falmouth, 508-548-2700;
www.capecodrestaurants.org

Seafood menu. Lunch, dinner. Bar. Children's menu. Casual attire. Outdoor seating. Closed late November-mid-March. **$$**

★★LANDFALL

2 Luscombe Ave., Woods Hole, 508-548-1758;
www.woodshole.com/landfall

Seafood menu. Lunch, dinner. Bar. Children's menu. Casual attire. Reservations recommended. Outdoor seating. Closed December-March. **$$**

★★THE NIMROD

100 Dillingham Ave., Falmouth, 508-540-4132; www.thenimrod.com

American menu. Lunch, dinner, brunch. Bar. Children's menu. Casual attire. Outdoor seating. **$$**

FOXBOROUGH

This town, located between Providence and Boston, is home to Gillette Stadium, which hosts the New England Patriots football team and the New England Revolution soccer club.

Information: Neponset Valley Chamber of Commerce, 190 Vanderbilt Ave.,
Norwood, 781-769-1126; www.nvcc.com

WHAT TO SEE AND DO
NEW ENGLAND PATRIOTS
60 Washington St., Foxboro, 800-543-1776; www.patriots.com
Frequent NFL Super Bowl contenders, the Patriots call Foxborough's Gillette Stadium home. Game tickets can be ultra pricey, but the arena's top-notch amenities and die-hard fans make up for its steep costs.

NEW ENGLAND REVOLUTION
60 Washington St., Foxboro, 877-438-7387; www.revolutionsoccer.net
One of the top teams in major league soccer, the Revolution plays its home games at Gillette stadium. The Netside Terrace, a special seating area south of the pitch, costs $300 and includes parking, food and drinks for four. Closed October-March.

HOTELS
★★ COURTYARD BOSTON
35 Foxborough Blvd., Foxborough, 508-543-5222, 877-773-5738;
www.marriott.com/hotels/travel/bosfb-courtyard-boston-foxborough
161 rooms. Complimentary High-speed Internet access. Restaurant, bar. $

★★HOLIDAY INN
31 Hampshire St., Mansfield, 508-339-2200, 888-465-4329;
www.holiday-inn.com/bos-mansfield
202 rooms. Restaurant, bar. Whirlpool. High-speed Internet access. Indoor pool. $

RESTAURANT
★★LAFAYETTE HOUSE
109 Washington St., Foxborough, 508-543-5344; www.lafayettehouse.com
Continental, seafood menu. Lunch, dinner. Bar. Children's menu. $$

GLOUCESTER
Thanks to George Clooney's tough-talking sea captain character ("Are we men, or are we Gloucestermen?") in the *Perfect Storm,* this blue-collar seaside city has experienced a recent renaissance. Tourists now crowd the streets of this growing summer resort and embark on whale-watching cruises from its harbor. Fishing is still big business here—a rumored 10,000 local men have been lost at sea in the last three centuries.
Information: Cape Ann Chamber of Commerce, 33 Commercial St.,
Gloucester, 978-283-1601, 800-321-0133; www.capeannvacations.com

WHAT TO SEE AND DO
BEAUPORT, THE SLEEPER-MCCANN HOUSE
75 Eastern Point Blvd., Gloucester, 978-283-0800; www.spnea.org
(1907-1934) Henry Davis Sleeper, an early 20th-century interior designer, first built a 26-room house here in 1907. With the help of local architect Halfdan Hanson, he kept adding rooms until decades later, there were 40. Twenty-five are now on view and contain collections of antique furniture, rugs, wallpaper, ceramics and glass. Mid-May-mid-September, Monday-Friday; mid-September-mid-October, daily.

MASSACHUSETTS

★
★
★
☆
☆

CAPE ANN HISTORICAL MUSEUM

27 Pleasant St., Gloucester, 978-283-0455; www.capeannhistoricalmuseum.org

This museum has paintings by Fitz Hugh Lane, decorative arts and furnishings, and exhibitions on Cape Ann's history. Tuesday-Saturday 10 a.m-5 p.m, Sunday 1 p.m-4 p.m; closed on February.

HAMMOND CASTLE MUSEUM

80 Hesperus Ave., Gloucester, 978-283-2080; www.hammondcastle.org

Built by inventor Dr. John Hays Hammond, Jr. to resemble a medieval castle, this museum contains a rare collection of art objects, including an 8,200-pipe organ. Memorial Day-Labor Day, daily; after Labor Day-Columbus Day, Thursday-Sunday; rest of year, Saturday-Sunday.

SARGENT HOUSE MUSEUM

49 Middle St., Gloucester, 978-281-2432; www.sargenthouse.org

This late 18th-century Georgian residence was built for Judith Sargent, an early feminist writer and sister of Governor Winthrop Sargent. Period furniture, china, glass, silver, needlework, Early American portraits and paintings by John Singer Sargent are on display. Memorial Day-Columbus Day, Friday-Monday noon-4 p.m.

174 HOTELS

★BASS ROCKS OCEAN INN

107 Atlantic Road, c 978-283-7600, 800-780-7234;
www.bassrocksoceaninn.com

51 rooms. Complimentary full breakfast. Closed December-March. **$$**

★THE MANOR INN

141 Essex Ave., Gloucester, 978-283-0614; www.themanorinnofgloucester.com

10 rooms. Closed November-April. Complimentary continental breakfast. Free wireless Internet access. **$**

★★OCEAN VIEW INN AND RESORT

171 Atlantic Road, Gloucester, 978-283-6200, 800-315-7557;
www.oceanviewinnandresort.com

62 rooms. Restaurant. Free wireless Internet access. **$**

RESTAURANT

★★GLOUCESTER HOUSE RESTAURANT

63 Rogers St., Gloucester, 978-283-1812, 888-283-1812;
www.thegloucesterhouse.com

Seafood menu. Lunch, dinner. Bar. Children's menu. Outdoor seating. **$$**

GREAT BARRINGTON

The once tiny, locals-only town of Great Barrington has slowly become the dining, shopping and cultural center of the Southern Berkshires. Tourists mob the streets and restaurants on summer weekends, leaving residents at once miffed at the crowds and grateful for the tourism dollars. The country spot has also become popular with the New York City summerhouse set, which means things quiet down considerably in the winter. Hiking, biking, walking, skiing, snowshoeing and other outdoor activities abound here, as do music, theater and dance events.

Information: Southern Berkshire Chamber of Commerce, 362 Main St.,
Great Barrington, 413-528-1510; www.greatbarrington.org

WHAT TO SEE AND DO
CATAMOUNT SKI AREA
Highway 23, Great Barrington, 518-325-3200; www.catamountski.com
Night skiing is popular at this mountain, which has four double chairlifts, a ski school, equipment rentals, a cafeteria, bar and nursery. The longest run is two miles with a vertical drop of 1,000 feet. December-March, daily. Monday-Friday 9 a.m.-4 p.m., Saturday and Sunday 10 a.m.-2 p.m.

COLONEL ASHLEY HOUSE
117 Cooper Hill Road, Sheffield, 413-229-8600; www.thetrustees.org
The elegance of this home reflects Colonel Ashley's prominent place in society. One political meeting he held here produced the Sheffield Declaration, the forerunner to the Declaration of Independence. July-August, Wednesday-Sunday; Memorial Day-June and September-Columbus Day, weekends; open on Monday. Fee: adults $5, children $3.

OTIS RIDGE
159 Monterey Road, Otis, 413-269-4444; www.otisridge.com
This ski resort has a double chairlift, T-bar, J-bar, three rope tows, ski patrol and school, rentals, plus a cafeteria. The longest run is one mile with a vertical drop of 400 feet. December-March, daily.

SKI BUTTERNUT
380 State Road, Great Barrington, 413-528-2000, 800-438-7669;
www.butternutbasin.com
The family-friendly Butternut has a quad, triple and four double chairlifts, plus a pomalift and a rope tow. The cafeteria and wine room are better than the average ski resort's and the slalom race course frequently attracts experts. The longest run is approximately 1½ miles; its vertical drop is 1,000 feet. There are also seven miles of cross-country trails. December-March, daily.

SPECIAL EVENT
BERKSHIRE CRAFT FAIR
Monument Mountain Regional High School, 600 Stockbridge Road,
Great Barrington, 413-528-3346; www.berkshirecraftsfair.org
This annual juried fair typically attracts more than 100 artisans. Mid-August. Admission: adults $6, children 12 and under free.

HOTELS
★MONUMENT MOUNTAIN MOTEL
247 Stockbridge Road, Great Barrington, 413-528-3272;
www.monumentmountainmotel.com
17 rooms. Free High-speed Internet access. Free local calls. **$**

MASSACHUSETTS

★
★
★
★
☆

SPECIALTY LODGINGS

THE EGREMONT INN

10 Old Sheffield Road, South Egremont, 413-528-2111, 800-859-1780;
www.egremontinn.com

20 rooms. Complimentary continental breakfast. Restaurant. Complimentary high-speed Internet access. Outdoor pool. Two tennis court. Outdoor dinning. Pets not accepted. **$**

RACE BROOK LODGE

864 S. Undermountain Road, Sheffield, 413-229-2916, 888-725-6343;
www.rblodge.com

32 rooms. Complimentary full breakfast. Bar. Pool. Restaurant. Meeting room. **$$**

THORNEWOOD INN & RESTAURANT

453 Stockbridge Road, Great Barrington, 413-528-3828, 800-854-1008;
www.thornewood.com

13 rooms. Children over 12 years only. Complimentary full breakfast. Restaurant. **$$**

WINDFLOWER INN

684 S. Egremont Road, Great Barrington, 413-528-2720, 800-992-1993;
www.windflowerinn.com

On 10 acres of Berkshire hillside, this white clapboard country inn has a screened-in porch and antique-filled rooms. The estate dates back to the 1850s and is near the famous Tanglewood music center. 13 rooms. Complimentary full breakfast. **$$**

RESTAURANTS

★★★CASTLE STREET CAFÉ

10 Castle St., Great Barrington, 413-528-5244; www.castlestreetcafe.com

Chef/owner Michael Ballon's lively restaurant is divided into two parts: a fine-dining room and the more casual Celestial Bar. White tablecloths and candles decorate the former, while live music and multicolored pendant lamps set the tone in the (often very noisy) bar. The eatery's classic American food (think burgers and salads) is consistently fresh. American menu. Dinner. Bar. Closed Tuesday. Daily. **$$**

★★JOHN ANDREW'S RESTAURANT

Highway 23, South Egremont, 413-528-3469; www.jarestaurant.com

American menu. Dinner. Bar. Children's menu. Outdoor seating. Closed Wednesday. **$$**

★★THE OLD MILL

53 Main St., South Egremont, 413-528-1421

American menu. Dinner. Bar. Children's menu. **$$**

★★★SPENCER'S

453 Stockbridge Road, Great Barrington, 413-528-3828, 800-854-1008;
www.thornewood.com

Located in the turn-of-the-century Thornewood Inn, Spencer's is a mellow, cozy restaurant favored by the area's many retirees. All produce is provided by the inn's own gardens, making dishes very seasonal and flavorful. American menu. Dinner Thursday-Saturday. Bar. Outdoor seating. **$$**

HARWICH

Like many Massachusetts towns, Harwich has been immortalized in some of the country's best-known books. The pretty Cape Cod spot stars in Joseph C. Lincoln's novels, Whittier poems and James Fenimore Cooper's novel *The Spy*. Most of the area's seaside houses are owned by city dwellers who visit on weekends.

Information: Harwich Chamber of Commerce, Harwich,
508-432-1600; www.capecodchamber.org

WHAT TO SEE AND DO
CAPE COD BASEBALL LEAGUE
11 North Road, Harwich, 508-432-3878; www.capecodbaseball.org
This is baseball as it should be: local, passionate, affordable and played only with wooden bats. The 10 teams are made up of college players from around the country who live with host families for the summer. Spectators sit on wooden benches, pack picnic lunches and cheer for their favorite players during each of the season's 44 games. Mid-June-mid-August.

HARWICH HISTORICAL SOCIETY
80 Parallel St., Harwich, 508-432-8089; www.harwichhistoricalsociety.org
The society has Native American artifacts, a marine exhibit, cranberry industry articles and early newspapers and photographs. It's also the site of one of the first schools of navigation in the United States. Usually mid-June-mid-October, Wednesday-Friday; schedule may vary.

SPECIAL EVENT
CRANBERRY HARVEST FESTIVAL
Highway, 58 N. and Rochester Road, Harwich, 508-430-2811;
www.harwichcranberryfestival.org
A family day with an antique car show, music, arts and crafts, fireworks, carnival and parade. One weekend in mid-September.

HOTELS
★★THE COMMODORE INN
30 Earle Road, West Harwich, 508-432-1180, 800-368-1180;
www.commodoreinn.com
27 rooms. Complimentary continental breakfast. Restaurant, bar. Pool. Closed November-April. Wireless Internet access. **$**

★THE SANDPIPER BEACH INN
16 Bank St., Harwich Port, 508-432-0485, 800-433-2234;
www.sandpiperbeachinn.com
20 rooms. Beach. Continental breakfast. Pets not accepted. **$**

★
★
★
★
★

★SEADAR INN

1 Braddock Lane, Harwich Port, 508-432-0264, 800-888-5250; www.seadarinn.com

20 rooms. Complimentary continental breakfast. Near beach. Closed mid-October-late May. **$**

SPECIALTY LODGINGS
CAPE COD CLADDAGH INN

77 Main St., West Harwich, 508-432-6333, 877-602-6333; www.capecodcladdaghinn.com

Nine rooms. Complimentary full breakfast. Restaurant. Closed January-March. Pub. **$**

COUNTRY INN

86 Sisson Road, Harwich Port, 508-432-2769

Six rooms. Complimentary continental breakfast. Restaurant. Beach. **$**

DUNSCROFT BY THE SEA

24 Pilgrim Road, Harwich Port, 508-432-0810, 800-432-4345;
www.dunscroftbythesea.com

Eight rooms. Children over 12 years only. Complimentary full breakfast. Whirlpool. Wireless Internet access. Pets not accepted. **$$**

RESTAURANTS
★400 EAST

1421 Orleans Road, Harwich, 508-432-1800; www.the400.com/East

American menu. Lunch, dinner, late-night. Bar. Children's menu. Casual attire. **$**

★★AY! CARAMBA CAFÉ

703 Main St., Harwich, 508-432-9800; www.aycarambacafe.com

Mexican menu. Lunch, dinner. Bar. Children's menu. Casual attire. Outdoor seating. **$**

★★BISHOP'S TERRACE

Route 28, West Harwich, 508-432-0253; www.bishopsterrace.com

American menu. Dinner. Bar. Children's menu. Casual attire. Outdoor dining, June-October. Closed Monday; also Thanksgiving-Memorial Day. **$$**

★★L'ALOUETTE

787 Main St., Harwich Port, 508-430-0405; www.lalouettebistro.com

French menu. Dinner. Reservations recommended. **$$$**

HYANNIS AND BARNSTABLE

The gateway to Cape Cod, Hyannis sees some six million visitors each year. Its seaside streets are well prepared, with multitudes of antique and specialty boutiques, fancy and casual eateries, libraries, museums and of course, the Kennedy Compound. In the surrounding area are tennis courts, golf courses, arts and crafts galleries and theaters. Tourists stream in and out by Amtrak rail, commuter flights, and ferries, giving this bustling city of 14,000 a very transient feel although those in the know stay put to decompress on the town's laid-back beaches.

Information: Chamber of Commerce, 1481 Highway 132, Hyannis,
508-362-5230, 877-492-6647; www.hyannis.com

WHAT TO SEE AND DO

CAPE COD PATHWAYS

3225 Highway 6A, Barnstable, 508-362-3828; www.capecodcommission.org/pathways

This network of walking and hiking trails is composed of a perfect mix of dirt, sand and gravel. It links to most Cape towns, thanks to the Cape Cod Commission, which oversees the trails and produces a detailed map. In early June, hearty souls hike from one end of the cape to the other on the Cape Walk; during the October Walking Weekend, guides lead groups on short and long hikes. Daily.

CAPE COD POTATO CHIP COMPANY

100 Breed's Hill Road, Hyannis, 508-775-3358; www.capecodchips.com

Cape Cod chips, now sold all over the world, may be the area's most recognizable food product. Perhaps the best part about the onsite self-guided tour is the free samples, though seeing the chips cook in huge kettles is a close second. Monday-Friday 9 a.m.-5 p.m. Free admission. Closed on holidays.

HYANNIS WHALE WATCHER CRUISES

Barnstable Harbor, 269 Mill Way, Barnstable, 508-362-6088,
888-942-5392; www.whales.net

View whales aboard the *Whale Watcher*, a 297-passenger super-cruiser, custom designed and built specifically for whale-watching. An onboard naturalist narrates. April-October, daily. Admission: adults $45, seniors 62 and over $40, children (4-12) $26, children 3 and under free.

JOHN F. KENNEDY HYANNIS MUSEUM

397 Main St., Hyannis, 508-790-3077; www.jfkhyannismuseum.org

Here, photographic exhibits and a seven-minute video narrated by Walter Cronkite focus on President Kennedy's relationship with Cape Cod. Mid-April-October: Monday-Saturday 9 a.m.-5 p.m., Sunday and holidays noon-5 p.m.; rest of year: Thursday-Saturday 10 a.m.-4 p.m., Sunday and holidays noon-4 p.m. Closed in January. Admission: adults $5, children 10-17 $2.50, children under 10 free.

OSTERVILLE HISTORICAL SOCIETY MUSEUM

155 W. Bay Road, Osterville, 508-428-5861; www.osterville.org

A sea captain's house with 18th- and 19th-century furnishings and a boat-building museum. Mid-June-September, Thursday-Sunday 1:30-4:30 p.m.; and by appointment.

STEAMSHIP AUTHORITY

Ocean Street, Hyannis, 508-477-8600, 508-693-9130; www.steamshipauthority.com

Catch ferries to Woods Hole, Martha's Vineyard and Nantucket from the South Street dock.

WEST PARISH MEETINGHOUSE

2049 Meetinghouse Road, West Barnstable, 508-362-4445; www.westparish.org

This building is said to be the oldest Congregational church in the country. Regular Sunday services are held here all year. Worship Sundays 10 a.m. Music programs.

MASSACHUSETTS

★
★
★
★
★

SPECIAL EVENTS
CAPE COD OYSTER FESTIVAL
20 Independence Drive, Hyannis, 508-775-4746;
www.capdecodclash.org
It's all you can eat at the Cape Cod Oyster fest and, thanks to local vineyards, all you can drink, too. Held at the Naked Oyster restaurant under a big tent, the event draws locals and tourists alike. Late September.

FIGAWI SAILBOAT RACE AND CHARITY BALL
486 W. Hyannisport, 508-737-2987; www.figawi.com
The largest regatta on the East Coast, Figawi features 200 sailboats racing from Hyannis to Nantucket on Saturday, then back again in a Return Race on Monday. A black-tie charity ball precedes the event by one week. Held in Hyannis (and also celebrated on Nantucket) and featuring live bands, dancing and a big feast, it's a major social event. Memorial Day weekend.

POPS BY THE SEA
Town Green, Hyannis, 508-362-0066;
www.artsfoundationcapecod.org
In early August, the Boston Pops makes its way to the Cape for a concert on the Hyannis Town Green. Each year brings a new celebrity guest conductor, from actors to poets to famous chefs. The performance serves as a fundraiser that supports the Arts Foundation of Cape Cod.

WILLOWBEND CHILDREN'S CHARITY PRO-AM
100 Willowbend Drive, Mashpee, 508-539-5030;
www.shark.com/sharkwatch/news
The biggest names in professional golf pair up with celebrities for this annual charity golf event on Willowbend's course. The $20 fee is among the lowest you can pay to watch professional golf; the proceeds benefit a variety of children's charities. Early July.

HOTELS
★ANCHOR-IN
One South St., Hyannis, 508-775-0357; www.anchorin.com
43 rooms. Complimentary breakfast. Heated outdoor pool.

★★CAPE CODDER RESORT & SPA
1225 Iyanough Road, Hyannis, 508-771-3000, 888-297-2200;
www.capecodderresort.com
257 rooms. Wireless Internet access. Two restaurants. Two bars. Children's activity center. Airport transportation available. $$

★CENTERVILLE CORNERS INN
1338 Craigville Beach Road, Centerville, 508-775-7223,
800-242-1137; www.centervillecorners.com
48 rooms. Complimentary continental breakfast. Wireless Internet access. Closed November-April. Pets accepted with fee. Indoor heated pool. $

MASSACHUSETTS

★
★
★
★
☆

★★COURTYARD BY MARRIOTT

707 Highway, 132, Hyannis, 508-775-6600, 800-321-2211;
www.marriott.com

119 rooms. High-speed Internet access. Restaurant. Bar. Airport transportation available. **$$**

★★INTERNATIONAL INN

662 Main St., Hyannis, 508-775-5600, 877-528-3353;
www.cuddles.com

141 rooms. Restaurant, bar. High-speed Internet access. **$**

SPECIALTY LODGINGS

ACWORTH INN

4352 Old King's Highway, Cummaquid, 508-362-6363, 800-362-3330;
www.acworthinn.com

Five rooms. Children over 12 years only. Complimentary full breakfast. Daily newspaper. **$**

ASHLEY MANOR

3660 Olde King's Highway, Barnstable, 508-362-8044, 888-535-2246;
www.ashleymanor.net

A lovely garden and gazebo adorn this beautiful inn. Unwind with a book in the library or with afternoon tea in front of the fire. Wireless Internet access. Six rooms. Children over 14 years only. Complimentary full breakfast. **$**

BEECHWOOD INN

2839 Main St., Barnstable, 508-362-6618, 800-609-6618;
www.beechwoodinn.com

Situated near Barnstable Village, the Beechwood coordinates biking, whale-watching and golf trips for its guests. Those looking for total relaxation can remain in their plush rooms or hang out in the porch's rocking chairs. Six rooms. Children over 12 years only. Complimentary full breakfast. Wireless Internet access. **$**

CAPTAIN DAVID KELLEY HOUSE

539 Main St., Centerville, 508-775-4707, 888-815-5700;
www.captaindavidkelleyhouse.com

Five rooms. Complimentary full breakfast. **$**

HONEYSUCKLE HILL BED AND BREAKFAST

591 Old King's Highway, West Barnstable, 508-362-8418, 866-444-5522;
www.honeysucklehill.com

Five rooms. Children over 12 years only. Complimentary full breakfast. Wireless Internet access. Spa. Pets not accepted. **$**

SEA BREEZE INN

270 Ocean Ave., Hyannis, 508-771-7213; www.seabreezeinn.com

14 rooms. Complimentary continental breakfast. Restaurant. Theater. Golf. Island boats. Beach. Pets not accepted. **$**

MASSACHUSETTS

★
★
★
★
★

RESTAURANTS

★★DOLPHIN RESTAURANT

3250 Main St., Barnstable, 508-362-6610; www.thedolphinrestaurant.com

American, seafood menu. Lunch, dinner. Bar. Children's menu. Casual attire. Reservations recommended. $$

★EGG & I

521 Main St., Hyannis, 508-771-1596

American menu. Breakfast. Children's menu. Casual attire. Closed November-March. $

★★FIVE BAYS BISTRO

825 Main St., Osterville, 508-420-5559; www.fivebaysbistro.com

American menu. Dinner. Bar. Casual attire. Daily dinner. $$$

★★★NAKED OYSTER

20 Independence Drive, Hyannis, 508-778-6500; www.nakedoyster.com

Seafood menu. Lunch, dinner. Bar. Casual attire. Closed on Sunday. $$

★ORIGINAL GOURMET BRUNCH

517 Main St., Hyannis, 508-771-2558; www.theoriginalgourmetbrunch.com

American menu. Breakfast, lunch. Casual attire. Daily. $

★★★THE PADDOCK

20 Scudder Ave., Hyannis, 508-775-7677; www.paddockcapecod.com

Pressed linens and abundant flowers add sophistication to this family-friendly restaurant, while equestrian paintings and antiques lend a classic look and feel. The menu is full of fresh seafood (though poultry, steak and pasta also make appearances). Private parties and weddings. American, seafood menu. Lunch, dinner. Bar. Children's menu. Casual attire. Reservations recommended. Valet parking. Closed mid-November-March. $$

★★★THE REGATTA OF COTUIT

4631 Falmouth Road, Cotuit, 508-428-5715; www.regattaofcotuit.com

This 1790 stagecoach inn is run by chef Heather Allen, who cooks with French, American and Asian themes. The lacquered duck is a neatly Americanized version of Peking duck; and the Vietnamese-style fish and chips tempura is made from whatever the local fishermen catch that day. Owners Wendy and Brantz Bryan have accrued a nearly legendary wine list over the last three decades, making the Regatta a must-stop for wine lovers. American menu. Dinner. Bar. Business casual attire. Reservations recommended. Closed on Sunday, November-April. $$

★★ROADHOUSE CAFÉ

488 South St., Hyannis, 508-775-2386; www.roadhousecafe.com

Italian, seafood menu. Dinner. Bar. Casual attire. Reservations recommended. Valet parking. Jazz. Dessert. $$

★SAM DIEGO'S
950 Iyanough Road, Hyannis, 508-771-8816; www.samdiegos.com
Mexican, Southwestern menu. Lunch, dinner. Bar. Children's, Desserts menu. Casual attire. Outdoor seating. $

★YING'S
59 Center St., Hyannis, 508-790-2432; www.yings.net
Asian menu. Lunch, dinner. Casual attire. Reservations recommended. Outdoor seating. $$

IPSWICH

Ipswich is a summer resort town and home of Crane beach, one of the most beautiful stretches of sand in the state. The historic village has nearly 50 houses built before 1725, and many are from the 17th century.
Information: Ipswich Visitors Center-Hall Haskell House, 36 S. Main St.,
Ipswich, 978-356-8540; www.ipswichchamber.org

WHAT TO SEE AND DO
CLAM BOX OF IPSWICH
246 High St., Ipswich, 978-356-9707; www.ipswichma.com/clambox
This quirky roadside clam shack (the building is in the shape of an open box) is renowned for its perfectly prepared, deliciously greasy fried clams and superb lobster rolls.

CRANE BEACH
290 Argilla Road, Ipswich, 978-356-4354;
www.ipswichma.com/directory/castle.asp
Among the best beaches on the Atlantic coast, Crane has five miles of sand, lifeguards, bathhouses, a refreshment stand and walking trails. Daily 8 a.m.-sunset.

JOHN HEARD HOUSE
54 S. Main St., Ipswich, 978-356-2811; www.ipswichmuseum.net/homes.php
Bought as a memorial to Thomas F. Waters, this house has Chinese furnishings from the China sea trade. May-mid-October, Wednesday-Saturday 10 a.m.-4 p.m., Sunday from 1 p.m.

THE JOHN WHIPPLE HOUSE
1 S. Village Green, Ipswich, 978-356-2811; www.ipswichmuseum.net
The 1640 house has 17th- and 18th-century furniture and a garden. May-mid-October, Wednesday-Saturday 10 a.m.-4 p.m., Sunday from 1 p.m.

HOTEL
★COUNTRY GARDEN INN AND MOTEL
101 Main St., Rowley, 978-948-7773, 800-287-7773;
www.countrygardenmotel.com
24 rooms. Pets not accepted. $

MASSACHUSETTS

★
★
★
★

SPECIALTY LODGING
MILES RIVER COUNTRY INN BED AND BREAKFAST
823 Bay Road, Hamilton, 978-468-7206; www.milesriver.com
This 200-year-old rambling colonial is set on 30 acres that adjoin meadows, woodlands and marshes. Six rooms. Complimentary full breakfast. **$**

RESTAURANT
★★★1640 HART HOUSE
51 Linebrook Road, Ipswich, 978-356-1640; www.1640harthouse.com
Twenty years after the Pilgrims landed in the town of Ipswich, they built this now-restored property. The original room has since been sold to the Metropolitan Museum of Art. American menu. Lunch, dinner. Bar. Children's menu. Reservations recommended. **$$**

LEE

Once an underappreciated Berkshire village, Lee has finally been discovered by summer and winter tourists. Its proximity to major cultural festivals and outdoor recreation makes it an ideal town in which to book an (often less-expensive) area room.

WHAT TO SEE AND DO
OCTOBER MOUNTAIN STATE FOREST
256 Woodland Road, Lee, 413-243-1778; www.mass.gov/dcr/parks/western/octm.htm
The forest provides fine mountain scenery overlooking 16,000 acres of hiking, hunting and snowmobiling.

SANTARELLA
75 Main Road, Tyringham, 413-243-2819, 760-212-1577;
www.santarella.us
The former studio of sculptor Sir Henry Kitson, creator of the *Minuteman* statue in Lexington, was built in the early 1920s. The roof was designed to look like the rolling hills of the Berkshires in autumn; the fronting rock pillars and grottoes are fashioned after similar edifices in Europe. Unique and charming setting on a four-acre estate.

SPECIAL EVENT
JACOB'S PILLOW DANCE FESTIVAL
358 George Carter Road, Becket, 413-243-0745;
www.jacobspillow.org
America's oldest and most prestigious dance festival includes performances by international dance companies in the Ted Shawn Theatre and the Doris Duke Theatre. Tuesday-Saturday, some Sundays. Late June-August.

HOTEL
★★BEST WESTERN BLACK SWAN INN
435 Laurel St., Lee, 413-243-2700, 800-876-7926;
bestwestern.worldexecutive.com/directory/usa/lee/hotels
52 rooms. Restaurant, bar. Outdoor pool. Exercise room. Free parking. **$**

SPECIALTY LODGINGS

APPLEGATE

279 W. Park St., Lee, 413-243-4451, 800-691-9012;
www.applegateinn.com

This Georgian Colonial is a charming bed and breakfast built in the 1920s. Each room is individually decorated, and guests can stroll through six acres of rose gardens, perennial beds and apple trees. 11 rooms. Children over 12 years only. Complimentary full breakfast. Pool. Wireless Internet access. **$**

CHAMBERY INN

199 Main St., Lee, 413-243-2221, 800-537-4321; www.chamberyinn.com

This property was once the county's first parochial school. The owners saved it from destruction and kept the unique structure and original blackboards. Guests get the "menu selected" breakfasts delivered to their doors in a country basket. Free wireless Internet access. Nine rooms. Children over 16 years only. **$$**

DEVONFIELD INN

85 Stockbridge Road, Lee, 413-243-3298, 800-664-0880; www.devonfield.com

Located in the heart of the Berkshires, this Federal-era manor house offers a comfortable stay. 10 rooms. Children over 10 years only. Complimentary full breakfast. **$$**

FEDERAL HOUSE INN

1560 Pleasant St., South Lee, 413-243-1824, 800-243-1824;
www.federalhouseinn.com

This 1824 inn borders the Housatonic River and the Beartown State Forest. The rooms have a casual, country-style décor. Guests have access to golf and tennis at nearby Stockbridge Country Club. 10 rooms. Children over 12 years only. Complimentary full breakfast. Bar. Pets not accepted. **$$**

HISTORIC MERRELL INN

1565 Pleasant St., South Lee, 413-243-1794, 800-243-1794;
www.merrell-inn.com

Listed on the National Register of Historic Places, this old stagecoach inn sits on two acres of picturesque Housatonic River-front property and is close to the Berkshire Mountains. All rooms have private baths; a country breakfast is included. 10 rooms. Complimentary full breakfast. Pets not accepted. **$**

MORGAN HOUSE

33 Main St., Lee, 413-243-3661, 877-571-0837;
www.morganhouseinn.com

11 rooms. Complimentary full breakfast. Restaurant, bar. **$**

RESTAURANTS

★★CORK N' HEARTH

Route 20 Laurel Lake, Lee, 413-243-0535; www.corknhearth.com

Three dining rooms. Seafood, steak menu. Dinner. Bar. Children's menu. Closed Monday. **$$**

★★SULLIVAN STATION RESTAURANT

109 Railroad St., Lee, 413-243-2082; www.sullivanstationrestaurant.com

American menu. Lunch, dinner. Bar. Outdoor seating. Closed two weeks in late February-early March. **$$**

LENOX

Lenox is the Berkshires' most talked-about town. Its name has become synonymous with rambling summer homes, fine cuisine and intellectual pursuits. The Boston Symphony orchestra calls Tanglewood its summer base, and the literati find inspiration in Edith Wharton's former grand manse, the Mount. But because not everyone can afford a second residence, many inns, bed and breakfasts and full-service resorts have opened in the surrounding hills.

Information: Chamber of Commerce, 65 Main St.,
Lenox, 413-637-3646; www.lenox.org

WHAT TO SEE AND DO

EDITH WHARTON ESTATE (THE MOUNT)

Second Plunkett St., Lenox, 413-551-5104, 888-637-1902;
www.edithwharton.org

Edith Wharton's summer estate was planned from a book she coauthored in 1897, *The Decoration of Houses,* and built in 1902. The enormous Classical Revival house is continuously being restored. May-October, daily 9 a.m.-5 p.m.

PLEASANT VALLEY WILDLIFE SANCTUARY

472 W. Mountain Road, Lenox, 413-637-0320;
www.massaudubon.org/Nature_Connection

A sanctuary of the Massachusetts Audubon Society has 1,500 acres with seven miles of trails and a beaver colony. Dogs not accepted. Mid-June-Columbus Day. Admission: $4 for nonmember adults, $3 for nonmember children (3-12).

TANGLEWOOD

197 W. St., Lenox, 413-637-1600; www.bso.org

Nathaniel Hawthorne planned *Tanglewood Tales* here. Many of the 526 acres, developed into a gentleman's estate by William Aspinwall Tappan, take the form of formal gardens. Well-known today as the summer home of the Boston Symphony Orchestra, the outdoor music venue stages concerts—rock, country and classical—all season long. Daily; free except during concerts.

SPECIAL EVENT

SHAKESPEARE & COMPANY

70 Kemble St., Lenox, 413-637-1199; www.shakespeare.org

The professional theater company performs plays by Shakespeare and Edith Wharton on four stages (one is outdoor). The main season runs late June-early September. Tuesday-Sunday. Free parking. Pets accepted.

HOTELS

★★★★★BLANTYRE

16 Blantyre Road, Lenox, 413-637-3556; www.blantyre.com

Gilded Age charm abounds at this Tudor-style mansion in the Berkshire Mountains. Blantyre's rooms maintain a decidedly British country style, with floral fabric, over-stuffed furniture, and in some, fireplaces. Activities include croquet, tennis, swimming and the cultural festivals of Tanglewood and Jacob's Pillow. Dining at Blantyre is a special occasion. The chef even packs gourmet picnics. 25 rooms. Children over 12 years only. Complimentary continental breakfast. High-speed Internet access. Spa. Restaurant, bar. $$$$

★★★CRANWELL RESORT SPA AND GOLF CLUB

55 Lee Road, Lenox, 413-637-1364, 800-272-6935; www.cranwell.com

This historic 100-year-old country hotel is set on a hill surrounded by 380 acres and a 60-mile view of the southern Berkshires. The 18-hole championship golf course is host to Beecher's golf school. Inside the sprawling mansion are an enormous new spa and fitness center, complete with yoga studios and a pool. 108 rooms. High-speed Internet access. Three restaurants, three bars. Spa. Children's activity center. Fitness center. Complimentary bottle water. Complimentary parking. $$$

★★★GATEWAYS INN

51 Walker St., Lenox, 413-637-2532, 888-492-9466; www.gatewaysinn.com

11 rooms. Complimentary full breakfast. Restaurant, bar. $$

★★★WHEATLEIGH

Hawthorne Road, Lenox, 413-637-0610; www.wheatleigh.com

Wheatleigh is a country house hotel of the finest order. The 19th-century Italian-ate palazzo is set on 22 acres of hills and Frederick Law Olmsted-designed gardens, and the estate shares in the grand Gilded Age heritage of the region. Guest rooms are comfortably elegant with English soaking tubs, exclusive bath amenities from Ermenegildo Zegna, raw silk coverlets and CD players. Details make the difference here, from the dazzling Tiffany windows to the ornate fireplace in the Great Hall. The restaurant, with its updated French dishes, draw gourmands. 19 rooms. Children over 9 years only. Wireless Internet access. Two restaurants, bar. $$$$

★YANKEE INN

461 Pittsfield Road, Lenox, 413-499-3700, 800-835-2364; www.yankeeinn.com

96 rooms. Complimentary continental breakfast. Bar. Outdoor and indoor pool. $$

SPECIALTY LODGINGS

APPLE TREE INN

10 Richmond Mountain Road, Lenox, 413-637-1477;
www.appletree-inn.com

Just outside the center of town, the Apple Tree Inn sits on 22 hilltop acres and affords beautiful views of the Berkshires. 34 rooms. Complimentary full breakfast (off-season). Restaurant, bar. $$

BIRCHWOOD INN

7 Hubbard St., Lenox, 413-637-2600, 800-524-1646;
www.birchwood-inn.com

This bed and breakfast is decorated with antiques and collectibles, and features meticulously kept rooms and gardens. 11 rooms. Complimentary full breakfast. Wireless Internet access. Children 12 and over only. Free High-speed Internet access. Pets accepted, fee. **$$**

BROOK FARM INN

15 Hawthorne St., Lenox, 413-637-3013, 800-285-7638;
www.brookfarm.com

An impressive library of poetry, fiction collection and history lends a literary feel. The Victorian inn is close to Tanglewood and the area's many other cultural and outdoor activities. Children 15 and over only. Complimentary full breakfast. Wireless Internet access. Pets not accepted. **$$**

HARRISON HOUSE

174 Main St., Lenox, 413-637-1746; www.harrison-house.com

The immaculate porch of this country inn overlooks Tanglewood and is directly across from Kennedy Park. Six rooms. No children allowed. Complimentary full breakfast. **$$**

★
★
★
★
★

KEMBLE INN

2 Kemble St., Lenox, 413-637-4113, 800-353-4113; www.kembleinn.com

Located on three acres in the center of historic Lenox, this inn features magnificent views of the Berkshire Mountains. The guest rooms are named after American authors. 14 rooms. Children over 12 years only. Complimentary continental breakfast. **$$**

ROOKWOOD INN

11 Old Stockbridge Road, Lenox, 413-637-9750, 800-223-9750;
www.rookwoodinn.com

This 1885 Victorian inn is furnished with English antiques and is located in the center of Lenox, close to the art, music and theater of Tanglewood. 21 rooms. Complimentary full breakfast. Pets accepted. **$$**

THE SUMMER WHITE HOUSE

17 Main St., Lenox, 413-637-4489, 800-382-9401;
www.thesummerwhitehouse.com

This inn is a former original Berkshire cottage built in 1885. Guest rooms feature private baths and air conditioning. Six rooms. Children over 12 years only. Complimentary continental breakfast. **$$**

THE VILLAGE INN

16 Church St., Lenox, 413-637-0020, 800-253-0917;
www.villageinn-lenox.com

32 rooms. Complimentary full breakfast. Restaurant, bar. Smoke free. Whirlpool tub. **$$**

WHISTLER'S INN

5 Greenwood St., Lenox, 413-637-0975, 866-637-0975;
www.whistlersinnlenox.com

This inn was once the home of Ross Whistler, a railroad tycoon and nephew of the legendary American painter, James Abbott McNeil Whistler. Big library. Music room. 14 rooms. Children over 10 years only. Complimentary full breakfast. Closed November-May. $$

RESTAURANTS

★★★BISTRO ZINC

56 Church St., Lenox, 413-637-8800;
www.bistrozinc.com

This lively hotspot is a good choice for a preconcert meal. The contemporary décor features black-and-white herringbone tile, tin ceilings, pale yellow walls, burgundy banquettes and a large copper bar. French-American fusion standouts include ginger-encrusted salmon and entrecote aux oignons. French bistro menu. Lunch, dinner, late-night. Bar. Casual attire. Reservations recommended. $$$

★★★BLANTYRE

16 Blantyre Road, Lenox, 413-637-3556; www.blantyre.com

Dining at the 1902 mansion is a rare culinary experience. Diners enjoy predinner champagne and canapes on the terrace or in the Music Room before feasting on chef Christopher Brooks' rich, out-of-this-world fare. Antique glassware and place settings combine to create a romantic atmosphere, and the service is impeccable. French menu. Breakfast, lunch, dinner. Jacket required. Reservations recommended. Valet parking. Spa. Bar. $$$

★★CAFÉ LUCIA

80 Church St., Lenox, 413-637-2640;
www.cafelucialenox.com

Italian, seafood menu. Dinner. Bar. Casual attire. Outdoor seating. Tuesday-Saturday. Open Sundays on holiday weekends and in summer. $$$

★CAROL'S

8 Franklin St., Lenox, 413-637-8948

American menu. Breakfast, lunch, brunch. Casual attire. $

★★CHURCH STREET CAFÉ

65 Church St., Lenox, 413-637-2745;
www.churchstreetcafe.biz

American, International menu. Lunch, dinner. Bar. Children's menu. Casual attire. Reservations recommended. Outdoor seating. Closed March-April; also Sunday-Monday in May-June and September-February. $$$

★★★GATEWAYS INN

51 Walker St., Lenox, 413-637-2532, 888-492-9466; www.gatewaysinn.com

At the Gateways, the chefs use locally grown produce and dairy products in each dish on their seasonal menu. The best seat in the house is in the main dining room: Its

MASSACHUSETTS

★
★
★
★
★

French doors and terra cotta painted walls recall a Tuscan country inn. American menu. Breakfast, lunch, dinner. Bar. Casual attire. Reservations recommended. Closed Monday in September-June. **$$$**

★PANDA HOUSE CHINESE RESTAURANT
506 Pittsfield Road, Lenox, 413-499-0660
Chinese menu. Lunch, dinner. Bar. Children's menu. Casual attire. **$$**

★★★WHEATLEIGH
Hawthorne Road, Lenox, 413-637-0610; www.wheatleigh.com
Polished mahogany doors lead to the hotel's regal dining room, which was modeled in 1893 after a 16th-century Florentine palazzo. Dine on contemporary French cuisine in a sun-drenched room filled with oil paintings, hand-carved Chippendale chairs and a large wood-burning fireplace. Favorites on the menu include roasted Maine lobster and sweet corn soufflé with cassis ice cream. 19 rooms. French menu. Dinner, Sunday brunch. Bar. Business casual attire. Reservations recommended. Valet parking. **$$$$**

★★★THE WYNDHURST RESTAURANT
55 Lee Road, Lenox, 413-637-1364, 800-272-6935; www.cranwell.com
Cranwell Resort's main dining room is on the first floor of the 100-year-old Tudor mansion. Large windows offer vistas of the Berkshire Hills and the fireplace keeps the room warm on cold New England nights. The French and American cuisine highlights local produce, including game and cheeses. American, French menu. Lunch, dinner. Business casual attire. Reservations recommended. Valet parking. **$$$**

LEXINGTON
Lexington is often referred to as the birthplace of American liberty. On its town green, on April 19, 1775, eight Minutemen were killed in what is sometimes considered the first organized fight of the War for Independence. As the British approached, American Captain John Parker told his men: "Stand your ground. Don't fire unless fired upon. But if they mean to have a war, let it begin here!" And so it did.
Information: Chamber of Commerce Visitors Center, 1875 Massachusetts Ave., Lexington, 781-862-1450; www.lexingtonchamber.org

WHAT TO SEE AND DO
BATTLE GREEN
Center of town
The Old Monument, the *Minuteman* statue and the Boulder mark the line of the Minutemen, seven of whom are buried here.

BUCKMAN TAVERN
1 Bedford St., Lexington, 781-862-1703; www.lexingtonhistory.org
The minutemen assembled here before the battle. Mid-April-May: weekends only; June-October: daily 10 a.m.-4 p.m.

HANCOCK-CLARKE HOUSE

36 Hancock St., Lexington, 781-862-1703;
www.lexingtonhistory.org

Here, John Hancock and Samuel Adams were awakened by Paul Revere's alarm on April 18, 1775. Mid-April-May: weekends only; June-October: daily; tours hourly 11 a.m.-2 p.m.

LEXINGTON HISTORICAL SOCIETY

1332 Massachusetts Ave., Lexington, 781-862-1703;
www.lexingtonhistory.org

Revolutionary period houses and guided tours. Admission: for one house $6 adults, $4 children; for two houses $8 adults, $5 children.

MUNROE TAVERN

1332 Massachusetts Ave., Lexington, 781-862-1703;
www.lexingtonhistory.org

This was the site of the British hospital after the battle. George Washington dined here in 1789. Mid-April-October: tour at 3 p.m. daily.

NATIONAL HERITAGE MUSEUM

33 Marrett Road, Lexington, 781-861-6559, 781-457-4142; www.monh.org

The museum features exhibits on American history, including that of Lexington and the Revolutionary War. Monday-Saturday 10 a.m.-5 p.m., Sunday from noon. Closed Thanksgiving Day, Christmas Day and Easter Day.

SPECIAL EVENT
REENACTMENT OF THE BATTLE OF LEXINGTON AND CONCORD

Lexington Green, Lexington, 781-862-1450; www.battleroad.org

The yearly reenactment of the opening battle of the Revolutionary War takes place at dawn on Patriots Day and includes a parade. Monday nearest April 19.

HOTELS
★QUALITY INN AND SUITES

440 Bedford St., Lexington, 781-861-0850;
www.qualityinnlexington.com

204 rooms. Complimentary continental breakfast. Fitness center. Free High-speed Internet access. Pets accepted. Outdoor heated pool. $

★★★SHERATON LEXINGTON INN

727 Marrett Road, Lexington, 781-761-1700; www.sheraton.com

Fifteen miles from Boston, this inn has 5,000 square feet of meeting space and an outdoor pool. 121 rooms. Restaurant. Bar. Pets accepted. Complimentary High-speed Internet access. $

MASSACHUSETTS

LOWELL

In the 19th century, the powerful Merrimack River and its canals helped transform Lowell from a handicraft center to an industrial city. The Francis Floodgate, near Broadway and Clare Streets, was called "Francis's Folly" when it was built in 1848, but it saved the city from flood in 1936. A restoration of the historic canal system is currently underway, and the revitalized downtown district is sprouting urban chic stores and cafés.

Information: Greater Lowell Chamber of Commerce, 77 Merrimack St., Lowell, 978-459-8154; www.greaterlowellchamber.org

WHAT TO SEE AND DO

AMERICAN TEXTILE HISTORY MUSEUM

491 Dutton St., Lowell, 978-441-0400; www.athm.org

The site's permanent exhibit, "Textiles in America," features 18th- to 20th-century textiles, artifacts and machinery that show the impact of the Industrial Revolution on labor. Tuesday-Sunday. Admission: $8 for adults, $6 for seniors. Free parking. Closed Monday-Wednesday.

LOWELL HERITAGE STATE PARK

160 Pawtucket Blvd, Lowell, 978-458-8750; www.mass.gov

Six miles of canals and two miles of park on the bank of the Merrimack River offer boating, a boathouse, a concert pavilion and interpretive programs. Schedule varies. Free parking.

LOWELL NATIONAL HISTORICAL PARK

246 Market St., Lowell, 978-970-5000; www.nps.gov/lowe

The nation's first large-scale center for the mechanized production of cotton cloth, Lowell became a model for 19th-century industrial development. This park was established to commemorate Lowell's unique legacy as the most important planned industrial city in America. It includes mill buildings and a five-and-a-half-mile canal system. May-Columbus Day weekend.

NEW ENGLAND QUILT MUSEUM

18 Shattuck St., Lowell, 978-452-4207;
www.nequiltmuseum.org

Changing exhibits feature antique, traditional and contemporary quilts. Tuesday-Saturday 10 a.m.-4 p.m. Closed on Mondays and major holidays. Admission: adults $5, seniors and students $4.

WHISTLER HOUSE MUSEUM OF ART

243 Worthen St., Lowell, 978-452-7641;
www.whistlerhouse.org

The birthplace of the painter James Abbott McNeill Whistler. Exhibits include several of his etchings. Wednesday-Saturday 11 a.m.-4 p.m. Admission: seniors $5, students $4.

MASSACHUSETTS

HOTELS

★BEST WESTERN CHELMSFORD INN
187 Chelmsford St., Chelmsford, 978-256-7511, 888-770-9992;
www.bestwestern.com/chelmsfordinn
114 rooms. High-speed Internet access. Pets not accepted. Spa. Free parking. $

★COURTYARD BY MARRIOTT
30 Industrial Ave. East, Lowell, 978-458-7575, 888-236-2427; www.courtyard.com
120 rooms. High-speed Internet access. Restaurant. Complimentary onsite parking. $

★★DOUBLETREE HOTEL
50 Warren St., Lowell, 978-452-1200, 800-876-4586; www.doubletree.com
252 rooms. Wireless Internet access. Restaurant. Bar. Pets not accepted. Pool. Fitness center, business center. $

★★RADISSON HOTEL AND SUITES CHELMSFORD
10 Independence Drive, Chelmsford, 978-256-0800, 800-333-3333;
www.radisson.com
214 rooms. Restaurant, bar. Complimentary high-speed Internet access. Fitness center. Pool. $

★★★STONEHEDGE INN
160 Pawtucket Blvd., Tyngsboro, 978-649-4400, 888-649-2474;
www.stonehedgeinn.com
This contemporary inn is an American imitation of an English country manor. Large, comfortable rooms have spacious bathrooms with heated towel racks. Set on the grounds of a horse farm, the out-of-the-way spot is perfect for a romantic rendezvous or a corporate retreat. Complimentary parking. 30 rooms. Restaurant, bar. $$

★★WESTFORD REGENCY INN AND CONFERENCE CENTER
219 Littleton Road, Westford, 978-692-8200, 800-543-7801;
www.westfordregency.com
193 rooms. Restaurant, bar. Free wireless Internet access. Pets not accepted. $$

MASSACHUSETTS

★
★
★
★

RESTAURANTS

★★COBBLESTONES
91 Dutton St., Lowell, 978-970-2282; www.cobblestonesoflowell.com
American menu. Lunch, dinner, late-night. Bar. Children's menu. Casual attire. Closed Sunday; one week in August. Open Monday-Saturday. $$

★★★LA BONICHE
143 Merrimack St., Lowell, 978-458-9473; www.laboniche.com
Though the food is upscale, the dress is casual at this fine restaurant. International menu. Lunch, dinner. Closed Sunday-Monday first week of July. Bar. Casual attire. $$

★★★SILKS

160 Pawtucket Blvd., Tyngsboro, 978-649-4400, 888-649-2474;
www.stonehedgeinn.com

Said to have one of the world's most impressive wine caves, this out-of-the-way restaurant is an oenophile retreat. On 36 acres of horse country farm, the Stonehedge
Inn's eatery proffers nearly 2,000 wines (its cellar alledgedly houses more than 90,000
bottles). The food is equally impressive. Thankfully the service is anything but snooty.
French menu. Breakfast, lunch, dinner, Sunday brunch. Closed Monday. Outdoor
seating. **$$$**

MARBLEHEAD

Marblehead sits on a pretty peninsula 17 miles north of Boston. The town was settled
in 1629 by hardy fishermen from England's West counties. It now boasts a beautiful
harbor and a number of busy boatyards. Beaches, boating, fishing, art exhibits, and
antique and curio shops abound—all combine to offer either quiet relaxation or active
recreation.

Information: Chamber of Commerce, 62 Pleasant St.,
Marblehead, 781-631-2868; www.marbleheadchamber.org

WHAT TO SEE AND DO

ABBOT HALL

188 Washington St., Marblehead, 781-631-0000;
www.abbothall.org

On display here are the "Spirit of '76" painting and the town's original deed. Last
weekend in May-last weekend in October: daily; rest of year: Monday-Friday.

JEREMIAH LEE MANSION

170 Washington St., Marblehead, 781-631-1768;
www.marbleheadmuseum.org

Run by the Marblehead Historical Society, this mansion is where Generals Glover, Lafay-
ette and Washington were entertained. June-October, Tuesday-Saturday 10 a.m.-4 p.m.

KING HOOPER MANSION

8 Hooper St., Marblehead, 781-631-2608;
www.marbleheadarts.org

A restored house with a garden and art exhibits. Mansion rooms include parlor, dining
room, wine cellar. Tuesday-Saturday 10 a.m.-4 p.m., Sunday 1-5 p.m.

SPECIALTY LODGINGS

HARBOR LIGHT INN

58 Washington St., Marblehead, 781-631-2186;
www.harborlightinn.com

Each room at this inn has a fireplace, canopy bed and Jacuzzi. Continental breakfast
and fresh-baked cookies are served in the colonial dining room. 21 rooms. Children
over 8 years only. Complimentary continental breakfast. Airport transportation avail-
able. Pets not accepted. **$**

★
★
★
★
☆

MARBLEHEAD INN

264 Pleasant St., Marblehead, 781-639-9999, 800-399-5843;
www.marbleheadinn.com

10 rooms. Children over 10 years only. Complimentary continental breakfast. Wireless Internet access. Pets not accepted. Nonsmoking inn. **$$**

SEAGULL INN

106 Harbor Ave., Marblehead, 781-631-1893; www.seagullinn.com

Six rooms. Complimentary continental breakfast. Wireless Internet access. Complimentary bottled water. Smoke free. **$$**

RESTAURANTS

★★MARBLEHEAD LANDING

81 Front St., Marblehead, 781-639-1266;
www.thelandingrestaurant.com

Seafood menu. Lunch, dinner, Sunday brunch. Bar. Children's menu. Outdoor seating. **$$**

★★PELLINO'S

261 Washington St., Marblehead, 781-631-3344; www.pellinos.com

Italian menu. Dinner. Bar. Reservations recommended. Daily. **$$**

MARTHA'S VINEYARD

For an island less than 10 miles long and 20 miles wide, Martha's Vineyard has an outsized reputation. Along with neighboring Nantucket, the isle began as a whaling center and morphed into an offshore resort for the rich and fabulous. Its acres of soft, white-sand beaches, grassy dunes, craggy cliffs and cultivated farmland are almost *too* postcard-perfect. Not quite as ideal are the island's lofty prices—housing, shopping and dining here all come with hefty fees. Nevertheless, tourists continually pack the streets of Edgartown, Oak Bluffs and Vineyard Haven in the summer.

Information: Chamber of Commerce, Beach Road, Vineyard Haven,
508-693-0085; www.mvy.com

WHAT TO SEE AND DO

AQUINNAH CLIFFS

230 Jones Road, Falmouth Aquinnah, 508-540-0448, 508-444-0173;
www.aquinnahcliffs.com

These cliffs are national landmarks and the most photographed attraction on Martha's Vineyard. More than 150 feet tall and brilliantly colored, they were formed over millions of years by glaciers. Today, the cliffs are owned by the Wampanoag Indians, who hold them sacred. At their peak sits the Aquinnah Light lighthouse, commissioned by President John Adams in 1798. At the bottom of the cliffs is a beach where nude sunbathing is permitted. April-November.

BLACK DOG BAKERY

3 Water St., Vineyard Haven, 508-693-4786; www.theblackdog.com

The Black Dog is more than just a bakery: it's a cultural phenomenon. Its logo—a black Labrador retriever—is omnipresent on T-shirts, hats, mugs and belts. The company's General Store has four Vineyard locations. All sell souvenirs and even dog treats.

MASSACHUSETTS

★
★
★
★
★

The bakery serves coffee, pastries, torts, truffles and other treats. Not to be outdone, the nearby Black Dog Tavern has tasty seafood and other island-appropriate dishes. Daily 5:30 a.m.-5 p.m., till 9 p.m. in summer.

CHICAMA VINEYARDS

Stoney Hill Road, West Tisbury, www.chicamavineyards.com

The Vineyard was once a winemaking mecca; today Chicama is reviving the tradition. It produces a variety of wines, including merlot, chardonnay and cabernet. The onsite store also sells vinegars and salad dressings, mustards and chutneys, and jams and jellies. Tours and wine tastings are available. Hours vary; call ahead.

FEATHERSTONE MEETING HOUSE FOR THE ARTS

Barnes Road, Oak Bluffs, 508-693-1850; www.featherstonearts.org

This arts center offers tourists the hourly use of studios, as well as photography, woodworking, pottery, weaving and stained-glass classes. The Meeting House also includes a gallery of works from local artists and a camp for kids. Daily; call for studio availability.

FELIX NECK SANCTUARY

Edgartown-Vineyard Haven Road, Vineyard Haven, 508-627-4850; www.massaudubon.org

★
★
★
★
★

This 350-acre wildlife preserve is a haven for kids and bird-lovers alike. Six miles of trails (guided or self-guided) meander through meadows, woods, salt marshes and beaches. The visitor center has exhibits and a gift shop. In the summer, kids enroll in the site's Fern & Feather Day Camp. Daily 8 a.m.-4 p.m.; closed Monday in September-May.

FLYING HORSE CAROUSEL

33 Oak Bluffs Ave., Oak Bluffs, 508-693-9481; www.mvpreservation.org/carousel.html

This carousel is the oldest in the country and a national historic landmark. Its flying horses are gorgeous, hand-carved and lifelike. Grasping the center brass ring earns you your next ride for free.

MENEMSHA FISHING VILLAGE

North Street, Menemsha

Menemsha is a picturesque fishing village, full of cedar-sided clam shacks, fishermen in waterproof gear and lobster traps strewn about. The movie *Jaws* was filmed here, and the main street has a few cute clothing shops.

MYTOI

Dike Road, Chappaquiddick, 508-693-7662; www.thetrustees.org

Although the Vineyard may not be a logical location for a Japanese garden, Mytoi has won praises for its mix of azaleas, irises, dogwood, daffodils, rhododendron and Japanese maple. The 50-year-old garden's centerpiece is a pond filled with goldfish and koi. Daily.

OAK BLUFFS

www.ci.oak-bluffs.ma.us

In 1835, this Methodist community served as the site of annual summer camp meetings for church groups. The communal tents gave way to family tents, which in turn became wooden cottages designed to look like tents. Today, visitors to the community take in the town's resulting famous "gingerbread cottages."

OLD WHALING CHURCH

89 Main St., Edgartown, 508-627-4442;
www.mvpreservation.org/whale.html

Built in 1843, this is a fine example of Greek Revival architecture. It's now a performing arts center with seating for 500.

VINCENT HOUSE

Pease's Point Way, Edgartown, 508-627-4440

Built in 1672, the oldest known house on the island has been carefully restored to allow visitors to see how buildings were constructed 300 years ago. June-early October, daily 11 a.m.-3 p.m.; rest of year, by appointment.

VINEYARD HAVEN AND EDGARTOWN SHOPPING

508-693-0085; www.mvy.com

Vineyard Haven is where most of the island's year-round residents live, so its shops are a bit less upscale than those in ritzy Edgartown, where you could spend an afternoon or even an entire day opening your wallet. In both towns you'll find clothing boutiques (including midnight Farm in Vineyard Haven, which is owned by Carly Simon), bookstores, jewelry shops, home accessories stores and gourmet boîtes.

VINEYARD MUSEUM

59 School St., Edgartown, 508-627-4441;
www.marthasvineyardhistory.org

Four buildings dating back to pre-Revolutionary War times join together to form the Vineyard Museum. The Thomas Cooke House, a historic colonial home, specializes in antiques and folk art; the Foster Gallery displays exhibits from the whaling industry; the Pease Galleries specialize in Native American exhibits; the Gale Huntington Library is a useful tool for genealogy.

THE YARD

Middle Road, Chilmark, 508-645-9662; www.dancetheyard.org

For 30 years, the Yard has hosted dance performances throughout the summer. The 100-seat theater makes its home in a renovated Chilmark barn and offers community dance classes and free performances for children and seniors. June-September. Admission: premium seating $50, general seating $25, seniors and under 30 $15.

MASSACHUSETTS

★
★
★
★
★

SPECIAL EVENT
STRIPED BASS & BLUEFISH DERBY

1A Dock St., Edgartown, 508-693-0085; www.mvderby.com

Just after midnight on the first day of the Derby, fishing enthusiasts seek out their favorite spots and cast off, hoping to land the big one. Whenever contestants haul in striped bass, bluefish, bonito or false albacore, the catch is weighed and measured at Edgartown Harbor. Prizes are awarded daily for big fish. A grand prize awaits the contestant who nets the largest catch caught during the tournament. Mid-September-mid-October.

HOTELS
★★★BEACH PLUM INN

50 Beach Plum Lane, Menemsha, 508-645-9454, 877-645-7398;
www.beachpluminn.com

This Vineyard inn was built in 1890 from the salvage of a shipwreck. Set on a hilltop, it overlooks the ocean. A stone drive and garden-like path lead to the main house. Several other cottages dot the seven-acre property. 11 rooms. Complimentary full breakfast. Restaurant. $$

★★★★CHARLOTTE INN

27 S. Summer St., Edgartown (Martha's Vineyard), 508-627-4751

Charlotte Inn is a quietly posh bastion of Edwardian splendor, is an oasis of tranquility even though it's located in the middle of the busiest town on Martha's Vineyard. Once you walk along the garden paths under the linden and chestnut trees, you just know this is a place coveted by those with a penchant for privacy and peace. Inside, the rooms are outfitted in elegant 19th-century art and original antiques. The guest rooms continue the luxe treatment with flatscreen TVs, down pillows and comforters, and Bulgari toiletries. 23 rooms, 2 suites. Restaurant. $$$$

★★★HARBOR VIEW HOTEL

131 N. Water St., Edgartown, 508-627-7000, 800-225-6005;
www.harbor-view.com

The renovated Harbor View combines the island's heritage with modern amenities. Rooms are bright, airy and clean, and the service is top-notch. The hotel's lengthy veranda has many rocking chairs and overlooks Edgartown Harbor, making it the perfect perch from which to watch ships roll in. 124 rooms. Restaurant, bar. High-speed Internet access. Outdoor heated pool. Kids program. Golf. Spa. $

★★★KELLEY HOUSE

23 Kelley St., Edgartown, 508-627-7900, 800-225-6005;
www.kelley-house.com

53 rooms. Complimentary continental breakfast. Restaurant. Deep-sea fishing. Outdoor pool. Kids club. Golf. $$

★★MANSION HOUSE HOTEL & HEALTH CLUB

9 Main St., Vineyard Haven, 508-693-2200, 800-332-4112;
www.mvmansionhouse.com

40 rooms. High-speed Internet access. Restaurant, bar. Pets not accepted. Health club. Spa. Restaurant. $$

★THE NASHUA HOUSE HOTEL

30 Kennebec Ave., Oak Bluffs, 508-693-0043, 888-343-0043;
www.nashuahouse.com

16 rooms. 10-acre public park. No children under 4. Pets not accepted. **$**

★★★THE WINNETU INN & RESORT

31 Dunes Road, Edgartown, 508-627-4747; www.winnetu.com

This family-friendly resort has a prime location on the beautiful, uncrowded South Beach just outside Edgartown. The cheery rooms are decorated with beachy prints and feature kitchens that can be stocked with the inn's grocery service. Activities include weekly clambakes, movie nights and rides around the property on the restored fire engine. 52 rooms. Restaurant, bar. Children's activity center. Yoga and fitness classes. Outdoor heated pool. Tennis. **$$**

SPECIALTY LODGINGS

THE ARBOR INN

222 Upper Main St., Edgartown, 508-627-8137, 888-748-4383;
www.arborinn.net

10 rooms. Children over 12 years only. Complimentary continental breakfast. Closed November-April. **$$**

ASHLEY INN

129 Main St., Edgartown, 508-627-9655; www.ashleyinn.net

10 rooms. Children over 12 years only. Complimentary continental breakfast. Restaurant. **$**

COLONIAL INN OF MARTHA'S VINEYARD

38 N. Water St., Edgartown, 508-627-4711, 800-627-4701;
www.colonialinnmvy.com

43 rooms. Closed January-mid-April. Complimentary continental breakfast. Restaurant. Pets accepted. Fitness room. Spa. **$**

DOCKSIDE INN

Circuit Avenue Extension, Oak Bluffs, 508-693-2966, 800-245-5979;
www.vineyardinns.com/dockside.html

This gingerbread-style inn overlooks the harbor in the seaside village of Oak Bluffs and is walking distance to beaches and shopping areas. 22 rooms. Complimentary continental breakfast. Closed December-March. **$**

THE EDGARTOWN INN

56 N. Water St., Edgartown, 508-627-4794; www.edgartowninn.com

The inn is based in a 1798 sea captain's home. It has been a hotel of sorts since 1820. 12 rooms. Restaurant. Closed November-March. **$**

GREENWOOD HOUSE

40 Greenwood Ave., Vineyard Haven, 508-693-6150, 866-693-6150;
www.greenwoodhouse.com

Five rooms. Complimentary full breakfast. Pets not accepted. **$$**

THE HANOVER HOUSE

28 Edgartown Road, Vineyard Haven, 508-693-1066, 800-696-8633;
www.hanoverhouseinn.com

Set on a half-acre of land, this cozy bed and breakfast is walking distance to the ferry, shopping, restaurants and the library. Shuttles are available for travel to Edgartown and Oak Bluffs. 15 rooms. Complimentary continental breakfast. High-speed Internet access. Children are welcome. No smoking. **$$**

HOB KNOB INN

128 Main St., Edgartown, 508-627-9510, 800-696-2723; www.hobknob.com

The Hob Knob feels like it could be in a mountainside forest—its cozy guest rooms, many fireplaces and old-school dining room all recall a secluded country hideaway. 17 rooms. Complimentary full breakfast. Spa. Fitness center. Business center. **$$**

LAMBERT'S COVE COUNTRY INN

Lambert's Cove Road, Vineyard Haven, 508-693-2298, 866-526-2466;
www.lambertscoveinn.com

15 rooms. Complimentary full breakfast. Restaurant (public by reservation). High-speed Internet access. **$$**

THE OAK HOUSE

79 Seaview and Pequot Aves., Oak Bluffs, 508-693-4187, 866-693-5805;
www.vineyardinns.com/oakhouse.html

10 rooms. Closed mid-October-April. Children over 10 years only. Complimentary continental breakfast. Pets not accepted. No smoking. **$$**

OUTERMOST INN

171 Lighthouse Road, Chilmark, 508-645-3511; www.outermostinn.com

The inn's picture windows provide excellent views of Vineyard Sound and the Elizabeth Islands. Seven rooms. Children over 12 years only. Complimentary full breakfast and coffee. Restaurant, bar. Restaurant. **$$**

★
★
★
★
★

PEQUOT HOTEL

19 Pequot Ave., Oak Bluffs, 508-693-5087, 800-947-8704;
www.bnblist.com/ma/pequothotel

29 rooms. Closed November-April. Complimentary continental breakfast. Pets not accepted. High-speed Internet access. **$**

THORNCROFT INN

460 Main St., Vineyard Haven, 508-693-3333; www.thorncroft.com

Secluded on a tree-lined, three-acre peninsula, this charming, white-shuttered house has romantic guest rooms with hot tubs and fireplaces. A full country breakfast can be eaten in the dining room or bed. 14 rooms. Complimentary full breakfast. Afternoon tea and pastries. High-speed Internet access. No smoking. Pets not accepted. **$$$**

RESTAURANTS

★★★ALCHEMY

71 Main St., Edgartown, 508-627-9999

A smart, casual crowd, including the occasional celebrity, frequents Edgartown's popular Alchemy. The American bistro offers upscale dining—don't miss the fried risotto balls—in a relaxing, two-story atmosphere. The happening bar and lounge are packed with local revelers after hours. American menu. Lunch, dinner. Bar. Casual attire. Outdoor seating. Closed January. **$$$**

★★THE AQUINNAH SHOP

State Road, Aquinnah, 508-645-3142

American menu. Breakfast, lunch, dinner. Children's menu. Casual attire. Outdoor seating. Closed mid-October-Easter. **$$**

★★★BALANCE

9 Oak Bluff Ave., Oak Bluffs, 508-696-3000; www.balancerestaurant.com

Balance adds a contemporary splash to Martha's Vineyard, and the flavors that come from its kitchen are bold. The chef is something of a local celebrity, and his creativity is evident in his inventive dishes. The bar attracts fashionable A-listers. American menu. Dinner. Bar. Casual attire. **$$**

★★★BEACH PLUM INN RESTAURANT

50 Beach Plum Lane, Menemsha, 508-645-9454; www.beachpluminn.com

Every table at the renowned, out-of-the-way Beach Plum has an ocean view, making the eatery one of the most romantic places on the island. The seafood-heavy menu is nearly flawless and the four-course prix fixe menu is a delicious extravagance. American menu. Dinner. Casual attire. Outdoor seating. High-speed Internet access. Closed January-early May. **$$$**

★★CAFÉ MOXIE

48 Main St., Vineyard Haven, 508-693-1484; www.cafemoxie.com

American menu. Lunch, dinner. Casual attire. Closed Tuesday; fall-winter. **$$$**

★★★COACH HOUSE

131 N. Water St., Edgartown, 508-627-7000, 800-225-6005; www.harbor-view.com

Casual refinement is the calling card of the Coach House. The breezy Harbor View Hotel restaurant looks out over the Edgartown Harbor. An upscale crowd comes here for modern twists on old standbys at breakfast and lunch, while fresh seafood and shellfish dominate the dinner menu. The wine list is comprehensive, providing the perfect complement to an exceptional meal. American menu. Breakfast, lunch, dinner, Sunday brunch. Bar. Children's menu. Casual attire. Reservations recommended. Valet parking. Closed Sunday-Monday evenings. **$$$**

★COOP DE VILLE

Dockside Marketplace, Oak Bluffs, 508-693-3420; www.coopdevillemv.com

Seafood menu. Lunch, dinner. Bar. Outdoor seating. No smoking. **$$**

MASSACHUSETTS

★
★
★
★
★

★ESPRESSO LOVE CAFÉ

17 Church St., Edgartown, 508-627-9211; www.espressolove.com
International menu. Breakfast, lunch, dinner. Children's menu. Casual attire. Reservations recommended. Outdoor seating. **$$**

★★HOME PORT

512 North Road, Menemsha, 508-645-2679; www.homeportmv.com
Seafood menu. Dinner. Children's menu. Casual attire. Reservations recommended. Outdoor seating. Closed Labor Day-Memorial Day. **$$$**

★★JIMMY SEA'S

32 Kennebec Ave., Oak Bluffs, 508-696-8550
Italian menu. Dinner. Casual attire. Outdoor seating. **$$**

★★★L'ETOILE

22 N. Water St., Edgartown, 508-627-5187; www.letoile.net
L'Etoile moved last year from the stuffy Charlotte Inn to a more relaxed location on North Water Street. The food is still served in a very formal atmosphere—and still costs a pretty penny—but the overall experience is now focused on the menu, not the staff's pomp. A new brightly colored bar adjoins the restaurant; either room is a worthy place to dine in style. French menu. Dinner. Bar. Jacket required. Reservations recommended. Closed Monday-Thursday off-season. **$$$$**

★LATTANZI'S PIZZERIA

Old Post Office Square, Edgartown, 508-627-9084, 508-627-8854;
www.lattanzis.com
Italian, pizza menu. Dinner. Children's menu. Casual attire. Reservations recommended. Outdoor seating. Sunday, Monday holiday. **$**

★★LE GRENIER FRENCH RESTAURANT

82 Main St., Vineyard Haven, 508-693-4906;
www.legrenierrestaurant.com
French menu. Dinner. Casual attire. Reservations recommended. Daily. Available for special functions. **$$$**

★LINDA JEAN'S

34 Circuit Ave., Oak Bluffs, 508-693-4093
American menu. Breakfast, lunch, dinner. Children's menu. Casual attire. Outdoor seating. **$**

★★LOLA'S SOUTHERN SEAFOOD

Beach Road, Oak Bluffs, 508-693-5007;
www.lolassouthernseafood.com
American, seafood menu. Dinner, late-night, Sunday brunch. Outdoor bar. Music and entertainment. Casual attire. **$$**

★LOOKOUT TAVERN
8 Seaview Ave., Oak Bluffs, 508-696-9844
Seafood menu. Lunch, dinner. Bar. Casual attire. Outdoor seating. Closed November-April. $$

★★LURE
31 Dunes Road, Edgartown, 508-627-3663; www.winnetu.com
Seafood menu. Dinner. High-speed Internet access. Pets not accepted. Labor Day-Columbus Day: closed Monday-Tuesday; Columbus Day-Thanksgiving: closed Monday-Thursday; closed Thanksgiving-May. $$$

★THE NEWES FROM AMERICA
23 Kelly St., Edgartown, 508-627-4397;
www.kelley-house.com/dining
American menu. Lunch, dinner. $

★★★OUTERMOST INN
81 Lighthouse Road, Aquinnah, 508-645-3511;
www.outermostinn.com
Dining here is a serene experience, thanks to the refined inn's clifftop location and relaxed elegance. Fresh herbs and vegetables grown on the property influence the creative prix fixe menu. Wine lovers, take note: The restaurant is strictly BYOB. American menu. Dinner. Reservations recommended. Closed Wednesday; also mid-October-mid-May. $$$

★★SEASONS EATERY
19 Circuit Ave., Oak Bluffs, 508-693-7129
American menu. Lunch, dinner. Bar. Children's menu. Casual attire. $

★★SQUARE RIGGER
235 State Road, Edgartown, 508-627-9968
Seafood menu. Dinner. Bar. Casual attire. Reservations recommended. Closed January. $$

★★SWEET LIFE CAFÉ
63 Circuit Ave., Oak Bluffs, 508-696-0200
Seafood menu. Dinner. Reservations recommended. Outdoor seating. Closed January-March. $$

★★THEO'S AT THE INN AT BLUEBERRY HILL
74 North Road, Chilmark, 508-645-3322, 800-356-3322;
www.blueberryinn.com
American menu. Dinner. Casual attire. $$

★THE WHARF PUB & RESTAURANT
Lower Main Street, Edgartown, 508-627-9966; www.wharfpub.com
Seafood menu. Lunch, dinner. Bar. Children's menu. Reservations recommended (six or more people). Closed March. $$

MASSACHUSETTS

★
★
★
★
★

NANTUCKET

Generally regarded as even *more* exclusive than Martha's Vineyard, Nantucket is a small island full of sprawling cottages, endless soft-sand beaches, first-rate restaurants and breathtaking ocean vistas. In the peak summer season, the island's population skyrockets to nearly overcrowded proportions, as day-trippers and weekenders stream from the Steamship Authority ferries. Somehow, though, the island retains its charm and its flush residents take the tourists in stride. A plethora of outdoor activity can be explored here, from biking to swimming to sailing to tennis and golf. Siasconset (Sconset to natives) and Nantucket Town are the isle's shopping and dining hubs, though many small stores and eateries are sprinkled over the land's 49 square miles.

Information: Chamber of Commerce, 48 Main St., Nantucket,
508-228-1700; Information Bureau, 25 Federal St., Nantucket,
508-228-1700; www.nantucketchamber.org

WHAT TO SEE AND DO

1800 HOUSE
8 Mill St., Nantucket, 508-228-1894; www.nha.org
This early 19th-century house has period furnishings, a large, round cellar and a kitchen garden.

ALTAR ROCK
Off Polpis Road, Nantucket
Altar Rock rises 90 feet above sea level and affords stunning views of Nantucket and the surrounding Cape. Go at dawn or dusk for the best views.

BARTLETT'S FARM
33 Bartlett Farm Road, Nantucket, 508-228-9403;
www.bartlettsfarm.com
The Bartlett family has tilled the land of Nantucket's largest farm for nearly 200 years. Stop by for fresh vegetables, milk, eggs, cheese, freshly baked bread and cut flowers. A handful of prepared foods such as salads, pies, snacks, jams and chutneys are also available. Daily 8 a.m.-6 p.m.

CISCO BREWERS
5 Bartlett Farm Road, Nantucket, 508-325-5929; www.ciscobrewers.com
Local beer-makers Cisco Brewers concoct dozens of micro-specialties such as Whales Tales Pale Ale, Baileys Ale, Moor Porter, Capn' Swains Extra Stout, Summer of Lager and Baggywrinkle Barleywine. Onsite are guided tours of the brewery, vineyard and distillery. Summer, Monday-Saturday 10 a.m.-6 p.m., Sunday till 5 p.m.; fall-spring: Saturday 10 a.m.-5 p.m.

ENDEAVOR SAILING ADVENTURES
Straight Wharf, Nantucket, 508-228-5585; www.endeavorsailing.com
U.S. Coast Guard Captain James Genthner built his sloop, the *Endeavor*, and has been sailing it for more than 20 years. Take a 90-minute sail around Nantucket Sound and let Genthner and his wife, Sue, introduce you to Nantucket's sights, sounds and history. May-October.

FIRST CONGREGATIONAL CHURCH

62 Centre St., Nantucket, 508-228-0950; www.nantucketfcc.org

Also called the Old North Church, this spot arguably offers Nantucket's best view of the island and surrounding ocean. To enjoy it, you'll have to climb the 120-foot-tall steeple's 94 steps. Mid-June-mid-October, Monday-Saturday.

FOLGER-FRANKLIN MEMORIAL FOUNTAIN

Madaket Road, Nantucket, 508-228-1894

The birthplace of Abiah Folger, Benjamin Franklin's mother.

HADWEN HOUSE

96 Main St., Nantucket, 508-228-1894; www.nha.org

A Greek Revival mansion with furnishings from the whaling period. Monday-Saturday 10 a.m.-5 p.m., Sunday from noon.

JETHRO COFFIN HOUSE (OLDEST HOUSE)

16 Sunset Hill Lane, Nantucket, 508-228-1894

Built in 1686, Oldest House is, true to its name, one of the oldest houses in the United States. The building was a wedding present given to the children of two feuding families (the Gardners and the Coffins) by their in-laws, who reconciled after the happy event. Thursday-Monday, 11 a.m.-4 p.m. Closed December 1-4. Admission: adults $6, children 6-17 $3.

JETTIES BEACH

Bathing Beach Road, Nantucket, 508-228-2279; thejettiesnantucket.com

Kid-friendly Jetties is the best bet for beach-going families. There are restrooms, showers, changing rooms, a snack bar, lifeguards, rental chairs, a playground, volleyball and tennis courts, and a skateboarding park. You can also rent kayaks, sailboards and sailboats through Nantucket Community Sailing (508-228-5358). Daily.

LOINES OBSERVATORY

59 Milk St., Nantucket, 508-228-9273; mmo.org

Named for the first professional female astronomer, the observatory lets guests peek through a telescope to view the star-filled Cape Cod skies. Monday, Wednesday, Friday evenings in summer, Saturday evenings year-round; closed Tuesday, Thursday, Sunday in summer, Sunday-Friday year-round.

MIACOMET GOLF COURSE

12 W. Miacomet Road, Nantucket, 508-228-9764, 508-325-0333; www.miacometgolf.com

Nantucket's only public golf course offers nine holes (two are Par-fives). Reserve a tee time at least a week in advance; the chances of playing in the summertime without a reservation are zero. Daily.

MURRAY'S TOGGERY

62 Main St., Nantucket, 508-228-0437, 800-368-2134; www.nantucketreds.com

Murray's Toggery was the first store on the island to sell Nantucket Reds, the casual pink khaki pants that have since invaded every nook of preppiness in America.

Monday-Saturday 9 a.m.-7 p.m., Sunday 10 a.m.-6 p.m.; winter, Monday-Saturday 9 a.m.-5 p.m.

NANTUCKET HISTORICAL ASSOCIATION WHALING MUSEUM

15 Broad St., Nantucket, 508-228-1894; www.nha.org

This museum, redesigned and reopened in 2005, is the premier institution devoted to the history of the whaling industry. Inside are a 46-foot preserved sperm whale skeleton (the whale washed ashore in 1998) and many artifacts from the island's heyday as a center for whale oil production. Mid-May-mid-October, daily 10 a.m.-5 p.m.; mid-October-mid-December, Thursday-Monday 11 a.m.-4 p.m.; closed mid-December-May.

NANTUCKET MARIA MITCHELL ASSOCIATION

4 Vestal St., Nantucket, 508-228-9198; www.mmo.org

The scientific library has historical documents, science journals and Mitchell family memorabilia. There's also a natural science museum with local wildlife, and an aquarium is nearby at 28 Washington Street. Mid-June-August, Tuesday-Saturday; library also open rest of year, Wednesday-Saturday.

NANTUCKET TOWN

Nantucket, 508-228-1700; www.nantucketchamber.org/directory/merchants

Nantucket Town is a shopper's dream. A walk down its main street involves passing by home, clothing, culinary, boat, jewelry, art and antique shops, most of which are tasteful and well-edited.

OLD MILL

50 Prospect St., Nantucket, 508-228-1894; www.nha.org/sites/oldmill.html

Believed to be the oldest windmill in the United States, this Dutch-style structure is impressive in its beauty and sheer vertical height of 50 feet. It was built in 1746 with salvaged oak that washed up on shore from shipwrecks. Inside are a research center and whaling museum. June-August: daily; call for off-season hours.

RAFAEL OSONA AUCTIONS

21 Washington St., Nantucket, 508-228-3942; www.rafaelosonaauction.com

This spot hosts estate auctions on selected weekends (call for exact dates and times) that feature treasured pieces from both the United States and Europe. Late May-early December.

SIASCONSET VILLAGE

East end of Nantucket Island

Siasconset lies seven miles from Nantucket Town and can be reached by bicycle or shuttle bus (driving often takes twice as long due to traffic). This 18th-century fishing village features quaint cottages, grand mansions, restaurants, a few shops and a summer cinema.

SOMETHING NATURAL

50 Cliff Road, Nantucket, 508-228-0504; www.somethingnatural.com

Those looking for a casual breakfast or lunch should check out. This off-the-beaten-path shop that makes healthy sandwiches, breads, bagels, salads and cookies. May-October.

THE STRAIGHT WHARF

Straight Wharf, Nantucket

Built in 1723, the wharf is Nantucket's launching area for sailboats, sloops and kayaks, but it's also a great shopping and eating area. Loaded with restaurants and quaint, one-room cottage shops, the wharf also features an art gallery, museum and outdoor concert pavilion.

STRONG WINGS SUMMER CAMP

9 Nobadeer Farm RoadRd., Nantucket, 508-228-1769; www.strongwings.org

Open for just two months every year, the Strong Wings Summer Camp enrolls kids ages 5-15 in three- or five-day sessions, where they explore the area, mountain bike, hike, kayak, snorkel, rock climb and boogie board. Older kids learn search-and-rescue techniques. Late June-late August: daily.

THE SUNKEN SHIP

12 Broad St., Nantucket, 508-228-9226; www.sunkenship.com

The Sunken Ship is a full-service dive shop that offers lessons and rentals. The general store offers an eclectic array of maritime goods. Daily; call for closures.

THEATRE WORKSHOP OF NANTUCKET

2 Centre St., Nantucket, 508-228-4305; www.theatreworkshop.com

The theater has staged comedies, dramas, plays and dance concerts since 1985. Both professionals and amateurs make up the company, which offers between 6 and 10 performances each summer.

WINDSWEPT CRANBERRY BOG

Polpis Road, Siasconset

To see how cranberries are grown and harvested, visit this 200-acre bog during the fall harvest (late September-October from dawn-dusk). At other times of the year, the bog is a peaceful place to walk and bike. Daily dawn-dusk.

SPECIAL EVENTS

NANTUCKET ARTS FESTIVAL

508-325-8588; www.nantucketartscouncil.org

This weeklong festival celebrates a full range of arts on the island: films, poetry and fiction, acting, dance, paintings, photography and many other forms. Look for the wet-paint sale in which you can bid on works completed just that day. Early October.

NANTUCKET FILM FESTIVAL

508-228-6648; www.nantucketfilmfestival.org

Like other film fests, this one screens new independent movies that may not otherwise garner attention. It's attended by screenwriters, actors, film connoisseurs and occasionally, big-name celebrities. A daily event called Morning Coffee showcases a panel of the above participating in Q&As. Mid-June.

MASSACHUSETTS

NANTUCKET WINE FESTIVAL

508-228-1128; www.nantucketwinefestival.com

The Great Wine in Grand Houses event allows you to visit a private mansion, sip fine vintages drawn from nearly 100 wineries and dine on food prepared by some of the area's finest chefs. Reservations are required. Mid-May.

HOTELS

★★THE BEACHSIDE AT NANTUCKET

30 N. Beach St., Nantucket, 508-228-2241, 800-322-4433; www.thebeachside.com

93 rooms. Complimentary continental breakfast. Restaurant. Bar. Closed November-April. Pool. $

★★CLIFFSIDE BEACH CLUB

46 Jefferson Ave., Nantucket, 508-228-0618; www.cliffsidebeach.com

27 rooms, all suites. Closed November-April. Restaurant, bar. Beach. Spa. Pool. Pets not accepted. Complimentary continental breakfast. Wireless Internet access. Exercise facility. $$

★★HARBOR HOUSE VILLAGE

99 S. Beach St., Nantucket, 508-325-1000, 866-325-9300;
www.nantucketislandresorts.com

104 rooms. Restaurant, bar. Beach. Wireless Internet access. Pool. Pets accepted (fee). $

★★★JARED COFFIN HOUSE

29 Broad St., Nantucket, 508-228-2400; www.jaredcoffinhouse.com

60 rooms. Restaurant, bar. Spa. Pets not accepted. Wireless Internet access. Pool. $

★★NANTUCKET INN

1 Miller's Way, Nantucket, 508-228-6900, 800-321-8484; www.nantucketinn.net

100 rooms. Closed December-March. Restaurant, bar. Airport transportation available. Pool. Fitness center. Wireless Internet access. Business center. Complimentary continental breakfast. $

★★★WHITE ELEPHANT RESORT

50 Easton St., Nantucket, 508-228-2500, 800-445-6574;
www.whiteelephanthotel.com

Step back in time for a game of croquet on a sweeping, manicured lawn at this harborfront resort. Rooms are comfortable with plush beds and luxurious bath amenities. Guests can stay in the main inn or in one of the many onsite cottages. 66 rooms. Restaurant, bar. Closed mid December-March. Complimentary High-speed Internet access. Exercise room. $$$

★★★★THE WAUWINET

120 Wauwinet Road, Nantucket, 508-228-0145, 800-426-8718;
www.wauwinet.com

Staying at the Wauwinet is akin to being marooned on a remote island with impeccable service. Built in 1876 by ship captains, the Wauwinet is a grand resort, with sophisticated rooms and suites, and private beaches fronting the harbor and Atlantic Ocean. Its

★
★
★
★

clay tennis courts are well maintained, and its restaurant has a 20,000-bottle wine cellar. 36 rooms. Closed late October-early May. Children over 18 only. Complimentary full breakfast. Restaurant. Tennis. Spa. Complimentary wireless Internet access. Pets not accepted. **$$$$**

SPECIALTY LODGINGS

CARLISLE HOUSE INN
26 N. Water St., Nantucket, 508-228-0720; www.carlislehouse.com
The structure was built in 1765, and now houses an inn with rooms featuring fireplaces and four poster beds. 17 rooms. Closed January-March. Children over 10 years only. Complimentary continental breakfast. Pets not accepted. **$**

CENTERBOARD GUEST HOUSE
8 Chester St., Nantucket, 508-228-9696; www.centerboardguesthouse.com
The updated, modern rooms at this bed and breakfast have flatscreen TVs, down duvets and full baths with Caswell and Massey bath products. Eight rooms. Closed January-February, Complimentary continental breakfast. Free Wi-Fi. **$**

CENTRE STREET INN
78 Centre St., Nantucket, 508-228-0199, 800-298-0199;
www.centrestreetinn.com
Rooms in this cozy inn are named after holidays and feature antique furniture and fireplaces. 14 rooms. Complimentary continental breakfast. Closed January-April. Pets not accepted. **$**

COBBLESTONE INN
5 Ash St., Nantucket, 508-228-1987; www.nantucket.net
The petite rooms at this cozy inn have fireplaces, private baths, colorful quilts and private baths. Five rooms. Closed January-March. Complimentary full breakfast. **$**

MARTIN HOUSE INN
61 Centre St., Nantucket, 508-228-0678; www.martinhouseinn.net
Located in a house built in 1803, this historic inn has rooms with four-poster or canopy beds and fireplaces. 13 rooms. Complimentary continental breakfast. Restaurant. **$**

ROBERTS HOUSE INN
11 India St., Nantucket, 508-228-0600, 800-872-6830;
www.robertshouseinn.com
Restored in 2003, this inn has rooms furnished with antiques and reproductions and private baths. 45 rooms. Complimentary continental breakfast. Free wireless Internet access. **$**

SEVEN SEA STREET INN
7 Sea St., Nantucket, 508-228-3577; www.sevenseastreetinn.com
Spread over three historic houses, this inn has rooms with canopy beds, high-definition TV and Jacuzzi tubs. 11 rooms. Children over 5 years only. Complimentary continental breakfast. Closed January-mid April. Spa. **$$**

MASSACHUSETTS

★
★
★
★
☆

SHERBURNE INN

10 Gay St., Nantucket, 508-228-4425, 888-577-4425; www.sherburneinn.com

Built by whaling captatin Obed Starbuck in 1831, this small inn has rooms decorated in cheerful colors. Breakfast and afternoon tea are served daily. Eight rooms. Children over 6 years only. Complimentary continental breakfast. Complimentary wireless Internet access. **$**

SHIPS INN

13 Fair St., Nantucket, 508-228-0040; www.shipsinnnantucket.com

12 rooms. Closed November-April. Complimentary continental breakfast. Restaurant, bar. **$$**

VANESSA NOEL HOTEL

5 Chestnut St., Nantucket, 508-228-5300; www.vanessanoelhotel.com

This petite inn opened by a New York-based designer is housed above her eponymous shoe boutique. Rooms are simple but luxurious with plush beds, Frette linens and Bulgari bath products. Eight rooms. Complimentary continental breakfast. Highspeed Internet access. Bar. **$$$**

RESTAURANTS

★★★21 FEDERAL

21 Federal St., Nantucket, 508-228-2121; www.21federal.com

Historic charm and contemporary panache come together at this stylishly clubby spot—a favorite of the islands Who's-Who, both for its delectable New American cuisine and convivial bar. The well-rounded menu has a wide selection of meat, poultry and seafood, while the award-winning wine list delights oenophiles. American menu. Dinner. Bar. Business casual attire. Reservations recommended. Outdoor seating. Closed January-April. **$$$**

★★★AMERICAN SEASONS

80 Center St., Nantucket, 508-228-7111; www.americanseasons.com

American Seasons' menu is refreshingly varied, if perhaps a bit gimmicky. The menu is divided to reflect regional cuisines: New England, Down South, the Wild West and the Pacific Coast. Thanks to meticulous attention to detail and fresh, local produce, the themed meals are a success. Regulars rave about the cooking and the folk-art-decorated, romantic dining room and patio. American menu. Dinner. Bar. Business casual attire. Reservations recommended. Outdoor seating. Closed January-March. **$$$**

★ATLANTIC CAFÉ

15 S. Water St., Nantucket, 508-228-0570; www.atlanticcafe.com

American, seafood menu. Lunch, dinner, late-night. Bar. Children's menu. Closed late December-early January. **$**

★★BLACK EYED SUSAN'S

10 India St., Nantucket, 508-325-0308; www.black-eyedsusans.com

International menu. Breakfast, dinner. Casual attire. Reservations recommended. Outdoor seating. Closed Sunday; also November-March. **$$**

★★★BOARDING HOUSE

12 Federal St., Nantucket, 508-228-9622; www.boardinghouse-pearl.com

The restaurant's nouveau cuisine and sexy, youthful scene make the long waits worth it. Those in the know book a table outdoors to people-watch and stargaze as they eat. Others prefer the dimly lit downstairs dining room. Seafood and beef are the main inspirations behind the creative Asian-influenced menu; a comprehensive wine list ensures perfect pairings. American menu. Lunch, dinner. Bar. Reservations recommended. Outdoor seating. **$$$**

★CAMBRIDGE STREET RESTAURANT

12 Cambridge St., Nantucket, 508-228-7109

American menu. Dinner. Bar. Casual attire. Closed January-April. **$$**

★★★CLUB CAR

1 Main St., Nantucket, 508-228-1101; www.theclubcar.com

The Club Car lounge is housed in a renovated train club car that once ran between Steamboat Wharf and Siasconset Village. Lunches and dinners offer sophisticated menus, and a pianist performs nightly. French menu. Lunch, dinner. Bar. Business casual attire. Reservations recommended. Closed November-late May. **$$$$**

★★★COMPANY OF THE CAULDRON

7 India St., Nantucket, 508-228-4016;
www.companyofthecauldron.com

From its ivy-covered exterior to the soft glow of its candlelit dining room to its gentle harp soundtrack, this restaurant seems crafted straight from a romance novel. The menu features New American dishes and changes nightly. International menu. Dinner. Business casual attire. Reservations recommended. Closed Monday; also Mid-December-April. **$$$**

★DOWNYFLAKE

18 Sparks Ave., Nantucket, 508-228-4533

Breakfast, lunch. Casual attire. **$**

★FOG ISLAND CAFÉ

7 S. Water St., Nantucket, 508-228-1818; www.fogisland.com

American menu. Breakfast, Lunch, dinner. Bar. Children's menu. Casual attire. Closed January-February. **$**

★★LE LANGUEDOC

24 Broad St., Nantucket, 508-228-2552; www.lelanguedoc.com

French menu. Lunch, dinner. Bar. Casual attire. Reservations recommended. Outdoor seating. Closed February-March. **$$$**

★★NANTUCKET LOBSTER TRAP

23 Washington St., Nantucket, 508-228-4200;
www.nantucketlobstertrap.com

Seafood menu. Dinner. Bar. Children's menu. Casual attire. Outdoor seating. Closed October-April. **$$$**

MASSACHUSETTS

★
★
★
★
★

★★★ORAN MOR

2 S. Beach St., Nantucket, 508-228-8655; www.oranmorbistro.com

Climb the stairs to Oran Mor and discover a foodlover's heaven. The eclectic menu echoes the restaurant's accessible elegance. Organic ingredients and fresh seafood dominate the complex dishes. A friendly, knowledgeable staff caps off a fine-dining experience. International menu. Dinner. Bar. Business casual attire. Reservations recommended. Closed January-March. **$$$**

★★★THE PEARL

12 Federal St., Nantucket, 508-228-9701;
www.boardinghouse-pearl.com

This spot was among the first to bring city chic to Nantucket, appealing to a young, fashionable clientele that crowds the bar area on weekend nights. Asian flavors punctuate the Pearl's seafood dishes, while the drink menu is decidedly metropolitan, with various takes on martinis, cosmos and sake in addition to a complete wine and champagne list. There are only two seatings per evening, so reserve early. International menu. Dinner, late-night. Bar. Casual attire. Reservations recommended. Outdoor seating. Closed October-April. **$$$$**

★★ROPEWALK

1 Straight Wharf, Nantucket, 508-228-8886; www.theropewalk.com

Seafood menu. Lunch, dinner. Bar. Children's menu. Casual attire. Outdoor seating. Closed mid-October-mid-May. **$$**

★★SEAGRILLE

45 Sparks Ave., Nantucket, 508-325-5700; www.theseagrille.com

Seafood menu. Lunch, dinner. Children's menu. Business casual attire. Reservations recommended. Outdoor seating. **$$**

★★★SUMMER HOUSE

17 Ocean Ave., Nantucket, 508-257-9976; www.thesummerhouse.com

The Summer House seduces with oceanfront seating and superb cuisine. White wicker furnishings and ceiling fans set the scene for the refined New American cuisine. A more casual poolside lunch is also served. American menu. Dinner. Bar. Casual attire. Outdoor seating. Closed mid-October-mid-May. **$$$$**

★★★★TOPPER'S

120 Wauwinet Road, Nantucket, 508-228-0145, 800-426-8718; www.wauwinet.com

Chef David Daniels lends his extensive New England-honed skills to Toppers. Regulars know to order the seasonal prix fixe menu, which has locally inspired treats like lobster and chestnut soup, roasted sirloin of venison and housemade ice cream. His signature dishes, such as maple-glazed foie gras, potato-crusted Maine scallops and roasted New York duckling, are all outstanding. All meals can be paired with a selection from the award-winning 900-bottle wine list. American menu. Lunch, dinner, Sunday brunch. Bar. Business casual attire. Reservations recommended. Outdoor seating. Closed late October-early May. **$$$$**

★
★
★
★

★★WEST CREEK CAFÉ
11 W. Creek Road, Nantucket, 508-228-4943
American menu. Dinner. Bar. Reservations recommended. Outdoor seating. Closed Tuesday. $$$

★WESTENDER
326 Madaket Road, Nantucket, 508-228-5100
American menu. Lunch, dinner. Bar. Closed in winter. $$

SPA
★★★SPA BY THE SEA
120 Wauwinet Road, Nantucket, 508-228-0145, 800-426-8718; www.wauwinet.com
Indulge all your senses at this luxury spa located in the Nantucket cozy seaside retreat The Wauwinet. Signature treaments, including the Garden facial and Atlantic Seaweed Wrap, use local and sea-inspired ingredients. While the spa herb garden, comfortable chaise lounges and sounds of rolling waves enhance the serene atmosphere.

NEW BEDFORD
Herman Melville once said every house in New Bedford was harpooned, then reeled in from the bottom of the sea. His metaphor held some truth: In his time, the city was the greatest whaling port in the world. But in 1857, when miners struck oil in Pennsylvania, this bustling sea-dependent spot became a veritable ghost town. It was eventually rebuilt around manufacturing but never quite recaptured the flourish of its earlier era. Today, the city is mostly urban and slight gritty. Its past can be glimpsed in its monuments and museums, and in the sea captains' homes that still line its better streets.

Information: Bristol County Convention & Visitors Bureau, 70 N. Second St., New Bedford, 508-997-1250, 800-288-6263; www.bristol-county.org

WHAT TO SEE AND DO
BUTTONWOOD PARK & ZOO
425 Hawthorn St., New Bedford, 508-991-6178; www.bpzoo.org
The park has a greenhouse, ball fields, tennis courts, a playground, a picnic area and a fitness circuit. Zoo exhibits include elephants, lions, deer, bears, buffalo and a seal pool. Daily 10 a.m.-5 p.m.

NEW BEDFORD WHALING MUSEUM
18 Johnny Cake Hill, New Bedford, 508-997-0046;
www.whalingmuseum.org
The museum features an 89-foot half-scale model of the whale ship *Lagoda*. Galleries are devoted to scrimshaw, local artists, murals and a whale skeleton. Daily 9 a.m.-5 p.m.

ROTCH-JONES-DUFF HOUSE AND GARDEN MUSEUM
396 County St., New Bedford, 508-997-1401;
www.rjdmuseum.org
This Greek Revival mansion has been maintained to reflect the lives of three families that lived in the house. Daily.

MASSACHUSETTS

★
★
★
★

SEAMEN'S BETHEL

15 Johnny Cake Hill, New Bedford, 508-992-3295;
www.rixsan.com/nbvisit/attract/bethel1.htm

(1832) Here is the "Whaleman's Chapel" referred to by Melville in *Moby Dick*. The prow-shaped pulpit was later built to represent Melville's description. Daily.

SPECIAL EVENT
FEAST OF THE BLESSED SACRAMENT

50 Madeira Ave., Hathaway St.,
and Tinkham Street, New Bedford, 508-992-6911;
www.portuguesefeast.com

This is the largest Portuguese feast in North America and features three days of entertainment, parades and amusement rides. First weekend in August.

HOTEL
★★DAYS INN

500 Hathaway Road, New Bedford, 508-997-1231, 800-329-7466;
www.daysinn.com

151 rooms. Restaurant, bar. Airport transportation available. Free wireless Internet access. Pets accepted. Pool. Free continental breakfast. **$**

RESTAURANTS
★ANTONIO'S

267 Coggeshall St., New Bedford, 508-990-3636

American, Spanish menu. Lunch, dinner. Bar. Children's menu. Casual attire. **$$**

★★FREESTONE'S CITY GRILL

41 William St., New Bedford, 508-993-7477; www.freestones.com

Seafood menu. Lunch, dinner. Bar. Children's menu. Casual attire. **$$**

★★★OCEANNA

95 William St., New Bedford, 508-997-8465;
www.oceannarestaurant.com/oceanna.htm

Seafood menu. Lunch, dinner. Bar. Children's menu. Casual attire. Closed Sunday. **$$**

NEWBURYPORT

One of Massachusetts's best-kept secrets, Newburyport might be the ideal New England town. Smaller than a city but bigger than a village, this north shore spot is quaint without being saccharine, manageable without being boring. Its clean, safe streets exude history, especially those lined with stately Federalist ship captain's houses. Locals have an easy commute to Boston but rarely bother making the trip—everything they need, from sweet clothing boutiques to first-rate dining to the sandy shores of Plum Island, is right here.

Information: Greater Newburyport Chamber of Commerce & Industry, 29 State St.,
Newburyport, 978-462-6680; www.newburyport.chamber.org

WHAT TO SEE AND DO

COFFIN HOUSE

14 High Road, Newburyport, 978-462-2634; www.historicnewengland.org

This old home features 17th- and 18th-century kitchens, a buttery and parlor with early 19th-century wallpaper. June-mid-October, first Saturday of the month 11 a.m.-5 p.m.

CUSHING HOUSE MUSEUM

98 High St., Newburyport, 978-462-2681; www.newburyhist.com

This Federalist-style mansion was once the home of Caleb Cushing, the first U.S. envoy to China. May-November, Tuesday-Friday 10 a.m.-4 p.m., Saturday from noon.

CUSTOM HOUSE MARITIME MUSEUM

25 Water St., Newburyport, 978-462-8681;
www.customhousemaritimemuseum.org

Collections of marine artifacts, ship models and navigational instruments are on display here. April-late-December, Monday-Saturday 11 a.m.-4 p.m., Sunday noon-4 p.m.

PARKER RIVER NATIONAL WILDLIFE REFUGE

6 Plum Island Turnpike, Newburyport, 978-465-5753;
www.fws.gov/northeast/parkerriver/contact.html

This breathtaking natural barrier beach is six and a half miles long and the home of many species of birds, mammals, reptiles, amphibians and plants. Available are hiking, bicycling, waterfowl hunting and a nature trail. Daily.

HOTEL

★★GARRISON INN

11 Brown Square, Newburyport, 978-499-8500; www.garrisoninn.com

24 rooms. Restaurant, bar. Children's activity center. Wireless Internet access. Pool. Fitness center. Spa. **$**

SPECIALTY LODGINGS

CLARK CURRIER INN

45 Green St., Newburyport, 978-465-8363; www.clarkcurrierinn.com

Seven rooms. Complimentary full breakfast. **$**

ESSEX STREET INN

7 Essex St., Newburyport, 978-465-3148; www.essexstreetinn.com

19 rooms. Complimentary continental breakfast. Spa. Bar. **$**

MORRILL PLACE

209 High St., Newburyport, 978-462-2808

Nine rooms. Complimentary continental breakfast. **$**

RESTAURANTS

★★★DAVID'S

11 Brown Square, Newburyport, 978-462-8077; www.davidstavern.com

A favorite of locals and visitors alike, this restaurant serves a wide variety of global fare. International menu. Dinner. Bar. Children's menu. **$$$**

★★GLENN'S GALLEY

44 Merrimac St., Newburyport, 978-465-3811;
www.glennsrestaurant.com
Seafood menu. Dinner. Bar. Children's menu. Closed Monday. **$$**

★THE GROG

13 Middle St., Newburyport, 978-465-8008; www.thegrog.com
International menu. Lunch, dinner. Bar. **$$**

★★MICHAEL'S HARBORSIDE

1 Tournament Wharf, Newburyport, 978-462-7785;
www.michaelsharborside.com
Seafood menu. Lunch, dinner. Bar. Outdoor seating. **$$**

★★TEN CENTER STREET

10 Center St., Newburyport, 978-462-6652;
www.tencenterstreet.com
American menu. Lunch, dinner, Sunday brunch. Bar. Outdoor seating. Closed Monday. **$$**

216 NEWTON

Right outside Boston, the city of Newton is made up of 13 small suburban villages best known for their well-moneyed citizens and much-envied addresses. The various main streets have become shopping and dining destinations for the family sets, while the city's five big schools—including Boston College—lend youthful energy to the area.
Information: Chamber of Commerce, 199 Wells Ave., Newton, 617-244-5300;
www.nnchamber.com

WHAT TO SEE AND DO

CHARLES RIVER CANOE & KAYAK CENTER

2401 Commonwealth Ave., Newton, 617-965-5110;
www.ski-paddle.com/cano/canoe.htm
Tourists who aren't afraid of getting a little wet love this Charles River entry point. Kayaks and canoes are available for rent. April-October: daily.

JACKSON HOMESTEAD MUSEUM

527 Washington St., Newton, 617-552-7238; www.ci.newton.ma.us
(1809) Once a station on the Underground Railroad, the home of the Newton Historical Society has changing exhibits and a children's gallery. Tuesday-Saturday and Sunday afternoon.

HOTELS

★★★BOSTON MARRIOTT NEWTON

2345 Commonwealth Ave., Newton, 617-969-1000, 800-228-9290; www.marriott.com
Ideal for business travelers, the Newton Marriot has a 24-hour, self-serve business center and more than 16,000 square feet of meeting space. Its prime location along the Charles River offers a great view. 430 rooms. Restaurant, bar. High-speed Internet access. Pets not accepted. Fitness center. **$**

★★★SHERATON NEWTON HOTEL

320 Washington St., Newton, 617-969-3010, 800-325-3535; www.sheraton.com

All rooms and suites at this recently renovated property have a contemporary décor with sleek white bedding, well-designed work areas and warm, mustard-colored walls. Those not wanting to shell out for Boston rates can stay here and hop the downtown express, which departs for Faneuil Hall every 20 minutes. 270 rooms. High-speed Internet access. Restaurant, bar. Pool. Fitness facility. $

RESTAURANT
★★★LUMIERE

1293 Washington St., West Newton, 617-244-9199; www.lumiererestaurant.com

The words "warm" and "whimsical" best sum up the ambiance at this suburban French spot. The front door opens by spoon, and Scrabble tiles line the restroom doors. But the contemporary French cuisine doesn't fool around—it's fresh and straightforward, making this spot the best bistro for miles around. French, Mediterranean, Pacific menu. Dinner. $$$

NORTH ADAMS

No town in the Berkshires has gone through a more dramatic transformation than North Adams (well, at least not recently). Thanks to Mass MoCA, the biggest modern art museum in the world, the former factory city suddenly finds itself a booming tourist center. Boutiques and eateries have followed suit, as has a crowd of young culture vultures eager to invest in the locale's emerging spirit.

Information: Northern Berkshire Chamber of Commerce, 75 North St., Pittsfield, 413-663-3735; www.berkshirebiz.org

WHAT TO SEE AND DO
KIDSPACE

87 Marshall St., North Adams, 413-664-4481

The museum's children's gallery presents contemporary art in a manner that is interesting and accessible, and has hands-on activity stations where kids can create their own art. June-early September: daily noon-4 p.m.; rest of year: limited hours.

MASS MOCA

1040 Mass MoCA Way, North Adams, 413-664-4481; www.massmoca.org/kidspace

The center for visual, performing and media arts features unconventional exhibits and performances by renowned artists and cultural institutions. July-early September: daily 10 a.m.-6 p.m.; rest of year: Wednesday-Monday 11 a.m.-5 p.m.

MOHAWK TRAIL STATE FOREST

175 Mohawk Trail/Route 2, Charlemont, 413-339-5504; www.mass.gov/dcr/parks/western/mhwk.htm

The forest has spectacular scenery and swimming, fishing, hiking, winter sports, picnicking, camping and log cabins.

★
★
★
★
★

MOUNT GREYLOCK STATE RESERVATION
Rockwell Road, North Adams, 413-499-4262;
www.mass.gov/dcr/parks/mtGreylock
At 3,491 vertical feet, Mount Greylock is the highest point in the state. Fishing, hunting, cross-country skiing, picnicking and snowmobiles are allowed. Mid-May-mid-October.

NATURAL BRIDGE STATE PARK
McCauley Road, off Route 8 North Adams, 413-663-6392;
www.mass.gov/dcr/parks/western/nbdg.htm
This park has a water-eroded marble bridge and 550-million-year-old rock formations popularized by Nathaniel Hawthorne. Picnicking. Mid-May-mid-October.

WESTERN GATEWAY HERITAGE STATE PARK
115 State St., North Adams, 413 663-6312;
www.mass.gov/dcr/parks/western/wghp.htm
A restored freight yard with six buildings surround a cobbled courtyard and detailed historic exhibits on the construction of the Hoosac Railroad Tunnel. Daily.

SPECIAL EVENT

FALL FOLIAGE FESTIVAL
6 West Main St, North Adams, 413-664-6180; www.fallfoliageparade.com
Parade, entertainment, dancing and children's activities. Late September-early October.

HOTELS

★★HOLIDAY INN BERKSHIRES
40 Main St., North Adams, 413-663-6500; www.holiday-inn.com
86 rooms. Wireless Internet access. Restaurant, bar. Whirlpool. $

★★★THE PORCHES INN
231 River St., North Adams, 413-664-0400; www.porches.com
Directly across from Mass MoCA, this inn is housed in a row of vividly painted Victorian buildings, each of which has been restored and decorated with sleek, modern furnishings. There are porches and rocking chairs, but most guests ignore them in favor of the pool and luxe amenities. 52 rooms. Complimentary continental breakfast. Fitness room. $$

NORTHAMPTON

Thanks to Jonathan Edwards, a Puritan who was once regarded as the greatest preacher in New England, Northampton was the scene of a frenzied religious revival movement in the early 18th century. However, the fervor had little lasting impact on the town, which is now full of first-class theaters and restaurants, antique shops and art galleries, and up-to-date hotels and inns. The area's thriving arts scene can be partly credited to its close proximity to five colleges: Mount Holyoke, Amherst, Hampshire, Smith and the University of Massachusetts.
Information: Chamber of Commerce and Visitor Center, 99 Pleasant St.,
Northampton, 413-584-1900; www.northamptonuncommon.com

WHAT TO SEE AND DO

ARCADIA NATURE CENTER AND WILDLIFE SANCTUARY, MASSACHUSETTS AUDUBON SOCIETY

127 Combs Road, Easthampton, 413-584-3009; www.massaudubon.org

On these 550 acres are an ancient oxbow of the Connecticut River, self-guided nature trails and an observation tower. Tuesday-Sunday 9 a.m.-3 p.m.

CALVIN COOLIDGE MEMORIAL ROOM

20 West St., Northampton, 413-587-1011;
www.forbeslibrary.org/coolidge/coolidge.shtml

On display are the local son and the late president's papers and correspondence. Monday-Thursday, Saturday; schedule may vary.

HADLEY FARM MUSEUM

208 Middle St., Hadley, 413-584-1160; www.hadleyonline.com/farmmuseum

A restored 1782 barn houses agricultural implements, tools and domestic items dating back to the 1700s. May-October, Wednesday-Saturday 11 a.m.-4 p.m., Sunday 1-4 p.m.

HISTORIC NORTHAMPTON MUSEUM HOUSES

46-66 Bridge St., Northampton, 413-584-6011;
www.historic-northampton.org/aboutus.html

These include the 1820 Damon House and the 1730 Parsons House. Tuesday-Friday 10 a.m.-4 p.m., Saturday-Sunday from noon.

LOOK PARK

300 N. Main St., Florence, 413-584-5457; www.lookpark.org

In the park are a miniature train, the Christenson Zoo, boating, tennis, picnicking, playgrounds, ball fields and the Pines Theater.

SMITH COLLEGE

33 Elm St., Northampton, 413-584-2700; www.smith.edu

With 2,700 women, this is the largest private women's liberal arts college in the United States. On campus are Paradise Pond, the Helen Hills Chapel and the William Allan Neilson Library that has more than one-million volumes.

MUSEUM OF ART

Elm Street, Northampton, 413-585-2760; www.smith.edu/artmuseum/#start

This spot has a fine collection with emphasis on American and European art of the 19th and 20th centuries. September-May, Tuesday-Sunday; rest of year, Tuesday-Saturday.

SPECIAL EVENT

THREE-COUNTY FAIR

Three-County Fairgrounds, Damon Road and Highway 9,
Northampton, 413-584-2237; www.3countyfair.com

The nation's oldest agricultural fair has agricultural exhibits, horse racing and pari-mutuel betting. Labor Day week.

★
★
★
★

HOTELS

★★CLARION HOTEL AND CONFERENCE CENTER

1 Atwood Drive, Northampton, 413-586-1211, 800-582-2929; www.clarionhotel.com

122 rooms. Wireless Internet access. Restaurant, bar. Business center. Free wireless Internet access. Pool. Pets accepted. **$**

★★★THE HOTEL NORTHAMPTON

36 King St., Northampton, 413-584-3100, 800-547-3529; www.hotelnorthampton.com

Built in 1927, this brick Colonial Revival building sits on a busy street opposite the restored Calvin Theater. A narrow glass greenhouse enwraps half the building, and the hotel's public areas are adorned with Norman Rockwell prints and Japanese woodcuts. Colonial furnishings lend most guest rooms a stately vibe, while the hotel's two restaurants round out the experience. 106 rooms. Complimentary continental breakfast. Wireless Internet access. Two restaurants, two bars. **$$**

SPECIALTY LODGINGS

AUTUMN INN

259 Elm St., Northampton, 413-584-7660; www.hampshirehospitality.com

This hotel sits in an old residential area within walking distance from the main gates of Smith College and a mile from downtown Northampton, The 1960s brick property was built to resemble a colonial-era inn with a sweeping, well-manicured lawn. Its huge, wood-burning lobby has lots of copper kettles and cast-iron fixtures on display, giving the whole room the rustic feel of a bygone era. 32 rooms. Complimentary continental breakfast. Free Wireless Internet access. Pool. **$**

RESTAURANT

★★EASTSIDE GRILL

19 Strong Ave., Northampton, 413-586-3347; www.eastsidegrill.com

American menu. Dinner. Bar. **$$**

ORLEANS

Orleans was supposedly named in honor of the French Duke of Orleans. Its history also includes the dubious distinction of being the only town in America to have been fired upon by the Germans during World War I. Today, tourists pass through this commercial hub along the way to Nauset Beach and the outer Cape.

Information: Cape Cod Chamber of Commerce, Highways 6 and 132, Hyannis, 508-362-3225, 888-227-3263; www.capecodchamber.org

WHAT TO SEE AND DO

ACADEMY OF PERFORMING ARTS

120 Main St., Orleans, 508-255-1963; www.apa1.org

The theater presents comedies, dramas, musicals, dance and workshops for all ages.

FRENCH CABLE STATION MUSEUM

41 S. Orleans Road, Orleans, 508-240-1735; www.frenchcablestationmuseum.org

Built in 1890 as the American end of the transatlantic cable from Brest, France, the museum has original submarine cable equipment. July-Labor Day, Tuesday-Saturday afternoons.

★
★
★
★
★

NAUSET BEACH

Beach Road, Orleans, 508-255-1386; www.capecod-orleans.com

One of the most spectacular ocean beaches on the Atlantic coast sits within the boundaries of Cape Cod National Seashore. Swimming, surfing, fishing and lifeguards. Parking fee.

HOTELS

★THE COVE

13 S. Orleans Road, Orleans, 508-255-1203, 800-343-2233;
www.thecoveorleans.com

47 rooms. Wireless Internet access. Airport transportation available. Pool. **$**

★NAUSET KNOLL MOTOR LODGE

237 Beach Road, East Orleans, 508-255-2364;
www.capecodtravel.com/nausetknoll

12 rooms. Closed late October-mid-April. Pets not accepted. **$**

★SEASHORE PARK MOTOR INN

24 Canal Road, Orleans, 508-255-2500, 800-772-6453;
www.seashoreparkinn.com

62 rooms. Complimentary continental breakfast. Wireless Internet access. Airport transportation available. Closed November-mid-April. Pets accepted. **$**

SPECIALTY LODGINGS

THE PARSONAGE INN

202 Main St., East Orleans, 508-255-8217, 888-422-8217;
www.parsonageinn.com

Built around 1770, this inn features cozy rooms with canopy beds and colorful quilts. Eight rooms. Children over 6 years only. Complimentary full breakfast. **$**

SHIP'S KNEES INN

186 Beach Road, East Orleans, 508-255-1312;
www.shipskneesinn.com

This inn is a restored sea captain's house and is just steps from the ocean. The rooms are individually decorated in a nautical style and are furnished with antiques and four-poster beds. 16 rooms. Children over 12 years only. Complimentary continental breakfast. **$**

RESTAURANTS

★★BARLEY NECK INN

5 Beach Road, East Orleans, 508-255-0212, 800-281-7505;
www.barleyneck.com

American menu. Dinner. Bar. Casual attire. Reservations recommended. **$$**

★THE BEACON ROOM

23 West Road, Orleans, 508-255-2211; www.beaconroom.com

American menu. Lunch, dinner. Bar. Casual attire. Outdoor seating. **$$**

★★★CAPTAIN LINNELL HOUSE

137 Skaket Beach Road, Orleans, 508-255-3400; www.linnell.com

Chef/owner Bill Conway delivers a delightful dining experience at this romantic restaurant. The yard sets the scene with a Victorian gazebo, lavender bushes and ocean breezes. Oil lamps and fresh flowers add to the main room's cozy, peaceful atmosphere. The skillfully prepared menu has highlights like veal with crab, bouillabaisse and pork tenderloin, and an extensive wine list is offered. American menu. Dinner. Bar. Children's menu. Business casual attire. Reservations recommended. Closed Monday; also mid-February-March. $$$

★DOUBLE DRAGON INN

Highways, 6A and 28, Orleans, 508-255-4100

Chinese menu. Lunch, dinner, late-night. Bar. Casual attire. $

★LOBSTER CLAW

Highway 6A, Orleans, 508-255-1800; www.lobsterclaw.com

American, seafood menu. Lunch, dinner. Bar. Children's menu. Casual attire. Closed mid-November-March. $$

★★MAHONEY'S ATLANTIC BAR AND GRILL

28 Main St., Orleans, 508-255-5505; www.mahoneysatlantic.com

American menu. Dinner. Bar. Casual attire. $$

★★NAUSET BEACH CLUB RESTAURANT

222 E. Main St., East Orleans, 508-255-8547;
www.nausetbeachclub.com

Italian menu. Dinner. Bar. Casual attire. Reservations recommended. $$$

★★OLD JAILHOUSE TAVERN

28 West Road, Orleans, 508-255-5245

American menu. Lunch, dinner, late-night, Sunday brunch. Bar. Children's menu. Casual attire. Outdoor seating. $$

★SIR CRICKET'S FISH AND CHIPS

38 Route 6A, Orleans, 508-255-4453

Seafood menu. Lunch, dinner. Children's menu. Casual attire. $

★THE YARDARM

48 Highway 28 Orleans, 508-255-4840;
www.yardarmrestaurant.com

American menu. Lunch, dinner. Bar. Children's menu. Casual attire. $$

PITTSFIELD

Once widely regarded as the unwelcoming, gritty epicenter of the Berkshires, Pittsfield has recently started to return to its busy, beautiful small-town roots. The city's revitalized North Street once again boasts fine restaurants and shops, and its museums and theaters have also undergone facelifts. Instead of being a place that visitors drive through on their way elsewhere, Pittsfield is becoming a veritable destination.

Information: Berkshire Visitors Bureau, Berkshire Common,
413-443-9186, 800-237-5747; www.berkshires.org

WHAT TO SEE AND DO
ARROWHEAD
780 Holmes Road, Pittsfield, 413-442-1793; www.mobydick.org
(1780) Herman Melville wrote *Moby Dick* while living here from 1850-1863. It's now the headquarters of the Berkshire County Historical Society. Memorial Day weekend-October, daily.

BERKSHIRE MUSEUM
39 South St., Pittsfield, 413-443-7171; www.berkshiremuseum.org
This is a museum of art, natural science and history, featuring American 19th- and 20th-century paintings; works by British and European masters; artifacts from ancient civilizations; exhibits on Berkshire County history; and children's programs. July-August: daily; rest of year: Tuesday-Sunday.

BOUSQUET
101 Dan Fox Drive, Pittsfield, 413-442-8316; www.bousquets.com
The ski area has two double chairlifts, three rope tows, snowmaking, ski school, rentals, a cafeteria, bar and daycare. The longest run is one mile with a vertical drop of 750 feet. Night skiing. December-March, daily.

HANCOCK SHAKER VILLAGE
Highways 20 and 41, Pittsfield, 413-443-0188; www.hancockshakervillage.org
A Shaker site from 1790-1960, this is now a living history museum of Shaker life, crafts and farming. A large collection of furniture and artifacts is housed in 20 restored buildings, including the Round Stone Barn.

JIMINY PEAK
37 Corey Road, Hancock, 413-738-5500; www.jiminypeak.com
This ski area has a six-passenger lift, three double chairlifts, a J-bar, two quads, three triple chairs, a ski school, rentals, a restaurant, two cafeterias, a bar and a lodge. The longest run is two miles with a vertical drop 1,140 feet. Thanksgiving-early April, daily. In the summer, the mountain has trout fishing, 18-hole miniature golf course and an Alpine slide and tennis center. Memorial Day-Labor Day.

HOTELS
★★CROWNE PLAZA HOTEL
1 West St., Pittsfield, 413-499-2000, 800-227-6963; www.berkshirecrowne.com
179 rooms. High-speed Internet access. Restaurant, bar. Pool. Fitness center. Business center. Spa. $

★★JIMINY PEAK MOUNTAIN RESORT
37 Corey Road, Hancock, 413-738-5500, 800-882-8859; www.jiminypeak.com
96 rooms. Restaurant. Children's activity center. Ski-in/ski-out. Pool. Fitness center. Whirlpools. Spa. $

★
★
★
★
★

RESTAURANT
★★DAKOTA
1035 South St., Pittsfield, 413-499-7900; www.dakotarestaurant.com
American menu. Lunch, dinner, Sunday brunch. Bar. Children's menu. Casual attire. Reservations recommended. $$

PLYMOUTH
On December 21, 1620, 102 people stepped off the *Mayflower* to found the first permanent European settlement north of Virginia: Plymouth. Plagued by exposure, cold, hunger and disease during its first American winter, the colony was nearly wiped out. But the next year, the settlers were firmly established. Their landing site is memorialized by Plymouth Rock. Today, the town doubles as a summer resort oasis and fishing village, with tourists and locals going about their days together in ways those early citizens could hardly have imagined.
Information: Destination Plymouth, 170 Water St., Plymouth,
508-747-7525, 800-872-1620; www.visit-plymouth.com

WHAT TO SEE AND DO
HARLOW OLD FORT HOUSE
119 Sandwich St., Plymouth, 508-746-0012
(1677) A Pilgrim household with crafts, candle-dipping demonstrations and an herb garden. July-August, Tuesday-Friday.

HEDGE HOUSE
126 Water St., Plymouth, 508-746-0012;
www.visit-plymouth.com/hedgehouse.htm
This 1809 house has period furnishings and special exhibits. June-October, Thursday-Saturday.

HOWLAND HOUSE
33 Sandwich St., Plymouth, 508-746-9590;
www.pilgrimjohnhowlandsociety.org/howland_house.shtml
This restored 1666 Pilgrim house has 17th- and 18th-century furnishings. Memorial Day-mid-October, Monday-Saturday.

MAYFLOWER SOCIETY HOUSE MUSEUM
4 Winslow St., Plymouth, 508 746-3188;
www.themayflowersociety.com/museum.htm
This is the national headquarters of the General Society of Mayflower Descendants. July-Labor Day: daily; Memorial Day weekend-June and early September-October: Friday-Sunday.

MYLES STANDISH STATE FOREST
194 Cranberry Road, South Carver, 508-866-2526;
www.mass.gov/dcr/parks/southeast/mssf.htm
The park consists of approximately 15,000 acres with swimming, fishing, boating, hiking, riding, hunting, picnicking and camping.

★
★
★
★
★

NATIONAL MONUMENT TO THE FOREFATHERS

Allerton Street, and Highway 44, Plymouth, 508-746-1790

This site was built between 1859 and 1889—at a cost of $155,000—to depict the virtues of the Pilgrims. At 81 feet high, it is the tallest solid granite monument in the United States. May-October, daily.

PILGRIM HALL MUSEUM

75 Court St., Plymouth, 508-746-1620;
www.pilgrimhall.org

Decorative arts and possessions of first Pilgrims and their descendants, plus the only known portrait of a *Mayflower* passenger, are on display here. Daily; closed January.

PLIMOTH PLANTATION/MAYFLOWER II

137 Warren Ave., Plymouth, 508-746-1622;
www.plimoth.org

No, it's not a typo. The Plimoth Plantation, a re-creation of the 1627 Pilgrim village, uses the colony's old-fashioned spelling. Onsite actors pretend to have zero knowledge of the 21st—or even the 18th—century; they wear and use only the clothing, equipment, tools and cookware the early settlers would have employed. The *Mayflower II* is a full-scale reproduction of the original built by J. W. & A. Upham with oak timbers, hand-forged nails, linen canvas sails and hemp rope. April-November, daily; closed December-March.

PLYMOUTH COLONY WINERY

56 Pinewood Road, Plymouth, 508-747-3334;
www.plymouthcolonywines.com

These working cranberry bogs are open to the public and give a good insight into cranberry harvest activities. April-late December, daily; March, Friday-Sunday; also holidays.

PROVINCETOWN FERRY

10 Town Wharf, Plymouth, 508-746-2643, 800-242-2469;
www.provincetownferry.com

A round-trip passenger ferry departs State Pier in the morning and returns in the evening. Mid-June-Labor Day, daily; May-mid-June and after Labor Day-October, weekends.

RICHARD SPARROW HOUSE

42 Summer St., Plymouth, 508-747-1240; www.sparrowhouse.com

Dating to 1640, this is Plymouth's oldest restored home. Memorial Day weekend-Thanksgiving, Monday-Tuesday, Thursday-Sunday; gallery open till late December.

SPOONER HOUSE

27 North St., Plymouth, 508-746-0012;
www.visit-plymouth.com/spoonerhouse.htm

This 1747 home was occupied by the Spooner family for five generations and is furnished with its heirlooms. June-October, Thursday-Saturday.

225

MASSACHUSETTS

★
★
★
★

AUTUMNAL FEASTING

137 Warren Ave., Plymouth, 508-746-1622; www.plimoth.org

At Plimoth Plantation's 1627 Pilgrim Village, this is a harvest celebration with Dutch colonists from Fort Amsterdam re-creating a 17th-century event. Activities, feasting, games.

HOTEL

★★RADISSON HOTEL PLYMOUTH HARBOR

180 Water St., Plymouth, 508-747-4900, 800-333-3333; www.radisson.com

175 rooms. High-speed Internet access. Restaurant, bar. Pool. Fitness center. Whirlpool. **$**

SPECIALTY LODGINGS

THE COLONIAL HOUSE INN

207 Sandwich St., Plymouth, 508-747-4274, 866-747-4274;
www.thecolonialhouseinn.com

Four rooms. Complimentary continental breakfast. Beach. **$$**

JOHN CARVER INN

25 Summer St., Plymouth, 508-746-7100, 800-274-1620;
www.johncarverinn.com

79 rooms. Restaurant, bar. Spa. Pool. Exercise room. **$$**

THE MABBETT HOUSE

7 Cushman St., Plymouth, 508-747-1044, 888-622-2388; www.mabbetthouse.com

Three rooms. Children over 12 years only. Complimentary full breakfast. **$**

RESTAURANT

★HEARTH AND KETTLE

25 Summer St., Plymouth, 508-746-7100;
www.johncarverinn.com

Seafood, steak menu. Breakfast, lunch, dinner. Children's menu. **$$**

PROVINCETOWN

Though its thunder has been stolen by Plymouth and that town's famous rock, Provincetown was actually the Mayflower's first docking site. Artists of all kinds converge in P'town, as those in the know call it, for the bustling—often too crowded—summer season.

Information: Chamber of Commerce, 307 Commercial St., Provincetown,
508-487-3424; www.ptownchamber.com

WHAT TO SEE AND DO

COMMERCIAL STREET

Commercial Street., Provincetown

Stretching more than three miles in length, this narrow street sports art galleries, shops, clubs, restaurants and hotels. When it was constructed in 1835, all houses faced the harbor. Today, most homes have been turned 180 degrees to face the street (or have had a new front door crafted on the opposite side).

226

MASSACHUSETTS

EXPEDITION WHYDAH'S SEA LAB & LEARNING CENTER

16 MacMillan Wharf, Provincetown, 508-487-8899;
ww.whydah.com

This is the archaeological site of the sunken pirate ship *Whydah,* which was struck by storms in 1717. Learn about the recovery of the ship's pirate treasure, the lives and deaths of pirates and the history of the ship and its passengers. April-mid-October: daily; mid-October-December: weekends and school holidays.

PILGRIM MONUMENT & MUSEUM

1 High Pole Hill, Provincetown, 508-487-1310;
www.pilgrim-monument.org

This is a 252-foot granite tower commemorating the Pilgrims' 1620 landing in the New World. Exhibits include whaling equipment, scrimshaw, ship models, artifacts from shipwrecks and a Pilgrim Room with a scale-model diorama of the *Mayflower.* Summer: daily.

PROVINCETOWN ART ASSOCIATION & MUSEUM

460 Commercial St., Provincetown, 508-487-1750; www.paam.org
Late May-October: daily; rest of year: weekends.

WHALE WATCHING

306 Commercial St., Provincetown, 508-240-3636, 800-826-9300;
www.whalewatch.com

Visitors can take 3½- to 4-hour trips. Research scientists from the Provincetown Center for Coastal Studies are aboard each trip to lecture on the history of whales. Mid-April-October, daily.

SPECIAL EVENT
PROVINCETOWN PORTUGUESE FESTIVAL

MacMillian Wharf, Provincetown, 508-487-3424;
www.provincetownportuguesefestival.com

Provincetown's Portuguese community started this festival more than 50 years ago. Each year in late June, the local bishop says mass at St. Peter's Church and then leads a procession to MacMillan Wharf, where he blesses a parade of fishing boats. The festival that follows features fireworks, concerts, dancing, and Portuguese art and food. Last week in June.

HOTELS
★★★CROWNE POINTE HISTORIC INN

82 Bradford St., Provincetown, 508-487-6767, 877-276-9631;
www.crownepointe.com

Five of the buildings at this downtown P'town inn date back to the 1600s. Peaceful gardens, a fountain and a koi pond contribute to the mellow outdoor setting, while hardwood floors, antiques, crown molding and ceiling fans decorate the interiors. The guest rooms are large and offer extensive amenities; most rooms also have fireplaces and whirlpool tubs. Room stays include hearty breakfasts and evening cocktail receptions. 40 rooms. No children accepted. Complimentary full breakfast. Wireless Internet access. Restaurant, bar. Spa. Airport transportation available. $$$

MASSACHUSETTS

★
★
★
★
★

★THE MASTHEAD RESORT
31-41 Commercial St., Provincetown, 508-487-0523, 800-395-5095;
www.themasthead.com
21 rooms. Wireless Internet access. Beach. $

★★PROVINCETOWN INN
1 Commercial St., Provincetown, 508-487-9500, 800-942-5388;
www.provincetowninn.com
100 rooms. Complimentary continental breakfast. Restaurant, bar. Beach. $

★WATERMARK INN
603 Commercial St., Provincetown, 508-487-0165; www.watermark-inn.com
10 rooms, all suites. Wireless Internet access. Beach access. Airport transportation available. $$

SPECIALTY LODGINGS
FAIRBANKS INN
90 Bradford St., Provincetown, 508-487-0386, 800-324-7265;
www.fairbanksinn.com
14 rooms. Children over 15 years only. Complimentary continental breakfast. $

SNUG COTTAGE
178 Bradford St., Provincetown, 508-487-1616, 800-432-2334;
www.snugcottage.com
Eight rooms. Complimentary full breakfast. $$

SOMERSET HOUSE
378 Commercial St., Provincetown, 508-487-0383, 800-575-1850;
www.somersethouseinn.com
13 rooms. Complimentary full breakfast. Beach access. $$

WATERSHIP INN
7 Winthrop St., Provincetown, 508-487-0094, 800-330-9413;
www.watershipinn.com
15 rooms. Complimentary continental breakfast. $

★
★
★
★
☆

WHITE WIND INN
174 Commercial St., Provincetown, 508-487-1526, 888-449-9463;
www.whitewindinn.com
12 rooms. Complimentary continental breakfast. $

RESTAURANTS
★★★BISTRO AT CROWNE POINTE INN
82 Bradford St., Provincetown, 508-487-6767; www.crownepointe.com
Paintings, fresh flowers and gleaming wood floors set the tone at this bluff-top restaurant. The seasonal menu is skillfully served, and guests can substitute or order options made from scratch, without butter, cream or fatty oils. American menu. Dinner. Bar. Casual attire. Reservations recommended. Valet parking. Closed Tuesday. $$$

★FANIZZI'S BY THE SEA

539 Commercial St., Provincetown, 508-487-1964; www.fanizzisrestaurant.com

American, Italian menu. Lunch, dinner. Bar. Children's menu. Casual attire. Reservations recommended. $$$

★★FRONT STREET

230 Commercial St., Provincetown, 508-487-9715;
www.frontstreetrestaurant.com

Italian menu. Dinner. Bar. Casual attire. Reservations recommended. Closed January-April. $$

★★LOBSTER POT

321 Commercial St., Provincetown, 508-487-0842; www.ptownlobsterpot.com

Seafood menu. Lunch, dinner. Bar. Children's menu. Casual attire. Closed December-March. $$$

★★LORRAINE'S RESTAURANT

133 Commercial St., Provincetown, 508-487-6074; www.lorrainesrestaurant.com

Mexican menu. Dinner. Bar. Children's menu. Casual attire. Reservations recommended. Closed December-March. $$

★★MARTIN HOUSE

157 Commercial St., Provincetown, 508-487-1327; www.themartinhouse.com

American menu. Dinner, brunch. Bar. Reservations recommended. Outdoor seating. Closed Monday-Wednesday; also January. $$$

★★THE MEWS RESTAURANT & CAFÉ

429 Commercial St., Provincetown, 508-487-1500; www.mews.com

International menu. Dinner, Sunday brunch. Bar. Casual attire. $$

★★NAPI'S

7 Freeman St., Provincetown, 508-487-1145, 800-571-6274;
www.napis-restaurant.com

International menu. Dinner. Bar. Children's menu. Casual attire. Reservations recommended. $$

★★★RED INN RESTAURANT

15 Commercial St., Provincetown, 508-487-7334, 866-473-3466;
www.theredinn.com

One of the best parts about this restaurant is its view of the harbor, the bay, Long Point lighthouse and the shores of the Outer Cape. Diners get an eyeful of the panoramic display as they chomp on the house specialty—a tasty porterhouse steak. New American menu. Dinner, brunch. Bar. Business casual attire. Reservations recommended. $$$

★★SAL'S PLACE

99 Commercial St., Provincetown, 508-487-1279; www.salsplaceofprovincetown.com

Italian menu. Dinner. Children's menu. Casual attire. Reservations recommended. Outdoor seating. Closed November-April. $$

ROCKPORT

Rockport is a year-round artists' colony. A weather-beaten shanty on one of its many wharves has been the subject of so many paintings that it's now referred to as "Motif No. 1." Studios, galleries and summer cottages dot the shore of this quiet Cape Ann town, while tourists cruise its streets.

Information: Chamber of Commerce, Rockport, 978-546-6575, 888-726-3922;
www.rockportusa.com

WHAT TO SEE AND DO

OLD CASTLE

Granite and Curtis Streets, Rockport, 978-546-9533;
www.sandybayhistorical.org

This 1715 structure is a fine example of early 18th-century architecture and exhibits. July-August: daily; rest of year: by appointment.

THE PAPER HOUSE

52 Pigeon Hill St., Rockport, 978-546-2629; www.paperhouserockport.com

Newspapers were used in the construction of this house and its furniture. April-October.

SANDY BAY HISTORICAL SOCIETY & MUSEUMS

40 King St., Rockport, 978-546-9533;
www.sandybayhistorical.org

The museum has early American and 19th-century rooms and objects and exhibits on fishing, the granite industry and the Atlantic cable. Mid-June-mid-September: daily; rest of year: by appointment.

SPECIAL EVENT

ROCKPORT CHAMBER MUSIC FESTIVAL

35 Main St., Rockport, 978-546-7391; www.rcmf.org

Soloists and chamber ensembles of international acclaim have performed at this art colony since 1982. A lecture series and family concert are also featured. Four weekends in June or July.

HOTELS

★★★EMERSON INN BY THE SEA

1 Cathedral Ave., Rockport, 978-546-6321, 800-964-5550;
www.emersoninnbythesea.com

This traditional country inn has hosted guests at its Pigeon Cove location since 1846. From March to the end of December, visitors can take in ocean views from the pool, porch, restaurant and half the guest rooms. 36 rooms. Restaurant. Spa. $

★★★SEACREST MANOR

99 Marmion Way, Rockport, 978-546-2211; www.seacrestmanor.com

The staff at this country inn is amazingly attentive (without being annoying). Guests can have traditional afternoon tea at the manor or rent one of the onsite bicycles and take a ride. Seven rooms. Complimentary full breakfast. Restaurant for inn guests only. Closed December-March. $$

★★★SEAWARD INN & COTTAGES

44 Marmion Way, Rockport, 978-546-3471, 877-473-2927;
www.seawardinn.com

39 rooms. Complimentary full breakfast. Restaurant. Airport transportation available. **$**

★★TURK'S HEAD MOTOR INN

151 South St., Rockport, 978-546-3436;
www.turksheadinn.com

28 rooms. Restaurant. **$**

★★★YANKEE CLIPPER INN

127 Granite St., Rockport, 978-546-3407, 800-545-3699;
www.yankeeclipperinn.com

One of a few coastal inns open year-round, this seaside resort has rolling country gardens, a heated pool and a comfortable atmosphere. Its Veranda Restaurant features elegant American-Continental cuisine. 16 rooms. Complimentary full breakfast. Outdoor saltwater pool. Airport transportation available. Closed January-February. **$$**

SPECIALTY LODGINGS

ADDISON CHOATE INN

49 Broadway, Rockport, 978-546-7543, 800-245-7543;
www.addisonchoateinn.com

This Cape Ann bed and breakfast is less than an hour's drive north of Boston. Eight rooms. Children over 11 years only. Complimentary continental breakfast. **$**

THE INN ON COVE HILL

37 Mount Pleasant St., Rockport, 978-546-2701, 888-546-2701;
www.innoncovehill.com

This inn was built in 1791 from proceeds of pirates' gold found nearby. Eight rooms. Complimentary continental breakfast. Closed mid-October-mid-April. **$**

LINDEN TREE INN

26 King St., Rockport, 978-546-2494, 800-865-2122; www.lindentreeinn.com

12 rooms. Complimentary full breakfast. **$**

PEGLEG RESTAURANT AND INN

1 King St., Rockport, 978-546-2352, 800-346-2352;
www.cape-ann.com/pegleg

33 rooms. Complimentary continental breakfast. Restaurant. Closed November-March. **$**

ROCKY SHORES INN & COTTAGES

65 Eden Road, Rockport, 978-546-2823, 800-348-4003;
www.sandybayhistorical.org

11 rooms. Complimentary full breakfast. Closed mid-October-mid-April. **$**

THE TUCK INN BED AND BREAKFAST

17 High St., Rockport, 978-546-7260, 800-789-7260; www.thetuckinn.com

13 rooms. Complimentary continental breakfast. **$**

MASSACHUSETTS

★
★
★
★
★

RESTAURANT
★BRACKETT'S OCEANVIEW
25 Main St., Rockport, 978-546-2797; www.bracketts.com
Seafood menu. Lunch, dinner. Closed mid-October-March. **$$**

SALEM

Despite its picturesque, idyllic streets, famous native son Nathaniel Hawthorne, and its legacy as a major shipbuilding center, Salem will always be known for the brutal blip in its history. In 1692, at the peak of the town's infamous witch trials, 19 people were hanged on Gallows Hill, another was "pressed" to death and at least two others died in jail. A museum now memorializes the terrible events and much of the town's tourist trade revolves around the old trials.

Information: Chamber of Commerce, 63 Wharf St., Salem,
978-744-0004; www.salem-chamber.org

WHAT TO SEE AND DO
CROWNINSHIELD-BENTLEY HOUSE
126 Essex St., Salem, 978-745-9500
Reverend William Bentley, minister and diarist, lived here from 1791-1819. June-October, daily; rest of year, Saturday-Sunday, holidays.

DERBY HOUSE
174 Derby St., Salem, 978-740-1660;
www.nps.gov/sama/historyculture/derby.htm
This was the home of maritime merchant Elias Hasket Derby, one of the country's first millionaires. The Garden features roses, herbs and 19th-century flowers.

GARDNER-PINGREE HOUSE
128 Essex St., Salem, 978-745-9500
Designed by McIntire, this 1804 house has been restored and handsomely furnished. June-October: daily; rest of year: Saturday-Sunday, holidays.

HOUSE OF SEVEN GABLES
115 Derby St., Salem, 978-744-0991; www.7gables.org
Nathaniel Hawthorne's 1851 novel of the same name is said to have been inspired by this home. Daily; closed first three weeks in January.

JOHN WARD HOUSE
161 Essex St., Salem, 978-745-9500
17th-century furnishings. June-October, daily; rest of year, Saturday-Sunday, holidays.

PEABODY MUSEUM & ESSEX INSTITUTE
East India Square, Salem, 978-745-9500, 866-745-1876; www.pem.org/museum
The Peabody Museum, founded by sea captains in 1799, features five world-famous collections in 30 galleries. Daily.

PEIRCE-NICHOLS HOUSE

80 Federal St., Salem, 978-745-9500

One of the finest examples of McIntire's architectural genius, this 1782 home is authentically furnished. By appointment only.

PIONEER VILLAGE: SALEM IN 1630

Forest River Park off W. St., Salem, 978-740-9636; www.essexheritage.org

A reproduction of an early Puritan settlement, the village has dugouts, wigwams and thatched cottages peopled by costumed interpreters.

ROPES MANSION AND GARDEN

318 Essex St., Salem, 978-745-9500;
www.salemmass.com/houses/buildings2.html

This is a restored gambrel-roofed, Georgian and colonial mansion furnished with period pieces. The garden, laid out in 1912, is known for its beauty and variety. June-October: daily; limited hours Sunday.

SALEM MARITIME NATIONAL HISTORIC SITE

174 Derby St., Salem, 978-740-1660; www.nps.gov/sama

Nine acres of historic waterfront. Self-guided and guided tours. Daily.

SALEM WITCH MUSEUM

19½ Washington Square, Salem, 978-744-1692; www.salemwitchmuseum.com

The Salem witch trials of 1692 are re-created here with a 30-minute narrated presentation that uses special lighting and life-size figures. (The exhibit may be frightening for young children.) Slightly less gruesome is the town's October Salem's Haunted Happenings, a Halloween festival that features street merchants, plays, Witchy games and haunted houses. Daily.

WITCH DUNGEON MUSEUM

16 Lynde St., Salem, 978-741-3570; www.witchdungeon.com

Onsite is a reenactment of the witch trial of Sarah Good and a tour through a re-created dungeon where accused witches awaited trial. April-November, daily.

WITCH HOUSE

310 Essex St., Salem, 978-744-8815; www.salemweb.com/witchhouse

This was the home of witchcraft trial judge Jonathan Corwin; some of the accused witches may have been examined here. May-early November, daily 10 a.m.-5 p.m.

HOTEL

★★HAWTHORNE HOTEL

18 Washington Square West, Salem, 978-744-4080, 800-729-7829;
www.hawthornehotel.com

93 rooms. Restaurant. **$**

MASSACHUSETTS

★
★
★
★
★

SPECIALTY LODGING
SALEM INN
7 Summer St., Salem, 978-741-0680, 800-446-2995;
www.saleminnma.com
With individually appointed rooms and suites, many of which feature Jacuzzis, kitchenettes and fireplaces, this inn provides comfort and luxury without assaulting your wallet. Season packages available. 33 rooms. Complimentary continental breakfast. **$**

RESTAURANTS
★★GRAPE VINE
26 Congress St., Salem, 978-745-9335; www.grapevinesalem.com
American, Italian menu. Dinner. Bar. Outdoor seating. **$$$**

★★★LYCEUM
43 Church St., Salem, 978-745-7665; www.lyceumsalem.com
One of the area's best restaurants, this comfortable dining room is located in the building where Alexander Graham Bell made his first call in 1877. American menu. Lunch, dinner, Sunday brunch. Bar. **$$**

★VICTORIA STATION
86 Wharf St., Salem, 978-745-3400; www.victoriastationinc.com
Seafood, steak menu. Lunch, dinner. Bar. Children's menu. Outdoor seating. **$**

SANDWICH
Sandwich was the first established town on Cape Cod. Today, it's famous for its eponymous glass.
Information: Cape Cod Canal Region Chamber of Commerce, 70 Main St.,
Buzzards Bay, 508-759-6000; www.capecodcanalchamber.org

WHAT TO SEE AND DO
HERITAGE PLANTATION
67 Grove St., Sandwich, 508-888-3300; www.heritageplantation.org
The Heritage Plantation has an eclectic mix of beautiful gardens, folk art, antique cars and military paraphernalia. Highlights include the 1800-era Old East Windmill and a restored 1912 carousel. Call ahead to find out about unique exhibits, displays and concerts. May-October, daily; November-April, Wednesday-Sunday.

HOXIE HOUSE & DEXTER GRISTMILL
Water St., Sandwich, 508-888-1173
These are restored mid-17th-century buildings with an operating mill. Mid-June-mid-October, daily.

SANDWICH GLASS MUSEUM
129 Main St., Sandwich, 508-888-0251;
www.sandwichglassmuseum.org/glass_show
An internationally renowned collection of Sandwich Glass. April-October, daily.

HOTELS

★★★DAN'L WEBSTER INN

149 Main St., Sandwich, 508-888-3622, 800-444-3566; www.danlwebsterinn.com
48 rooms. Restaurant, bar. **$$**

★EARL OF SANDWICH MOTEL

378 Highway, 6A, East Sandwich, 508-888-1415, 800-442-3275;
www.earlofsandwich.com
24 rooms. Complimentary continental breakfast. **$**

★SHADY NOOK INN & MOTEL

14 Old Kings Highway, Sandwich, 508-888-0409, 800-338-5208;
www.shadynookinn.com
30 rooms. **$**

★SPRING HILL MOTOR LODGE

351 Highway 6A, East Sandwich, 508-888-1456, 800-647-2514;
www.springhillmotorlodge.com
24 rooms. **$**

SPECIALTY LODGINGS

THE BELFRY INN & BISTRO

8 Jarves St., Sandwich, 800-844-4542, 800-844-4542; www.belfryinn.com
14 rooms. Children over 10 years only. Complimentary full breakfast. Restaurant. **$$**

ISAIAH JONES HOMESTEAD

165 Main St., Sandwich, 508-888-9115, 800-526-1625; www.isaiahjones.com
An American flag and flower-lined porch adorn the exterior of this 1849 Victorian home. Decorated with antiques and country-patterned fabrics, the guest rooms are an ideal place from which to explore the Cape's many historic sites. Seven rooms. Children over 16 years only. Complimentary full breakfast. **$**

VILLAGE INN

4 Jarves St., Sandwich, 508-833-0363, 800-922-9989; www.capecodinn.com
This Federal-style building was constructed in 1830. Eight rooms. Children over 8 years only. Complimentary full breakfast. **$**

RESTAURANTS

★★AQUA GRILLE

14 Gallo Road, Sandwich, 508-888-8889; www.aquagrille.com
American, seafood menu. Lunch, dinner. Bar. Children's menu. Casual attire. Outdoor seating. Closed November-mid-April. **$$**

★★BEEHIVE TAVERN

406 Highway 6A, Sandwich, 508-833-1184; www.beehivetavern.com
American, seafood menu. Lunch, dinner. Bar. Children's menu. Casual attire. **$$**

MASSACHUSETTS

★
★
★
★
★

★★★THE DAN'L WEBSTER INN

149 Main St., Sandwich, 508-888-3623, 800-444-3566; www.danlwebsterinn.com

A former 1800s stagecoach inn once frequented by its namesake, this hotel offers both a tavern and a white-tablecloth dining room. Chef and co-owner Robert Catania buys some of his fish and hydroponic vegetables from a local aquafarm, and he has built his wine list around his culinary aspirations. American menu. Breakfast, lunch, dinner, Sunday brunch. Bar. Children's menu. Business casual attire. Reservations recommended. Valet parking. **$$**

SPRINGFIELD

Springfield has a fine library, museums and a symphony orchestra, but it's best known for being a serious industrial city on the Connecticut River.

Information: Greater Springfield Convention & Visitors Bureau, 1441 Main St.,
Springfield, 413-787-1548, 800-723-1548; www.myonlinechamber.com

WHAT TO SEE AND DO

BASKETBALL HALL OF FAME

1150 W. Columbus Ave., Springfield, 413-781-6500; www.hoophall.com

This sports spot includes exhibits on the game and its teams and players. Inside the ball-shaped building are free movies, video highlights and life-size action blow-ups of Hall of Famers. Major features include *Hoopla*, a 22-minute film, and *The Spalding Shoot-Out*, which allows visitors to try scoring baskets from a moving sidewalk. Daily.

INDIAN MOTORCYCLE MUSEUM

33 Hendee St., Springfield, 413-737-2624

This was part of the vast complex where Indian motorcycles were made until 1953. On display are historic bikes, an early snowmobile, and a 1928 roadster. Daily.

SPRINGFIELD ARMORY NATIONAL HISTORIC SITE

1 Armory Square, Springfield, 413-734-8551; www.nps.gov/spar

The old U.S. armory contains one of the largest collections of military small arms in the world. Exhibits include the "Organ of Guns," made famous by Longfellow's poem "The Arsenal at Springfield." Tuesday-Saturday.

SPRINGFIELD MUSEUMS AT THE QUADRANGLE

220 State St., Springfield, 413-263-6800; www.springfieldmuseums.org

The site includes four museums and a library. The **George Walter Vincent Smith Art Museum** houses a collection of Asian armor, arms, jade, bronzes and rugs. The **Connecticut River Valley Historical Museum** includes genealogy and a local history library. The **Museum of Fine Arts** has 20 galleries and an outstanding collection of American and European works. The **Science Museum** has an exploration center, early aviation exhibit, aquarium, planetarium, African hall and dinosaur hall. All buildings Wednesday-Sunday.

STORROWTON VILLAGE

Eastern States Exposition, 1305 Memorial Ave., West Springfield, 413-205-5051;
www.thebige.com/village/storrowton_village.html

This group of restored Early American buildings includes a meeting house, schoolhouse, and blacksmith shop. June-August, Tuesday-Saturday; rest of year, by appointment.

★
★
★
★
★

SPECIAL EVENT

EASTERN STATES EXPOSITION (THE BIG E)

1305 Memorial Ave., West Springfield, 413-737-2443;
www.thebige.com

The largest fair in the Northeast has entertainment, exhibits, an historic Avenue of States, Storrowton Village, a horse show, agricultural events and a "Better Living Center" exhibit. September.

HOTELS

★HAMPTON INN

1011 Riverdale St., West Springfield, 413-732-1300, 800-426-7866;
www.hamptoninn.com

125 rooms. Complimentary continental breakfast. Fitness room. Pool. Business center. High-speed Internet access. Pets accepted. **$**

★★HOLIDAY INN DOWNTOWN

711 Dwight St., Springfield, 413-781-0900, 888-465-4329;
www.holiday-inn.com

242 rooms. Wireless Internet access. Restaurant, bar. Pets accepted, fee. Indoor pool. Fitness center. **$**

★★★MARRIOTT SPRINGFIELD

1500 Main St., Springfield, 413-781-7111, 800-228-9290;
www.marriott.com

At the Marriot Springfield, it's all about the beds. With extra-thick mattresses, duvets, bed skirts and plush pillows, the sweet sleep spots are reason enough to book a room here. Rooms also come with flatscreen TVs and polished granite bathrooms. The hotel is connected via enclosed walkway to a mall and complex with restaurants, art galleries, an African-American history museum and a billiards parlor. 265 rooms. Wireless Internet access. Two restaurants, bar. **$$**

★★★SHERATON SPRINGFIELD MONARCH PLACE HOTEL

1 Monarch Place, Springfield, 413-781-1010; www.sheraton-springfield.com

Guest rooms in this contemporary, urban spot surround a 12-story atrium, and the public areas feature local touches such as a folk art mural of Springfield's historical highlights. The Sheraton's Athletic Club is the largest hotel health club west of Boston, and hotel spa services include everything from tanning to massages to manicures. Business travelers should ask for a smart room, which comes with a photocopier and fax machine. 325 rooms. Wireless Internet access. Two restaurants, bar. High-speed Internet access by request (charge). **$$**

RESTAURANT

★★STUDENT PRINCE & FORT

8 Fort St., Springfield, 413-788-6628; www.studentprince.com

German menu. Lunch, dinner. Bar. Casual attire. Reservations recommended. Valet parking. **$$**

STOCKBRIDGE

Stockbridge's main drag was made forever famous by small-town life chronicler Norman Rockwell. The fact that the town still looks much as it appeared in his drawings continuously delights tourists, who crowd the area's shops and eateries in the summertime. West Stockbridge, by contrast, is a completely restored market village. Its own Main Street is lined with renovated, well-kept storefronts.

Information: Stockbridge Chamber of Commerce, 6 Elm St., Stockbridge, 413-298-5200; www.stockbridgechamber.org

WHAT TO SEE AND DO
BERKSHIRE BOTANICAL GARDEN
Highways 102 and 183, Stockbridge, 413-298-3926; www.berkshirebotanical.org

This 15-acre botanical garden has perennials, shrubs, trees, antique roses, ponds, a wildflower exhibit, vegetable gardens and demonstration greenhouses. Garden shop; special events, lectures; picnicking. May-October, daily.

CHESTERWOOD
284 Main St., Stockbridge, 413-298-3579; www.chesterwood.org

This was the grand early 20th-century summer residence and studio of Daniel Chester French, sculptor of the *Minute Man* statue in Concord and the Lincoln Memorial in Washington, D.C. May-October, daily.

MISSION HOUSE
1 Sergeant St., Stockbridge, 413-298-3239;
www.thetrustees.org/pages/324_mission_house.cfm

The house built in 1739 for the missionary Reverend John Sergeant and his wife, Abigail Williams, is now a museum of colonial life. Memorial Day weekend-Columbus Day weekend, daily.

NAUMKEAG
1 Seargeant St., Stockbridge, 413-298-3239;
www.thetrustees.org/pages/335_naumkeag.cfm

Stanford White designed this Norman-style "Berkshire cottage" in 1886. The interior has antiques, Oriental rugs and a collection of Chinese export porcelain. The gardens include terraces of tree peonies, fountains and a birch walk. Memorial Day weekend-Columbus weekend, daily.

NORMAN ROCKWELL MUSEUM
9 Glendale Road, Stockbridge, 413-298-4100; www.nrm.org

His eponymous museum maintains and exhibits the nation's largest collection of original art by Norman Rockwell. Daily.

HOTELS
★★★THE RED LION INN
30 Main St., Stockbridge, 413-298-5545; www.redlioninn.com

Along with the street it sits on, the Red Lion Inn was immortalized by Norman Rockwell in his hearty, happy Stockbridge street scenes. Its guest rooms are well-appointed, though a bit snug. For roomier digs, book one of the inn's off-site suites, which are

★
★
★
★
★

sprinkled among a handful of buildings throughout town, such as the former studio of artist Daniel Chester French and the former home of the Stockbridge Volunteer Fire Department. 100 rooms. Two restaurants, bar. $$

★★★WILLIAMSVILLE INN
Highway 41, West Stockbridge, 413-274-6118;
www.williamsvilleinn.com
Run by a German husband-and-wife team, the Williamsville Inn is a cross between Shaker austerity and three-star comfort. Its blond-wood floors are spotless, as are its white bed linens and bath towels. Fresh flowers lightly scent each room, and guests can walk through the property's extensive gardens. 16 rooms. Complimentary full breakfast. Restaurant, bar. $

SPECIALTY LODGINGS
INN AT STOCKBRIDGE
Highway 7 N., Stockbridge, 413-298-3337; www.stockbridgeinn.com
An in-room decanter of port. Breakfast in a formal dining room. A large parlor with fireside chairs. A stroll through 12 secluded acres. Sound appealing? This 1906 Georgian-style inn has just eight guest rooms, allowing each visitor to savor the amenities. The Cottage House, added in 1997, has four junior suites. The Barn, built in 2001, provides four deluxe suites. 16 rooms. Children over 12 years only. Complimentary full breakfast. Fitness, spa. $$$

THE TAGGART HOUSE
18 W. Main St., Stockbridge, 413-298-4303, 800-918-2680;
www.taggarthouse.com
This lovingly restored 1800s country house fronts the Housatonic River. It is luxurious and intimate, and replete with fine antiques. Four rooms. Children not accepted. Complimentary full breakfast. $$$

RESTAURANTS
★MICHAEL'S RESTAURANT & PUB
5 Elm St., Stockbridge, 413-298-3530; www.michaelsofstockbridge.com
American, Italian menu. Lunch, dinner, late-night. Bar. Children's menu. Casual attire. Reservations recommended. $$

★★★THE RED LION
30 Main St., Stockbridge, 413-298-5545; www.redlioninn.com
This inn's candlelit dining room is filled with antiques, colonial pewter and crystal. The contemporary New England menu emphasizes local, seasonal produce and offers several vegetarian options. American menu. Lunch, dinner. Bar. Children's menu. Business casual attire. Reservations recommended. Outdoor seating. $$$

★★★WILLIAMSVILLE INN
Highway 41, West Stockbridge, 413-274-6118; www.williamsvilleinn.com
This cozy dining room has an open fireplace and plenty of candlelight. But what's really special about the German eatery is its open kitchen—guests can watch chef/owner Erhard Wendt at work in his yellow-walled space (he often invites diners back

239

MASSACHUSETTS

★
★
★
★

for a closer look). The food is rich and savory—don't pass up any of the desserts. French, German menu. Dinner, brunch. Bar. Casual attire. Reservations recommended. Outdoor seating. $$$

SUDBURY

This leafy northwestern Boston suburb was founded in 1638.

Information: Board of Selectmen, Loring Parsonage, 288 Old Sudbury Road, Sudbury, 978-443-8891; www.sudbury.org.uk

WHAT TO SEE AND DO

MARTHA MARY CHAPEL

72 Wayside Inn Road, Sudbury Center, 978-443-1776; www.sudburyjp.com/WMarthaMary.htm

Built and dedicated by Henry Ford in 1940, this was a nondenominational, nonsectarian chapel. It's now used primarily for weddings. By appointment.

HOTELS

★★BEST WESTERN ROYAL PLAZA HOTEL & TRADE CENTER

181 W. Boston Post Road, Marlborough, 508-460-0700, 888-543-9500; www.bestwestern.com

431 rooms. Restaurant, bar. Complimentary full breakfast. Heated indoor pool. Exercise facility. High-speed Internet access. Pets accepted. $$

★CLARION HOTEL

738 Boston Post Road, Sudbury, 978-443-2223, 800-637-0113; www.clarionhotel.com

37 rooms. Complimentary full breakfast. Free wireless Internet. Free hot breakfast buffet. Business center. Fitness center. Pets accepted. $$

★★RADISSON HOTEL MARLBOROUGH

75 Felton St., Marlborough, 508-480-0015, 800-333-3333; www.radisson.com
206 rooms. Restaurant, bar. $

SPECIALTY LODGINGS

THE ARABIAN HORSE INN

277 Old Sudbury Road, Sudbury, 978-443-7400, 800-272-2426; www.arabianhorseinn.com
Five rooms. Complimentary full breakfast. $$

LONGFELLOWS WAYSIDE INN

72 Wayside Inn Road, Sudbury, 978-443-1776, 800-339-1776; www.wayside.org

A literary shrine, this is America's oldest operating inn. Originally restored by Henry Ford, it was badly damaged by fire in December 1955 and restored again by the Ford Foundation. It's now a national historic site. On its grounds are the Wayside Gristmill and Redstone School. 10 rooms. Complimentary full breakfast. Restaurant, bar. $

★★LONGFELLOW'S WAYSIDE INN
72 Wayside Inn Road, Sudbury Center, 978-443-1776;
www.wayside.org
Seafood, steak menu. Lunch, dinner. Bar. Children's menu. **$$**

TRURO & NORTH TRURO
Truro is perhaps the most sparsely settled part of Cape Cod, with great stretches of rolling moorland dotted only occasionally by small cottages. On the hill above the Pamet River marsh are two early 19th-century churches—one is the town hall. The surrounding countryside is popular with artists and writers.
Information: Cape Cod Chamber of Commerce, Highways 6 and 132,
Hyannis, 508-362-3225, 888-227-3263; www.capecodchamber.org

WHAT TO SEE AND DO
HIGHLAND LIGHT/CAPE COD LIGHT
Highland Light Road, North Truro, 508-487-1121; www.lighthouse.cc/highland
This was the first lighthouse on Cape Cod. Built in 1798 and fueled with whale oil, it was rebuilt in 1853 and switched to an automated facility in 1986. It now shines for 30 miles, the longest visible range of any lighthouse on the Cape. Thoreau once stayed here. The museum next door, housed in a historic building, is open from June-September and highlights the area's fishing and whaling heritage. May-late October, daily.

TRURO HISTORICAL SOCIETY MUSEUM
6 Highland Road, North Truro, 508-487-3397; www.trurohistorical.org
The collection of artifacts from the town's past include shipwreck mementos, whaling gear, ship models, 17th-century firearms, a pirate chest and period rooms. June-September, Monday-Saturday 10 a.m.-4:30 p.m., Sunday from 1 p.m.

HOTEL
★CROW'S NEST RESORT
496 Shore Road, North Truro, 508-487-9031, 800-499-9799;
www.caperesort.com
33 rooms. Closed December-March. Beach. **$**

RESTAURANTS
★ADRIAN'S
535 Highway 6, North Truro, 508-487-4360; www.adriansrestaurant.com
Italian menu. Breakfast, dinner. Bar. Children's menu. Outdoor seating. Closed mid-October-mid-May. **$$**

★★MONTANO'S
481 Highway 6, North Truro, 508-487-2026; www.montanos.com
Italian, seafood menu. Dinner. Bar. Children's menu. Casual attire. **$$**

241

MASSACHUSETTS

★
★
★
★
★

WALTHAM

The name Waltham, taken from the English town of Waltham Abbey, means "a home in the forest." Indeed, this Boston suburb is based in a wooded area, but it's not completely countrified. The town is a mix of McMansions, industry and academia—Bentley, Brandeis and Regis colleges are based here.

Information: Waltham West Suburban Chamber of Commerce, 84 South St.,
Waltham, 781-894-4700; www.walthamchamber.com

WHAT TO SEE AND DO

BRANDEIS UNIVERSITY

415 South St., Waltham, 781-736-2000; www.brandeis.edu
(1948) This was the first Jewish-founded nonsectarian university in the United States. Its 250-acre campus includes Three Chapels, the Rose Art Museum (September-May, Tuesday-Sunday), the Spingold Theater Arts Center (plays presented October-May) and the Slosberg Music Center (September-May).

GORE PLACE

52 Gore St., Waltham, 781-894-2798; www.goreplace.org
A living history farm, Gore Place has changing exhibits and 40 acres of cultivated fields. The mansion, designed in Paris and built in 1805, has 22 rooms filled with examples of Early American, European and Asian antiques. Mid-April-mid-November: Thursday-Monday hourly tours 1-4 p.m.

LYMAN ESTATE

185 Lyman St., Waltham, 781-893-7232;
www.waltham-community.org/Lyman.html
Designed in 1793 by Samuel McIntire for Boston merchant Theodore Lyman, this home was enlarged and remodeled in the 1880s. Its five operating greenhouses contain grape vines, camellias, orchids and herbs. The house is open by appointment for groups only. Monday-Saturday, also Sunday afternoons.

HOTELS

★★DOUBLETREE HOTEL

550 Winter St., Waltham, 781-890-6767, 800-222-8733; www.doubletree.com
275 rooms, all suites. Restaurant, bar. Business center. High-speed Internet access. Pool. Pets not accepted. $

★★HOME SUITES INN

455 Totten Pond Road, Waltham, 781-890-3000, 866-335-6175;
www.homesuitesinn.com
116 rooms, all suites. Complimentary continental breakfast. Restaurant, bar. Free High-speed Internet access. Pets accepted. $

★★★THE WESTIN WALTHAM-BOSTON

70 Third Ave., Waltham, 781-290-5600, 800-228-3000; www.westin.com
Just 15 minutes from downtown Boston, this modern hotel has rooms geared toward the business traveler. 346 rooms. Restaurant, bar. Airport transportation available. High-speed Internet access in all guest rooms (charge). $$

RESTAURANTS
★★★GRILLE AT HOBBS BROOK
550 Winter St., Waltham, 781-487-4263; www.grilleathobbsbrook.com
Many of the Grille's menu ingredients come from its onsite garden. The plush setting is a quiet, relaxing place to dine. American menu. Breakfast, lunch, dinner. Bar. Children's menu. $$$

★★★IL CAPRICCIO
888 Main St., Waltham, 781-894-2234; www.ilcappricciowaltham.com
Gauzy drapes and glass partitions give this innovative restaurant a chic, urban look. Italian menu. Dinner. Bar. Closed Sunday. $$$

★★TUSCAN GRILL
361 Moody St., Waltham, 781-891-5486; www.tuscangrillwaltham.com
Italian menu. Dinner. Bar. $$

WELLFLEET
Once a fishing town, Wellfleet dominated the New England oyster business in the latter part of the 19th century. It is now a summer resort and an art gallery town, and there's still plenty of oysters.
Information: Chamber of Commerce, Wellfleet, 508-349-2510;
www.wellfleetchamber.com

WHAT TO SEE AND DO
HISTORICAL SOCIETY MUSEUM
266 Main St., Wellfleet, 508-349-9157;
www.wellfleethistoricalsociety.com
Marine items, whaling tools, Marconi memorabilia, needlecraft, photograph collection, marine and primitive paintings are on display here. Late June-early September, Tuesday-Saturday; schedule may vary.

WELLFLEET BAY WILDLIFE SANCTUARY
291 Highway 6, South Wellfleet, 508-349-2615; www.wellfleetbay.org
Operated by the Massachusetts Audubon Society, the sanctuary has self-guiding nature trails and a natural history summer day camp for children. Memorial Day-Columbus Day, daily; rest of year, Tuesday-Sunday.

WELLFLEET DRIVE-IN THEATER
Highway 6, Wellfleet, 508-349-7176; www.wellfleetdrivein.com
This is the only outdoor theater on the Cape. It projects a family-oriented double feature every evening under the stars. Mid-October-mid-April.

HOTEL
★★WELLFLEET MOTEL & LODGE
146 Highway 6, South Wellfleet, 508-349-3535, 800-852-2900;
www.wellfleetmotel.com
65 rooms. Restaurant, bar. $

MASSACHUSETTS

★
★
★
★
★

SPECIALTY LODGING
INN AT DUCK CREEK
70 Main St., Wellfleet, 508-349-9333; www.innatduckcreeke.com
25 rooms. Complimentary continental breakfast. Closed November-April. **$**

RESTAURANTS
★MOBY DICK'S
Highway 6, Wellfleet, 508-349-9795; www.mobydicksrestaurant.com
Seafood menu. Lunch, dinner. Children's menu. Casual attire. Outdoor seating. Closed mid-October-April. **$$**

★★VAN RENSSELAER'S RESTAURANT & RAW BAR
1019 Highway 6, South Wellfleet, 508-349-2127;
www.vanrensselaers.com
American, seafood menu. Breakfast, dinner. Bar. Children's menu. Casual attire. Outdoor seating. Closed late October-early April. **$$**

WILLIAMSTOWN
Most things in this Northern Berkshires town are centered around Williams College, one of the best-known liberal arts school in the country. The very quiet, very remote hamlet is a perfect setting for a school campus, and a drive through the area reveals myriad playing fields and students shuffling to class.

WHAT TO SEE AND DO
STERLING AND FRANCINE CLARK ART INSTITUTE
225 South St., Williamstown, 413-458-2303; www.clarkart.edu
This museum houses more than 30 paintings by Renoir and other French Impressionists, as well as English and American silver and works by American artists like Homer, Sargent, Cassatt and Remington. July-Labor Day, daily; rest of year, Tuesday-Sunday.

WILLIAMS COLLEGE
54 Sawyer Library Drive, Williamstown, 413-597-3131;
www.williams.edu
This private liberal arts college has a student body of 1,950 and an idyllic campus. Its Chapin Library of rare books is one of the nation's finest and houses the four founding documents of the United States. The Hopkins Observatory has planetarium shows and the Adams Memorial Theater presents plays.

WILLIAMS COLLEGE MUSEUM OF ART
15 Lawrence Hall Drive, Williamstown, 413-597-2429;
www.wcma.org
This spot is considered one of the finest college art museums in the country; it houses approximately 11,000 pieces. Tuesday-Saturday 10 a.m.-5 p.m., Sunday from 1 p.m. and Monday holidays.

HOTELS

★★★1896 HOUSE

910 Cold Spring Road, Williamstown, 413-458-1896, 888-999-1896;
www.1896house.com

Among other options, guests can choose to stay in a brook or pondside room at this old inn. The Brookside suite, hidden from the road by trees, features Cushman rock maple furniture, luxurious amenities and a beautiful gazebo. The Pondside room has slightly fewer frills. 29 rooms. Complimentary continental breakfast. Restaurant. **$**

★BERKSHIRE HILLS MOTEL

1146 Cold Spring Road, Williamstown, 413-458-3950, 800-388-9677;
www.berkshirehillsmotel.com

21 rooms. Complimentary buffet breakfast. **$**

★FOUR ACRES MOTEL

213 Main St., Williamstown, 413-458-8158;
www.fouracresmotel.com

31 rooms. Complimentary continental breakfast. **$**

★★★THE ORCHARDS

222 Adams Road, Williamstown, 413-458-9611, 800-225-1517;
www.orchardshotel.com

Grand gates of Vermont granite lead into this European chateau-style property just east of the village center. With bay windows and marble-floored baths, the rooms are reminiscent of those in an English countryside. Public spaces are plush with Oriental rugs and Austrian crystal chandeliers. The onsite restaurant serves a mix of continental and American cuisine; visitors can dine outdoors in the garden during summer months. 49 rooms. Wireless Internet access. Restaurant, bar. **$$**

★★★WILLIAMS INN

Highways 7 and 2, Williamstown, 413-458-9371, 800-828-0133; www.williamsinn.com

Because it's located on the college campus, the Williams Inn often hosts parents and families of students, as well as visiting professors and lecturers. The staff is friendly and creates an at-home feel, and the spot's live entertainment—from jazz to acoustic guitar to cabaret—is a community favorite. 125 rooms. High-speed Internet access. Restaurant, bar. **$$**

RESTAURANTS

★★★GALA RESTAURANT & BAR

222 Adams Road, Williamstown, 413-458-9611, 800-225-1517;
www.galarestaurant.com

Gold and red brocade chairs and white tablecloths dress the room's interior at Gala, in the Orchards hotel. The bar area has fireside couches and walls adorned with large nature photographs. The chef incorporates high-quality local ingredients in the classic American dishes, which include apple and cheddar-stuffed pork chop, merlot-braised New Zealand lamb shank and seared Atlantic salmon. A wine cellar with a tasting room is used for chef's tables and private functions. American menu. Breakfast, lunch, dinner, Sunday brunch. Bar. Casual attire. Reservations recommended. Outdoor seating. **$$**

★★JAE'S INN

777 Cold Spring Road, Williamstown, 413-458-8032;
www.jaesinn.com

Korean menu. Lunch, dinner. Bar. Children's menu. Casual attire. Reservations recommended. Outdoor seating. **$$**

★★WATER STREET GRILL

123 Water St., Williamstown, 413-458-2175

American menu. Lunch, dinner. Bar. Children's menu. Casual attire. **$$**

WORCESTER

One of the largest cities in New England, Worcester is an important industrial center. It's also another academic powerhouse—within city limits are 12 colleges.
Information: Worcester County Convention & Visitors Bureau, 30 Worcester
Center Blvd., Worcester, 508-753-2920; www.worcester.org

WHAT TO SEE AND DO

AMERICAN ANTIQUARIAN SOCIETY

185 Salisbury St., Worcester, 508-755-5221;
www.americanantiquarian.org

This research library has the largest collection of source materials pertaining to the first 250 years of American history. Monday-Friday; Guided tours Wednesday afternoons.

ECOTARIUM

222 Harrington Way, Worcester, 508-929-2700; www.ecotarium.org

This museum has environmental science exhibits, a solar/lunar observatory, a multimedia planetarium theater and an African Hall. Tuesday-Saturday 10 a.m.-5 p.m., Sunday from noon.

JOHN H. CHAFFY BLACKSTONE RIVER VALLEY NATIONAL HERITAGE CORRIDOR

414 Massasoit Road, Worcester, 508-755-8899; www.nps.gov/blac

This 250,000-acre region extends southward to Providence, Rhode Island and includes many points of historical and cultural interest.

SALISBURY MANSION

40 Highland St., Worcester, 508-753-8278;
www.worcesterhistory.org/mansion.html

This was the house of leading businessman and philanthropist Stephen Salisbury.

WORCESTER ART MUSEUM

55 Salisbury St., Worcester, 508-799-4406;
www.worcesterart.org

Fifty centuries of paintings, sculpture, decorative arts, prints, drawings and photography from America to ancient Egypt are on display here. Wednesday-Sunday.

★
★
★
★
☆

HOTELS

★★★BEECHWOOD HOTEL
363 Plantation St., Worcester, 508-754-5789, 800-344-2589;
www.beechwoodhotel.com
The hotel has a 24-hour fitness room and business center which makes it ideal for business travelers. A polished foyer with marble floors, a small fireside seating area, and antique, stained-glass windows spice up the lobby. 73 rooms, Wireless Internet access. Restaurant, bar. $$

★★★CROWNE PLAZA HOTEL
10 Lincoln Square, Worcester, 508-791-1600, 877-227-6963;
www.cpworcester.com
The Crowne Plaza is modern and close to shopping malls and the booksellers' marketplace and within 10 minutes of most area businesses. It also has a large indoor/outdoor pool and a courtyard landscaped with holly and flowering fruit trees. Ask for a room with a balcony, where you can enjoy morning coffee and a view of Lincoln Square. 243 rooms. Wireless Internet access. Restaurant, bar. $

RESTAURANT

★★★CASTLE
1230 Main St., Leicester, 508-892-9090; www.castlerestaurant.com
Owned and operated by the Nicas family since 1950, this "castle," complete with turrets, towers and a moat, always provides a unique dining experience. Choose from one of the two distinctly different dining rooms, the Crusader or the Camelot; each has its own creative menu. French menu. Lunch, dinner. Closed Monday. Bar. Children's menu. Outdoor seating. $$$

YARMOUTH

Much of the Yarmouth area was developed on the strength of its 19th-century seafaring and fishing industries. Well-preserved houses line Main Street, where well-preserved locals shop and stroll.
Information: Yarmouth Area Chamber of Commerce, Yarmouth,
800-732-1008; www.capecodchamber.org

WHAT TO SEE AND DO

CAPE SYMPHONY ORCHESTRA
712A Main St., Yarmouth Port, 508-362-1111;
www.capesymphony.org
This 90-member professional orchestra performs 15 indoor concerts throughout the year at Barnstable High School's 1,400-seat auditorium. Selections range from classical to pops to special children's events. September-May; also two concerts in summer.

HISTORIC NEW ENGLAND
250 Highway 6A, South Yarmouth, 617-227-3957
This is a Georgian house adorned with 17th-, 18th- and 19th-century furnishings collected in the early 20th century. June-October, first Saturday of the month.

HOTELS

★ALL SEASON MOTOR INN

1199 Main St., South Yarmouth, 508-394-7600, 800-527-0359;
www.allseasons.com
114 rooms. Restaurant. $

★★BEST WESTERN BLUE WATER ON THE OCEAN

291 S. Shore Drive, South Yarmouth, 508-398-2288, 800-367-9393;
www.bestwestern.com
106 rooms. Restaurant, bar. Children's activity center. Beach. Free parking. Heated indoor pool. Heated outdoor pool. Spa. High-speed Internet access. $$

★★BLUE ROCK RESORT

39 Todd Road, South Yarmouth, 508-398-6962, 800-780-7234;
www.redjacketresorts.com
44 rooms. Restaurant, bar. Closed late-October-March. $

★GULL WING SUITES

822 Main St., South Yarmouth, 508-394-9300, 877-984-9300; www.gullwinghotel.com
136 rooms. $

★★★LIBERTY HILL INN

77 Main St., Yarmouth Port, 508-362-3976, 800-821-3977;
www.libertyhillinn.com
The stately, whitewashed building that houses this charming inn was built in 1825. Rooms have antique furniture and oriental rugs and some bathrooms have original clawfoot tubs. Nine rooms. Complimentary full breakfast. Airport transportation available. $

★★RED JACKET BEACH

1 S. Shore Drive, South Yarmouth, 508-398-6941, 800-672-0500;
www.redjacketbeach.com
150 rooms. Restaurant, bar. Children's activity center. Closed late October-March. $$

★★RIVIERA BEACH RESORT

327 S. Shore Drive, South Yarmouth, 508-398-2273, 800-227-3263;
www.rivieraresort.com
125 rooms. Restaurant, bar. Children's activity center. Beach. Closed November-March. $$

SPECIALTY LODGINGS

CAPTAIN FARRIS HOUSE BED AND BREAKFAST

308 Old Main St., South Yarmouth, 508-760-2818, 800-350-9477;
www.captainfarris.com
This bed and breakfast has beautifully landscaped lawns and breathtaking views. Guests can take advantage of nearby sailing, canoeing, kayaking and windsurfing. Antique shopping, bird-watching and the John F. Kennedy Museum are also nearby. 10 rooms. Children over 10 years only. Complimentary full breakfast. Restaurant. Whirlpool. $

COLONIAL HOUSE INN & RESTAURANT

277 Main St., Yarmouth Port, 508-362-4348, 800-999-3416;
www.colonialhousecapecod.com

21 rooms. Complimentary full breakfast. Restaurant, bar. **$**

INN AT LEWIS BAY

57 Maine Ave., West Yarmouth, 508-771-3433, 800-962-6679;
www.innatlewisbay.com

Located in a quiet seaside neighborhood just one block from Lewis Bay, this Dutch colonial bed and breakfast serves a bountiful meal each morning and refreshments each afternoon. Six rooms. Children over 12 years only. Complimentary full breakfast. **$**

RESTAURANTS

★★ABBICCI

43 Main St., Yarmouth Port, 508-362-3501; www.abbicci.com

Mediterranean menu. Lunch, dinner. Bar. Business casual attire. Reservations recommended. **$$**

★★ARDEO

23V Whites Path, South Yarmouth, 508-760-1500; www.ardeocapecod.com

Mediterranean menu. Lunch, dinner. Bar. Children's menu. Casual attire. **$$**

★★INAHO

157 Route 6A Yarmouth Port, 508-362-5522

Japanese, sushi menu. Dinner. Casual attire. **$$**

★★RIVERWAY LOBSTER HOUSE

1338 Route 28, South Yarmouth, 508-398-2172; www.riverwaylobsterhouse.com

American menu. Dinner. Bar. Children's menu. Casual attire. Reservations recommended. Closed Monday in January-April. **$$**

★★SKIPPER RESTAURANT

152 S. Shore Drive, South Yarmouth, 508-394-7406; www.skipper-restaurant.com

Seafood menu. Lunch, dinner. Bar. Children's menu. Casual attire. Outdoor seating. Closed mid-October-mid-April. **$$**

★★YARMOUTH HOUSE

335 Main St., West Yarmouth, 508-771-5154; www.yarmouthhouse.com

Seafood, steak menu. Lunch, dinner. Bar. Children's menu. Casual attire. Reservations recommended. **$$**

NEW HAMPSHIRE

NEW HAMPSHIRE'S MOTTO, AS PROUDLY PROCLAIMED ON ITS LICENSE PLATES, IS "LIVE FREE or Die", a reference to the state's revolutionary spirit. Some from the surrounding states like to tease that the motto should be "Live Free *and* Die" because the granite state has markedly fewer laws restricting personal freedoms than any other state, from no helmet laws for motorcyclists over 18 to no seatbelts laws for car drivers and passengers over 18. But this atmosphere of free living is what is attracting more and more newcomers to New Hampshire, who come here for the low taxes and beautiful mountain scenery.

New Hampshire is famous for the important role it plays in national politics. The state traditionally holds the first presidential primary in the country, placing the laser focus of the media on its many small towns, their inhabitants and their voting habits.

The mountains in New Hampshire are known for their rugged "notches" (called "gaps" and "passes" elsewhere) and the old valley towns offer a serene beauty. Some of the best skiing in the East is available at several major resorts here. The state's many parks, antique shops, art and theater festivals and county fairs are also popular attractions, and more than half of New England's covered bridges are in New Hampshire.

In 1623, David Thomson and a small group of colonists settled on the New Hampshire coast near Portsmouth. These early settlements were part of Massachusetts. In 1679, they became a separate royal province under Charles the Second. In 1776, the Provincial Congress adopted a constitution making New Hampshire the first independent colony, seven months before the Declaration of Independence was signed. Although New Hampshire was the only one of the 13 original states not invaded by the British during the Revolution, its men fought long and hard on land and sea to bring about the victory. This strong, involved attitude continues in New Hampshire to this day.

FUN FACTS

Tupperware was invented in Berlin, New Hampshire in 1938.

The oldest ski club in America was formed by a group of Scandinavians in Berlin in 1882.

The first U.S. public library was opened in Peterborough in 1837.

Open since 1789, the John Hancock Inn in Hancock is the oldest operating tavern in New England.

BARTLETT

Bartlett is home to Attitash ski resort, popular in the area for its focus on snowboarding.
Information: Mount Washington Valley Chamber of Commerce, North Main Street, North Conway, 603-356-5701; www.mtwashingtonvalley.org

WHAT TO SEE AND DO
ATTITASH BEAR PEAK SKI RESORT
Highway 302, Bartlett, New Hampshire, 603-374-2368; www.attitash.com
Two high-speed quad, three quad, three triple, three double chairlifts; three surface lifts; patrol, school, rentals; snowmaking; nursery; cafeteria; bar. Longest run 1¾ mile;

vertical drop 1,750 feet. Mid-November-late April: daily. Summer recreation: Alpine slide, waterslides, scenic chairlift, horseback riding, mountain biking, hiking, driving range mid-June-Labor Day: daily; Memorial Day-mid-June and early September-mid-October:weekends; fees.

HOTEL
★★ATTITASH GRAND SUMMIT RESORT AND CONFERENCE CENTER
Highway 302, Bartlett, 603-374-1900, 800-862-1600; www.attitashmtvillage.com
350 rooms. Restaurant, bar. Indoor pool, two outdoor pools, whirlpool. Tennis. Ski-in/ski-out. $

BRETTON WOODS
Bretton Woods is located in the White Mountains on a long glacial plain next to Mount Washington and the Presidential Range. Mount Washington was first sighted in 1497; however, settlement around it did not begin until 1771 when the Crawford Notch, which opened the way through the mountains, was discovered. In the 1770s, Governor Wentworth named the area Bretton Woods for his ancestral home in England. This historic name was set aside in 1832 when all the tiny settlements in the area were incorporated under the name of Carroll. For a time, a railroad through the notch brought as many as 57 trains a day and the area grew as a resort spot. A string of hotels sprang up, each more elegant and fashionable than the last. In 1903, the post office, railroad station and express office reverted to the traditional name—Bretton Woods. Today, Bretton Woods is a resort area at the base of the mountain.

WHAT TO SEE AND DO
BRETTON WOODS SKI AREA
Highway 302, Bretton Woods, 603-278-1000; www.brettonwoods.com
Two high-speed quad, triple, two double chairlifts, three surface lifts; patrol, school, rentals, snowmaking; restaurant, cafeteria, bar; child care; lodge. Longest run two miles; vertical drop 1,500 feet. Thanksgiving-April: daily. Night skiing early December-March: Friday-Saturday. 48 miles of cross-country trails.

CRAWFORD NOTCH STATE PARK
Highway 302, Bretton Woods, 603-374-2272; www.nhstateparks.com
One of the state's most spectacular passes. Mounts Nancy and Willey rise to the west; Mounts Crawford, Webster and Jackson to the east. Park headquarters is at the former site of the Samuel Willey house. The family of six and two hired men died in a landslide in 1826 when they rushed out of their house, which was left untouched. Fishing, trout-feeding pond. Hiking, walking trails on the Appalachian system. Picnicking, concession. Camping. Interpretive center. Late-May-mid-October.

HOTEL
★★★MOUNT WASHINGTON HOTEL
Highway 302, Bretton Woods, 603-278-1000, 800-258-0330; www.mtwashington.com
This landmark hotel is a true retreat in every way. Enjoy golfing, horseback riding and bicycle riding during the day and live music, fine dining and dancing at night to live jazz or big band tunes. 200 rooms. Two restaurants, five bars. Children's activity center. Fitness room. Indoor pool, outdoor pool. Golf, 27 holes. Tennis. Business center. $$$

★
★
★
★
★

RESTAURANT
★FABYAN'S STATION
Highway 302, Bretton Woods, 603-278-2222; www.mtwashington.com
American menu. Lunch, dinner. Bar. Children's menu. Casual attire. **$$**

CONCORD

New Hampshire, one of the original 13 colonies, entered the Union in 1788, but its capital was in dispute for another 20 years. Concord finally won the honor in 1808. Building began for the state house immediately and finally finished in 1819. The legislature is the largest (more than 400 seats) of any state. Concord is the financial center of the state and offers a diverse range of industry as well.

Information: Chamber of Commerce, 40 Commercial St., 603-224-2508;
www.concordnhchamber.com

WHAT TO SEE AND DO
CANTERBURY SHAKER VILLAGE
288 Shaker Road, Canterbury, 603-783-9511; www.shakers.org
Pay homage to New Hampshire's Shaker heritage with a visit to this National Historic Landmark museum, which offers guided and self-guided tours and a variety of exhibits. Mid-May-late-October: daily 10 a.m.-5 p.m.; November-December: Saturday-Sunday 10 a.m.-4 p.m.

CHRISTA MCAULIFFE PLANETARIUM
2 Institute Drive, Concord, 603-271-7831; www.starhop.com
This living memorial to New Hampshire teacher Christa McAuliffe, who died aboard the U.S. space shuttle *Challenger* on January 28, 1986, offers a variety of shows designed for all ages in a 92-seat theater. Some shows are aimed at the very young while others boast 3-D computer graphic effects that are likely to impress all ages. Daily; call or visit Web site for show schedule.

GRANITE STATE CANDY SHOPPE
9-17 Warren St., Concord, 603-225-2591, 888-225-2531; www.nhchocolates.com
Founded in 1927 by a Greek immigrant, Granite State Candy Shoppe is an old-fashioned candy store with the motto, "We're in the happiness business." The candy shoppe is now owned by the founder's grandchildren, who still use many of his original copper kettles and dip each chocolate one by one.

MUSEUM OF NEW HAMPSHIRE HISTORY
6 Eagle Square, Concord, 603-228-6688; www.nhhistory.org
Historical museum (founded 1823) with permanent and changing exhibits, including examples of the famed Concord Coach; museum store. July 1-October 15 and December, Tuesday-Saturday 9:30 a.m.-5 p.m., Sunday noon-5 p.m.

PIERCE MANSE
14 Penacook St., Concord, 603-225-4555
Home of President Franklin Pierce from 1842 to 1848. Reconstructed and moved to the present site; contains many original furnishings and period pieces. Mid-June-mid-October Tuesday-Saturday 11 a.m.-3 p.m.; also by appointment.

STATE HOUSE

107 N. Main St., Concord, 603-271-2154

Hall of Flags; statues, portraits of state notables. Monday-Friday.

HOTELS

★★★COLBY HILL INN

The Oaks, Henniker, 603-428-3281, 800-531-0330; www.colbyhillinn.com

This classic New England country inn offers individually decorated rooms and fine-dining in a beautiful, wooded setting. 14 rooms. Children over 7 years only. Complimentary full breakfast. Wireless Internet access. Restaurant. Indoor pool, outdoor pool. Bar. Reservations recommended. **$$**

★COMFORT INN

71 Hall St., Concord, 603-226-4100, 877-424-6423; www.comfortinn.com

100 rooms. Pets accepted, some restrictions, fee. Complimentary continental breakfast. Indoor pool, whirlpool. High-speed Internet access. Fitness room. **$**

★HAMPTON INN

515 S. St., Bow, 603-224-5322, 800-426-7866; www.hamptoninn.com

145 rooms. Complimentary continental breakfast. Indoor pool, whirlpool. Fitness room. Business center. High-speed Internet access. **$**

RESTAURANTS

★★ANGELINA'S RISTORANTE ITALIANO

11 Depot St., Concord, 603-228-3313; www.angelinasrestaurant.com

American, Italian menu. Lunch, dinner. Casual attire. Reservations recommended. Lunch Monday-Friday, dinner Monday-Saturday; closed Sunday. **$$**

★ARNIE'S PLACE

164 Loudon Road, Concord, 603-228-3225; www.arniesplace.com

American menu. Lunch, dinner. Children's menu. Casual attire. Outdoor seating. No credit cards accepted. **$**

★BOAR'S TAVERN

Routes 106 and 129, Loudon, 603-798-3737; www.boarstavern.com

American menu. Lunch, dinner. Bar. Casual attire. **$$**

★★COLBY HILL INN

The Oaks, Henniker, 603-428-3281; www.colbyhillinn.com

14 rooms. Regional menu. Dinner. Business casual attire. Reservations recommended. Indoor pool, whirlpool. High-speed Internet access. **$$$**

★★LONGHORN STEAKHOUSE

217 Loudon Road, Concord, 603-228-0655; www.longhornsteakhouse.com

Steak menu. Lunch, dinner. Bar. Children's menu. Casual attire. **$$**

★
★
★
★
★

★MAKRIS LOBSTER AND STEAK HOUSE
354 Sheep Davis Road, Concord, 603-225-7665; www.eatalobster.com
Seafood, steak menu. Lunch, dinner, late-night. Bar. Children's menu. Casual attire.
Outdoor seating. **$$**

★RED BLAZER RESTAURANT
72 Manchester St., Concord, 603-224-4101; www.redblazer.cc
American menu. Lunch, dinner. Bar. Children's menu. Casual attire. Daily. **$$**

★SAL'S JUST PIZZA
80 Storrs St., Concord, 603-226-0297; www.sals-pizza.com
Pizza. Lunch, dinner. Children's menu. Casual attire. Outdoor seating. No credit cards
accepted. **$**

DIXVILLE NOTCH
The small village of Dixville Notch shares its name with the most northern White
Mountain passes. The Notch cuts through the mountain range between Kidderville
and Errol. At its narrowest point, east of Lake Gloriette, is one of the most impressive
views in the state. Every four years, Dixville Notch is invaded by the national news
media, who report the nation's first presidential vote tally shortly after midnight on
Election day.

WHAT TO SEE AND DO
BALSAMS/WILDERNESS SKI AREA
1000 Cold Spring Road, Dixville Notch, 603-255-3400, 877-225-7267;
www.thebalsams.com
Chairlift, two T-bars; patrol, school, rentals, snowmaking; restaurant, cafeteria, bar,
nursery, resort. Longest run one mile; vertical drop 1,000 feet. December-March:
daily. Cross-country trails.

HOTEL
★★★THE BALSAMS
1000 Cold Spring Road, Dixville Notch, 603-255-3400, 877-225-7267;
www.thebalsams.com
The Balsams has impressive architecture and a bucolic setting. Built just after the
Civil War, this 15,000-acre resort offers downhill skiing, cross-country skiing, snowboarding and ice skating, while warmer months are spent playing golf or tennis and
enjoying the great outdoors on nature walks. Operating on the all-inclusive American
plan, the Balsams makes gourmet dining an integral part of the experience here. 212
rooms. Two restaurants. Two bars. Fitness room. Outdoor pool. Golf, 27 holes. Tennis.
Ski-in/ski-out. Airport transportation available. **$$**

DOVER
With its historic trails and homes, Dover is the oldest permanent settlement in New
Hampshire. The town contains the only known existing colonial garrison.
Information: Chamber of Commerce, 299 Central Ave., 603-742-2218; www.dovernh.org

WHAT TO SEE AND DO
WOODMAN INSTITUTE
182-190 Central Ave., Dover, 603-742-1038; www.doverwasfirst.com

Garrison House (1675), the only garrison in New Hampshire now visible in nearly its original form. Woodman House (1818), residence of the donor, is now a natural history museum with collections of minerals, Native American artifacts and displays of mammals, fish, amphibians, reptiles, birds, insects; war memorial rooms. Senator John P. Hale House (1813) contains articles of Dover history and antique furniture. May-November, Wednesday-Sunday afternoons; December, Saturday-Sunday afternoons.

HOTEL
★DAYS INN
481 Central Ave., Dover, 603-742-0400, 800-329-7466;
www.dover-durham-daysinn.com

50 rooms. Pets accepted. Complimentary continental breakfast. Outdoor pool, whirlpool. Free Wireless Internet access. Fitness center. Business center. **$**

RESTAURANTS
★★★MAPLES
17 Newmarket Road, Durham, 603-868-7800, 888-399-9777;
www.threechimneysinn.com

This restaurant provides service in an old New England setting that includes dark wood tables and large, comfortable chairs. In the summertime, the patio is open for dining and in the winter, the fireplace provides a cozy atmosphere. American menu. Lunch, dinner. Outdoor seating. **$$$**

★NEWICK'S SEAFOOD
431 Dover Point Road, Dover, 603-742-3205; www.newicks.com
Seafood menu. Lunch, dinner. Daily. **$$**

EXETER

A respected preparatory school and colonial houses are a large part of Exeter's radical history. The town had its beginnings in religious nonconformity, led by Reverend John Wheelwright and Anne Hutchinson, both of whom were banished from Massachusetts for heresy. There was an antiBritish scuffle in 1734, and by 1774, Exeter was burning Lord North in effigy and talking of liberty. It was made the capital of the state during the Revolution. Exeter is the birthplace of Daniel Chester French and John Irving.

Information: Exeter Area Chamber of Commerce, 120 Water St.,
603-772-2411; www.exeterarea.org

WHAT TO SEE AND DO
AMERICAN INDEPENDENCE MUSEUM
1 Governors Lane, Exeter, 603-772-2622; www.independencemuseum.org
Site of Revolutionary War-era state treasury building; grounds house Folsom Tavern (1775). May-October, Wednesday-Saturday 10 a.m.-4 p.m. Free parking.

PHILLIPS EXETER ACADEMY

20 Main St., Exeter, 603-772-4311; www.exeter.edu

(1781) (990 students) A prestigious college preparatory school on 400 acres with more than 100 buildings. Coed school for grades 9-12. Founded by John Phillips, who sought a school for "students from every quarter." Exeter is known for its student diversity. On campus there is a contemporary library (1971), designed by Louis I. Kahn; the Frederick R. Mayer Art Center and the Lamont Art Gallery.

FRANCONIA

Franconia is the gateway to the White Mountains. From here, explore the area's best hiking and skiing and in the fall, leaf peeping, as the annual pilgrimage to view the changing colors of the leaves is affectionately called.

Information: Franconia Notch Chamber of Commerce, 603-823-5661, 800-237-9007; www.franconianotch.org

WHAT TO SEE AND DO

FROST PLACE

Ridge Road, Franconia, 603-823-5510; www.frostplace.org

Two furnished rooms of Robert Frost's home open to public; memorabilia; poetry trail; 25-minute video. July-Columbus Day, Wednesday-Monday afternoons; Memorial Day-June, Saturday-Sunday afternoons. Free admission to museum.

NEW ENGLAND SKI MUSEUM

Franconia Notch Parkway, Franconia, 603-823-7177, 800-639-4181; www.nesm.org

Details history of skiing in the East; exhibits feature skis and bindings, clothing, art and photographs; vintage films. Gift shop. Memorial Day-Columbus Day and December-March, daily 10 a.m.-5 p.m. Free admission.

HOTELS

★★★FRANCONIA INN

1300 Easton Road, Franconia, 603-823-5542, 800-473-5299; www.franconiainn.com

Located in the White Mountains but still close to the town center, this charming inn welcomes guests into an informal country-home atmosphere. The comfortable guest rooms are spacious and onsite activities include horseback riding, mountain biking, fishing and croquet. 34 rooms. Complimentary full breakfast. Restaurant, bar. Outdoor pool, whirlpool. Tennis. Closed April-mid-May. Reservations recommended. $

★★FRANCONIA VILLAGE HOTEL

87 Wallace Hill Road, Franconia, 603-823-7422, 888-669-6777; www.franconiahotel.com

60 rooms. Pets accepted, some restrictions; fee. Complimentary continental breakfast. Restaurant, bar. Fitness room. Indoor pool. Business center. High-speed Internet access. $

★★★LOVETTS INN

1474 Profile Road, Franconia, 603-823-7761, 800-356-3802; www.lovettsinn.com

Breathe in the fresh country air at this historic, romantic inn surrounded by the White Mountains. This rustic-like inn is well appointed and charming, and just a short drive away from the town center. 18 rooms. Pets accepted; fee. Complimentary full breakfast. Wireless Internet access. Restaurant, bar. Outdoor pool. Closed April. **$$**

★STONYBROOK MOTEL & LODGE

1098 Profile Road, Franconia, 603-823-5800, 800-722-3552; www.stonybrookmotel.com
23 rooms. Complimentary continental breakfast. Children's activity center. Indoor pool, outdoor pool. Pets not accepted. High-speed Internet access. **$**

★★SUGAR HILL INN

Highway 117, Franconia, 603-823-5621, 800-548-4748; www.sugarhillinn.com
15 rooms. Complimentary full breakfast. Wireless Internet access. Restaurant, bar. Spa. Closed one week in April. **$$**

SPECIALTY LODGINGS
HILLTOP INN

1348 Main St., Sugar Hill, 603-823-5695, 800-770-5695; www.hilltopinn.com
Built in 1895; rooms feature antiques, quilts. Six rooms. Pets accepted, some restrictions; fee. Complimentary full breakfast. Free High-speed Internet access. **$**

SUNSET HILL HOUSE–A GRAND INN

231 Sunset Hill Road, Sugar Hill, 603-823-5522, 800-786-4455; www.sunsethillhouse.com
Built in 1882; beautiful view of mountains. 28 rooms. Complimentary full breakfast. Restaurant. Outdoor pool. Golf. **$$$**

RESTAURANTS
★★★THE FRANCONIA INN

1300 Easton Road, Franconia, 603-823-5542, 800-473-5299; www.franconiainn.com
This restaurant nestled among hills and mountains offers New American cuisine, drawing on regional specialties and influenced by the rich heritage of the area. Main courses include filet mignon with crab cakes and pepper-seared Atlantic salmon. American menu. Breakfast, dinner. Closed April-mid-May. Bar. Children's menu. Casual attire. Reservations recommended. Pool. **$$**

★★HORSE & HOUND

205 Wells Road, Franconia, 603-823-5501, 800-450-5501;
www.horseandhoundnh.com
American menu. Dinner. Closed Sunday-Wednesday. Bar. Casual attire. Reservations recommended. Outdoor seating. Eight guest rooms. **$$**

★★LOVETTS INN BY LAFAYETTE BROOK

1474 Profile Road, Franconia, 603-823-7761; www.lovettsinn.com
American menu. Breakfast, dinner. Bar. Casual attire. Reservations recommended. Outdoor seating. **$$**

★★POLLY'S PANCAKE PARLOR

672 Highway 117, Sugar Hill, 603-823-5575; www.pollyspancakeparlor.com
American menu. Breakfast, lunch. Closed November-April. Children's menu. Reservations recommended. **$$**

★
★
★
★
☆

FRANCONIA NOTCH STATE PARK

This seven-mile pass and state park, a deep valley of 6,440 acres between the Franconia and Kinsman ranges of the White Mountains has been a top tourist attraction since the mid-19th-century. Mounts Liberty (4,460 feet), Lincoln (5,108 feet) and Lafayette (5,249 feet) loom in the east, and Cannon Mountain (4,200 feet) presents a sheer granite face. The Pemigewasset River follows the length of the Notch. The park offers various recreational activities, including swimming at Sandy Beach; fishing and boating on Echo Lake (junction Highway 18 and Interstate-93 exit 3); hiking; eight-mile paved bike path through the Notch; skiing; picnicking; camping. Fees for some activities.

Information: Franconia Notch State Park, Franconia, 603-823-5563

WHAT TO SEE AND DO
CANNON MOUNTAIN SKI AREA
Franconia Notch State Parkway, Franconia, 603-823-8800; www.cannonmt.com
Tramway, two quad, three triple, two double chairlifts, pony lift; patrol, school, rentals; snowmaking; cafeterias, bar (beer and wine); nursery. New England Ski Museum. Longest run is two miles, vertical drop is 2,146 feet. Late November-mid-April, daily. Tramway rising 2,022 feet vertically over a distance of one mile in six minutes. Also operates Memorial Day-mid-October, daily; rest of year, weekends (weather permitting).

FLUME GORGE & PARK INFORMATION CENTER
Franconia Notch State Parkway, Franconia, 603-745-8391; www.flumegorge.com
Narrow, natural gorge and waterfall along the flank of Mount Liberty, accessible by stairs and walks. Information center offers a 15-minute movie every half-hour introducing the park. Interpretive exhibits. Gift shop, cafeteria. Mid-May-late-October, daily 9 a.m.-5.30 p.m. Admission: adult $12, children 6-12 years $8, children under 5 free with adult.

OLD MAN OF THE MOUNTAIN HISTORIC SITE
1, 200 feet, above Profile Lake, Franconia, Notch State Parkway
Discovered in 1805, the craggy likeness of a man's face was formed naturally of five layers of granite and was 40 feet high. It tumbled down on May 3, 2003. It was also known as the "Great Stone Face."

GORHAM

Located near the Presidential Range of the White Mountains, at the north end of Pinkham Notch, Gorham is the center for summer and winter sports. The Peabody River merges with the Androscoggin River in a series of falls. The Ranger District office of the White Mountain National Forest is located here.

Information: Northern White Mountains Chamber of Commerce, 164 Main St.,
Berlin, 603-752-6060, 800-992-7480; www.northernwhitemountains.com

WHAT TO SEE AND DO
MOOSE BROOK STATE PARK
30 Jimtown Road, Gorham, 603-466-3860; www.nhstateparks.com/moose.html
Views of the Presidential Range of the White Mountains; good stream fishing area. Swimming, bathhouse; picnicking; camping. Hiking to Randolph Range. Late May-early-September.

★
★
★
★
★

HOTELS
★MT. MADISON MOTEL
365 Main St., Gorham, 603-466-3622, 800-851-1136; www.mtmadisonmotel.com
32 rooms. Pets accepted, some restrictions. Outdoor pool. Reservations recommended. **$**

★★ROYALTY INN
130 Main St., Gorham, 603-466-3312, 800-437-3529; www.royaltyinn.com
88 rooms. Pets accepted, some restrictions. Restaurant, bar. Fitness room. Indoor pool, outdoor pool. Reservations recommended. **$**

RESTAURANT
★★YOKOHAMA
288 Main St., Gorham, 603-466-2501
Japanese menu. Lunch, dinner. Children's menu. Closed Monday; also two weeks in spring and two weeks in fall. **$$**

HAMPTON BEACH
This beachfront town has an old-fashioned boardwalk and plenty of sandy beaches. An annual seafood festival, held the week after Labor Day, is the town's biggest event.
Information: Chamber of Commerce, 1 Park Ave., 603-926-8717,
800-438-2826; www.hamptonbeaches.com

WHAT TO SEE AND DO
FULLER GARDENS
10 Willow Ave., North Hampton, 603-964-5414; www.fullergardens.org
Former estate of the late Governor Alvan T. Fuller featuring extensive rose gardens, annuals, perennials, Japanese garden and conservatory. Mid-May-mid-October: daily 10 a.m.-5.30 p.m. Admission: adults $6.50, senior $5.50, student $3.50, children $2.50.

TUCK MEMORIAL MUSEUM
40 Park Ave., Hampton, 603-929-0781; www.hampton.lib.nh.us
Home of Hampton Historical Society. Antiques, documents, photographs, early postcards, tools and toys; trolley exhibit; memorabilia of Hampton history. Restored one-room schoolhouse; fire station. Mid-June-mid-September.

HOTELS
★★ASHWORTH BY THE SEA
295 Ocean Blvd., Hampton Beach, 603-926-6762, 800-345-6736;
www.ashworthhotel.com
98 rooms. Three restaurants, bar. Indoor pool. Wireless Internet access. Fitness room. Spa. **$$**

★HAMPSHIRE INN
20 Spur Road, Seabrook, 603-474-5700, 800-932-8520; www.hampshireinn.com
35 rooms. Complimentary continental breakfast. Fitness room. Indoor pool, whirlpool. Airport transportation available. Fitness room. Spa. **$**

★
★
★
★
★

★★HAMPTON FALLS INN

11 Lafayette Road, Hampton Falls, 603-926-9545, 800-356-1729;
www.hamptonfallsinn.com

47 rooms. Pets accepted, some restrictions. Wireless Internet access. Restaurant. Indoor pool, whirlpool. Free local calls. Free Parking. Fitness room. **$**

★★INN OF HAMPTON

815 Lafayette Road, Hampton, 603-926-6771, 800-423-4561; www.theinnofhampton.com

71 rooms. Restaurant, bar. Children's activity center. Fitness room. Indoor pool. Business center. Free breakfast. High-speed Internet access. **$**

★★LAMIE'S INN & OLD SALT RESTAURANT

490 Lafayette Road, Hampton, 603-926-0330, 800-805-5050; www.lamiesinn.com

32 rooms. Pets accepted, some restrictions; fee. Complimentary continental breakfast. Restaurant, bar. **$**

SPECIALTY LODGING

D. W.'S OCEANSIDE INN

365 Ocean Blvd., Hampton Beach, 603-926-3542, 866-623-2674; www.oceansideinn.com

This early-1900s beach house overlooking the Atlantic Ocean is an ideal getaway. The décor is colonial and some rooms have canopy beds. Nine rooms. No children accepted. Complimentary full breakfast. Beach. Closed mid-October-mid-May. **$$**

HANOVER

Established four years after the first settlers came here, Dartmouth College is an integral part of Hanover. Named for the Earl of Dartmouth, the school was founded by the Reverend Eleazar Wheelock "for the instruction of the youth of Indian tribes and others." An ivy league college famous for its party scene, Dartmouth was the inspiration for the film *Animal House*.

Information: Chamber of Commerce, 216 Nugget Bldg., Main St.,
603-643-3115; www.hanoverchamber.org

WHAT TO SEE AND DO

DARTMOUTH COLLEGE

Main and Wheelock Streets, Hanover, 603-646-1110; www.dartmouth.edu

(1769) This Ivy League school of 5,400 students is renowned for its business school and top-notch academics.

ENFIELD SHAKER MUSEUM

24 Caleb Dyer Lane, Enfield, 603-632-4346; www.shakermuseum.org

Museum devoted to Shaker culture on the site where the Shakers established their Chosen Vale in 1793. Includes exhibits, craft demonstrations, workshops, special programs and extensive gardens Monday-Saturday 10 a.m.-5 p.m. Sunday noon-5 p.m.

SAINT-GAUDENS NATIONAL HISTORIC SITE

139 Saint-Gaudens Road, Route 12A, Cornish, 603-675-2175; www.nps.gov/saga

Former residence and studio of sculptor Augustus Saint-Gaudens (1848-1907). Saint-Gaudens' famous works *The Puritan*, *Adams Memorial* and *Shaw Memorial* are among the 100 works on display. Also includes formal gardens and works by other artists; sculptor-in-residence; interpretive programs. Memorial Day-October, daily 9 a.m.-4:30 p.m. Pets accepted; some restrictions.

WEBSTER COTTAGE
32 N. Main St., Hanover, 603-643-6529
(1780) Residence of Daniel Webster during his last year as a Dartmouth College student; colonial and Shaker furniture and Webster memorabilia. Memorial Day-mid-October, Wednesday, Saturday-Sunday afternoons.

HOTELS
★★FIRESIDE INN & SUITES
25 Airport Road, West Lebanon, 603-298-5900, 877-258-5900; www.afiresideinn.com
126 rooms. High-speed Internet access. Fitness room. Indoor pool. Pets accepted. $$

★★★HANOVER INN
Main and Wheelock Streets, Hanover, 603-643-4300, 800-443-7024; www.hanoverinn.com
At this inn located just minutes from Dartmouth College, guest rooms are decorated with a colonial motif, and guests have access to athletic facilities at the university. 92 rooms. Pets accepted; fee. Wireless Internet access. Restaurant, bar. Fitness room. Airport transportation available. $$$

SPECIALTY LODGING
DOWD'S COUNTRY INN
On the Common, Lyme, 603-795-4712, 800-482-4712; www.dowdscountryinn.com
This charming New England inn surrounded by trees is located 10 miles north of Dartmouth College and is close to the Lyme commons. 23 rooms. Complimentary full breakfast. $$

RESTAURANTS
★★JESSE'S
Lebanon Road, Hanover, 603-643-4111; www.blueskyrestaurants.com
Steak menu. Lunch, dinner. Bar. Children's menu. Outdoor seating. $$

★MOLLY'S
43 S. Main St., Hanover, 603-643-2570; www.mollysrestaurant.com
American menu. Lunch, dinner. Bar. Daily. $$

HOLDERNESS
Holderness is the shopping center and post office for Squam Lake, the second-largest lake in the state, and neighboring Little Squam. Fishing, boating, swimming, water sports and winter sports are popular in this area. The movie *On Golden Pond* was filmed here.

WHAT TO SEE AND DO
SQUAM LAKES NATURAL SCIENCE CENTER
23 Science Center Road, Holderness, 603-968-7194; www.nhnature.org
If this attraction looks familiar, perhaps you'll recognize it as the site where the 1981 movie, *On Golden Pond,* with Henry Fonda and Katharine Hepburn was filmed.

Walking through the woods of this 200-acre wildlife sanctuary, you'll see black bears, deer, bobcats, otters, mountain lions, foxes and birds of prey in enclosed trailside exhibits. You can also take the Explore Squam boat tour. Picnicking. May-early November, daily 9:30 a.m.-4:30 p.m.

HOTEL

★★★MANOR ON GOLDEN POND

Manor Drive, Holderness, 603-968-3348, 800-545-2141;
www.manorongoldenpond.com

Modeled after an English country estate, this inn is located on the shore of Squam Lake. Activities include tennis, badminton, croquet and access to a private beach. 25 rooms. Children over 12 years only. Complimentary full breakfast. Wireless Internet access. Restaurant, bar. Indoor pool. Tennis. Pets not accepted. **$$$**

SPECIALTY LODGINGS

GLYNN HOUSE INN

59 Highland St., Ashland, 603-968-3775, 800-637-9599; www.glynnhouse.com

This restored 1896 Queen Anne/Victorian is conveniently located near Squam Lake in the White Mountains. The interior is tastefully decorated and guest rooms are nicely appointed. Lakes Region dining, attractions and activities are all nearby. 13 rooms. Children over 12 years only. Complimentary full breakfast. Whirlpool. Free Wireless Internet access. Pets accepted; fee. **$$**

INN ON GOLDEN POND

Route 25, Holderness, 603-968-7269; www.innongoldenpond.com

Built in 1879; fireplace; individually-decorated rooms. Eight rooms. Children over 10 years only. Complimentary continental breakfast. **$**

RESTAURANTS

★COMMON MAN

60 Main St., Ashland, 603-968-7030; www.thecman.com

American menu. Lunch, dinner. Bar. Children's menu. Casual attire. Outdoor seating. **$$**

★★CORNER HOUSE INN

22 Main St., Center Sandwich, 603-284-6219; www.cornerhouseinn.com

American menu. Lunch, dinner, brunch. Bar. Children's menu. Casual attire. Reservations recommended. **$$**

★★MANOR ON GOLDEN POND

Manor Drive, Holderness, 603-968-3348; www.manorongoldenpond.com

Dinner at this cozy inn on Squam Lake is a romantic experience. The location, high on a hill, provides spectacular views. The frequently changing à la carte menu includes New American dishes like duck hash Napoleon and sautéed mahi mahi. American menu. Dinner, bar. Business casual attire. Valet parking. **$$$**

JACKSON

At the south end of Pinkham Notch, Jackson is a center for skiing and a year-round resort. The Wildcat River rushes over rock formations in the village; Wildcat Mountain is to the north. A circa-1870 covered bridge spans the Ellis River.

Information: Chamber of Commerce, 603-383-9356; www.jacksonnh.com

WHAT TO SEE AND DO

BLACK MOUNTAIN

Highway 16B, Jackson, 603-383-4490; www.blackmt.com

Triple and double chairlifts, J-bar, patrol, school, rentals, cafeteria, nursery. Longest run is one mile; vertical drop 1,100 feet.

JACKSON SKI TOURING FOUNDATION

153 Main St., and Highway 16A, Jackson, 603-383-9355; www.jacksonxc.org

Maintains 95 miles of cross-country trails, connecting inns and ski areas. Instruction, rentals, rescue service. December-mid-April, daily.

HOTELS

★★EAGLE MOUNTAIN HOUSE

Carter Notch Road, Jackson, 603-383-9111, 800-966-5779; www.eaglemt.com

97 rooms. Wireless Internet access. Restaurant, bar. Fitness room. Outdoor pool, whirlpool. Golf, nine holes. Tennis. Ski-in/ski-out. Pets not accepted. Tennis. Fitness room.

★★★INN AT ELLIS RIVER

17 Harriman Road, Jackson, 603-383-9339, 800-233-8309; www.innatellisriver.com

This luxurious inn offers rooms with period furnishings and a wide variety of amenities. Some rooms have whirlpool tubs or balconies, most have fireplaces. The surrounding area offers year-round activities such as cross-country skiing, golf, fishing, swimming and kayaking. 21 rooms. Children over 12 years only. Complimentary full breakfast. Restaurant, bar. Outdoor pool. Reservations recommended. Pets not accepted. $

★★★INN AT THORN HILL

Thorn Hill Road, Jackson, 603-383-4242, 800-289-8990; www.innatthornhill.com

This historic inn puts a premium on luxury. Rooms have plush, down duvet-topped beds, Jacuzzi tubs and TV/DVD players. A full gourmet breakfast is served each morning at the inn's restaurant. 25 rooms. Children over 8 years only. Complimentary full breakfast. Wireless Internet access. Restaurant, bar. Fitness room. Spa. Outdoor pool, whirlpool. Ski-in/ski-out. Pets not accepted. $$$

★LODGE AT JACKSON VILLAGE

153 Highway 16, Jackson, 603-383-0999, 800-233-5634;
www.lodgeatjacksonvillage.com

32 rooms. Complimentary full breakfast. Wireless Internet access. Outdoor pool, whirlpool. Tennis. Pets not accepted. $$

★★STORYBOOK RESORT INN

Highways 302 and 16, Glen, 603-383-6800; www.storybookresort.com

78 rooms. Restaurant, bar. Fitness room. Indoor pool, two outdoor pools, children's pool. Tennis. $

NEW HAMPSHIRE

★
★
★
★
★

★★★WENTWORTH RESORT HOTEL

1 Carter Notch Road, Jackson, 603-383-9700, 800-637-0013; www.thewentworth.com

This elegant country inn, built in 1869, has been in continuous operation for more than a century. Located in the White Mountains, the year-round resort offers a fine-dining restaurant and recreational facilities. 51 rooms. Restaurant, bar. Outdoor pool. Golf, 18 holes. Tennis. Ski-in/ski-out. Airport transportation available. **$$**

SPECIALTY LODGINGS

DANA PLACE INN

Highway 16, Jackson, 603-383-6822, 800-537-9276; www.danaplace.com

30 rooms. Pets accepted, some restrictions. Complimentary full breakfast. Restaurant, bar. Indoor pool, children's pool, whirlpool. Golf. Tennis. Business center. **$$**

NESTLENOOK FARM RESORT

Dinsmore Road, Jackson, 603-383-9443, 800-659-9443;
www.luxurymountaingetaways.com

Located on the river, this restored Victorian building is one of the oldest in Jackson (1770). Furnishings include antiques, tiffany lamps and 18th-century parlor stoves. Seven rooms, all suites. No children accepted. Complimentary full breakfast. Outdoor pool, indoor pool. Closed two weeks in April. **$$**

RESTAURANTS

★★CHRISTMAS FARM INN

Highway 16B, Jackson, 603-383-4313, 800-443-5837; www.christmasfarminn.com

American menu. Breakfast, dinner. Bar. Children's menu. Casual attire. Reservations recommended. Fitness room. Pool. Pets not accepted. **$$$**

★★★INN AT THORN HILL

Thorn Hill Road, Jackson, 603-383-4242, 800-289-8990; www.innatthornhill.com

The dining room at this restaurant has a wood-burning fireplace and views of the countryside. The menu changes seasonally and serves dishes such as pan-seared tuna, grilled beef tenderloin and petite rack of veal. An extensive wine list is offered. American menu. Breakfast, dinner. Bar. Business casual attire. Reservations recommended. Outdoor seating. Fitness room. Pool. Pets not accepted. **$$$**

★RED PARKA PUB

Highway 302, Glen, 603-383-4344; www.redparkapub.com

Steak menu. Dinner. Bar. Children's menu. Outdoor seating. Casual attire. **$**

★★WILDCAT INN & TAVERN

Highway 16A, Jackson, 603-383-4245, 800-228-4245; www.wildcattavern.com

American menu. Lunch, dinner. Bar. Children's menu. Casual attire. Outdoor seating. Reservations recommended. **$$$**

KEENE

A modern commercial city, Keene is the chief community of the Monadnock region. Its industries manufacture many products including furniture, machinery, textiles and toys.

Information: Chamber of Commerce, 48 Central Square, 603-352-1303;
www.keenechamber.com

WHAT TO SEE AND DO

COLONY MILL MARKETPLACE

222 W. St., Keene, 603-357-1240; www.colonymill.com

Restored 1838 textile mill now transformed into regional marketplace with dozens of specialty shops, an antique center, numerous dining options and varied entertainment. Monday-Saturday 10 a.m.-9 p.m.; Sunday 11 a.m.-6 p.m.

HISTORICAL SOCIETY OF CHESHIRE COUNTY

339 Main St., Keene, 603-352-1895; www.hsccnh.org

The 1762 scene of the first meeting of Dartmouth College trustees in 1770; now furnished in 1820s style. June-September, Thursday-Saturday.

HORATIO COLONY HOUSE MUSEUM

199 Main St., Keene, 603-352-0460; www.horatiocolonymuseum.org

Stately Federalist home (1806) of the son of prominent Keene mill owners. Features treasures collected from Colony's world travels; books, art, antique furniture. May-mid-October: Wednesday-Sunday, 11 a.m.-4 p.m.; rest of year: by appointment.

HOTEL

★★BEST WESTERN SOVEREIGN HOTEL

401 Winchester St., Keene, 603-357-3038, 800-780-7234; www.bestwestern.com

131 rooms. Pets accepted; fee. Complimentary full breakfast. Restaurant, bar. Indoor pool. High-speed Internet access. $

RESTAURANT

★THE PUB

131 Winchester St., Keene, 603-352-3135; www.thepubrestaurant.com

American menu. Breakfast, lunch, dinner. Bar. Children's menu. Reservations recommended. $

LACONIA

On four lakes (Winnisquam, Opechee, Pauqus Bay and Winnipesaukee), Laconia is the commercial center of this area, known as the "Lakes Region." Besides the resort trade, it has numerous factories whose products include knitting machinery, hosiery, knitted fabrics, ball bearings and electronic components. The headquarters of the White Mountain National Forest is also located here.

Information: Chamber of Commerce, 11 Veterans Square,
603-524-5531; www.laconia-weirs.org

WHAT TO SEE AND DO

M/S MOUNT WASHINGTON

211, Lakeside Ave., Weirs Beach, 603-366-5531, 888-843-6686; www.cruisenh.com

Cruise the waters of Lake Winnipesaukee, the largest lake in New Hampshire, and enjoy scenic mountain views aboard the M/S *Mount Washington*, which offers daily scenic and dinner dance cruises. Ports of call include Weirs Beach, Wolfeboro, Meredith, Alton Bay and Center Harbor. Mid-May-October; check Web site or call for schedule.

HOTELS

★★B. MAE'S RESORT INN & SUITES

Routes 11 and 11B, Gilford, 603-293-7526, 800-458-3877; www.bmaesresort.com

82 rooms. Complimentary continental breakfast. Restaurant, bar. Fitness room. Indoor pool, outdoor pool, whirlpool. High-speed Internet access. $

★BARTON'S MOTEL

1330 Union Ave., Laconia, 603-524-5674; www.bartonsmotel.com

41 rooms. Beach. Outdoor pool. Reservations recommended. $

RESTAURANT

★NASWA BEACH BAR AND GRILL

1086 Weirs Blvd., Laconia, 603-366-4341; www.naswa.com

American menu. Lunch, dinner. Bar. Children's menu. Casual attire. Outdoor seating. $$

LINCOLN/WOODSTOCK

In a spectacular mountain setting, the villages of Lincoln and Woodstock lie at the junction of the road through Franconia Notch State Park and the Kancamagus Scenic Byway.

Information: Chamber of Commerce, Lincoln, 603-745-661, 800-227-4191; www.lincolnwoodstock.com

WHAT TO SEE AND DO

LOON MOUNTAIN RECREATION AREA

Highway 112, Lincoln, 603-745-8111; www.loonmtn.com

A 7,100-foot gondola, two triple and four double chairlifts, one high-speed quad chairlift, pony lift, patrol, school, rentals, shops, snowmaking, restaurant, bar, nursery, lodge. Longest run 2½ miles; vertical drop 2,100 feet. (Late November-mid-April, daily). Cross-country trails (December-March). Summer activities include mountain biking (rentals), bike tours, in-line skating, horseback riding, skate park, climbing wall. Gondola also operates Memorial Day-mid-October daily.

LOST RIVER GORGE

Lost River Road, North Woodstock, 603-745-8031; www.findlostriver.com

Natural boulder caves, largest known granite pothole in the eastern United States; Paradise Falls; boardwalks with 1,900-foot glacial gorge; nature garden with 300 varieties of native shrubs and flowers; geology exhibits. Cafeteria, picnicking. Mid-May-mid-October: daily. Appropriate outdoor clothing recommended.

SPECIAL EVENT

NEW HAMPSHIRE HIGHLAND GAMES

Loon Mountain, 603-229-1975, 800-358-7268; www.nhscot.org

Largest Scottish gathering in the eastern United States. Bands, competitions, concerts, workshops. Three days in September.

NEW HAMPSHIRE

★
★★
★★
★

HOTELS

★★INDIAN HEAD RESORT

664 U.S. Route 3, Lincoln, 603-745-8000, 800-343-8000;
www.indianheadresort.com

98 rooms. Restaurant, bar. Fitness room. Indoor pool, outdoor pool, whirlpool. Tennis. Restaurant. **$**

★★INNSEASON RESORTS SOUTH MOUNTAIN

Main St., Route 112, Lincoln, 603-745-9300, 800-654-6183;
www.innseasonresorts.com

84 rooms. Fitness room. Indoor pool, outdoor pool. **$**

★★MOUNTAIN CLUB ON LOON

90 Loon Mountain Road, Lincoln, 603-745-2244, 800-229-7829;
www.mtnclub.com

This ski area is located at the base of Loon Mountain on the scenic Kancamagus Highway and offers lifts, ski shops and shuttle services, along with many onsite activities. 234 rooms. Two restaurants. Bar. Children's activity center. Fitness room. Spa. Indoor pool, outdoor pool, children's pool, whirlpool. Ski-in/ski-out. **$$**

★★WOODWARDS RESORT

527 U.S. Route 3, Lincoln, 603-745-8141, 800-635-8968;
www.woodwardsresort.com

85 rooms. Restaurant, bar. Indoor pool. Outdoor pool. **$$**

SPECIALTY LODGING

WOODSTOCK INN

135 Main St., North Woodstock, 603-745-3951, 800-321-3985;
www.woodstockinnnh.com

Victorian house (1890). 33 rooms. Complimentary full breakfast. Restaurant, bar. Whirlpool. **$**

RESTAURANTS

★★COMMON MAN

Pollard Road, Lincoln, 603-968-9330; www.thecman.com

American menu. Dinner. Bar. Children's menu. **$$**

★★GORDI'S FISH & STEAK HOUSE

260 Main St., Kancamagus Highway, Lincoln, 603-745-6635

Seafood, steak menu. Lunch, dinner. Bar. Children's menu. Reservations recommended. **$$$**

★TRUANTS TAVERNE

96 Main St., North Woodstock, 603-745-2239

American menu. Lunch, dinner. Bar. Children's menu. **$$**

NEW HAMPSHIRE

★
★
★
★
★

LITTLETON

Littleton is a resort area a few miles northwest of the White Mountain National Forest, which maintains a Ranger District office in nearby Bethlehem. It is a regional commercial center, with industries that produce abrasives and electrical component parts. The Ammonoosuc River falls 235 feet on its way through the community.

Information: Chamber of Commerce, 120 Main St., 603-444-6561; www.littletonareachamber.com

WHAT TO SEE AND DO

LITTLETON HISTORICAL MUSEUM

1 Cottage St., Littleton, 603-444-6435

Photographs, arts and crafts, stereographs, local memorabilia. April-November: Wednesday, or by appointment.

HOTELS

★★★ADAIR COUNTRY INN

80 Guider Lane, Bethlehem, 603-444-2600, 888-444-2600; www.adairinn.com

Built in 1927, this inn is situated on 200 landscaped acres designed by the Olmsted Brothers. Guest rooms are furnished with antiques and original artwork and include afternoon tea and homemade desserts. 10 rooms. Children over 12 years only. Complimentary full breakfast. Wireless Internet access. Restaurant. Tennis. Closed three weeks in April and November. **$$**

★★EASTGATE MOTOR INN

335 Cottage St., Littleton, 603-444-3971, 866-640-3561; www.eastgatemotorinn.com

55 rooms. Pets accepted, some restrictions; fee. Complimentary continental breakfast. Restaurant, bar. Outdoor pool, children's pool. Internet access. Reservations recommended. **$**

★★WAYSIDE

3738 Main St., Bethlehem, 603-869-3364, 800-448-9557; www.thewaysideinn.com

26 rooms. Complimentary full breakfast. Restaurant, bar. Tennis. Closed April and November. Pets accepted. **$**

SPECIALTY LODGINGS

THAYER'S INN

111 Main St., Littleton, 603-444-6469, 800-634-8179; www.thayersinn.com

Historic inn (1843); antiques, library, sitting room. Cupola open to the public. 39 rooms. Pets accepted, some restrictions. Complimentary continental breakfast. Free Wireless Internet access. **$**

RESTAURANTS

★★CLAM SHELL

274 Dells Road, Littleton, 603-444-6445

American, seafood menu. Lunch, dinner. Bar. Children's menu. **$$**

NEW HAMPSHIRE

★
★★
★★★
★★★★
★★★★★

★EASTGATE
335 Cottage St., Littleton, 603-444-3971; www.eastgatemotorinn.com
American menu. Dinner. Bar. Casual attire. **$**

★★ITALIAN OASIS
106 Main St., Littleton, 603-444-6995
Italian menu. Lunch, dinner. Bar. Converted Victorian home (circa 1890). Outdoor seating. **$$**

★★ROSA FLAMINGOS
Main St., Bethlehem, 603-869-3111
Italian menu. Lunch, dinner, brunch. Bar. Children's menu. Casual attire. Reservations recommended. Outdoor seating. **$$**

MANCHESTER

Manchester is a city that has refused to bow to economic adversity. When the Amoskeag Manufacturing Company (cotton textiles), which had dominated Manchester's economy, failed in 1935, it left the city poverty-stricken. However, a group of citizens bought the plant for $5 million and revived the city. Now Manchester is northern New England's premier financial center.

Information: Chamber of Commerce, 889 Elm St., 603-666-6600;
www.manchester-chamber.org

WHAT TO SEE AND DO

CURRIER MUSEUM OF ART
150 Ash St., Manchester, 603-669-6144; www.currier.org
One of New England's leading small museums; 13th- to 20th-century European and American paintings and sculpture; New England decorative art; furniture, glass, silver and pewter; changing exhibitions, concerts, films, other programs. Tours of Zimmerman House, designed by Frank Lloyd Wright (call for reservations and times, fee). Wednesday-Monday 11 a.m.-5 p.m.

MANCHESTER HISTORIC ASSOCIATION MILLYARD MUSEUM
129 Amherst St., Manchester, 603-622-7531; www.manchesterhistoric.org
Museum and library with collections illustrating life in Manchester from precolonial times to present; permanent and changing exhibits; firefighting equipment; decorative arts, costumes, paintings. Wednesday-Saturday 10 a.m.-4 p.m.

SCIENCE ENRICHMENT ENCOUNTERS MUSEUM
200 Bedford St., Manchester, 603-669-0400; www.see-sciencecenter.org
More than 60 interactive, hands-on exhibits demonstrate basic science principles. Monday-Friday 10 a.m.-4 p.m., Saturday-Sunday 10 a.m.-5 p.m.

HOTELS

★★★BEDFORD VILLAGE INN
2 Olde Bedford Way, Bedford, 603-472-2001, 800-852-1166; www.bedfordvillageinn.com
This stately New England inn, a converted 1800s barn, offers all-suite accommodations and four-poster beds, Italian marble and whirlpool bathtubs. 14 rooms, all

NEW HAMPSHIRE

★
★
★
★
★

suites. Wireless Internet access. Restaurant, bar. Airport transportation available. Whirlpool. **$$$**

★★FOUR POINTS BY SHERATON

55 John Devine Drive, Manchester, 603-668-6110, 800-368-7764;
www.fourpoints.com/manchester

120 rooms. Pets accepted; fee. Wireless Internet access. Restaurant, bar. Fitness room. Indoor pool, whirlpool. Airport transportation available. **$**

★★QUALITY INN BEDFORD

121 S. River Road, Bedford, 603-622-3766, 800-424-6423; www.wayfarerinn.com

175 rooms. Pets accepted; fee. Complimentary continental breakfast. Restaurant, bar. Fitness room. Indoor pool, outdoor pool. Airport transportation available. Complimentary Wireless Internet access. **$**

★★RADISSON HOTEL MANCHESTER

700 Elm St., Manchester, 603-625-1000, 800-333-3333;
www.radisson.com/manchesternh

251 rooms. Pets accepted. Wireless Internet access. Restaurant, bar. Fitness room. Indoor pool, whirlpool. Airport transportation available. **$**

RESTAURANTS

★★★BEDFORD VILLAGE INN

2 Village Inn Way, Bedford, 603-472-2001, 800-852-1166; www.bedfordvillageinn.com

Originally part of a working farm (1810), this inn is surrounded by pristine gardens. Choose from eight separate dining rooms, each with its own distinct character (hand-painted murals, swag drapes, area rugs, or a roaring fireplace). The kitchen offers updated regional New England cuisine using only the freshest local ingredients. American menu. Breakfast, lunch, dinner. Business casual attire. Reservations recommended. Bar. **$$$**

★PURITAN BACKROOM

245 Hooksett Road, Manchester, 603-669-6890; www.puritanbackroom.com

American menu. Lunch, dinner. Bar. Children's menu. Casual attire. Outdoor seating. **$$**

MEREDITH

Between Lakes Winnipesaukee and Waukewan in the Lakes Region, Meredith is a year-round recreation area.

Information: Chamber of Commerce, 272 Daniel Webster Highway,
603-279-6121, 877-279-6121; www.meredithcc.org

WHAT TO SEE AND DO

LEAGUE OF NEW HAMPSHIRE CRAFTSMEN—MEREDITH/LACONIA ARTS & CRAFTS

279 Daniel Webster Highway, Meredith, 603-279-7920; www.nhcrafts.org

Work by some of New Hampshire's finest craftspeople. Daily.

WINNIPESAUKEE SCENIC RAILROAD

Meredith, 603-279-5253; www.hoborr.com

Scenic train rides along the shore of Lake Winnipesaukee. Board in Meredith or Weirs Beach. Memorial Day-October. Fall foliage trains to Plymouth.

HOTEL

★★★THE INN AT BAY POINT

312 Daniel Webster Highway, Meredith, 603-279-7006, 800-622-6455;
www.millfalls.com

Right on the edge of Lake Winnipesaukee, this inn offers guests views of the lake from the large, comfortable rooms and also from the dining area. Canoeing and other water sports are among the outdoor activities offered here, and there are plenty of shops and dining options in the surrounding area. 24 rooms. Complimentary continental breakfast. Restaurant, bar. Spa. Indoor pool, outdoor pool. Pets accepted; fee. Closed midweek in winter. $$

SPECIALTY LODGINGS

THE INN AT MILL FALLS

312 Daniel Webster Highway, Meredith, 603-279-7006, 800-622-6455;
www.millfalls.com

54 rooms. Two restaurants, bar. Fitness room. Spa. Indoor pool. $$

OLDE ORCHARD INN

108 Lee Road, Moultonborough, 603-476-5004, 800-598-5845;
www.oldeorchardinn.com

This quaint inn was built in 1790 and converted to a bed-and-breakfast 150 years later. The cozy lounge has a fireplace. Nine rooms. Complimentary full breakfast. $

RESTAURANTS

★HART'S TURKEY FARM

Highways 3 and 104, Meredith, 603-279-6212; www.hartsturkeyfarm.com

American menu. Breakfast, lunch, dinner, brunch. Children's menu. Casual attire. Reservations recommended. $$

★★MAME'S

8 Plymouth St., Meredith, 603-279-4631; www.mamesrestaurant.com

American, Italian menu. Lunch, dinner, brunch. Bar. Children's menu. Casual attire. Reservations recommended. $$

MOUNT WASHINGTON

Mount Washington is the central peak of the White Mountains and the highest point in the northeastern United States (6,288 feet). At the summit, there is a 54-acre state park with an information center, first-aid station, restaurant and gift shop. The mountain has the world's first cog railway, completed in 1869; a road to the top dates back to 1861. P. T. Barnum called the view from the summit "the second-greatest show on earth." The weather on Mount Washington is so violent that the timberline is at about 4,000 feet; in the Rockies it is nearly 10,000 feet. In the treeless zone are alpine plants and insects, some unique to the region. The weather station here recorded a wind speed of 231 miles per hour in April, 1934—a world record. The lowest temperature recorded was −49 F; the year-round average is below freezing. The peak gets nearly 15 feet of snow each year.

www.mountwashington.org

WHAT TO SEE AND DO
COG RAILWAY
Highway 302, Bretton Woods, 603-278-5404, 800-922-8825; www.thecog.com
Allow at least three hours for round trip. May-Memorial Day weekend: weekends; after Memorial Day weekend-November: daily.

GREAT GLEN TRAILS
Highway 16, Gorham, 603-466-2333; www.greatglentrails.com
Located at the base of Mount Washington, this all-season, nonmotorized recreational trails park features biking programs (rentals), hiking programs (guided or self-guided), kayak and canoe tours, and workshops in summer; cross-country skiing, snowshoeing and snow tubing in winter. Daily; closed April. Detailed map with trail information available on the Web site.

MOUNT WASHINGTON AUTO ROAD
Highway 16, Gorham, 603-466-3988; www.mt-washington.com
The trip to the summit of Mount Washington takes approximately 30 minutes each way. Make sure your car is in good condition; check brakes before starting. Mid-May-mid-October daily, weather permitting. Guided tour service available daily.

MOUNT WASHINGTON SUMMIT MUSEUM
Highway 302, Sargent's Purchase. Top of Mount Washington; 603-466-3388
Displays on life in the extreme climate of the summit; rare flora and fauna; geology, history. Memorial Day-Columbus Day: daily.

NASHUA
Originally a fur trading post, Nashua's manufacturing began with the development of Merrimack River water power early in the 19th-century. The city is the second largest in New Hampshire.
Information: Greater Nashua Chamber of Commerce, 151 Main St., 603-881-8333; www.nashuachamber.com

WHAT TO SEE AND DO
SILVER LAKE STATE PARK
Silver Lake Road, Hollis, 603-465-2342
One-thousand-foot beach on a 34-acre lake; swimming, bathhouse; picnicking. Late June-Labor Day 9 a.m.-8 p.m.

HOTELS
★★★CROWNE PLAZA
2 Somerset Parkway, Nashua, 603-886-1200, 800-962-7482; www.cpnashua.com
Just 15 miles from Manchester Airport and 40 miles from Boston's Logan Airport, this full-service hotel is in the heart of New Hampshire's high-tech area. 230 rooms. High-speed Internet access. Restaurant, bar. Fitness room. Indoor pool. Airport transportation available. **$$**

★FAIRFIELD INN
4 Amherst Road, Merrimack, 603-424-7500, 800-228-2800; www.fairfieldinn.com
116 rooms. Complimentary continental breakfast. Outdoor pool. Complimentary Wireless Internet access. $

★★HOLIDAY INN NASHUA
9 Northeastern Blvd., Nashua, 603-888-1551, 888-801-5661; www.holidayinn.com
208 rooms. Pets accepted; fee. Wireless Internet access. Restaurant, bar. Fitness room. Outdoor pool. Parking available.

★★★SHERATON NASHUA HOTEL
11 Tara Blvd., Nashua, 603-888-9970, 800-325-3535; www.sheraton.com
This contemporary hotel with Tudor-style architecture offers a comfortable stay for both business and leisure travelers. It is located near the highway in a corporate park with 16 acres of landscaped grounds. 336 rooms. Pets accepted, some restrictions. Wireless Internet access. Restaurant, bar. Indoor pool, outdoor pool, whirlpool. Airport transportation available. $$

NEW LONDON
Located in the Lake Sunapee recreational area, this town has a charming main street and is close to many cross-country skiing and hiking trails.
Information: Chamber of Commerce, Main St., 603-526-6575, 877-526-6575; www.newlondonareanh.com

HOTELS

★★★INN AT PLEASANT LAKE
853 Pleasant St., New London, 603-526-6271, 800-626-4907; www.innatpleasantlake.com
Situated between the lake and Mount Kearsarge, this gabled country inn is decorated like a comfortable house and has access to a private beach. 12 rooms. Complimentary full breakfast. Wireless Internet access. Restaurant. Beach. Closed one week in April and two weeks in November. Pets not accepted. $$

SPECIALTY LODGING

FOLLANSBEE INN
Highway 114, North Sutton, 603-927-4221, 800-626-4221; www.follansbeeinn.com
This homey 1840 country inn, located on the south shore of Keyzar Lake, has a wraparound porch and individually decorated rooms. 17 rooms. Children over 10 years only. Complimentary full breakfast. Pets not accepted. $

NEW LONDON INN
353 Main St., New London, 603-526-2791, 800-526-2791; www.newlondoninn.us
This historic inn is located on the main street of a quaint town. Each room is uniquely decorated, and some feature Jacuzzi tubs and TV/DVD players. 24 rooms. Pets accepted. Complimentary full breakfast. Wireless Internet access. Restaurant, bar. Closed one week in November. $

NEW HAMPSHIRE

★
★
★
★
☆

RESTAURANTS

★★MILLSTONE

74 Newport Road, New London, 603-526-4201; www.millstonerestaurant.com

American menu. Lunch, dinner, Sunday brunch. Bar. Children's menu. Casual attire. Daily. **$$**

★★NEW LONDON INN

353 Main St., New London, 603-526-2791, 800-526-2791; www.newlondoninn.net

American menu. Dinner, Sunday brunch. Bar. Children's menu. Casual attire. Reservations recommended. Outdoor seating. Closed Monday. **$$**

NORTH CONWAY

The heart of the famous Mount Washington Valley region of the White Mountains, this area also includes Bartlett, Glen, Jackson, Conway, Redstone, Kearsarge and Intervale. Mount Washington, seen from the middle of Main Street, is one of the great views in the East.

Information: Mount Washington Valley Chamber of Commerce, 2617 Main St., 603-356-5701, 800-367-3364; www.mtwashingtonvalley.org

WHAT TO SEE AND DO

CONWAY SCENIC RAILROAD

38 Norcross Circle, North Conway, 603-356-5251; www.conwayscenic.com

Steam and diesel trains depart from restored Victorian station (1874) for an 11-mile (55-minute) round trip. The Valley Train explores the Saco River valley. Mid-May-October: daily; mid-April-mid-May, November-December: weekends. The Notch Train travels through Crawford Notch Mid-September-mid-October: daily; late June-mid-September: Tuesday-Thursday, Saturday. Railroad museum.

ECHO LAKE STATE PARK

Highway 302, 603-356-2672

Mountain lake in the shadow of White Horse Ledge. Scenic road to 700-foot Cathedral Ledge, a dramatic rock formation; panoramic views of the White Mountains and the Saco River Valley. Swimming, picnicking. Late June-Labor Day.

MOUNT CRANMORE

Intersection of Route 16 and Kearsarge Street, 800-786-6754; www.cranmore.com

Express quad, triple, double chairlift to summit, three double chairlifts to north, south and east slopes, four surface lifts, patrol, school, rentals, snowmaking, Restaurant, bar, day care. Longest run 1¾ miles; vertical drop 1,200 feet. November-April: daily.

HOTELS

★★BEST WESTERN RED JACKET MOUNTAIN VIEW RESORT & CONFERENCE CENTER

Highway 16, North Conway, 603-356-5411, 800-752-2538; www.bestwestern.com

148 rooms. Wireless Internet access. Two restaurants, bar. Children's activity center. Fitness room. Spa. Indoor pool, outdoor pool, whirlpool. Tennis. Pets accepted. Restriction. **$$**

★
★
★
★
★

★COMFORT INN

2001 White Mountain Highway, North Conway, 603-356-8811, 866-647-8483;
www.comfortinnnh.com

59 rooms. Complimentary continental breakfast. Wireless Internet access. Children's activity center. Fitness room. Indoor pool. **$**

★★THE FOX RIDGE

White Mountain Highway; Highway 16, North Conway, 603-356-3151, 800-343-1804;
www.redjacketresorts.com

136 rooms. Wireless Internet access. Restaurant, bar. Children's activity center. Fitness room. Indoor pool, outdoor pool, whirlpool. Tennis. **$$**

★★GREEN GRANITE INN

Highways 16 and 302, North Conway, 603-356-6901, 800-468-3666;
www.greengranite.com

91 rooms. Complimentary full breakfast. Children's activity center. Fitness room. Indoor pool, outdoor pool, whirlpool. Reservations recommended. **$$**

★★NORTH CONWAY GRAND HOTEL

72 Common Court, North Conway, 603-356-9300, 800-648-4397;
www.northconwaygrand.com

200 rooms. Restaurant, bar. Children's activity center. Fitness room. Indoor pool, whirlpool. Tennis. Free Wireless Internet. Tennis Courts. **$$**

★NORTH CONWAY MOUNTAIN INN

Main St., North Conway, 603-356-2803, 800-319-4405;
www.northconwaymountaininn.com

32 rooms. Internet access. Pets accepted; fee. **$**

★SWISS CHALETS VILLAGE INN

Highway 16A, Intervale, 603-356-2232, 800-831-2727;
www.swisschaletsvillage.com

42 rooms. Pets accepted; fee. Complimentary continental breakfast. Outdoor pool. Reservations recommended. **$**

★★★WHITE MOUNTAIN HOTEL & RESORT

West Side Road, North Conway, 603-356-7100, 800-533-6301;
www.whitemountainhotel.com

Beneath the Whitehorse and Cathedral ledges and Echo State Park, this elegant English country inn offers outdoor activities including cross-country skiing, hiking and rock climbing. 80 rooms. Wireless Internet access. Restaurant, bar. Children's activity center. Fitness room. Outdoor pool, whirlpool. Golf, nine holes. Tennis. Ski-in/ski-out. Reservations recommended. Pets not accepted. **$$**

★
★
★
★
☆

SPECIALTY LODGINGS

1785 INN

3582 N. White Mountain Highway, North Conway, 603-356-9025, 800-421-1785;
www.the1785inn.com

This colonial-style building (1785) is located on six acres and features original fire-places and Victorian antiques. The inn has views of Mount Washington. 17 rooms. Complimentary full breakfast. Restaurant, bar. Reservations recommended. **$**

BUTTONWOOD INN ON MT. SURPRISE

Mt. Surprise Road, North Conway, 603-356-2625, 800-258-2625;
www.buttonwoodinn.com

Located on 17 wooded acres on the mountainside, this 1820s Cape Cod-style building features antiques and a library. 10 rooms. Children over 12 years only. Complimentary full breakfast. Outdoor pool. Pets not accepted. **$$**

CRANMORE MOUNTAIN LODGE

859 Kearsarge St., North Conway, 603-356-2044, 800-356-3596; www.cml1.com

Located on 12 acres, this historic guest house (1860) was once owned by Babe Ruth's daughter and son-in-law. There are farm animals and a duck pond on the grounds. 21 rooms. Outdoor pool. Pets accepted, restrictions. **$**

DARBY FIELD COUNTRY INN

185 Chase Hill Road, Albany, 603-447-2181, 800-426-4147; www.darbyfield.com

This inn has views of the Presidential Mountains. 13 rooms. Children over 8 years only. Complimentary full breakfast. Outdoor pool. **$$**

EASTMAN INN

2331 White Mountain Highway, North Conway, 603-356-6707, 800-626-5855;
www.eastmaninn.com

This classic three-story Victorian inn (1777) features a wraparound veranda and rich and tasteful décor. The central location is close to shopping and attractions in town. 14 rooms. Children over 15 years only. Complimentary full breakfast. **$$**

MERRILL FARM RESORT

428 White Mountain Highway, North Conway, 603-447-3866, 800-445-1017;
www.merrillfarm.com

Just south of the town's center, this converted farmhouse (1885) is located on the Saco River and has cottages for overnight stays. Nearby activities and attractions include skiing, golfing, covered bridges and shopping. 62 rooms. Complimentary continental breakfast. Indoor pool, whirlpool. **$**

SNOWVILLAGE INN

Stewart Road, Snowville, 603-447-2818, 800-447-4345; www.snowvillageinn.com

18 rooms. Pets accepted, some restrictions. Complimentary full breakfast. Restaurant, bar. **$$**

NEW HAMPSHIRE

★
★
★
★
★

RESTAURANTS

★★★1785 INN

3582 White Mountain Highway, North Conway, 603-356-9025, 800-421-1785;
www.the1785inn.com

This restaurant offers an extensive continental menu that includes creative veal chops with mushroom and cabernet sauvignon reduction and seared sea scallops with leeks and artichokes. American, continental menu. Dinner. Bar. Casual attire. **$$**

★BELLINI'S

1857 White Mountain Highway, North Conway, 603-356-7000; www.bellinis.com

American, Italian menu. Lunch, dinner. Bar. Children's menu. Casual attire. Outdoor seating. **$$**

★HORSEFEATHERS

2679 White Mountain Highway Main St., North Conway, 603-356-2687;
www.horsefeathers.com

American menu. Lunch, dinner, brunch. Bar. Children's menu. Casual attire. **$$**

PETERBOROUGH

This was the home of composer Edward MacDowell (1861-1908). Edward Arlington Robinson, Stephen Vincent Bent, Willa Cather and Thornton Wilder, among others, worked at the MacDowell Colony, a thriving artists' retreat, which made Peterborough famous.

Information: Greater Peterborough Chamber of Commerce,
603-924-7234; www.peterboroughchamber.com

WHAT TO SEE AND DO

MILLER STATE PARK

Route 101 E., Peterborough, 603-924-3672; www.nhstateparks.com/miller.html

Atop the 2,288-foot Pack Monadnock Mountain; walking trails on summit; scenic drive; picnicking. June-Labor Day, daily; May and Labor Day-November, Saturday-Sunday and holidays.

PETERBOROUGH HISTORICAL SOCIETY

19 Grove St., Peterborough, 603-924-3235

Exhibits on the history of the area; historical and genealogical library. Monday-Saturday.

HOTEL

★★★HANCOCK INN

33 Main St., Hancock, 603-525-3318, 800-525-1789; www.hancockinn.com

In operation since 1789, the interior of this country inn is reminiscent of 18th-century New England. Sit by the fire in the red-walled dining room and order the famous Shaker cranberry pot roast.15 rooms. Pets accepted. Complimentary full breakfast. Wireless Internet access. Restaurant, bar. **$$**

NEW HAMPSHIRE

★
★
★
★
☆

PLYMOUTH

Since 1795, Plymouth's varied industries have included lumber, pig iron, mattresses, gloves and sporting goods. It has been a resort center since the mid-19th-century.

Information: Chamber of Commerce, 603-536-1001, 800-386-3678; www.plymouthnh.org

WHAT TO SEE AND DO
MARY BAKER EDDY HISTORIC HOUSE

58 Stinson Lake Road, Rumney, 603-786-9943; www.longyear.org/houses/rumney.html
Residence of Mary Baker Eddy from 1860 to 1862, prior to the founding of the Christian Science Church. May-October Tuesday-Sunday.

HOTEL
★COBBLESTONE INN

304 Main St., Plymouth, 603-536-2330; www.cobblestoneinnh.com
38 rooms. Pets accepted. Complimentary continental breakfast. Outdoor pool. $

PORTSMOUTH

A tour of Portsmouth's historic houses reveals architecture from the Colonial and Federal periods into the 19th-century. The one-time capital of New Hampshire, Portsmouth was also the home port of a dynasty of merchant seamen who grew rich and built accordingly. The U.S. Navy Yard located in Kittery, Maine on the Piscataqua River has long been Portsmouth's major industry. The peace treaty ending the Russo-Japanese War was signed at the Portsmouth Navy Yard in 1905.

Information: Greater Portsmouth Chamber of Commerce, 500 Market St., 603-436-3988; www.portsmouthchamber.org

WHAT TO SEE AND DO
CHILDREN'S MUSEUM OF PORTSMOUTH

280 Marcy St., Portsmouth, 603-436-3853; www.childrens-museum.org
Arts and science museum featuring mock submarine, space shuttle, lobster boat, exhibits and gallery. Summer and school vacations, daily; rest of year, Tuesday-Sunday.

FORT CONSTITUTION

New Castle, 603-436-1552; www.nhstateparks.com/fortconstitution.html
(1808) The first cannon was placed on this site in 1632; in 1694, it was known as Fort William and Mary. Information about a British order to stop gunpowder from coming into the colonies, brought by Paul Revere on December 13, 1774, caused the Sons of Liberty from Portsmouth, New Castle and Rye to attack and capture a fort that held five tons of gunpowder the next day. Much of this powder was used at Bunker Hill by the Patriots. This uprising against the King's authority was one of the first overt acts of the Revolution. Little remains of the original fort except the base of its walls. Fort Constitution had been built on the same site by 1808; granite walls were added during the Civil War. Mid-June-early September: daily; late May-mid-June, late September-mid-October: weekends, holidays only.

★
★
★
★
★

FORT STARK STATE HISTORIC SITE

Wild Rose Lane, New Castle, 603-436-1552; www.nhstateparks.com/fortstark.html

A former portion of the coastal defense system dating to 1746, exhibiting many of the changes in military technology from the Revolutionary War through World War II. The fort is situated on Jerry's Point, overlooking the Piscataqua River, Little Harbor and Atlantic Ocean. Late May-mid-October daily.

GOVERNOR JOHN LANGDON HOUSE

143 Pleasant St., Portsmouth, 603-436-3205; www.spnea.org/visit/homes/langdon.htm

(1784) John Langdon served three terms as governor of New Hampshire and was the first president *pro tempore* of the U.S. Senate. The house's exterior proportions are monumental and the interior is embellished with excellent woodcarving and fine Portsmouth-area furniture. George Washington was entertained here in 1789. Surrounded by landscaped grounds with gazebo, rose and grape arbor and restored perennial garden beds. Tours: June-mid-October Friday-Sunday.

ISLES OF SHOALS

315 Market St., Portsmouth, 603-431-5500; www.islesofshoals.com

The M/V *Thomas Laighton* makes cruises to historic Isles of Shoals. Lobster clambake river cruises, fall foliage excursions and others. Party ship. Mid-June-Labor Day daily.

JOHN PAUL JONES HOUSE

43 Middle St., Portsmouth, 603-436-8420; www.portsmouthhistory.org/jpjhouse.html

(1758) Where the famous naval commander twice boarded; now a museum containing period furniture, collections of costumes, china, glass, documents, weapons. Guided tours: June-mid-October, daily.

MOFFATT-LADD HOUSE

154 Market St., Portsmouth, 603-436-8221, www.moffattladd.org

Built in 1763 by Captain John Moffatt; later the home of General William Whipple, his son-in-law and a signer of the Declaration of Independence. Many original 18th and 19th-century furnishings. Formal gardens. Mid-June-mid-October, daily.

RUNDLET-MAY HOUSE

364 Middle St., Portsmouth, 603-436-3205;
www.seacoastnh.com/houses/rundletmay/index.html

Federalist, three-story 1807 mansion. House sits on terraces and retains its original 1812 courtyard and garden layout; landscaped grounds. House contains family furnishings and accessories, including many fine examples of Federalist craftsmanship and the latest technologies of its time. Guided tours. Grounds available for rental. June-October first Saturday of the month.

STRAWBERY BANKE MUSEUM

454 Court St., Portsmouth, 603-433-1100; www.strawberybanke.org

Restoration of a 10-acre historic waterfront neighborhood; site of the original Portsmouth settlement. 42 buildings dating from 1695 to 1950. Includes nine houses: Captain Keyran Walsh House (1796), Governor Goodwin Mansion (1811), Chase House (1762), Captain John Wheelwright House (1780), Thomas Bailey Aldrich

NEW HAMPSHIRE

★
★
★
★
★

House (1790), Drisco House (1790s), Rider-Wood House (1840s), Abbott Grocery Store (1943) and the William Pitt Tavern (1766). Shops, architectural exhibits, pottery shop and demonstrations, family programs and activities, special events, tours. May-October, Monday-Saturday, Sunday afternoons; November-April, Thursday-Sunday; closed January.

WARNER HOUSE
150 Daniel St., Portsmouth, 603-436-5909; www.warnerhouse.org
(1716) One of New England's finest Georgian houses, with scagliola in the dining room, restored mural paintings on the staircase walls, a lightning rod on the west wall said to have been installed by Benjamin Franklin in 1762 and five portraits by Joseph Blackburn. Guided tours. June-mid-October Monday-Saturday, Sunday afternoons.

WENTWORTH-GARDNER HOUSE
50 Mechanic St., Portsmouth, 603-436-4406; www.wentworthgardnerandlear.org
(1760) Excellent example of Georgian architecture. Elaborate woodwork and main staircase. Mid-June-mid-October Tuesday-Saturday afternoons.

HOTELS
★FAIRFIELD INN
650 Borthwick Ave., Portsmouth, 603-436-6363, 800-228-2800; www.marriott.com/psmfi
105 rooms. Complimentary continental breakfast. Wireless Internet access. Outdoor pool. Pets not accepted. $

★★HOLIDAY INN
300 Woodbury Ave., Portsmouth, 603-431-8000, 888-465-4329; www.holiday-inn.com
130 rooms. Restaurant, bar. Fitness room. Indoor pool. $$

★THE PORT INN
505 Highway 1 Bypass South, Portsmouth, 603-436-4378, 800-282-7678;
www.theportinn.com
57 rooms. Complimentary continental breakfast. Wireless Internet access. Outdoor pool. Free continental breakfast. $

★★★SHERATON HARBORSIDE HOTEL PORTSMOUTH
250 Market St., Portsmouth, 603-431-2300, 800-325-3535;
www.sheratonportsmouth.com
This large New England-style hotel features a brick and granite exterior with large-paneled windows. The interior is inviting and stylish, and the location is in the downtown historic district on the Piscataqua River. 220 rooms. Pets accepted, some restrictions. Restaurant, bar. Fitness room. Indoor pool. Business center. $$

SPECIALTY LODGING
SISE INN
40 Court St., Portsmouth, 603-433-1200, 877-747-3466; www.siseinn.com
This Queen Anne-style home was built in 1881 for the prosperous businessman and merchant John E. Sise. 34 rooms. Complimentary full breakfast. Wireless Internet access. $$

SALEM

This southern New Hampshire town was once part of Massachusetts. Many of its residents commute to Boston.

Information: Greater Salem Chamber of Commerce, 224 N. Broadway, 603-893-3177; www.salemnhchamber.org

WHAT TO SEE AND DO

AMERICA'S STONEHENGE

105 Haverhill Road, North Salem, 603-893-8300; www.stonehengeusa.com

A megalithic calendar site dated to 2000 BC, with 22 stone buildings on more than 30 acres. The main site features a number of stone-constructed chambers and is surrounded by miles of stone walls containing large, shaped monoliths that indicate the rising and setting of the sun at solstice and equinox, as well as other astronomical alignments, including lunar. Daily.

ROBERT FROST FARM

Highway 28, Derry, 603-432-3091; www.robertfrostfarm.org

Home of poet Robert Frost from 1900 to 1911; period furnishings; audiovisual display; poetry-nature trail. Mid-June-Labor Day, Wednesday-Sunday; mid-May-mid-June:, weekends.

HOTELS

★FAIRFIELD INN

8 Keewaydin Drive, Salem, 603-893-4722, 800-228-2800; www.fairfieldinn.com

105 rooms. Pets accepted; fee. Complimentary continental breakfast. Outdoor pool. $

★★HOLIDAY INN

1 Keewaydin Drive, Salem, 603-893-5511, 888-465-4329; www.holiday-inn.com

109 rooms. Pets accepted; fee. Complimentary continental breakfast. Restaurant. Fitness room. Outdoor pool, indoor pool, whirlpool. Fitness center. High-speed Internet access. Business center. Pets not accepted. $

SUNAPEE

This is a year-round resort community on Lake Sunapee and a popular weekend and summer escape for Bostonians.

Information: New London Lake Sunapee Region Chamber of Commerce, 603-526-6575, 877-526-6575; www.lakesunapeenh.org

WHAT TO SEE AND DO

SNOWHILL AT EASTMAN SKI AREA

6 Club House Lane, Grantham, 603-863-4500; www.eastman-lake.com

Ski Touring Center has 30 kilometers of cross-country trails; patrol, school, rentals; bar, restaurant. Summer facilities include Eastman Lake (swimming, boating, fishing); 18-hole golf, tennis, indoor pool, hiking. December-March: daily.

NEW HAMPSHIRE

★
★
★
★
★

HOTEL
★BURKEHAVEN AT SUNAPEE
179 Burkehaven Hill Road, Sunapee, 603-763-2788, 800-567-2788;
www.burkehavenatsunapee.com
11 rooms. Outdoor pool. Tennis. Continental breakfast. **$**

SPECIALTY LODGINGS
CANDLELITE INN
5 Greenhouse Lane, Bradford, 603-938-5571, 888-812-5571; www.candleliteinn.com
Built in 1897; gazebo porch. Six rooms. Complimentary full breakfast. **$**

DEXTERS INN & TENNIS CLUB
258 Stagecoach Road, Sunapee, 603-763-5571, 800-232-5571; www.dextersnh.com
17 guest rooms, plus cottage on 20-acre estate. Pets accepted, some restrictions; fee.
Complimentary full breakfast. Outdoor pool. Tennis. **$$**

TWIN MOUNTAIN
Information: Chamber of Commerce, 800-245-8946; www.twinmountain.org

HOTELS
★FOUR SEASONS MOTOR INN
Birch Road, and Route 3, Twin Mountain, 603-846-5708, 800-228-5708;
www.4seasonsmotorinn.com
24 rooms. Outdoor pool. **$**

★SHAKESPEARE'S INN
675 Highway 3, Twin Mountain, 603-846-5562, 888-846-5562;
www.shakespearesinn.com
33 rooms. Restaurant. Outdoor pool. Tennis. **$**

SPECIALTY LODGING
NORTHERN ZERMATT INN & MOTEL
529 Highway 3 N., Twin Mountain, 603-846-5533, 800-535-3214; www.zermattinn.com
Former boarding house (circa 1900) for loggers and railroad workers. 17 rooms. Pets
accepted, some restrictions. Complimentary continental breakfast. Outdoor pool. **$**

WATERVILLE VALLEY
Although the resort village of Waterville Valley was developed in the late 1960s,
the surrounding area has attracted tourists since the mid-19th-century, when summer
vacationers stayed at the Waterville Inn. Completely surrounded by the White Moun-
tain National Forest, the resort, approximately 11 miles northeast of Campton, offers
a variety of winter and summer activities and spectacular views of the mountains.
Information: Waterville Valley Region Chamber of Commerce, Campton,
603-726-3804, 800-237-2307; www.watervillevalleyregion.com

WHITE MOUNTAIN NATIONAL FOREST

This national forest includes the Presidential Range and a large part of the White Mountains. With more than 100 miles of roads and 1,128 miles of foot trails, there is much to see. The Appalachian Trail, with eight hostels, winds over some spectacular peaks—eight tower more than a mile above sea level (the highest is Mount Washington at 6,288 feet). Twenty-two mountains rise more than 4,000 feet and there are several well-defined ranges, divided by deep "notches" and broader valleys. Clear streams, mountain lakes and ponds dot the landscape and deer, bears, moose and bobcats roam throughout the area.

There is lodging within the forest; for information and reservations, contact the Appalachian Mountain Club, Pinkham Notch, Gorham, New Hampshire 03581 (603-466-2727). There are also many resorts, camp-sites, picnicking and recreational spots in private and state-owned areas. A visitor center (daily) is located at the Saco Ranger Station at 33 Kancamagus Highway in Conway (603-447-5448). Information stations are also located at exits 28 and 32, off Interstate 93 and at Franconia Notch State Park Visitor Center. For further information, contact the Supervisor at the White Mountain National Forest Office. The following cities and villages in and near the forest are included in this book: Bartlett, Bretton Woods, Franconia, Franconia Notch State Park, Gorham, Jackson, Lincoln/Woodstock, Mount Washington, North Conway, Pinkham Notch, Twin Mountain and Waterville Valley.

Information: White Mountain National Forest Office, 719 N. Main Street, 603-528-8721; www.fs.fed.us/r9/forests/white_mountain/contact/

WHAT TO SEE AND DO
WATERVILLE VALLEY SKI AREA

1 Ski Area Road, Waterville Valley, 800-468-2553; www.waterville.com

Three double, two triple chairlifts, two quad chairlifts, T-bar, J-bar, four platter pulls, patrol, school, retail, rental and repair shops, snowmaking, restaurants, lounge and nursery. 52 ski trails; longest run three miles; vertical drop 2,020 feet. Half-day rates. Mid-November-mid-April, daily. Ski Touring Center with 46 miles of cross-country trails, rentals, school, restaurants. Summer facilities include nine-hole golf, 18 clay tennis courts, small boating, hiking, fishing, bicycling; entertainment. Indoor sports center (daily). Contact Waterville Valley Resort, Town Square.

HOTELS
★★SNOWY OWL INN

4 Village Road, Waterville Valley, 603-236-8383, 800-766-9969;
www.snowyowlinn.com

83 rooms. Pets accepted, some restrictions. Complimentary continental breakfast. Fitness room. Indoor pool, outdoor pool, whirlpool. $

★★VALLEY INN & TAVERN

1 Tecumseh Road, Waterville Valley, 603-236-8336, 800-343-0969; www.valleyinn.com

52 rooms. Complimentary continental breakfast. Restaurant, bar. Fitness room. Indoor pool, outdoor pool, whirlpool. **$**

RESTAURANT
★★WILLIAM TELL

Route 49, Thornton, 603-726-3618; www.nhwilliamtell.com

American, Continental menu. Dinner. Bar. Children's menu. Outdoor seating. Closed Wednesday. **$$**

WOLFEBORO

Wolfeboro has been a resort area for more than two centuries. It's the oldest summer resort in America, but come winter, it's a ski touring center with 40 miles of groomed trails.

Information: Chamber of Commerce, 312 Central Ave., 603-569-2200,
800-516-5324; www.wolfeborochamber.com

WHAT TO SEE AND DO
CLARK HOUSE

337 S. Main St., Wolfeboro, 603-569-4997;
www.wolfeborohistoricalsociety.org/clarkhouse.html

Wolfeboro Historical Society is housed in the Clark family homestead (1778), a one-room schoolhouse (circa 1820) and a firehouse museum. Clark House has period furnishings and memorabilia; the firehouse museum contains restored firefighting equipment dating to 1842. July-August, Wednesday-Saturday.

WRIGHT MUSEUM

77 Center St., Wolfeboro, 603-569-1212; www.wrightmuseum.org

Showcases American enterprise during World War II. Collection of tanks, Jeeps and other military vehicles, period memorabilia. May-October, daily; weekends only April and November; closed December-March.

HOTEL
★★★THE WOLFEBORO INN

90 N. Main St., Wolfeboro, 603-569-3016, 800-451-2389; www.wolfeboroinn.com

Built in 1812, this inn is located on Lake Winnipesaukee in one of America's oldest summer resort towns. Many rooms offer Wolfeboro Bay views and all include a boat ride and private beach access during summer months. 40 rooms. Complimentary continental breakfast. Restaurant, bar. **$$**

★
★★
★★
★

RHODE ISLAND

RHODE ISLAND'S MOTTO IS "HOPE," BUT A MORE APPROPRIATE MAXIM MIGHT BE "SIZE doesn't matter." Yes, the wee state is the smallest in the nation, more petite even than most neighboring state counties. But its pint size belies its influence as a historical, cultural and natural treasure trove—one that road trippers would be remiss to miss. For starters, the Ocean State has more than 400 miles of coastline, replete with sunning, swimming, sailing and fishing enclaves. Then there are the inland 1,000 or so square miles, studded with postcard-perfect working farms, quaint Colonial inns and protected nature reserves. Cities such as Providence and Newport supply the state with first-rate lodging and modern cuisine while isles like Block Island give the harried a place to unwind.

All of this would no doubt have blown the feather cap off explorer Giovanni da Verrazano, who landed in Narragansett Bay in 1524, but it might not have surprised Roger Williams. Like thousands after him, Williams moved to Rhode Island to get away from it all. True, the "all" in his case was the puritanical tyranny of Massachusetts but still, his tolerant 1636 settlement set the tone for times to come. The area quickly became known for its policy of religious and political freedom and, in 1663, King Charles II granted it a royal charter, creating the state of Rhode Island.

Since then, the region has become a seat of firsts: Rhode Islanders were among the first colonists to attack the British; on May 4, 1776, the state was the first to proclaim independence (a full two months before the Declaration of Independence was signed); resident Samuel Slater built America's first water-powered cotton mill in 1790; and, in 1876, Newport held the country's first polo match. And it may not have been the first watering hole ever built, but Newport's 1673 White Horse Tavern is the oldest operating pub in the United States. It's small, but sturdy and still going strong.

★ **FUN FACTS**

Rhode Island is the smallest state in the country.

In 1895, the state was home to the first open golf tournament. Rhode Island's eastern coastline.

Information: www.visitrhodeisland.com

BLOCK ISLAND
Twelve miles off the state mainland and a short ferry ride from Montauk, Block Island seems a world away. Blessedly absent from the 21-square-mile retreat are Long Island's social-climbing weekenders and Newport's summer hordes. The scene here just feels milder and, technically, it is—once named Rhode Island's "air conditioned" resort, the atoll is up to 15 degrees cooler than the rest of the state. Named for Dutch explorer Adriaen Block, who landed here in 1614, the island was once a low-key fishing and farming community. Today, it's still low-key, and draws burnt-out city slickers

and nature enthusiasts to its white-sanded shores. More than 40 rare and endangered species of plants and animals live here; most are protected by public land trusts like The Nature Conservancy, which designated Block Island "one of the twelve last great places in the Western Hemisphere."

Information: Chamber of Commerce, Water Street, Block Island, 401-466-2982, 800-383-2474; www.blockislandchamber.com

WHAT TO SEE AND DO

MOHEGAN BLUFFS
West of the Southeast Light lighthouse off Mohegan Trail, these grand 200-foot clay cliffs provide sightseers with an unparalleled ocean view.

NEW HARBOR
One mile west of the Mohegan Bluffs on Ocean Avenue, the mammoth New Harbor was formed when town planners cut through a sand bar to merge the sea with Great Salt Pond.

NORTH LIGHT
Built in 1867 at the tip of the island near Settler's Rock, this former lighthouse now houses a maritime museum. Its surrounding dunes host a seagull rookery and wildlife sanctuary.

RHODE ISLAND'S EASTERN COASTLINE

Summer in Rhode Island's South County means beaches, boating and basking in the sun. It also means tourists galore. Navigating Newport traffic in August can bring out road rage in the mildest-mannered of drivers; waiting in epic lines for ice cream can be a chore. Escape the crowds by taking a day trip along the state's quiet eastern coastline, through the (almost) untouched towns of Bristol, Tiverton and Little Compton. From downtown Providence, take Highway 195 east to exit 7, Highway 114 South. Drive through Barrington, Warren and Bristol. (Dozens of antique and second-hand shops line Warren's Main and Water streets.) Highway 114 becomes Hope Street in Bristol, where stately Federal-era houses (many of them now bed and breakfasts) hint at the town's pre-Civil War wealth. Continue over the Mount Hope Bridge into Portsmouth and turn left onto Highway 24. Cross the Sakonnet River Bridge into Tiverton, and turn right onto Highway 77 South. At the lone traffic light on 77, an intersection with Highway 179, is Tiverton Four Corners. Pause here for shopping and lunch at the town's boutiques and eateries, and don't miss a cone from1920s sweet shop Gray's Ice Cream. Continue south on 77 toward Little Compton, past open fields with panoramic views of Narragansett Bay. Once a productive agricultural area, Little Compton is now a wealthy summer community; the restored-farmhouses-cum-stately-estates are a sight to be seen. You can double back on the same route or turn right onto Highway 24 North in Tiverton and drive into Fall River, Mass., then head west to Providence on Highway 195. Approximately 40 miles.

HOTEL
★★SPRING HOUSE
52 Spring St., Block Island, 401-466-5844, 800-234-9263; www.springhousehotel.com
50 rooms. Closed in winter. Complimentary continental breakfast. Restaurant, bar. Airport transportation available. **$$**

SPECIALTY LODGING
THE 1661 INN & GUEST HOUSE
1 Spring St., Block Island, 401-466-2421, 800-626-4773; www.blockislandresorts.com
Nine rooms. Complimentary full breakfast. Airport transportation available. **$$$**

RESTAURANTS
★FINN'S SEAFOOD
212 Water St., Block Island, 401-466-2473
Seafood menu. Lunch, dinner. Bar. Children's menu. Casual attire. **$$**

★★★HOTEL MANISSES DINING ROOM
1 Spring St., Block Island, 401-466-2836; www.blockislandresorts.com
Often praised for its seafood-heavy contemporary American menu, romantics favor dining in the glass-enclosed garden room; sweet tooths adore rich homemade desserts like layered banana cream cake and Italian-style hot chocolate. A discreet, knowledgeable staff adds to the experience. American menu. Dinner. Closed November-April. Bar. Reservations recommended. Outdoor seating. **$$$**

★MOHEGAN CAFÉ
Water St., Block Island, 401-466-5911
American menu. Lunch, dinner. Bar. Casual attire. **$$**

BRISTOL
Quaint little Bristol's history is surprisingly rife with strife. In the late 1600s, the Native American rebel leader King Philip headquartered his Wampanoag troops in the area, preparing them for the country's first major Colonist vs. Indian battle. The resulting yearlong King Philip's War began and ended on the Bristol peninsula, between Mount Hope and Narragansett bays. Civil War officer—and later, state governor and senator—General Ambrose Burnside also earned his military stripes in Bristol, which by the turn of the 18th-century had become the fourth-busiest port in the United States. Today, the town is well known for its postcard-perfect, seaside feel and the storied Herreshoff Boatyard where many an America's Cup champion was built.
Information: East Bay County Chamber of Commerce,
654 Metacom Ave., Warren, 401-245-0750; www.eastbaychamber.org

★
★
★
★
★

WHAT TO SEE AND DO
BLITHEWOLD MANSION AND GARDENS
101 Ferry Road, Bristol, 401-253-2707; www.blithewold.org
With its manicured trees, flowers and gardens combine with a sweeping sea view to put visitors' aesthetic senses into overdrive. Concerts are held on the grounds of this 45-room mansion in the summer. Mansion, mid-April-Columbus Day, Wednesday-Sunday 10 a.m.-4 p.m.; grounds, daily 10 a.m.-5 p.m.

COGGESHALL FARM MUSEUM, COLT STATE PARK

Poppasquash Road, Bristol, 401-253-9062

Set in the middle of Colt State Park, this working 18th-century farm has fresh vegetables and herbs as well as colonial craft demonstrations. Visitors with extra time can cruise the park's three-mile scenic drive around the former Colt family estate on Narrangansett Bay, or take advantage of area fishing, boating, hiking, picnicking and seasonal concerts in Stone Barn. Farm museum: March-September: daily 10 a.m.-6 p.m.; October-February: daily 10 a.m.-dusk.

HERRESHOFF MARINE MUSEUM

1 Burnside St., Bristol, 401-253-5000; www.herreshoff.org

The Herreshoff Manufacturing Company produced some of the world's greatest yachts, including eight winners of the America's Cup. Permanent exhibits include big boats, steam engines, and photographs and memorabilia from the "golden age of yachting." May-October: daily 10 a.m.-5 p.m., closed Monday. Admission: adults 21 and older $8, seniors over 65 $7, student with student card $4, children under 12 no charge, members free.

SPECIALTY LODGINGS

ROCKWELL HOUSE INN

610 Hope St., Bristol, 401-253-0040, 800-815-0040;
www.rockwellhouseinn.com

One block from Bristol Harbor, this 1809 inn is set on a half-acre of land that boasts the state's largest tulip tree and is within walking distance to Narragansett Bay and Bristol's many antiques shops and restaurants. The restored property features a mix of architectural styles—Federal, Georgian, Victorian—and guest rooms are filled with antique furniture and cooled by new ceiling fans. Four rooms. Children over 12 years only. Complimentary full breakfast. **$$**

WILLIAMS GRANT INN

154 High St., Bristol, 401-253-4222, 800-596-4222; www.wmgrantinn.com

Five rooms. Children over 12 years only. Complimentary full breakfast. **$**

RESTAURANT

★★LOBSTER POT

119 Hope St., Bristol, 401-253-9100; www.lobsterpotri.com

American, seafood menu. Lunch, dinner. Closed Monday; also two weeks in March. Bar. Business casual attire. Reservations recommended. Outdoor seating. **$$**

KINGSTON

Home to the University of Rhode Island, Kingston is a melting pot of enterprising students and laid-back old-timers. The city's early settlers were farmers, and their legacy lives on in the Biscuit City neighborhood's water-powered mill. Legal eagles love Kingston for its legislative lore—the state constitution and an early antislavery law were ratified here. A fertile flood plain lies on the outskirts of town; geologists believe it was once an ancient river.

Information: Chamber of Commerce, 328 Main St.,
Wakefield; 401-783-2801; www.southcountyri.com

WHAT TO SEE AND DO
KINGSTON LIBRARY
2605 Kingston Road, Kingston, 401-783-8254;
www.skpl.org, web.provlib.org/SkiLib/skk.html
Once visited by George Washington and Benjamin Franklin, the library housed the Rhode Island General Assembly when the British occupied Newport. Monday-Saturday.

SPECIAL EVENT
WAKEFIELD ROTARY BALLOON FESTIVAL
University of Rhode Island, 404 Wordens Pond Road, Kingston, 401-783-1770;
www.wakefieldrotary.com/BalloonFestival.cfm
The two-day event features hot air balloon rides, parachute demonstrations, arts and crafts, and music. There is also an exhibit of vintage cars to admire. Late July or early August.

NARRAGANSETT
Before there was Monte Carlo, there was Narragansett. The southern Rhode Island city was once home to a lavish McKim, Mead and White-designed casino. Several summer "cottages" and hotels were built to house the well-heeled who flocked here to hobnob and gamble in the late 19th and early 20th centuries. The casino was devastated by fire in 1900, but its Tower still stands on Ocean Road. Today, Narragansett—named for its indigenous people—counts fishing and tourism as its leading industries. The city is also home to the University of Rhode Island's renowned Graduate School of Oceanography.

Information: Narragansett Chamber of Commerce, The Towers Narragansett Visitors Center, Ocean Road, Narragansett, 401-783-7121; www.narragansettri.com/chamber

WHAT TO SEE AND DO
BLOCK ISLAND FERRY
Galilee State Pier, 304 Great Island Road, Point Judith,
401-783-4613; www.blockislandferry.com
Automobile ferries to Block Island from Point Judith and Newport. Daily.

POINT JUDITH
1460 Ocean Road, Narragansett, 401-789-0444
The lighthouse and station are closed to the public, but strolling Point Judith's historical grounds is free.

SOUTH COUNTY MUSEUM
Strathmore St., Narragansett, 401-783-5400; www.southcountymuseum.org
The museum exhibits 19th-century Rhode Island antique costumes, vehicles, toys and nautical equipment, as well as farm and blacksmithing displays. Also see a historic country kitchen, general store, cobbler's shop and a complete turn-of-the-century letterpress print shop. May-June, September-October: Friday-Saturday 10 a.m.-4 p.m., Sunday noon-4 p.m.; July-August: Wednesday-Saturday 10 a.m.-4 p.m., Sunday noon-4 p.m.

THE TOWERS

35 Ocean Road, Narragansett, 401-782-2597; www.thetowersri.com

In 1900, McKim, Mead and White's grandiose casino—the landmark that solidified Narragansett as a summer destination for the rich and fashionable—was destroyed by fire. This Romanesque arch entryway, flanked by conical towers, is the only structural element that remains. Various public events throughout summer.

SPECIAL EVENT

MID-WINTER NEW ENGLAND SURFING CHAMPIONSHIP

Narragansett Town Beach, 170 Clarke Road, Narragansett,
401-723-8795; www.sne.surfesa.org

For information, contact the Northeastern Surfing Association, 126 Sayles Ave., Pawtucket. Third Saturday in February.

RESTAURANT

★★COAST GUARD HOUSE

40 Ocean Road, Narragansett, 401-789-0700; www.thecoastguardhouse.com

American, seafood menu. Lunch, dinner, Sunday brunch. Bar. Children's menu. Casual attire. Outdoor seating. Closed early January-mid-February. $$

NEWPORT

Had Jay Gatsby had a second summer home, it might have been in Newport. The laid-back resort town was once the epicenter of East Coast summer society, where the rich and fabulous—August Belmont, Ward McAllister, William Astor, Stuyvesant Fish—built megamansions along the city's now-public Cliff Walk. Their lavish and often outrageous soirees, some costing upwards of $300,000, were the talk of early-20th-century Rhode Island. World War I dampened the revelry considerably, though many modern-day bluebloods still flock here for various seasonal affairs.

Social registries aside, Newport is home to Rhode Island's first school and newspaper, as well as the country's earliest Quaker and Jewish communities. During the Revolutionary War, it was occupied by the British for two years before being recaptured by French allies. Throughout its history, the city has been famous for its boating and yachting culture—shipbuilders and sailors still abound in town.

Information: Newport County Convention & Visitors Bureau, 23 America's
Cup Ave., Newport, 401-849-8048, 800-976-5122; www.gonewport.com

WHAT TO SEE AND DO

ASTOR'S BEECHWOOD

580 Bellevue Ave., Newport, 401-846-3772; www.astorsbeechwood.com

Italianate summer residence of Mrs. Caroline Astor—that's *the* Mrs. Astor. A theatrical tour of house includes actors portraying Mrs. Astor's servants and society guests. Mid-May-mid-December: daily; rest of year: weekends only.

BELCOURT CASTLE

657 Bellevue Ave., Newport, 401-846-0669; www.belcourtcastle.com

Designed by Richard Morris Hunt in French château style, this 1891-era 62-room house was the residence of Oliver Hazard Perry Belmont and his wife, Alva Vanderbilt Belmont. Belmont loved horses and his stables sit inside the main structure.

The castle contains the largest collection of antiques and objets d'art in Newport. Tea served. Special events scheduled throughout year. Daily; closed January.

BREAKERS

44 Ochre Point Ave., Newport, 401-847-1000;
www.newportmansions.org/page7016.cfm

With 70 rooms, the Northern Italian palazzo designed by Richard Morris Hunt is the largest of all Newport cottages. The children's playhouse cottage has a scale-size kitchen, fireplace and playroom. The mansion was built for Mr. and Mrs. Cornelius Vanderbilt in 1895. Daily.

BRICK MARKET

121 Thames St., Newport, 401-846-0813; www.brickmarketnewport.com

Home of the Newport Historical Society, the Brick Market was built by Touro Synagogue architect Peter Harrison in 1762. The restored building, which once served as a market and granary, is now full of boutiques and restaurants. Daily.

CHATEAU-SUR-MER

474 Bellevue Ave., Newport, 401-847-1000;
www.newportmansions.org/page7016.cfm

This 1852 Victorian mansion was remodeled in 1872 by Richard Morris Hunt and has landscaped grounds with a Chinese moon gate. Built for William S. Wetmore, who made his fortune in the China trade. Late June-early October, daily.

CLIFF WALK

Memorial Blvd., Newport, 401-847-1355; www.cliffwalk.com

This scenic walk overlooking the Atlantic Ocean adjoins many of Newport's famous cottages. It was designated a National Recreational Trail in 1975.

EDWARD KING HOUSE

Aquidneck Park, 35 King St., Newport, 401-846-7426, 866-878-6954;
www.edwardkinghouse.com

Richard Upjohn's 1895 mansion is considered one of the finest Italianate houses in the country. It's now used as senior citizens' center. Monday-Friday.

ELMS

367 Bellevue Ave., Newport, 401-847-1000; www.newportmansions.org/page7016.cfm

Modeled after the 18th-century Chateau d'Asnieres near Paris, this restored cottage from Newport's gilded age boasts elaborate interiors and formal, sunken gardens. The 1901 home was built for Edward J. Berwind, a Philadelphia coal magnate. May-October: daily; November-March: Saturday-Sunday.

FRIENDS MEETING HOUSE

82 Touro St., Newport, 401-846-0813; www.newporthistorical.org

The site of the New England Yearly Meeting of the Society of Friends from 1699-1905. The expanded meeting house spans three centuries of architecture and construction. Guided tours through Newport Historical Society. Mid-June-August: Thursday-Saturday. Tours hourly 10 a.m.-3 p.m.; also by appointment.

★
★
★
★
★

HISTORIC MANSIONS AND HOUSES

Combination tickets to the Elms, the Breakers, Rosecliff, Marble House, Hunter House, Château-sur-Mer, Kingscote and Green Animals topiary gardens are available at any of these houses.

HUNTER HOUSE

54 Washington St., Newport, 401-847-1000;
www.newportmansions.org/page7016.cfm

An outstanding example of Colonial architecture, the 1748 Hunter House features a gambrel roof, 12-on-12 panel windows and a broken pediment doorway. It's furnished with pieces by famous 18th-century cabinetmakers Townsend and Goddard. Late June-late September daily.

INTERNATIONAL TENNIS HALL OF FAME & MUSEUM

194 Bellevue Ave., Newport, 401-849-3990, 800-457-1144;
www.tennisfame.org/museum

The world's largest tennis museum features interactive and dynamic exhibits detailing the history of the sport. Tennis equipment, fashions, trophies and memorabilia are on display in the famous Newport Casino, built in 1880 and designed by McKim, Mead and White. Daily. Grass courts available May-October.

KINGSCOTE

253 Bellevue Ave., Newport, 401-847-1000;
www.newportmansions.org/page7016.cfm

A Gothic Revival cottage designed by Richard Upjohn. In 1881, McKim, Mead and White added the "aesthetic" dining room, which features a Tiffany-glass wall and Chinese paintings and porcelains. Built for George Noble Jones of Savannah, Georgia, Kingscote is considered the nation's first true summer "cottage." June-October daily.

MARBLE HOUSE

596 Bellevue Ave., Newport, 401-847-1000;
www.newportmansions.org/page7016.cfm

The front gates, entrance and central hall of this 1892 house are modeled after Versailles. It's named for the many kinds of marble used on its interior, which also features lavish use of gold. Original furnishings include dining room chairs made of gilded bronze. It was built for Mrs. William K. Vanderbilt. On display are yachting memorabilia and a restored Chinese teahouse where Mrs. Vanderbilt held suffragette meetings. April-October: daily; rest of year weekends.

NEWPORT ART MUSEUM AND ART ASSOCIATION

76 Bellevue Ave., Newport, 401-848-8200; www.newportartmuseum.com

Changing exhibitions of contemporary and historical art are housed in the 1864 mansion designed by Richard Morris Hunt in the "Stick-Style" and in the 1920 Beaux-Arts building. Available are lectures, performing arts events, evening musical picnics and tours. Columbus Day-Memorial Day: Tuesday-Saturday 10 a.m.-4 p.m., Sunday noon-4 p.m.; rest of the year: Monday-Saturday 10 a.m.-5 p.m., Sunday noon-5 p.m.

OLD STONE MILL

Touro Park, Mill St., and Bellevue Ave., Newport, 401-846-1398; www.quahog.org

The origin of this circular stone tower supported by arches is unknown. Although excavations (1948-1949) have disproved it, some people still believe it was built by Norsemen.

REDWOOD LIBRARY AND ATHENAEUM

50 Bellevue Ave., Newport, 401-847-0292; www.redwoodlibrary.org

Designed by master Colonial architect Peter Harrison, this is thought to be oldest library building (1750) in continuous use in United States. It was used by English officers as a club during Revolution. Collections include original books and early portraits. Monday, Friday-Saturday 9:30 a.m.-5:30 p.m.; Tuesday-Thursday until 8 p.m.; Sunday 1-5 p.m.

ROSECLIFF

548 Bellevue Ave., Newport, 401-847-6543;
www.newportmansions.org/page7016.cfm

Modeled by Stanford White after the Grand Trianon at Versailles, Rosecliff has the largest private ballroom in Newport and a famous heart-shaped staircase. It was built for socialite Mrs. Hermann Oelrichs in 1902. April-early November daily.

SAMUEL WHITEHORNE HOUSE

416 Thames St., Newport, 401-849-7300; www.newportrestoration.org

The 1811 house has exquisite furniture, silver and pewter made by 18th-century artisans, plus Chinese porcelain, Irish crystal, Pilgrim-era furniture and a garden. May-October, Monday, Thursday-Friday 11 a.m.-4 p.m.; Saturday-Sunday 10 a.m.-4 p.m.; winter by appointment.

293

TOURO SYNAGOGUE NATIONAL HISTORIC SITE

85 Touro St., Newport, 401-847-4794; www.tourosynagogue.org

The first synagogue (1763) in America, a Georgian masterpiece by the country's first architect, Peter Harrison, the Touro contains the oldest Torah in North America, examples of 18th-century crafts and a letter from George Washington. Free admission.

TRINITY CHURCH

Queen Anne Square, Newport, 401-846-0660; www.trinitynewport.org

The first Anglican parish in the state (1698), the Trinity has been in continuous use since it was built. George Washington and philosopher George Berkeley were communicants. Interior features Tiffany windows and an organ tested by Handel before being shipped from London. Tours.

WANTON-LYMAN-HAZARD HOUSE

17 Broadway, Newport, 401-846-0813; www.newporthistorical.org

This 1675 house is the oldest in Newport and one of the finest Jacobean homes in New England. It was the site of the 1765 Stamp Act riot. Its 18th-century garden has been restored. Guided tours. Mid-June-late August: Thursday-Saturday; five tours daily; closed holidays.

RHODE ISLAND

WHITEHALL MUSEUM HOUSE

311 Berkeley Ave., Middletown, 401-846-3116; www.whitehallmuseumhouse.org

A restored, 1729 hip-roofed country house built by Bishop George Berkeley, the British philosopher and educator. July-Labor day: Tuesday-Sunday 10 a.m.-5 p.m.; also by appointment.

SPECIAL EVENTS

NEWPORT MUSIC FESTIVAL

Newport, 401-849-0700; www.newportmusic.org

Chamber music held in Newport's fabled mansions. Three concerts daily. Mid-July.

NEWPORT WINTER FESTIVAL

28 pelham St., Newport, 401-847-7666, 800-326-6030;
www.newportevents.com/winterfest

Ten days of food, festivities and music with more than 200 cultural and recreational events and activities. Mid-February.

HOTELS

★★BEECH TREE INN

34 Rhode Island Ave., Newport, 401-847-9794, 800-748-6565;
www.beechtreeinn.com

Eight rooms. Wireless Internet access. **$$**

★★★CASTLE HILL INN & RESORT

590 Ocean Drive, Newport, 401-849-3800, 888-466-1355; www.castlehillinn.com

This colossal city landmark is located right off the famous Ocean Drive. Converted in 1974, the resort spans the main house, the adjacent Harbor House, a guest chalet and renovated private cottages, and it offers ocean views. Romantic and quiet (no kids allowed in the lobby), most rooms are filled with original antiques, gas fireplaces, marble baths and canopy beds. If you can tear yourself away from your suite, don't miss the lobby's evening fireside s'mores. 35 rooms. Complimentary full breakfast. Wireless Internet access. Restaurant, two bars. Beach. Airport transportation available. **$$$$**

★★★THE CHANLER AT CLIFF WALK

117 Memorial Blvd., Newport, 401-847-1300; www.thechanler.com

Manicured grounds, gardens and antique paintings epitomize Newport's charm at this mansion-turned-hotel. Each of Chanler's rooms is uniquely designed to represent a different historical period or theme. Its Ocean Villas have private water views, saunas and whirlpools. If you're feeling particularly indulgent, request a butler-drawn bath or in-room massage treatment. 20 Rooms. Wireless Internet access. Restaurant, bar. **$$$$**

★★COURTYARD MARRIOTT

9 Commerce Drive, Middletown, 401-849-8000, 888-686-5067;
www.courtyard.com

148 rooms. High-speed Internet access. Restaurant. Airport transportation available. **$$**

★★★THE FRANCIS MALBONE HOUSE
392 Thames St., Newport, 401-846-0392, 800-846-0392; www.malbone.com

At the Malbone House, decorum still reigns with complimentary daily tea service and better yet, a full gourmet breakfast. The rooms are spacious, immaculate and tasteful, with Jacuzzis, fireplaces and fluffy comforters. The house dates back to 1760 and is within a convenient walking distance of Newport's shops and eateries. 20 rooms. Complimentary full breakfast. Wireless Internet access. Airport transportation available. $$$

★★★HOTEL VIKING
1 Bellevue Ave., Newport, 401-847-3300, 800-556-7126; www.hotelviking.com

First built in 1926, the Hotel Viking, in Newport's Historic Hill neighborhood, is listed on the National Register of Historic Places. It has four-poster beds and antique-looking furniture, and is also home to a modern, full-service spa. The Viking's vistas are sweeping, thanks to its off-the-beaten-path hilltop location far away from tourists, yet close enough to attractions like the Tennis Hall of Fame. 222 rooms. High-speed Internet access. Restaurant, bar. Airport transportation available. $$$

★★★HYATT REGENCY NEWPORT
1 Goat Island, Newport, 401-851-1234, 888-591-1234; www.newport.hyatt.com

On the tip of Goat Island, the Hyatt Regency overlooks Newport's harbor, Narragansett Bay and Jamestown Bridge. Pillow-top mattresses, plush duvets and Portico toiletries lend each room a home-away-from-home feel while a kid-friendly outdoor pool reminds guests they're on vacation (though business travelers can still sit in on conferences in the hotel's wired work center). No seaside trip is complete without a clambake and the Hyatt delivers this, too with two do-it-yourself waterfront fire pits. 264 rooms. Wireless Internet access. Two restaurants, bar. Airport transportation available. Outdoor pool, indoor pool. Fitness center, spa. $$$

★★HYDRANGEA HOUSE INN
16 Bellevue Ave., Newport, 401-846-4435, 800-945-4667; www.hydrangeahouse.com

Six rooms. Complimentary full breakfast. Free long distance phone calls and Internet access. Spa. $$$

★★IVY LODGE
12 Clay St., Newport, 401-849-6865, 800-834-6865; www.ivylodge.com

Eight rooms. Complimentary full breakfast. Wireless Internet access. Airport transportation available. Business center. $$$

★★★MARRIOTT NEWPORT
25 America's Cup Ave., Newport, 401-849-1000, 800-458-3066;
www.newportmarriott.com

The nautical-themed Marriott Newport seamlessly blends big-city service with small-town charm. Massive suspended sails hover over a lounge in the waterfront-facing, multilevel lobby; upstairs, sailboat-patterned quilts lay across white guestroom duvets. 319 rooms. Internet access. Restaurant, bar. Airport transportation available. Fitness center. Indoor pool, whirlpool. Unlimited U.S. calls. $$$

RHODE ISLAND

★
★
★
★

★★MELVILLE HOUSE

39 Clarke St., Newport, 401-847-0640, 800-711-7184; www.melvillehouse.com

Six rooms. Children over 12 years only. Complimentary full breakfast. Wireless Internet access. Airport transportation available. No disabled facilities. **$$**

★★MILL STREET INN

75 Mill St., Newport, 401-849-9500, 800-392-1316; www.millStreetinn.com

23 rooms, all suites. Complimentary full breakfast. Wireless Internet access. **$$$**

★★★NEWPORT HARBOR HOTEL AND MARINA

49 America's Cup Ave., Newport, 401-847-9000, 800-955-2558;
www.newporthotel.com

Want to live like the Astors but lacking a seaside manse? Check in to the Newport Harbor Hotel. The Queen Ann Square spot overlooks its own 60-slip marina off Narragansett Bay. The surrounding acres include first-rate restaurants and shops, 19th-century mansions, a golf course, tennis courts and local wineries. Low-key blue and gray furniture decorates the hotel's lobby and guest rooms are stocked with televisions, DVDs and video games. 133 rooms. High-speed Internet access. Restaurant, bar. Airport transportation available. Parking is available. **$$$$**

★★PILGRIM HOUSE

123 Spring St., Newport, 401-846-0040, 800-525-8373;
www.pilgrimhouseinn.com

11 rooms. Children over 12 years only. Homemade continental breakfast. Wireless Internet access. Airport transportation available. **$$**

RESTAURANTS

★★★CANFIELD HOUSE

5 Memorial Blvd., Newport, 401-847-0416; www.canfieldhousenewport.com

This elegant restaurant once housed Newport's only gambling casino. Today, it is a place where both locals and tourists come for traditional American fare such as steaks, lamb and local seafood. High ceilings, dark wood paneling, crystal chandeliers, a prominent stained-glass window and other refined touches make any meal here a celebration. Alfresco dining is available on the covered porch during the warmer months, and more casual meals are available in the cellar pub. American menu. Dinner. Bar. Children's menu. Business casual attire. Reservations recommended. Valet parking. Outdoor seating. Closed Monday. **$$**

★★LA FORGE CASINO RESTAURANT

186 Bellevue Ave., Newport, 401-847-0418; www.laforgenewport.com

American menu. Lunch, dinner, Sunday brunch. Bar. Children's menu. Casual attire. Outdoor seating. No disabled facilities. **$$**

★★RHODE ISLAND QUAHOG COMPANY

250 Thames St., Newport, 401-848-2330; www.riquahogco.com

Seafood menu. Lunch, dinner. Bar. Children's menu. Casual attire. Reservations recommended. Outdoor seating. Closed January-February. **$$**

★★★WHITE HORSE TAVERN
26 Marlborough St., Newport, 401-849-3600
If walls could talk, the White Horse Tavern's dark wooden planks would have much to say. Built in 1673, the downtown tavern is America's oldest watering hole. Its litany of owners have thankfully left the pub's brown clapboard exterior, stone fireplaces and exposed ceiling beams, all smack filled with centuries-old character. The only thing updated is the food, which highlights a menu of well-executed regional New England entrées. American menu. Lunch, dinner, Sunday brunch. Bar. Business casual attire. Reservations recommended. Outdoor seating. **$$$**

PROVIDENCE
Grateful that God's providence had led him to this spot, Roger Williams founded a town and named it accordingly. The early 1636 settlement, more farm town than urban center, soon morphed into an important port and industrial hub. Clipper ships left the harbor to explore China and the West Indies. Silver and jewelry artisans set up shop along the city's Colonial-lined streets.

Today, Rhode Island's capital is the biggest metropolis in the state—which, with 160,000 residents isn't saying too much—and best-known for its outstanding universities: the liberal, Ivy League Brown, and the funky, alternative Rhode Island School of Design. Students are fixtures in the myriad coffee shops and bars of bustling Thayer Street, while local Goodfellas frequent the trattorias of Federal Hill, Providence's Little Italy. The up-and-coming downtown now has an upscale mall, modern convention center and a booming nightlife scene. Still, perhaps in deference to the deferential Roger Williams himself, the city has maintained much of its old charm—contemporary hotels and office buildings share streets with historic houses, and the views of Narragansett Bay are as striking as ever.

Information: Providence Warwick Convention & Visitors Bureau, 1 W. Exchange St., Providence, 401-274-1636, 800-233-1636; www.pwcvb.com

WHAT TO SEE AND DO
ARCADE
65 Weybosset St., Providence, 401-273-9700
America's first indoor shopping mall, built in 1828, has national landmark status and more than 35 specialty shops and restaurants.

BROWN UNIVERSITY
45 Prospect St., Providence, 401-863-1000; www.brown.edu
Founded as Rhode Island College in 1764, the school was renamed for major benefactor Nicholas Brown in 1804. The 7,500-student Ivy is the seventh-oldest university in the country; its many libraries are free and open to the public.

CULINARY ARCHIVES & MUSEUM
315 Harborside Blvd., Providence, 491-598-2805; www.culinary.org
Dubbed the "Smithsonian of the food service industry," this museum contains more than 200,000 items related to the culinary arts. Tuesday-Sunday 10 a.m.-5 p.m.

★
★
★
★
★

FIRST UNITARIAN CHURCH

1 Benevolent St., Providence, 401-421-7970; www.firstunitarianprov.org

At the top of this 1816 building is the largest bell ever cast by Paul Revere.

GOVERNOR STEPHEN HOPKINS HOUSE

15 Hopkins St., Providence, 401-421-0694; www.stephenhopkins.org

The 10-time governor of Rhode Island (he signed the Declaration of Independence) lived here. April-December Wednesday, Saturday 1-4 p.m.; also by appointment.

JOHN BROWN HOUSE

52 Power St., Providence, 401-273-7507; www.rihs.org

George Washington was once a guest at this Georgian manse that now houses a museum of 18th-century china, glass and paintings, as well as John Brown's chariot, the oldest surviving American-made vehicle. January-April, Friday-Saturday 10:30 a.m.-4:30 p.m.; May-December, Tuesday-Saturday 10:30 a.m.-4:30 p.m.

MUSEUM OF NATURAL HISTORY AND CORMACK PLANETARIUM

1000 Elmwood Ave., Providence, 401-785-9450; www.rogerwilliamsparkzoo.org

Anthropology, geology, astronomy and biology displays; educational and performing arts programs. Daily 10 a.m.-5 p.m.; planetarium September-June Saturday-Sunday, July-August Tuesday.

OLD STATE HOUSE

150 Benefit St., Providence, 401-222-2678; www.preservation.ri.gov

The state General Assembly met here between 1762 and 1900. Independence was proclaimed in the State House two months before the Declaration was signed in Philadelphia. Monday-Friday.

PROVIDENCE ATHENAEUM LIBRARY

251 Benefit St., Providence, 401-421-6970; www.providenceathenaeum.org

Housed in a Greek Revival building designed by William Strickland, this is one of the oldest subscription libraries in the United States. The rare book room includes original Audubon elephant folios and a small art collection. September-May: Monday-Thursday 9 a.m.-7 p.m., Friday-Saturday until 5 p.m., Sunday 1-5 p.m.; June-Labor Day: Monday-Thursday 9 a.m.-7 p.m., Friday until 5 p.m., Saturday until 1 p.m.; closed first two weeks in August.

PROVIDENCE CHILDREN'S MUSEUM

100 South St., 401-273-5437; www.childrenmuseum.org

Many hands-on exhibits, including a time-travel adventure through Rhode Island's multicultural history, a wet-and-wild exploration of water and a hands-on geometry lab, entertain kids at the museum. September-March, Tuesday-Sunday 9 a.m.-6 p.m.; April-Labor Day, daily 9 a.m.-6 p.m.

RHODE ISLAND SCHOOL OF DESIGN

2 College St., Providence, 401-454-6100; www.risd.edu

Nearly 2,200 are enrolled here at one of the country's leading art and design schools.

RHODE ISLAND

★
★
★
★
☆

RHODE ISLAND STATE HOUSE

82 Smith St., Providence, 401-222-2357; www.rilin.state.ri.us

Inside the 1901 capitol, designed by McKim, Mead and White, is an original Gilbert Stuart portrait of George Washington. Monday-Friday 9-11 a.m.; closed second Monday in August.

ROGER WILLIAMS NATIONAL MEMORIAL

282 N. Main St., Providence, 401-521-7266; www.nps.gov

At the site of the old town spring, this 4½-acre park commemorates Roger Williams and the founding of Providence. Daily.

ROGER WILLIAMS PARK

1000 Elmwood Ave., Providence, 401-785-9450;
www.rogerwilliamsparkzoo.org/visit/ParkCarousel.cfm

The park has 430 acres of woodlands, waterways and winding drives, plus greenhouses and a Japanese garden. Daily.

ROGER WILLIAMS PARK ZOO

1000 Elmwood Ave., Providence, 401-785-3510; www.rogerwilliamsparkzoo.org

Ideal for kids, the zoo has a nature center, tropical building, African plains and Marco Polo exhibits, and more than 600 animals. Daily.

SPECIAL EVENTS
SPRING FESTIVAL OF HISTORIC HOUSES

21 Meeting St., Providence, 401-831-7440; www.ppsri.org

Sponsored by the Providence Preservation Society, the festival runs tours of grand old private houses and gardens. Third weekend in June.

WATERFIRE

Waterplace Park, 101 Regent Ave., Providence, 401-272-3111; www.waterfire.org

Floating bonfires in the Providence River are accompanied by music. Weekends, late May-late October.

HOTELS
★★CHRISTOPHER DODGE HOUSE

11 W. Park St., Providence, 401-351-6111; www.providence-hotel.com

14 rooms. Complimentary full breakfast. High-speed Internet access. Airport transportation available. $

★★COURTYARD BY MARRIOTT PROVIDENCE DOWNTOWN

32 Exchange Terrace, Providence, 401-272-1191, 800-321-2211; www.courtyard.com

216 rooms. High-speed Internet access. Two restaurants. Bar. Airport transportation available. $$

★★★MARRIOTT PROVIDENCE

1 Orms St., Providence, 401-272-2400, 800-937-7768; www.marriottprovidence.com

Located just off Interstate 95 (I-95), the Marriott can't be beat for convenience. Well-appointed rooms—think cushy armchairs, stately desks and a pillow menu—make it hard to beat for hospitality as well. Even kids get special treatment here in the form of poolside sand competitions and hotel-run scavenger hunts. Rows of classic Rhode Island Colonial homes, as well as plenty of shopping and eating options are nearby. 346 rooms. High-speed Internet access. Restaurant, bar. Airport transportation available. $$

★★RADISSON HOTEL PROVIDENCE HARBOR

220 India St., Providence, 401-272-5577, 800-333-3333;
www.radisson.com/providenceri

136 rooms. High-speed Internet access. Restaurant, bar. Whirlpool. Airport transportation available. Free parking. $

★★★THE WESTIN PROVIDENCE

1 W. Exchange St., Providence, 401-598-8000, 800-301-1111;
www.westin.com/providence

The downtown Westin is attached—via sky bridge—to Providence Place, the city's major mall. If browsing hundreds of boutiques isn't your thing, the modern two-tower hotel also provides plenty of other distractions, including a pool, fitness classes and extensive in-suite entertainment. Each room is outfitted with Starwood's signature "Heavenly Bed" and offers a flatscreen TV, cordless phone, dual-head shower and better-than-average minibar. Canine guests are welcome, and they get their own bowls, treats and "Heavenly" dog beds, too. 364 rooms. High-speed Internet access. Two restaurants, two bars. Airport transportation available. $$$

★
★
★
☆
☆

RESTAURANTS

★★ADESSO

161 Cushing St., Providence, 401-521-0770; www.zerotosixfigures.com/adesso
California, Italian menu. Lunch, dinner, late-night. Bar. Casual attire. Reservations recommended. Valet parking. $$$

★★★AL FORNO

577 S. Main St., Providence, 401-273-9760; www.alforno.com
Local favorite Al Forno has turned out primo pasta dishes for nearly three decades. Chef-owners (and cookbook authors) Johanne Killeen and George Germon preside over their rustic, two-story waterfront spot and infuse their Italian menu with Tuscan and Provençal flair. Housemade gnocchi with spicy sausage and the baked pasta with cream and four cheeses are among many mouthwatering must-eat dishes. Italian menu. Dinner. Bar. Casual attire. Valet parking. Outdoor seating. Closed Sunday-Monday. $$$

★THE CACTUS GRILLE

800 Allens Ave., Providence, 401-941-0004
Mexican menu. Lunch, dinner. Bar. Children's menu. Casual attire. $$

★★HEMENWAY'S SEAFOOD GRILL

121 South main St., Providence, 401-351-8570; www.hemenwaysrestaurant.com
Seafood menu. Lunch, dinner. Bar. Outdoor seating. $$

★★★★MILL'S TAVERN

101 N. Main St., Providence, 401-272-3331; www.merchantcircle.com

From its smart design and young, energetic vibe to its appealing menu, this winning restaurant housed in a former mill turns tradition on its head. The menu echoes the classic-contemporary sentiment offering a wide variety of creatively prepared American seasonal dishes, many of which are cooked in the kitchen's wood-burning oven, wood grill and rotisserie. The warm, knowledgeable staff provides professional and thorough service without being stuffy or intrusive. Contemporary American menu. Dinner. Bar. Business casual attire. Reservations recommended. Valet parking. $$$

★★★NEW RIVERS

7 Steeple St., Providence, 401-751-0350; www.newriversrestaurant.com

Fake fruit and wall-mounted plates have the potential to turn a good kitchen into kitsch. But while both Lucite pears and Majolica pottery are incorporated into New Rivers' décor, the overall ambiance is comfortable, not cheesy. The colorful downtown American bistro's seasonal menu is full of fresh, local ingredients; standout dishes include poached rabbit loin in sweet pea broth and roasted trout with cracked wheat and beets. American menu. Dinner. Bar. Business casual attire. Reservations recommended. Closed Sunday. $$$

★★PANE E VINO

365 Atwells Ave., Providence, 401-223-2230; www.panevino.net

Italian menu. Dinner. Bar. Business casual attire. Reservations recommended. Valet parking. $$$

301

★★★POT AU FEU

44 Custom House St., Providence, 401-273-8953; www.potaufeuri.com

A formal, upstairs salon and a relaxed downstairs bistro make up Pot Au Feu, a traditional French bistro in the heart of Providence. The classic and regional French dishes—onion soup, salade niçoise, sweet and savory crepes—are authentic and delicious. The exposed brick walls and candlelit tables create a warm and cozy atmosphere. French bistro menu. Lunch, dinner. Bar. Business casual attire. Reservations recommended. Closed Sunday. $$

RHODE ISLAND

WARWICK

Sometimes pretty, sometimes gritty, Warwick often (unfairly) gets a bad rap. The state's second-largest city is home to T.F. Green International airport and countless industrial warehouses, *but* it also has 39 miles of Narragansett Bay coastline and more than 15 picturesque marinas. Less populated than Providence, Warwick still has plenty of shopping and eating destinations, and its decentralized geography has given rise to a number of postcard-perfect villages such as Pawtuxet, Cowesett and Conanicut.

Information: City Hall, 3275 Post Road, 401-738-2000, 800-492-7942; www.warwickri.com

★
★
★
★
★

WHAT TO SEE AND DO
HISTORIC PONTIAC MILLS
334 Knight St., Warwick, 401-737-2700; www.visitwarwickri.com
A restored 1863 mill complex houses nearly 80 small businesses, artisans and shops, with an open-air market on weekends. Daily.

WALKING TOUR OF HISTORIC APPONAUG VILLAGE
3275 Post Road, Warwick, 401-738-2000, 800-492-7942; www.visitwarwickri.com
More than 30 historic and architecturally interesting buildings comprise this walking tour; brochure available through Warwick City.

SPECIAL EVENTS
GASPEE DAYS
Warwick, 401-781-1772, 800-492-7942; www.gaspee.com
A celebration of the capture and burning of the British schooner Gaspee by Rhode Island patriots includes arts and crafts, concerts, footraces, battle reenactments, parades and contests. May-June.

WARWICK HERITAGE FESTIVAL
Warwick City Park, Warwick, 401-738-2000, 800-492-7942; www.visitwarwickri.com
A weekend reenactment of the city's history. November, Veterans Day weekend.

HOTELS
★★★CROWNE PLAZA
801 Greenwich Ave., Warwick, 401-732-6000, 800-227-6963; www.crowneplaza.com
Stranded travelers breathe a sigh of relief when checking into the Crowne Plaza. Three miles from the airport. At this tastefully decorated hotel, rooms come with marble baths, dark wooden desks, CD players, bathrobes and upscale toiletries, making overnights a genuine pleasure. For the travel weary, there is a sleep amenity package that includes an eye mask, drape clip, ear plugs, lavender spray and a night light. 266 rooms. High-speed Internet access. Restaurant, bar. Airport transportation available. Pets accepted. Car parking. $$

★★RADISSON AIRPORT HOTEL
2081 Post Road, Warwick, 401-739-3000, 800-333-3333;
www.radisson.com/warwickri
111 rooms. Complimentary continental breakfast. High-speed Internet access. Restaurant, bar. Airport transportation available. $$

WESTERLY
Tourists looking for Newport's panache without its crowds would do well to look toward Westerly. The quiet seaside city and surrounding hamlets, including the very WASPy Watch Hill, are full of grand old-money cottages and quaint small-town streets. Founded in 1669, Westerly is among the state's oldest settlements and the seat of once-booming granite quarries. Today, the southwestern Rhode Island locale counts tourism and fishing gear among its top industries.
Information: Westerly-Pawcatuck Area Chamber of Commerce, 1 Chamber Way, Westerly, 401-596-7761, 800-732-7636; www.westerlychamber.org

RHODE ISLAND

★
★
★
★
★

WHAT TO SEE AND DO
BABCOCK-SMITH HOUSE
124 Granite St., Westerly, 401-596-5704; www.babcock-smithhouse.com
This 1732 two-story, gambrel-roofed Georgian mansion was once home to Dr. Joshua Babcock, Westerly's first physician. Today, its furniture collection spans 200 years. Late May-October, Saturday 2-5 p.m.; July-August, Friday 2-5 p.m.; also by appointment.

MISQUAMICUT STATE BEACH
319 Atlantic Ave., Westerly, 401-596-9097; www.misquamicut.org
Soft sands and gentle waves make Misquamicut the perfect place to lay a towel. Swimming, bathhouse, fishing, picnicking, concession. Memorial Day-Labor Day daily 9 a.m.-6 p.m.

WATCH HILL
Watch Hill, Westerly, 401-596-7761; www.westerlychamber.org
A Newport-like historic community of handsome summer houses, many of which date back to the 1870s.

WATCH HILL LIGHTHOUSE
Watch Hill, 14 Lighthouse Road, Westerly, 401-596-7761; www.lighthouse.cc
The granite lighthouse was built in 1856 to replace the wooden 1807 structure. Museum exhibits. July-August Tuesday, Thursday 1-3 p.m.

HOTELS

★BREEZEWAY RESORT
70 Winnapaug Road, Misquamicut Beach, 401-348-8953, 800-462-8872; www.breezewayresort.com
50 rooms. Complimentary continental breakfast. Bar. Free beach parking. Heated pool. $

★★SHELTER HARBOR INN
10 Wagner Road, Westerly, 401-322-8883, 800-468-8883; www.shelterharborinn.com
24 rooms. Complimentary full breakfast. Restaurant, bar. Tennis Courts. $

★WINNAPAUG INN
169 Shore Road, Westerly, 401-348-8350, 800-288-9906; www.winnapauginn.com
49 rooms. Complimentary continental breakfast. High-speed Internet access. Restaurant, bar. Pool. $$

SPECIALTY LODGING
VILLA BED & BREAKFAST
190 Shore Road, Westerly, 401-596-1054, 800-722-9240; www.thevillaatwesterly.com
This bed and breakfast doubles as a romantic hideaway complete with flower gardens, Italian porticos and verandas. Alfresco diners are fans of the Villa's complimentary poolside breakfast; beachgoers love its proximity to Misquamicut Beach. Block Island, Foxwoods Casino and the Mystic Aquarium are all short rides away. Eight rooms. Complimentary continental breakfast. $

RHODE ISLAND

★
★
★
★
☆

VERMONT

GREEN ROLLING HILLS, PICTURE-PERFECT VILLAGES, FIELDS DOTTED WITH BLACK-AND-WHITE
cows. Vermont is every bit as bucolic as most imagine. But under that peaceful surface
is an independent spirit that makes Vermont one of the most progressive, liberal states
in the country. Vermonters are proudly individualist and even retain a bit of the '60s
hippie spirit—recently, one town threatened to secede from the U.S. over the Iraq war,
and several towns have fought fiercely (but unsuccessfully) to stop Wal-Mart from
opening in the state. And while modern Vermont is progressively leftist (it was one of
the first states to sanction civil unions), that independent spirit is nothing new.

In 1724, Vermont became the last New England state to be settled. Ethan Allen and
his Green Mountain Boys made Vermont famous when they took Fort Ticonderoga from
the British in 1775. Claimed by both New York and New Hampshire, Vermont framed a
constitution in 1777. It was the first state to prohibit slavery and the first state to provide
universal male suffrage, regardless of property or income. For 14 years, Vermont was an
independent republic, running its own postal service, coining its own money, natural-
izing citizens of other states and countries and negotiating with other states and nations.
In 1701, Vermont became the 14th state.

Tourism is a driving force in Vermont, with every town sprinkled with quaint bed
and breakfasts, inns and restaurants. The state's many ski resorts often get top marks
by national publications. A strong organic and environmentalist movement exists
here, and chains are rare. It's not unusual to buy your gas from an independent gas
station, or turn to a local bookshop for the
latest bestseller.

That kind of grassroots populism is refresh-
ing in an ever-homogenous America. Here
you'll find tiny villages, outstanding fresh,
organic food, top-notch skiing and the best
maple syrup in the country. Burlington is a
funky, artsy college town, while Montpelier is
one of the country's prettiest state capitals. In
between is a delightful landscape of adorable
villages, each with a unique and proud character of its own.

Information: www.travel-vermont.com

FUN FACTS

Vermonter Calvin
Coolidge was the only
U.S. president to be
born on the Fourth
of July.

More people in Vermont live in a rural
setting than an urban setting.

Vermont produces more than
500,000 gallons of maple syrup
each year.

ARLINGTON

Arlington, located in Southwestern Vermont, lies between the Green Mountains and
the Taconic range. There are five mountain peaks located in the town.

www.townofarlington.org

WHAT TO SEE AND DO
NORMAN ROCKWELL EXHIBITION

3772 Highway 7A, Arlington, 802-375-6423;
www.vmga.org/bennington/normrockwell.html

Hundreds of magazine covers, illustrations, advertisements, calendars and other printed works are displayed in a historic 1875 church in the illustrator's hometown. Hosts are Rockwell's former models. Daily.

HOTELS
★★★ARLINGTON INN

3904 Highway 7A and 313W, Arlington, 802-375-6532, 800-443-9442;
www.arlingtoninn.com

Built in 1848, this Greek Revival-style mansion has been an inn since 1888 and is listed on the National Register of Historic Places. Spread throughout the main house and several converted outbuildings, the guest rooms feature antiques, double-sided fireplaces and Jacuzzi tubs. If you'd like a more historic room, opt for the main house; the carriage house and parsonage have been renovated with modern architectural details, such as cathedral ceilings and skylights. The three-acre grounds include a walking path, gazebo and small stone fountain with waterfall. 18 rooms. Complimentary full breakfast. Restaurant, bar. **$$**

★★★ARLINGTON'S WEST MOUNTAIN INN

144 W. Mountain Inn Road, and Highway 313, Arlington, 802-375-6516;
www.westmountaininn.com

This historic white, seven-gabled inn was built in 1849 and opened as an inn in 1978. Located on a mountainside overlooking the Battenkill River, the interior of the inn is furnished with a mix of antiques and country classics (pine paneling, fireplace, books, chess and checkers). Nearby activities include hiking, snowshoeing, canoeing, tubing, tennis and golf. 20 rooms. Complimentary full breakfast. Restaurant, bar. **$$**

★CANDLELIGHT MOTEL

4893 Highway 7A, Arlington, 802-375-6647, 800-348-5294;
www.candlelightmotel.com

17 rooms. Complimentary continental breakfast. Outdoor pool. **$**

SPECIALTY LODGING
HILL FARM INN

458 Hill Farm Road, Arlington, 802-375-2269, 800-882-2545; www.hillfarminn.com

North of Arlington's town center on 50 acres fronting the Battenkill River lies this charming inn, which has sheep, goats and chickens wander about outside to amuse kids and adults alike. There is a a historic guest house (1790), a classic white farmhouse (1830) and several outlying cottages housing family suites and efficiencies. Sheep, goats and chickens wander about outside to amuse kids and adults alike. Inside, the guest rooms have simple country charm—there are no phones, but some rooms have televisions. 15 rooms. Complimentary full breakfast. **$**

VERMONT

★
★
★
★
★

RESTAURANT
★★★ARLINGTON INN

3904 Highway 7A, Arlington, 802-375-6532, 800-443-9442;
www.arlingtoninn.com

This historic landmark inn was built in 1848 as a private home and has been in operation since 1888. The Victorian dining room serves classic dishes such as beef stroganoff and filet mignon. American menu. Dinner. Bar. Children's menu. Business casual attire. Reservations recommended. Closed Monday; last week in April-first week in May; also Sunday in off-season. **$$$**

BENNINGTON

Bennington headquartered Ethan Allen's Green Mountain Boys—known to New Yorkers as the "Bennington Mob"—in Vermont's long struggle with New York. On August 16, 1777, this same "mob" won a decisive battle in the Revolutionary War. Bennington has three separate areas of historic significance: the Victorian and turn-of-the-century buildings downtown; the colonial houses, church and commons in Old Bennington (1 mile west) and the three covered bridges in North Bennington.

Information: Information Booth, 100 Veterans Memorial Drive,
802-447-3311, 800-229-0252; www.bennington.com

WHAT TO SEE AND DO
BENNINGTON BATTLE MONUMENT

15 Monument Circle, Old Bennington, 802-447-0550;
www.dhca.state.vt.us

A 306-foot monolith commemorates a Revolutionary War victory. Elevator to observation platform Mid-April-October, daily 9 a.m.-5 p.m.

BENNINGTON COLLEGE

Highway 67A and One College Drive, Bennington, 802-442-5401;
www.bennington.edu

(1932) Introduced progressive methods of education; became coeducational in 1969. The Visual and Performing Arts Center has special exhibits. Summer programs and performances.

BENNINGTON MUSEUM

75 Main St., Bennington, 802-447-1571;
www.benningtonmuseum.org

Early Vermont and New England historical artifacts, including American glass, paintings, sculpture, silver, furniture; Bennington pottery, Grandma Moses paintings, 1925 "Wasp" luxury touring car. Schoolhouse Museum contains Moses family memorabilia, Bennington flag, other Revolutionary War collections. Thursday-Tuesday 10 a.m.-5 p.m. Genealogical library by appointment.

OLD BURYING GROUND

1 Veterans Memorial Drive, Bennington, 802-447-3311;
www.bennington.com

Poet Robert Frost and those who died in the Battle of Bennington are all buried here.

OLD FIRST CHURCH

One Monument Circle, Old Bennington, Vt. Route 9 and Monument Avenue,
Old Bennington, 802-447-1223; www.oldfirstchurchbenn.org

(1805) Example of early colonial architecture; original box pews; Asher Benjamin steeple. Guided tours. Memorial Day-June: weekends; July-mid-October: Monday-Saturday 10 a.m.-noon, 1-4 p.m., Sunday 1-4 p.m.

PARK-MCCULLOUGH HOUSE MUSEUM

One Park and West Street, North Bennington, 802-442-5441;
www.parkmccullough.org

A 35-room 1865 Victorian mansion with period furnishings, stable with carriages. Costume collection, Victorian gardens, child's playhouse. Special events are held throughout the year. Mid-May-mid-October: daily, tours 10 a.m.-3 p.m.

WOODFORD STATE PARK

142 State Park Road, Woodford, 802-447-7169; www.vtstateparks.com

At 2,400 feet, this 400-acre park has the highest elevation of any park in the state. Swimming, fishing, boating (no motors; rentals), nature and hiking trails, picnicking, tent and trailer sites (dump station). Memorial Day-Columbus Day.

HOTELS

★BEST WESTERN

220 Northside Drive, Bennington, 802-442-6311, 800-780-7234;
www.bestwestern.com

58 rooms. Complimentary continental breakfast. Outdoor pool. Near Bennington College. High-speed Internet access. $

★★★FOUR CHIMNEYS INN

21 W. Road, Bennington, 802-447-3500; www.fourchimneys.com

Guest rooms blend modern amenities with an Old -World feel at this elegant 1783 inn that is set on 11 acres of trees and rolling grass fields. 11 rooms. Complimentary full breakfast. Restaurant, bar. $$

★HAMPTON INN

51 Hannaford Square, Bennington, 802-440-9862, 800-426-7866;
www.hamptoninn.com

Complimentary breakfast. Fitness center. Pets not accepted. High-speed Internet access. Pool, whirlpool. $

SPECIALTY LODGING

SOUTH SHIRE INN

124 Elm St., Bennington, 802-447-3839, 888-201-2250;
www.southshire.com

This inn is reminiscent of the Victorian era from its shingled façade to the mahogany paneling, leaded glass doors and ornate moldings of its common rooms. All rooms have period furnishings. Nine rooms. Children over 12 years only. Complimentary full breakfast. High-speed Internet access. $$

★
★
★
★

BRANDON

Brandon is a resort and residential town located at the western edge of the Green Mountains. The first U.S. electric motor was made in nearby Forestdale by Thomas Davenport.

Information: Brandon Area Chamber of Commerce, 802-247-6401; www.brandon.org

WHAT TO SEE AND DO
MOUNT INDEPENDENCE

Highways 22A and 73 West, Orwell, 497 Mount Independence Road, Orwell,
802-759-2412; www.historicvermont.org/sites

Wooded bluff on shore of Lake Champlain, part of the Revolutionary War defense complex. Fort built in 1776 across from Fort Ticonderoga to house 12,000 troops and protect colonies from northern invasion; evacuated in 1777. Least disturbed major Revolutionary War site in the country; four marked trails show ruins of fort complex. Late May-mid-October, daily 9:30 a.m.-5 p.m.

STEPHEN A. DOUGLAS BIRTHPLACE

2 Grove St. (Highway 7), Brandon, 802-247-6401; www.brandon.org

Cottage where the "Little Giant," once the Democratic nominee for president who lost to Abraham Lincoln, was born in 1813. Douglas attended Brandon Academy before moving to Illinois in 1833. By appointment.

HOTEL

★★★LILAC INN

53 Park St., Brandon, 802-247-5463, 800-221-0720; www.lilacinn.com

This colonial home, built in 1909, is on the National Register of Historic Places. Decorated in Victorian style, rooms feature antiques, historical prints and artwork. Extensive gardens are found in back, along with a patio and gazebo. Enjoy a book in the library, practice on the putting green or take a drive to nearby historic Fort Ticonderoga. Nine rooms. Pets accepted; fee. Children over 12 permitted. Complimentary full breakfast. Restaurant, bar. $$

SPECIALTY LODGING
THE BRANDON INN

20 Park St., Brandon, 802-247-5766, 800-639-8685; www.historicbrandoninn.com

Built in 1786. 37 rooms. Restaurant, bar. Outdoor pool. $$

BRATTLEBORO

The first settlement in Vermont was at Fort Dummer (two miles south) in 1724.

Information: Brattleboro Area Chamber of Commerce, 180 Main St.,
802-254-4565; www.brattleboro.com

WHAT TO SEE AND DO
BRATTLEBORO MUSEUM & ART CENTER

10 Vernon St., Brattleboro, 802-257-0124; www.brattleboromuseum.org

Exhibits change periodically and feature works by New England artists; frequent performances and lecture programs. May-February: Wednesday-Monday 11 a.m.-5 p.m.; closed July 4, November 25; also August 2-5, November 1-4.

CREAMERY BRIDGE

Guilford Street, and Route 9 West, Brattleboro, 802-254-4565;
www.brattleborochamber.org
(1879) One of Vermont's best-preserved covered bridges.

HARLOW'S SUGAR HOUSE

563 Bellows Falls Road, Putney, 802-387-5852;
www.vermontsugar.com
Observe working sugarhouse (March-mid-April). Maple exhibit and products. Pick your own fruit in season: strawberries, blueberries, raspberries, apples; cider in fall. Daily; closed January-February.

HOTELS

★LATCHIS HOTEL

50 Main St., Brattleboro, 802-254-6300, 800-254-6304, 800-798-6301;
www.latchis.com
30 rooms. Complimentary continental breakfast. Wireless Internet access. $

★★QUALITY INN

1380 Putney Road, Brattleboro, 802-254-8701, 800-228-5151;
www.qualityinnbrattleboro.com
98 rooms. Complimentary continental breakfast. Wireless Internet access. Restaurant, bar. Fitness room. Indoor pool, outdoor pool. $

BURLINGTON

Located on Lake Champlain, Burlington is the largest city in Vermont. It's the site of the oldest university and the oldest daily newspaper (1848) in the state, the burial place of Ethan Allen and the birthplace of philosopher John Dewey. It has a diverse range of industries and the lakefront area offers a park, dock and restaurants.
Information: Lake Champlain Regional Chamber of Commerce, 60 Main St.,
802-863-3489, 877-686-5253; www.vermont.org

WHAT TO SEE AND DO

BOLTON VALLEY SKI/SUMMER RESORT

4302 Bolton Access Road, Bolton Valley, 877-926-5866;
www.boltonvalleyvt.com
Resort has quad, four double chairlifts, one surface lift, school, patrol, rentals, snow-making, cafeteria, restaurants, bar, nursery. Forty-three runs, longest run over three miles, vertical drop 1,600 feet. November-April: daily. Sixty-two miles of cross-country trails. Also summer activities.

CHURCH STREET MARKETPLACE

2 Church St., Suite 2A, Burlington, 802-863-1648;
www.churchstmarketplace.com
Four traffic-free blocks, from the Unitarian Church, (designed in 1815 by Peter Banner), to City Hall at the corner of Main Street. Buildings are a mix of Art Deco and 19th-century architectural styles and house more than 100 shops, restaurants, galleries and cafés. The brick promenade offers vendors and street entertainers.

VERMONT

★
★★
★★
★★

ETHAN ALLEN HOMESTEAD AND MUSEUM

1 Ethan Allen Homestead, Burlington, 802-865-4556;
www.ethanallenhomestead.org

Ethan Allen had a colorful history as a frontiersman, military leader, land speculator, suspected traitor and prisoner of war. This preserved pioneer homestead was Allen's last home. Here you'll find a re-created hayfield and kitchen gardens, plus the 1787 farmhouse. One-hour guided tours are available. Monday-Saturday 10 a.m.-4 p.m., Sunday 1-4 p.m.; tours available June-October.

ETHAN ALLEN PARK

1006 N. Ave Burlington and Ethan Allen Parkway, Burlington,
802-863-3489; www.enjoyburlington.com/Parks/EthanAllenPark.cfm

Part of Ethan Allen's farm. Ethan Allen Tower, Memorial Day-Labor Day: Wednesday-Sunday afternoons and evenings with view of Adirondacks and Lake Champlain to the west, Green Mountains to the east. Picnicking.

LAKE CHAMPLAIN CHOCOLATES

750 Pine St., Burlington, 802-864-1808, 800-465-5909;
www.lakechamplainchocolates.com

Large glass windows give visitors a view of the chocolate-making process at this small-scale factory. The gift shop onsite usually features in-store chocolate-making demonstrations on Saturdays, when the factory itself is closed. Tours: Monday-Friday 9 a.m.-2 p.m. on the hour; factory store: Monday-Saturday 9 a.m.-6 p.m., Sunday noon-5 p.m.

UNIVERSITY OF VERMONT

Waterman Building, 85 S. Prospect St., Burlington, 802-656-3480;
www.uvm.edu

(1791) (10,000 students) Fifth-oldest university in New England. Graduate and under-graduate programs. On campus is the Billings Center, the Bailey-Howe Library, the largest in the state, the Georgian-designed Ira Allen Chapel, named for the founder, and the Old Mill, a classroom building with cornerstone laid by General Lafayette in 1825.

SPECIAL EVENTS

DISCOVER JAZZ FESTIVAL

187 St. Paul St., Suite One, Burlington, 802-863-7992;
www.discoverjazz.com

A jazz extravaganza with more than 150 live performances taking place in city parks, clubs and restaurants. Ten days in early June.

VERMONT MOZART FESTIVAL

3 Main St., Suite 217, Burlington, 802-862-7352;
www.vtmozart.com

Features 26 chamber concerts in picturesque Vermont settings including the Trapp Family Meadow, Basin Harbor Club in Vergennes and Shelburne Farms on Lake Champlain. Mid-July-early August.

HOTELS

★★BEST WESTERN WINDJAMMER INN & CONFERENCE CENTER
1076 Williston Road, South Burlington, 802-863-1125, 800-371-1125;
www.bestwestern.com/windjammerinn
159 rooms. Pets accepted, some restrictions; fee. Complimentary continental breakfast. Restaurant. Fitness room. Indoor pool, outdoor pool, whirlpool. Airport transportation available. High-speed Internet access. **$**

★COMFORT INN
1285 Williston Road, South Burlington, 802-865-3400,
877-424-6423; www.comfortinn.com
105 rooms. Pets accepted, some restrictions; fee. Complimentary continental breakfast. Fitness room. Outdoor pool. **$**

★★DOUBLETREE HOTEL
1117 Williston Road, South Burlington, 802-658-0250,
800-222-8733; www.doubletree.com
130 rooms. Pets accepted, some restrictions; fee. Restaurant, bar. Fitness room. Indoor
pool, children's pool. Airport transportation available. High-speed Internet access. **$**

★HOLIDAY INN EXPRESS
1720 Shelburne Road, South Burlington, 1-800-874-1554,
802-860-6000; www.innvermont.com
121 rooms, all suites. Complimentary continental breakfast. Airport transportation
available. **$**

★★★THE INN AT ESSEX—A SUMMIT HOTEL
70 Essex Way, Essex, 802-878-1100, 800-727-4295;
www.innatessex.com
Each room at this inn is individually decorated with 18th-century period-style furniture. The meals are prepared by the New England Culinary Institute. 120 rooms. Pets
accepted, some restrictions; fee. Restaurant. Airport transportation available. High-
speed Internet access. **$$**

★★★SHERATON BURLINGTON HOTEL AND CONFERENCE CENTER
870 Williston Road, South Burlington, 802-865-6600, 800-677-6576;
www.sheratonburlington.com
This full-service hotel is the only Sheraton located in Vermont. Rooms are comfortable
with plush beds and Wireless Internet access. 309 rooms. Pets accepted. Restaurant,
bar. Fitness room. Indoor pool, whirlpool. Airport transportation available. Business
center. **$**

RESTAURANTS

★DAILY PLANET
15 Center St., Burlington, 802-862-9647; www.dailyplanet15.com
International menu. Dinner, late-night. Bar. Children's menu. Casual attire. Reserva-
tions recommended. Outdoor seating. **$$**

VERMONT

★
★
★
★
★

★★ICE HOUSE RESTAURANT AND BAR

171 Battery St., Burlington, 802-864-1800

American menu. Lunch, dinner. Bar. Children's menu. Casual attire. Reservations recommended. Outdoor seating. **$$**

★★★PAULINE'S

1834 Shelburne Road, South Burlington, 802-862-1081; www.paulinescafe.com

This two-story restaurant serves fresh seasonal ingredients and a seafood-heavy menu. A $30 two-course dinner-for-two menu is offered at opening Sunday-Thursday. American menu. Lunch, dinner, Sunday brunch. Bar. Children's menu. Outdoor seating. **$$**

DORSET

This charming village is surrounded by hills that are 3,000 feet high. In 1776, the Green Mountain Boys voted for Vermont's independence here, and in 1785, the first marble quarry in the country was opened on nearby Mount Aeolus.

Information: Dorset Chamber of Commerce, 802-867-2450; www.dorsetvt.com

SPECIAL EVENT

DORSET THEATRE FESTIVAL

Dorset Playhouse, 104 Cheney Road, Dorset, 802-867-2223;
www.dorsettheatrefestival.com

Professional theater company presents six productions each season. Mid-June-Labor Day.

★
★
★
☆

HOTELS

★★★DORSET INN

8 Church St. and Route 30, Dorset, 802-867-5500, 877-367-7389;
www.dorsetinn.com

Established in 1796, this is the oldest continuously operating inn in Vermont, and it is rich with history—the Green Mountain Boys plotted their fight against the British here. Guest rooms feature private baths, antique furnishings and wall-to-wall carpet. There are no telephones in guest rooms, but some offer televisions. The onsite restaurant serves high-end comfort food, made from locally farmed products—dishes include smoked salmon and Asian spiked shrimp skewers. 29 rooms. Pets accepted, some restrictions; fee. Complimentary full breakfast. Wireless Internet access. Restaurant, bar. Spa. **$$**

★★★INN AT WEST VIEW FARM

2928 Highway 30, Dorset, 802-867-5715, 800-769-4903;
www.innatwestviewfarm.com

This restored farmhouse overlooks the Vermont countryside. Beds are topped with down duvets and bathrooms have Caswell Masey bath products. 10 rooms. Complimentary full breakfast. Restaurant, bar. **$**

SPECIALTY LODGING

BARROWS HOUSE INN

3156 Highway 30, Dorset, 802-867-4455, 800-639-1620; www.barrowshouse.com

28 rooms. Pets accepted, some restrictions; fee. Restaurant, bar. Outdoor pool. Tennis. **$$**

RESTAURANTS
★★★BARROWS HOUSE INN
3156 Highway 30, Dorset, 802-867-4455, 800-639-1620; www.barrowshouse.com

Choose to sit in the clubby tavern, the bright greenhouse, on the small outdoor patio or in the more formal dining room while enjoying the regional cuisine served at this inn. American menu. Breakfast, dinner. Bar. Children's menu. Casual attire. Reservations recommended. Outdoor seating. **$$**

★★INN AT WEST VIEW FARM
2928 Route 30, Dorset, 802-867-5715, 800-769-4903;
www.innatwestviewfarm.com

American menu. Dinner. Bar. Business casual attire. Reservations recommended. Closed Tuesday-Wednesday. **$$$**

FAIRLEE

This town is located near the New Hampshire border and on Lake Morley.
Information: Town Offices, Main Street, 802-333-4363; www.fairleevt.org

HOTEL
★★LAKE MOREY RESORT
1 Clubhouse Road, Fairlee, 802-333-4311, 800-423-1211;
www.lakemoreyresort.com

144 rooms. Restaurant, bar. Children's activity center. Fitness room. Indoor pool, outdoor pool, whirlpool. Golf. Tennis. Spa. **$**

313

GRAFTON

This New England village is a blend of houses, churches, galleries, antiques shops—all circa 1800. Founded in pre-Revolutionary times under the patronage of George III, Grafton became a thriving mill town and modest industrial center after the damming of the nearby Saxton River. When water power gave way to steam, the town declined. Rescued, revived and restored by the Windham Foundation, its beauty remains intact. A creek runs through the picturesque town, a favorite among photographers.
Information: Great Falls Regional Chamber of Commerce, 55 Village Square,
Bellows Falls, 802-463-4280; www.gfrcc.org

WHAT TO SEE AND DO
GRAFTON PONDS CROSS-COUNTRY SKI CENTER
Townshend Road, Grafton, 800-843-1801, 802-843-2400; www.graftonponds.com

Featuring more than 16 miles of groomed trails, a skiing school, rentals, concessions and a warming hut. December-March: daily. In summer: walking and fitness trails (no fee).

THE OLD TAVERN AT GRAFTON
92 Main St., Grafton, 800-843-1801; www.old-tavern.com

(1801) Visited by many famous guests over the years, including several presidents and authors; names inscribed over the desk. Furnished with antiques and colonial décor. Former barn converted to lounge; annex is restored from two houses; dining by reservations. May-March daily.

VERMONT

★
★
★
★
★

HOTEL

★★★OLD TAVERN AT GRAFTON

92 Main St., Grafton, 802-843-2231, 800-843-1801; www.old-tavern.com

This New England inn features guest rooms with antique Chippendale and Windsor furnishings. Guests will enjoy the afternoon tea, tennis courts and bicycles. 46 rooms. Closed April. Children over 7 years only. Complimentary full breakfast. Restaurant, bar. Tennis. **$**

SPECIALTY LODGING

INN AT WOODCHUCK HILL FARM

Middletown Road, Grafton, 802-843-2398; www.woodchuckhill.com

First farmhouse in town (1790). On 200 acres with a pond. 10 rooms. Complimentary full breakfast. **$**

JEFFERSONVILLE

This village, located in the mountains of Vermont's Northern Kingdom, has a population of less than 600. Smugglers' Notch ski resort is located here.

Information: Smugglers' Notch Area Chamber of Commerce; www.smugnotch.com

WHAT TO SEE AND DO

SMUGGLERS' NOTCH

4323 Highway 108 South, Jeffersonville, 802-644-8851,
800-451-8752; www.smuggs.com

Resort has five double chairlifts, three surface lifts, school, rentals, snowmaking, concession area, cafeteria, restaurants, a nursery and a lodge. Sixty runs, longest run over three miles; vertical drop 2,610 feet. Thanksgiving-mid-April, daily. More than 25 miles of cross-country trails (December-April: daily; rentals), ice skating. Summer activities include 10 swimming pools, three water slides, tennis, miniature golf, driving range.

HOTEL

★★SMUGGLERS' NOTCH RESORT

4323 Highway 108 South, Jeffersonville, 802-644-8851,
800-451-8752; www.smuggs.com

525 rooms. Restaurant, bar. Children's activity center. Fitness room. Eight outdoor pools, whirlpool. Tennis. Ski-in/ski-out. Airport transportation available. **$**

SPECIALTY LODGING

SINCLAIR INN BED & BREAKFAST

389 Highway 15, Jericho, 802-899-2234, 800-433-4658; www.sinclairinnbb.com

This restored Queen Anne Victorian inn was built in 1890. Six rooms. Children over 12 years only. Complimentary full breakfast. **$**

KILLINGTON

One of New England's most popular ski towns, Killington attracts scores every year thanks to its reliable and early-season snowmaking. The bars and lounges around Killington become a lively singles scene for skiing Bostonians come winter.

Information: Killington Chamber of Commerce, 802-773-4181,
800-337-1928; www.killingtonchamber.com

★
★
★
★
☆

WHAT TO SEE AND DO

GIFFORD WOODS STATE PARK

34 Gifford Woods, Killington, 802-775-5354; www.vtstateparks.com

This 114-acre park has fishing and boat access to Kent Pond. Foot trails (Appalachian Trail passes through park). Virgin forest with picnic facilities. Tent and trailer sites (dump station). Standard fees. Memorial Day-Columbus Day.

KILLINGTON RESORT

4763 Killington Road, Killington, 802-422-3261, 800-621-6867;
www.killington.com

Comprises 1,200 acres with seven mountains (highest elevation 4,241 feet). Two gondolas, six high-speed quad, six quad, six triple, four double chairlifts, eight surface lifts, patrol, school, rentals, snowmaking, mountaintop restaurant (with observation decks), six cafeterias, bars, children's center, nursery and lodging. More than 200 runs, with the longest run 10 miles, with a vertical drop 3,150 feet. Snowboarding; snow tubing. October-June daily.

PICO ALPINE SLIDE AND SCENIC CHAIRLIFT

4763 Killington Road, Killington, 866-667-7426;
www.killington.com/summer/events/adventure_center/alpine_slides/index.html

Chairlift to top of mountain slope; control speed of own sled on the way down. Sports center and restaurant below. Late May-mid-October.

HOTELS

★★CASCADES LODGE

58 Old Mill Road, Killington Village, 802-422-3731, 800-345-0113;
www.cascadeslodge.com

46 rooms. Pets accepted, some restrictions; fee. Complimentary full breakfast. Restaurant, bar. Fitness room. Indoor pool, whirlpool. Ski-in/ski-out. **$**

★★★CORTINA INN AND RESORT

103 Highway 4, Killington, 802-773-3333, 800-451-6108;
www.cortinainn.com

Open year-round, this inn offers a perfect weekend retreat. Rooms are cozy and offer Wireless Internet access and Direct TV. 97 rooms. Pets accepted; fee. Complimentary full breakfast. Restaurant, bar. Fitness room. Indoor pool, whirlpool. Tennis. Airport transportation available. **$**

★ECONO LODGE KILLINGTON AREA

51 Route 4, Mendon, 800-992-9067, 800-553-2666; www.econolodge.com

30 rooms. Pets accepted. Complimentary continental breakfast. Children's activity center. Outdoor pool, whirlpool. **$**

★★GREY BONNET INN

831 Highway 100, Killington, 802-775-2537, 800-342-2086;
www.greybonnetinn.com

40 rooms. Restaurant, bar. Fitness room. Indoor pool, outdoor pool, whirlpool. Tennis. Closed April-May, late October-late November. **$**

VERMONT

★
★
★
★
★

★★INN OF THE SIX MOUNTAINS

2617 Killington Road, Killington, 802-422-4302, 800-228-4676;
www.sixmountains.com

Located close to Killington ski resort, this inn offers an easy location from which to hit the slopes early in the morning. Cedars restaurant serves breakfast and the lounge is a great place for an après-ski drink. 100 rooms. Complimentary full breakfast. Restaurant, bar. Fitness room. Indoor pool, outdoor pool, whirlpool. Tennis. Spa. Private tennis court (seasonal). $

★★KILLINGTON PICO MOTOR INN

64 Highway 4, Killington, 802-773-4088, 800-548-4713; www.killingtonpico.com

28 rooms. Complimentary full breakfast. Restaurant, bar. Outdoor pool, whirlpool. $

★★★RED CLOVER INN

7 Woodward Road, Mendon, 802-775-2290, 800-752-0571;
www.redcloverinn.com

This 1840s country inn features views of the Green Mountains. Some rooms have fireplaces and four-poster beds. 14 rooms. Children over 12 years only. Complimentary full breakfast. Wireless Internet access. Restaurant, bar. $$

★SHERBURNE-KILLINGTON MOTEL

1946 Highway 4, Killington, 802-773-9535, 800-366-0493;
www.lodgingkillington.com

20 rooms. Complimentary continental breakfast. Outdoor pool. Wi-Fi Internet access. $

★★SUMMIT LODGE

Killington Mountain Road, Killington, 802-422-3535, 800-635-6343;
www.summitlodgevermont.com

45 rooms. Complimentary full breakfast. Wireless Internet access. Restaurant, bar. Two outdoor pools, whirlpool. Tennis. Spa. Golfing. $

SPECIALTY LODGING

VERMONT INN

H.C. 34 Box 37J Highway 4, Killington, 802-775-0708, 800-541-7795;
www.vermontinn.com

18 rooms. Children over 6 years only. Restaurant, bar. Fitness room. Outdoor pool, whirlpool. Tennis. Closed mid-April-late May. $$

RESTAURANTS

★★★HEMINGWAY'S

4988 Highway 4, Killington, 802-422-3886; www.hemingwaysrestaurant.com

Housed in a charming 19th-century house, Hemingway's offers a six-course menu, a four-course vegetable menu and a three-course prix fixe menu. Everything is prepared with seasonal ingredients, regional seafood and farm-raised poultry and game. Known for its robust American fare, the menu features dishes such as pecan-crusted Vermont lamb with crispy potatoes and green beans, and wood-grilled quail with cheddar corn cakes and black-eyed pea vinaigrette. Everything is prepared with seasonal ingredients, regional seafood and farm-raised poultry and game. International

★
★
★
★
★

menu. Dinner. October-mid-November. Bar. Casual attire. Closed Monday-Tuesday; also mid-April-mid-May. **$$$$**

★★★RED CLOVER

7 Woodward Road, Mendon, 802-775-2290, 800-752-0571; www.redcloverinn.com

This 19th-century farmhouse inn offers sophisticated dining in four candlelit rooms. The menu changes frequently and entrées include oven-roasted quail on a Tuscan bean salad and cider-marinated-salmon. American menu. Breakfast, dinner. Bar. Business casual attire. Reservations recommended. Closed Monday-Wednesday. **$$$**

★★VERMONT INN

Highway 4, Killington, 802-775-0708, 800-541-7795; www.vermontinn.com

Located in the Vermont Inn, this restaurant features a large wood-burning fireplace, exposed beams and views of the front lawn and mountains. American menu. Dinner. Bar. Children's menu. Casual attire. Reservations recommended. Closed three weeks in April and May. **$$**

LONDONDERRY

A tiny town of less than 2,000 residents, this village is located close to Magic Mountain ski resort.

Information: Londonderry Area Chamber of Commerce Mountain Marketplace, 802-824-8178; www.londonderryvt.org

HOTEL

★★DOSTAL'S RESORT LODGE

441 Magic Mountain Access Road, Londonderry, 802-824-6700, 800-255-5373; www.dostals.com

50 rooms. Pets accepted; fee. Restaurant, bar. Indoor pool, outdoor pool, whirlpool. Tennis. Closed November-mid-December. **$**

SPECIALTY LODGINGS

FROG'S LEAP INN

7455 Highway 100, Londonderry, 802-824-3019, 877-376-4753; www.frogsleapinn.com

This historic building (1842) is situated on 32 wooded acres. 17 rooms. Pets accepted; fee. Restaurant. Outdoor pool. Tennis. Closed three weeks in April and one week in November. **$**

LONDONDERRY INN

8 Melendy Hill Road, Londonderry, 802-824-5226, 800-644-5226; www.londonderryinn.com

Built in 1826, this inn used to be a farmhouse. 25 rooms. Complimentary continental breakfast. Restaurant. Outdoor pool. **$**

SWISS INN

249 Highway 11, Londonderry, 802-824-3442, 800-847-9477; www.swissinn.com

19 rooms. Complimentary full breakfast. Restaurant, bar. Outdoor pool. Tennis. Free Wireless Internet access. **$**

VERMONT

★
★
★
☆

LUDLOW

This southwestern Vermont town is close to Okemo Mountain and Ascutney Mountain ski resorts.

Information: Ludlow Area Chamber of Commerce, Okemo Market Place, 802-228-5830; www.ludlow.org.uk

WHAT TO SEE AND DO
CROWLEY CHEESE FACTORY

14 Crowley Lane, Healdville, 802-259-2340, 800-683-2606; www.crowleycheese-vermont.com

(1882) Oldest cheese factory in the United States that still makes cheese by hand. Display of tools used in early cheese factories and in home cheesemaking. Watch the process and sample the product. Monday-Friday.

GREEN MOUNTAIN SUGAR HOUSE

820 Highway 100 North, Ludlow, 800-643-9338; www.gmsh.com

Working maple sugar producer on shore of Lake Pauline.

HOTEL
★★★THE GOVERNOR'S INN

86 Main St., Ludlow, 802-228-8830, 800-468-3766; www.thegovernorsinn.com

The building dates back to 1890 and is a Victorian masterpiece. Many rooms have period antiques and gas-lit stoves or fireplaces. Diners taken with the cuisine at the restaurant can participate in one of the Culinary Magic Cooking Seminars. The challenging slopes of Okemo Mountain are just a short distance from the Governor's Inn. A shuttle is available to the base of the mountain from the inn. Nine rooms. Children over 12 years only. Complimentary full breakfast. Restaurant. Closed late December; also two weeks in April and two weeks in November. **$$**

SPECIALTY LODGINGS
ANDRIE ROSE INN

13 Pleasant St., Ludlow, 802-228-4846, 800-223-4846; www.andrieroseinn.com

Built in 1829, this inn is at the base of Okemo Mountain. 23 rooms. Complimentary full breakfast. **$**

COMBES FAMILY INN

953 E. Lake Road, Ludlow, 802-228-8799, 800-822-8799; www.combesfamilyinn.com

This restored farmhouse (1891) is situated on 50 acres of land near Lake Rescue. 11 rooms. Pets accepted. Restaurant. Closed mid-April-mid-May. Golf. **$**

GOLDEN STAGE INN

399 Depot St., Proctorsville, 802-226-7744, 800-253-8226; www.goldenstageinn.com

Nine rooms. Restaurant (public by reservation), bar. Outdoor pool. Pets not accepted. **$$**

INN AT WATER'S EDGE

45 Kingdom Road, Ludlow, 802-228-8143, 888-706-9736; www.innatwatersedge.com

11 rooms. Complimentary full breakfast. **$$**

★
★★
★★
★★

LYNDONVILLE

Lyndonville, located in the valley of the Passumpsic River, is home to several small industries and a trading center for the surrounding dairy and stock raising farms. Five covered bridges, the earliest dating to 1795, are found within the town limits.

Information: Lyndon Area Chamber of Commerce, 802-626-9696;
www.lyndonvermont.com

WHAT TO SEE AND DO
BURKE MOUNTAIN SKI AREA
Route 114 E. & E. Burke, Lyndonville, 802-626-7300,
888-287-5388; www.skiburke.com

Area has two chairlifts, one Pomalift, J-bar, school, rentals and snowmaking; two cafeterias, two bars, nursery. Forty-three runs, longest run approximately 2 1/2 miles, with a vertical drop of 2,000 feet. More than 57 miles of cross-country trails. Thanksgiving-early April, daily.

HOTEL
★COLONNADE INN
28 Back Center Road, Lyndonville, 802-626-9316, 877-435-5688;
www.nekchamber.com

40 rooms. Complimentary continental breakfast. $

SPECIALTY LODGING
THE WILDFLOWER INN
2059 Darling Hill Road, Lyndonville, 802-626-8310, 800-627-8310;
www.wildflowerinn.com

Family-oriented inn on 500 acres; barns, farm animals, sledding slopes. Art gallery. 25 rooms. Complimentary full breakfast. Restaurant. Children's activity center. Outdoor pool, children's pool, whirlpool. Tennis. Closed two weeks in April and November. $

MANCHESTER

Manchester and Manchester Center have been among Vermont's best-loved year-round resorts for 100 years. The surrounding mountains and the ski business add to their popularity. Bromley Mountain, Stratton Mountain and other areas lure thousands each year and a Ranger District office of the Green Mountain National Forest is located here.

Information: Manchester and the Mountains Regional Chamber of Commerce,
5046 Main St., 802-362-2100, 800-362-4144; www.manchestervermont.net

WHAT TO SEE AND DO
AMERICAN MUSEUM OF FLY FISHING
410 Main St., Manchester, 802-362-3300; www.amff.com

Founded in 1968 by fishermen who wanted to ensure that the history of their sport would not be lost, this museum is a hotspot for anglers of all ages. Collection of fly-fishing memorabilia and tackle of many famous persons, including Dwight D. Eisenhower, Ernest Hemingway, Andrew Carnegie, Winslow Homer, Bing Crosby and others. Monday-Friday 10 a.m.-4 p.m.

VERMONT

★
★
★
★
★

EMERALD LAKE STATE PARK

65 Emerald Lake Lane, North Dorset, 802-362-1655; www.vtstateparks.com

This 430-acre park has rich flora in a limestone-based bedrock. Swimming beach, bathhouse, fishing (also in nearby streams), boating (rentals), nature and hiking trails, picnicking, concession. Tent and trailer sites (dump station). Standard fees. Memorial Day-Columbus Day.

EQUINOX SKY LINE DRIVE

1A St. and Bruno Drive, Manchester and Manchester Center, 802-362-1114,
802-362-1115; www.equinoxmountain.com/skylinedrive

A spectacular five-mile paved road that rises from 600-3,835 feet. Parking and picnic areas are along the road and a view from top of Mount Equinox. Fog or rain may make mountain road dangerous and travel inadvisable. May-October: daily. No large camper vehicles.

HISTORIC HILDENE

1005 Hildene Road, Manchester, 802-362-1788, 800-578-1788; www.hildene.org

(1904) The 412-acre estate of Robert Todd Lincoln (Abraham Lincoln's son) includes a 24-room Georgian manor house, held in the family until 1975. Original furnishings, carriage barn, formal gardens, nature trails. Tours. Mid-May-October: daily 9:30 a.m.-3 p.m.; November-May: Thursday-Monday 11 a.m.-3 p.m.

MANCHESTER DESIGNER OUTLETS

Highways 11 and 30, Manchester Center, 802-362-3736;
www.manchesterdesigneroutlets.com

Many outlet stores can be found in this area, mainly along Highway 11/30 and at the intersection of Highway 11/30 and Highway 7A. Contact the Chamber of Commerce (802-362-2100) for a complete listing of stores. Monday-Saturday 10 a.m.-7 p.m., Sunday 10 a.m.-6 p.m.

HOTELS

★ASPEN MOTEL

5669 Main St., Manchester Center, 802-362-2450; www.theaspenatmanchester.com

24 rooms. Outdoor pool. Free Wireless Internet access. $

★★★THE EQUINOX

3567 Main St., Manchester Village, 802-362-4700, 866-346-7625;
www.equinox.rockresorts.com

Open since 1769, this premier resort has long been a favorite of notables, including the Lincolns, Tafts and Roosevelts, and is listed on the National Register of Historic Places. Located in the shadow of Mount Equinox, there is a lot to do. From world-class golf at the Gleneagles golf course, skiing at nearby Stratton and Bromley mountains, Orvis fly fishing and shooting schools, and its very own falconry center, this place is a paradise for sports enthusiasts. A luxe new spa is located onsite, as are three restaurants. 180 rooms. Pets accepted, some restrictions; fee. Wireless Internet access. Three restaurants, two bars. Fitness room, fitness classes available. Spa. Indoor pool, whirlpool. Golf, 18 holes. Tennis. Ski-in/ski-out. Airport transportation available. Business center. $$$

★MANCHESTER VIEW

Highway 7A and High Meadow Way, Manchester Center, 802-362-2739,
800-548-4141; www.manchesterview.com

35 rooms. Complimentary continental breakfast. Outdoor pool. Wireless Internet access. Spa. **$**

★★★RELUCTANT PANTHER INN AND RESTAURANT

39 W. Road, Manchester, 802-362-2568, 800-822-2331;
www.reluctantpanther.com

This inn was built in 1850 by a wealthy blacksmith. The owners have refurbished the property, retaining two of the original fireplaces. 21 rooms. Children over 14 years only. Complimentary full breakfast. Restaurant, bar. **$$**

SPECIALTY LODGINGS

1811 HOUSE

Main Street, Manchester, 802-362-1811, 800-432-1811;
www.1811house.com

Each guest room at this inn is named for individuals who were prominent in the history of Manchester. Gardens surround around the inn. 13 rooms. Children over 16 years only. Complimentary full breakfast. Bar. Tennis. **$$**

INN AT MANCHESTER

3967 Main St., Manchester, 802-362-1793, 800-273-1793;
www.innatmanchester.com

This 19th-century Victorian structure has been beautifully restored to its original grandeur. 18 rooms. Children over 8 years only. Complimentary full breakfast. Wireless Internet access. Outdoor pool. **$$**

THE INN AT ORMSBY HILL

1842 Main St., Manchester, 802-362-1163, 800-670-2841;
www.ormsbyhill.com

Hospitality and relaxation await at this tranquil location surrounded by views of the Green Mountains. The common areas feature a collection of china and unique fireplaces. 10 rooms. Complimentary full breakfast. Wireless Internet access. **$$**

MANCHESTER HIGHLANDS INN

216 Highland Ave., Manchester Center, 802-362-4565, 800-743-4565;
www.highlandsinn.com

Views of Mount Equinox can be seen from this Victorian inn. Plenty of outlet shopping is nearby. 15 rooms. Complimentary full breakfast. Wireless Internet access. Outdoor pool. Pets not accepted. **$$**

PALMER HOUSE

5383 Main St., Manchester Center, 802-362-3600, 800-917-6245;
www.palmerhouse.com

50 rooms. Children over 12 years only. Complimentary continental breakfast. Fitness room. Indoor pool, outdoor pool, whirlpool. Golf, 9 holes. Tennis. **$**

VERMONT

★
★
★
★

WILBURTON INN
River Road, Manchester Village, 802-362-2500, 800-648-4944; www.wilburton.com
Set on a hill that overlooks the Battenkill Valley, this 20-acre Victorian estate offers guests numerous onsite activities as well as nearby shopping. 36 rooms. Complimentary full breakfast. Outdoor pool. Fitness center. **$$**

SPA
★★★AVANYU SPA AT THE EQUINOX RESORT
3567 Main St., Manchester Village, 802-362-4700; www.equinoxresort.com
This recently constructed 13,000-square-foot spa has a 75-foot heated indoor pool, state-of-the-art fitness center, 10 treatment rooms, saunas and steam baths. Treatments include the Gentle Rain body treatment, where a sea salt, maple or citrus scrub is followed with a warm waterfall shower and an application of a rich body cream. Massage therapies like Flowing Water, Rolling Thunder and Dancing Wind simulate nature's energies through effleurage, deep tissue and gentle massage techniques.

MIDDLEBURY
Benjamin Smalley built the first log house here just before the Revolution. In 1800, the town had a full-fledged college and, by 1803, there was a flourishing marble quarry and a women's academy run by Emma Hart Willard, a pioneer in education for women. Today, Middlebury is known for Middlebury College. A Ranger District office of the Green Mountain National Forest is also located here, and a map and guides for day hikes on Long Trail are available.

Information: Addison County Chamber of Commerce Information Center,
2 Court St., 802-388-7951, 800-733-8376; www.midvermont.com

WHAT TO SEE AND DO
BREAD LOAF
121A S. Main St., Middlebury College, Freeman International Center,
Middlebury, 802-443-5418; www.middlebury.edu
Site of nationally known Bread Loaf School of English in June and annual Writers' Conference in August. Also site of Robert Frost's cabin. In winter, it is the Carroll and Jane Rikert Ski Touring Center.

CONGREGATIONAL CHURCH
27 N. Pleasant St., Middlebury, 802-388-7634; www.midducc.org
(1806-1809) Built after a plan in the *Country Builder's Assistant* and designed by architect Lavius Fillmore. Architecturally, one of the finest in Vermont.

MIDDLEBURY COLLEGE
Middlebury College, Route 30, Middlebury, 802-443-5000; www.middlebury.edu
(1800) (1,950 students) Famous for the teaching of arts and sciences, summer language schools; Bread Loaf School of English and Writers' Conference.

MIDDLEBURY COLLEGE SNOW BOWL
Route 125, Middlebury, 802-388-4356; www.middlebury.edu
Area has triple, two double chairlifts, patrol, school, rentals, snowmaking, cafeteria. Fourteen runs. Early December-early April, daily.

VERMONT
★
★
★
★
★

VERMONT STATE CRAFT CENTER AT FROG HOLLOW

1 Mill St., Middlebury, 802-388-3177, 888-388-3177;
www.froghollow.org

Restored mill overlooking Otter Creek Falls houses an exhibition and sales gallery with works of more than 300 Vermont artists. Special exhibitions, classes and workshops. Spring-fall, daily; rest of year, Monday-Saturday.

SPECIAL EVENTS
FESTIVAL ON THE GREEN

Middlebury Green, Main Street and Highway 7, Middlebury,
802-388-0216; www.festivalonthegreen.com

Village green. Classical, modern and traditional dance; chamber and folk music; theater and comedy presentations. Early July.

WINTER CARNIVAL

Middlebury College, Highway 30, Middlebury, 802-443-3100,
802-443-5483; www.middlebury.edu

The oldest and largest student-run carnival in the country includes fireworks, an ice show and ski competitions; held on the campus of Middlebury College. Late February.

HOTELS
★★MIDDLEBURY INN

14 Court House Square, Middlebury, 802-388-4961, 800-842-4666;
www.middleburyinn.com

70 rooms. Pets accepted, some restrictions. Complimentary continental breakfast Restaurant, bar. **$$**

★★★SWIFT HOUSE INN

25 Stewart Lane, Middlebury, 802-388-9925, 866-388-9925;
www.swifthouseinn.com

This inn has three separate buildings, each with its own character and charm. Rooms are individually decorated and feature four-poster beds and handmade quilts. Pets accepted, some restrictions; fee. Complimentary continental breakfast. Restaurant. **$$**

SPECIALTY LODGING
WAYBURY INN

457 E. Main, East Middlebury, 802-388-4015, 800-348-1810;
www.wayburyinn.com

Constructed as a stagecoach stop; an inn since 1810. Near Middlebury College. 14 rooms. Pets accepted. Complimentary full breakfast. Restaurant, bar. **$**

MONTPELIER

Vermont's capital is one of the nation's most picturesque, located on the banks of the Winooski River and made up of quaint brick buildings. A popular summer vacation area, Montpelier absorbs the overflow from the nearby ski areas in winter.

Information: Central Vermont Chamber of Commerce, Barre,
802-229-5711; www.central-vt.com

VERMONT

WHAT TO SEE AND DO

MORSE FARM
1168 County Road, Montpelier, 802-223-2740, 800-242-2740;
www.morsefarm.com
Maple sugar and vegetable farm in rustic, wooded setting. Tour of sugar house; view sugar-making process in season March-April. Slide show explains process off-season. Gift shop. Daily.

STATE HOUSE
115 State St., Montpelier, 802-828-2228, 802-828-1411;
www.leg.state.vt.us/sthouse/sthouse.htm
(1859) Made of Vermont granite; dome covered with gold leaf. Monday-Friday 8 a.m.-4 p.m.; guided tours, July-mid-October, Monday-Friday 10 a.m.-3:30 p.m., Saturday 11 a.m.-2:30 p.m.

THOMAS WATERMAN WOOD ART GALLERY
36 College St., Montpelier, 802-828-8743; www.twwoodgallery.org
Oils, watercolors and etchings by Wood and other 19th-century American artists. Also, American artists of the 1920s and '30s changing monthly exhibits of works of contemporary local and regional artists. Tuesday-Wednesday, Friday-Sunday noon-4 p.m.; Thursday until 8 p.m.

VERMONT HISTORICAL SOCIETY MUSEUM

109 State St., Montpelier, 802-828-2291; www.vermonthistory.org
Historical exhibits. Tuesday-Saturday 10 a.m.-4 p.m., Sunday noon-4 p.m., May-October; closed holidays.

HOTELS

★★★CAPITOL PLAZA HOTEL AND CONFERENCE CENTER
100 State St., Montpelier, 802-223-5252, 800-274-5252;
www.capitolplaza.com
Across the street from the historic State House, this hotel has served Vermont's lawmakers and tourists since the 1930s. 56 rooms. Restaurant, bar. High speed Internet access. **$**

★COMFORT INN
213 Paine Turnpike North, Montpelier, 802-229-2222, 800-424-6423;
www.choicehotels.com
89 rooms. Complimentary continental breakfast. Bar. Airport transportation available. Pets not accepted. Free Wireless Internet access. **$**

★★★INN AT MONTPELIER
147 Main St., Montpelier, 802-223-2727; www.innatmontpelier.com
Revisit the early 1800s at this historic inn comprised of two stately buildings showcasing Greek and Colonial Revival woodwork, numerous fireplaces and a spectacular front staircase. 19 rooms. Complimentary continental breakfast. Pets not accepted. **$**

★★★THE INN ON THE COMMON

1162 N. Craftsbury Road, Craftsbury Common, 802-586-9619, 800-521-2233;
www.innonthecommon.com

This inn is made up of three restored Federal-style houses that feature colorful gardens and wooded hillsides. 16 rooms. Pets accepted, some restrictions; fee. Restaurant, bar. Outdoor pool. Tennis. Horseback riding. **$$**

SPECIALTY LODGING
NORTHFIELD INN

228 Highland Ave., Northfield, 802-485-8558;
www.thenorthfieldinn.com

This inn was built in 1901 and is furnished with period pieces. 28 rooms. Children over 15 years only. Complimentary full breakfast. **$**

RESTAURANT
★★CHEF'S TABLE

118 Main St., Montpelier, 802-229-9202, 802-223-3188;
www.neci.edu/restaurants.html

International menu. Dinner. Bar. Closed Sunday-Monday. **$$$**

NEWFANE

Originally settled high on Newfane Hill, this postcard-perfect Vermont town was a favorite vacation spot for American poet Eugene Field.

Information: Town Clerk, 802-365-7772; www.newfanevt.com

WHAT TO SEE AND DO
SCOTT COVERED BRIDGE

Route 30, Townshend, 802-257-0292

Longest single span bridge in the state (166 feet), built with lattice-type trusses. Together the three spans total 276 feet. Other two spans are of king post-type trusses.

TOWNSHEND STATE FOREST

2755 State Forest Road, Townshend, 802-365-7500;
www.vtstateparks.com

A 1,690-acre area with foot trail to Bald Mountain (1,580 feet). Swimming at nearby Townshend Reservoir Recreation Area, hiking trails, picnic sites, tent and trailer sites. Standard fees. May-Columbus Day.

HOTEL
★★★WINDHAM HILL INN

311 Lawrence Drive, West Townshend, 802-874-4080, 800-944-4080;
www.windhamhill.com

This charming and elegant 1825 country estate features rooms with fireplaces, spa or soaking tubs and plush beds. The onsite restaurant serves full country breakfasts and simple, well-prepared dinners. 21 rooms. Children over 12 years only. Restaurant. Outdoor pool. Tennis. **$$**

SPECIALTY LODGING

FOUR COLUMNS INN

21 W. St., Newfane, 802-365-7713, 800-787-6633;
www.fourcolumnsinn.com

Located in the center of Newfane and at the foot of a private mountain, this 16-room inn combines historic charm with modern flair. The décor is old-fashioned, with sleigh and iron four-poster beds. Many suites have two-sided fireplaces and most rooms have whirlpools or soaking tubs. While some rooms are without TVs, all have Wireless Internet access. 16 rooms. Pets accepted, some restrictions; fee. Complimentary continental breakfast. Restaurant, bar. Outdoor pool. **$$$**

RESTAURANTS

★★★FOUR COLUMNS

21 W. St., Newfane, 802-365-7713, 800-787-6633; www.fourcolumnsinn.com

Chef Greg Parks offers innovative and contemporary cuisine and an award-winning wine list at this welcoming inn. Dinner often features dishes such as grilled angus tenderloin with green peppercorn vinaigrette. American menu. Breakfast for inn guests only, dinner. Bar. Casual attire. Reservations recommended. Outdoor seating. Closed Tuesday. Pets accepted, some restrictions; fee. **$$$**

★★★OLD NEWFANE INN

Highway 30, Newfane, 802-365-4427, 800-784-4427; www.oldnewfaneinn.com

Timbered ceilings and brick fireplaces add to the colonial charm of this historic 1787 landmark specializing in European classics such as chateaubriand and veal goulash. Continental, French menu. Dinner, bar. Casual attire. Reservations recommended. Closed Monday; April-mid-May, November-mid-December. **$$**

NORTH HERO

This far northern Vermont town borders Lake Champlain and is close to both New York State and Quebec, Canada.

Information: Champlain Islands Chamber of Commerce, 802-372-8400,
800-262-5226; www.champlainislands.com

WHAT TO SEE AND DO

NORTH HERO STATE PARK

3803 Lakeview Drive, North Hero, 802-372-8727; www.vtstateparks.com

A 399-acre park located in the north part of the Champlain Islands; extensive shoreline on Lake Champlain. Swimming, fishing, boating (ramps), hiking trails, playground, tent and trailer sites (dump station). Standard fees. Memorial Day-Labor Day.

SPECIAL EVENT

ROYAL LIPPIZAN STALLIONS OF AUSTRIA

Knight Point State Park, 44 Knight Point Road, North Hero, 802-372-8400,
800-262-5226; www.champlainislands.com

Summer residence of the stallions. Performances Thursday and Friday evenings, Saturday and Sunday afternoons. For ticket prices, contact Chamber of Commerce. July-August.

326

VERMONT

★
★
★
★

m o b i l t r a v e l g u i d e . c o m

HOTELS
★★★NORTH HERO HOUSE INN
Highway 2, North Hero, 802-372-4732, 888-525-3644; www.northherohouse.com
This inn, built in 1800, is surrounded by spectacular views of the Green Mountains and Mount Mansfield. Activities are available year-round. 26 rooms. Complimentary continental breakfast. Restaurant, bar. Tennis. Pets not accepted. Internet access. **$$**

★★SHORE ACRES INN
237 Shore Acres Drive, North Hero, 802-372-8722; www.shoreacres.com
23 rooms. Pets accepted; fee. Restaurant, bar. Tennis. Wirless Internet Access. **$**

SPECIALTY LODGING
THOMAS MOTT ALBURG HOMESTEAD BED AND BREAKFAST
63 Blue Rock Road, Alburg, 802-796-4402, 800-348-0843; www.thomas-mott-bb.com
This restored farmhouse (1838) overlooks the lake. Four rooms. Children over 6 years only. Complimentary full breakfast. Pets accepted. **$**

RESTAURANT
★★NORTH HERO HOUSE
Highway 2, North Hero, 802-372-4732, 888-525-3644; www.northherohouse.com
American menu. Breakfast for inn guests only, dinner, Sunday brunch. Bar. Outdoor seating. Pets not accepted. Internet access. **$$**

PLYMOUTH

This town hasn't changed much since July 4, 1872, when Calvin Coolidge was born in the back of the village store (which is still in business today). A country road leads to the cemetery where the former president and six generations of his family are buried. Nearby is the Coolidge Visitors Center and Museum, which displays historical and presidential memorabilia.
Information: Town of Plymouth, 802-672-3655; www.plymouth-ma.gov

VERMONT

WHAT TO SEE AND DO
PRESIDENT CALVIN COOLIDGE HOMESTEAD
Coolidge Memorial Drive, Plymouth Notch, 802-672-3773; www.dhca.state.vt.us
In 1923, Calvin Coolidge was sworn in by his father in his house's sitting room, which has been restored to its early 20th-century appearance. The Plymouth Historic District also includes the General Store that was operated by the president's father, the house where the president was born, the village dance hall that served as the 1924 summer White House office, the Union Church with its Carpenter Gothic interior, the Wilder House (birthplace of Coolidge's mother), the Wilder Barn with 19th-century farming equipment, a restaurant and a visitor center with museum. Late May-mid-October, daily 9:30 a.m.-5 p.m.

★
★
★
★
★

HOTELS
★FARMBROOK MOTEL
706 Highway 100A, Plymouth, 802-672-3621; www.farmbrookmotel.net
12 rooms. **$**

★★★HAWK INN AND MOUNTAIN RESORT

Route 100 South, Plymouth, 802-672-3811, 800-685-4295; www.hawkresort.com

From rooms at the inn to luxurious mountainside villas on the resort's nearly 1,200 acres, guests will enjoy privacy and a variety of onsite activities including a spa and stables. 200 rooms. Restaurant, bar. Children's activity center. Fitness room. Indoor pool, outdoor pool, whirlpool. Tennis. Airport transportation available. Pets not accepted. Wireless Internet access. Spa. $$$

RUTLAND

This is Vermont's second-largest city. Its oldest newspaper, the *Rutland Herald*, has been published continuously since 1794. The world's deepest marble quarry is in West Rutland and the office of the supervisor of the Green Mountain National Forest is located here.

Information: Chamber of Commerce, 256 N. Main St., 802-773-2747;
www.rutlandvermont.com

WHAT TO SEE AND DO

HUBBARDTON BATTLEFIELD AND MUSEUM

5696 Monument Hill Road, East Hubbardton, 802-759-2412;
www.historicvermont.org

On July 7, 1777, the Green Mountain Boys and colonial troops from Massachusetts and New Hampshire stopped British forces pursuing the American Army from Fort Ticonderoga. This was the only battle of the Revolution fought on Vermont soil and the first in a series of engagements that led to the capitulation of Burgoyne at Saratoga. Visitor Center with exhibits. Battle monument, trails, picnicking. Memorial Day-Columbus Day: Wednesday-Sunday 9:30 a.m.-5 p.m.

NEW ENGLAND MAPLE MUSEUM

Highway 7, Pittsford, 802-483-9414, 800-639-4280; www.maplemuseum.com

One of the largest collections of antique maple sugaring artifacts in the world; two large dioramas featuring more than 100 hand-carved figures; narrated slide show; demonstrations, samples of Vermont foodstuffs; craft and maple-product gift shop. Late May-October, daily 8:30 a.m.-5:30 p.m.; November-December, mid-March-late May, daily 10 a.m.-4 p.m.; closed January-February.

NORMAN ROCKWELL MUSEUM

654 Highway 4 E., Rutland, 802-773-6095; www.normanrockwellvt.com

More than 2,000 pictures and Rockwell memorabilia spanning 60 years of the artist's career. Includes the Four *Freedoms*, Boy Scout series, many magazine covers, including all 323 from the *Saturday Evening Post* and nearly every illustration and advertisement. Daily.

WILSON CASTLE

West Proctor Road, Center Rutland, 802-773-3284; www.wilsoncastle.com

This 32-room 19th-century mansion features 19 open proscenium arches, 84 stained-glass windows, 13 imported tile fireplaces, a towering turret and parapet; European and Asian furnishings; art gallery; sculpture; 15 other buildings. Picnic area. Guided tours. Late May-late October: daily 9 a.m.-6 p.m.; Christmas tours.

★
★
★
★
☆

HOTELS

★BEST WESTERN INN & SUITES RUTLAND/KILLINGTON

One Route 4 East, Rutland, 802-773-3200, 800-720-7234; www.bestwestern.com

56 rooms. Complimentary continental breakfast. Wireless Internet access. Fitness room. Outdoor pool. Tennis. **$$**

★★COMFORT INN

19 Allen St., Rutland, 802-775-2200, 800-432-6788; www.choicehotels.com

104 rooms. Pets accepted, some restrictions; fee. Complimentary continental breakfast. Wireless Internet access. Restaurant, bar. Indoor pool, whirlpool. Business center. **$**

★★HOLIDAY INN RUTLAND/KILLINGTON

2111 Highway 7 South, Rutland, 802-775-1911, 800-462-4810;
www.ichotelsgroup.com/h/d/6c/1/en/hd/rutvt

151 rooms. Pets accepted; fee. Wireless Internet access. Restaurant, bar. Fitness room. Indoor pool, whirlpool. Airport transportation available. Business center. **$$**

★★★MOUNTAIN TOP INN

195 Mountain Top Road, Chittenden, 800-445-2100, 800-445-2100,
802-483-2311; www.mountaintopinn.com

Located in the Green Mountains of Vermont close to Killington ski resort, the guest rooms at this inn are rustic and cozy, with down duvets and rich toiles and chintzes. 60 rooms. Closed April and first three weeks in November. Pets accepted; fee. Restaurant, bar. Outdoor pool. Golf. Tennis. **$$**

SPECIALTY LODGINGS

INN AT RUTLAND

70 N. Main St., Rutland, 802-773-0575, 800-808-0575; www.innatrutland.com

This Victorian mansion was built in 1893 and has been completed restored to its former elegance. 11 rooms. Complimentary full breakfast. **$**

MAPLEWOOD INN

1108 S. Main St., Fair Haven, 802-265-8039, 800-253-7729; www.maplewoodinn.net

Listed on the National Register of Historic Places, this Greek Revival inn has rooms with period décor and is perfect for a romantic getaway. Five rooms. Pets accepted, some restrictions. Complimentary full breakfast. **$**

SHELBURNE

With the Adirondack Mountains on the west and the Green Mountains on the east, Shelburne is a small, friendly town that borders Lake Champlain. The Shelburne Museum has one of the most comprehensive exhibits of early American life.

Information: Town Hall, 5420 Shelburne Road, 802-985-5110; www.shelburnevt.org

WHAT TO SEE AND DO

SHELBURNE FARMS

1611 Harbor Road, Shelburne, 802-985-8686; www.shelburnefarms.org

Built at the turn of the 20th-century, this is the former estate of Dr. Seward Webb and his wife, Lila Vanderbilt. Located on the shores of Lake Champlain, the grounds,

★
★
★
★

landscaped by Frederick Law Olmsted and forested by Gifford Pinchot, once totaled 3,800 acres. Structures include the Webbs' mansion, Shelburne House, a 110-room summer "cottage" built in the late 1800s on a bluff overlooking the lake, a five-story farm barn, and the coach barn, once the home of prize horses. Tours Memorial Day-mid-October, daily 9 a.m.-5:30 p.m.; off-season, daily 10 a.m.-5 p.m. Also, hayrides, walking trail. Visitor center 802-985-8442. Cheese shop daily. Overnight stays available.

SHELBURNE MUSEUM

5555 Shelburne Road, Shelburne, 802-985-3346; www.shelburnemuseum.org
Founded by Electra Webb, daughter of Sugar King H. O. Havemeyer, this collection of Americana art is located on 45 acres with 37 historic buildings containing items such as historic circus posters, toys, weather vanes, trade signs and an extensive collection of wildfowl decoys and dolls. American and European paintings and prints (including works by Monet and Grandma Moses) are on display as well. Also here is the 220-foot side-wheel steamboat *Ticonderoga*, which carried passengers across Lake Champlain in the early part of the century and is now the last vertical beam passenger and freight side-wheel steamer intact in the United States. There is a working carousel and a 5,000-piece hand-carved miniature traveling circus, a fully intact lighthouse, a one-room schoolhouse, an authentic country store, the only two-lane covered bridge with footpath in Vermont, blacksmith shop, printing and weaving demonstrations, farm equipment and more than 200 horse-drawn vehicles on display. May-October, daily 10 a.m.-5 p.m.

VERMONT TEDDY BEAR COMPANY

6655 Shelburne Road, Shelburne, 802-985-1319; www.vermontteddybear.com
The guided tour at this factory shows the process of handcrafting these famous stuffed animals. The onsite gift shop ensures that you won't go home empty handed—the Bear Shop opens at 9 a.m. daily. Call for a tour schedule.

VERMONT WILDFLOWER FARM

4750 Shelburne Ave., Shelburne, 802-425-3641; www.vermontwildflowerfarm.com
Acres of wildflower gardens, flower fields and woodlands, pond and brook. April-October, daily 10 a.m.-5 p.m.

HOTEL

★DAYS INN

3229 Shelburne Road, Shelburne, 802-985-3334, 800-329-7466; www.daysinn.com
58 rooms. Complimentary continental breakfast. Outdoor pool. Free High-speed Internet access. **$**

SPRINGFIELD

The cascades of the Black River once provided power for the machine tool plants that stretch along Springfield's banks. Lord Jeffrey Amherst started the Crown Point Military Road to Lake Champlain from here in 1759. Springfield has been the home of many New England inventors and is also the headquarters of the Amateur Telescope Makers who meet at Stellafane, an observatory site west of Highway 11.
Information: Chamber of Commerce, 14 Clinton St., 802-885-2779;
www.springfieldvt.com

WHAT TO SEE AND DO
EUREKA SCHOOLHOUSE
Charlestown Road, Springfield, 802-885-2779; www.HistoricVermont.org
Oldest schoolhouse in the state, built in 1790. Nearby is a 100-year-old lattice-truss covered bridge. Memorial Day-Columbus Day: Wednesday-Monday 10 a.m.-4 p.m.

REVEREND DAN FOSTER HOUSE & OLD FORGE
2656 Weathersfield Center Road, Weathersfield, 802-263-5230;
www.weathersfieldvt.org
Historic parsonage (1785) contains antique furniture, textiles, utensils, farm tools; old forge has working machinery and bellows. Guided tours. For further information contact the Chamber of Commerce. Mid-June-October: Thursday-Monday 2-5 p.m., or by appointment.

SPRINGFIELD ART AND HISTORICAL SOCIETY
Miller Art Center, 9 Elm Hill, Springfield, 802-885-2415
American art and artifacts. Collections include Richard Lee pewter, Bennington pottery, 19th-century American paintings, costumes, dolls and toys. Springfield historical items. Changing exhibits. Mid-April-October, Tuesday-Friday 10 a.m.-4 p.m., Saturday 10 a.m.-1 p.m.

HOTELS
★HOLIDAY INN EXPRESS
818 Charlestown Road, Springfield, 802-885-4516, 800-465-4329;
www.vermonthi.com
88 rooms. Pets accepted; fee. Complimentary continental breakfast. Wireless Internet access. Fitness room. Indoor pool. Business center. $$

★★★THE INN AT WEATHERSFIELD
1342 Highway 106, Weathersfield, 802-263-9217; www.weathersfieldinn.com
This colonial countryside inn is full of charm and tranquility. Gourmet, candlelit dinners are served in a dining room that includes an eclectic mix of original wood beams and rustic tables. A natural amphitheater on the grounds is used in summer for performances by local musicians, and also for weddings. And shopping, state parks, hiking, skiing and sleigh and carriage rides are just minutes away. 12 rooms. Children over 14 years only. Complimentary full breakfast. Wireless Internet access. Restaurant, bar. Airport transportation available. $$

SPECIALTY LODGINGS
HARTNESS HOUSE
30 Orchard St., Springfield, 802-885-2115, 800-732-4789; www.hartnesshouse.com
This lodging is part historic inn, part aviation museum and working observatory. A former Vermont governor, James Hartness was an inventor who built a series of underground tunnels where he could work without being disturbed. He was also an aviation pioneer fascinated with astronomy and telescope-making. Today three of the workrooms in Hartness' underground tunnels have been turned into a museum. The underground tunnels also lead to the original 1903 Hartness House, containing 14 guest rooms above. Two wings wrap around the pool, one with eight rooms, the

VERMONT

★
★
★
★
★

other with 24. The Hartness House is surrounded by woods and winding nature trails—the innkeepers will be happy to make you a sack lunch to take along on a hike. 43 rooms. Pets accepted, some restrictions; fee. Complimentary full breakfast. Wireless Internet access. Restaurant, bar. Outdoor pool. **$**

STONE HEARTH INN

698 Highway 11 West, Chester, 802-875-2525, 888-617-3656;
www.thestonehearthinn.com
Restored farm house (1810); antiques. 10 rooms. Complimentary full breakfast. Bar. **$$**

ST. JOHNSBURY

This town was named for Ethan Allen's French friend, John Hector St. John de Crevecoeur, author of *Letters from an American Farmer*. The town gained fame when Thaddeus Fairbanks invented the platform scale in 1830. Fairbanks scales, maple syrup and manufacturing are among this town's major industries.

Information: Northeast Kingdom Chamber of Commerce, 51 Depot Square
St. Johnsbury, 802-748-3678, 800-639-6379; www.nekchamber.com

WHAT TO SEE AND DO

FAIRBANKS MUSEUM AND PLANETARIUM

1302 Main St., St. Johnsbury, 802-748-2372; www.fairbanksmuseum.org
Exhibits and programs on natural science, regional history, archaeology, anthropology, astronomy and the arts. More than 4,500 mounted birds and mammals, antique toys, farm, village and craft tools; Northern New England Weather Broadcasting Center; planetarium; Hall of Science; special exhibitions in Gallery Wing. Monday-Saturday, also Sunday afternoons. Planetarium (July-August, daily; rest of year, Saturday-Sunday only).

MAPLE GROVE FARMS OF VERMONT FACTORY
TOURS & MAPLE MUSEUM

1052 Portland St., St. Johnsbury, 802-748-5141, 800-525-2540;
www.maplegrove.com
Learn about Vermont's maple syrup industry on this factory tour, which offers glimpses into the process of making pure syrup and maple candy. Also, taste the various grades of syrup available in the Cabin Shop. May-December, Monday-Friday 8 a.m.-2 p.m.

SPECIAL EVENT

ST. JOHNSBURY TOWN BAND

Courthouse Park, St. Johnsbury, 802-748-8891
One of the oldest continuously performing bands (since 1830) in the country plays weekly outdoor evening concerts. Contact the Chamber of Commerce for further information. Monday, mid-June-late August.

HOTELS

★THE FAIRBANKS INN

401 Western Ave., St. Johnsbury, 802-748-5666; www.stjay.com
46 rooms. Pets accepted; fee. Complimentary continental breakfast. Outdoor pool. **$**

★
★
★
☆
☆

★HOLIDAY MOTEL
222 Hastings St., St. Johnsbury, 802-748-8192
34 rooms. Pets accepted, some restrictions; fee. Outdoor pool. **$**

★★★RABBIT HILL INN
48 Lower Waterford Road, Lower Waterford, 802-748-5168, 800-762-8669;
www.rabbithillinn.com
Rooms are decorated in a crisp, colonial style at this old-fashioned inn that dates back to 1795. Befitting of a bed and breakfast, there is a lavish morning buffet, afternoon tea and five-course dinners. 19 rooms. Children over 13 years only. Complimentary full breakfast. Restaurant, bar. Closed first two weeks of April and first two weeks of November. **$$**

RESTAURANT
★★★RABBIT HILL
48 Lower Waterford Road, Lower Waterford, 802-748-5168, 800-762-8669;
www.rabbithillinn.com
This charming country inn has an acclaimed restaurant where fresh seasonal ingredients are the focus. Roasted rack of lamb comes with thyme-whipped potatoes, while seared duck breast is served with currant and pear-laced bulgur wheat, Brussels sprouts and peach chutney. American menu. Breakfast, dinner. Bar. Reservations recommended. **$$$**

STOWE

Stowe is a year-round resort area, with more than half of its visitors coming during the summer. Mount Mansfield, Vermont's highest peak (4,393 feet), offers skiing, snowboarding, snowshoeing and skating in the winter. Summer visitors can experience outdoor concerts, hiking, biking, golf, tennis and many events and attractions, including a Ben & Jerry's ice cream factory tour.
Information: Stowe Area Association, Main St., 802-253-7321, 877-467-8693;
www.gostowe.com

WHAT TO SEE AND DO
ALPINE SLIDE
Stowe Mountain Resort, Spruce Peak, 5781 Mountain Roadm, Stowe,
802-253-3000, 800-253-4754; www.stowe.com
Chairlift takes riders to a 2,300-foot slide that runs through the woods and open field. Speed controlled by rider. Late June-Labor Day, daily 10 a.m.-5 p.m.; September-mid-October, weekends.

MOUNT MANSFIELD GONDOLA
Stowe Mountain Resort, 5781 Mountain Road, Stowe, 802-253-3000, 800-253-4754
An eight-passenger enclosed gondola ride to the summit of Vermont's highest peak. Spectacular view of the area. Restaurant and gift shop. Mid-June-mid-October, daily 10 a.m.-5 p.m.

MOUNT MANSFIELD STATE FOREST
This 38,000-acre forest can be reached from Underhill Flats, off Highway 15, or from Stowe through Smugglers' Notch, north on Highway 108. The Long Trail leads

to the summit of Mount Mansfield from the north and south. There are three state recreation areas in the forest. **Smugglers' Notch** (802-253-4014 or 802-479-4280) and **Underhill** (802-899-3022 or 802-879-5 674) areas offer hiking, skiing, snowmobiling, picnicking, camping (dump station). **Little River Camping Area** (802-244-7103 or 802-479-4280), northwest of Waterbury, offers swimming, fishing, boating (rentals for campers only), hiking, camping. Memorial Day-Columbus Day. www.vtstateparks.com

STOWE MOUNTAIN RESORT
5781 Mountain Road, Stowe, 802-253-3000, 800-253-4754; www.stowe.com
Resort has quad, triple and six double chairlifts, Mighty-mite handle tow, patrol, school, rentals, snowmaking, cafeterias, restaurants, bar, entertainment, nursery. Forty-seven runs, longest run more than 3½ miles; vertical drop 2,360 feet. Night skiing. Mid-November-mid-April, daily. Summer activities include three outdoor swimming pools, alpine slide (mid-June-early September, daily), mountain biking (rentals), gondola rides, in-line skate park, fitness center, spa, recreation trail, tennis, golf.

SPECIAL EVENT
STOWEFLAKE BALLOON FESTIVAL
Stoweflake Mountain Resort & Spa, 1746 Mountain Road, Stowe,
800-253-2232, 802-253-7355; www.stoweflake.com
Stoweflake Resort Field, Highway 108. More than 20 balloons launched continuously. Second weekend in July.

HOTELS
★★EDSON HILL MANOR
1500 Edson Hill Road, Stowe, 802-253-7371, 800-621-0284;
www.edsonhillmanor.com
25 rooms. Pets accepted, some restrictions. Complimentary full breakfast. Restaurant, bar. Indoor pool. Ski-in/ski-out. $$

★★GOLDEN EAGLE RESORT
511 Mountain Road, Stowe, 802-253-4811, 800-626-1010;
www.goldeneagleresort.com
94 rooms. Restaurant. Children's activity center. Fitness room. Indoor pool, two outdoor pools, whirlpool. Tennis. $$

★★★GREEN MOUNTAIN INN
18 S. Main St., Stowe, 802-253-7301, 800-253-7302; www.greenmountaininn.com
This historic (yet modern) colonial inn is surrounded by charming stores, galleries and restaurants. 104 rooms. Wireless Internet access. Restaurant, bar. Fitness room. Outdoor pool. $$

★★GREY FOX INN AND RESORT
990 Mountain Road, Stowe, 802-253-8921, 800-544-8454;
www.stowegreyfoxinn.com
38 rooms. Complimentary full breakfast. Restaurant, bar. Children's activity center. Fitness room. Indoor pool, outdoor pool, whirlpool. $

★★★STOWEFLAKE MOUNTAIN RESORT & SPA

1746 Mountain Road, Stowe, 802-253-7355, 800-253-2232; www.stoweflake.com

This resort, the oldest in Stowe, recently underwent a major renovation and also added a 50,000-square-foot spa. Rooms are decorated in country quilts and feature pillow-top beds and down duvets. The restaurant serves innovative takes on American cuisine. 117 rooms. High-speed Internet access. Restaurant, bar. Fitness room, fitness classes available. Spa. Indoor pool, outdoor pool, whirlpool. Golf, 9 holes. **$$$**

★★★TOPNOTCH RESORT AND SPA

4000 Mountain Road, Stowe, 888-460-5567,800-451-8686;
www.topnotchresort.com

This classic New England ski resort underwent a complete renovation in Spring 2008. Guests will enjoy the resort's sprawling new spa and onsite restaurant Norma's. 126 rooms. High-speed Internet access. Restaurant, bar. Fitness center. Spa. Pool, whirlpool. Business center. Pets accepted. **$$$**

★★TRAPP FAMILY LODGE

700 Trapp Hill Road, Stowe, 802-253-8511, 800-826-7000; www.trappfamily.com

Channel your inner Julie Andrews at this Tyrolean resort run by the Von Trapp family, the inspiration for the movie *The Sound of Music*. The rustic lodge overlooks a beautiful mountain range and is accented with hand-carved balustrades, pitched gables and a cedar shake roof. Activities include croquet, hiking, horse-drawn sleigh rides, pastry classes and cross-country skiing. 96 rooms. Wireless Internet access. Restaurant, bar. Fitness room. Indoor pool, outdoor pool. Tennis. **$$**

★★★YE OLDE ENGLAND INNE

433 Mountain Road, Stowe, 802-253-7558, 800-477-3771; www.englandinn.com

This elegant 1893 English inn offers rooms decorated in English chintzes and antiques. Mr. Pickwick's Polo Pub is a great spot to grab a meal. 30 rooms. Complimentary full breakfast. Wireless Internet access. Restaurant, bar. Outdoor pool, whirlpool. **$$**

SPECIALTY LODGINGS

FITCH HILL INN

258 Fitch Hill Road, Hyde Park, 802-888-3834, 800-639-2903; www.fitchhillinn.com

This tranquil setting is 15 minutes north of Stowe and is located on three acres of woods and gardens. Guest rooms are decorated in a country style featuring quilts and lace curtains. Six rooms. Complimentary full breakfast. Whirlpool. **$$**

STONE HILL INN

89 Houston Farm Road, Stowe, 802-253-6282; www.stonehillinn.com

This inn is close to all the antique shops, restaurants and activities the town has to offer. Trails, snowshoes, tobogganing and sledding are offered onsite. Nine rooms. Closed April; also mid-November-mid-December. Children not allowed. Complimentary full breakfast. Wireless Internet access. Whirlpool. **$$$**

STRATTON

Stratton Mountain is the main attraction in this central Vermont town. The ski resort has a reputation as a superb mountain for families.

Information: www.stratton.com

VERMONT

WHAT TO SEE AND DO
STRATTON MOUNTAIN
Stratton Mountain Road, Londonderry, 802-297-4211; www.stratton.com

A high-speed gondola, two high-speed six-passenger chairlifts, three quads, one triple and two double chairlifts, two surface lifts, patrol, school, rentals, snowmaking, cafeterias, restaurants, bars, nursery, sports center. Ninety runs, longest run three miles; vertical drop 2,003 feet. Mid-November-mid-April, daily. More than 17 miles of cross-country trails (December-March, daily), rentals, snowboarding. Summer activities include gondola ride, horseback riding, tennis, golf (school), festivals, concert series.

SPECIAL EVENT
VERMONT ARTS & FINE CRAFTS FESTIVAL
Stratton Mountain Ski Resort, Stratton Mountain Road, Stratton Mountain

Paintings, photography, sculpture and crafts; special performing arts events, craft demonstrations. Labor Day Weekend.

HOTEL
★★THE INN AT STRATTON MOUNTAIN
61 Middle Ridge Road, Stratton, 802-297-2500, 800-787-2886;
www.stratton.com

119 rooms. Children's activity center. Fitness room. Indoor pool, three outdoor pools, whirlpool. Golf. Tennis. Ski-in/ski-out. $

SWANTON
The location of this town, just two miles east of Lake Champlain, makes it a popular resort spot.
Information: Chamber of Commerce, 802-868-7200;
www.swantonchamber.com

WHAT TO SEE AND DO
MISSISQUOI NATIONAL WILDLIFE REFUGE
29 Tabor Road, Swanton, 802-868-4781; www.fws.gov

More than 6,400 acres, including much of the Missisquoi River delta on Lake Champlain. Primarily a waterfowl refuge (best in April, September and October), but other wildlife and birds may be seen. Fishing, hunting, hiking and canoe trails. Daily.

HOTEL
★★TYLER PLACE FAMILY RESORT
1 Old Dock Road, Highgate Springs, 802-868-4000; www.tylerplace.com

39 rooms. Restaurant, bar. Children's activity center. Fitness room. Indoor pool, outdoor pool, children's pool. Tennis. Closed Labor Day-late May. $

VERGENNES
The oldest city in Vermont and the third oldest in New England, Vergennes is one of the smallest incorporated cities in the nation (one square mile).
Information: Vergennes Chamber of Commerce, 802-877-0080

WHAT TO SEE AND DO
BUTTON BAY STATE PARK
5 Button Bay State Park Road, Vergennes, 802-475-2377;
www.vtstateparks.com/htm/buttonbay.cfm

This 236-acre park on a bluff overlooking Lake Champlain was named for the button-like formations in the clay banks. Spectacular views of Adirondack Mountains. Swimming pool, fishing, boating (rentals), nature and hiking trails, picnicking, tent and trailer sites (dump station). Naturalist museum. Memorial Day-Columbus Day.

JOHN STRONG MANSION
6656 Highway 17 West, West Addison, 802-759-2309;
www.vmga.org/addison/jstrong.html

(1795) Federalist house, restored and furnished in the period. Memorial Day-Labor Day, Saturday-Sunday 10 a.m.-5 p.m.

ROKEBY MUSEUM
4334 Highway 7, Ferrisburgh, 802-877-3406; www.rokeby.org

(Circa 1785) The ancestral home of abolitionist Rowland T. Robinson was a station for the Underground Railroad. Artifacts and archives of four generations of the Robinson family. Set on 85 acres, the farmstead includes an ice house, a creamery and a stone smokehouse. Special events are offered year-round. Tours. Mid-May-mid-October, house tours: Thursday-Sunday 11 a.m., 12:30 p.m., 2 p.m.; grounds: Tuesday-Sunday 10 a.m.-4 p.m.

HOTEL
★★★BASIN HARBOR CLUB
4800 Basin Harbor Road, Vergennes, 802-475-2311;
www.basinharbor.com

Located on Lake Champlain, this hotel offers accommodations in the lodge or in the cottages spread out over the property. Fresh local ingredients are used to prepare the breakfast and dinner served in the main dining room. 117 rooms. Pets accepted, some restrictions; fee. Restaurant, bar. Children's activity center. Fitness room. Beach. Outdoor pool. Golf. Tennis. Airport transportation available. Closed November-mid-May. $$

SPECIALTY LODGING
STRONG HOUSE INN
94 W. Main St., Vergennes, 802-877-3337; www.stronghouseinn.com

This historic Federal-style inn is furnished in period furniture and antiques and is set on six acres of walking trails, gardens and ponds. Hiking, golfing, cycling and fishing are nearby. 14 rooms. Children over 8 years only. Complimentary full breakfast. $$

WAITSFIELD

This region, known as "the Valley," is a popular area in summer as well as in the winter ski season. Rolling hills and bucolic farms dot the countryside.

Information: Sugarbush Chamber of Commerce, General Wait House, Highway 100, 802-496-3409, 800-828-4748; www.sugarbushchamber.org

★
★
★
★
★

WHAT TO SEE AND DO
MAD RIVER GLEN SKI AREA
Highway 17, Waitsfield, 802-496-3551; www.madriverglen.com

This ski resort has the country's oldest single chairlift, which was fully restored in 2006. Mad River Glen does not make snow, so conditions here depend on the weather. Area has three double and two single chairlifts, patrol, school, rentals, cafeterias, restaurant, bar, nursery. Forty-four runs, longest run three miles; vertical drop 2,000 feet. December-April, daily.

HOTEL
★★TUCKER HILL INN
65 Marble Hill Road, Waitsfield, 802-496-3983, 800-543-7841; www.tuckerhill.com

18 rooms. Restaurant, bar. Outdoor pool. Tennis. **$$**

SPECIALTY LODGING
1824 HOUSE INN BED AND BREAKFAST
2150 Main St., Waitsfield, 802-496-7555, 800-426-3986; www.1824house.com

This restored 1824 farmhouse features feather beds, Oriental rugs and down quilts. Eight rooms. Complimentary full breakfast. Whirlpool. **$**

THE INN AT THE ROUND BARN
1661 E. Warren Road, Waitsfield, 802-496-2276; www.theroundbarn.com

Located on more than 200 acres of mountains, ponds and meadows, this inn has a round barn that is fully restored and is the setting for weddings, meetings and other functions. 12 rooms. Complimentary full breakfast. Indoor pool. **$$**

LAREAU FARM COUNTRY INN
48 Lareau Road, Waitsfield, 802-496-4949, 800-833-0766; www.lareaufarminn.com

Farmhouse and barn built by the area's first physician. 13 rooms. Complimentary full breakfast. **$**

THE WAITSFIELD INN
5267 Main St., Waitsfield, 802-496-3979, 800-758-3801; www.waitsfieldinn.com

14 rooms. Closed April, November. **$**

RESTAURANT
★★THE STEAK PLACE AT TUCKER HILL
65 Marble Hill Road, Waitsfield, 802-496-3983, 800-543-7841; www.tuckerhill.com

American menu. Breakfast, dinner. Bar. Children's menu. Outdoor seating. Closed Sunday-Monday. **$$**

WARREN

This northern Vermont town is close to two ski areas, Sugarbush and Mad River Glen. The town has several small bed and breakfasts and quaint restaurants that feed and house skiers at the end of a day on the mountain.

Information: Sugarbush Chamber of Commerce, Waitsfield, 802-496-3409, 800-828-4748; www.sugarbushchamber.org

WHAT TO SEE AND DO

SUGARBUSH RESORT

1840 Sugarbush Access Road, Warren, 802-583-6300,
800-583-7669; www.sugarbush.com

Area has seven quad, three triple and six double chairlifts, four surface lifts, patrol, school, rentals, concession area, cafeteria, restaurant, bar, nursery. More than 100 runs, longest run more than two miles, vertical drop 2,650 feet. Early November-late April, daily.

HOTELS

★★★THE PITCHER INN

275 Main St., Warren, 802-496-6350, 800-735-2478; www.pitcherinn.com

Rustic, yet rich and elegant guest accommodations in the main house capture Vermont's colonial history, while two suites in the adjacent barn are perfect for families. The inn's restaurant serves breakfast and dinner and boasts a 6,500-bottle wine cellar. This inn also offers a locker room for ski storage and a boot and glove warmer. 11 rooms. Complimentary full breakfast. Wireless Internet access. Restaurant, bar. **$$$$**

★★★SUGARBUSH INN

1840 Sugarbush Access Road, Warren, 802-583-6114,
800-537-8427; www.sugarbush.com

Surrounded by slopes, hills and trails, this activity-oriented inn is between the towns of Waitsfield and Warren. Snowshoeing, snow tubing, ice skating and horse-drawn sleigh rides are available on the property. 143 rooms. Complimentary full breakfast. Three restaurants, bar. Children's activity center. Fitness room. Indoor pool, outdoor pool, whirlpool. Golf, 18 holes. Tennis. Ski-in/ski-out. **$$**

SPECIALTY LODGING

SUGARTREE INN

2440 Sugarbush Access Road, Warren, 802-583-3211,
800-666-8907; www.sugartree.com

Nine rooms. Pets accepted, some restrictions. Children over 12 years only. Complimentary full breakfast. Restaurant. Closed three weeks in April. **$**

RESTAURANT

★★★THE COMMON MAN

3209 German Flats Road, Warren, 802-583-2800;
www.commonmanrestaurant.com

Located in Vermont's Mad River Valley, this 1880s restored barn houses a casual dining spot. American menu. Dinner. Bar. Children's menu. Casual attire. Reservations recommended. Closed Sunday-Monday; two-four weeks in spring and November. **$$**

WATERBURY

Close to many outstanding ski resorts, including Stowe, Mad River Valley and Bolton Valley, this area is also popular in the summer for hiking, backpacking and bicycling.
Information: Central Vermont Chamber of Commerce, Barre, 802-229-5711

★
★
★
★
★

WHAT TO SEE AND DO

BEN & JERRY'S ICE CREAM FACTORY TOUR

Route 100, Waterbury, 866-258-6877;
www.benjerry.com

This half-hour guided tour, offered every 30 minutes (and even more frequently in summer, spring and fall), takes visitors through the ice cream factory that cranks out such beloved flavors as Cherry Garcia and Chunky Monkey. The tour includes a seven-minute "moovie," views of the production line (except on weekends) and free samples in the FlavoRoom. There's also a gift shop, where you can pick up one of those famous tie-dyed cow T-shirts and a few pints to take home. Daily.

CAMEL'S HUMP MOUNTAIN

Long Trail, Waterbury, 802-244-7037;
www.mountainzone.com/mountains

State's third-highest mountain, the trail is quite challenging. Weather permitting, Canada can be seen from the top.

COLD HOLLOW CIDER MILL

3600 Waterbury-Stowe Road, Waterbury Center, 802-244-8771,
800-327-7537; www.coldhollow.com

One of the largest cider mills in New England features a 43-inch rack-and-cloth press capable of producing 500 gallons of cider an hour. Also, jelly-making operations (fall). Samples are served.

LONG TRAIL

802-244-7037; www.greenmountainclub.org

A 22-mile segment of backpacking trail connects Camel's Hump with Mount Mansfield, the state's highest peak. Primitive camping is allowed on both mountains. Recommended for the experienced hiker.

HOTEL

★★BEST WESTERN WATERBURY-STOWE

45 Blush Hill Road, Waterbury, 802-244-7822, 800-621-7822;
www.bestwesternwaterburystowe.com

79 rooms. Restaurant, bar. Fitness room. Indoor pool. Tennis. **$**

SPECIALTY LODGINGS

BIRDS NEST INN

5088 Waterbury-Stowe Road, Waterbury Center, 802-244-7490,
800-366-5592; www.birdsnestinn.com

Surrounded by black locust trees, this restored 1832 farmhouse has rooms with private baths and down comforters. A hearty three-course breakfast made with local produce is served daily. In the evening, complimentary wines and hot and cold hors d'oeuvres are offered. The inn is close to all major ski areas. Five rooms. Children over 15 years only. Complimentary full breakfast. **$**

THATCHER BROOK INN
1017 Waterbury Stowe Road, Waterbury, 802-244-5911,
800-292-5911; www.thatcherbrook.com
Built in 1899; twin gazebos with front porch. 22 rooms. Complimentary full breakfast. Restaurant. **$**

WEST DOVER

A south central Vermont village, West Dover is located in the Green Mountains and near several ski resorts.

Information: Mount Snow Valley Region Chamber of Commerce, West Main Street, Wilmington, 802-464-8092, 877-887-6884; www.visitvermont.com

WHAT TO SEE AND DO
MOUNT SNOW SKI AREA
12 Pisgah Road, West Dover, 802-464-2151, 800-498-0479; www.mountsnow.com
Area has two quad, six triple and nine double chairlifts, patrol, school, rentals, snowmaking, cafeterias, restaurant, bars, entertainment and nursery. More than 100 trails spread over five interconnected mountain areas. Longest run is 2 1/2 miles, with a vertical drop of 1,700 feet. Half-day rates. November-early May: daily.

SPECIAL EVENTS
OKTOBERFEST & CRAFT SHOW
Mount Snow Resort, 12 Pisgah Road, West Dover, 802-464-2151,
800-498-0479; www.mountsnow.com
New England artisans exhibit pottery, jewelry, glass, graphics, weaving and other crafts; German-style entertainment. Chairlift rides and foliage. Columbus Day weekend.

SHIMANO NORBA NATIONAL MOUNTAIN BIKE SERIES FINALS
Mount Snow Ski Area, 12 Pisgah Road, West Dover, 802-464-4191, 800-451-4211;
www.mountsnow.com/summer/norba
More than 1,500 cyclists from throughout the world compete in downhill, dual slalom and circuit racing events. Late August.

HOTELS
★★★FOUR SEASONS INN
145 Route 100, West Dover, 802-464-8303; www.thefourseasonsinn.com
18 rooms. Children not allowed. Complimentary full breakfast. Wireless Internet access. Restaurant, bar. Spa. Outdoor pool. **$$**

★★★THE INN AT SAWMILL FARM
Highway 100 and 7 Crosstown Road, West Dover, 802-464-8131,
800-493-1133; www.theinnatsawmillfarm.com
This inn is housed in a converted barn, and the location is perfect for skiers looking to hit the slopes of nearby Mount Snow. Rustic, yet polished, weathered floors and hand-hewn posts and beams hint at the original construction, while the restaurant offers haute cuisine that rivals many of its city competitors. 21 rooms. Restaurant, bar. Fitness room. Outdoor pool. Tennis. Closed April-May. **$$$$**

★★WEST DOVER INN

108 Highway 100, West Dover, 802-464-5207; www.westdoverinn.com

Built in 1846, this inn was once a stagecoach stop and a general store. 12 rooms. Children over 12 years only. Complimentary full breakfast. Restaurant, bar. **$$**

RESTAURANT
★★★THE INN AT SAWMILL FARM

Highway 100 and Crosstown Road, West Dover, 802-464-8131, 800-493-1133; www.theinnatsawmillfarm.com

Exposed beams and chandeliers create a perfect place to relax and enjoy delicious home-style cooking. The seasonal American menu features locally farmed game such as quail, pheasant, rabbit and venison. The impressive wine list offers a selection of 1,285 wines in the 30,000-bottle cellar. American menu. Breakfast, dinner. Bar. Business casual attire. Reservations recommended. Closed April-May. **$$$**

WILMINGTON

This town is located in central Vermont's Green Mountains and is close to several area ski resorts.

Information: Mount Snow Valley Region Chamber of Commerce, West Main Street, 802-464-8092, 877-887-6884; www.visitvermont.com

WHAT TO SEE AND DO
MOLLY STARK STATE PARK

705 Highway 9 East, Wilmington, 802-464-5460; www.vtstateparks.com/htm/mollystark.cfm

A 158-acre park named for the wife of General John Stark, hero of the Battle of Bennington (1777); on west slope of Mount Olga (2,438 feet). Fishing in nearby lake, hiking trails, tent and trailer sites (dump station). Fire tower with excellent views. Standard fees. Memorial Day-Columbus Day.

HOTELS
★★HORIZON INN

861 Highway 9 East, Wilmington, 802-464-2131, 800-336-5513; www.horizoninn.com

28 rooms. Complimentary continental breakfast. Wireless Internet access. Restaurant, bar. Fitness room. Indoor pool, whirlpool. **$**

★★★WHITE HOUSE OF WILMINGTON

178 Highway 9 East, Wilmington, 802-464-2135, 800-541-2135; www.whitehouseinn.com

Built in 1915 as a summer home for a wealthy lumber baron, this historic inn was restored in 1978, but many of its original details were left intact (including a secret staircase, a favorite of guests). The original house has nine guest rooms, some with fireplaces and some with both fireplaces and whirlpool tubs. An adjoining guest house has eight additional rooms designed to accommodate families. 25 rooms. Children over 8 years only. Complimentary full breakfast. Restaurant, bar. Fitness room. Indoor pool, outdoor pool, steamroom, sauna. Ski-in/ski-out. Closed April. **$$**

SPECIALTY LODGING
TRAIL'S END - A COUNTRY INN
5 Trail's End Lane, Wilmington, 802-464-2727, 800-859-2585;
www.trailsendvt.com
Located near Mount Snow ski resort, this country inn has rooms with four-poster beds. Five rooms. Complimentary full breakfast. Outdoor pool. Tennis. **$**

RESTAURANT
★★WHITE HOUSE
178 Highway 9 East, Wilmington, 802-464-2135, 800-541-2135;
www.whitehouseinn.com
Located in the White House of Wilmington, the restaurant is easily accessible from Routes 9 and 100.Dine in one of the three dining rooms of this 1915 mansion. The menu changes seasonally and includes local Vermont cheeses and entrées such as roasted Vermont duckling and Wiener schnitzel. A wine list with a 100-plus selection is also offered. American menu. Dinner, bar. Casual attire. Reservations recommended. Closed Monday-Tuesday; April; first two weeks in May. **$$$**

WINDSOR
Situated on the Connecticut River in the shadow of Mount Ascutney, Windsor was once the political center of the Connecticut Valley towns. The name "Vermont" was adopted, and its constitution was drawn up here. Many notable inventors (and inventions) were developed here in the 19th-century, including the hydraulic pump, sewing machine, coffee percolator and various refinements in firearms.
Information: White River Area Chamber of Commerce,
White River Junction, 802-295-6200

WHAT TO SEE AND DO
CONSTITUTION HOUSE
16 N. Main St., Windsor, 802-672-3773;
www.historicvermont.org
An 18th-century tavern where the constitution of the Republic of Vermont was signed on July 8, 1777. Museum. Late May-mid-October: Wednesday-Sunday 11 a.m.-5 p.m.

MOUNT ASCUTNEY STATE PARK
1826 Back Mountain Road Windsor, Vermon, 802-674-2060;
www.vtstateparks.com
This 1,984-acre park has a paved road to the summit of Mount Ascutney (3,144 feet). Hiking trails, picnicking, tent and trailer sites (dump station). Memorial Day-Columbus Day.

VERMONT STATE CRAFT CENTER AT WINDSOR HOUSE
54 Main St., Windsor, 802-674-6729;
www.vmga.org/windsor/vsscwindsor.html
Restored building features works of more than 250 Vermont craftspeople. January-May: Thursday-Saturday 10 a.m.-6 p.m., Sunday 11 a.m.-5 p.m.; June-December: Monday-Saturday 10 a.m.-6 p.m., Sunday 11 a.m.-5 p.m.

343

VERMONT

★
★
★
★
★

HOTEL

★★★JUNIPER HILL INN

153 Pembroke Road, Windsor, 802-674-5273, 800-359-2541;
www.juniperhillinn.com

This 1902 Classical Revival mansion is perched atop 14 acres of hillside. A 30- by 40-foot Great Hall features a floor-to-ceiling fireplace, and the library in the west wing of the inn offers a great place to read or play board games. Past visitors include Teddy Roosevelt. 16 rooms. Children over 12 years only. Complimentary full breakfast. Restaurant. Outdoor pool. Closed two weeks in November; three weeks in late March-early April. $$

WOODSTOCK

The historic charm of Woodstock has been preserved, at least in part, by determination. Properties held for generations by descendants of original owners provided built-in zoning long before historic district status was achieved. When the iron bridge that crosses the Ottauquechee River at Union Street was condemned in 1968, it was replaced by a covered wooden bridge. The nearby town of Quechee is equally charming and is home to the famed Simon Pearce glass and pottery studio and restaurant.
Information: Chamber of Commerce, 18 Central St., 802-457-3555;
www.woodstockvt.com

WHAT TO SEE AND DO

KEDRON VALLEY STABLES

Highway 106 South, South Woodstock, 802-457-1480,
800-225-6301; www.kedron.com

Hayrides, sleigh rides, picnic trail rides, indoor ring rides and riding lessons by appointment.

MARSH-BILLINGS-ROCKEFELLER NATIONAL HISTORIC PARK

54 Elm St., Woodstock, 802-457-3368; www.nps.gov/mabi

Includes Marsh-Billings-Rockefeller mansion, which contains an extensive collection of American landscape paintings. Mansion is surrounded by 550-acre Mount Tom forest. Interpretive tours are available. Reservations recommended. Park also offers hiking, nature study and cross-country skiing. Memorial Day-October, daily 10 a.m.-5 p.m.

SUICIDE SIX SKI AREA

South Pomfret Road, Woodstock, 802-457-1100; www.skivermont.com

Area has two double chairlifts, J-Bar, patrol, PSIA school, rentals, snowmaking, cafeteria, wine and beer bar, lodge. Twenty-two runs, longest run is one mile, with a vertical drop of 650 feet. Site of the first ski tow in the United States (1934). Early December-late March, daily.

VERMONT INSTITUTE OF NATURAL SCIENCE

Route 4, Quechee, 802-359-5000; www.vinsweb.org

Property includes a 47-acre mixed habitat site with trails. VINS Nature Center includes the Raptor Museum, which has 26 species of hawks, owls and eagles May-October, daily 9 a.m.-5:30 p.m.; November-April, daily 10 a.m.-4 p.m.

VERMONT

★
★
★
★

WOODSTOCK COUNTRY CLUB

14 The Green, Woodstock, 802-457-1100, 800-448-7900; www.woodstockinn.com

An 18-hole championship golf course, 10 tennis courts, paddle tennis, cross-country skiing center with more than 35 miles of trails, rentals, instruction, tours. Restaurant, lounge. Fee for activities. Daily; closed April and November.

WOODSTOCK HISTORICAL SOCIETY

26 Elm St., Woodstock; www.woodstockhistoricalsociety.org

Dana House (1807) has 11 rooms spanning 1750-1900, including a children's room; also silver, glass, paintings, costumes, furniture and research library; Woodstock-related artifacts, photographs. Farm and textile equipment. Gift shop. Late May-late October: Monday-Saturday 10 a.m.-4 p.m., Sunday noon-4 p.m.

HOTELS

★★★KEDRON VALLEY INN

10671 S. Road, South Woodstock, 802-457-1473, 800-836-1193;
www.kedronvalleyinn.com

Located five miles outside Woodstock, this small historic inn is a great home base for guests focused on antique shopping or checking out the local shops. 26 rooms. Pets accepted, some restrictions. Restaurant, bar. Closed April. **$$**

★POND RIDGE MOTEL

506 Highway 4 West, Woodstock, 802-457-1667; www.pondridgemotel.com

20 rooms. **$**

★★★QUECHEE INN AT MARSHLAND FARM

1119 Quechee Main St., Quechee, 802-295-3133, 800-235-3133;
www.quecheeinn.com

This inn was built in 1793 and has simply decorated rooms, complete with many modern conveniences. 24 rooms. Complimentary full breakfast. Restaurant, bar. **$$**

★THE SHIRE RIVERVIEW

46 Pleasant St., Woodstock, 802-457-2211; www.shiremotel.com

42 rooms. Wireless Internet access. **$**

★★★★★TWIN FARMS

452 Royalton Turnpike, Barnard, 802-234-9999, 800-894-6327; www.twinfarms.com

This secluded, exclusive hideaway in central Vermont offers one of the most uniquely sybaritic lodging experiences to be had in America. With 10 private cottages and 10 sumptuous guest rooms, Twin Farms is designed to cater to the individual experience. Each room is decorated to reflect a different theme by renowned interior designer Jed Johnson—the Moroccan-influenced Meadow has Persian rugs and a mosaic-tiled fireplace, while the Scandinavian Barn has bleached pine floors, walls and rafters and crisp white and blue fabrics and upholstery. Meals are made to order and can be taken in the main dining room or the privacy of your cottage. The cost is all-inclusive. 16 rooms. Children not allowed. Complimentary full breakfast. Wireless Internet access. Restaurant (guests only), two bars. Fitness room. Spa. Tennis. Ski-in/ski-out. Airport transportation available. **$$$$**

★★★WOODSTOCK INN & RESORT

14 The Green, Woodstock, 802-457-1100, 800-448-7900; www.woodstockinn.com

The Woodstock Inn & Restaurant, the centerpiece of Woodstock, has been around since the 18th-century. The rooms and suites capture traditional Vermont style, with handmade quilts, built-in alcoves and original prints. Downhill and cross-country skiing are two of the resort's most popular winter activities, while the Woodstock Country Club's prestigious course attracts golfers. Other popular activities include biking, canoeing, fishing, horseback riding and nature walks, and the town's shops are within walking distance. Three restaurants serve everything from gourmet cuisine to casual fare and traditional tavern-style food. 142 rooms. Wireless Internet access. Restaurant, bar. Fitness room, fitness classes available. Spa. Indoor pool, outdoor pool, whirlpool. Golf, 18 holes. Tennis. Ski-in/ski-out. Business center. $$$

SPECIALTY LODGINGS

APPLEBUTTER INN

Happy Valley Road, Woodstock, 802-457-4158; www.applebutterinn.com

Built in 1846, this inn used to be a stagecoach stop and a general store. Six rooms. Complimentary full breakfast. $

CANTERBURY HOUSE BED AND BREAKFAST

43 Pleasant St., Woodstock, 802-457-3077, 800-390-3077; www.thecanterburyhouse.com

Victorian home built in 1880; antiques. Seven rooms. Children not allowed. Complimentary full breakfast. Restaurant. $

CHARLESTON HOUSE

21 Pleasant St., Woodstock, 802-457-3843; www.charlestonhouse.com

Greek Revival house built in 1835. Nine rooms. Complimentary full breakfast. $$

THE LINCOLN INN AT THE COVERED BRIDGE

530 Woodstock Road, Woodstock, 802-457-3312; www.lincolninn.com

This renovated farmhouse's property (circa 1869) is bordered by the Ottauquechee River and a covered bridge. Six rooms. Complimentary full breakfast. Restaurant. $

MAPLE LEAF INN

Highway 12, Barnard, 802-234-5342, 800-516-2753; www.mapleleafinn.com

This property is located on 16 acres of maple and birch trees near the quaint town of Woodstock, where antique stores, unique shops and outdoor recreations abound. Seven rooms. $$

PARKER HOUSE INN

1792 Quechee Main St., Quechee, 802-295-6077; www.theparkerhouseinn.com

Victorian house (1857); former senator's residence. Seven rooms. Pets accepted, some restrictions; fee. Complimentary full breakfast. Restaurant. $

WOODSTOCKER BED AND BREAKFAST

61 River St., Woodstock, 802-457-3896, 866-662-1439; www.woodstockervt.com

Built in 1830. Nine rooms. Complimentary full breakfast. Whirlpool. $

★
★
★
★
★

RESTAURANTS

★★★BARNARD INN

5518 Highway 12, Barnard, 802-234-9961; www.barnardinnrestaurant.com

Built in 1796, this inn is quaint and simple in a charming New England way. The restaurant serves dishes prepared with French technique, such as steamed mussels with saffron and garlic. French menu. Dinner. Bar. Children's menu. Closed Sunday-Monday. **$$**

★★★KEDRON VALLEY INN

Highway 106, South Woodstock, 802-457-1473, 800-836-1193;
www.kedronvalleyinn.com

This inn, located just outside Woodstock, is a local favorite for its cheerful rooms and reasonable prices. The menu at the inn's restaurant features Vermont-raised produce and meat. American menu. Breakfast, dinner. Bar. Children's menu. Closed Tuesday-Wednesday, November-July, week of December 25. **$$**

★★★PRINCE AND THE PAUPER

24 Elm St., Woodstock, 802-457-1818; www.princeandpauper.com

Chef and owner Chris Balce offers a menu that changes seasonally. The house specialty is boneless rack of lamb in puff pastry with spinach and mushroom duxelles. American menu. Dinner. Bar. Business casual attire. Reservations recommended. **$$$**

★★★QUECHEE INN AT MARSHLAND FARM

1119 Quechee Main St., Quechee, 802-295-3133, 800-235-3133;
www.quecheeinn.com

The restaurant is in the main house of this inn, which dates back to 1793 and overlooks the Ottauquechee River. The cuisine is served in a casual but sophisticated setting, with a wine list to match. American menu. Breakfast, dinner. Bar. Children's menu. Business casual attire. Reservations recommended. Outdoor seating. **$$**

★★★SIMON PEARCE

1761 Main St., Quechee, 802-295-1470; www.simonpearce.com

Part of the glass-blowing and pottery complex that has become an emblem of Vermont, this spacious, contemporary restaurant has beautiful, forested views of the Ottauquechee River and a covered bridge. The cuisine is innovative American with Asian accents, and the breads and soups are homemade. American menu. Lunch, dinner. Bar. Casual attire. Reservations recommended. Outdoor seating. **$$$**

★★★WOODSTOCK INN

14 The Green, Woodstock, 802-457-1100, 800-448-7900; www.woodstockinn.com

Nightly piano entertainment perfectly suits the romantic atmosphere at this quaint restaurant in the Woodstock Inn. The kitchen makes full use of local and seasonal produce with offerings like organic field greens with Vermont chevre, raspberries and maple mustard vinaigrette and char-grilled black Angus filet mignon with a Vermont gorgonzola crust and a cider reduction. American menu. Dinner, Sunday brunch. Bar. Children's menu. Business casual attire. Reservations recommended. Valet parking. **$$$**

VERMONT

★
★
★
★
★

INDEX

Symbols

124 Cottage Street (Bar Harbor, ME), *55*

1640 Hart House (Ipswich, MA), *184*

The 1661 Inn & Guest House (Block Island, RI), *287*

1785 Inn (North Conway, NH), *276*

1785 Inn (North Conway, NH), *277*

1800 House (Nantucket, MA), *204*

1811 House (Manchester, VT), *321*

1824 House Inn Bed and Breakfast (Waitsfield, VT), *338*

1830 Admiral's Quarters Inn (Boothbay Harbor, ME), *62*

1896 House (Williamstown, MA), *245*

21 Federal (Nantucket, MA), *210*

400 East (Harwich, MA), *178*

88 Grandview (Boothbay Harbor, ME), *62*

98 Provence (Ogunquit, ME), *93*

A

A Cambridge House Bed and Breakfast Inn (Cambridge, MA), *153*

Abbe Museum (Bar Harbor, ME), *52*

Abbicci (Yarmouth Port, MA), *249*

Abbot Hall (Marblehead, MA), *194*

Abe & Louie's (Boston, MA), *137*

Abigail Adams House (Weymouth, MA), *147*

Academy of Performing Arts (Orleans, MA), *220*

Acadia Inn (Bar Harbor, ME), *53*

Accursed Tombstone (near Verona Island Bridge, Bucksport, ME), *65*

Acworth Inn (Cummaquid, MA), *181*

Adair Country Inn (Bethlehem, NH), *268*

Addison Choate Inn (Rockport, MA), *231*

Adesso (Providence, RI), *300*

Admiral Peary House (Fryeburg, ME), *72*

Adrian's (North Truro, MA), *241*

Al Forno (Providence, RI), *300*

Alchemy (Edgartown, MA), *201*

Aldrich Contemporary Art Museum (Ridgefield, CT), *40*

All Season Motor Inn (South Yarmouth, MA), *248*

Allen House Victorian Inn (Amherst, MA), *119*

Allis-Bushnell House and Museum (Madison, CT), *26*

Alpine Slide (Stowe, VT), *333*

Altar Rock (Nantucket MA), *204*

America's Stonehenge (North Salem, NH), *281*

American Antiquarian Society (Worcester, MA), *246*

American Independence Museum (Exeter, NH), *255*

American Museum of Fly Fishing (Manchester, VT), *319*

American Seasons (Nantucket, MA), *210*

American Textile History Museum (Lowell, MA), *192*

Amherst College (Amherst, MA), *118*

Amistad Memorial (New Haven, CT), *31*

Anchor Watch Bed AND Breakfast (Boothbay Harbor, ME), *62*

Anchorage By The Sea (Ogunquit, ME), *92*

Anchorage Motor Inn (York Beach, ME), *115*

Anchor-In (Hyannis, MA), *180*

Andover Inn (Andover, MA), *119*

Andover Wyndham Hotel (Andover, MA), *119*

Andrew's Harborside Restaurant (Boothbay Harbor, ME), *63*

Andrie Rose Inn (Ludlow, VT), *318*

Angelina's Ristorante Italiano (Concord, NH), *253*

Antonio's (New Bedford, MA), *214*

Apple Tree Inn (Lenox, MA), *187*

Applebutter Inn
(Woodstock, VT), *346*

Applegate (Lee, MA),
185

Apricot's (Farmington,
CT), *17*

Aqua Grille (Sandwich,
MA), *235*

Aquinnah Cliffs
(Falmouth Aquinnah,
MA), *195*

The Aquinnah Shop
(Aquinnah, MA), *201*

Aquitaine (Boston, MA),
137

The Arabian Horse Inn
(Sudbury, MA), *240*

The Arbor Inn
(Edgartown, MA), *199*

Arcade (Providence, RI),
297

Arcadia Nature
Center and Wildlife
Sanctuary,
Massachusetts
Audubon Society
(Easthampton,
MA), *219*

Ardeo (South Yarmouth,
MA), *249*

Arlington Inn (Arlington,
VT), *305, 306*

Arlington's West
Mountain Inn
(Arlington, VT), *305*

Arnie's Place (Concord,
NH), *253*

Arrowhead (Pittsfield,
MA), *223*

Arrows (Ogunquit, ME),
94

Arts and Crafts Show
(Old Saybrook, CT),
39

Arundel, Meadows Inn
(Kennebunk, ME), *81*

Ashley Inn (Edgartown,
MA), *199*

Ashley Manor
(Barnstable, MA), *181*

Ashumet Holly &
Wildlife Sanctuary
(Falmouth, MA), *170*

Ashworth By The Sea
(Hampton Beach,
NH), *259*

Aspen Motel
(Manchester Center,
VT), *320*

Asticou Inn (Northeast
Harbor, ME), *91*

Astor's Beechwood
(Newport, RI), *290*

Atlantic Birches Inn
(Old Orchard Beach,
ME), *96*

Atlantic Café (Nantucket,
MA), *210*

Atlantic Seal Cruises
(South Freeport.
Depart from Town
Wharf, ME), *77*

Atlantica (Camden,
ME), *70*

atre Workshop of
Nantucket (Nantucket,
MA), *207*

Attitash Bear Peak
Ski Resort (New
Hampshire, NH), *250*

Attitash Grand
Summit Resort And
Conference Center
(Bartlett, NH), *251*

Audubon Center
(Greenwich, CT), *17*

Aujourd'hui (Boston,
MA), *137*

Aura (Boston, MA), *137*

Autumn Inn
(Northampton, MA),
220

Autumnal Feasting
(Plymouth, MA),
226

Avanyu Spa at the
Equinox Resort
(Manchester Village,
VT), *322*

Avon Old Farms Hotel
(Avon, CT), *11*

Avon Old Farms Inn
(Avon, CT), *11*

Ay! Caramba Café
(Harwich, MA), *178*

B

B & G Oysters Ltd
(Boston, MA), *137*

B. Mae's Resort Inn &
Suites (Gilford, NH),
266

Babcock-Smith House
(Westerly, RI), *303*

Back Bay Grill (Portland,
ME), *101*

The Back Eddy
(Westport, MA), *169*

Balance (Oak Bluffs,
MA), *201*

Balance Rock Inn (Bar
Harbor, ME), *54*

The Balsams (Dixville
Notch, NH), *254*

Balsams/Wilderness Ski
Area (Dixville Notch,
NH), *254*

Bangor Museum and
Center for History
(Bangor, ME), *51*

Bar Harbor Grand Hotel
(Bar Harbor, ME), *54*

Bar Harbor Historical
Society Museum
(Bar Harbor, ME), *52*

Bar Harbor Hotel-
Bluenose Inn (Bar
Harbor, ME), *53*

Bar Harbor Inn (Bar
Harbor, ME), *53*

Bar Harbor Motel (Bar
Harbor, ME), *53*

Bar Harbor Whale
Watch Company (Bar
Harbor, ME), *52*

Barley Neck Inn (East
Orleans, MA), *221*

Barnacle Billy's
(Ogunquit, ME), *94*

Barnard Inn (Barnard,
VT), *347*

Barnum Festival
(Bridgeport, CT), *12*

Barnum Museum
(Bridgeport, CT), *12*

Barracks Museum
(Eastport, ME), *75*

Barrows House Inn
(Dorset, VT), *312*

INDEX

★
★
★
★

Barrows House Inn
  (Dorset, VT), *313*
Bartlett Arboretum and
  Gardens (Stamford,
  CT), *41*
Bartlett's Farm
  (Nantucket, MA), *204*
Bartley's Dockside
  (Kennebunkport,
  ME), *85*
Barton's Motel (Laconia,
  NH), *266*
Basin Harbor Club
  (Vergennes, VT), *337*
Basketball Hall of Fame
  (Springfield, MA),
  236
Bass Rocks Ocean Inn,
  174
Bates College (Lewiston,
  ME), *88*
Battle Green (Center of
  town MA), *190*
Battleship Cove (Fall
  River, MA), *168*
Bay Chamber Concerts
  (Rockport, ME), *68*
The Bayview (Bar
  Harbor, ME), *53*
The Beach House
  (Kennebunk Beach,
  ME), *81*
Beach Plum Inn
  (Menemsha, MA),
  198
Beach Plum Inn
  Restaurant
  (Menemsha, MA),
  201
The Beachmere Inn
  (Ogunquit, ME), *92*
The Beachside at
  Nantucket (Nantucket,
  MA), *208*
The Beacon Room
  (Orleans, MA), *221*
Beal's Lobster Pier
  (Southwest Harbor,
  ME), *110*
Beauport, the Sleeper-
  McCann House
  (Gloucester, MA), *173*

Bedford Village Inn
  (Bedford, NH), *269,
  270*
Bee and Thistle Inn (Old
  Lyme, CT), *38*
Beech Tree Inn
  (Newport, RI), *294*
Beechwood Hotel
  (Worcester, MA), *247*
Beechwood Inn
  (Barnstable, MA), *181*
Beehive Tavern
  (Sandwich, MA), *235*
Belcourt Castle
  (Newport, RI), *290*
Belfast Harbor Inn
  (Belfast, ME), *58*
The Belfry Inn & Bistro
  (Sandwich, MA), *235*
Bell Buoy Restaurant
  (Old Orchard Beach,
  ME), *96*
Bellini's (North Conway,
  NH), *277*
The Belvidere Room
  (Kennebunkport,
  ME), *85*
Ben & Jerry's Ice
  Cream Factory Tour
  (Waterbury, VT), *340*
Bennington Battle
  Monument (Old
  Bennington, VT), *306*
Bennington College
  (Bennington, VT), *306*
Bennington Museum
  (Bennington, VT), *306*
Berkshire Botanical
  Garden (Stockbridge,
  MA), *238*
Berkshire Craft Fair
  (Great Barrington,
  MA), *175*
Berkshire Hills Motel
  (Williamstown, MA),
  245
Berkshire Museum
  (Pittsfield, MA), *223*
Best Value Heritage
  Motor Inn-Millinocket
  (Millinocket, ME), *89*

Best Value Inn-
  Manchester
  (Manchester, CT), *27*
Best Western
  (Bennington, VT), *307*
Best Western at Historic
  Concord (Concord,
  MA), *162*
Best Western Black Swan
  Inn (Lee, MA), *184*
Best Western Blue Water
  on the Ocean (South
  Yarmouth, MA), *248*
Best Western Camden
  Riverhouse Hotel
  (Camden, ME), *68*
Best Western Camelot
  Inn (Wethersfield,
  CT), *45*
Best Western Chelmsford
  Inn (Chelmsford,
  MA), *193*
Best Western Freeport
  Inn (Freeport, ME), *78*
Best Western Hotel Tria
  (Cambridge, MA), *153*
Best Western Inn &
  Suites Rutland/
  Killington (Rutland,
  VT), *329*
Best Western Inn (Bar
  Harbor, ME), *53*
Best Western Red Jacket
  Mountain View Resort
  & Conference Center
  (North Conway, NH),
  274
Best Western
  Roundhouse Suites
  (Boston, MA), *130*
Best Western Royal Plaza
  Hotel & Trade Center
  (Marlborough, MA),
  240
Best Western Senator
  Inn & Spa (Augusta,
  ME), *49*
Best Western Sovereign
  Hotel (Keene, NH),
  265

Best Western Waterbury-Stowe (Waterbury, VT), *340*

Best Western Waterville Inn (Waterville, ME), *111*

Best Western Windjammer Inn & Conference Center (South Burlington, VT), *311*

Best Western, MErry Manor Inn (South Portland, ME), *99*

Bethel Inn & Country Club (Bethel, ME), *59*

Big G's Deli (Winslow, ME), *111*

Billy's Etc. (Ogunquit, ME), *94*

Birchwood Inn (Lenox, MA), *188*

Birds Nest Inn (Waterbury Center, VT), *340*

Bishop's Terrace (West Harwich, MA), *178*

Bistro at Crowne Pointe Inn (Provincetown, MA), *228*

Bistro Zinc (Lenox, MA), *189*

Black Dog Bakery (Vineyard Haven, MA), *195*

Black Eyed Susan's (Nantucket, MA), *210*

Black Friar Inn (Bar Harbor, ME), *54*

Black Horse Tavern (Bridgton, ME), *64*

Black Mountain (Jackson, NH), *263*

Black Point Inn (Scarborough, ME), *99*

Blaine House (Augusta, ME), *49*

Blantyre (Lenox, MA), *187*

Blantyre (Lenox, MA), *189*

Blithewold Mansion and Gardens (Bristol, RI), *287*

Block Island Ferry (Point Judith, RI), *289*

Blue Elephant (Ogunquit, ME), *94*

Blue Grass Festival (Preston, CT), *37*

Blue Harbor House, A Village Inn (Camden, ME), *68*

Blue Hill Inn (Blue Hill, ME), *60*

Blue Iris Motor Inn (Rumford, ME), *106*

Blue Moon Café (Boothbay Harbor, ME), *63*

Blue Rock Resort (South Yarmouth, MA), *248*

Blue Room (Cambridge, MA), *155*

Boar's Tavern (Loudon, NH), *253*

Boarding House (Nantucket, MA), *211*

Bob's Best Sandwiches (Dennisport, MA), *167*

Bob's Southern Bistro (Boston, MA), *137*

Bolton Valley Ski/Summer Resort (Bolton Valley, VT), *309*

Bonfire (Boston, MA), *138*

Boothbay Railway Village (Boothbay, ME), *61*

Boothbay Region Historical Society Museum (Boothbay Harbor, ME), *61*

Boston African American National Historic Site (Boston, MA), *120*

Boston Ballet (Boston, MA), *121*

Boston Bruins (Boston, MA), *121*

Boston Celtics (Boston, MA), *121*

Boston College (Chestnut Hill, MA), *121*

Boston Common (Boston MA), *121*

Boston Harbor Hotel (Boston, MA), *130*

Boston Harbor Islands National Recreation Area (Boston, MA), *121*

Boston Marathon, *129*

Boston Marriott Cambridge (Cambridge, MA), *153*

Boston Marriott Copley Place (Boston, MA), *130*

Boston Marriott Long Wharf (Boston, MA), *130*

Boston Marriott Newton (Newton, MA), *216*

boston Public Garden (Boston, MA), *122*

Boston Public Library (Boston, MA), *122*

Boston Red Sox (Boston, MA), *122*

Boston Symphony Orchestra/Boston Pops (Boston, MA), *122*

Boston Tea Party Ship and Museum (Boston, MA), *122*

Boston University (Boston, MA), *122*

Bousquet (Pittsfield, MA), *223*

Bowdoin College (Brunswick, ME), *64*

Brackett's Oceanview (Rockport, MA), *232*

The Bradford of Chatham (Chatham, MA), *157*

Bradley House Museum (Woods Hole, MA), *170*

The Bradley Inn (New Harbor, ME), *74*

Bramble Inn (Brewster, MA), *149*

Bramble Inn (Brewster, MA), *149*

Brandeis University (Waltham, MA), *242*

The Brandon Inn (Brandon, VT), *308*

The Brannon Bunker Inn (Walpole, ME), *74*

Brasserie Jo (Boston, MA), *138*

Brattleboro Museum & Art Center (Brattleboro, VT), *308*

Bravo Bravo (Mystic, CT), *30*

Bravo Restaurant (Boston, MA), *138*

Bread Loaf (Middlebury, VT), *322*

Breakers (Newport, RI), *291*

The Breakwater Inn and Hotel (Kennebunkport, ME), *82*

Breezeway Resort (Misquamicut Beach, RI), *303*

Bretton Woods Ski Area (Bretton Woods, NH), *251*

Brewster by the Sea (Brewster, MA), *149*

Brewster Fish House (Brewster, MA), *149*

Brewster House Bed & Breakfast (Freeport, ME), *78*

Brewster Inn and Chowder House (Brewster, MA), *150*

The Briar Lea Inn and Restaurant (Bethel, ME), *59*

Brick Market (Newport, RI), *291*

Brick Store Museum (Kennebunk, ME), *81*

Brook Farm Inn (Lenox, MA), *188*

Brown Sugar Café-Fenway (Boston, MA), *138*

Brown University (Providence, RI), *297*

Brown's Wharf Motel (Boothbay Harbor, ME), *61*

Bruce Museum (Greenwich, CT), *18*

Buckman Tavern (Lexington, MA), *190*

Bufflehead Cove (Kennebunkport, ME), *83*

Bunker Hill Monument (Charlestown, MA), *123*

Burke Mountain Ski Area (Lyndonville, VT), *319*

Burkehaven at Sunapee (Sunapee, NH), *282*

Bush-Holley House (Cos Cob, CT), *18*

The Butcher Shop (Boston, MA), *138*

Butler-McCook Homestead and Main Street History Center (Hartford, CT), *22*

Butterfly (West Hartford, CT), *24*

Buttolph-Williams House (Wethersfield, CT), *44*

Button Bay State Park (Vergennes, VT), *337*

Buttonwood Inn on Mt. Surprise (North Conway, NH), *276*

Buttonwood Park & Zoo (New Bedford, MA), *213*

By The Sea Guests (Dennisport, MA), *166*

C

The Cactus Grille (Providence, RI), *300*

Café Allegre (Madison, CT), *27*

Café Lucia (Lenox, MA), *189*

Café Moxie (Vineyard Haven, MA), *201*

Caffe Bella (Randolph, MA), *147*

Calvin Coolidge Memorial Room (Northampton, MA), *219*

Cambridge Antique Mall (Cambridge, MA), *151*

Cambridge Street Restaurant (Nantucket, MA), *211*

Camden Harbour Inn (Camden, ME), *68*

Camden Hills State Park (Camden, ME), *67*

Camden Opera House (Camden, ME), *67*

Camden Snow Bowl (Camden, ME), *67*

Camden Windward House (Camden, ME), *69*

Camel's Hump Mountain (Waterbury, VT), *340*

Can Am Crown Sled Dog Races (Fort Kent, ME), *77*

Candlelight Motel (Arlington, VT), *305*

Candlelite Inn (Bradford, NH), *282*

Candlewood Lake (Danbury, CT), *14*

Canfield House (Newport, RI), *296*

Cannon Mountain Ski Area (Franconia, NH), *258*

Canterbury House Bed and Breakfast (Woodstock, VT), *346*

Canterbury Shaker Village (Canterbury, NH), *252*

Cap'n Simeon's Gallery (Kittery Point, ME), *88*

Cape Ann Historical Museum (Gloucester, MA), *174*

Cape Arundel Inn (Kennebunkport, ME), *83*

Cape Cod Baseball League (Harwich, MA), *177*

Cape Cod Claddagh Inn (West Harwich, MA), *178*

Cape Cod Kayak (Cataumet, MA), *170*

Cape Cod Museum of Natural History (Brewster, MA), *148*

Cape Cod Oyster Festival (Hyannis, MA), *180*

Cape Cod Pathways (Barnstable, MA), *179*

Cape Cod Potato Chip Company (Hyannis, MA), *179*

Cape Cod Repertory Theater Company (Brewster, MA), *148*

CAPE COD, *156*

Cape Codder Resort & Spa (Hyannis, MA), *180*

Cape Playhouse (Dennis, MA), *165*

Cape Symphony Orchestra (Yarmouth Port, MA), *247*

The Capital Grille (Boston, MA), *138*

Capitol Plaza Hotel and Conference Center (Montpelier, VT), *324*

Captain Daniel Stone Inn (Brunswick, ME), *65*

Captain David Kelley House (Centerville, MA), *181*

Captain Fairfield Inn (Kennebunkport, ME), *83*

Captain Farris House Bed and Breakfast (South Yarmouth, MA), *248*

Captain Freeman Inn (Brewster, MA), *149*

The Captain Jefferds Inn (Kennebunkport, ME), *84*

Captain Lindsey House Inn (Rockland, ME), *104*

Captain Linnell House (Orleans, MA), *222*

The Captain Lord Mansion (Kennebunkport, ME), *84*

Captain Nick's Seafood House (Bangor, ME), *51*

Captain Tom Lawrence House (Falmouth, MA), *171*

Captain's Galley Restaurant (Old Orchard Beach, ME), *96*

Captain's House Inn (Chatham, MA), *159*

Captain's Quarters, *168*

Carbone's (Hartford, CT), *24*

Caribou Historical Center (Caribou, ME), *71*

Caribou Inn & Convention Center (Caribou, ME), *71*

Carlisle House Inn (Nantucket, MA), *209*

Carmen (Boston, MA), *138*

Carol's (Lenox, MA), *189*

Carrabassett Valley Ski Area (Kingfield, ME), *86*

Carter's X-Country Ski Center (Bethel, ME), *59*

Casa Romero (Boston, MA), *138*

Casablanca (Cambridge, MA), *155*

Cascade Inn (Saco, ME), *107*

Cascades Lodge (Killington Village, VT), *315*

Casco Bay Inn (Freeport, ME), *78*

Casco Bay Lines (Portland, ME), *73*

Castelmaine (Bar Harbor, ME), *54*

Castine Inn (Castine, ME), *66*

Castle (Leicester, MA), *247*

Castle Hill Inn & Resort (Newport, RI), *294*

Castle Street Café (Great Barrington, MA), *176*

Catamount Ski Area (Great Barrington, MA), *175*

Cavey's French Restaurant (Manchester, CT), *28*

Cavey's Italian Restaurant (Manchester, CT), *28*

Cedar Crest Motel (Camden, ME), *68*

Centennial Inn Suites (Farmington, CT), *17*

Centerboard Guest House (Nantucket, MA), *209*

Centerville Corners Inn (Centerville, MA), *180*

Centre Street Inn (Nantucket, MA), *209*

Chalet Moosehead Lakefront Motel (Greenville, ME), *80*

Chamard Vineyards (Clinton, CT), *13*

Chambery Inn (Lee, MA), *185*

The Chanler at Cliff Walk (Newport, RI), *294*

Chapman-Hall House (Damariscotta, ME), *73*

Charles Hotel (Cambridge, MA), *153*

★
★
★
★

Charles Ives Center for the Arts (Danbury, CT), *14*

Charles River Canoe & Kayak Center (Newton, MA), *216*

Charles River Esplanade, *123*

Charles Street Inn (Boston, MA), *136*

Charleston House (Woodstock, VT), *346*

Charlotte Inn (Edgartown, Martha's Vineyard, MA), *198*

Chateau-sur-Mer (Newport, RI), *291*

Chatfield Hollow State Park (Killingworth, CT), *13*

Chatham Bars Inn (Chatham, MA), *157*

Chatham Light (Chatham, MA), *157*

The Chatham Motel (Chatham, MA), *158*

Chatham Seafarer (Chatham, MA), *158*

Chatham Squire (Chatham, MA), *159*

Chatham Wayside Inn (Chatham, MA), *158*

Chau Chow City (Boston, MA), *139*

Chebeague Transportation (Chebeague Island, ME), *73*

Cheers (Boston, MA), *139*

Chef's Table (Montpelier, VT), *325*

Cheney Homestead (Manchester, CT), *27*

Chesterwood (Stockbridge, MA), *238*

Chez Henri (Cambridge, MA), *155*

Chicama Vineyards (West Tisbury, MA), *196*

Children's Museum of Boston (Boston, MA), *123*

Children's Museum of Maine (Portland, ME), *97*

Children's Museum of Portsmouth (Portsmouth, NH), *278*

Chillingsworth (Brewster, MA), *150*

China Blossom (North Andover, MA), *120*

China by the Sea (Boothbay Harbor, ME), *63*

Chowder House, (Boothbay Harbor), *63*

Christ Church (Cambridge, MA), *151*

Christa McAuliffe Planetarium (Concord, NH), *252*

Christmas Farm Inn (Jackson, NH), *264*

Christmas Torchlight Parade (Old Saybrook, CT), *39*

Christopher Dodge House (Providence, RI), *299*

Church Street Café (Lenox, MA), *189*

Church Street Marketplace (Burlington, VT), *309*

Ciao Bella (Boston, MA), *139*

Ciao Café and Wine Bar (Danbury, CT), *14*

Cisco Brewers (Nantucket, MA), *204*

Clam Box of Ipswich (Ipswich, MA), *183*

Clam Festival (Yarmouth, ME), *114*

Clam Shell (Littleton, NH), *268*

Clancy's (Dennisport, MA), *167*

Clarion Hotel (Manchester, CT), *28*

Clarion Hotel (Sudbury, MA), *240*

Clarion Hotel and Conference Center (Northampton, MA), *220*

Clark Currier Inn (Newburyport, MA), *215*

Clark House (Wolfeboro, NH), *284*

The Clark Point Inn (Southwest Harbor, ME), *110*

Clarke's Turn of the Century (Boston, MA), *139*

Classic Connecticut, *11*

Clay Hill Farm (Cape Neddick, ME), *94*

Cleftstone Manor (Bar Harbor, ME), *54*

Cliff Walk (Newport, RI), *291*

Cliffside Beach Club (Nantucket, MA), *208*

Clinton Motel (Clinton, CT), *13*

Clio (Boston, MA), *139*

Club Car (Nantucket, MA), *211*

Coach House (Edgartown, MA), *201*

Coachman Inn (Kittery, ME), *88*

Coast Guard House (Narragansett, RI), *290*

Cobb's Mill Inn (Weston, CT), *44*

Cobblestone Inn (Nantucket, MA), *209*

Cobblestone Inn (Plymouth, NH), *278*

Cobblestones (Lowell, MA), *193*

Cod Cove Inn (Edgecomb, ME), *113*

Codman House (Lincoln, MA), *160*

Coffin House (Newburyport, MA), *215*

Cog Railway (Bretton Woods, NH), *272*

Coggeshall Farm Museum, Colt State Park (Bristol, RI), *288*

Colby College (Waterville, ME), *110*

Colby Hill Inn (Henniker, NH), *253*

Colby Hill Inn (Henniker, NH), *253*

Cold Hollow Cider Mill (Waterbury Center, VT), *340*

Cole Land Transportation Museum (Bangor, ME), *51*

Colonel Ashley House (Sheffield, MA), *175*

Colonial House Inn & Restaurant (Yarmouth Port, MA), *249*

The Colonial House Inn (Plymouth, MA), *226*

Colonial Inn (Concord, MA), *162*

Colonial Inn (Concord, MA), *163*

Colonial Inn Of Martha's Vineyard (Edgartown, MA), *199*

Colonial Pemaquid State Park (New Harbor, ME), *73*

The Colonnade Hotel (Boston, MA), *130*

Colonnade Inn (Lyndonville, VT), *319*

The Colony Hotel (Kennebunkport, ME), *82*

Colony Mill Marketplace (Keene, NH), *265*

Combes Family Inn (Ludlow, VT), *318*

Comfort Inn (Augusta, ME), *50*

Comfort Inn (Brunswick, ME), *65*

Comfort Inn (Concord, NH), *253*

Comfort Inn (Montpelier, VT), *324*

Comfort Inn (Mystic, CT), *29*

Comfort Inn (North Conway, NH), *275*

Comfort Inn (Rutland, VT), *329*

Comfort Inn (South Burlington, VT), *311*

Commercial Street (Provincetown MA), *226*

The Commodore Inn (West Harwich, MA), *177*

Common Man (Ashland, NH), *262*

Common Man (Lincoln, NH), *267*

The Common Man (Warren, VT), *339*

Community Boating (Boston, MA), *123*

Company of the Cauldron (Nantucket, MA), *211*

Concord Museum (Concord, MA), *160*

Congregational Church (Middlebury, VT), *322*

Connecticut Firemen's Historical Society Fire Museum (Manchester, CT), *27*

Connecticut River Museum (Essex, CT), *15*

Connecticut Storytelling Festival (New London, CT), *34*

Connecticut's Beardsley (Bridgeport, CT), *12*

Constitution House (Windsor, VT), *343*

Conway Homestead-Cramer Museum (Camden, ME), *67*

Conway Scenic Railroad (North Conway, NH), *274*

Cook's Lobster House (Bailey Island, ME), *50*

Coonamessett Inn (Falmouth, MA), *170*

Coop de Ville (Oak Bluffs, MA), *201*

Copley Place (Boston, MA), *123*

Copley Square Hotel (Boston, MA), *131*

Copp's Hill Burying Ground (Boston, MA), *123*

Copper Beech Inn (Ivoryton, CT), *15, 16*

Cork N' Hearth (Lee, MA), *185*

Corner House Inn (Center Sandwich, NH), *262*

Corsair and CrossRip Oceanfront (Dennisport, MA), *166*

Corsican (Freeport, ME), *79*

Cortina Inn and Resort (Killington, VT), *315*

Country Club Inn (Rangeley, ME), *103*

Country Garden Inn And Motel (Rowley, MA), *183*

Country Inn (Harwich Port, MA), *178*

Courtyard Boston (Foxborough, MA), *173*

Courtyard by Marriott (Danvers, MA), *163*

Courtyard by Marriott (Hyannis, MA), *181*

Courtyard by Marriott (Lowell, MA), *193*

Courtyard by Marriott (New Haven, CT), *32*

Courtyard by Marriott Providence Downtown (Providence, RI), *299*

★
★
★
★

Courtyard Marriott (Middletown, RI), *294*

Courtyard Marriott Boston Tremont Hotel (Boston, MA), *131*

The Cove (Orleans, MA), *221*

Crab Shell (Stamford, CT), *42*

Craigie on Main (Cambridge, MA), *155*

Craignair Inn (Spruce Head, ME), *105*

Cranberry Cove Boating Company, *109*

Cranberry Harvest Festival (Harwich, MA), *177*

Cranberry Inn (Chatham, MA), *158*

Crane Beach (Ipswich, MA), *183*

Cranmore Mountain Lodge (North Conway, NH), *276*

Cranwell Resort Spa and Golf Club (Lenox, MA), *187*

Crawford Notch State Park (Bretton Woods, NH), *251*

Creamery Bridge (Brattleboro, VT), *309*

Crow's Nest Resort (North Truro, MA), *241*

Crowley Cheese Factory (Healdville, VT), *318*

Crowne Plaza (Hartford, CT), *23*

Crowne Plaza (Nashua, NH), *272*

Crowne Plaza (Warwick, RI), *302*

Crowne Plaza Hotel (Pittsfield, MA), *223*

Crowne Plaza Hotel (Worcester, MA), *247*

Crowne Pointe Historic Inn (Provincetown, MA), *227*

Crowninshield-Bentley House (Salem, MA), *232*

Culinary Archives & Museum (Providence, RI), *297*

Currier Museum of Art (Manchester, NH), *269*

Cushing House Museum (Newburyport, MA), *215*

Custom House Maritime Museum (Newburyport, MA), *215*

D

D. W.'s Oceanside Inn (Hampton Beach, NH), *260*

Daily Planet (Burlington, VT), *311*

Dakota (Avon, CT), *12*

Dakota (Pittsfield, MA), *224*

Dan'l Webster Inn (Sandwich, MA), *235*

The Dan'l Webster Inn (Sandwich, MA), *236*

Dana Place Inn (Jackson, NH), *264*

Darby Field Country Inn (Albany, NH), *276*

Darby's (Belfast, ME), *58*

Dartmouth College (Hanover, NH), *260*

David's (Newburyport, MA), *215*

Davide (Boston, MA), *139*

Davio's (Boston, MA), *139*

Days Inn (Danvers, MA), *164*

Days Inn (Dover, NH), *255*

Days Inn (New Bedford, MA), *214*

Days Inn (Shelburne, VT), *330*

DeCordova Museum & Sculpture Park (Lincoln, MA), *160*

Deep River Ancient Muster and Parade (Main street, Deep River, CT), *15*

Deerfield Inn (Deerfield, MA), *164*, *165*

The Delamar (Greenwich, CT), *18*

Denison Homestead (Mystic, CT), *28*

Derby House (Salem, MA), *232*

Devonfield Inn (Lee, MA), *185*

Dexters Inn & Tennis Club (Sunapee, NH), *282*

Di Millo's Floating Restaurant (Portland, ME), *101*

Dinosaur State Park (Rocky Hill, CT), *44*

Discover Jazz Festival (Burlington, VT), *310*

Discovery Museum and Planetarium (Bridgeport, CT), *12*

Dock and Dine (Old Saybrook, CT), *39*

Dockside (York, ME), *116*

Dockside Guest Quarters (York, ME), *115*

Dockside Inn (Oak Bluffs, MA), *199*

Docksider (Northeast Harbor, ME), *91*

Dolphin Restaurant (Barnstable, MA), *182*

Dorset Inn (Dorset, VT), *312*

Dorset Theatre Festival (Dorset, VT), *312*

Dostal's Resort Lodge (Londonderry, VT), *317*

Double Dragon Inn (Orleans, MA), *222*

Doubletree Club Hotel (Norwalk, CT), *35*

356

INDEX

★
★
★
★
★

Doubletree Guest Suites (Boston, MA), *131*

Doubletree Hotel (Lowell, MA), *193*

Doubletree Hotel (South Burlington, VT), *311*

Doubletree Hotel (Waltham, MA), *242*

Doubletree Hotel (Windsor Locks, CT), *46*

Dowd's Country Inn (Lyme, NH), *261*

Down Easter Inn (Damariscotta, ME), *74*

Downyflake (Nantucket, MA), *211*

Dr. Moses Mason House Museum (Bethel, ME), *59*

Drumlin Farm Education Center (Lincoln, MA), *160*

Duck Tours (Boston, MA), *124*

Dunscroft By the Sea (Harwich Port, MA), *178*

Durgin Park (Boston, MA), *139*

Dyer Library & Saco Museum (Saco, ME), *107*

E

Eagle Mountain House (Jackson, NH), *263*

Earl of Sandwich Motel (East Sandwich, MA), *235*

Eartha (Yarmouth, ME), *114*

East Coast Grill & Raw Bar (Cambridge, MA), *155*

East Rock Park (New Haven, CT), *31*

Eastern Standard (Boston, MA), *140*

Eastern States Exposition (The Big E) (West Springfield, MA), *237*

Eastgate (Littleton, NH), *269*

Eastgate Motor Inn (Littleton, NH), *268*

Eastham Historical Society (Eastham, MA), *167*

Eastham Windmill (Eastham, MA), *168*

Eastland Park Hotel (Portland, ME), *99*

Eastman Inn (North Conway, NH), *276*

Eastside Grill (Northampton, MA), *220*

Echo Lake State Park, *274*

Econo Lodge Killington Area (Mendon, VT), *315*

EcoTarium (Worcester, MA), *246*

The Edgartown Inn (Edgartown, MA), *199*

The Edgewater (Old Orchard Beach, ME), *95*

Edith Wharton Estate (The Mount) (Lenox, MA), *186*

Edson Hill Manor (Stowe, VT), *334*

Edward King House (Newport, RI), *291*

Edwards Harborside Inn (York Harbor, ME), *115*

Egg & I (Hyannis, MA), *182*

Eggspectation (South Portland, ME), *101*

The Egremont Inn (South Egremont, MA), *176*

The Elephant Walk (Cambridge, MA), *155*

The Eliot Hotel (Boston, MA), *131*

Elm Arch Inn (Falmouth, MA), *171*

Elms (Newport, RI), *291*

The Elms (Ridgefield, CT), *40*

Elms Bed and Breakfast (Camden, ME), *69*

The Elms Inn (Ridgefield, CT), *40*

Embassy Suites (Portland, ME), *99*

Emerald Lake State Park (North Dorset, VT), *320*

Emerson Inn by the Sea (Rockport, MA), *230*

Emerson-Wilcox House (York, ME), *114*

Emily Dickinson Museum: the Homestead and the Evergreens (Amherst, MA), *118*

Endeavor Sailing Adventures (Nantucket, MA), *204*

Enfield Shaker Museum (Enfield, NH), *260*

English, MEadows Inn (Kennebunkport, ME), *84*

The Equinox (Manchester Village, VT), *320*

Equinox Sky Line Drive (Manchester and Manchester Center, VT), *320*

Eric Carle Museum of Picture Book Art (Amherst, MA), *118*

Espresso Love Café (Edgartown, MA), *202*

Essex Street Inn (Newburyport, MA), *215*

Ethan Allen Homestead and Museum (Burlington, VT), *310*

Ethan Allen Hotel (Danbury, CT), *14*

Ethan Allen Park (Burlington, VT), *310*

Eugene O'Neill Theater Center (Waterford, CT), *33*

Eureka Schoolhouse (Springfield, VT), *331*

Excelsior (Boston, MA), *140*

Expedition Whydah's Sea Lab & Learning Center (Provincetown, MA), *227*

F

Fabyan's Station (Bretton Woods, NH), *252*

Factory Outlet Stores (Freeport, ME), *78*

Fairbanks Inn (Provincetown, MA), *228*

The Fairbanks Inn (St. Johnsbury, VT), *332*

Fairbanks Museum and Planetarium (St. Johnsbury, VT), *332*

Fairfield Inn (Bangor, ME), *51*

Fairfield Inn (Merrimack, NH), *273*

Fairfield Inn (Portsmouth, NH), *280*

Fairfield Inn (Salem, NH), *281*

Fairfield Inn (Scarborough, ME), *107*

The Fairmont Copley Plaza Boston (Boston, MA), *131*

Fall Foliage Festival (North Adams, MA), *218*

Fall River Historical Society (Fall River, MA), *169*

Falmouth Restaurant (Falmouth, MA), *172*

Falmouth Road Race (Falmouth, MA), *170*

Faneuil Hall Marketplace (Fifth floor Boston, MA), *124*

Fanizzi's by the Sea (Provincetown, MA), *229*

Farmbrook Motel (Plymouth, VT), *327*

Farmington Antiques Weekend (Farmington, CT), *16*

The Farmington Inn of Greater Hartford (Farmington, CT), *17*

Farmington Valley Arts Center (Avon, CT), *10*

Farnsworth Art Museum and Wyeth Center (Rockland, ME), *104*

Fazio's Italian (York, ME), *116*

Feast of the Blessed Sacrament (New Bedford, MA), *214*

Featherstone Meeting House For the Arts (Oak Bluffs, MA), *196*

Federal House Inn (South Lee, MA), *185*

Federal Jack's Restaurant and Brew Pub (Kennebunk, ME), *81*

Felix Neck Sanctuary (Vineyard Haven, MA), *196*

Ferry Service (Cranberry Isles, ME), *90*

Ferry Service to Yarmouth, Nova Scotia (Bar Harbor, ME), *52*

Festival de Joie (Lewiston, ME), *88*

Festival on the Green (Middlebury, VT), *323*

Figawi Sailboat Race and Charity Ball, *180*

Filippo (Boston, MA), *140*

Finn's Seafood (Block Island, RI), *287*

Fio's Ristorante (Stamford, CT), *42*

The Fireplace (Brookline, MA), *150*

Fireside Inn & Suites (West Lebanon, NH), *261*

First Congregational Church (Nantucket, MA), *205*

First Night Boston, *129*

First Unitarian Church (Providence, RI), *298*

Fisherman's Wharf Inn (Boothbay Harbor, ME), *61, 63*

Fitch Hill Inn (Hyde Park, VT), *335*

Five Bays Bistro (Osterville, MA), *182*

Five Gables Inn (East Boothbay, ME), *62*

Flood Tide (Mystic, CT), *30*

Florence Griswold Museum (Old Lyme, CT), *37*

Flume Gorge & Park Information Center (Franconia, NH), *258*

The Flying Bridge (Falmouth, MA), *172*

Flying Horse Carousel (Oak Bluffs, MA), *196*

Fog Island Café (Nantucket, MA), *211*

Folger-Franklin Memorial Fountain (Nantucket, MA), *205*

Follansbee Inn (North Sutton, NH), *273*

Fore Street (Portland, ME), *101*

Formaggio Kitchen (Cambridge, MA), *152*

Fort Constitution, *278*

Fort Foster Park, *87*

Fort Griswold Battlefield State Park (Groton, CT), *20*

Fort Kent Blockhouse, *77*

Fort Kent Historical Society Museum and Gardens (Fort Kent, ME), *77*

Fort Nathan Hale Park and Black Rock Fort (New Haven, CT), *31*

Fort Popham Memorial (Highway 209, ME), *57*

Fort Saybrook Monument Park (Saybrook Point, Old Saybrook, CT), *38*

Fort Stark State Historic Site (New Castle, NH), *279*

Fort William Henry State Memorial, *73*

Four Acres Motel (Williamstown, MA), *245*

Four Chimneys Inn (Bennington, VT), *307*

Four Columns (Newfane, VT), *326*

Four Columns Inn (Newfane, VT), *326*

Four Points by Sheraton (Eastham, MA), *168*

Four Points by Sheraton (Manchester, NH), *270*

Four Points by Sheraton (Norwalk, CT), *36*

Four Seasons Hotel Boston (Boston, MA), *132*

Four Seasons Inn (West Dover, VT), *341*

Four Seasons Motor Inn (Twin Mountain, NH), *282*

The Fox Ridge (North Conway, NH), *275*

The Francis Malbone House (Newport, RI), *295*

Franconia Inn (Franconia, NH), *256*

The Franconia Inn (Franconia, NH), *257*

Franconia Village Hotel (Franconia, NH), *256*

Franklin Café (Boston, MA), *140*

Franklin Park Golf Course (William J. Devine Golf Course) (Dorchester, MA), *124*

Franklin Park Zoo (Dorchester, MA), *124*

Freedom Trail (Suite 401 MA), *124*

Freeport Clipper Inn (Freeport, ME), *78*

Freestone's City Grill (New Bedford, MA), *214*

French Cable Station Museum (Orleans, MA), *220*

Friends and Company (Madison, CT), *27*

Friends Meeting House (Newport, RI), *291*

Frog's Leap Inn (Londonderry, VT), *317*

Front Street (Provincetown, MA), *229*

Frost Place (Franconia, NH), *256*

Fruitlands Museums (Harvard, MA), *161*

Fugakyu (Brookline, MA), *151*

Fuller Gardens (North Hampton, NH), *259*

G

Gala Restaurant & Bar (Williamstown, MA), *245*

Galen C. Moses House (Bath, ME), *57*

Gardner-Pingree House (Salem, MA), *232*

Garrison Inn (Newburyport, MA), *215*

Garrison Suites (Wells, ME), *112*

Gaspee Days (Warwick, RI), *302*

Gateways Inn (Lenox, MA), *187*, *189*

General William Hart House (Old Saybrook, CT), *39*

Giant Staircase, *50*

Gibbs Avenue Museum (Bridgton, ME), *63*

Gifford Woods State Park (Killington, VT), *315*

Gilbert Bean Museum (Braintree, MA), *147*

Ginza (Boston, MA), *140*

Glen Cove Motel (Glen Cove, ME), *105*

Glen Magna Farms (Danvers, MA), *163*

Glenn's Galley (Newburyport, MA), *216*

Gloucester House Restaurant (Gloucester, MA), *174*

Glynn House Inn (Ashland, NH), *262*

Go Fish (Mystic, CT), *30*

Golden Eagle Resort (Stowe, VT), *334*

Golden Stage Inn (Proctorsville, VT), *318*

Goodwin Hotel (Hartford, CT), *23*

Goose Cove Lodge (Sunset, ME), *75*

Gordi's Fish & Steak House (Lincoln, NH), *267*

Gore Place (Waltham, MA), *242*

Gorges Grant Hotel (Ogunquit, ME), *92*

Governor John Langdon House (Portsmouth, NH), *279*

★
★
★
★

Governor Stephen
Hopkins House
(Providence, RI), *298*
The Governor's Inn
(Ludlow, VT), *318*
Grafton Inn (Falmouth,
MA), *171*
Grafton Notch State
Park, *59*
Grafton Ponds Cross-
Country Ski Center
(Grafton, VT), *313*
Granary Burying Ground
(Boston, MA), *124*
The Grand Hotel
(Ogunquit, ME), *92*
Grand Summit Resort
Hotel (Kingfield,
ME), *86*
Granite State Candy
Shoppe (Concord,
NH), *252*
Grape Vine (Salem,
MA), *234*
Great Glen Trails
(Gorham, NH), *272*
Great Impasta
(Brunswick, ME), *65*
Great Meadows National
Wildlife Refuge
(Sudbury Center,
MA), *161*
Green Granite Inn (North
Conway, NH), *275*
Green Mountain Inn
(Stowe, VT), *334*
Green Mountain Sugar
House (Ludlow, VT),
318
Greenville Inn
(Greenville, ME), *80*
Greenwood House
(Vineyard Haven,
MA), *199*
Grey Bonnet Inn
(Killington, VT), *315*
Grey Fox Inn and Resort
(Stowe, VT), *334*
Grey Gull (Wells, ME),
112
Grill 23 & Bar (Boston,
MA), *140*

Grille at Hobbs Brook
(Waltham, MA), *243*
Grissini (Kennebunk,
ME), *81*
Griswold Inn (Essex,
CT), *16*
Gritty McDuff's
(Freeport, ME), *79*
The Grog (Newburyport,
MA), *216*
Gropius House (Lincoln,
MA), *161*
Grove Street Cemetery
(New Haven, CT), *31*
Gryphon House (Boston,
MA), *136*
The Gull Motel Inn
& Cottages1 (Old
Orchard Beach, ME),
95
Gull Wing Suites (South
Yarmouth, MA), *248*
Gypsy Sweethearts
(Ogunquit, ME), *94*

H

Hadley Farm Museum
(Hadley, MA), *219*
Hadwen House
(Nantucket, MA),
205
Haight-Brown Vineyard
and Winery
(Litchfield, CT), *25*
Hamersley's Bistro
(Boston, MA), *140*
Hamilton House (South
Berwick, ME), *87*
Hammonasset Beach
State Park (Madison,
CT), *27*
Hammond Castle
Museum (Gloucester,
MA), *174*
Hampshire Inn
(Seabrook, NH), *259*
Hampton Falls Inn
(Hampton Falls, NH),
260
Hampton Inn
(Bennington, VT), *307*

Hampton Inn (Bow, NH),
253
Hampton Inn (South
Portland, ME), *99*
Hampton Inn (West
Springfield, MA),
237
Hampton Inn (Westport,
MA), *169*
Hancock Inn (Hancock,
NH), *277*
Hancock Shaker Village
(Pittsfield, MA), *223*
Hancock-Clarke House
(Lexington, MA), *191*
The Hanover House
(Vineyard Haven,
MA), *200*
Hanover Inn (Hanover,
NH), *261*
Harbor House Inn (Old
Greenwich, CT), *19*
Harbor House Village
(Nantucket, MA), *208*
Harbor Light Inn
(Marblehead, MA),
194
Harbor View
(Thomaston, ME),
105
Harbor View Hotel
(Edgartown, MA), *198*
Harborside Hotel &
Marina (Bar Harbor,
ME), *54*
Harborside Inn of Boston
(Boston, MA), *132*
Harbour Towne Inn
on the Waterfront
(Boothbay Harbor,
ME), *62*
The Hardcover (Danvers,
MA), *164*
Harlow Old Fort House
(Plymouth, MA), *224*
Harlow's Sugar House
(Putney, VT), *309*
Harraseeket Inn
(Freeport, ME), *78*
Harriet Beecher Stowe
Center (Hartford,
CT), *22*

Harrison House (Lenox, MA), *188*

Hart's Turkey Farm (Meredith, NH), *271*

Hartford Marriott Farmington (Farmington, CT), *17*

Hartness House (Springfield, VT), *331*

Hartwell House (Ogunquit, ME), *93*

Harvard Museum of Natural History (Cambridge, MA), *152*

Harvard University (Cambridge, MA), *152*

Harvard University Art Museums (Cambridge, MA), *152*

Harvest (Cambridge, MA), *155*

Harwich Historical Society (Harwich, MA), *177*

Hawk Inn and Mountain Resort (Plymouth, VT), *328*

Hawthorn Inn (Camden, ME), *69*

Hawthorne Hotel (Salem, MA), *233*

Hawthorne Inn (Concord, MA), *162*

Hayloft (Moody, ME), *112*

Haymarket (Boston MA), *124*

Head of the Charles Regatta (Cambridge, MA), *153*

The Hearth (Brookfield, CT), *15*

Hearth and Kettle (Plymouth, MA), *226*

Hedge House (Plymouth, MA), *224*

Helmand (Cambridge, MA), *156*

Hemenway's Seafood Grill (Providence, RI), *300*

Hemingway's (Killington, VT), *316*

Henry Whitfield State Museum (Guilford, CT), *21*

The Herbert Grand Hotel (Kingfield, ME), *87*

Heritage House (Skowhegan, ME), *109*

Heritage Plantation (Sandwich, MA), *234*

Herreshoff Marine Museum (Bristol, RI), *288*

Highland Light/Cape Cod Light (North Truro, MA), *241*

Hill Farm Inn (Arlington, VT), *305*

Hill-Stead Museum (Farmington, CT), *16*

Hilltop Inn (Sugar Hill, NH), *257*

Hilton Boston Back Bay (Boston, MA), *132*

Hilton Boston Logan Airport (Boston, MA), *132*

Hilton Mystic (Mystic, CT), *29*

Historic Deerfield (Deerfield, MA), *164*

Historic Hildene (Manchester, VT), *320*

Historic Mansions and Houses, *292*

Historic Merrell Inn (South Lee, MA), *185*

Historic New England (South Yarmouth, MA), *247*

Historic Northampton Museum Houses (Northampton, MA), *219*

Historic Pontiac Mills (Warwick, RI), *302*

Historic Ship Nautilus and Submarine Force Museum (Groton, CT), *20*

Historic South Norwalk (SoNo) (South Norwalk, CT), *34*

Historical Museum of Gunn Memorial Library (Washington, CT), *42*

Historical Society Museum (Wellfleet, MA), *243*

History House (Skowhegan, ME), *108*

Hob Knob Inn (Edgartown, MA), *200*

Holiday Inn (Bangor, ME), *51*

Holiday Inn (Bar Harbor, ME), *54*

Holiday Inn (Bath, ME), *57*

Holiday Inn (Boxborough, MA), *163*

Holiday Inn (Bridgeport, CT), *12*

Holiday Inn (Danbury, CT), *14*

Holiday Inn (East Hartford, CT), *23*

Holiday Inn (Ellsworth, ME), *76*

Holiday Inn (Mansfield, MA), *173*

Holiday Inn (Portland, ME), *99*

Holiday Inn (Portsmouth, NH), *280*

Holiday Inn (Randolph, MA), *147*

Holiday Inn (Salem, NH), *281*

Holiday Inn (Stamford, CT), *41*

Holiday Inn (Waterville, ME), *111*

Holiday Inn Berkshires (North Adams, MA), *218*

Holiday Inn Downtown (Springfield, MA), *237*

★
★
★
★
★

Holiday Inn Express (Rockland, MA), *147*

Holiday Inn Express (South Burlington, VT), *311*

Holiday Inn Express (Springfield, VT), *331*

Holiday Inn Nashua (Nashua, NH), *273*

Holiday Inn Rutland/ Killington (Rutland, VT), *329*

Holiday Inn Select-Government Center (Boston, MA), *132*

Holiday Motel (St. Johnsbury, VT), *333*

Holley-Williams House (Lakeville, CT), *24*

Holt House (Blue Hill, ME), *60*

Home Port (Menemsha, MA), *202*

Home Port Inn (Lubec, ME), *89*

Home Port Inn (Lubec, ME), *89*

Home Suites Inn (Waltham, MA), *242*

Homestead Inn (Greenwich, CT), *18*

The Homestead Inn (New Milford, CT), *14*

Homewood Suites (Windsor Locks, CT), *46*

Honeysuckle Hill Bed AND Breakfast (West Barnstable, MA), *181*

Horatio Colony House Museum (Keene, NH), *265*

Horizon (Old Orchard Beach, ME), *95*

Horizon Inn (Wilmington, VT), *342*

Horse & Hound (Franconia, NH), *257*

Horsefeathers (North Conway, NH), *277*

Hot Tomatoes (Hartford, CT), *24*

Hotel 140 (Boston, MA), *132*

Hotel Commonwealth (Boston, MA), *133*

Hotel Manisses Dining Room (Block Island, RI), *287*

Hotel Marlowe (Cambridge, MA), *154*

The Hotel Northampton (Northampton, MA), *220*

Hotel Viking (Newport, RI), *295*

House of Seven Gables (Salem, MA), *232*

Howard House Lodge (Boothbay Harbor, ME), *62*

Howard Johnson (Hadley, MA), *118*

Howland House (Plymouth, MA), *224*

Hoxie House & Dexter Gristmill (Sandwich, MA), *234*

Hubbardton Battlefield and Museum (East Hubbardton, VT), *328*

The Hungry I (Boston, MA), *141*

Hunter House (Newport, RI), *292*

Huntsman Motor Lodge (West Dennis, MA), *166*

Hurlburt-Dunham House (Wethersfield, CT), *45*

Hyannis Whale Watcher Cruises (Barnstable, MA), *179*

Hyatt Harborside (Boston, MA), *133*

Hyatt Regency Boston Financial District (Boston, MA), *133*

Hyatt Regency Cambridge (Cambridge, MA), *154*

Hyatt Regency Greenwich (Old Greenwich, CT), *18*

Hyatt Regency Newport (Newport, RI), *295*

Hydrangea House Inn (Newport, RI), *295*

Hyland House (Guilford, CT), *21*

I

Icarus (Boston, MA), *141*

Ice House Restaurant and Bar (Burlington, VT), *312*

Il Capriccio (Waltham, MA), *243*

Il Falco (Stamford, CT), *42*

Impudent Oyster (Chatham, MA), *159*

Inaho, *249*

Indian Head Resort (Lincoln, NH), *267*

Indian Hill Motel (Greenville, ME), *80*

Indian Leap (Norwich, CT), *36*

Indian Motorcycle Museum (Springfield, MA), *236*

Indochine Pavilion (New Haven, CT), *32*

Inn At Bay Ledge (Bar Harbor, ME), *55*

The Inn At Bay Point (Meredith, NH), *271*

Inn at Duck Creek (Wellfleet, MA), *244*

Inn at Ellis River (Jackson, NH), *263*

The Inn at Essex—A Summit Hotel (Essex, VT), *311*

The Inn at Harvard (Cambridge, MA), *154*

Inn at Iron Masters (Lakeville, CT), *25*

★
★
★
★
★

Inn at Lewis Bay (West Yarmouth, MA), *249*

The Inn at Long Lake (Naples, ME), *64*

The Inn at Longshore (Westport, CT), *44*

Inn at Manchester (Manchester, VT), *321*

The Inn at Mill Falls (Meredith, NH), *271*

Inn At Montpelier (Montpelier, VT), *324*

Inn at Mystic (Mystic, CT), *29*

Inn at National Hall (Westport, CT), *43*

Inn at Ocean's Edge (Camden, ME), *69*

The Inn at Ormsby Hill (Manchester, VT), *321*

Inn at Pleasant Lake (New London, NH), *273*

Inn at Rutland (Rutland, VT), *329*

Inn at Saint John (Portland, ME), *100*

The Inn at Sawmill Farm (West Dover, VT), *341*, *342*

Inn at Stockbridge (Stockbridge, MA), *239*

The Inn at Stratton Mountain (Stratton, VT), *336*

Inn At Sunrise Point (Camden, ME), *69*

The Inn at the Oaks (Eastham, MA), *168*

The Inn at the Round Barn (Waitsfield, VT), *338*

Inn At Thorn Hill (Jackson, NH), *263*

Inn at Thorn Hill (Jackson, NH), *264*

Inn at Water's Edge (Ludlow, VT), *318*

The Inn at Weathersfield (Weathersfield, VT), *331*

Inn at West View Farm (Dorset, VT), *312*

Inn at West View Farm (Dorset, VT), *313*

Inn At Woodchuck Hill Farm (Grafton, VT), *314*

Inn By The Sea (Cape Elizabeth, ME), *99*

Inn Of Hampton (Hampton, NH), *260*

Inn Of The Six Mountains (Killington, VT), *316*

Inn on Carleton (Portland, ME), *101*

The Inn On Cove Hill (Rockport, MA), *231*

Inn On Golden Pond (Holderness, NH), *262*

The Inn On The Common (Craftsbury Common, VT), *325*

Inn on the Sound (Falmouth, MA), *171*

InnSeason Resorts South Mountain (Lincoln, NH), *267*

Institute for American Indian Studies (Washington, CT), *42*

Institute of Contemporary Art (Boston, MA), *125*

InterContinental Boston (Boston, MA), *133*

Interlaken Inn (Lakeville, CT), *25*

International Festival Week, *66*

International Inn (Hyannis, MA), *181*

International In-Water Boat Show (Norwalk, CT), *35*

International Tennis Hall of Fame & Museum (Newport, RI), *292*

Isabella Stewart Gardner Museum (Boston, MA), *125*

Isaiah Clark House (Brewster, MA), *149*

Isaiah Hall Bed and Breakfast Inn (Dennis, MA), *166*

Isaiah Jones Homestead (Sandwich, MA), *235*

Isle au Haut Boat Services (Stonington, ME), *75*

Isle au Haut, *75*

Isles of Shoals (Portsmouth, NH), *279*

Islesford Historical Museum (Cranberry Isles, ME), *73*

Italian Oasis (Littleton, NH), *269*

Ivy Lodge (Newport, RI), *295*

J

Jackson Homestead Museum (Newton, MA), *216*

The Jackson Laboratory (Bar Harbor, ME), *52*

Jackson Ski Touring Foundation (Jackson, NH), *263*

Jacob's Pillow Dance Festival (Becket, MA), *184*

Jade Palace (Caribou, ME), *71*

Jae's Inn (Williamstown, MA), *246*

Jameson Tavern (Freeport, ME), *79*

Jared Coffin House (Nantucket, MA), *208*

Jasper White's Summer Shack (Boston, MA), *141*

Jean-Louis (Greenwich, CT), *19*

Jeremiah Lee Mansion (Marblehead, MA), *194*

Jesse's (Hanover, NH), *261*

Jethro Coffin House
(Oldest House)
(Nantucket, MA), *205*

Jetties Beach (Nantucket, MA), *205*

Jiminy Peak (Hancock, MA), *223*

Jiminy Peak Mountain Resort (Hancock, MA), *223*

Jimmy Sea's (Oak Bluffs, MA), *202*

Jimmy's Harborside (Boston, MA), *141*

John Andrew's Restaurant (South Egremont, MA), *176*

John Brown House (Providence, RI), *298*

John Carver Inn (Plymouth, MA), *226*

John F. Kennedy Hyannis Museum (Hyannis, MA), *179*

John F. Kennedy National Historic Site (Brookline, MA), *150*

John H. Chaffy Blackstone River Valley National Heritage Corridor (Worcester, MA), *246*

John Hancock Warehouse (York, ME), *115*

John Heard House (Ipswich, MA), *183*

John Martin's Manor (Waterville, ME), *111*

John Paul Jones House (Portsmouth, NH), *279*

John Strong Mansion (West Addison, VT), *337*

John Ward House (Salem, MA), *232*

The John Whipple House (Ipswich, MA), *183*

Jonathan's (Ogunquit, ME), *94*

Joseph's by the Sea (Old Orchard Beach, ME), *96*

Joshua Hempstead House (New London, CT), *33*

Joshua L. Chamberlain Museum (Brunswick, ME), *64*

Josiah Dennis Manse (Dennis, MA), *165*

Juniper Hill Inn (Ogunquit, ME), *93*

Juniper Hill Inn (Windsor, VT), *344*

K

Kashmir (Boston, MA), *141*

Katahdin Inn (Millinocket, ME), *90*

Kedron Valley Inn (South Woodstock, VT), *345*, *347*

Kedron Valley Stables (South Woodstock, VT), *344*

Keeler Tavern Museum (Ridgefield, CT), *40*

Kelley House (Edgartown, MA), *198*

Kemble Inn (Lenox, MA), *188*

Kendall Tavern Bed AND breakfast (Freeport, ME), *79*

The Kennebunk Inn (Kennebunk, ME), *81*

The Kennebunk Inn (Kennebunk, ME), *81*

Kennebunkport Inn (Kennebunkport, ME), *82*

Kenniston Hill Inn (Boothbay, ME), *62*

Kensington (Norwich, CT), *37*

Kidspace (North Adams, MA), *217*

Killington Pico Motor Inn (Killington, VT), *316*

Killington Resort (Killington, VT), *315*

King Hooper Mansion (Marblehead, MA), *194*

King's Chapel and Burying Ground (Boston, MA), *125*

Kingscote (Newport, RI), *292*

Kingsleigh Inn (Southwest Harbor, ME), *110*

Kingston Library (Kingston, RI), *289*

Kittery Historical and Naval Museum (Kittery, ME), *87*

L

L'Alouette (Harwich Port, MA), *178*

L'Arte Di Cucinare (Boston, MA), *125*

L'Escale (Greenwich, CT), *19*

L'Etoile (Edgartown, MA), *202*

La Boniche (Lowell, MA), *193*

La Bretagne (Stamford, CT), *42*

La Forge Casino Restaurant (Newport, RI), *296*

La Quinta Inn & Suites Andover (Andover, MA), *120*

La Scala (Dennisport, MA), *167*

Lafayette House (Foxborough, MA), *173*

Lake Champlain Chocolates (Burlington, VT), *310*

Lake Morey Resort (Fairlee, VT), *313*

Lake St. George State Park (Liberty, ME), *58*

Lakeshore Inn (Rockland, ME), *105*

364

INDEX

★
★
★
★
★

Lala Rokh (Boston, MA), *142*

Lambert's Cove Country Inn (Vineyard Haven, MA), *200*

Lamie's Inn & Old Salt Restaurant (Hampton, NH), *260*

Lamoine State Park (Ellsworth, ME), *76*

Landfall (Woods Hole, MA), *172*

The Landing Hotel & Restaurant (Kennebunkport, ME), *85*

The Langham Boston (Boston, MA), *133*

Lareau Farm Country Inn (Waitsfield, VT), *338*

Latchis Hotel (Brattleboro, VT), *309*

Lattanzi's Pizzeria (Edgartown, MA), *202*

Le Garage (Wiscasset, ME), *113*

Le Grenier French Restaurant (Vineyard Haven, MA), *202*

Le Languedoc (Nantucket, MA), *211*

Le Meridien (Cambridge, MA), *154*

Le'Espalier (Boston, MA), *141*

League of New Hampshire Craftsmen—Meredith/ Laconia Arts & Crafts (Meredith, NH), *270*

Lenox Hotel (Boston, MA), *134*

Les Zygomates (Boston, MA), *142*

Levitt Pavilion for the Performing Arts (Westport, CT), *43*

Lexington Historical Society (Lexington, MA), *191*

Liberty Hill Inn (Yarmouth Port, MA), *248*

Lighthouse Inn (West Dennis, MA), *166*

Lighthouse Point Park (New Haven, CT), *31*

Lilac Inn (Brandon, VT), *308*

Lincoln County Museum and Old Jail (Wiscasset, ME), *113*

The Lincoln Inn at the Covered Bridge (Woodstock, VT), *346*

Linda Jean's (Oak Bluffs, MA), *202*

Linden Tree Inn (Rockport, MA), *231*

List Visual Arts Center at MIT (Cambridge, MA), *152*

Litchfield History Museum (Litchfield, CT), *25*

Litchfield Inn (Litchfield, CT), *26*

Litchfield's (Wells, ME), *112*

Littleton Historical Museum (Littleton, NH), *268*

Lizzie Borden Bed and Breakfast (Fall River, MA), *169*

Lobster Claw (Orleans, MA), *222*

Lobster Cooker (Freeport, ME), *79*

Lobster Hatchery (Bar Harbor, ME), *53*

Lobster Pot (Bristol, RI), *288*

Lobster Pot (Provincetown, MA), *229*

The Lobster Pound (Lincolnville Beach, ME), *70*

Locke-Ober (Boston, MA), *142*

Lockwood-Mathews Mansion Museum (Norwalk, CT), *34*

The Lodge and Cottages at Camden Hills (Camden, ME), *69*

Lodge at Jackson Village (Jackson, NH), *263*

The Lodge at Moosehead Lake (Greenville, ME), *80*

Log Cabin Island Inn (Bailey Island, ME), *50*

Log Cabin Restaurant and Lounge (Clinton, CT), *13*

Loines Observatory (Nantucket, MA), *205*

Lola's Southern Seafood (Oak Bluffs, MA), *202*

Londonderry Inn (Londonderry, VT), *317*

Lonesome Pine Trails (Fort Kent, ME), *77*

Long Trail, *340*

Longfellow National Historic Site (Cambridge, MA), *152*

Longfellow's (Kingfield, ME), *87*

Longfellow's Wayside Inn (Sudbury Center, MA), *241*

Longfellows Wayside Inn (Sudbury, MA), *240*

Longhorn Steakhouse (Concord, NH), *253*

Look Park (Florence, MA), *219*

Lookout Tavern (Oak Bluffs, MA), *203*

Loon Mountain Recreation Area (Lincoln, NH), *266*

Lord Jeffery Inn (Amherst, MA), *119*

365

INDEX

★
★
★
★
☆

Lord's Harborside (Wells, ME), *112*

Lorraine's Restaurant (Provincetown, MA), *229*

Lost River Gorge (North Woodstock, NH), *266*

Louis Boston (Boston, MA), *125*

Louisburg Square (Beacon Hill MA), *125*

Lovetts Inn (Franconia, NH), *256*

Lovetts Inn by Lafayette Brook (Franconia, NH), *257*

Lowell Heritage State Park (Lowell, MA), *192*

Lowell National Historical Park (Lowell, MA), *192*

The Lucerne Inn (Dedham, ME), *51*

Lucia (Boston, MA), *142*

Lumiere (West Newton, MA), *217*

Lure (Edgartown, MA), *203*

Lyceum (Salem, MA), *234*

Lyman Allyn Art Museum (New London, CT), *33*

Lyman Estate (Waltham, MA), *242*

M

M/S Mount Washington (Weirs Beach, NH), *265*

The Mabbett House (Plymouth, MA), *226*

Mabel's Lobster Claw (Kennebunkport, ME), *85*

Mad River Glen Ski Area (Waitsfield, VT), *338*

Madison Beach Hotel (Madison, CT), *27*

Mae's Café and Bakery (Bath, ME), *57*

Maggie's (Bar Harbor, ME), *55*

Mahoney's Atlantic Bar and Grill (Orleans, MA), *222*

Maine Diner (Wells, ME), *112*

The Maine Dining Room (Freeport, ME), *79*

Maine History Gallery (Portland, ME), *97*

Maine Lighthouse Museum (Rockland, ME), *104*

Maine Lobster Festival (Rockland, ME), *104*

Maine Maritime Museum (Bath, ME), *57*

Maine State Ferry Service (Bass Harbor, ME), *109*

Maine State Ferry Service (Lincolnville Beach, ME), *67*

Maine State Ferry Service (Rockland, ME), *104*

Maine State Museum (Augusta, ME), *49*

Maine Stay Bed and Breakfast (Camden, ME), *69*

Maine Stay Inn & Cottages at the, MElville Walker House (Kennebunkport, ME), *84*

Maison Suisse Inn (Northeast Harbor, ME), *91*

Makris Lobster and Steak House (Concord, NH), *254*

Mame's (Meredith, NH), *271*

Mamma Maria (Boston, MA), *142*

Manchester Designer Outlets (Manchester Center, VT), *320*

Manchester Highlands Inn (Manchester Center, VT), *321*

Manchester Historic Association Millyard Museum (Manchester, NH), *269*

Manchester View (Manchester Center, VT), *321*

Manor House Inn (Bar Harbor, ME), *55*

The Manor Inn (Gloucester, MA), *174*

Manor on Golden Pond (Holderness, NH), *262*

Manor On Golden Pond (Holderness, NH), *262*

Mansion House Hotel & Health Club (Vineyard Haven, MA), *198*

Maple Grove Farms of Vermont Factory Tours & Maple Museum (St. Johnsbury, VT), *332*

Maple Leaf Inn (Barnard, VT), *346*

Maples (Durham, NH), *255*

Maplewood Inn (Fair Haven, VT), *329*

Marble House (Newport, RI), *292*

Marblehead Inn (Marblehead, MA), *195*

Marblehead Landing (Marblehead, MA), *195*

Margarita's (Orono, ME), *97*

Maritime Aquarium at Norwalk (Norwalk, CT), *35*

Mark Twain House (Hartford, CT), *22*

Marrett House and Garden (Standish, ME), *108*

Marriott Newport (Newport, RI), *295*

Marriott Providence (Providence, RI), *299*

Marriott Springfield (Springfield, MA), *237*

Marsh-Billings-Rockefeller National Historic Park (Woodstock, VT), *344*

Martha Mary Chapel (Sudbury Center, MA), *240*

Martin House (Provincetown, MA), *229*

Martin House Inn (Nantucket, MA), *209*

Mary Baker Eddy Historic House (Rumney, NH), *278*

Masa (Boston, MA), *142*

MASS MoCA (North Adams, MA), *217*

Massachusetts Institute of Technology (Cambridge, MA), *152*

Mast Landing Sanctuary (Falmouth, ME), *78*

The Masthead Resort (Provincetown, MA), *228*

Maurice Restaurant Francais (South Paris, ME), *92*

Max Downtown (Hartford, CT), *24*

The Mayflower Inn (Washington, CT), *43*

Mayflower Society House Museum (Plymouth, MA), *224*

The Mayflower Spa (Washington, CT), *43*

MDC Memorial Hatch Shell, *125*

Meadowmere (Ogunquit, ME), *93*

Melville House (Newport, RI), *296*

Memorial Hall Museum (Deerfield, MA), *164*

Menemsha Fishing Village (Menemsha MA), *196*

Meritage (Boston, MA), *142*

Merrill Farm Resort (North Conway, NH), *276*

The Metropolitan Club (Chestnut Hill, MA), *143*

The Mews Restaurant & Café (Provincetown, MA), *229*

Miacomet Golf Course (Nantucket, MA), *205*

Michael's Harborside (Newburyport, MA), *216*

Michael's Restaurant & Pub (Stockbridge, MA), *239*

Middlebury College (Middlebury, VT), *322*

Middlebury College Snow Bowl (Middlebury, VT), *322*

Middlebury Inn (Middlebury, VT), *323*

Mid-Winter New England Surfing Championship (Narragansett, RI), *290*

Miel (Boston, MA), *143*

Migis Lodge (South Casco, ME), *108*

Mike's City Diner (Boston, MA), *143*

Miles River Country Inn Bed AND Breakfast (Hamilton, MA), *184*

The Milestone (Ogunquit, ME), *93*

Mill Hill Historic Park (Norwalk, CT), *35*

Mill Street Inn (Newport, RI), *296*

Mill's Tavern (Providence, RI), *301*

Millennium Bostonian Hotel (Boston, MA), *134*

Miller State Park (Peterborough, NH), *277*

Millstone (New London, NH), *274*

Minute Man National Historical Park (Concord, MA), *161*

Minuteman Commuter Bikeway, *126*

Mira Monte Inn & Suites (Bar Harbor, ME), *55*

Misquamicut State Beach (Westerly, RI), *303*

Mission House (Stockbridge, MA), *238*

Missisquoi National Wildlife Refuge (Swanton, VT), *336*

Mistral (Boston, MA), *143*

MIT Museum (Cambridge, MA), *153*

Moby Dick's (Wellfleet, MA), *244*

Moffatt-Ladd House (Portsmouth, NH), *279*

Mohawk Trail State Forest (Charlemont, MA), *217*

Mohegan Bluffs, *286*

Mohegan Café (Block Island, RI), *287*

Molly Stark State Park (Wilmington, VT), *342*

Molly's (Hanover, NH), *261*

Monhegan Lighthouse/Museum (Monhegan Island, ME), *90*

Monomoy National Wildlife Refuge (Chatham, MA), *157*

Montano's (North Truro, MA), *241*

Monte Cristo Cottage (New London, CT), *33*

367

INDEX

★
★
★
★
★

Monument Mountain Motel (Great Barrington, MA), *175*

Monument to Paul Bunyan (Bangor, ME), *51*

Moose Brook State Park (Gorham, NH), *258*

Moosehead Marine Museum (Greenville, ME), *80*

Moosehead Motel (Rockwood, ME), *106*

Moosehorn National Wildlife Refuge (Calais, ME), *66*

Morgan House (Lee, MA), *185*

Morrill Place (Newburyport, MA), *215*

Morse Farm (Montpelier, VT), *324*

Moses Nickerson House Inn (Chatham, MA), *159*

Mostly Hall (Falmouth, MA), *172*

Mother Church, the First Church of Christ, Scientist Christian Science Center (Boston, MA), *126*

Mount Ascutney State Park (Vermon, VT), *343*

Mount Blue State Park (Weld, ME), *106*

Mount Cranmore, *274*

Mount Desert Oceanarium (Southwest Harbor, ME), *109*

Mount Greylock State Reservation (North Adams, MA), *218*

Mount Independence (Orwell, VT), *308*

Mount Mansfield Gondola (Stowe, VT), *333*

Mount Mansfield State Forest, *333*

Mount Snow Ski Area (West Dover, VT), *341*

Mount Washington Auto Road (Gorham, NH), *272*

Mount Washington Hotel (Bretton Woods, NH), *251*

Mount Washington Summit Museum (Top of Mount Washington, NH), *272*

Mountain Club on Loon (Lincoln, NH), *267*

Mountain Top Inn (Chittenden, VT), *329*

Mt. Madison Motel (Gorham, NH), *259*

Munroe Tavern (Lexington, MA), *191*

Murray's Toggery (Nantucket, MA), *205*

Museum at the John Fitzgerald Kennedy Library, *126*

Museum of Afro American History (Boston, MA), *126*

Museum of Art (Northampton, MA), *219*

Museum of Connecticut History (Hartford, CT), *22*

Museum of Fine Arts (Boston, MA), *126*

Museum of Natural History and Cormack Planetarium (Providence, RI), *298*

Museum of New Hampshire History (Concord, NH), *252*

Museum of Science (Boston, MA), *126*

Music Mountain Summer Music Festival (Falls Village, CT), *25*

Myles Standish State Forest (South Carver, MA), *224*

Mystic Aquarium (Mystic, CT), *28*

Mystic Marriott Hotel and Spa (Groton, CT), *20*

Mystic Pizza (Mystic, CT), *30*

Mystic Seaport (Mystic, CT), *29*

Mytoi (Chappaquiddick, MA), *196*

N

Naked Oyster (Hyannis, MA), *182*

Nantucket Arts Festival, *207*

Nantucket Film Festival, *207*

Nantucket Historical Association Whaling Museum (Nanutcket, MA), *206*

Nantucket Inn (Nantucket, MA), *208*

Nantucket Lobster Trap (Nantucket, MA), *211*

Nantucket Maria Mitchell Association (Nantucket, MA), *206*

Nantucket Town (Nantucket, MA), *206*

Nantucket Wine Festival, *208*

Napi's (Provincetown, MA), *229*

The Nashua House Hotel (Oak Bluffs, MA), *199*

Naswa Beach Bar and Grill (Laconia, NH), *266*

Natalie's (Camden, ME), *70*

Nathaniel Hempstead House (New London, CT), *33*

National Heritage Museum (Lexington, MA), *191*

National Monument to the Forefathers (Plymouth, MA), *225*

Natural Bridge State Park, (North Adams), *218*

Naumkeag (Stockbridge, MA), *238*

Nauset Beach (Orleans, MA), *221*

Nauset Beach Club Restaurant (East Orleans, MA), *222*

Nauset Knoll Motor Lodge (East Orleans, MA), *221*

Nautilus Motor Inn (Woods Hole, MA), *170*

Neptune Oyster (Boston, MA), *143*

Nestlenook Farm Resort (Jackson, NH), *264*

New Bedford Whaling Museum (New Bedford, MA), *213*

New England Air Museum (Windsor Locks, CT), *45*

New England Aquarium (Boston, MA), *127*

New England Aquarium Whale Watches (Boston, MA), *127*

New England Fire & History Museum (Brewster, MA), *148*

New England Maple Museum (Pittsford, VT), *328*

New England Patriots (Foxboro, MA), *173*

New England Quilt Museum (Lowell, MA), *192*

New England Revolution (Foxboro, MA), *173*

New England Ski Museum (Franconia, NH), *256*

New Hampshire Highland Games, *266*

New Harbor, *286*

New Haven Green (New Haven, CT), *31*

New Haven Symphony Orchestra (New Haven, CT), *32*

New London Inn (New London, NH), *273*

New London Inn (New London, NH), *274*

New Rivers (Providence, RI), *301*

New Seabury Resort and Conference Center (New Seabury, MA), *171*

New Year's Eve Portland (Portland, ME), *98*

Newbury Guest House (Boston, MA), *136*

Newbury Street (Boston, MA), *126*

Newcastle Inn (Newcastle, ME), *74*

The Newes from America (Edgartown, MA), *203*

Newick's Seafood (Dover, NH), *255*

Newick's Seafood (South Portland, ME), *101*

Newport Art Museum and Art Association (Newport, RI), *292*

Newport Harbor Hotel and Marina (Newport, RI), *296*

Newport Music Festival (Newport, RI), *294*

Newport Winter Festival (Newport, RI), *294*

Nichols House Museum (Boston, MA), *127*

Nickels-Sortwell House (Wiscasset, ME), *113*

Nickerson State Park (Brewster, MA), *148*

The Nimrod (Falmouth, MA), *172*

Nine Zero Hotel (Boston, MA), *134*

Nistico's Red Barn (Westport, CT), *44*

No. 9 Park (Boston, MA), *143*

No. Five-O (Ogunquit, ME), *94*

Noah Webster Foundation and Historical Society (West Hartford, CT), *22*

Noden-Reed House & Barn (Windsor Locks, CT), *45*

Nonantum Resort (Kennebunkport, ME), *83*

Norman Rockwell Exhibition (Arlington, VT), *305*

Norman Rockwell Museum (Rutland, VT), *328*

Norman Rockwell Museum (Stockbridge, MA), *238*

Norseman Inn (Bethel, ME), *59*

North Conway Grand Hotel (North Conway, NH), *275*

North Conway Mountain Inn (North Conway, NH), *275*

North Hero House (North Hero, VT), *327*

North Hero House Inn (North Hero, VT), *327*

North Hero State Park (North Hero, VT), *326*

North Light, *286*

Northern Outdoors, Inc. (Rockwood, ME), *106*

Northern Zermatt Inn & Motel (Twin Mountain, NH), *282*

Northfield Inn (Northfield, VT), *325*

Norumbega Inn (Camden, ME), *70*

★
★
★
★
★

Nunan's Lobster Hut (Kennebunkport, ME), 85

Nylander Museum (Caribou, ME), 71

O

o's at the Inn at Blueberry Hill (Chilmark, MA), 203

Oak Bluffs, 197

The Oak House (Oak Bluffs, MA), 200

The Oak Room (Boston, MA), 144

Oarweed Cove (Ogunquit, ME), 95

Ocean Beach Park (New London, CT), 33

Ocean Edge Golf Course (Brewster, MA), 148

Ocean Edge Resort (Brewster, MA), 148

Ocean View Inn and Resort (Gloucester, MA), 174

Oceanna (New Bedford, MA), 214

Oceanside Grille at the Brunswick (Old Orchard Beach, ME), 96

Octagon (Groton, CT), 21

October Mountain State Forest (Lee, MA), 184

Ogunquit Lobster Pound (Ogunquit, ME), 95

Ogunquit Museum of American Art (Ogunquit, ME), 92

Ogunquit Playhouse (Northeast Harbor, ME), 92

Oktoberfest & Craft Show (West Dover, VT), 341

Old Burying Ground (Bennington, VT), 306

Old Castle (Rockport, MA), 230

Old First Church (Old Bennington, VT), 307

Old Fort Inn (Kennebunkport, ME), 84

Old Fort Western (Augusta, ME), 49

Old Gaol (York, ME), 115

Old Harbor Inn (Chatham, MA), 159

Old Jailhouse Tavern (Orleans, MA), 222

Old Lyme Inn (Old Lyme, CT), 38

Old Man of the Mountain Historic Site (Notch State Parkway, NH), 258

Old Manse (Concord, MA), 161

The Old Manse Inn (Brewster, MA), 149

Old Mill (Nantucket, MA), 206

The Old Mill (South Egremont, MA), 176

The Old Mystic Inn (Old Mystic, CT), 30

Old Newfane Inn (Newfane, VT), 326

Old Newgate Prison (East Granby, CT), 45

Old North Church (Boston, MA), 127

Old Port Festival (Portland, ME), 98

Old Sea Pines Inn (Brewster, MA), 149

Old South Church (Boston, MA), 127

Old South Meeting House (Boston, MA), 127

Old Sow Whirlpool, 75

Old State House (Hartford, CT), 23

Old State House (Providence, RI), 298

Old State House/Site of Boston Massacre (Boston, MA), 128

Old Stone Mill (Newport, RI), 293

The Old Tavern at Grafton (Grafton, VT), 313

Old Tavern At Grafton (Grafton, VT), 314

Old Village Inn (Ogunquit, ME), 95

Old Whaling Church (Edgartown, MA), 197

Old York Historical Society (York, ME), 115

Olde Orchard Inn (Moultonborough, NH), 271

Oleana (Cambridge, MA), 156

Omni New Haven Hotel (New Haven, CT), 32

Omni Parker House (Boston, MA), 134

Oran Mor (Nantucket, MA), 212

Orchard House (Concord, MA), 161

The Orchards (Williamstown, MA), 245

Original Gourmet Brunch (Hyannis, MA), 182

Osterville Historical Society Museum (Osterville, MA), 179

Otis Ridge (Otis, MA), 175

Outermost Inn (Aquinnah, MA), 203

Outermost Inn (Chilmark, MA), 200

Oxford House Inn (Fryeburg, ME), 72

Oxford House Inn (Fryeburg, ME), 72

Oyster Festival (East Norwalk, CT), 35

P

The Paddock (Hyannis, MA), 182

The Palm (Boston, MA), *144*

Palmer House (Manchester Center, VT), *321*

The Palmer House Inn (Falmouth, MA), *172*

Pamola Motor Lodge (Millinocket, ME), *90*

Panda House Chinese Restaurant (Lenox, MA), *190*

Pane E Vino (Providence, RI), *301*

The Paper House (Rockport, MA), *230*

Pardee-Morris House (New Haven, CT), *31*

Park Kitchen (Portland, ME), *101*

Park Street Church (Boston, MA), *128*

Parker House Inn (Quechee, VT), *346*

Parker River National Wildlife Refuge (Newburyport, MA), *215*

Parker's (Boston, MA), *144*

Park-McCullough House Museum (North Bennington, VT), *307*

The Parsonage Inn (East Orleans, MA), *221*

Passamaquoddy Indian Reservation (Perry, ME), *75*

Pasta Nostra (South Norwalk, CT), *36*

Pate's (Chatham, MA), *159*

Patriot's Day Parade Bn (Concord, MA), *162*

Paul Revere House (Boston, MA), *128*

Pauline's (South Burlington, VT), *312*

Peabody Museum & Essex Institute (Salem, MA), *232*

Peabody Museum (Andover, MA), *119*

Peabody Museum of Archaeology and Ethnology (Cambridge, MA), *153*

Peabody Museum of Natural History (New Haven, CT), *32*

The Pearl (Nantucket, MA), *212*

Peary-MacMillan Arctic Museum (Brunswick, ME), *64*

Pegleg Restaurant and Inn (Rockport, MA), *231*

Peirce-Nichols House (Salem, MA), *233*

Pejepscot Historical Society Museum (Brunswick, ME), *65*

Peking Tom's (Boston, MA), *144*

Pellino's (Marblehead, MA), *195*

Pemaquid Point Lighthouse Park (New Harbor, ME), *74*

Pennesseewassee Lake, *91*

The Penny House Inn (Eastham, MA), *168*

Penobscot Bay Inn (Belfast, ME), *58*

Penobscot Marine Museum (Searsport, ME), *108*

Pentagoet Inn (Castine, ME), *66*

Peppercorn's Grill (Hartford, CT), *24*

Pequot Hotel (Oak Bluffs, MA), *200*

Peter Ott's (Camden, ME), *70*

Peterborough Historical Society (Peterborough, NH), *277*

Phillips andover Academy (Andover, MA), *119*

Phillips Exeter Academy (Exeter, NH), *256*

Pho Republique (Boston, MA), *144*

Pico Alpine Slide and Scenic Chairlift (Killington, VT), *315*

The Pier, *95*

Pierce Manse (Concord, NH), *252*

Pilgrim Hall Museum (Plymouth, MA), *225*

Pilgrim House (Newport, RI), *296*

Pilgrim Monument & Museum (Provincetown, MA), *227*

Pilgrims Inn (Deer Isle, ME), *75*

The Pine Hill Inn (Ogunquit, ME), *93*

Pioneer Village: Salem in 1630 (Salem, MA), *233*

The Pitcher Inn (Warren, VT), *339*

Pleasant Bay Village Resort (Chatham, MA), *158*

Pleasant Valley Wildlife Sanctuary (Lenox, MA), *186*

Plimoth Plantation/ Mayflower II (Plymouth, MA), *225*

Plymouth Colony Winery (Plymouth, MA), *225*

Point Judith (Narragansett, RI), *289*

Polly's Pancake Parlor (Sugar Hill, NH), *257*

Pomegranate Inn (Portland, ME), *101*

Pond Ridge Motel (Woodstock, VT), *345*

Popham Colony, *57*

Pops by the Sea (Hyannis, MA), *180*

The Porches Inn (North Adams, MA), *218*

371

INDEX

★
★
★
★
☆

The Port Inn (Portsmouth, NH), *280*

Portland Harbor Hotel (Portland, ME), *100*

Portland Head Lighthouse Museum (Cape Elizabeth, ME), *97*

Portland Marriott at Sable Oaks (South Portland, ME), *100*

Portland Museum of Art (Portland, ME), *97*

Portland Observatory (Portland, ME), *98*

Portland Regency Hotel & Spa (Portland, ME), *100*

Pot Au Feu (Providence, RI), *301*

Pownalborough Courthouse (Dresden, ME), *113*

President Calvin Coolidge Homestead (Plymouth Notch, VT), *327*

Primo (Rockland, ME), *105*

Prince and the Pauper (Woodstock, VT), *347*

Providence Athenaeum Library (Providence, RI), *298*

Providence Children's Museum, *298*

Provincetown Art Association & Museum (Provincetown, MA), *227*

Provincetown Ferry (Plymouth, MA), *225*

Provincetown Inn (Provincetown, MA), *228*

Provincetown Portuguese Festival (Provincetown, MA), *227*

The Pub (Keene, NH), *265*

Puritan Backroom (Manchester, NH), *270*

Putnam Cottage/Knapp Tavern (Greenwich, CT), *18*

Quality Inn (Bar Harbor, ME), *54*

Quality Inn (Brattleboro, VT), *309*

Quality Inn (Somerset, MA), *169*

Quality Inn and Suites (Lexington, MA), *191*

Quality Inn Bedford (Bedford, NH), *270*

Quality Inn & Suites (Augusta, ME), *50*

Quechee Inn at Marshland Farm (Quechee, VT), *345*, *347*

Queen Anne Inn (Chatham, MA), *158*

Quisisana Lodge (Center Lovell, ME), *72*

R

Rabbit Hill (Lower Waterford, VT), *333*

Rabbit Hill Inn (Lower Waterford, VT), *333*

Race Brook Lodge (Sheffield, MA), *176*

Rachel Carson National Wildlife Refuge (Wells, ME), *111*

Rackliffe Pottery (Blue Hill, ME), *60*

Radcliffe College's Schlesinger Library Culinary Collection (Cambridge, MA), *153*

Radisson Airport Hotel (Warwick, RI), *302*

Radisson Hotel and Suites Chelmsford (Chelmsford, MA), *193*

Radisson Hotel Manchester (Manchester, NH), *270*

Radisson Hotel Marlborough (Marlborough, MA), *240*

Radisson Hotel New London (New London, CT), *34*

Radisson Hotel Plymouth Harbor (Plymouth, MA), *226*

Radisson Hotel Providence Harbor (Providence, RI), *300*

Radius (Boston, MA), *144*

Rafael Osona Auctions (Nantucket, MA), *206*

Ralph Waldo Emerson House (Concord, MA), *161*

Ramada Inn (Boston, MA), *134*

Ramada Inn (Falmouth, MA), *171*

Ramada Inn (Lewiston, ME), *89*

Rangeley Inn (Rangeley, ME), *103*

Rangeley Lake State Park (Rangeley, ME), *103*

Reading Room (Bar Harbor, ME), *55*

Rebecca Nurse Homestead (Danvers, MA), *163*

Red Blazer Restaurant (Concord, NH), *254*

Red Clover (Mendon, VT), *317*

Red Clover Inn (Mendon, VT), *316*

The Red Fez (Boston, MA), *145*

Red Horse Inn (Falmouth, MA), *171*

Red Inn Restaurant (Provincetown, MA), *229*

Red Jacket Beach (South Yarmouth, MA), *248*

The Red Lion (Stockbridge, MA), *239*

The Red Lion Inn (Stockbridge, MA), *238*

Red Parka Pub (Glen, NH), *264*

Red Pheasant Inn (Dennis, MA), *167*

Redington Museum (Waterville, ME), *110*

Redwood Library and Athenaeum (Newport, RI), *293*

Reenactment of the Battle of Lexington and Concord (Lexington, MA), *191*

The Regatta of Cotuit (Cotuit, MA), *182*

Reluctant Panther Inn and Restaurant (Manchester, VT), *321*

Reno's (Caribou, ME), *72*

Restaurant Bricco (West Hartford, CT), *24*

Reverend Dan Foster House & Old Forge (Weathersfield, VT), *331*

Rhode Island Quahog Company (Newport, RI), *296*

Rhode Island School of Design (Providence, RI), *298*

Rhode Island State House (Providence, RI), *299*

Rhumb Line Motor Lodge (Kennebunkport, ME), *83*

Rialto (Cambridge, MA), *156*

Ribolita (Portland, ME), *102*

Richard Sparrow House (Plymouth, MA), *225*

Ristorante Toscano (Boston, MA), *145*

The Ritz-Carlton, Boston Common (Boston, MA), *135*

Riverside (Ogunquit, ME), *93*

Riverway Lobster House (South Yarmouth, MA), *249*

Riviera Beach Resort (South Yarmouth, MA), *248*

Road Racing Classic (Lakeville, CT), *25*

Roadhouse Café (Hyannis, MA), *182*

Robert Frost Farm (Derry, NH), *281*

Roberts House Inn (Nantucket, MA), *209*

Rockport Chamber Music Festival (Rockport, MA), *230*

Rockwell House Inn (Bristol, RI), *288*

Rocky Shores Inn & Cottages (Rockport, MA), *231*

Roger Williams National Memorial (Providence, RI), *299*

Roger Williams Park (Providence, RI), *299*

Roger Williams Park Zoo (Providence, RI), *299*

Rokeby Museum (Ferrisburgh, VT), *337*

The Roma Café (Portland, ME), *102*

Rookwood Inn (Lenox, MA), *188*

Roosevelt Campobello International Park (New Brunswick, ME), *89*

Ropes Mansion and Garden (Salem, MA), *233*

Ropewalk (Nantucket, MA), *212*

Rosa Flamingos (Bethlehem, NH), *269*

Rosecliff (Newport, RI), *293*

Rotch-Jones-Duff House and Garden Museum (New Bedford, MA), *213*

Round Hill Highland Games (Norwalk, CT), *35*

Route 66 (Bar Harbor, ME), *56*

Rowantrees Pottery (Union, ME), *60*

Royal Anchor Resort (Old Orchard Beach, ME), *96*

Royal Lippizan Stallions of Austria (North Hero, VT), *326*

Royal Mohegan Burial Grounds (Norwich, CT), *36*

Royal River Grillhouse (Yarmouth, ME), *114*

Royal Sonesta Hotel Boston (Cambridge, MA), *155*

Royalsborough Inn at Bagley House (Durham, ME), *79*

Royalty Inn (Gorham, NH), *259*

Rubin's Kosher Delicatessen (Brookline, MA), *151*

Rundlet-May House (Portsmouth, NH), *279*

S

S. S. Milton (Bethel, ME), *60*

S. W. Swan Bistro (Ogunquit, ME), *95*

Sage (Boston, MA), *145*

Sage American Bar & Grill (Chester, CT), *16*

Sailfest (New London, CT), *34*

373

INDEX

★
★
★
★

Saint-Gaudens National Historic Site (Cornish, NH), *260*

Sal's Just Pizza (Concord, NH), *254*

Sal's Place (Provincetown, MA), *229*

Salem Inn (Salem, MA), *234*

Salem Maritime National Historic Site (Salem, MA), *233*

Salem Witch Museum (Salem, MA), *233*

Salisbury Mansion (Worcester, MA), *246*

Salts (Cambridge, MA), *157*

Sam Diego's (Hyannis, MA), *183*

Samoset Resort (Rockport, ME), *105*

Samuel Adams Brewery (Boston, MA), *128*

Samuel Whitehorne House (Newport, RI), *293*

The Sandpiper Beach Inn (Harwich Port, MA), *177*

Sandrine's (Cambridge, MA), *157*

Sandwich Glass Museum (Sandwich, MA), *234*

Sandy Bay Historical Society & Museums (Rockport, MA), *230*

Santarella (Tyringham, MA), *184*

Sarah Orne Jewett House (South Berwick, ME), *87*

Sargent House Museum (Gloucester, MA), *174*

Saybrook Point Inn and Spa (Old Saybrook, CT), *39*

Sayward-Wheeler House (York Harbor, ME), *115*

Scarborough Marsh Audubon Center (Scarborough, ME), *107*

Scargo Café (Dennis, MA), *167*

School House (Kennebunkport, ME), *82*

Schooner Days & North Atlantic Blues Festival, *104*

Science Enrichment Encounters Museum (Manchester, NH), *269*

Scott Covered bridge, (Townshend), *325*

Sea Breeze Inn (Hyannis, MA), *181*

Sea Crest Resort (North Falmouth, MA), *171*

Seacrest Manor (Rockport, MA), *230*

Seadar Inn (Harwich Port, MA), *178*

SeaGrille (Nantucket, MA), *212*

Seagull Inn (Marblehead, MA), *195*

Seamen's Bethel (New Bedford, MA), *214*

Seamen's Inne (Mystic, CT), *30*

Seaport Hotel (Boston, MA), *135*

Seashore Park Motor Inn (Orleans, MA), *221*

Seasons (Bar Harbor, ME), *56*

Seasons Eatery (Oak Bluffs, MA), *203*

Seaward Inn & Cottages (Rockport, MA), *231*

Senor Panchos (Litchfield, CT), *26*

Sesuit Harbor (East Dennis, MA), *166*

Seven Sea Street Inn (Nantucket, MA), *209*

Shady Nook Inn & Motel (Sandwich, MA), *235*

Shakespeare & Company (Lenox, MA), *186*

Shakespeare's Inn (Twin Mountain, NH), *282*

Shaw Perkins Mansion (New London, CT), *34*

Shawnee Peak Ski Area (Bridgton, ME), *64*

Shelburne Farms (Shelburne, VT), *329*

Shelburne Museum (Shelburne, VT), *330*

Shelter Harbor Inn (Westerly, RI), *303*

Sheraton Boston Hotel (Boston, MA), *135*

Sheraton Bradley Airport Hotel (Windsor Locks, CT), *46*

Sheraton Braintree Hotel (Braintree, MA), *147*

Sheraton Burlington Hotel and Conference Center (South Burlington, VT), *311*

Sheraton Danbury Hotel (Danbury, CT), *14*

Sheraton Ferncroft Resort (Danvers, MA), *164*

Sheraton Harborside Hotel Portsmouth (Portsmouth, NH), *280*

Sheraton Hartford Hotel (East Hartford, CT), *23*

Sheraton Lexington Inn (Lexington, MA), *191*

Sheraton Nashua Hotel (Nashua, NH), *273*

Sheraton Newton Hotel (Newton, MA), *217*

Sheraton Springfield Monarch Place Hotel (Springfield, MA), *237*

Sheraton Stamford Hotel (Stamford, CT), *41*

Sherburne Inn (Nantucket, MA), *210*

Sherburne-Killington Motel (Killington, VT), *316*

Shimano NORBA National Mountain Bike Series Finals (West Dover, VT), *341*

Ship's Knees Inn (East Orleans, MA), *221*

Ships Inn (Nantucket, MA), *210*

The Shire Riverview (Woodstock, VT), *345*

The Shops at the Prudential Center (Boston, MA), *128*

Shore Acres Inn (North Hero, VT), *327*

Siasconset Village (East end of Nantucket Island MA), *206*

Sidewalk Art Show (Portland, ME), *98*

Sienna (Deerfield, MA), *165*

Silks (Tyngsboro, MA), *194*

Silver Lake State Park (Hollis, NH), *272*

Silvermine Tavern (Norwalk, CT), *36*

The Silvermine Tavern (Norwalk, CT), *36*

Simon Pearce (Quechee, VT), *347*

Sinclair Inn Bed & Breakfast (Jericho, VT), *314*

Sir Cricket's Fish and Chips (Orleans, MA), *222*

Sise Inn (Portsmouth, NH), *280*

Ski Butternut (Great Barrington, MA), *175*

Skipper Restaurant (South Yarmouth, MA), *249*

Skolfield-Whittier House (Brunswick, ME), *65*

Skowhegan State Fair (Skowhegan, ME), *109*

Sleepy Hollow Cemetery (Concord; MA), *162*

Smith College (Northampton, MA), *219*

Smugglers' Notch (Jeffersonville, VT), *314*

Smugglers' Notch Resort (Jeffersonville, VT), *314*

Snowhill at Eastman Ski Area (Grantham, NH), *281*

Snowvillage Inn (Snowville, NH), *276*

Snowy Owl Inn (Waterville Valley, NH), *283*

Snug Cottage (Provincetown, MA), *228*

Somerset House (Provincetown, MA), *228*

Something Natural (Nantucket, MA), *206*

SoNo Arts Celebration (South Norwalk, CT), *35*

Sonsie (Boston, MA), *145*

Sorrelina (Boston, MA), *145*

Soundings Seaside Resort (Dennisport, MA), *166*

South County Museum (Narragansett, RI), *289*

South Shire Inn (Bennington, VT), *307*

The Spa at Norwich Inn (Norwich, CT), *37*

Spa at White Barn Inn (Kennebunkport, ME), *85*

Spa by the Sea (Nantucket, MA), *213*

Spencer's (Great Barrington, MA), *176*

Spooner House (Plymouth, MA), *225*

Spring Festival of Historic Houses (Providence, RI), *299*

Spring Hill Motor Lodge (East Sandwich, MA), *235*

Spring House (Block Island, RI), *287*

Springfield Armory National Historic Site (Springfield, MA), *236*

Springfield Art and Historical Society (Springfield, VT), *331*

Springfield Museums at the Quadrangle (Springfield, MA), *236*

Spruce Point Inn (Boothbay Harbor, ME), *61*

Squam Lakes Natural Science Center (Holderness, NH), *261*

Square Rigger (Edgartown, MA), *203*

Squire Tarbox Inn (Westport Island, ME), *113*

St. Croix Island International Historic Site (St. Croix River; accessible only by boat, ME), *66*

St. Johnsbury Town Band (St. Johnsbury, VT), *332*

Stage Neck Inn (York Harbor, ME), *115*

Stamford Marriott Hotel & Spa (Stamford, CT), *41*

Stanley-Whitman House (Farmington, CT), *16*

Stanton House (Clinton, CT), *13*

Stanton House Inn (Greenwich, CT), *19*

Stanwood Sanctuary (Birdsacre) and

Homestead Museum (Ellsworth, ME), *76*

State Capitol (Hartford, CT), *23*

State House (Augusta, ME), *49*

State House (Boston, MA), *128*

State House (Concord, NH), *253*

State House (Montpelier, VT), *324*

The Steak Place at Tucker Hill (Waitsfield, VT), *338*

Steakhouse (Wells, ME), *112*

Steamship Authority (Hyannis, MA), *179*

Stephen A. Douglas Birthplace (Brandon, VT), *308*

Sterling and Francine Clark Art Institute (Williamstown, MA), *244*

Stone Hearth Inn (Chester, VT), *332*

Stone Hill Inn (Stowe, VT), *335*

Stonehedge Inn (Tyngsboro, MA), *193*

Stonehenge (Ridgefield, CT), *40*

Stonehenge Inn (Ridgefield, CT), *40*

Stonewell (Farmington, CT), *17*

Stonybrook Motel & Lodge (Franconia, NH), *257*

Storrowton Village (West Springfield, MA), *236*

Storybook Resort Inn (Glen, NH), *263*

Stowe Mountain Resort (Stowe, VT), *334*

Stoweflake Balloon Festival (Stowe, VT), *334*

Stoweflake Mountain Resort & Spa (Stowe, VT), *335*

The Straight Wharf (Nantucket MA), *207*

Stratton Mountain (Londonderry, VT), *336*

Strawbery Banke Museum (Portsmouth, NH), *279*

Street & Co. (Portland, ME), *102*

Striped Bass & Bluefish Derby (Edgartown, MA), *198*

Stripers (Kennebunkport, ME), *85*

Strong House Inn (Vergennes, VT), *337*

Strong Wings Summer Camp (Nantucket, MA), *207*

Student Prince & Fort (Springfield, MA), *237*

Suffolk Downs (East Boston, MA), *129*

Sugar Hill Inn (Franconia, NH), *257*

Sugarbush Inn (Warren, VT), *339*

Sugarbush Resort (Warren, VT), *339*

Sugarloaf Inn (Kingfield, ME), *87*

Sugarloaf/USA Ski Area (Kingfield, ME), *86*

Sugartree Inn (Warren, VT), *339*

Suicide Six Ski Area (Woodstock, VT), *344*

Sullivan Station Restaurant (Lee, MA), *186*

Summer House (Nantucket, MA), *212*

The Summer White House (Lenox, MA), *188*

Summit Lodge (Killington, VT), *316*

Sunday River Ski Resort (Bethel, ME), *59*

The Sunken Ship (Nantucket, MA), *207*

Sunset Hill House–A Grand Inn (Sugar Hill, NH), *257*

Swan River Seafood (Dennisport, MA), *167*

Sweet Life Café (Oak Bluffs, MA), *203*

Swift House Inn (Middlebury, VT), *323*

Swiss Chalets Village Inn (Intervale, NH), *275*

Swiss Inn (Londonderry, VT), *317*

T

The Taggart House (Stockbridge, MA), *239*

Taj Boston (Boston, MA), *135*

Tanglewood (Lenox, MA), *186*

Tantaquidgeon Indian Museum (Uncasville, CT), *37*

Tapeo (Boston, MA), *145*

Tapping Reeve House (Litchfield, CT), *26*

Taranta (Boston, MA), *145*

Taste of Greater Danbury (Danbury, CT), *14*

Taste of Maine (Woolwich, ME), *57*

Tate House (Portland, ME), *98*

Ten Center Street (Newburyport, MA), *216*

Terra Ristorante Italiano (Greenwich, CT), *19*

The Terrace By The Sea (Ogunquit, ME), *93*

Terramia (Boston, MA), *146*

That Little Italian Restaurant (Greenwich, CT), *19*

Thatcher Brook Inn (Waterbury, VT), *341*

Thayer's Inn (Littleton, NH), *268*

Thomas Griswold House Museum (Guilford, CT), *21*

Thomas Henkelmann (Greenwich, CT), *20*

Thomas Mott Alburg Homestead Bed AND Breakfast (Alburg, VT), *327*

Thomas Point Beach (Brunswick, ME), *65*

Thomas Waterman Wood Art Gallery (Montpelier, VT), *324*

Thorncroft Inn (Vineyard Haven, MA), *200*

Thornewood Inn & Restaurant (Great Barrington, MA), *176*

Thornhedge Inn (Bar Harbor, ME), *55*

Three Chimneys (New Haven, CT), *32*

Three Seasons Motor Lodge (Dennisport, MA), *166*

Three-County Fair (Northampton, MA), *219*

Tides Inn by the Sea (Kennebunkport, ME), *84*

Todd House (Eastport, ME), *76*

Top of the Hub (Boston, MA), *146*

Topnotch Resort and Spa (Stowe, VT), *335*

Topper's (Nantucket, MA), *212*

Topsmead State Forest (Litchfield, CT), *26*

Touro Synagogue National Historic Site (Newport, RI), *293*

Tower Suites Motel (Guilford, CT), *21*

The Towers (Narragansett, RI), *290*

Towneplace Suites By Marriott Portland Scarborough (Scarborough, ME), *107*

Townshend State Forest (Townshend, VT), *325*

Trail's End - A Country Inn (Wilmington, VT), *343*

Trapp Family Lodge (Stowe, VT), *335*

Tremont 647/Sister Sorel (Boston, MA), *146*

Trinity Church (Boston, MA), *129*

Trinity Church (Newport, RI), *293*

Troquet (Boston, MA), *146*

Truants Taverne (North Woodstock, NH), *267*

Trumbull Marriott Merritt Parkway (Trumbull, CT), *12*

Truro Historical Society Museum (North Truro, MA), *241*

The Tuck Inn Bed and Breakfast (Rockport, MA), *231*

Tuck Memorial Museum (Hampton, NH), *259*

Tucker Hill Inn (Waitsfield, VT), *338*

Tugboat Inn (Boothbay Harbor, ME), *61*

Turk's Head Motor Inn (Rockport, MA), *231*

Tuscan Grill (Waltham, MA), *243*

Twenty-Eight Atlantic (Chatham, MA), *159*

Twin Farms (Barnard, VT), *345*

Two Steps Downtown Grille (Danbury, CT), *15*

Two-Cent Footbridge (Waterville, ME), *110*

Tyler Place Family Resort (Highgate Springs, VT), *336*

Typhoon! On Broadway (Portland, ME), *102*

U

Union Bar and Grille (Boston, MA), *146*

Union Oyster House (Boston, MA), *146*

University of Hartford (West Hartford, CT), *23*

University of Maine-Orono (Orono, ME), *96*

University of Massachusetts (Amherst, MA), *118*

University of Vermont (Burlington, VT), *310*

US Coast Guard Academy (New London, CT), *34*

USS Constitution (Boston, MA), *129*

V

Valley Inn & Tavern (Waterville Valley, NH), *284*

Valley Railroad (Essex, CT), *15*

Van Rensselaer's Restaurant & Raw Bar (South Wellfleet, MA), *244*

Vanessa Noel Hotel (Nantucket, MA), *210*

Venice Restaurant (Ridgefield, CT), *41*

Vermont Arts & Fine Crafts Festival, *336*

Vermont Historical Society Museum (Montpelier, VT), *324*

Vermont Inn (Killington, VT), *316*

377

INDEX

Vermont Inn (Killington, VT), *317*

Vermont Institute of Natural Science (Quechee, VT), *344*

Vermont Mozart Festival (Burlington, VT), *310*

Vermont State Craft Center at Frog Hollow (Middlebury, VT), *323*

Vermont State Craft Center at Windsor House (Windsor, VT), *343*

Vermont Teddy Bear Company (Shelburne, VT), *330*

Vermont Wildflower Farm (Shelburne, VT), *330*

Via Matta (Boston, MA), *146*

Victoria Mansion (Portland, ME), *98*

Victoria Station (Salem, MA), *234*

The Victorian By The Sea (Lincolnville, ME), *70*

Villa Bed & Breakfast (Westerly, RI), *303*

Village By The Sea (Wells, ME), *112*

The Village Inn (Lenox, MA), *188*

Village Inn (Sandwich, MA), *235*

Village Restaurant (Litchfield, CT), *26*

Vincent House (Edgartown, MA), *197*

Vincent's (Camden, ME), *71*

Vines (Groton, CT), *21*

Vineyard Haven and Edgartown Shopping, *197*

Vineyard Museum (Edgartown, MA), *197*

Vining's Bistro (Chatham, MA), *160*

W

Wadsworth Atheneum Museum of Art (Hartford, CT), *23*

Wadsworth-Longfellow House (Portland, ME), *98*

The Waitsfield Inn (Waitsfield, VT), *338*

Wake Robin Inn (Lakeville, CT), *25*

Wakefield Rotary Balloon Festival (Kingston, RI), *289*

Walden Pond State Reservation (Concord, MA), *162*

Walking Tour of Historic Apponaug Village (Warwick, RI), *302*

Walter's Café (Portland, ME), *102*

Wang Theater/The Shubert Theater (Boston, MA), *129*

Wanton-Lyman-Hazard House (Newport, RI), *293*

Warner House (Portsmouth, NH), *280*

Warren's Lobster House (Kittery, ME), *88*

Warwick Heritage Festival (Warwick, RI), *302*

Washington Square Tavern (Brookline, MA), *151*

Watch Hill (Westerly, RI), *303*

Watch Hill Lighthouse (Westerly, RI), *303*

Water Street Grill (Williamstown, MA), *246*

Water's Edge Resort and Conference Center (Westbrook, CT), *39*

WaterFire (Providence, RI), *299*

Waterford Inne (Waterford, ME), *91*

Waterfront (Camden, ME), *71*

Watermark Inn (Provincetown, MA), *228*

Watership Inn (Provincetown, MA), *228*

Waterville Valley Ski Area (Waterville Valley, NH), *283*

The Wauwinet (Nantucket, MA), *208*

Waybury Inn (East Middlebury, VT), *323*

Wayside (Bethlehem, NH), *268*

Wayside (Concord; MA), *162*

Weathervane (Waterville, ME), *111*

Webb-Deane-Stevens Museum (Wethersfield, CT), *45*

Webster Cottage (Hanover, NH), *261*

Wellfleet Bay Wildlife Sanctuary (South Wellfleet, MA), *243*

Wellfleet Drive-In Theater (Wellfleet, MA), *243*

Wellfleet Motel & Lodge (South Wellfleet, MA), *243*

Wells Natural Estuarine Research Reserve (Wells, ME), *111*

Wendell Gilley Museum (Southwest Harbor, ME), *109*

Wentworth Resort Hotel (Jackson, NH), *264*

Wentworth-Gardner House (Portsmouth, NH), *280*

Wequassett Inn (Chatham, MA), *158*

West Creek Café (Nantucket, MA), *213*

West Dover Inn (West Dover, VT), *342*

378

INDEX

★
★
★
★
★

West Lane Inn (Ridgefield, CT), *40*

West Parish Meetinghouse (West Barnstable, MA), *179*

West Street Grill (Litchfield, CT), *26*

Westender (Nantucket, MA), *213*

Western Gateway Heritage State Park (North Adams, MA), *218*

Westford Regency Inn and Conference Center (Westford, MA), *193*

Westin Copley Place (Boston, MA), *135*

The Westin Providence (Providence, RI), *300*

The Westin Stamford (Stamford, CT), *42*

The Westin Waltham-Boston (Waltham, MA), *242*

Weston House Bed AND Breakfast (Eastport, ME), *76*

Westport Inn (Westport, CT), *44*

Whale Watching (Provincetown, MA), *227*

Whaler's Inn (Mystic, CT), *29*

The Whalewalk Inn (Eastham, MA), *168*

The Wharf Pub & Restaurant (Edgartown, MA), *203*

Wheatleigh (Lenox, MA), *187, 190*

Whistler House Museum of Art (Lowell, MA), *192*

Whistler's Inn (Lenox, MA), *189*

The White Barn Inn (Kennebunkport, ME), *83*

The White Barn Inn Restaurant (Kennebunkport, ME), *85*

White Cedar Inn (Freeport, ME), *79*

White Elephant Resort (Nantucket, MA), *208*

White Horse Tavern (Newport, RI), *297*

White House (Wilmington, VT), *343*

White House of Wilmington (Wilmington, VT), *342*

White Mountain Hotel & Resort (North Conway, NH), *275*

White Wind Inn (Provincetown, MA), *228*

White's of Westport (Wesport, MA), *169*

Whitehall Inn (Camden, ME), *70*

Whitehall Museum House (Middletown, RI), *294*

Wickachee (Calais, ME), *67*

Wilburton Inn (Manchester Village, VT), *322*

Wildcat Inn & Tavern (Jackson, NH), *264*

Wilderness Expeditions, Inc., *106*

Wildflower Inn (Falmouth, MA), *172*

The Wildflower Inn (Lyndonville, VT), *319*

Wilhelm Reich Museum (Rangeley, ME), *103*

William Tell (Thornton, NH), *284*

Williams College (Williamstown, MA), *244*

Williams College Museum of Art (Williamstown, MA), *244*

Williams Grant Inn (Bristol, RI), *288*

Williams Inn (Williamstown, MA), *245*

Williamsville Inn (West Stockbridge, MA), *239*

Willowbend Children's Charity Pro-Am (Mashpee, MA), *180*

Wilson Castle (Center Rutland, VT), *328*

Wilson Museum (Castine, ME), *66*

Windflower Inn (Great Barrington, MA), *176*

Windham Hill Inn (West Townshend, VT), *325*

Windjammer Days (Boothbay Harbor, ME), *61*

Windjammer Sailing (Camden Harbor, ME), *68*

Windjammer Weekend (Camden Harbor, ME), *68*

Windjammers, *104*

Windows on the Water (Kennebunk, ME), *82*

Windswept Cranberry Bog (Siasconset MA), *207*

Wings Hill Inn (Rome, ME), *50*

Winnapaug Inn (Westerly, RI), *303*

The Winnetu Inn & Resort (Edgartown, MA), *199*

Winnipesaukee Scenic Railroad (Meredith, NH), *271*

Winter Carnival (Middlebury, VT), *323*

Witch Dungeon Museum (Salem, MA), *233*

Witch House (Salem, MA), *233*

Witchcraft Victims Memorial (Danvers, MA), *163*

INDEX

★
★
★
★
★

The Wolfeboro Inn
(Wolfeboro, NH), *284*

Wonder View Inn (Bar
Harbor, ME), *54*

Woodford State Park
(Woodford, VT), *307*

Woodlawn Museum
(The Black House)
(Northeast Harbor,
ME), *90*

Woodman Institute
(Dover, NH), *255*

Woodstock Country
Club (Woodstock,
VT), *345*

Woodstock Historical
Society (Woodstock,
VT), *345*

Woodstock Inn & Resort
(Woodstock, VT), *346*

Woodstock Inn (North
Woodstock, NH),
267

Woodstock Inn
(Woodstock, VT), *347*

Woodstocker Bed and
Breakfast (Woodstock,
VT), *346*

Woodwards Resort
(Lincoln, NH), *267*

Worcester Art Museum
(Worcester, MA), *246*

Wright Museum
(Wolfeboro, NH), *284*

The Wyndhurst
Restaurant (Lenox,
MA), *190*

XV Beacon (Boston,
MA), *136*

Y

Yachtsman Lodge
& Marina
(Kennebunkport,
ME), *85*

Yale Repertory Theater
(New Haven, CT), *32*

Yale University (New
Haven, CT), *32*

Yankee Clipper Inn
(Rockport, MA), *231*

Yankee Inn (Lenox, MA),
187

The Yard (Chilmark,
MA), *197*

The Yardarm, *222*

Yarmouth Historical
Society Museum
(Yarmouth, ME),
114

Yarmouth House (West
Yarmouth, MA), *249*

Ye Olde England Inne
(Stowe, VT), *335*

Ying's (Hyannis, MA),
183

Yokohama (Gorham,
NH), *259*

York Harbor Inn (York
Harbor, ME), *116*

York Harbor Inn (York
Harbor, ME), *116*

Young's Lobster Pound
(Belfast, ME), *58*

380

INDEX

★
★
★
★
★

NOTES

NOTES

INDEX